Support for asylu

a guide to legal and welfare rights

second edition

Sue Willman is a solicitor at Pierce Glynn solicitors, specialist in housing, community care and social security law. She has developed a specialism in welfare law as it affects asylum-seekers, through her litigation, writing, training and policy development work.

Stephen Knafler is a barrister at Two Garden Court, who formerly practised as a solicitor and transferred to the bar in 1993. He specialises in housing, community care and support for asylum-seekers and has acted in many of the leading cases in these areas. He is the general editor of *Community Care Law Reports* (Legal Action Group, quarterly) and co-author of *Remedies for Disrepair and other Building Defects* (Sweet & Maxwell, 1996) and *Repairs: Tenants' Rights* (Legal Action Group, 3rd edn) and has acted in many of the leading cases in this area.

Stephen Pierce is a partner at Pierce Glynn solicitors, specialist in housing, community care and social security law. He has written and lectured in these areas and is an editorial board member of the *Community Care Law Reports*.

Support for asylum-seekers

a guide to legal and welfare rights

SECOND EDITION

Sue Willman, Stephen Knafler
and Stephen Pierce
with Alison Stanley

Legal Action Group
2004

This edition published in Great Britain 2004
by LAG Education and Service Trust Limited
242 Pentonville Road, London N1 9UN
www.lag.org.uk

© Sue Willman, Stephen Knafler and Stephen Pierce 2004

First published 2001

British Library Cataloguing in Publication Data
a CIP catalogue record for this book is available from the British Library.

Crown copyright material is produced with the permission of the Controller of HMSO and the Queen's Printer for Scotland.

ISBN-10 1 903307 24 4
ISBN-13 978 1 903307 24 4

Typeset by Regent Typesetting, London.
Printed by Biddles Ltd, Kings Lynn, Norfolk.

Foreword

by Malcolm Smart
Director of the Medical Foundation for the Care of Victims of Torture

I became the director of the Medical Foundation in September 2002 following the retirement of the founder and first director of the Medical Foundation for the Care of Victims of Torture, Helen Bamber, who wrote the foreword to the 2001 first edition of this now indispensable work.

In her foreword, Helen referred to our report of October 1997 entitled *Past Misery, Present Muddle*. The title remains no less valid in 2004 than when the report was published in 1997.

> Although the then Government claimed that genuine asylum-seekers would not suffer as a result of these measures, that was not the experience of over 100 Medical Foundation clients initially left destitute when their benefits were withdrawn. The removal of the means to provide the basics of life made it impossible to do any useful rehabilitation work with the clients affected. While we tried to protect our core work with torture victims, a particularly susceptible group of asylum-seekers, we had to use great effort and ingenuity to meet their essential needs.
>
> The Medical Foundation still finds its work disrupted by the inadequacy and confusion surrounding provision ... We still supplement what our clients are getting ... Without this, our clients would be unable to benefit much from the medical and other therapeutic help we can offer. Often our first intervention with clients has to be to ensure that they are getting the basic subsistence to which they are entitled but which may be hard for them to get. Only then can we turn to the essential rehabilitation work of helping them to come to terms with their experience of torture.

Of course the Government can no longer claim that 'genuine asylum-seekers would not suffer as a result of these measures'. As Helen said in 2001, 'the misery continues'. Indeed, for a time it seemed to grow considerably with the introduction of s55 of the Nationality, Immigration and Asylum Act 2002. This was no mere 'muddle' but Government policy designed to use the weapon of destitution as deterrent, or 'Destitution by Design' as it was described in the Court of Appeal, and as a weapon s55 is a decidedly blunt instrument. It makes no distinction between the refugee and the economic migrant for, in order to gain entry into fortress Britain, both must often use means which (sometimes unwittingly when placed at the mercy and under the control of traffickers) evade immigration control. A respite from the worst effects of s55 has been brought about by the Court of Appeal in the case of Limbuela, Tesema and Adam (Mr Adam was the subject of a medico-legal report by the Medical Foundation). We await with concern the final outcome of the case in the House of Lords.

Before the misery of s55 came to an end, perhaps temporarily, a new NASS muddle arose concerning individuals claiming asylum from those states newly joining the European Union. It was proposed that, over this year's May bank holiday, their status would change to that of persons entitled to work in the UK but that all NASS support and accommodation would be peremptorily withdrawn. Eviction notices were met with injunctions and the matter was resolved, again, initially, by recourse to law, when the Administrative Court (no doubt scarcely recovered from the onslaught of s55 cases) requested the parties to resolve the matter by other means. NASS, it seems, had not considered the impact of these new measures by reference to individual assessments and Article 3 of the European Convention on Human Rights.

As I write, NASS has decided to inflict further misery and muddle by moving the goal posts so that children of school age who have lived in London for 12 months or more and who are accommodated and supported by NASS must now face dispersal unless they are in an exam preparatory year. Has NASS learnt any lessons from s55 and the 'Accession cases'? Apparently not. This dispersal programme, beginning 13 August, must be completed before the school term begins in September 2004. No sensitivity to pressing needs and the best interests of children (of school age and otherwise) appears to have been taken into account. For example, the announcement of policy change makes no reference to the child's psychological need for continuity or her need to integrate into the host culture including learning the language, the ways to behave to be accepted and how to fit into the social and education systems.

Thus, as Helen said in 2001 'the muddle has increased' and, it would appear, continues to do so. The provisions surrounding support for asylum-seekers were complex in 1997 and more so in 2001. It was 'difficult to know where to start' in 2001. The watch words for 2004 may perhaps be 'it is difficult to see where it will end'.

The Medical Foundation believes that this second edition will continue to provide a guide through the muddle. Whether helping individual clients or shaping a strategy to change the legal framework, all of us need a clearer understanding of the relevant law in this often-impenetrable area. *Support for Asylum-seekers* meets that purpose and is an effective tool for change to be used to challenge both misery and muddle.

Malcolm Smart
August 2004

Acknowledgements

The authors would like to thank the following for their direct or indirect contributions to this edition:

Diane Astin, the Asylum Support Adjudicators, Rosie Brennan, Jerry Clore, Simon Cox (Doughty Street Chambers), Nic Alderson, Tim Crowley and Bharti Patel (Refugee Council), Richard Dunstan (Citizen's Advice), Nancy Fancott, Deborah Gellner, Polly Glynn, Nick Goss (Wandsworth Law Centre), the Housing and Immigration Group (HIG), the Immigration Law Practitioners' Association (ILPA), Angela Jackman, Tim Kell, Kat Lorenz (Refugee Action), Jan Luba QC, Pip Salvador-Jones (Hackney Community Law Centre), Duran Seddon, Joanna Thomson, Shelter, Solange Valdez and Sheona York (Hammersmith and Fulham Community Law Centre), Two Garden Court Chambers, and the staff at Legal Action Group.

We are particularly grateful to Alison Stanley of Bindman and Partners solicitors who contributed chapter 1.

We have endeavoured to state the law as 1st July 2004.

Sue Willman
Stephen Knafler
Stephen Pierce

July 2004

Contents

APPENDICES

Table of cases

Table of statutes

Sections higlighted in **bold** are reproduced in full, as amended, in appendix A.

Table of statutory instruments

Statutory instruments higlighted in **bold** are reproduced in appendix A.

Table of European legislation

Table of international legislation

Table of decisions

Abbreviations

ACD	Asylum Casework Directorate
ARC	Application registration card
ASA	Asylum Support Adjudicator
ASU	Asylum screening unit
CESC	Council of Europe Social Charter
CIO	Chief immigration officer
CLS	Community Legal Service
CPS	Crown Prosecution Service
CTA	Common Travel Area
DLR	Discretionary leave to remain
DWP	Department for Work and Pensions
EA	Emergency accommodation
EC	European Community
ECHR	European Convention on Human Rights
ECJ	European Court of Justice
ECO	Entry clearance officer
ECSMA	European Convention on Social and Medical Assistance
EEA	European Economic Area
EHO	Environmental Health Officer
ELR	Exceptional leave to remain
EU	European Union
FACN	Framework for the Assessment of Children in Need; 'the lilac book'
HIG	Housing and Immigration Group
HLPA	Housing Law Practitioners Group
HOPO	Home Office Presenting Officer
HP	Humanitarian protection
HRT	Habitual residence test
IAA	Immigration Appellate Authority
IAP	Inter-Agency Partnership
IAT	Immigration Appeal Tribunal
ILR	Indefinite leave to remain
IND	Immigration and Nationality Directorate
INEB	Immigration and Nationality Enquiry Bureau
JCWI	Joint Council for the Welfare of Immigrants
LSC	Legal Services Commission

NASS	National Asylum Support Service
NEAT	NASS Eligibility and Assessment Team
NIAA 2002 Guidance	Nationality, Immigration and Asylum Act 2002 section 54 and Schedule 3 and the Withholding and Withdrawal of Support (Travel Assistance and Temporary Accommodation) Regulations 2002: Guidance to Local Authorities and Housing Authorities
NINO	National insurance number
PFA	Person from abroad
PSIC	Persons subject to immigration control
RANS	Restricted Access to NASS Support
RAP	Refugee Arrivals Project
RTR	Right to reside
SAL	Standard acknowledgement letter
SEF	Statement of evidence form
UCP	Urgent cases payments

Statutes

AIA 1996	Asylum and Immigration Act 1996
AI(TC)A 2004	Asylum and Immigration (Treatment of Claimants, etc) Act 2004
CA 1989	Children Act 1989
HA 1996	Housing Act 1996
HRA 1998	Human Rights Act 1998
HSPHA 1968	Health Services and Public Health Act 1968
IA 1971	Immigration Act 1971
IAA 1999	Immigration and Asylum Act 1999
NAA 1948	National Assistance Act 1948
NIAA 2002	Nationality, Immigration and Asylum Act 2002
NHSA 1977	National Health Services Act 1977
PFEA 1977	Protection from Eviction Act 1977
SPCA 2002	State Pension Credit Act 2002
SSA 1998	Social Security Act 1998
SSAA 1992	Social Security Administration Act 1992
SSCBA 1992	Social Security Contributions and Benefits Act 1992

Statutory instruments

AS Regs	Asylum Support Regulations 2000 SI No 704
CTB Regs	Council Tax Benefit Regulations 1992 SI No 1814
EEA Regs	Immigration (European Economic Area) Regulations 2000 SI No 2326
HB Regs	Housing Benefit (General) Regulations SI No 1971
Interim Regs 1999	Asylum Support (Interim Provisions) Regulations 1999
IS Regs	Income Support (General) Regulations 1987 SI No 1967
JSA Regs	Jobseeker's Allowance Regulations 1996 SI No 207
SPC Regs	State Pension Credit Regulations 2002 SI No 1792

SPC(TMP)A Regs	State Pension Credit (Transitional and Miscellaneous Provisions) Amendment Regulations 2003 SI No 2274
SS(AA) Regs	Social Security (Attendance Allowance) Regulations 1991 SI No 2740
SS(CP) Regs	Social Security (Claims and Payments) Regulations 1987 SI No 1968
SS(DLA) Regs	Social Security (Disability Living Allowance) Regulations 1991 SI No 2890
SS(IA)CA Regs	Social Security (Immigration and Asylum) Consequential Amendments Regulations 2000 SI No 636
SS(IB) Regs	Social Security (Incapacity Benefit) Regulations 1994 SI No 2946
SS(ICA) Regs	Social Security (Invalid Care Allowance) Regulations 1976 SI No 409
SS(PFA)MA Regs	Social Security (Persons from Abroad) Miscellaneous Amendments Regulations 1996 SI No 30
SSCS(DA) Regs	Social Security and Child Support (Decisions and Appeals) Regulations 1999 SI No 991
TC(I) Regs	Tax Credits (Immigration) Regulations 2003 SI No 653
VOLO	Immigration (Variation of Leave) Order 1976 SI No 1572
WWS(TATA)R 2002	Withholding and Withdrawal of Support (Travel Assistance and Temporary Accommodation) Regulations 2002

Benefits
Means-tested benefits
CTC	Child Tax Credit
CTB	Council Tax Benefit
HB	Housing Benefit
IS	Income Support
MIG	Minimum Income Guarantee[1]
SF	Social Fund payments
SPC	State Pension Credit
WTC	Working Tax Credit

Non-means-tested benefits
AA	Attendance Allowance
BA	Bereavement Allowance
CA	Carers' Allowance
CB	Child Benefit
DLA	Disability Living Allowance
IB	Incapacity Benefit

---

1 Note that from 6 October 2003, the Minimum Income Guarantee has been replaced by State Pension Credit; SPCs administered by the Pension Service.

MA   Maternity Allowance
RP   Retirement Pension
SDA   Severe Disablement Allowance[2]

2 Note that Severe Disablement Allowance has been abolished for new claimants with
   effect from 6 April 2001, but remains in payment to existing claimants.

Asylum and immigration law

continued

Introduction

1.1 Immigration law is the starting point for most decisions about an asylum-seeker's legal or welfare rights. This chapter aims to provide non-immigration specialists with a background in asylum and immigration law and practice to inform their advice about welfare law issues.[1]

1.2 The chapter begins with an outline of the legal framework and an explanation of common immigration law terms and concepts. It is then divided into three parts: the asylum process, decisions/remedies, and rights/duties during the process. The first part explains the meaning of 'asylum-seeker' and the different stages in an asylum claim, both at the port of entry and 'in-country'. In the second part, favourable and unfavourable decisions are considered, as is the appeals process. Finally, the rights of the asylum-seeker pending a decision, and problems such as access to immigration advice and documentation are discussed.

1.3 Asylum law and the appeals process has been significantly changed by the Nationality, Immigration and Asylum Act 2002. Further changes are introduced by the Asylum and Immigration (Treatment of Claimants, etc) Act 2004 which received Royal Assent on 22 July 2004. Among other changes, the system for appeals has been radically overhauled again, introducing a single-tier appeal, the details of which are not clear.

1.4 Immigration documents referred to in this chapter are reproduced in the appendices. Reference materials relied on by immigration practitioners include Butterworths' Immigration Law Service, a comprehensive looseleaf volume containing the legislative and policy materials, and Macdonald's Immigration Law and Practice.[2] The Joint Council for the Welfare of Immigrants (JCWI) publishes accessible handbooks on immigration and asylum law. The Legal Action Group publishes handbooks on specific topics.

The administration of asylum and immigration decisions

1.5 The Home Secretary is responsible for immigration policy and asylum decision-making through the Home Office's Immigration and

---

1 The provision of immigration advice is an offence unless a person is registered, authorised or exempt under IAA 1999 Part 5.
2 Butterworths, 5th edn, 2001.

Nationality Directorate (IND). The IND is based at Croydon but has regional offices where decisions are also made.

1.6   The National Asylum Support Service (NASS) is also part of the IND with its main offices in Croydon, although some functions are being transferred to the regions.[3]

Leave to enter and leave to remain

1.7   It is the Home Secretary, through the IND, who has the power under Immigration Act (IA) 1971 s4(1) to grant or refuse leave to remain in the UK. Immigration officers have the power to grant leave to enter the UK (IA 1971 s4(1)). The Immigration and Asylum Act (IAA) 1999 introduced the power for entry clearance officers (ECOs) based outside the UK to grant leave to enter the UK.[4]

1.8   The immigration rules[5] explain the relationship between the powers of the immigration service and the Home Office in asylum applications. Only the Home Secretary can decide asylum applications. An asylum application made to an immigration officer at the port should be referred to the IND for a decision.[6]

The immigration service

1.9   The immigration service employs immigration officers, who are appointed by the Home Secretary, at 'ports of entry' to the UK. These include Waterloo International railway station, airports such as Heathrow and Gatwick, and sea-ports such as Dover. The administrative provisions governing control of entry to the UK are found in IA 1971 Sch 2, which provides for immigration officers to detain and/or to give directions for removal to illegal entrants and people refused leave to enter. The powers of immigration officers were extended by IAA 1999 ss1 and 2. If asylum-seekers claim asylum at the port, an immigration officer can either detain them or grant 'temporary admission'. The immigration officer must refer applicants to the IND

---

3   See appendix G for addresses.
4   See IA 1971 s3A introduced by IAA 1999 ss1 and 2, and the Immigration (Leave to Enter and Remain) Order 2000 SI No 1161. The statement of changes in immigration rules laid down on 28 July 2000 allows immigration officers to vary leave.
5   HC 395 paras 328–333. See para 1.9 below.
6   HC 395 para 328.

for a decision on the asylum claim. In these 'port cases', if the IND decides to recognise an asylum-seeker as a refugee, or to grant humanitarian protection or discretionary leave,[7] it will advise the immigration service at the port of entry. An immigration officer will then formally grant leave to enter. If asylum is refused or an appeal dismissed, the immigration officer must reconsider the original application for leave to enter. If that is refused, the immigration officer may start removal proceedings.[8]

The legal framework

1.10   The Immigration Act 1971 forms the framework of domestic immigration law. Section 3(2) gives the Home Secretary power to make 'rules' about when 'leave to enter or remain' in the UK is needed and when it will be granted by laying a 'statement of changes in immigration rules' before Parliament. The current immigration rules are HC 395. They are amended by statements of changes, for example, Cmnd 4851 which came into force on 2 October 2000, amending the rules to take account of the Human Rights Act (HRA) 1998 and by later amendments which, for example, incorporate some earlier concessions into the rules. The immigration rules are not a statutory instrument and are amended to accommodate legislative changes and political developments. In addition to the rules there are a number of extra-statutory 'concessions' which are matters of policy outside the immigration rules, for example, the seven-year residence for families concession provides (with exceptions) for indefinite leave to remain to be granted to families with children under 18 years of age who face removal. The government had announced its intention to review existing concessions with a view to incorporating them into the rules. Only some of the concessions were included in the October 2000 changes.[9]

1.11   An asylum-seeker applies to be recognised as a refugee within the meaning of the 1951 United Nations Convention and 1967 Protocol

---

7   In the past, a person refused asylum but granted a lesser status was granted 'exceptional leave to enter or remain'. This has been abolished see paras 1.115–1.120 below.

8   Normally, the decision to refuse asylum to a port applicant is accompanied by a decision to refuse leave to enter. Older cases, however, may have two separate decisions.

9   For example, the concession granting leave to enter or remain to unmarried, cohabiting partners of two years' standing is now part of the rules after the Statement of Changes in Immigration Rules, 2 October 2000 amended HC 395, para 295.

relating to the Status of Refugees. An asylum-seeker (or other 'person subject to immigration control') may also claim that to return him or her to his or her country of origin would be a breach of article 3 or other articles of the European Convention for the Protection of Human Rights and Fundamental Freedoms ('Human Rights Convention'). The Human Rights Convention is now incorporated into UK law by the HRA 1998.[10] IAA 1999 s167 refers to the UN Convention as 'the Refugee Convention' and the European Convention as 'the Human Rights Convention' and so the same terms are used in this book.

1.12   In reaching a decision on an asylum claim, the IND should have regard to other international human rights instruments to which the UK is a party, as a matter of international law.[11] These include, in particular, the UN Convention against Torture and other Cruel, Inhuman or Degrading Treatment or Punishment 1984 and the International Covenant on Civil and Political Rights 1966.

1.13   The domestic law governing an asylum claim is derived from the Asylum and Immigration Appeals Act (AIAA) 1993, the Asylum and Immigration Act (AIA) 1996, the Immigration and Asylum Act 1999 and the Nationality, Immigration and Asylum Act 2002. These statutes, referred to here as 'the Asylum Acts', are supplemented by the immigration rules, concessions, and internal IND policy. Some of this material is published on the Home Office website, although the policy section in particular is frequently out of date.[12] The website publishes an IND 'country assessment' of each of the main asylum producing countries. This should be treated as a relevant consideration when the Home Secretary decides an asylum claim.

1.14   The NIAA 2002 amended the previous Asylum Acts and the IA 1971. The most significant changes include:

- Changes to the process by which individuals acquire British citizenship and can have citizenship revoked.
- The introduction of an 'authority-to-carry scheme'. This is a completely new scheme which requires airlines and other carriers to obtain authority from the Immigration Service before bringing certain classes of passenger to the UK. The grant or refusal of authority to carry would not determine whether a person is permitted to enter the UK. At the time of writing, the Home Office has not made or publicised any scheme.

---

10 See appendix A.
11 These instruments are not currently incorporated into domestic law or referred to in the immigration rules or IND instructions.
12 www.homeoffice.gov.uk/ind/hpg.htm.

- Extension of the juxtaposed controls – the arrangements under which UK immigration controls are operated in another European Economic Area (EEA) State and, on a reciprocal basis, that other State operates its own frontier controls within the UK. Prior to NIAA 2002, the Immigration Service already operated immigration controls at the Eurotunnel site at Coquelles and at three Eurostar stations (Paris Nord, Lille Europe and Calais Frethun). The NIAA 2002 gives the Home Office a new power to exercise British immigration controls at other EEA ports.
- Changes designed to provide a seamless system of support by the National Asylum Support Service for asylum-seekers from the point at which they initially make their claim until the time at which their application is finally determined and they have exhausted their statutory appeal rights. The system includes the introduction of 'induction', 'accommodation', and 'removal' centres.
- Changes to the appeals system including removal of the right of appeal against:
  - Refusal of asylum where leave to remain (such as humanitarian protection) is granted for one year or less. Once a second year's leave has been granted, there will be a right of appeal.
  - Decisions taken outside the rules (that is, under concessions and policies).
  - The destination to which the person is to be removed.
  - The validity of removal directions.
- The introduction of non-supensive appeal rights (that is, no right of appeal from within the UK) if the Home Office certifies that an asylum or human rights claim is 'clearly unfounded'.
- Refusal to grant permission to appeal to the tribunal or to challenge the grant of permission is by way of statutory review (not judicial review as previously).
- Changes in immigration procedure.
- The introduction of further criminal offences.

Immigration law concepts

'Subject to immigration control'

1.15   The IA 1971 distinguishes between people who have the 'right of abode' in the UK and those whose right to live, work and settle here is subject to regulation and control under the Act. A person who is subject to immigration control needs permission to enter the UK and remain here. These permissions are known as 'leave to enter' and 'leave to remain'. The meaning of 'subject to immigration control' in the context of the IA 1971 is different from the definition of 'person subject to immigration control' (PSIC) in Part VI of the IAA 1999. Section 115(9) of the 1999 Act introduced a definition of PSIC for welfare purposes, excluding PSICs from social security benefits and other forms of assistance.

'Person from abroad'

1.16   The term 'person from abroad' (PFA) was previously used in social security law to refer to certain persons subject to immigration control as well as persons who were not subject to immigration control but who were not 'habitually resident' in the UK, such as British citizens who had recently arrived in the UK after living abroad. The IAA 1999 and Social Security (Immigration and Asylum) Consequential Amendments (SSIA) Regs[13] have amended various social security regulations to replace PFA with the new s115(9) definition[14] of 'person subject to immigration control'. The term PFA now applies only to those who have failed the habitual residence test.

1.17   British citizens under the British Nationality Act 1981, Commonwealth citizens with the right of abode, and citizens of the Republic of Ireland are not subject to immigration control under the IA 1971.

1.18   A citizen of a country within the European Economic Area (EEA) is not a PSIC for the purposes of welfare provision according to the s115(9) definition, and so is not excluded from social security benefits. The exception to this are nationals of the ' Accession 8' or 'A8' countries who can be excluded – this is discussed fully in chapter 2.

1.19   Immigration control of citizens of the EEA[15] is derived from

---

13 SI 2000 No 636. See appendix A.

14 See chapter 2, para 2.28.

15 The EEA consists of the states which are contracting parties to the Economic Area Agreement, signed at Oporto on 2 May 1992. They are the countries of the European Union: Austria, Belgium, Denmark, Finland, France, Germany, Greece, Italy, Luxembourg, the Netherlands, the Republic of Ireland, Portugal, Spain, Sweden, and the UK, together with Iceland, Liechtenstein and Norway. From 1 May 2004 the 10 'Accession Countries' have freedom of movement within the EU, but only limited access to work and benefits. The Accession Countries are: Cyprus, Czech Republic, Estonia, Hungary, Latvia, Lithuania, Malta, Poland, Slovakia and Slovenia The UK has permitted limited working rights and access to benefits apart from to Cypriot and Maltese nationals. See chapter 2.

European law. The Treaty on European Union 1992 (the Maastricht Treaty) provides freedom of movement to an EEA national if he or she is a 'worker', self-employed, providing or receiving services. The Immigration (EEA) Regulations 2000[16] (the EEA Regs) interpret the European law position, that is, that EEA nationals and their family members are entitled to remain in the UK provided they are here to exercise their EU Treaty rights. Certain EEA nationals should be regarded as having the right to remain in the UK without any restriction on the period for which they may remain.[17] Extended family members may fall within the regulations' definition of 'family member'. The EEA provisions are relevant to some asylum-seeker households. An asylum-seeker may have the right to live in the UK, and access to benefits and housing, if he or she is the family member of an EEA national, for example, if the asylum-seeker is married to a French citizen who is working in the UK.[18]

1.20   The EU has entered into agreements with various countries of Central and Eastern Europe, and the Magreb. These are known as 'Association Agreements'. Many of the Association Agreement countries (known as the 'accession countries')[19] joined the EU on 1 May 2004. Initially, the UK stated that nationals of these countries should have full freedom of movement rights in the UK, including access to welfare benefits. This decision has been changed and while nationals of the accession countries have access to the UK employment market, apart from nationals of Cyprus and Malta, these nationals only have limited access to benefits. This is discussed fully in chapter 2.

1.21   Everyone not mentioned in the above categories, is 'subject to immigration control', and so needs leave to enter or remain in the UK under the IA 1971 and immigration rules. The category includes other specified types of British citizen (for example, British Overseas citizens), Commonwealth citizens without the right of abode, and citizens of other non-EEA countries (who are known as 'aliens').

'Leave to enter or remain' and 'public funds'

1.22   The length of leave to enter or remain in the UK may be 'limited' or 'indefinite' (IA 1971 s3(1)(b)). Limited leave and indefinite leave are defined by IA 1971 s33. Indefinite leave to remain is also known as

---

16 SI No 2326.
17 EEA Regs, reg 8.
18 See EEA Regs and para 2.28 below.
19 See note 15 above.

settled status, or in ordinary English 'permanent residency'. Where limited leave is granted to a person, it may be subject to conditions:[20]

i) a condition restricting his employment or occupation in the UK;

ii) a condition requiring him to maintain and accommodate himself, and any dependants of his, without recourse to public funds; and

iii) a condition requiring him to register with the police.[21]

1.23 A breach of a condition may lead to prosecution, detention or removal from the UK.

Variation of leave

1.24 A person who has 'limited leave' or 'exceptional leave' can apply to the IND to vary it, before it expires. So a person with humanitarian protection leave which is due to expire could apply for another period of humanitarian protection or indefinite leave, as appropriate. The original leave then continues until 28 days after a decision has been made. The authority for this was previously the Immigration (Variation of Leave) Order (VOLO) 1976[22] and is now IAA 1999 s3 amending IA 1971 s3C.[23] Any entitlement to benefits would continue on the same basis. If leave is refused and an appeal is then entered, the leave will continue until the determination of the appeal.[24] Local authorities and the Job Centre should accept (as evidence of immigration status) the original leave, combined with evidence that an application to vary has been made before the expiry of the original leave to enter or remain. In practice, many authorities demand confirmatory letters from the Home Office. These can be difficult to obtain.

Sponsorship and recourse to public funds

1.25 Leave to enter the UK may be granted subject to a condition or requirement that the person coming here will be able to maintain and accommodate him or herself 'without recourse to public funds'. In the case of elderly dependent relatives coming to live with relatives in

---

20 The Home Secretary has power to add to these conditions (IA 1971, inserted by IAA 1999 ss1 and 2).

21 IA 1971 ss3 and 4 and Immigration Rules para 8.

22 SI No 1572.

23 See also the Immigration (Variation of Leave) (Amendment) Order 2000 SI No 2445.

24 IAA 1999 Sch 4 para 17.

the UK, for example, there is a requirement that a 'sponsor' will maintain and accommodate them.[25]

1.26   A sponsor of a person seeking leave to enter or remain in the UK
may be asked 'to give an undertaking in writing to be responsible for
that person's maintenance and accommodation for the period of any
leave granted . . .'[26] If such an undertaking has been signed (currently on form RON 112 or SET(F)), the dependant falls within the IAA
1999 s115 definition of PSIC and is not entitled to benefits.[27]

1.27   Recourse to public funds means 'additional public funds' so the
rule does not prevent the sponsor from claiming benefits for him or
herself, provided that he or she is not claiming additional funds for
the person he or she is sponsoring.[28]

1.28   'Public funds' are defined by Immigration Rules para 6, as amended. They include attendance allowance, severe disabled person's
allowance, invalid care allowance, child benefit, council tax benefit,
disability living allowance, housing benefit, income-based jobseeker's
allowance, income support, carer's allowance, severe disablement
allowance (abolished for new claimants from 6 April 2001), social
fund payments and housing as homeless or public housing (provided
under Housing Act 1996 Parts VI and VII). Working tax credit, child
tax credit and pension credit are likely to added to the list.

Common travel area

1.29   A person who is resident in or a citizen of the UK, the Channel
Islands and the Isle of Man or the Republic of Ireland may travel
freely within this area, which is defined by IA 1971 as the 'common
travel area'. Anyone who is subject to immigration control, but passes
through Ireland on the way to the UK, is still subject to immigration
control at the UK border.

'Pre-entry' immigration control and 'visa nationals'

1.30   'Immigration control' is classified as 'pre-entry', 'on-entry' and 'after
entry' control.

1.31   The IA 1971 categorises countries as 'visa national' or 'non-visa
national' countries. The immigration rules list the countries that

25 HC 395 para 317(iv).
26 HC 395 para 35.
27 But see further chapter 2, para 2.57 below (death of sponsor).
28 HC 395 para 6A.

come within these categories.[29] A citizen of a visa national country needs to get a visa (which may be referred to as 'entry clearance') from a British Entry Clearance Officer (ECO) outside the UK, in order to enter the UK lawfully. A grant of 'entry clearance' may include leave to enter.[30] The IAA 1999 empowers ECOs to grant leave to enter the UK, but since there is no 'asylum visa' for most asylum-seekers, the majority of asylum-seekers will continue to apply for asylum on or after arrival in the UK.[31]

1.32   A citizen of a non-visa national country does not need to obtain entry clearance before entering the UK if the visit is for certain temporary purposes, such as for a holiday or to study. If he or she wishes to settle in the UK, for example, on grounds of marriage, entry clearance must be obtained. A visitor or student from a non-visa national country can apply for entry clearance before entry and may wish to do so if he or she thinks that there is a chance the immigration service will refuse entry. There is a right of appeal against refusal from within the UK if an entry clearance visa has been obtained pre-entry. Anyone entering the UK without entry clearance, who is refused entry, has to leave the UK to exercise a right of appeal. There is no right of appeal for visitors from visa national countries who are refused entry except for family visitors, who can only exercise the right of appeal from outside the UK.[32]

Asylum-seekers, illegal entrants and overstayers

1.33   The Home Office treats some asylum-seekers as 'illegal entrants'. IA 1971 s33(1) defines 'illegal entrant' as:

a person
(a) unlawfully entering or seeking to enter [the UK] in breach of a deportation order or the immigration laws; or
(b) entering or seeking to enter by means which include deception by another person.

29 Appendix 1 of the Immigration Rules, which is periodically updated.
30 See IA 1971 s3A introduced by IAA 1999 s1 and Immigration (Leave to Enter and Remain) Order 2000 SI No 1161.
31 In the past, the UK has accepted for settlement 'mandate refugees' where the determination of status is made abroad by the UNHCR (for example, from Vietnam) and the government has announced a further scheme, but details have not been published. See note 33 below.
32 IAA 1999 s60, Immigration Appeals (Family Visitor) (No 2) Regulations 2000 SI No 2446, as amended by Immigration Appeals (Family Visitor) (Amendment) Regulations 2001 SI No 52 and Immigration Appeals (Family Visitor) Regulations 2003 SI No 518.

1.34   An asylum-seeker cannot usually obtain entry clearance from his or her country of origin to enter the UK as a refugee or asylum-seeker. An asylum-seeker in another country would be expected to claim asylum there unless it was not a 'safe third country'.[33]

1.35   The term 'illegal entrant' is most commonly used to refer to people who come to the UK clandestinely, for example, hidden in a lorry. It is also used to refer to those who have used forged documents or who misrepresented the purpose of their visit, for example, someone who entered the UK with a student visa and then claimed asylum and to those who enter while a deportation order is in existence. The Refugee Convention provides that receiving countries should not 'impose penalties' on refugees who enter illegally.[34]

1.36   Illegal entry, assisting illegal entry and 'harbouring an illegal entrant' are all offences under IA 1971 ss24 and 25.[35] The Immigration (Carriers Liability) Act 1987 introduced fines for airlines which transport people to the UK without a valid visa. IAA 1999 Part II extended this to lorries and ships.

1.37   The ability of an asylum-seeker to enter the UK legally has increasingly been restricted. The immigration rules' list of 'visa national' countries whose citizens need a visa to enter the UK includes most of the countries which are seen as 'generating' asylum-seekers. Home Office airport liaison officers are stationed at strategic overseas airports to 'advise' airlines about prospective illegal entrants who are attempting to be passengers.[36] 'Juxtaposed controls' – immigration control at strategic channel ports takes place in France and the NIAA 2002 gives the power to extend this to other EU countries.[37] Document checks by airlines and other carriers mean that it is difficult for asylum-seekers to travel to the UK unless they enter clandestinely using an agent and/or obtain forged documents. As a result many obtain entry by using forged documents or otherwise enter illegally (for example, in container lorries).

1.38   An illegal entrant can be removed from the UK after removal directions have been issued by an immigration officer (IA 1971 Sch 2). Directions should not be acted on if there is an outstanding

---

33   The main exception is the 'Gateway Protection Programme' for the resettlement of 500 refugees through the UNHCR. See http://www.ind. homeoffice.gov.uk/default.asp?PageId=4835

34   Article 31(1). See also para 1.48 below.

35   As amended by IAA 1999 ss28 and 29 and NIAA 2002 ss143 and 156.

36   See White Paper 'Fairer, Faster and Firmer – A Modern Approach to Immigration and Asylum' July 1998, Cm 4018, chapter 11.

37   NIAA 2002 s141. See para 1.14 above.

claim under the Human Rights Act 1998 or an asylum claim[38] (or if those claims have been refused but there is an appeal or judicial review application to challenge the refusal).

1.39   An 'overstayer' is a person who originally had limited leave to enter or remain in the UK, but whose leave has expired. Before the IAA 1999 became law, the normal procedure for expelling an over-stayer from the UK began when the Home Office served a notice of intention to make a deportation order under IA 1971 Sch 3, which allowed a right of appeal. Since 2 October 2000, overstayers have no right of appeal before removal except on asylum, human rights or discrimination grounds.[39] An illegal entrant or overstayer who is challenging removal must be served with a 'one-stop' notice to allow him or her to raise any grounds for remaining in the UK, including Human Rights Convention points, before removal.

The asylum application – law and procedure

Meaning of 'asylum-seeker' and 'refugee'

1.40   A 'refugee' is 'a person who has a well-founded fear of persecution for reasons of race, religion, nationality, membership of a particular social group or political opinion and who is outside the country of his nationality or former habitual residence and is unable or, owing to such fear, is unwilling to avail himself of the protection of that country or return to it'.[40]

1.41   The UK is a signatory to the 1951 Refugee Convention, and to its 1967 Protocol. The approach to considering whether an asylum-seeker should be recognised as a refugee stems from the principle of non-return or 'non-refoulement'.[41] A 'refugee' cannot be lawfully returned to his or her country of origin except in very limited circumstances. The government is allowed to return the refugee to the country of origin where he or she has committed a serious crime and is a danger to the community, or presents a serious security risk.[42]

---

38   IAA 1999 s10 as amended by NIAA 2002 s77.
39   IAA 1999 s10. The 'Regularisation Scheme for Overstayers' preserved the right of appeal against deportation for those who applied under the scheme before the deadline on 2 October 2000.
40   Refugee Convention art 1A(2).
41   Refugee Convention art 33(1).
42   Refugee Convention art 33(2).

Domestic law now incorporates Human Rights Convention obligations, prohibiting the removal or return of a refugee even in these circumstances, if he or she has a valid Human Rights Convention claim, usually under article 3.[43]

1.42   The immigration rules provide that an 'asylum applicant' is a person (of any age) who claims that it would be contrary to the UK's obligations under the Convention and Protocol for him or her to be removed from or required to leave the UK.[44] In very simple terms, an asylum-seeker needs to show that he or she is:

- in the UK;
- a refugee as defined by the Convention and Protocol; and
- 'refusing his application would result in his being required to go ... in breach of the Convention and Protocol, to a country in which his life or freedom would be threatened on account of his race, religion, nationality, political opinion or membership of a particular social group'.[45]

1.43   The definition of 'asylum-seeker' for the purposes of entitlement to asylum support is wider than the immigration law definition. Under IAA 1999 Part VI, for example, if the asylum-seeker has a dependent child, the applicant continues to be defined as 'an asylum-seeker' for support purposes for as long as they both remain in the UK and the child is under the age of 18 (IAA 1999 s94(5)).

1.44   The Refugee Convention is interpreted by case law and by IND instructions. Case law makes reference to the UNHCR's International Handbook on Procedures and Criteria for Determining Refugee Status 1988. The Immigration Rules contain the separate procedure for claiming asylum, the factors which the IND must consider in decision-making, and the appeals process. The IND should consider the facts of each application and grant asylum, that is, recognise the applicant as a refugee, if the Home Secretary is satisfied that the Convention criteria are met. If the Home Secretary considers the criteria are not met, but forcing the applicant to return to his or her country would be a breach of the UK's obligations under the European Convention on Human Rights, then humanitarian protection

---

43   See paras 1.10 and 1.51. Removal may be prohibited if it interferes with other Human Rights Convention rights such as the art 8 right to family life, but unlike art 3 claims, art 8 allows a balancing exercise. This book focuses on art 3 claims because they provide access to Part VI support, unlike a claim under the other Convention articles.

44   HC 395 para 328.

45   HC 395 para 334.

will be granted. If there are other compelling reasons why an asylum-seeker should not be forced to return to the country of origin at that time, discretionary leave to remain may be granted. In rare cases, leave outside the rules may be granted.[46]

1.45 Until 1 April 2003 where an asylum-seeker was refused refugee status, but there were compelling reasons why he or she should not be removed from the UK, exceptional leave to remain (ELR) was granted. Usually for a period of four years, but for certain nationals for shorter periods. The Home Office policy of granting indefinite leave to remain to those with ELR who have completed four years on this status remains in place, provided the applicant has a continuing fear of return to his or her country of origin.[47]

1.46 It is useful for those advising about support to be aware of the decision-making criteria because the asylum-seeker's actions in relation to a support claim may have an impact on the asylum claim. The immigration rules outline the factors which may lead to a refusal of an asylum claim: a failure without reasonable explanation to make a prompt and full disclosure of material factors, either orally or in writing, or otherwise to assist the Secretary of State in establishing the facts of the case may lead to the refusal of an asylum application.[48]

1.47 IAA 1999 s20 provides that information held by contractors providing housing or support under the asylum/interim support scheme may be supplied to the Home Secretary 'for use for immigration purposes'. Supported asylum-seekers should be aware that this allows information provided to NASS to be used by the Home Office in relation to their asylum claim.

1.48 An asylum-seeker's credibility is central to the success or failure of his or her asylum claim. The actions which the immigration rules state may damage credibility include:

a) delay in making a prompt asylum application unless the claim is based on events occurring after arrival in the UK,

b) making false oral or written representations,

c) destroying or disposing of documents relevant to the claim,

d) undertaking activities which are inconsistent with previous beliefs and behaviour and which are intended to strengthen the asylum claim,

e) making concurrent applications for asylum in or outside the UK.[49]

46 See paragraphs 1.115– 1.120.
47 See paras 1.115– 1.120 for the replacement statuses.
48 HC 395 para 340.
49 HC 395 para 341.

The above must be read in conjunction with article 31(1) of the Refugee Convention:

> The contracting states shall not impose penalties, on account of their illegal entry or presence, on refugees, who coming directly from a territory where their life or freedom was threatened in the sense of Article 1, enter or are present in a territory without authorisation, provided they present themselves without delay to the authorities and show good cause for their illegal entry or presence.

1.49   In *R v Uxbridge Magistrates' Court ex p Adimi*[50] the High Court decided that to convict an asylum-seeker for using false documents would be in breach of article 31.

1.50   In the context of social security law, *Adimi* was considered by a commissioner who was evaluating the meaning of 'on arrival'. He decided that to exclude from income support an asylum-seeker who applied for asylum shortly after entry in the UK could constitute 'a penalty' within the meaning of article 31(1).[51] The 'penalty' argument is relevant in other asylum support contexts.

Article 3 of the European Convention on Human Rights

1.51   An asylum-seeker who would suffer torture or inhuman or degrading treatment or punishment (within the meaning of article 3) if returned to his or her country of origin, should not be expelled from the UK. This applies even if he or she does not meet the Refugee Convention criteria, as in cases where the applicant is likely to be tortured for a 'non-Convention' reason. An article 3 claim is normally made concurrently with an ordinary asylum claim under the Refugee Convention, but where an asylum claim has been made before October 2000 when the ECHR was incorporated into UK law it can be made at a later stage, for example, where asylum has been refused.[52]

1.52   In *D v United Kingdom*[53] the European Court of Human Rights held that it would be a breach of article 3 to return a person with AIDS (who was on temporary admission with a conviction for serious drugs offences) to St Kitts because vital medical treatment was not available

---

50 [2000] 4 All ER 520.
51 Commissioner's Decision CIS 4439/98.
52 But see para 1.139 below.
53 (1997) 24 EHRR 423.

there and his removal would expose him to a real risk of dying in circumstances which would amount to inhuman treatment. If an article 3 claim is pending, whether at first decision stage or at appeal stage, the applicant for asylum support or interim support must be treated as an 'asylum-seeker' entitled to support for the purposes of IAA 1999 s94.

1.53   The IAA 1999 requires an asylum-seeker to raise any article 3 or other Human Rights Convention points at the earliest opportunity. For new applicants this is at the same time as the asylum application. For applications that pre-date the introduction of the Human Rights Act 1998, this is usually when grounds of appeal are entered, no later than within ten working days of the 'one-stop notice' being served. The one-stop notice and appeal procedure is explained below at paragraph 1.139.[54] Article 3 grounds may arise after the determination of the appeal, for example, if the appellant's health deteriorates dramatically or if conditions in the country of origin change suddenly. If an applicant is prevented from raising new article 3 grounds after the determination, this may violate the Human Rights Convention.

Unaccompanied minors[55]

1.54   There is a special regime for asylum-seekers under 18 who come to the UK without a parent or guardian. The immigration rules state that a child who appears to be under 18 should be treated as a minor, unless there is documentary evidence to suggest he or she is 18 or over. Where there is a doubt, it is the role of the Home Secretary to establish the age of a young adult. This is an issue that is often disputed and it may be that the Home Office's assessment will need to be challenged.[56] From October 2003 the Home Office have run a pilot programme to interview minors from the age of 12 upwards about the substance of their claim.[57] Those who have had applications pending for some time and who completed a SEF self-completion application

---

54 NIAA 2002 s120

55 For further discussion on unaccompanied minor asylum-seekers see chapter 6, paras 6.128–6.153.

56 This is a specialist area and specialist immigration advice should be obtained. At the time of writing ILPA is drafting *Working with Children and Young People subject to Immigration Control: Guidelines for Best Practice* which deals with the subject of age disputes in the immigration context. The guidelines should be published by the end of 2004.

57 HC 395 para 352.

form are being 'invited' to attend for interview. An individual decision should be made about whether an individual child or young person should attend. New child applicants will be called for an interview. A revised statement of evidence form (SEF) has also been produced for child applicants which is very similar to that used for adults. The form and content of the questions do very little to assist a child's understanding about the information required of him or her.

1.55   Unlike most other immigration interviews, the Legal Services Commission (LSC) will fund a legal representative at interviews of children. A 'responsible adult' (whose function is different from that of a legal representative, being to provide support and advocacy to the child, not to give legal advice) must be present at any interview including the screening unit interview. Minors should be referred to a social services department and should not be detained. The Home Office should refer asylum-seekers who claim to be minors and are unaccompanied to the Refugee Council's Children's Panel of Advisers for assistance.

1.56   Home Office policy is not to seek to remove an unaccompanied minor unless it is possible to put in place acceptable reception and care arrangements in their country of origin. Frequently minors are granted leave to remain until their 18th birthday, when they can be removed without this precondition being necessary. Careful consideration should be given to whether children granted only limited leave should appeal against the refusal of asylum. At the time of writing, the Home Office is actively seeking to return minors to Kosovo, Macedonia and Albania. The Home Office does not intend to concentrate on reuniting these children with their families of origin. Instead the aim will be to ensure there are reception facilities for them. It is proposed to ask social workers to give their opinion on whether it would be in the children's best interests to be returned, despite the fact that in many cases, the local authority in question will not have any parental responsibility for the child and the question will never have been considered by a family court.

1.57   Specific issues concerning the financial support of unaccompanied minor asylum-seekers are dealt with in chapter 6.

1.58   If the child is still awaiting the determination of his or her asylum application at 18, NASS will pay the relevant local authority to continue to accommodate him or her within their area and will not disperse them.

1.59   Children who have been looked after are also deemed to be in priority need for housing if they are homeless under article 4 of the

Homelessness (Priority Need for Accommodation) (England) Order 2002.[57a]

The procedure for claiming asylum

1.60 A person who claims that it would be contrary to the Refugee Convention for him or her to be removed from the UK is an 'asylum applicant'.[58] An asylum claim can be made either 'in-country' or at the port of entry but all applications are decided by the Home Office.

1.61 An asylum-seeker may present him or herself to the immigration officer at the port of entry while passing through immigration control at, for example, Heathrow airport. If the word 'refugee' or 'asylum' is not used, the asylum-seeker should at least have indicated a fear of returning home. This may be relevant at a later stage to demonstrate that asylum was claimed 'on arrival' for benefit purposes (in pre-3 April 2000 asylum claims or in NIAA 2002 s55 cases). There are cases where an asylum applicant who is treated as 'in-country' by the Home Office for immigration purposes is an 'on-arrival' applicant entitled to benefit for social security law purposes.[59]

1.62 Alternatively, an asylum claim can be made 'in-country' by an application in person to the Home Office at the Asylum Screening Units in Croydon or Liverpool. Applications can no longer be made by post.

1.63 An asylum applicant has to have his or her claim for asylum recorded by the Home Office 'as soon as reasonably practicable' after arrival in the UK.[60] The asylum claim has to be made at a designated place.[61] Failure to do so can result in the person being denied financial support from NASS. The changes in where an applicant can make his or her application for asylum have caused great difficulties for a number of asylum-seekers who have not been able to afford to travel the large distances necessary to make an application. This is discussed further in chapter 3. A late claim for asylum can also impact on the applicant's credibility.

57a SI No 2051
58 HC 395 para 327.
59 If an asylum claim was made before 3 April 2000 and is not yet determined. See para 2.51.
60 NIAA 2002 s55(1)(b).
61 See chapter 3, paragraph 3.60.

When is an asylum claim recorded?[62]

1.64   Eligibility for support under the Asylum Support Regulations 2000[63] ('AS Regs') or Asylum Support (Interim Provisions) Regulations 1999[64] ('Interim Regs') starts when a claim for asylum under the Refugee Convention or a claim under ECHR article 3 has been recorded but not determined.[65] A claim is recorded when it is notified to the Home Office in person, at the Asylum Screening Unit.[66] It has been argued that evidence of a solicitor's letter making a claim under article 3 of the Human Rights Convention that it would be contrary to the UK's obligations under that Convention for the claimant to be removed from the UK should be sufficient evidence that the claimant is an 'asylum-seeker' for support purposes.[67]

1.65   Having claimed asylum, there are a number of stages in the process of seeking asylum in the UK. The process varies slightly depending on whether the asylum-seeker is a port or in-country applicant, whether she or he has been put into an induction centre or into the Oakington procedure, or some other special project. The options are:

- induction centre process; and/or
- screening and registration of the application;
- return to another 'safe third country' without the application being considered; or
- 'detention' in Oakington or other 'removal centre' or detention under the fast track process in Harmondsworth; or
- grant of temporary admission or release;
- referral of destitute asylum applicants to reception assistants for asylum support under IAA 1999 Part VI;
- completion of the statement of evidence form (SEF) – self-completion; and/or
- interview and completion of the SEF – interview; and/or
- other special project;
- decision by the Asylum Casework Group within the Home Office IND leading to
- grant of refugee or other status or appeal or removal.

---

62   See chapter 3 for a detailed discussion.
63   SI No 704.
64   SI No 3056.
65   IAA 1999 s94(1).
66   IND open letter, Chris Hudson, 15 September 2000.
67   See chapter 3. See also *R (Nigatu) v SSHD* [2004] EWHC 1806 (Admin).

1.66   There are a number of pilot programmes within this general scheme. For example, a SEF-less procedure, whereby the person is interviewed without first completing a SEF. Minors have been treated slightly differently, but are now interviewed about the substantive nature of their claim.

Screening interview

1.67   In order to apply for asylum the applicant (and his or her spouse and any dependants) have to go through a screening process at the Asylum Screening Unit (ASU). Queues at the ASU can be very lengthy.

1.68   The first part of the screening process involves completion of basic information about the applicant's identity and means of travel to the UK. The Home Office will provide an interpreter, if necessary. At the first stage, a 14 page questionnaire is completed called 'Screening Form Level 1'. No questions about the substantive asylum claim should be asked. One aim is to identify those applicants who can be removed to another country who will examine the asylum claim instead of the United Kingdom. This is known as a 'safe third country'. Screening an applicant will be concluded at this level only if the applicant's claimed nationality, identity and route to the UK are supported by a passport and a ticket, and there is no possibility of excluding the applicant on safe third country grounds. Some applicants also undergo level 2 screening interviews, which is where a decision is made as to whether the applicant has complied with Nationality, Immigration and Asylum Act (NIAA) 2002 s55(1).

1.69   Usually on the same day as the initial claim for asylum, the applicant (and dependants) will be fingerprinted and photographed.

Fingerprinting[68]

1.70   Fingerprints may be taken from an asylum-seeker and any dependants if an asylum claim is made.[69] Fingerprints may not be taken from a child under 16 unless a parent, guardian or responsible adult is present.[70] The police and immigration officers have a power to arrest

---

68 IAA 1999 ss141–144. The Immigration (PACE Codes of Practice No 2 and Amendment) Direction 2000 governs the fingerprinting procedures.

69 IAA 1999 s141(1).

70 IAA 1999 s141(3).

without a warrant anyone who claims asylum and refuses to supply fingerprints. The fingerprints may be held on a computerised central database and circulated to other EEA member states.[71] The fingerprints should usually be destroyed after ten years or within a month of the grant of indefinite leave to remain but some could be held permanently.[72] A refusal of fingerprinting could prejudice the asylum claim. Fingerprinting takes place at ports or at the Asylum Screening Unit (ASU) interview.

1.71   An 'Application Registration Card' (ARC) will be issued. This is a plastic card the same size as a credit card. It includes the applicant's photograph and is endorsed with a prohibition on employment. A permanent Home Office reference number is issued.[73]

1.72   The applicant will also be assessed for eligibility for NASS support. A second 'Screening Form Level 2' form is completed.[74] If it is accepted that the applicant made his or her application for asylum 'as soon as reasonably practicable after arrival' then he or she will be given an endorsed 'Grant Letter' which will facilitate access to emergency accommodation and should be attached to the NASS application form.

1.73   If the ASU is very busy, full screening at level 2 will not take place, and the applicant will be told to return later (usually one week later). Until a full screening has taken place and a decision under NIAA 2002 s55 has been made, the applicant can access emergency accommodation under IAA 1999 s98 from the voluntary sector suppliers, and he or she will be given an endorsed letter which confirms this.

1.74   There are two further possible screening interviews: level 3 and level 4. Level 3 interviews are less structured than level 1 and 2 interviews and enable the interviewing officer to challenge an applicant's credibility. If the applicant is disbelieved he or she should be told this and given an opportunity to expand or clarify matters.

1.75   Level 4 interviews are conducted if at any time during earlier screening interviews it is considered that an immigration or criminal offence might have occurred. The interview is conducted under PACE.[75]

---

71 See para 1.77 below.

72 IAA 1999 s143.

73 Older asylum claimants may still have a 'Standard Acknowledgement Letter' – SAL 1 or SAL 2. The Home Office have stated that these will be replaced by ARCs, but no timetable for this is available.

74 At the time of writing NIAA 2002 s55 level 2 interviews were under review.

75 Police and Criminal Evidence Act 1984.

1.76   The Legal Services Commission has agreed to finance legal representatives' attendance at screening interviews involving unaccompanied minors and those suffering a 'mental incapacity'. Where there is a possibility of a level 4 interview under PACE being conducted, it may be possible to get authority for legal representation under the Legal Help scheme. Otherwise, no funding is available. The applicant should be given a copy of the notes of the screening interview(s).

Removal to a 'safe third country'[76]

1.77   If an asylum applicant has travelled through a 'safe third country' he or she may be returned to that country without consideration of the asylum claim and will have very limited rights of appeal against the removal directions.[77] For port applicants, the decision is usually made at the port in the initial interview with the applicant. The decision is made by the Home Office in 'in-country' cases. The asylum-seeker can only apply for judicial review if the country is not one which is deemed to be safe, and if it can be shown that the country is not 'safe', for example, that it might return the applicant to his or her country of origin, or if he or she has close relatives living in the UK. The Dublin II Regulation 2003,[78] to which the UK is a signatory, is based on the principle that asylum applicants should have their claim considered in the first EU country that they reach. An EEA member state is automatically treated as a safe third country.[79]

1.78   An asylum-seeker may appeal on limited grounds in relation to a third country removal under IAA 1999 ss11 or 12. If that appeal is unsuccessful, there may be a judicial review or appeal under IAA 1999 s65 on Human Rights Convention grounds.

Temporary admission and detention

1.79   A person liable to detention or detained under IA 1971 Sch 2 para 16 above may, under written authority of an immigration officer, be

76 IAA 1999 s11.
77 IAA 1999 s12(1).
78 This came into force on 1 September 2003 and replaced the Dublin Convention – the Convention determining the state responsible for examining applications for asylum lodged in one of the member states of the European Communities, signed in Dublin on 15 June 1990 (ratified by the UK and all member states).
79 IAA 1999 s12(1)(a).

temporarily admitted to the UK without being detained or be released from detention; but this shall not prejudice a later exercise of the power to detain him.[80]

1.80   When an asylum claim is made at the port, the immigration officer will consider whether to grant 'temporary admission', or whether to detain the applicant under IA 1971 Sch 2 para 16 pending a decision on the asylum claim. Detention should be a last resort, to be considered where there are doubts about the asylum applicant's identity or a fear that he or she may abscond. UNHCR Guidelines[81] state that as a general principle asylum-seekers should not be detained and there is a presumption against detention. Detention appears to be used mostly in relation to single adult males and the male head of household, with some nationalities more commonly detained than others. Families can be detained at Harmondsworth and Oakington Detention Centre (see para 1.90 below). At the time of writing it is usual practice for immigration officers to grant asylum applicants temporary admission, documented by form IS96. However, this may change, if the arrangements for Reception and Removal centres set out in the NIAA 2002 are introduced.

1.81   Temporary admission usually include restrictions preventing the asylum-seeker from working, as well as requirements about where he or she must live and to report to a specified immigration office or police station.[82] A breach of these conditions can lead to detention (and withdrawal of support). In order to be granted temporary admission, the asylum-seeker must usually provide an address in the UK, although this can be an address provided by NASS.

1.82   The IAA 1999 provides for regulations (which must be laid before and approved by Parliament) prohibiting asylum-seekers from living in certain parts of the UK as a condition of their temporary admission. Such regulations could also require asylum-seekers to live, for example, at accommodation provided under IAA 1999 s4 and prohibit them from leaving that accommodation at certain times or at all. The regulations[83] may, among other things, provide for the inclusion of provisions:

(a) prohibiting residence in one or more particular areas;
(b) requiring the person concerned to reside in accommodation

---

80   IA 1971 Sch 2 para 21(1).
81   UNHCR's Guidelines on applicable Criteria and Standards relating to the Detention of Asylum-seekers, 1999.
82   IA 1971 Sch 2 para 21(2A).
83   At the time of writing, no regulations have yet been laid before Parliament.

> provided under section 4 of the Immigration and Asylum
> Act 1999 and prohibiting him from being absent from that
> accommodation except in accordance with the restrictions
> imposed on him . . .[84]

1.83 When a person subject to immigration control applies for asylum 'in-country', there is a risk that the conditions of any current leave to enter or remain in the UK may be varied, the leave may be curtailed or the applicant treated as an illegal entrant. Apart from those nationalities on the Oakington list and those being 'fast tracked', temporary admission or release is normally granted, although there is the power to detain under the IA 1971.

1.84 Asylum-seekers and their dependants may be held in removal centres such as Campsfield, or in ordinary prisons such as Holloway. The Home Office describes the regime in removal centres as less restrictive than a prison. The IAA 1999 extended the use of detention of asylum-seekers, and the routine bail hearings contained in Part III of the IAA 1999 have never been introduced and have now been repealed by the NIAA 2002. Bail can be applied for, and public funding is available to make bail applications.[85]

1.85 Temporary admission, which is evidenced by form IS96, is not the same as leave to enter. The Home Office has suggested that it is a form of 'licence' to be in the UK. Whether temporary admission amounts to 'lawful presence' in the UK affects the question of whether nationals of north African countries, Turkey, Poland, Cyprus and countries which have ratified the European Social Charter are eligible for benefits and housing.[86]

Bail

1.86 There have been a number of government pronouncements over the years that detention will only be authorised where there is no alternative. The UNHCR take the view that detention of asylum-seekers is inherently undesirable. Despite this the number of people being detained is increasing and now also includes minors whose age is disputed or who appear to be vulnerable. Bail can be applied for by anyone who is detained under immigration powers. If someone is

---

84 IA 1971 Sch 2 para 21(2B) as amended by IAA 1999 Sch 14 para 62.
85 See 'Challenging Immigration Detention – a best practice guide', Emily Burnham, ILPA, The Law Society and Bail for Immigration Detainees, October 2003.
86 See chapter 2.

currently serving a prison sentence bail cannot be obtained using immigration procedures.

1.87   The Immigration Service policy on detention and temporary release used to be set out in chapter 38 of the Service's Operation Enforcement Manual. This is no longer available on the Home Office website although a section of it is in the ILPA/Law Society/Bail for Immigration Detainees best practice guide.[87]

1.88   Chief Immigration Officers (CIOs) have the power to grant bail subject to sureties. This is rarely used, due to the high level of sureties demanded by the Immigration Service. Alternatively, bail can be applied for from an immigration adjudicator. An application for bail has to be submitted using the correct form fully completed. The Immigration Appellate Authority (IAA) guidelines on bail (May 2003) state that a hearing will be listed within three days of submission of the form. Although the bail application form includes space for sureties' details, it is not essential to have a surety.

1.89   If bail by either the CIO or the IAA is granted it is usually subject to residence and reporting conditions. If bail is refused there is no prohibition on further applications being made although it is advisable to be able to identify a change of circumstances to increase the chances of bail being granted. If bail is refused a written notice of the decision will be given including the reasons for refusal.[88] NASS Policy Bulletin 64 describes NASS's approach to support for an asylum-seeker leaving detention or who is granted bail.

Oakington[89]

1.90   Some adults who apply for asylum at the port of entry are detained, with (or without) their families, including young children, at Oakington detention centre, a former military barracks in Cambridgeshire. When the IAA 1999 was debated in Parliament, it was initially understood that Oakington was to be established under section 4 of that Act. This empowers the Home Secretary to provide for facilities for asylum-seekers with temporary admission or who are released from

---

87   'Challenging Immigration Detention – a best practice guide', Emily Burnham, ILPA, The Law Society and Bail for Immigration Detainees, October 2003.

88   It is strongly recommended that guidance is sought from either a specialist adviser or the BID/ILPA/Law Society/BID best practice guide before submitting an application.

89   See chapter 4, para 4.47.

detention. The Home Office later stated that detention at Oakington would be under existing powers contained in the IA 1971. In law and practice, Oakington constitutes a detention centre although the Home Office still refers to it as a 'reception centre'.

1.91   Detention at Oakington is initially for a short period of about seven to ten days to enable an interview and an accelerated initial decision. Immigration advice is available at the site from the Immigration Advisory Service and the Refugee Legal Centre before and after the substantive interview. Other advisers can also be funded to advise individuals. After a period of detention, the possible outcomes are:

- grant of refugee status (humanitarian protection, or discretionary leave);
- refusal of asylum;
- grant of temporary admission or transfer to another detention centre while the IND further considers the application (or while any appeal is pending).

1.92   If asylum is refused, the applicant may appeal, leave the UK voluntarily, or be removed from the UK. If the asylum-seeker is granted temporary admission pending a first asylum decision or appeal, he or she may apply for NASS support. Voluntary sector reception assistants are on site at Oakington to assist the applicant in making appropriate support arrangements.

Referral of asylum-seekers to reception assistants

1.93   Voluntary sector organisations are funded by NASS to provide emergency accommodation for new asylum applicants while a claim for asylum support is being considered. The immigration officer at the port should refer an asylum applicant and any dependants who are in need of support to a voluntary sector reception assistant who acts as an agent for NASS and can arrange 'temporary support' under IAA 1999 s98.[90] A similar procedure applies to new 'in-country' applicants who are destitute and homeless and who make their application for asylum promptly.[91] See chapter 3, para 3.137 for further details of the role of reception assistants.

1.94   Temporary support includes emergency accommodation pending

---

90   See appendix F for list of one-stop services where voluntary sector reception assistants are employed.

91   NIAA 2002 s55.

a decision about eligibility for full asylum support. The reception assistants should assist asylum-seekers to obtain resources by putting them in touch with relatives or relevant services and helping them to complete an application for asylum support where necessary.[92]

1.95   Where an asylum-seeker has a disability or special need, NASS should also make a referral to social services. There is some dispute as to where the dividing line in providing for disabled asylum-seekers falls. The notes which form a Schedule to the Asylum Support Regulations suggest that NASS will provide support to meet needs related to a disability. For further discussion on the local authority/NASS division of responsibility in relation to community care see chapter 6.

1.96   The Court of Appeal has confirmed that social services have a duty to carry out a community care assessment and assist in cases where the need for residential accommodation does not arise solely as a result of destitution, or where the applicant has other community care needs.[93]

Asylum questionnaires, interviews and 'non-compliance'

1.97   Usually an asylum-seeker who applies at a port will be called back to the port at a later date for an asylum interview. If no substantive interview is carried out initially, the immigration officer issues a 'statement of evidence form' (SEF) previously known as a 'self-completion questionnaire' or 'political asylum questionnaire', which the applicant has to return within a short period, currently ten working days. In some ports the asylum-seeker may have a substantive interview on arrival or soon after arrival, depending on interpreting facilities. Ten days is a short period for an asylum applicant who has not had a substantive interview to get help to complete the SEF in English and return it with all supporting documents, particularly if he or she has been sent to an area where interpreters and immigration advisers are in short supply. The Home Office has discretion to extend the period but this is rarely used. At the same time, the asylum applicant usually has to complete a 'statement of additional grounds' setting out any other reasons, including under the Human Rights Act 1998, why he or she should be permitted to remain in the UK.

1.98   An asylum-seeker who applies 'in-country' may be interviewed

92   See chapter 3, para 3.143 onwards.
93   *R v Wandsworth LBC ex p O* (2000) 3 CCLR 237, CA. See further para 7.53.

immediately or may be given or sent a SEF, which again must be completed and returned within a short period, currently ten working days.

1.99   It is Home Office practice to allow applicants to be accompanied at the substantive interview by a representative. However, the Legal Services Commission no longer fund a legal representative or independent interpreter unless the applicant is a child, is mentally incapacitated, there is a possibility that the applicant will be interviewed under caution as an illegal entrant, where it is alleged that the applicant may pose a threat to national security or if the applicant is subjected to fast track processes. The Home Office have introduced a protocol[94] for representatives attending interviews in which it is stated that the representative should not intervene during the interview. Instead, the representative is asked to wait until the end of the interview to inform the interviewing officer of any concerns and ask for a note to be made, for example, if the interview was not conducted properly or the interpreting was inadequate. Obviously, the representative should not follow this request if the interview is being conducted inadequately. The asylum applicant is entitled to a copy of the asylum interview record or notes. The Immigration Service sends interview notes or questionnaires completed at the port to the IND which makes the substantive decision on the claim in the same way as for an 'in-country' applicant.

1.100   The government has stated that after the substantive interview the asylum applicant has a limited period, currently seven days, to submit any further evidence.[95] In practice, no time is usually allowed if a completed SEF has been returned.

1.101   In January 2001 the press reported that as many as 40 per cent of asylum claims were being refused on the grounds of technical 'non-compliance', that is, alleged failure to submit the SEF within the time limit. In many of these cases the SEF had been submitted within the time limit but the Home Office had not linked it to the correct file. In other cases the applicant may be unable to comply due to other difficulties such as language barriers. Erroneous non-compliance cases are no longer a major issue, but may still arise and are usually overturned on appeal.

1.102   Procedures for asylum applications are subject to change. Eventually it is intended that all asylum-seekers will have to attend an induction centre for up to 14 days to undergo identity screening and health

94   Published at http://www.ind.homeoffice.gov.uk/default.asp?PageId=3328.
95   HC Written Answers cols 263–264, Barbara Roche MP, 16 March 2000.

checks before being dispersed elsewhere. At present this is only operated to a limited extent in Dover. Before being dispersed applicants
will be given a SEF for self-completion or interviewed. They will not
be provided with legal advice but will be inducted into the application
procedure and access to support. There is nothing to prevent a legal
adviser being instructed at this stage.

Favourable and unfavourable decisions

What is the 'date of determination' of the asylum claim?

1.103   The 'date of determination' is crucial to those advising about welfare
entitlements because the right to receive asylum or interim support
ends after a prescribed period beginning with the date of determination. The date also affects entitlement to social security benefits and
the time limits for an asylum appeal.[96] In simple terms, an asylum-
seeker remains an asylum-seeker, entitled to asylum or interim
support under IAA 1999 Part VI until he or she receives a decision
refusing a grant of refugee status with full reasons for the refusal, or
an appeal decision. There is a different test of date of determination
for asylum-seekers who lose entitlement to social security benefits
after a negative asylum decision (see chapter 2).

1.104   The definition of when a claim is determined for the purposes of
support is due to be amended but at the time of writing, this is provided under Part VI of the IAA 1999, section 94(3)[97] states:

> (3) A claim for asylum shall be determined at the end of such period
>   beginning –
>   (a) on the day on which the Secretary of State notifies the
>   claimant of his decision on the claim, or
>   (b) if the claimant has appealed against the Secretary of State's
>   decision, on the day on which the appeal is disposed of, as
>   may be prescribed.
> (4) An appeal is disposed of when it is no longer pending for the
>   purposes of the Immigration Acts or the Special Immigration
>   Appeals Commission Act 1997.

1.105   The prescribed period is 21/28 days beginning with the date of the
notice for the purposes of support under both the AS Regs and the
Interim Regs. The determination must be in writing and if it is posted

---

96 See chapter 2, para 2.98.
97 As amended by NIAA 2002.

either to the asylum-seeker or his or her representative, 'it is to be taken to have been received by the asylum-seeker on the second day after the day on which it was posted'.[98]

1.106 NIAA 2002 s104 provides:

(1) An appeal under section 82(1) is pending during the period –
   (a) beginning when it is instituted, and
   (b) ending when it is finally determined, withdrawn or abandoned (or when it lapses under section 99).
(2) An appeal under section 82(1) is not finally determined for the purposes of subsection (1)(b) while a further appeal or an application under section 101 (2) –
   (a) has been instituted and is not yet finally determined, withdrawn or abandoned, or
   (b) may be brought (ignoring the possibility of an appeal out of time with permission).

Grant of asylum or other immigration status

1.107 An asylum-seeker who is granted refugee status, humanitarian protection, discretionary leave or leave outside the immigration rules may not receive accurate documents granting refugee or other immigration status until some time after 'the date of determination'. In such cases they may be eligible for community care help from local authorities (see chapter 6). Tactics for ensuring that social security benefits are processed as soon as possible are discussed in chapter 2.

The concession for asylum seeking families

1.108 On 24 October 2003 the Home Office announced a concession which effectively gave an amnesty to some asylum applicants. The 'amnesty' only applies to asylum applicants who satisfy the following criteria:

- the application for asylum must have been made before 2 October 2000; and
- the applicant must have at least one child in the United Kingdom who is still aged under 18 years and who has been living here since 2 October 2000; and
- no decision has been made on the initial asylum application; or
- the case is under appeal; or

98 IAA 1999 s94(9).

- the appeal rights have been exhausted, but removal from the UK has not been effected.

1.109   The concession will not apply to principal applicants or any of their dependants who:

- have committed a criminal offence in the UK; or
- have had an anti-social behaviour order or sex offender order made; or
- have made (or attempted to make) multiple asylum applications in more than one identity; or
- have travelled to the UK through a safe European country and could thus be sent back to that European country in order to have the asylum application assessed there;
- present a security risk; or
- are excluded from the protection of the Refugee Convention under Article 1F that is:
  - have committed a crime against peace, or a war crime against humanity;
  - have committed a serious non-political crime outside the UK prior to coming here;
  - are guilty of acts contrary to the purposes and principles of the United Nations; or
- whose presence in the UK is not conducive to the public good.

1.110   Asylum-seekers and their dependants who qualify under the concession will be granted indefinite leave to remain. On announcing the concession the Home Office stated that they expected to deal with all those eligible by April 2004, but this has not occurred. The process is that the Home Office will write to those who are eligible for leave to remain under the concession and send a questionnaire to be completed. Those eligible will be expected to withdraw any outstanding applications and appeals. This may have family reunion implications for those who might have expected to be recognised as refugees. Although initially, the Home Office asked that applicants should not write directly, some families who might benefit under the concession have not been contacted. If in doubt, an application should be made for consideration under the concession.[99]

---

99   The Home Office ILR integration project will confirm if an individual is being considered under the family concession. Contact: ILRIP@homeoffice.gsi.gov.uk.

Refugee status

1.111 Where an asylum applicant is recognised as a refugee under the Refugee Convention, he or she will receive a decision letter giving indefinite leave to enter or remain (ILR) in the UK. The document is currently in form ICD 0725.[100] A UK residence permit endorsed on an Immigration Status Document (number ACD.2161) will be issued to the applicant and to his or her dependants.[101] The Refugee Convention provides for recognised refugees to have civil rights and duties such as rights to work or receive welfare provision on the same terms as UK nationals, eg, refugees qualify for student grants on the same terms as home students without the need to reside in the UK for a qualifying period.

1.112 It would be incompatible with the grant of refugee status for the refugee to travel with his or her own national passport. He or she can apply to the Home Office for a Refugee Convention travel document, which is an entitlement under the Refugee Convention.

1.113 If a refugee is receiving interim support or asylum support, the support will end after a period of 28 days from the date the determination is received (see paragraph 1.24 above and chapter 3). The exception is where the Home Office appeals against an appeal decision, in which case support should continue.

1.114 At the time of writing refugees can claim backdated social security benefits for the whole period from their claim for asylum until their grant of refugee status.[102] They only have 28 days from the date of the Home Office decision in which to make the claim for backdated income support, as well as housing benefit and council tax benefit if appropriate.[103] Also, refugees can still claim backdated child benefit and child tax credit (see chapter 2).

Humanitarian protection and discretionary leave to remain

1.115 The system for granting leave to enter or remain outside the immigration rules on an exceptional basis has changed significantly. Prior to

---

100 Previously known as GEN 23.
101 Immigration Status Documents were introduced from 15 March 2004.
102 IAA 1999 s123. The Asylum and Immigration (Treatment of Claimants, etc) Act 2004 proposes to abolish this right in relation to means-tested benefits.
103 See further chapter 2, para 2.136.

1 April 2003, an asylum-seeker who was not recognised as a refugee under the Refugee Convention criteria may have been granted exceptional leave to enter or remain (ELR) in the UK outside the immigration rules. This has now been replaced by two different types of leave, known as 'humanitarian protection' (HP) and 'discretionary leave' (DL).

1.116   HP is leave granted to a person who would, if removed from the UK, face in the country of return a serious risk to life or person arising from a death penalty, unlawful killing, or torture or degrading treatment or punishment. This reflects the UK's obligations under article 2 (right to life) and article 3 (prohibition of torture) of the Human Rights Convention and protocol 6 to the Convention (against the death penalty). A person who qualifies for HP will usually, but not always, be granted leave for three years and may apply for settlement after three years. Settlement is not granted automatically: the applicant is subjected to an active review of his or her application and settlement will only be granted where the circumstances continue to justify further leave. Those granted HP can access public funds and are entitled to work. A UK residence permit will be endorsed in the applicant's national passport. If the applicant does not have one, this will be endorsed on an Immigration Status Document (number ACD.2152 or ACD.2150 for those granted HP on non-asylum grounds).[104]

1.117   HP will not be granted to those who meet criteria for exclusion from the UK, including where the person's presence is not conducive to the public good for criminal or security reasons. Such cases may qualify for discretionary leave.

1.118   DL can be granted in a number of circumstances:

- Where removal would breach article 8 of the Human Rights Convention (the right to respect for private and family life). In marriage cases, the standard period of leave granted is two years, in line with the qualifying period for settlement in marriage cases within the immigration rules. In other article 8 cases, the standard period granted is three years.
- Where removal would lead to torture, inhuman or degrading treatment or punishment where the claimant is excluded from HP. The standard period granted is six months. This period applies to the first grant and any subsequent grants of leave.
- Where removal would breach article 3 of the Human Rights Convention for health reasons or other severe humanitarian factors in

104 Immigration Status Documents were introduced from 15 March 2004.

the country of return (such as the absence of food or shelter). The threshold for this category is very high. The usual period granted is three years.

- In cases of unaccompanied asylum seeking children, where there are inadequate reception arrangements in their own country. The usual period of leave granted is three years or until the child reaches 18 years of age, whichever is shorter. This is under review, and is likely to change in the near future. In particular, the Home Office is actively considering the removal of refused minors from certain countries.

- Where there are individual circumstances, which do not meet any of the categories above, but which are so compelling that it is considered appropriate to grant some form of leave. This will be rare. The standard period of leave granted is three years.

1.119   DL will not be granted merely because there is no practical means of removing the person from the UK. DL may be granted for a shorter period of time depending on the circumstances of a case. Applications for an extension of DL will normally be subject to an active review. Only after a minimum of six years of DL will a person become eligible for settlement. Any time spent in prison does not count towards settlement. Those granted DL will have access to public funds and entitled to work. A UK residence permit will be endorsed in the applicant's national passport. If the applicant does not have one, this will be endorsed on an Immigration Status Document (number ACD.2373).[105]

1.120   Those people granted ELR in the past may normally apply for settlement once they have completed four years on this status.

Leave outside the Rules

1.121   The Home Office has retained the discretion to permit a person to remain in the UK even though he or she does not meet the criteria of the immigration rules or of the HP or DL policies. This could be when an individual is granted leave to remain under other policies outside the rules. This is rare.

1.122   If any form of leave is granted, this will be endorsed either in the person's passport (unless they have been recognised as a refugee) or, if there is no passport available, then on an 'immigration status

---

105 Immigration Status Documents were introduced from 15 March 2004.

document'.[106] In addition, the person will be given a letter confirming the type of status granted, and the implications of it.

Travel documents

1.123   Recognised refugees can apply for a Refugee Convention travel document (dark blue). Those granted other forms of leave to remain can apply for a Home Office travel document (brown), but this is only issued in limited circumstances. New criteria for the issuing of travel documents applied from the 27 March 2003.

1.124   Any person granted HP, DL or ELR in the past now has to show that they have been 'formally and unreasonably' refused a passport by their own national authorities. The Home Office will expect to see evidence of this in the form of a letter from the relevant Embassy or High Commission. Where permission to stay was granted on the basis of a fear of the authorities in the home country, or where the Home Office know that a person cannot access consular facilities, this requirement will be waived.

1.125   In addition, for people granted limited leave to remain, a travel document will only be issued if:

1) The country or countries the person wishes to visit, including any countries they may need to pass through in transit, are specified. The document will be valid only for travel for those countries;
2) Travel is necessary for one of the following four reasons:
   a) Essential employment/business reasons.
   b) Exceptional compassionate circumstances which will include:
      i)   serious illness of a close relative;
      ii) funeral of close relative;
      iii) medical treatment.
   c) Study reasons, that is organised educational visits; or courses of further and higher education.
   d) Religious reasons or other reasons of conscience for instance wishing to travel on pilgrimage.

1.126   The travel document is issued only for one year and is not valid for the country of origin.

1.127   People with HP, DL or ELR have leave to enter or remain in the UK so they are not 'persons subject to immigration control' excluded

---

106 Immigration Status Documents were introduced from 15 March 2004. See appendix D.

from benefits for the purposes of Part VI of the IAA 1999.[107] However-
er, they are subject to immigration control for ordinary immigration
law purposes, for example, HP, DL or ELR might be curtailed if they
return to the UK after a visit to their home country. Anyone with HP,
DL or ELR is entitled to work or receive social security benefits, housing and community care help on the same basis as a refugee. He or
she is entitled to income support and housing benefit backdated only
to the date of the grant of HP, DL or ELR, rather than the application.
This is because HP, DL or ELR is granted from the date of the Home
Office decision whereas the 'recognition' of refugee status dates back
to the original asylum application.

Leave 'in line'

1.128   If a child is born in the UK to parents with limited leave to enter or
remain in the UK such as HP, DL or ELR, he or she does not automatically become a British citizen by virtue of being born here. (A
separate application for leave to remain in line with the parents' leave
can be made if this is to the advantage of the child. Such leave would
usually be granted.) The immigration rules state that such a child
does not need to obtain leave to remain unless he or she is travelling
outside the UK and intends to return.[108] It has been suggested that
such a child is therefore not a person subject to immigration control
within the IAA 1999 s115(9) definition because he or she does not
need leave to enter or remain in the UK. Similarly, in a homelessness
application under the Housing Act 1996, such a child could be an
eligible person who could give the parent priority. Newly-arrived
dependants from outside the UK will need leave to enter until they are
granted leave in line with their sponsor. In either case, a local authority (social services) can be approached for housing and support under
Children Act 1989 s17 if there is a child in need and housing or
benefits have not been provided, because no such exclusion applies.

Cases where limited leave has expired

1.129   A person who has been granted limited leave to enter or remain in the
UK such as a spouse during the first year of marriage, a student, or

---

107 IAA 1999 s115(9)(a).
108 HC 395 paras 304–309.

someone with HP, DL or ELR can apply to the Home Office for such leave to be extended or varied. The application must be made before the leave expires in order to retain a right of appeal under IA 1971. These applicants have leave to stay in the UK (on the same terms as their previous leave) while the application is being considered. For example, if they previously had DL, they retain it until 28 days after a further decision is made.[109] Such applicants are not persons subject to immigration control (PSICs) within the meaning of IAA 1999 s115(9)(a). The letter with the original grant of leave and proof that they have applied for a variation in time (for example, a solicitor's letter) should be sufficient evidence to demonstrate that they have leave and that they retain any entitlement to social security benefits and housing as homeless people.

Indefinite leave to remain

1.130   Indefinite leave to remain (ILR), which is also known as 'settled status', 'settlement' or in ordinary English, 'permanent residence' can be granted in cases where the applicant had some other form of limited leave to enter or remain for a specified period. ILR is also granted to asylum-seekers who are recognised as refugees under the Refugee Convention.

Family reunion

1.131   If a husband or wife, or child under 18, who is outside the UK, wants to join someone who has been recognised as a refugee in the UK, he or she has a right to leave to enter or remain in the UK under the immigration rules, on proof of identity and of a relationship predating the asylum claim. Other members of an extended family may be granted leave to enter or remain if the relationship is recognised by the Home Office. This is not required by the Refugee Convention but is part of the 'principle of family unity' contained in the UNHCR Handbook's guidelines. If the marriage post-dates the grant of refugee status, the refugee may also need to consider the ordinary rules for a spouse who wants leave, for example, that he or she can be maintained and accommodated without recourse to public funds. In

109 See paragraph 1.24 above.

limited leave cases, there is no right to family reunion and it is difficult to achieve before the person has settlement. Family reunion can be applied for on Human Rights Convention grounds. The applicant would usually need to satisfy all the requirements of the immigration rules other than settlement. In exceptional compassionate circumstances the maintenance and accommodation rules may be waived. The family should be entitled to benefits and other welfare provision on arrival in the UK. In practice, the documentation may mistakenly include a condition prohibiting recourse to public funds. In such cases, it is advisable to refer them back to the port to amend it immediately.

Unfavourable decisions

Refusal of asylum

1.132   If the Home Office considers that the asylum-seeker does not meet the Refugee Convention criteria, a decision that asylum is refused ('the pre-decision letter') will be sent to the applicant and any legal representative. This may be dated some time before service, with a determination letter with reasons for the decision (see para 1.103 above). Alternatively, he or she may be advised of the decision at a Home Office/Immigration Service interview. Together with information about appeal rights, the applicant is given information about the impact of the decision on his or her financial support and the possibility of making a voluntary return to his or her country of origin. The appeal form (form N1) requires grounds to be lodged on both asylum and human rights bases.

1.133   Refusal of refugee status results in asylum support or interim support ending 21 days after the asylum determination being received (after allowing two days for delivery by first class post), unless the supported person appeals or makes an ECHR article 3 claim.[110] Families continue to receive support as long as there is a dependent child under 18 in the UK.

1.134   Usually, the asylum-seeker has 10 working days from the date of receiving the determination within which to appeal. The time limit is five working days for those in detention. Some cases are 'fast tracked'. These are applications from specific countries where the applicant is detained in Harmondsworth detention centre. The appeal has to be

110 IAA 1999 s94.

lodged within two days[111] and heard within two days. The LSC has set up a duty solicitor scheme to represent applicants processed through the fast track. Only those solicitors on the scheme can be paid out of public funds.

1.135   There is no longer a right of appeal from within the UK or those whose asylum or human rights claims the Home Office certifies as 'clearly unfounded'.[112] These are known as 'non-suspensive appeals'. NIAA 2002 s94(3) sets out a list of safe countries from which applications will normally be 'clearly unfounded'. The list can be added to. In addition, an application from any country can be certified as 'clearly unfounded'. An appeal can only be lodged once the applicant has left the UK and must be lodged within 28 days.

1.136   'In-country' applicants may have any existing leave to enter or remain in the UK curtailed. If the asylum-seeker enters an appeal, the immigration service will consider whether to detain or grant temporary admission. If temporary admission is granted, a form IS96 is issued. If temporary admission is refused, he or she will be detained under IA 1971.

1.137   Directions for the removal of the applicant from the UK may be issued by the Immigration Service. Unless the case is certified as 'clearly unfounded' the effect of an appeal against a refusal of asylum is that no removal directions may be given and that any existing directions are suspended pending the determination of the appeal.[113]

Remedies

Appeals

1.138   Unless the applicant is in detention, when the time limit is five working days, there is usually a time limit of 10 working days (from receiving the determination containing reasons for refusal of refugee status) within which to appeal to the adjudicator. The other exception to this is those detained cases certified 'clearly unfounded', where the time limit is two working days. Time runs from the second day following the date of determination. If that appeal is unsuccessful there is a further appeal on a point of law to the Immigration Appeal Tribunal (IAT), with permission, on a point of law. Again, the time

---

111 The Immigration and Asylum Appeals (Fast Track Procedure) Rules 2003, para 6.
112 NIAA 2002 s94(2).
113 NIAA 2002 Sch 4 para 10.

limit is 10 working days, unless the appellant is in detention, when the time limit is five working days.

1.139   The law and procedure governing asylum and immigration appeals was overhauled by the NIAA 2002 which repealed the earlier scheme set out in IAA 1999 Part 4 and Sch 4. The scheme retains a one-stop appeal at which all arguments relating to removal and human rights must be raised. At the same time as being issued with a statement of evidence form (SEF) the applicant is served with a 'one-stop' notice. The applicant and dependants have 10 working days to serve a statement of additional grounds on the Home Office. This must include all their reasons for seeking to remain in the UK (including any asylum or Human Rights Act (HRA) 1998 reasons).

1.140   The intention is to prevent a series of appeals. If a person who has been refused asylum fails to raise HRA 1998 arguments at the appeal stage, he or she should not be allowed to raise them at a later stage. If the adjudicator dismisses the appeal, there is a further appeal to the IAT.[114] There may then be an application for judicial review or, in a limited number of cases, an appeal to the Court of Appeal.

1.141   The effect of an appeal to the adjudicator against a refusal of asylum in 'in-country' cases is that the appellant's leave and conditions of leave are extended (see paragraph 1.24 above). Port applicants are entitled to have temporary admission extended until their appeal is determined. Asylum support and interim support continue pending the appeal determination. An asylum-seeker who enters an appeal may be detained or granted temporary admission pending the appeal.

1.142   The Asylum and Immigration (Treatment of Claimants, etc) Act 2004 proposes further changes to the appeal scheme, including changes to the second tier of appeal to the Immigration Appeal Tribunal (from the adjudicator) and limitations on access to the higher courts. At the time of writing these changes (which are controversial) have not been finalised.

Removal directions

1.143   The circumstances in which a person who is not a British citizen may be removed from the UK are set out in IAA 1999 s10. A person who is subject to immigration control may be removed from the UK with no

---

114 The Asylum and Immigration (Treatment of Claimants, etc) Act 2004 proposes the abolition of the IAT. It is probable that it will be replaced with some form of High Court review.

right to appeal if he or she is a port applicant, or entered the UK as an illegal entrant or has breached a condition of limited leave. Before making any such directions, the Immigration Service should take the HRA 1998 and compassionate circumstances into consideration.[115]

Unsuccessful asylum appeals

1.144   Where an appeal to the adjudicator is unsuccessful, an application for permission to appeal to the IAT can be made on a point of law.[116] If the application for permission is refused, this decision can be challenged through an application to the High Court for statutory review.[117] This application is determined on the papers only, without a hearing, and the decision of the High Court is final. If permission to appeal to the IAT is granted, but the substantive appeal is dismissed, an asylum-seeker may be able to apply for permission to appeal to the Court of Appeal.[118] An asylum-seeker without a dependent child stops being treated as an 'asylum-seeker' for the purposes of receiving asylum or interim support 14 days after 'the day on which the appeal is disposed of'.[119] 'Appeal' includes any appeal to the Court of Appeal. Childless asylum-seekers who remain in the UK to pursue a judicial review or otherwise may be eligible for NASS 'hard cases' support provided under IAA 1999 s4.[120] Those who have a need for care and attention arising for a reason other than their destitution, for example, age or ill-health, may be entitled to community care help.[121] An asylum-seeker with a dependent child is classed as an 'asylum-seeker' entitled to receive asylum or interim support, for as long as the child is under 18 and in the UK, subject to the NIAA 2002 Sch 3 exclusions explained in chapter 6.[122]

Complaints

1.145   The main sources of complaint by immigration specialists on behalf of their clients are delay and poor decision-making. The IND Complaints Unit will not consider complaints about these issues; instead

115 HC 395 paras 395A–D, as amended.
116 NIAA 2002 s101(1).
117 NIAA 2002 s101(2).
118 NIAA 2002 s103.
119 IAA 1999 s94(3).
120 See chapter 3, para 3.291.
121 See chapter 6 and *R v Wandsworth LBC ex p O* (2000) 3 CCLR 237, CA.
122 IAA 1999 s94(3A).

it investigates formal complaints about the conduct of IND staff. Despite this, practitioners may find it helpful to make a formal complaint about delay as this can galvanise the particular caseworking group into making a decision.

1.146   If there is no response to complaints about delays, the asylum-seeker's MP could be asked to write to the Home Secretary. A further complaint can be made to the Parliamentary Ombudsman via the MP by completing an application form.[123] The Ombudsman upheld a complaint by Bosnian refugees who were prevented from travelling to see her dying mother or attending her funeral by delay in the processing of applications for travel documents and ILR. The IND made an ex gratia payment to cover the family's administrative costs and paid £750 for the distress caused.[124]

1.147   There have been successful judicial reviews of delay in decision-making in certain circumstances where there is substantial delay and real prejudice has resulted.[125] The High Court decided that the Home Office's delay was unlawful in a case where an asylum appeal had been allowed, but for over six months the IND had not issued documents confirming refugee status and indefinite leave to remain.

1.148   The Race Relations Act (RRA) 1976 has been amended by the Race Relations (Amendment) Act 2000 to make racial discrimination by government departments unlawful and impose a positive duty to promote racial equality. There is an exemption for immigration purposes which limits the definition of racial discrimination to cases of discrimination on grounds of race or colour only. However, the legislation does not make it unlawful for a relevant person to discriminate against another person on grounds of nationality or ethnic or national origins in carrying out immigration and nationality origins functions. The exemption of the Home Office from liability for race discrimination was controversial and so RRA 1976 s19E provides for the appointment of a person to monitor the operation of the exemption.

1.149   The IAA 1999 extended appeal rights to cover racial discrimination. The provision is maintained in the NIAA 2002 s84(1)(b) which provides for a right to appeal to the special adjudicator where the Home Office or immigration service has racially discriminated in a decision about a person's right to enter or remain in the UK. If racial

---

123 Office of the Parliamentary Commissioner for Administration, Mill Bank Tower, Mill Bank, London SW1P 4QP; tel: 0845 015 4033; email:opca-enquombudsman.org.uk.

124 Parliamentary Ombudsman Complaint C1141/00/95.

125 *R v Secretary of State for the Home Department ex p Mersin* CO/4433/99, 25 May 2000 (unreported).

discrimination is proven, a claim for damages can be made in the county court.

Rights and duties of asylum-seekers pending a decision

Monitoring and offences

1.150   IAA 1999 Part VI introduced a number of new criminal penalties connected to the provision of support. These are discussed in more detail in chapter 4 at para 4.141. There is some common ground between the responsibilities of an asylum-seeker in relation to the asylum claim and those which relate to the support claim. It may be an offence not to notify NASS of a change of address.[126] In the same way, a failure to notify the IND of a change of address may jeopardise the asylum claim, for example, it may prevent the applicant from responding to requests for further information and lead to a negative decision.

1.151   The 1999 Act also introduced further powers for information sharing and monitoring of asylum-seekers. These are discussed in chapter 4 at para 4.141.

Right to work

1.152   A long standing concession outside the immigration rules allowed an asylum-seeker permission to work if he or she was still awaiting a decision six months after the asylum application. A similar concession was extended to asylum applicants whose appeals were pending. The concession has been withdrawn, but there may be some older cases still pending where the permission to work has not been revoked. When an asylum-seeker's status changes (for example, if the asylum application is refused) the Immigration Service routinely revokes the permission to work. If permission had been given in the past then this can be restored.

1.153   On 22 July 2003 the Home Office confirmed that if an asylum application remained outstanding for over one year without a decision, there remained discretion to grant permission to work. Permission to work is usually only granted to the principal asylum-seeker. A dependant will need to show particular circumstances to justify a

126 See chapters 3 and 4 for rights to IAA 1999 Part VI support.

grant of the right to work, for example, he or she has a useful skill or the main applicant is unable to work.

1.154 Where the asylum-seeker has a job offer, permission may be granted during the first 12 months if the asylum-seeker has special skills, particularly those that are in short supply in the UK. In this case, consideration should be given to making an application under another category of the immigration rules, for example, work permits. The difficulties which asylum-seekers face in obtaining National Insurance numbers are discussed in chapter 2 at paras 2.121–2.126.

1.155 AIA 1996 s8 made it a criminal offence to employ anyone who does not have the right to work in the UK. It is a defence for the employer to show that he or she has obtained evidence of the right to work. AIA 1996 s8A requires the Home Secretary to issue a statutory 'code of practice' to advise employers how to comply with section 8 without discriminating on grounds of race. An amendment to section 8 introduced by NIAA 2002 s147 (see Commencement Order No 6) from 1 May 2004 limits the documents which satisfy the statutory defence that the employer has obtained evidence of the right to work so that a National Insurance number is no longer sufficient. New guidance has been issued to employers as to what evidence is acceptable in order to comply with section 8.[127]

1.156 Since AIA 1996 s8 was introduced, a number of asylum-seekers and other immigrants have complained that they believe they have been discriminated against when seeking employment. There is no explicit provision to make less favourable treatment on grounds of immigration status unlawful. Under RRA 1976 s4(1) racial discrimination in recruitment, whether in refusing to offer a job or in recruitment procedures, is unlawful.[128] Racial discrimination may be direct discrimination 'on racial grounds'[129] or indirect discrimination, applying a condition or requirement which an employer 'cannot show to be justifiable irrespective of the colour, race, nationality or ethnic or national origins of the person to whom it is applied'.[130] An employer who only applied the AIA 1996 s8 requirements to black staff would be directly discriminating. The Court of Appeal has decided that it is not

---

127 'Changes on the law on preventing illegal working: short guidance for United Kingdom employers' (Home Office, April 2004). See www.ind.homeoffice.gov.uk/default.asp?pageid=17.

128 The Commission for Racial Equality (CRE) provides advice and pursues complaints about race discrimination in the provision of services, see appendix G.

129 RRA 1976 s1(1)(a).

130 RRA 1976 s1(1)(b).

unlawful racial discrimination to ask all non-British or non-EEA citizens to produce evidence of the right to work.[131] Thus the requirement to produce a National Insurance number, for example, which indirectly discriminates against asylum-seekers, can be justified because of section 8 and other statutory requirements. This may be a potential area for HRA 1998 challenges.

Common problems

Legal advice and access to immigration advisers

1.157   Asylum-seekers are entitled to obtain immigration advice and representation from any source, but there is a shortage of competent advice. Part V of the IAA 1999 was introduced to protect asylum-seekers and other immigrants from unscrupulous advisers. It is an offence for anyone to provide immigration advice in the course of business, whether or not for profit unless he or she is exempted by or registered with the Immigration Services Commissioner,[132] or authorised to do so by a body such as the Law Society or the Bar Council.[133] Organisations advising about asylum support issues should ensure that they do not give advice on immigration issues unless they are registered or are exempted from doing so. The Asylum and Immigration (Treatment of Claimants, etc) Act 2004 will further limit access to public funds for asylum appeals.

1.158   The Immigration Advisory Service and the Refugee Legal Centre are funded by the Legal Services Commission (LSC) to provide legal advice and representation to asylum-seekers. The LSC also funds solicitors and other voluntary organisations to provide advice and controlled representation in asylum and immigration cases through exclusive contracting arrangements. Regulations introduced in March 2004 give greater control to the LSC over the number of hours an adviser can be paid for advising asylum applicants under the Legal Help and Controlled Legal Representation schemes.

Advice for those considering an asylum or article 3 claim

1.159   People in the UK who are making a claim for asylum or under article 3 of the Human Rights Convention, should be referred to an immi-

---

131 *Dhatt v McDonalds Hamburgers Ltd* (1991) IRLR 130, CA.

132 See Commissioner's website for code of practice and complaints procedure: www.oisc.org.uk.

133 IAA 1999 s84.

gration specialist. A destitute single adult who is subject to immigration control but is not an asylum-seeker is not entitled to benefits or other welfare provision unless he or she has community care needs.[134] Advisers should be cautious of proposing an asylum or article 3 claim as a solution to homelessness or the lack of any income. Although it may be a route to support for a temporary period, an inappropriate claim may lead to existing leave being terminated, detention or removal from the UK. An asylum claim could damage credibility in relation to any other Home Office application for leave to remain in the UK, for example, through HP or DL. With the widening of the European Union, it may be that a failed application for asylum in the UK will negatively effect an individual's ability to travel elsewhere within the EU. Alternatives to consider are a National Assistance Act 1948 application following *R v Wandsworth LBC ex p O*[135] and/or a HRA 1998 challenge (see para 3.287 below).

Immigration advice pending a decision or appeal

1.160 It is important for non-immigration specialists to be aware of the short deadlines for producing evidence in support of an asylum claim and the risk of a refusal of asylum on technical 'non-compliance' grounds. Without quick access to competent immigration advice, an asylum-seeker may be unable to present an application that demonstrates that refugee status, HP or DL should be granted. The short appeal deadlines and the fast tracking of certain appeals further reduce the chance of a fair consideration of the claim. Dispersal and/or difficulty financing travel to advisers may indirectly violate asylum-seekers' human rights by preventing them from effectively exercising their rights under the Refugee Convention or the various articles of the Human Rights Convention.

Contacting the Home Office

1.161 Non-immigration specialists should be cautious about contact with the IND because inappropriate contact may delay the processing of a claim or prejudice an application. It is appropriate for the client's immigration adviser to contact the IND rather than an adviser dealing with support only. The main public contact point is the Public Enquiry

---

134 IAA 1999 Part VI.
135 (2000) 3 CCLR 237, CA.

Office or Immigration and Nationality Enquiry Bureau (INEB).[136] In the past, it has been notoriously difficult to get a reply within a reasonable time or at all, but improvements have now been made, although the telephonists only have access to limited computer-held data. Local authorities, statutory agencies and MPs have dedicated contact numbers.

Documentation and problems with proving identity or age

1.162   IND documents are often misunderstood or rejected by council officers or other officials who are not trained in immigration law. If there is evidence that an asylum claim has been made, a local authority has a duty to provide emergency support under the Interim Regs reg 4[137] while further enquiries are being made. Although the Secretary of State has a duty to enquire into and establish age under IAA 1999 s94(7), social services may need to consider age to fulfil their duties under Children Act 1989 ss17 or 20. The Home Office can make a 'without prejudice' agreement to treat an asylum-seeker as a minor until it has concluded its enquiries.

1.163   If the applicant has no evidence of identity at all, a letter with a signed photo attached confirming that a solicitor is acting for the person in the photograph may ensure that the local authority makes a decision. Arguably, there is no legal requirement to provide this as a pre-condition of IAA 1999 Part VI support.

1.164   Immigration documents often contain mistakes relating to the applicant's name or date of birth. If these are contained in the final grant of refugee status, HP or DL, it may take some time for the Home Office to correct them, causing delay before the applicant can get access to benefits. If mistakes are not remedied, the applicant is likely to have difficulty getting a National Insurance number and may face accusations of fraud if the Home Office document is inconsistent with other documents. Therefore, any mistakes spotted before the final decision should be drawn to the Home Office's attention. A judicial review or complaint about IND delay in remedying mistakes could be considered where the applicant is prejudiced.

1.165   Limited evidence of identity, before or after an asylum decision, combined with short residence in the UK inhibits the ability to obtain a driving licence or bank account and interferes with other rights

136   See appendix G.
137   See further chapter 4, para 4.7 below.

which British nationals have. In the case of driving licences, where the asylum-seeker, refugee or person with ELR, HP or DL does not have the relevant identification documents, write to the Driving Vehicle Licensing Agency (DVLA), to ask the secretary of state to exercise discretion in the stipulation of acceptable documents.[138] The Home Office will usually return a passport to an applicant for the sole purpose of obtaining a driving license. In the case of other public authorities, there may be scope for a request to exercise discretion to accept more limited evidence of identity in view of the Human Rights Convention 'anti-discrimination' article 14 combined with other relevant articles, for example, if article 8 rights are being interfered with. Internal complaints procedures could be considered.

Variation of leave

1.166   If a person subject to immigration control with limited leave has applied to vary the original leave to enter or remain in the UK, he or she will not be issued with new documentation. However, he or she will have valid leave to enter/remain in the UK on the same terms as the original leave until the application has been processed (see paragraph 1.24). It may save time for the immigration representative to provide a letter explaining this if the local authority or Job Centre are in doubt.

'Mixed' families[139]

1.167   Members of the same family may have a mixture of immigration applications and decisions. A husband may be granted HP, DL or full refugee status but the wife or dependants who have arrived in the UK separately may have an outstanding asylum claim. It is worth checking the immigration documents to work out the status of each family member before advising about their potential support entitlements. One family member may be entitled to claim benefits or asylum support for the whole household. The question of 'mixed families' is discussed in more detail in the support chapters.

1.168   Where an asylum-seeker is granted HP or DL or in the past, ELR, the grant will include any dependent children. If those children reach 18 years of age after leave is granted, evidence of identity, relationship and that the parent has been granted HP, DL or ELR should be

138   Road Traffic Act 1988 s97(1).
139   See also chapter 2, para 2.84 and chapter 3, para 3.20.

accepted as evidence that the child also has leave in line and is not a person subject to immigration control for the purposes of IAA 1999 s115. On reaching 18 the child does not need a separate document to prove immigration status and is entitled to claim social security and other benefits.

Common Home Office documents

Letter of appointment at the ASU

1.169   Delays in issuing ARCs (see below) have meant that some asylum-seekers only have a letter inviting them to an interview about the asylum claim. If Home Office staff or immigration officers do not have time to establish identity at the port, the asylum-seeker will receive an appointment to visit the asylum screening unit (ASU) or substantive asylum interview at a later date.

IS96

1.170   A form indicating a grant of temporary admission. It will usually give the asylum-seeker's full name and date of birth and the date when temporary admission ends. It is given to those who do not have any other valid leave to enter or remain in the UK such as port applicants and illegal entrants.

Application Registration Cards (ARCs)

1.171   These are credit card-sized plastic cards, with the applicant's photograph and other identity details, as well as biodata stored on a magnetic strip. They are usually endorsed with a statement that the individual does not have a right to work. ARCs are issued to new applicants for asylum.

Standard Acknowledgement Letter (SAL 1)

1.172   SALs are no longer issued, having been replaced by ARCs. However, many long-standing applicants still have SALs. The SAL 1 shows that the asylum-seeker has applied for asylum at the port of entry. If he or she has not satisfied the immigration officer as to identity, the form will state 'claims to be' before the name of the applicant. It will have a photograph of the asylum-seeker attached to the front of it and the photographs of any dependants attached to the back. A SAL 1 or SAL

2 shows that the Home Office has recorded a claim for asylum. It is generally accepted by other bodies as evidence of identity. Prior to 3 April 2000, a SAL 1 was treated as evidence that the asylum-seeker claimed asylum 'on arrival' and was entitled to income support. In practice, an asylum-seeker may have claimed 'on arrival' for benefit purposes but have a SAL 2 and vice versa. It is usual for the asylum-seeker to surrender his or her SAL when a favourable or unfavourable decision on the claim has been made.

SAL 2

1.173 An asylum-seeker who has applied for asylum 'in-country' should be given this. For asylum-seekers who arrived in the UK on or after 3 April 2000, the distinction between a SAL 1 and SAL 2 has no significance for the purposes of entitlement to benefits.

Statement of evidence form (SEF)

1.174 A self-completion questionnaire for the asylum-seeker to give details of the ground(s) on which he or she is applying for asylum.

Immigration status documents

1.175 • ICD.0725: a grant of refugee status.
   • ACD.2151: Immigration status document endorsed with UK residence permit issued to those granted refugee status and their dependants.
   • ACD.2152: Immigration status document endorsed with UK residence permit issued to those asylum applicants granted Humanitarian Protection and their dependants where a national passport is not available.
   • ACD.2373: Immigration status document endorsed with UK residence permit issued to those asylum applicants granted Discretionary Leave and their dependants, where a national passport is not available.
   • ACD.2150: Immigration status document endorsed with UK residence permit issued to those granted leave to remain other than on asylum grounds, without a national passport.

Benefits

continued

Introduction

2.1 Most asylum-seekers are not entitled to state benefits because successive legislation has removed their rights to such benefits and, instead, substituted forms of support specifically for them. A few asylum-seekers remain entitled to state benefits and, if they qualify, they will receive those benefits instead of the specific forms of asylum support detailed in chapters 3 and 4. Asylum-seekers who are granted refugee status or humanitarian protection/discretionary leave to remain (HP/DLR) cease to qualify for asylum support and become entitled to state benefits. This chapter covers:

- those asylum-seekers and other persons subject to immigration control who qualify for state benefits;
- the issue of who can claim benefit for whom, and the effect of the receipt of state benefits by one household member on the support available to another. Asylum-seekers may belong to a household where some members qualify for state benefits and some do not;
- the circumstances in which benefit entitlement for asylum-seekers ends;
- steps to be taken by asylum-seekers who are granted status.

Entitlement and disqualification

The legal framework

2.2 The remaining rights of asylum-seekers and other immigrants to state benefits come from three main sources:

- domestic social security legislation,
- European Community (EC) law,[1] and
- reciprocal agreements[2] entered into by the UK and other countries.

These provisions should be interpreted in the light of the Human Rights Act (HRA) 1998, which incorporates the European Convention on Human Rights (ECHR). The UK has ratified the European Convention on Social and Medical Assistance (ECSMA) and the

---

1   EC Council Reg 1408/71 co-ordinates social security systems within the European Economic Area (EEA), prohibiting discrimination against EEA nationals who are exercising their rights to freedom of movement to work. This allows certain EEA nationals and their family members to qualify for benefits in the UK on the same basis as British nationals. See para 2.30 onwards.

2   Department for Work and Pensions (DWP) Overseas Benefits Section, tel: 0191 218 7777 for details of reciprocal agreements.

Council of Europe Social Charter (CESC), which are reflected in domestic legislation.[3]

2.3   The principal relevant social security statutes are the Social Security Contributions and Benefits Act 1992 (for rules of entitlement), the Social Security Administration Act 1992 and the Social Security Act 1998 (for the administration of the scheme). The bulk of social security law, however, is contained in secondary legislation and the detailed rules relating to each benefit are contained in regulations. Decisions of the social security commissioners are binding on the decision-maker and form part of social security law.

2.4   Social security law restricts the availability of state benefits to people who come to the UK from abroad. This is achieved in the following way. First, all claimants of means-tested benefits (including UK citizens) must satisfy the 'habitual residence test' (HRT), which includes a requirement that a claimant has a 'right to reside' (RTR).[4] Those who do not satisfy the HRT are classified as 'persons from abroad'. Second, and additionally, claimants are excluded from entitlement if they are 'persons subject to immigration control'. On to this structure of exclusions is grafted a series of further rules, which provide for exemptions from the HRT requirement and which bring back into eligibility sub-groups of persons within the excluded categories. The habitual residence test is dealt with in detail below (at para 2.67 onwards). Most asylum-seekers are excluded from eligibility for benefits by being 'persons subject to immigration control' (PSIC).

2.5   The category of PSIC is defined[5] as a person who is not an EEA national and who:

a) requires leave to enter or remain in the UK but does not have it;[6]
b) has leave to enter or remain in the UK subject to a condition that he or she does not have recourse to public funds;[7]
c) has leave to enter or remain in the UK given as a result of a maintenance undertaking;

---

3 See para 2.62 below.
4 Social Security (Habitual Residence) Amendment Regulations 2004 SI No 1232. See appendix A.
5 IAA 1999 s115(9).
6 This includes most asylum-seekers – temporary admission does not amount to leave to enter or remain for the purposes of Immigration Act 1971 s3.
7 For example, visitors, students, au pairs, work permit holders, business and self-employed people, fiancé(e)s, artists and writers. The provision only applies if the Home Office actually imposed a condition. If leave was granted before 1997 there may be no condition. See paras 1.27–1.28 for a definition of 'recourse to public funds'.

d) has leave to enter or remain only as a result of leave being extended while he or she appeals against a refusal to grant or vary leave.[8]

2.6 The category of 'person subject to immigration control' does not include EEA nationals. It does not include British citizens, Commonwealth citizens with right of abode, or citizens of the Republic of Ireland. It does not include those granted refugee status, nor those granted humanitarian protection/discretionary leave to remain – unless, exceptionally, HP/DLR has been granted subject to a condition of no recourse to public funds. Those who are not PSICs will, nonetheless, be excluded from entitlement to benefit unless they can satisfy the habitual residence test, or are exempted from it: such excluded persons are classified as 'persons from abroad' for benefit purposes.[9]

2.7 PSICs are (subject to exceptions) excluded by IAA 1999 s115 from entitlement to:

- Income Support (IS)
- Income-based Jobseeker's Allowance (income-based JSA)
- Attendance Allowance (AA)
- Severe Disablement Allowance (SDA)
- Carers' Allowance (CA)
- Disability Living Allowance (DLA)
- Social Fund payments (SFP)
- Child Benefit (CB)
- Housing Benefit (HB), and
- Council Tax Benefit (CTB).

PSICs are (subject to exceptions) excluded by Tax Credits Act 2002 s42 and Tax Credit (Immigration) 2003 Regs reg 3(1) from entitlement to Working Tax Credit (WTC) and Child Tax Credit (CTC). PSICs are (subject to exceptions) excluded from entitlement to State Pension Credit (SPC) by State Pension Credit Act 2002 s4(2).

2.8 PSICS are not excluded from benefits that depend for entitlement upon a record of National Insurance contributions, because IAA 1999 s115 does not apply to them, that is, contribution-based Jobseeker's Allowance (contributory JSA), Incapacity Benefit (IB), Retirement Pension (RP) and Maternity Allowance (MA). In practice, few asylum-seekers will have worked for long enough to have been paid or credited with sufficient contributions to qualify for these insurance-based benefits.

8   IAA 1999 s115(9) and Sch 4 para 17.
9   IS Regs reg 21(3).

2.9   Regulations make provision to take some sub-groups of the PSIC category out of the general exclusion in IAA 1999 s115. Social Security (Immigration and Asylum) Consequential Amendments Regulations 2000 (SS(IA)CA Regs)[10] reg 2 sets out the persons who are not excluded from specified benefits. These are:

- persons specified in the Schedule to the regulations;[11]
- others covered by reciprocal agreements;[12]
- transitional cases.[13]

2.10   Those who are not 'persons subject to immigration control', as defined by IAA 1999 s115, are excluded from entitlement to benefits unless they are:

- EEA nationals who are 'workers' (see paras 2.33–2.37);
- EEA nationals who have a right to reside (see paras 2.77–2.80);
- habitually resident (see paras 2.67–2.76);
- refugees;
- persons with humanitarian protection, discretionary leave to remain or indefinite leave to remain.[14]

Categories of persons entitled to benefits

2.11   The principal categories of persons who come from abroad who are entitled to some state benefits are:

a) asylum-seekers who had subsisting claims for asylum in February 1996 and fall within transitional protection (1996 transitional protection cases);

b) asylum-seekers who had subsisting claims for asylum in April 2000 and fall within transitional protection (2000 transitional protection cases);

c) EEA citizens who are present in the UK exercising treaty rights or who are habitually resident in the UK;

d) those (apart from EEA citizens) who are not subject to immigration control, ie, British citizens, commonwealth citizens with right of

---

10 SI No 636.
11 SS(IA)CA Regs reg 2(1) and (2).
12 SS(IA)CA Regs reg 2(3). DMG para 070310 or the DSS Overseas Benefits Directorate (tel: 0191 218 7777) can provide an up-to-date list.
13 SS(IA)CA Regs reg 2(5).
14 For PC, by SPCA 2002 s1(2)(a) and SPC Regs reg 2.

abode, citizens of the Republic of Ireland (there are smaller categories dependent on special circumstances);

e) those who have acquired a record of National Insurance contributions;

f) those who have entered under sponsorship arrangements;

g) those whose funding from abroad is interrupted;

h) asylum-seekers from upheaval countries;

i) citizens of ECSMA and CESC countries;

j) those relying on reciprocal agreements with the EC;

k) persons deported or removed to the UK from other countries.

Each category carries eligibility for specific benefits. We will look at each group in turn, describing the qualifying conditions, and the resulting benefit eligibility.

1996 Transitional Protection cases

Who falls into the category?

2.12 Asylum-seekers who were entitled to or receiving benefits both on 4 February 1996 (or 6 October 1996 in the case of child benefit) and on 3 April 2000 have transitional protection. This means they are entitled to continue receiving benefit until the first negative decision on their asylum claim or until the award of benefit is revised or superseded if that happens first.[15] With the passage of time, few asylum-seekers still fall into this category. A first negative decision occurs when the Home Secretary records an asylum claim as having been decided and that decision is notified to the applicant or the claim is abandoned.[16] In cases where an appeal was entered before 5 February 1996, a first negative decision may be the first decision refusing the appeal. If a first negative decision is overturned on appeal, for example, if the Immigration Appeal Tribunal quashes a decision and refers it back to another adjudicator for reconsideration, entitlement to benefit does not revive.[17]

2.13 In the case of non-means-tested benefits (attendance allowance, disability living allowance, carers' allowance, severe disablement

15 SS(PFA)MA Regs reg 12; SS(IA)CA Regs regs 2(4) and 12(10).

16 SS(IA)CA Regs reg 12(10); *R (Anufrijeva) v Secretary of State for the Home Department and Secretary of State for Social Security* [2003] UKHL 36 (overruling the Court of Appeal decision in *R v Home Secretary ex p Salem* [1999] 1 AC 450; [1999] QB 805.

17 CIS/3418/1998, Starred Decision No 31/00.

allowance, child benefit), entitlement also ends if the benefit award is revised or superseded.[18] This has been interpreted to include the expiry of a time-limited award, even where the award would otherwise be renewed.[19] For these benefits, any break in the claim means that entitlement is lost.[20] In the case of means-tested benefits (income support, housing benefit, council tax benefit), entitlement survives a break in the claim.[21] Therefore, for example, an asylum-seeker may end the benefit claim to work and reclaim at a later date.

2.14   The transitional protection also covers persons who were members of the asylum-seeker's family on 5 February 1996 and 3 April 2000.[22] Thus, for example,

– a child who leaves school can make a claim for income support in his/her own right;
– in a case of relationship breakdown where one partner was receiving income support on 4 February 1996, the other can claim.

What benefits may be claimed?

2.15   This protection applies to asylum-seekers receiving or entitled to IS, HB, CTB, AA, DLA, CA or SDA on 4 February 1996. It does not apply to income-based JSA. IS is paid at the urgent cases rate[23] (see 2.81– 2.83).

2.16   It is not possible for claimants with this transitional protection to claim benefits additional to those they were receiving on the qualifying day. Thus, for example, an asylum-seeker entitled to IS and HB on 4 February 1996 who subsequently becomes disabled cannot claim DLA. However, an asylum-seeker receiving IS who reaches the age of 60 will qualify for SPC.[24]

2000 Transitional Protection cases

Who falls into the category?

2.17   Asylum-seekers who were entitled to or receiving means-tested benefits (income-based JSA, IS, HB, CTB) on 2 April 2000 retain

18 SS(IA)CA Regs reg 12(10).
19 *R (B) v Chief Adjudication Officer* [2001] UKHL 35, [2001] 4 All ER 41; *M (a minor) v Secretary of State for Social Security* (2001) *Times* 6 July, HL.
20 *R v Chief Adjudication Officer ex p B* [1999] 1 WLR 1695.
21 *Yildiz v Secretary of State for Social Security* (2001) 28 February, unreported, CA.
22 SS(PFA)MA 1996 Regs reg 12(1), as amended by SS(IA)CA Regs reg 12(11).
23 IS Regs reg 70(2A); JSA Regs reg147(2A).
24 SS(IA)CA Regs reg 2, as amended by SPC(TMP)A Regs reg 6.

entitlement until the first negative decision on their asylum claim.[25] The regulations build on the existing transitional protection provided by the Asylum and Immigration Act 1996.[26] It applies to those who are defined as 'asylum-seekers' within the meaning of the IS, HB and CTB Regs: that is, an asylum-seeker who made a claim for asylum 'on arrival' (see para 2.20 below) in the UK on or before 2 April 2000 and whose claim has been recorded by the Home Secretary.[27]

2.18   Note that the requirement is an *asylum* claim before 3 April, not a *benefit* claim. The asylum-seeker may claim benefit for the first time after 2 April 2000. Entitlement survives a break in the claim, so that, for example, an asylum-seeker may end the benefit claim to work and reclaim at a later date. Entitlement does not extend to family members who make their own claim for benefit, for example, on death or separation.

2.19   Benefit entitlement ends when the claim for asylum is recorded by the Home Secretary as decided (other than on appeal) and notified to the asylum-seeker, or it is abandoned.[28] Therefore, it ends if an asylum-seeker withdraws the asylum claim or receives a decision refusing asylum.

2.20   The term 'on arrival' is not defined in the legislation and has been the subject of much litigation. Rival interpretations have found approval before the Social Security Commissioners: it has been taken to mean 'on passing through immigration control at the port of entry', or 'while still within the perimeter of the port of entry'. The notion of application 'as soon as reasonably practicable' has also been canvassed. Recently, the Court of Appeal has added some guidance.

2.21   Commissioner Howell QC attempted to tackle the problem of a series of inconsistent commissioners' decisions by reviewing all of them in 1999.[29] He adopted the 'factual test' of 'on arrival'. He decided that commissioners who applied a test of whether the claim for asylum had been made within the port of entry, even if this was after

---

25 SS(IA)CA Regs regs 2 and 12.
26 SS(PFA)MA Regs, which also amended the substantive regulations.
27 SS(IA)CA Regs reg 12(4).
28 SS(IA)CA Regs reg12(5); *R (Anufrijeva) v Secretary of State for the Home Department and Secretary of State for Social Security* [2003] UKHL 36 (overruling the Court of Appeal decision in *R v Home Secretary ex p Salem* [1999] 1 AC 450; [1999] QB 805 and the High Court in *R (Paulo) v Secretary of State for the Home Department and Secretary of State for Social Security* [2001] EWHC Admin 480).
29 CIS 3867/98, 30 September 1999.

passing through immigration control,[30] were mistaken and the appropriate test was an 'immigration control' test.[31]

> It follows in my judgment that the reference in reg 70(3A)(a)[32] to a person submitting a claim for asylum on his arrival (other than on his re-entry) in the United Kingdom is concerned with the nature of the application made to be allowed into the United Kingdom at the point where a recently-arrived passenger submits, or should submit, himself to examination by an immigration officer at his or her port of first entry into this country.

The commissioner found in both this case and later in 2000[33] that clandestine entrants who had claimed asylum after passing through the port in a lorry had not claimed 'on arrival'.

2.22   However, Commissioner Sanders decided that where a Libyan asylum-seeker was too ill to claim asylum when he reached Heathrow due to torture in Libya, this was an exceptional case in which he might fall within the 'on arrival' definition if the facts of his illness could be proven.[34]

2.23   In another case, an applicant for asylum had passed through immigration control at Gatwick with an agent without claiming asylum but attempted to claim asylum two hours later with the help of a man from the Third World Refugee Bureau, after waiting in the arrivals hall.[35] Commissioner Williams rejected the 'as soon as reasonably practicable' test but, applying a measure of flexibility to the test of 'on arrival',[36] found that the claimant had claimed 'on arrival'. The DWP *Decision-makers' Guidance* accepts that an asylum-seeker who is prevented by ill-health from applying for asylum at immigration control but applies as soon as reasonably practicable falls within the 'on arrival definition'.[37]

2.24   The Court of Appeal has considered the situation of an applicant who does not claim asylum on passing through immigration control because he or she has placed themselves in the hands of or are fol-

---

30 CIS 1137/97 and CIS 4341/98.
31 CIS 143/97 and CIS 3231/97.
32 Now contained in SS(IA)CA Regs reg 12(4).
33 CIS 3646/98, 5 January 2000.
34 CIS 3803/98, 7 July 1999.
35 50/99, CIS 4341/98.
36 See also CIS 2719/97, 4117/97 and CIS/43/2000.
37 *Decision-maker's Guidance* 31041.

lowing the directions of an agent.[38] The court held that such a person voluntarily places him/herself in the control of the agent and adopts their actions, and so fails the test. The court specifically declined to approve or disapprove the 'immigration control', 'port perimeter' or 'as soon as reasonably practicable' approaches.

2.25   The conflicting decisions leave representatives to argue from fact and principle. There is still scope to argue that 'on arrival' includes claims made within the port of entry after clearing immigration control or, to a very limited extent, that it means 'as soon as reasonably practicable' following the exceptional circumstances test.[39] There is less authority for arguing that clandestine entrants, for example, travelling out of the port hidden in a lorry, have claimed 'on arrival'.

What benefits may be claimed?

2.26   The protection applies to income-based JSA, IS, HB, CTB and a social fund payment. IS and income-based JSA are paid at the urgent cases rate[40] (see paras 2.81–2.83). An asylum-seeker receiving IS or income-based JSA who reaches the age of 60 will qualify for state pension credit (SPC).[41] A claimant may have a choice whether to claim IS or income-based JSA.

Whether to claim IS or income-based JSA

2.27   Where a new claim is being made under 2000 Transitional Protection – for example, by a claimant who has stopped working in employed earner's employment due to loss of the job – a decision needs to be made whether to claim IS or income-based JSA. The decision has important consequences, although the rate of payment is the same for both benefits.

Advantages of claiming income-based JSA

2.28   An asylum-seeker can claim income-based JSA if he or she has permission from the Home Office to work.[42] He or she will need to

---

38 *Shire v Secretary of State for Work and Pensions* [2003] EWCA 1465, (2003) *Times* 14 October; the decision concerned the provisions as to claims made 'on arrival' in IS Regs reg 70(3A), since repealed. The position was confirmed by the Court of Appeal in *Kola and Mirzajani v Secretary of State for Work and Pensions* [2004] EWCA Civ 638.

39 CIS 3803/98.

40 IS Regs reg 70(2A); JSA Regs reg 147(2A).

41 SS(IA)CA Regs regs 2 and 12, as amended by SPC(TMP)A Regs reg 6.

42 JSA Regs reg 147(3).

comply with a jobseeker's agreement and show that he or she is actively seeking work. There is also the requirement to sign on fortnightly at the local job centre. An advantage of claiming JSA is that if the asylum-seeker finds work and then stops working due to unemployment, sickness or pregnancy, he or she will be credited with National Insurance contributions. This will allow him/her to start or continue a record of National Insurance contributions. There is no immigration test for contributory benefits and so an asylum-seeker with sufficient contributions could receive IB or contributory JSA even after a negative decision on his/her asylum claim. An asylum-seeker who is granted leave to remain in the UK will also benefit from starting to build up a contribution record. This is most likely to benefit single asylum-seekers or childless couples who have no difficulty in presenting themselves as actively seeking work.

Advantages of claiming IS

2.29   Unless an asylum-seeker has been granted the right to work by the Home Office, he or she will not be eligible to claim income-based JSA and will have to claim IS in any event. Where there is a choice, the advantage of a claim for IS is that the asylum-seeker will not have to sign on or demonstrate that he or she is actively seeking work. Complying with the jobseeker's agreement may be difficult for those who are beginning to learn spoken and written English. The cost of seeking work may also be problematic, since benefit is being paid at the lower urgent cases payments rate (see paras 2.81–2.83). If the claimant has no realistic prospect of obtaining work and so will not develop a contribution record, the administrative burden of claiming income-based JSA is unlikely to outweigh any advantage.

European Economic Area citizens

Who falls into the category?

2.30   Nationals of an EEA country and their family members in the UK are not treated as PSICs excluded from benefits by IAA 1999 s115. Specific rules regulate their eligibility for benefits. The EEA[43] includes the countries of the European Union (Austria, Belgium, Denmark, Finland, France, Germany, Greece, Italy, Luxembourg, the Netherlands, Portugal, Republic of Ireland, Spain, Sweden, the UK) plus Iceland,

43   An EEA state is defined by IAA 1999 s167 as 'a State which is a contracting Party to the Agreement on the European Economic Area signed at Oporto on 2nd May 1992 as it has effect for the time being'.

Liechtenstein and Norway. Since 1 May 2004, membership is enlarged to include Poland, Hungary, the Czech Republic, Slovenia, Slovakia, Estonia, Latvia, Lithuania, Cyprus and Malta, and the same rules apply to these countries, with modifications (see paras 2.43–2.44).

2.31   Whether an EEA citizen (or a family member of such a citizen) is entitled to benefits depends on whether he or she falls within a category of 'worker', or has a 'right to reside' in the UK. The Immigration (European Economic Area) Regulations 2000[44] outline the scheme under which EEA nationals and their family members can claim rights of entry into or residence in the UK.

2.32   An EEA national who is classified as a 'worker' can claim benefits under the ordinary rules, and does not have to satisfy the 'habitual residence' test (see paras 2.67–2.80). An EEA national who falls outside the class of 'worker' but has a 'right to reside' must satisfy the 'habitual residence' test to qualify for non-contributory benefits (see paras 2.77–2.80 for those who have a right to reside). An EEA national whose right to reside is as a person who is economically inactive is substantially rendered ineligible for non-contributory benefits because their right is contingent upon having sufficient resources to avoid becoming an unreasonable burden on the state.

Meaning of 'worker'

2.33   To qualify for benefits in the UK on the basis of being a 'worker', a person must be working or have been working in the UK for an employer in part-time or full-time work, provided it is not so irregular and limited that it is a 'marginal and ancillary' activity. If he or she has stopped work, it must be due to involuntary unemployment/lay-off or in order to undertake relevant training.[45] Work need not necessarily be of long duration: an au pair who had worked for five weeks, with pay of £35 for a 13-hour week plus board and lodging was found to be a worker.[46]

---

44 SI 2000 No 2326 came into force on 2 October 2000 replacing the Immigration (European Economic Area) Order 1994 SI No 1895.

45 For further discussion of 'worker' see *Levin v Secretary of State for Justice (Case 53/81)* [1982] ECR 1035; *Kempf v Staatssecretaris van Justitie (Case 139/85)* [1986] CR 1741; *Raulin v Minister van Onderwijs en Wetenschappen (Case 357/89)* [1992] ECR I–1027 and *DMG* para 071916.

46 CIS 12909/1996; see also *Ninni-Orasche v Bundesminister fur Wissenschaft, Verkehr und Kunst* (EC Case C–413/01): temporary work for two and a half months.

2.34   A person will not qualify as a worker simply by being a work-seeker, where he or she has not worked in the UK before.[47] See para 2.41 below for the position of work-seekers.

2.35   Some former workers also qualify as 'workers'. These include those retiring at pension age who have resided in the UK for three years and have been employed for at least one of those years, or who have a British spouse. Also included are those permanently incapable of work, where incapacity results from industrial injury or disease, or follows two years' residence in the UK, or where the person has a British spouse.[48]

2.36   These definitions of 'worker' derive from EC caselaw and the application by the court of EC 1612/68, which provides for freedom of movement and equal treatment of EEA nationals who are 'workers'. The right to equal treatment for workers in social security matters under co-operation agreements between the EEA and other states extends to Turkish nationals by virtue of the EEC-Turkey Association Agreement and EEA Council Decision 3/80.[49]

2.37   European Court of Justice judgments have established a wide definition of 'worker' in the context of the co-operation agreements, which covers most of those who have stopped lawfully working for a valid reason.[50] Nationals of Algeria, Morocco, Slovenia, Tunisia or Turkey are to be treated as 'workers' (eligible for benefits) if:

– they have permission to enter Britain and are working here with no restriction on their right to work; or

---

47 *Collins v Secretary of State for the Department of Work and Pensions*, EC Case C–138/02, 23 March 2004.

48 These provisions derive from EC Council Regulation 1251/70.

49 In *Surul* (Case C–262/96), the ECJ considered the principle of equal treatment and co-ordination in social security matters, which apply to EEA workers by virtue of EEC Reg 1408/71. It decided that the same 'freedom of movement' principles applied to Turkish workers, their families and survivors by virtue of Council Decision 3/80. The definition of 'worker and 'family member' was considered, and the court noted that the Decision 3/80 definition of 'worker' corresponds to the concept of worker contained in Reg 1408/71 art 1(a) and that the term 'member of family' has the meaning given to it by Reg 1408/71 art 1(f). See also social security commissioner's decision CFC/2613/1997.

50 See *Kziber* (Case C–18/90) [1991] ECR I–199; *Yousfi v Belgium* (Case C–58/93) [1994] ECR I–1353; *Krid v Caisse Nationale d'Assurance Veillesse des Travailleurs Salariés* (Case C–103/94) [1995] ECR I–719; *Hallouzi-Choho v Bestuur van de Sociale Verzekeringsbank* (Case C–126/95) [1996] ECR I–4807; *Babahenini* (Case C–113/97) [1998] ECR I–183.

- they have stopped working in the UK due to sickness, pregnancy, reaching pension age, widowhood, a work-related accident or disease, unemployment or to look after children.

Meaning of 'right to reside'

2.38 The meaning of this term and the categories of persons with a right to reside are described at paras 2.76–2.80.

Family members of EEA nationals[51]

2.39 A person who is a family member of an EEA national (but who may or may not themselves be an EEA national) has the same rights of freedom of movement and, therefore, is not a person subject to immigration control. They are thus not excluded from entitlement to benefits by IAA 1999 s115, but unless they are themselves 'workers' or have residence permits will have to satisfy the habitual residence test if making a benefit claim in their own right. 'Family member' includes spouse or partner, children up to the age of 21, and others who are mainly dependent on a person (which may include parents and others in the ascending line), even if not living in that person's household.

2.40 Other aspects of entitlement to benefits for EEA nationals go beyond the scope of this book, but mention is made of the following:

- EEA nationals who are insured persons in their state of origin may be able to receive income protection benefits in another EEA state. Thus, for example, a person who has paid into a state national insurance scheme in another EEA state may be able to claim in the UK benefits that are designed to replace earnings;[52] family benefits;[53] and 'special non-contributory benefits'.[54] EEA nationals qualifying under these provisions may be able to avoid having to satisfy the habitual residence test.[55]
- An EEA national may be able to receive a family benefit (such as child benefit) in respect of a family member who is not living in the UK.

51 EC Council Reg 1408/71, art 1(f).
52 These include IB, MA, SSP, SMP, SDA, RP and contributory JSA.
53 These include CB and CTC.
54 These include AA, DLA, CA, IS and income-based JSA.
55 These provisions derive from EC Council Regulation 1408/71. This is EC law directly applicable in the UK and designed to support the freedom of movement of EEA nationals. For further information, see *Migration and Social Security Handbook* (CPAG, 3rd edn, 2002).

The position of work-seekers

2.41   It has been noted that an EEA national present in the UK who has not
actually been in employed or self-employed work in the UK is not
within the category or 'worker'. Such persons are entitled to reside in
the UK for six months while seeking work,[56] and may not be removed
after three months if they can show that they are continuing to seek
work and that there is a genuine prospect of their obtaining it.[57] During this period, an EEA national has a right to reside in the UK and is
not subject to a condition that he or she be self-sufficient (but see
paras 2.43–2.44 below for the position of EEA nationals from the
eight east European states, which acceded to the European Union on
1 May 2004). Under UK domestic legislation, such work-seekers will
not qualify for benefit (or for social housing) unless they satisfy the
habitual residence test. However, in *Collins v Secretary of State for the
Department of Work and Pensions*,[58] the European Court has criticized
the application of the test to work-seekers. The court ruled that while
it might be appropriate for a member state to have a residence test,
such a test would be reasonable and proportionate (and therefore lawful) only if: (1) it was directed at and confined to establishing a link
between the person seeking work and the employment market in the
member state, (2) it did not discriminate on the basis of the nationality of persons concerned, and (3) it was based on clear criteria, with
judicial redress available in case of dispute. The court observed that
the other rules of the JSA scheme enabled the UK government to satisfy itself as to (1), with the implication that the (additional) habitual
residence test was disproportionate. It also observed that a test was to
be considered discriminatory if it was inherently more likely to be
satisfied by the member state's own citizens than by other EEA citizens. These rulings of the court are a fundamental challenge to the
lawfulness of the habitual residence test in its application to work-
seekers.

New rules affecting all EEA nationals from 1 May 2004

2.42   Before 1 May 2004, EEA nationals who were not 'workers' and/or did
not have the 'right to reside' could acquire entitlement to benefits by
satisfying the habitual residence test. As part of legislative changes
introduced as a result of the accession of new countries to the EU on
1 May 2004, the government changed the position so that no person

56   EC Treaty art 39.
57   *Antonissen* [1991] ECR I–745 and *Commission v Belgium* [1997] ECR I–1035.
58   Case C–138/02, 23 March 2004.

will be treated as habitually resident unless they also have a right to reside in the Common Travel Area.[59] In effect, to qualify for benefits, EEA nationals have either (a) to be 'workers', or (b) to have the 'right to reside' *and* satisfy the habitual residence test. There is transitional protection for those EEA nationals already in the UK and entitled to benefit on 30th April 2004 for so long as their claim for benefit lasts (including the period of a repeat claim or a claim to another benefit in succession to the first, provided there is no break). For the 'habitual residence test' and the 'right to reside', see paras 2.67–2.80.

New rules affecting nationals of 'Accession States' from 1 May 2004

2.43   From 1 May 2004, 10 countries joined the European Union. They are Poland, Hungary, the Czech Republic, Slovenia, Slovakia, Estonia, Latvia, Lithuania, Cyprus and Malta. The UK government introduced regulations[60] to restrict access to benefits for nationals of the eight eastern European countries (but not Cyprus and Malta, whose nationals will be treated the same as those of the existing 16 EEA states). The restriction on nationals of these states (referred to as 'Accession 8' or 'A8' nationals) applies by curtailing the benefit entitlement of employed 'workers' from these countries: they are required to register under a workers' registration scheme, and remain registered until they have been in continuous employment for a period of 12 months. Those registered are able to claim 'in-work' benefits – CB, WTC, CTC, HB and CTB and to have access to social housing. But if they lose their job within the 12 months period, they are barred from claiming IS, income-based JSA, SPC, HB and CTB and cease to be eligible for social housing.[61] There is bar to DLA, AA and CA, beyond the present

59 That is, the United Kingdom, Channel Islands, Republic of Ireland and the Isle of Man; the changes are made by the Social Security (Habitual Residence) Amendment Regulations 2004 SI No 1232.

60 Social Security (Habitual Residence) Amendment Regulations 2004 SI No 1232 reg 6.

61 The worker registration scheme is given effect by the Accession (Immigration and Worker Registration) Regulations 2004 SI No 1219. The disqualification from benefits is given effect by the Social Security (Habitual Residence) Amendment Regulations 2004 SI No 1232. Note that there are rules which allow a worker who loses a first job during the 12 month period to link employment in a second job to the first in calculating the 12 month period, providing the first and second jobs are not separated by more than 30 days (Accession (Immigration and Worker Registration) Regulations 2004 SI No 1219, reg 2(4), 2(8)). This concession does not apply if a second job is lost. Also, it applies only for the purpose of calculating the 12-month period: entitlements to HB, CTB, WTC, CB and social housing are lost as soon as the first job is lost and do not recommence until the second job starts.

26-week residence test. After the period of 12 months continuous employment, registration is no longer required, and the rights of an A8 national become the same as those of other EEA nationals. The position of the self-employed is that they are not required to register and are eligible for in-work benefits, but if they cease work, they cease to have a right to reside (unless they have applied for and obtained a residence permit), and thereupon lose entitlement. The position of work-seekers is that they are considered to have the right to reside only so long as they can support themselves, and so are debarred from all benefits until they find work. Those who are economically inactive are – like other EEA nationals – also considered to have the right to reside only so long as they are self-sufficient, and so remain debarred from means-tested benefits.

2.44   At the time of writing these changes are new. Possible lines of challenge that have emerged are as follows:

– it may be argued that the 12-month restriction on claims for non-work benefits may be in conflict with EC Reg 1408/71, which specifies no minimum period of employment in a member state, and with EC Reg 1612/68 in that a member state may not derogate from article 7(2) of the regulation which guarantees an EEA work-er the same rights as UK nationals in relation to tax and 'social advantage', a term which has been interpreted to include eligibility for means-tested non-work benefits

– for self-employed people it is arguable that their right to reside would continue if they ceased trading because of illness or accident

– for work-seekers, the bar on entitlement to benefits may breach rights under article 39 of the EU treaty, having regard to the judgment in *Collins v Secretary of State for Work and Pensions.*[62]

What benefits may be claimed?

2.45   All EEA citizens are entitled to claim benefits that depend on a record of National Insurance contributions (IB, contributory JSA, MA and RP). It is also possible to qualify for these benefits on the basis of equivalent or similar contributions made in other EEA states, however, the applicable rules are beyond the scope of this book.

2.46   All EEA citizens are eligible for the following non-means-tested benefits: AA, CA, DLA and social fund payments.

2.47   Family members of EEA citizens who are not themselves EEA citizens are also eligible for AA, CA, DLA and SF payments.[63]

---

62 Case C-138/02, 23 March 2004.
63 SS(IA)CA Regs reg 2(2) and Sch part II.

2.48 Note that for AA, DLA and CA eligibility depends on being present in the UK for 26 weeks and being ordinarily resident here.[64] EEA citizens who have worked in other EEA countries can count time spent in those countries towards the 26 weeks' presence.

2.49 EEA citizens who are workers or who meet the habitual residence test (see paras 2.67–2.80), and their family members, are eligible for the full range of benefits under the ordinary rules. For the restrictions on entitlement that apply to EEA citizens from the eight east European states acceded to the European Union on 1 May 2004, see paras 2.43–2.44 above.

Other persons not subject to immigration control

Who falls into the category?

2.50 The remaining broad category of persons who come to the UK who have entitlement to benefits are the following:

- British citizens (as defined by the British Nationality Act 1981);
- Commonwealth citizens with right of abode;
- Citizens of the Republic of Ireland.

Such persons are not subject to immigration control and have a right to reside in the Common Travel Area, but they must satisfy the habitual residence test (see paras 2.67–2.80) for most benefits, unless they fall into an exempt category.

What benefits may be claimed?

2.51 Persons in this category are entitled to claim benefits that depend on a record of National Insurance contributions, whether or not they satisfy the habitual residence test (IB, contributory JSA, MA and RP).

2.52 Persons in this category who satisfy (or are exempt from) the habitual residence test, and their family members, are eligible for the full range of benefits under the ordinary rules.

Special categories

2.53 There are certain special categories of persons for whom benefit entitlement is allowed or preserved by the regulations. The numbers of persons falling into these groups is generally small.

---

64 SS(AA) Regs reg 2(1); SS(DLA) Regs reg 2(1); SS(ICA) Regs reg 9(1); SS(IB) Regs reg 16.

Persons who have acquired a record of National Insurance contributions

2.54   Where a person has been in paid employment in the UK, or has paid national insurance as a self-employed person, they may have built up a sufficient contribution record to qualify for certain contributory benefits (IB, MA, contributory JSA and RP). Such benefits are paid irrespective of immigration status. Such persons will have National Insurance numbers. If you think a person may have a sufficient contribution record (and otherwise meets the conditions of entitlement) a claim should be made.

Persons entering the UK subject to sponsorship arrangements

2.55   Specific provision is made for a person whose leave to enter or remain in the UK is given as a result of an undertaking by a sponsor.[65] In considering the following rules, advisers should bear in mind that sponsored persons may have leave subject to a requirement that they do not have recourse to public funds, and that claiming benefits may jeopardize their entitlement to remain in the UK. Unless it is clear that a person is not subject to such a requirement, immigration advice should be sought before making a claim for benefit. It should also be borne in mind that a sponsor who fails to maintain in accordance with their undertaking may be prosecuted.[66]

2.56   A sponsored person is entitled to claim AA, SDA, CA, DLA and social fund payments.[67] Note that for AA, DLA and CA, eligibility depends on being present in the UK for 26 weeks and being ordinarily resident here.[68]

2.57   A sponsored person who has been here for more than five years or whose sponsor has died is entitled to claim income-based JSA, IS, social fund payments, HB, CTB,[69] CTC and WTC.[70] The five years run from the date of the original grant of leave to enter the UK or of the undertaking, whichever is the later. Only periods of residence in the UK count towards the five years, although it may be made up of

---

65   IAA 1999 s115(9)(c); it is sufficient if the undertaking contributed to the decision of the immigration authorities to grant leave to remain or enter: CIS/3508/2001.

66   IAA 1999 s108; see para 4.159.

67   S(IA)CA Regs reg 2(2) and Sch Part II.

68   SS(AA) Regs reg 2(1); SS(DLA) Regs reg 2(1); SS(ICA) Regs reg 9(1); SS(IB) Regs reg 16.

69   SS(IA)CA Regs reg 2 and Sch Part I.

70   TC(I) Regs 2003 reg 3.

aggregated shorter periods interspersed with periods of absence.[71] The undertaking may continue to run even if a person subsequently leaves and re-enters the UK and is given leave to enter without reference to sponsorship.[72] IS and income-based JSA are paid at the urgent cases rate[73] (see para 2.81–2.83). Sponsored persons who have been here for longer than five years are entitled to ordinary benefits.[74]

2.58 'Sponsorship' here is limited to a written undertaking given by another person under the Immigration Rules para 6 to be responsible for that person's maintenance and accommodation. The undertaking must be signed and dated by the sponsor and must refer to the immigration rules. The Home Office provides a form for the purpose (currently RON 112 or SET(F)), but use of the form is not essential if the above requirements are met.[75]

Persons funded from abroad whose funding is interrupted

2.59 A person whose leave to enter or remain in the UK is subject to a condition that they have 'no recourse to public funds', but whose funding from abroad has stopped temporarily is entitled to claim income-based JSA, IS, SPC, a social fund payment, HB, CTB,[76] CTC or WTC.[77] Benefit can only be paid under this heading for a maximum of 42 days in any one period of leave. IS and income-based JSA are paid at the urgent cases rate[78] (see paras 2.81–2.83). Again, advisers should bear in mind that claiming benefits may jeopardize such persons' entitlement to remain in the UK. Immigration advice should be sought before making a claim for benefit.

Asylum-seekers from designated 'upheaval' countries

2.60 The Home Secretary has power to declare as 'upheaval' countries states where changes in political conditions mean that it becomes unsafe for persons already in the UK to return. Where nationals of

---

71 CIS/1077/1999 and CIS/6608/1999.
72 *Shah v Secretary of State for Social Security* [2002] EWCA Civ 285.
73 IS Regs reg 70 (2A); JSA Regs reg 147(2A).
74 IS Regs reg 70 (2A); JSA Regs reg 147(2A).
75 CIS/47/2002; CIS/2474/1999; *R (Begum) v Social Security Commissioner* (2003) 6 November, unreported.
76 SS(IA)CA Regs reg 2(1) and Sch Part I, as amended by SPC(TMP)A Regs 2003 reg 6.
77 TC(I) Regs 2003 reg 3.
78 IS Regs reg 70(2A); JSA Regs reg147(2A).

such states claim asylum, special rules of entitlement to benefits apply. The only claims for asylum currently affected are those made by Sierra Leone nationals between 16 May 1997 and 16 August 1997, and those made by Democratic Republic of Congo nationals between 1 July 1997 and 1 October 1997.

2.61   A person from an upheaval country who claimed asylum within three months of the Home Secretary's declaration can claim IS, HB and CTB.[80] Entitlement to benefit continues until the first negative asylum decision. Entitlement does not extend to family members who make their own claim for benefit, for example, on death or separation.

Persons who are citizens of ECSMA and CESC countries

2.62   This category comprises nationals from countries that have ratified the European Convention on Social and Medical Assistance and Protocol 1953 or Council of Europe Social Charter 1961, ie, all EEA countries (Austria, Belgium, Denmark, Finland, France, Germany, Greece, Iceland, Ireland, Italy, Liechtenstein, Luxemburg, Nether-lands, Norway, Portugal, Spain, Sweden and the UK) plus Cyprus, Czech Republic, Hungary, Latvia, Malta, Poland, Slovakia and Turkey. Note that since 1 May 2004, all these countries are EEA coun-tries except Turkey, so that the commentary that follows will only be of relevance to Turkish nationals.

2.63   Nationals of these countries are entitled to claim IS at ordinary benefit rates[81] for themselves and any dependant provided that they are (for nationals of non-EEA countries) 'lawfully present' and (where they are not asylum-seekers) that they meet the 'habitual residence' test (see paras 2.67–2.80).

'Lawfully present'

2.64   Asylum-seekers who are EEA nationals are 'lawfully present' because of their EEA national status. For asylum-seeker nationals of the remaining participating state, Turkey, the meaning of 'lawfully pres-ent' is a key issue. Asylum-seekers are granted temporary admission to the UK. It has been argued that a grant of temporary admission means that an asylum-seeker is 'lawfully present' and so entitled to IS, income-based JSA, HB and CTB (and housing as homeless). How-ever, this has been rejected by the Court of Appeal in *Szoma v Secretary*

---

80 SS(IA)CA Regs reg 12(4).
81 IS Regs reg 70(2A).

of State for the Department for Work and Pensions,[82] and that decision is binding, pending an appeal to the House of Lords.

Persons entitled through reciprocal agreements

2.65　'A person who is lawfully working in Great Britain and is a national of a state with which the EEC has concluded an agreement under Article 310 of the Treaty of Amsterdam . . .'[83] (or a family member who is living with him/her) is eligible to claim certain benefits. The EEA has agreements with Algeria, Morocco, Slovenia, Tunisia and Turkey. UK regulations recognise these agreements as giving entitlement to AA, CA, DLA and social fund payments. Note that for AA, DLA and CA, eligibility depends on being present in the UK for 26 weeks and being ordinarily resident here.[84] However, the agreements also guarantee equal treatment and this extends eligibility to a wider range of social security benefits,[85] including income-based JSA, SPC, WTC, RP, MA and, possibly, IS.[86] In the context of reciprocal agreements, 'lawfully working' is interpreted by the DWP to mean working or having previously worked in the UK without restrictions on employment and with permission to enter: temporary admission such as is granted to asylum-seekers is not sufficient.[87] However, it has been held in the case of a Turkish national who had worked elsewhere in the EEA that he was eligible even though he had not been employed in the UK.[88] Family member has the same meaning as for EEA citizens (see 2.39–2.40).

Deportation or removal to the UK

2.66　Persons who are not subject to immigration control and who have been deported, expelled or removed from another country to the UK are eligible for IS, income-based JSA, HB and CTB and they are not subject to the habitual residence test.[89]

82　[2003] EWCA Civ 1131.
83　SS(IA)CA Regs Sch Part II.
84　SS(AA) Regs reg 2(1); SS(DLA) Regs reg 2(1); SS(ICA) Regs reg 9(1); SS(IB) Regs reg 16.
85　Those covered by EC Regulation 1408/71; see also CJSA/4705/1999.
86　Following the ECJ case of *Babahenini* C113/97.
87　CJSA/4705/1999.
88　*Surul* (Case C–262/96); R(FC)1/01.
89　IS Regs reg 21(3); JSA Regs reg 85; HB Regs reg 7A; CTB Regs reg 4A; as amended by the Income-Related Benefits and JSA (Amendment) Regulations 2000 SI No 979.

Habitual residence test and right to reside

2.67   The requirement that a benefit claimant is either habitually resident
or treated as habitually resident in the Common Travel Area (the UK,
Isle of Man, Republic of Ireland or the Channel Islands) applies to the
following benefits: IS, income-based JSA, HB, CTB and SPC.[90] Different rules apply to contributory benefits, which go beyond the scope of
this book.[91] A claimant who satisfies the habitual residence test is not
prevented from claiming for a partner or dependents who do not
themselves satisfy the test. Thus, where only one of two partners
satisfies, or is exempt from, the test, that partner should be the
claimant.

Those subject to the test and those exempt from it

2.68   The DWP applies the habitual residence test to claimants who have
not lived in the UK (or the Common Travel Area[92]) throughout the
past two years. The test is applied when a claim is made for IS,
income-based JSA, SPC, HB or CTB. A claimant will be treated as satisfying the test, if he or she falls into one of these exempt categories:

- people who have been granted humanitarian protection (HP) or
  discretionary leave to remain (DLR) (formerly exceptional leave to
  enter or remain (ELR)) in the UK or are recognised as refugees in
  the UK.[93] It would follow that asylum-seekers are also exempt and,
  in practice, the test is not applied to them unless they are EEA
  nationals;
- people who left Montserrat after 1 November 1995 due to the
  volcanic eruption there;
- EEA nationals who come within the definition of 'a worker', and
  their family members[94] – an EEA national who is not a 'worker' is
  subject to the test;

90 IS Regs reg 21(3); JSA Regs reg 85(4); HB Regs reg 7A(4)(e); CTB Regs reg
4A(4); SPC Regs reg 2.
91 See *Migration and Social Security Handbook* (CPAG, 3rd edn, 2002), chapters
24–27.
92 The Common Travel Area is the UK, Republic of Ireland, Channel Islands and
Isle of Man.
93 IS Regs reg 21(3) and (3F), 85(4) and (4A), JSA Regs reg 7A(4)(e) and (5), HB
Regs.
94 See paras 2.33–2.37, 2.39–2.40.

- people deported or legally removed to the UK from another country.[95]

Meaning of 'habitual residence'

2.69 The test is imprecise, as the term is not defined in domestic law and has a different meaning in EEA law.

2.70 The following factors should be taken into account:

- The claimant must have a 'settled intention' to reside in the UK. Events before and after arrival here can be used to demonstrate this. These would include circumstances and arrangements made before arrival in the UK and steps taken after arrival to settle here, for example, children attending school, registering with GPs and other organisations.
- A claimant will need to be resident in UK for an 'appreciable period' unless he or she is returning to the UK after a temporary absence abroad, in which case he or she is 'habitually resident' on the first day back in the UK.

Each claim should be considered on its own merits, taking account of the facts at the date of the claim. A claimant who fails the test may with the passage of time or changes of circumstances come to satisfy it, so that, where a claimant fails the test, consider repeat applications at regular intervals and an appeal against each individual negative decision.

2.71 The meaning of habitual residence (HR) has been reviewed by the ECJ in *Swaddling v Adjudication Officer*[96] and by the House of Lords in *Nessa*.[97]

2.72 In *Swaddling,* the ECJ decided that an EEA national who has come to the UK after working in Europe should not need to be in the UK for an appreciable period before being able to establish HR. The DSS (as it then was) then issued guidance,[98] which states that the national of any country who is returning to the UK to 'pick up the pieces of their former life' is habitually resident as soon as he or she arrives in the UK, that is, does not need to be in the UK for an appreciable period. Commissioner Mesher has commented that the guidance incorrectly

---

95 Income-related Benefits and JSA (Amendment) Regs 2000 SI No 979.
96 (Case C90/97) [1999] All ER (EC) 217.
97 *Nessa v Chief Adjudication Officer* [1999] 1 WLR 1937.
98 AM(AOG) 109.

interprets *Swaddling*.[99] He confirmed that an EEA national who has worked/been insured in the EEA and so falls within EC Reg 1408/71 cannot be excluded from benefit on the basis that the 'appreciable period' requirement is not met. He confirmed that the length of a person's residence in the UK will merely be one factor to consider in deciding whether he or she has a settled intention to remain here, and that in some circumstances other factors could mean that the person concerned was habitually resident on arrival.

2.73   In *Nessa*, the claimant came to the UK after living in Bangladesh all her life and appealed against a DWP decision that she was not habitually resident. The House of Lords attempted to distinguish her circumstances from those in *Swaddling*. The court held that a period of actual residence can be required for those who do not fall within *Swaddling*, that is, who have not worked in the EEA, although the appreciable period could be as short as one month. Lord Slynn stated:

> . . . as a matter of ordinary language a person is not habitually resident in any country unless he has taken up residence and lived here for a period . . . It is a question of fact to be decided on the date when the determination has to be made on the circumstances of each case whether and when the habitual residence had been established. Bringing possessions, doing everything necessary to establish residence before coming, having a right of abode, seeking to bring family, 'durable ties' with the country of residence have to be taken into account. The requisite period is not a fixed period. It may be longer when there are doubts. It may be short.

2.74   Commissioner Jacobs has accepted in the case of two appellants that no appreciable period is necessary to establish habitual residence.[100] An argument that the approach in *Swaddling* – being a decision of the ECJ – should prevail over that of the House of Lords in *Nessa* in a case involving a person who had not spent time in another EEA country before arriving in the UK was unsuccessful before the Court of Appeal.[101]

2.75   The European Court has recently, in the case of *Collins v Secretary of State for the Department of Work and Pensions*,[102] criticised the application of the habitual residence test in excluding EEA citizens who are in the UK as work-seekers from entitlement to JSA (see para 2.41

---

99   CIS 15484/96, 20 July 1999.

100 CIS/1304/1997 and CJSA/5394/1998.

101 *Gingi v Secretary of State for the Department of Work and Pensions* [2001] EWCA Civ 1685.

102 Case C–138/02, 23 March 2004.

above). The criticisms are based on the right of freedom of movement under the EC Treaty,[103] which right is guaranteed to EEA citizens[104] without discrimination.[105] The court found that such a test was potentially unlawful, since it was likely to be discriminatory and disproportionate to its objects. The ruling is likely to give rise to challenges to the lawfulness of the test in other contexts.

2.76   As part of legislative change occasioned by the accession of the ten states to the European Union on 1 May 2004, the government has proposed changes to the habitual residence test which affect all who are subject to it. From 1 May 2004, the habitual residence test is not satisfied by any person who does not also have a 'right to reside' (RTR) in the Common Travel Area (CTA). This marks a significant change, especially for EEA nationals: previously, all EEA nationals could satisfy the habitual residence test by an 'appreciable period' of residence in the CTA; now they will only be able to do so if they have RTR. Those who fall within the exempt categories described at para 2.70 above are unaffected by this extension of the test.

2.77   The following categories of people have a right to reside:

- UK citizens,[106] and citizens of the Channel Islands, Isle of Man and Republic of Ireland;
- EEA nationals who are 'workers'[107] (see paras 2.33–2.37 above);
- EEA workers who have retired from employment in the UK;[108]
- EEA nationals who are work-seekers for six months and thereafter for so long as they are genuinely seeking work;[109]
- EEA nationals who are self-employed[110] while they are providing services. A self-employed person's right to reside ends if they cease trading, but not if the person is temporarily incapable of work as a result of an illness or accident;[111]
- EEA nationals who are 'economically inactive' have a right to reside,[112] however, for the purposes of establishing eligibility for means-tested benefits, it is substantially nullified by being subject

103 EC Treaty art 39.
104 EC Treaty art 17.
105 EC Treaty art 12.
106 By virtue of Immigration Act 1971 s1.
107 Under EC Treaty art 39, EC reg 1612/68 and EC Directive 68/360.
108 EC reg 1251/70.
109 By EC Treaty art 39 and EC reg 1612/68; *Antonissen* [1991] ECR I–745.
110 By EC Treaty art 43 and EC Directive 73/148.
111 EC Directive 73/148.
112 Derived from EC Treaty art 18 and EC Directives 90/364, 90/365 and 93/96.

to a condition that they have sufficient resources to avoid becoming an unreasonable burden on the UK social assistance system. This category includes, for example, the sick and those who have retired other than from employment in the UK; it also includes others who are unlikely to qualify as workers, such as students, single parents and disabled people.

2.78 A person has a 'right to reside' if they have been issued with a residence permit, and residence permits are to be issued to persons on production of the document by which they entered the member state and proof of employment or engagement by an employer. However, a person also has a right to reside without the issue of a residence permit, if they fall within the category of 'worker'.[113]

2.79 Family members of EEA citizens in the above categories will have the same right to reside (paras 2.39–2.40).

2.80 It is to be noted that nationals of countries outside the UK and the EEA would also have to establish a right to reside to qualify for benefits, although, as has been seen (paras 2.4–2.7), most are disqualified by IAA 1999 s115 as 'persons subject to immigration control'. There is to be detailed guidance issued on establishing who does and who does not have a 'right to reside'. It is intended that the entitlement to benefit given to those special categories described above (paras 2.53–2.66) will be unaffected by the rule.

The urgent cases rate

2.81 Asylum-seekers and other persons subject to immigration control who are eligible for IS or income-based JSA are paid at a reduced rate known as urgent cases payments (UCP).[114] The applicable amount is calculated as 90 per cent of the personal allowance plus full personal allowances for children, any premiums and housing costs.[115]

2.82 The income and capital rules which apply to UCPs are stricter than those which usually apply to IS and income-based JSA.[116] If the claimant has any capital, he or she will not be eligible – the normal capital limit and rules about disregarded capital do not apply. This

---

113 The right of residence of 'workers' derives directly from the right of freedom of movement guaranteed to EEA citizens by the EC Treaty, rather than from EC Council Directive 68/360.

114 IS Regs reg 70(2A); JSA Regs reg 147(2A).

115 IS Regs reg 71; JSA Regs reg 148.

116 IS Regs reg 72; JSA Regs reg 149.

means that if a claimant receives arrears of disability benefits or has savings, he or she will not be entitled to any UCP until the money has been spent or accounted for. Arrears of UCPs or concessionary UCPs are not taken into account as capital.

2.83 Those who will be paid at the UCP rate are:

- asylum-seekers entitled to benefit by virtue of transitional protection (see paras 2.12–2.26);
- PSICs (such as students and visitors) who have limited leave but are temporarily without funds (see para 2.59);
- PSICs (such as elderly dependent relatives) whose sponsor has died within five years of their date of entry or the date of the undertaking, whichever is later (see paras 2.55–2.58).

Those entitled to IS or income-based JSA because they are nationals of an EEA country or because of a reciprocal agreement are not subject to UCPs and receive benefit at the normal rate.

Mixed households[117]

2.84 Problems arise frequently where there are households in which some family members are entitled to benefits and some are not. In such households, there is often a mix of sources of income including the DWP, the local authority and NASS. In practice, there is plenty of scope for errors to be made by each of these bodies as to who is responsible for supporting whom. Where there is a dispute about whether persons should be supported by benefits or by asylum support, it should be recalled that persons entitled to social security benefits are excluded from entitlement to asylum support.[118]

Who can be included in the benefit claim?

2.85 The usual position where benefit is claimed is that the claimant claims for him/herself and for any partner and dependent children. However, special rules apply to persons subject to immigration control. These rules are different for asylum-seekers and other persons subject to immigration control from those for persons receiving ordinary benefits.

---

117 See also para 3.20.
118 IAA 1999 s95(7); Asylum Support Regs 2000 reg 4(4); Asylum Support (Interim Provisions) Regs 1999 reg 7.

Where the household includes a person subject to immigration control entitled to benefits

2.86   In most cases, the entitlement to benefit of such persons derives from transitional protection (see 2.12–2.26). The rules differ depending on whether transitional protection derives from entitlement to benefit before 5 February 1996 (or in the case of CB, 6 October 1996), or from a claim for asylum made on arrival before 3 April 2000.[119]

1) Where there is a claimant who is entitled to benefit because they were entitled to benefit on 4 February 1996 and there has been no adverse decision on their asylum claim, and no revision or super-session of the benefit award, the rules are as follows. Where there is such a claimant in the household, the entitlement to benefit is preserved not only for the claimant but for all persons who were family members as at 5 February 1996 (including family members who are PSICs).[120] Thus, dependants will be included in the assessment, and such family members are able to make claims in their own right. IS and income-based JSA will be paid at the urgent cases rate (see para 2.81 above). Family members who joined the claimant after 5 February 1996 (except for children born in the UK) cannot be included in the assessment, nor are they able to make claims in their own right. Where they are asylum-seekers or dependants of an asylum-seeker they should apply to NASS. Where a person is receiving child benefit because of transitional protection, and another child is born or joins the family after 6 October 1996, additional child benefit can be claimed for the new child. Such a claim is treated as a new claim, and not a review or supersession of the existing claim.[121]

2) Where there is a claimant who is entitled to benefit[122] because he or she applied for asylum 'on arrival' before 3 April 2000 or on the basis of seeking refuge from an upheaval country (see para 2.60), the rules are as follows. The claimant's partner and dependants will be included in the assessment (including partners or depen-dants who are PSICs).[123] The DWP accepts partners and depend-ent children as included in the assessment in such cases only

119 See paras 2.12–2.26.
120 SS(PFA)MA Regs reg 12(1).
121 CF/1015/1995.
122 SS(PFA)MA Regs reg 12(1).
123 SS(IA)CA 2000 Regs regs 2(5), (6) and 12; IS Regs regs 70 and 71; see Asylum Support Adjudicator decision ASA 00/08/0037.

where they were part of the assessment before 3 April 2000. However, it is arguable that a claimant under this transitional protection should be able to include in the assessment a partner and dependent children joining the household after 2 April 2000. Family members of the claimant cannot make claims in their own right. This form of transitional protection applies only to IS, income-based JSA, HB and CTB. IS and income-based JSA will be paid at the urgent cases rate. Family members not included in the assessment who are asylum-seekers or dependants of an asylum-seeker should apply to NASS.

Where the household includes a person entitled to claim ordinary benefits

2.87   Such a claimant who has a partner who is a PSIC cannot receive benefit for that partner or for any children who are themselves PSICs[124] (except in the case of WTC and CTC – see para 2.89). Such a claimant can claim for any children born in the UK. Thus, for example, where one member of a couple is granted refugee status but the other partner and the children of the family still have pending applications for asylum, the refugee partner cannot claim for his/her partner or the children while they are excluded from benefits by IAA 1999 s115.

2.88   It can be seen from this example that where a partner has been receiving UCPs, the grant of status to that partner can have the effect of ending entitlement to benefit in respect of the other partner and children. Where this happens, an application should be made to NASS for support for the other partner and children.

2.89   In the case of WTC and CTC, a claimant who is entitled to tax credits can claim for a partner who is a PSIC.[125]

2.90   Where both partners in a couple are entitled to claim benefits, they can claim benefit for any dependent children, whether or not the children are PSICs.

2.91   Where the household includes a single parent who is entitled to claim benefits, he or she is able to claim benefit for dependent children, whether or not the children are PSICs.

2.92   Where the household comprises a single parent or a couple who are PSICs and dependent children who are not PSICs, it is not possible for the parents to claim benefit for the children.

---

124 IS Regs reg 21(3) and Sch 7 para 16A; SPC Regs 2002 SI 1792 reg 5(1), as amended by State Pension Credit (Consequential, Miscellaneous and Transitional Provisions) (No 2) Regs 2002 SI 3197 Sch para 2.
125 TC(I) Regs reg 3(2).

Where the household includes a child born in the UK

2.93   A child born in the UK will not be a British citizen unless one of the parents is British or has ILR. Such a child does not need to obtain leave to enter or remain in the UK unless he or she leaves the UK with an intention to re-enter.[126] It seems that such a child is not excluded from any benefit claim because he or she does not fall within the IAA 1999 s115 definition of PSIC.

Treatment of resources when assessing benefit entitlement

2.94   Where one partner to a couple is entitled to benefits and the other is not because they are a PSIC, the resources of both are taken into account in assessing benefit. The claimant will be able to receive the full amount of any housing costs included in the IS/JSA assessment and, where there are children, will also receive the family premium (even if the children are PSICs).[127]

Treatment of asylum/interim support as income in assessing benefit

2.95   Where a claimant receives means-tested benefits and his/her partner receives asylum support in kind rather than cash for essential living needs, the asylum support does not count as income for the purposes of income-based JSA or IS.[128] Asylum support paid in cash is treated as income.

2.96   Asylum support is treated as income for the purposes of HB and CTB.[129] The full asylum support payment whether in cash or in kind will be treated as income when assessing the amount of benefit. This even includes the payments of £50 in cash vouchers, which an asylum-seeker can claim every six months.

Housing benefit non-dependant deductions[130]

2.97   There is no provision to exempt asylum-seekers or those they live with from non-dependant deductions. This means that where an asylum-seeker stays as the guest of someone claiming HB or CTB, the

---

126   HC 395 paras 305–308, see para 1.128.
127   IS Regs reg 21(3) and Sch 7 para 16A.
128   IS Regs reg 40(2) and Sch 9 para 21; JSA Regs reg 103(2) and Sch 7 para 22.
129   HB Regs reg 33(4)(b) as amended by SS(IA)CA Regs reg 6(4); CTB Regs reg 24(5) as amended by SS(IA)CA Regs reg 7(4)(b).
130   See para 5.167 for council tax liability of supported persons.

host will be subject to a reduction in his/her benefit, assuming a contribution from the asylum-seeker. This applies whether the asylum-seeker household is in receipt of asylum support for living expenses, of interim support or has no income at all. There is an argument that non-dependant deductions should not be levied because an asylum-seeker is 'temporary' according to government statements (see paras 4.72–4.75). The claimant affected could apply to the local authority to exercise its discretion to award a discretionary housing payment.[131] A discretionary housing payment is an additional payment to recipients of HB/CTB over and above HB/CTB paid under the ordinary rules. A local authority may make such a payment where the claimants 'appear to such an authority to require some further financial assistance (in addition to the benefit or benefits to which they are entitled) in order to meet housing costs'.[132] In this context, 'housing costs' includes council tax. Where a discretionary housing payment is refused, the remedy is an internal review only.

End of entitlement to benefit

2.98   A person subject to immigration control who is entitled to state benefits will lose that entitlement in any of the following circumstances:

a) the first decision on asylum application for those entitled on the basis of transitional protection. If the decision is favourable it will, nonetheless, amount to a change of circumstances, which should immediately be reported to the DWP and (for HB/CTB) to the local authority (see paras 2.99–2.100 if the decision is unfavourable);

b) limited leave to remain (ELR/HP/DLR) expires without an application for extension or variation having been made (see paras 2.102–2.104);

c) in the case of non-contributory benefits, where entitlement to benefit is 'reviewed' (see para 2.105).

---

131 See the Child Support, Pensions and Social Security Act 2000 ss69 and 70 and the Discretionary Financial Assistance Regulations 2000. A detailed explanation of discretionary housing payments is beyond the scope of this book. Advisers should refer to *Welfare Benefits and Tax Credits Handbook* (CPAG, 2004/5).

132 Discretionary Financial Assistance Regulations 2000 reg 2(1)(b).

Unfavourable Home Office decisions

2.99   Entitlement to benefit ends with the first unfavourable decision on a pending asylum claim. Such a decision may be a first decision by the Home Office, or – less usually – in cases where there has been a long-outstanding appeal, a decision of the Special Adjudicator or Immigration Appeal Tribunal. Precisely, entitlement ends when the Home Secretary records the asylum claim as having been refused *and* the asylum applicant is notified of the decision.[133]

2.100   An asylum-seeker whose application for asylum is refused, and who is not granted any other form of leave such as ELR/HP/DLR, loses any entitlement to benefit unless he or she falls within a class of PSICs that is not excluded from benefits (see paras 2.30–2.66 above), for example, family members of EEA nationals. Asylum-seekers may be eligible for asylum support or interim support pending an asylum appeal or, in the case of families, for as long as they have dependent children under 18 living with them in the UK. The procedure is for 'disbenefited' claimants to obtain a form to claim NASS support.[134] NASS have made arrangements with local authorities to assist with the completion of these forms in the case of families with dependent children. Childless asylum-seekers who lose IS after an unsuccessful asylum appeal, and other unsuccessful applicants for leave to enter or remain in the UK, may be entitled to help under the community care provisions explained in chapter 6.

Expiry of limited leave to remain

2.101   Humanitarian protection (HP) and discretionary leave to remain (DLR) (both formerly known as exceptional leave to remain (ELR)) are granted for a specified limited period. Unless granted subject to a condition that there be no recourse to public funds, they carry with them entitlement to benefits, but that entitlement ends with the expiry of the period of leave. However, entitlement will not expire if an application is made for it to be extended or varied *before the expiry of the existing period of leave.*

---

133 SS(IA)CA Regs reg 12(5) and (10); *R (Anufrijeva) v Secretary of State for the Home Department and Secretary of State for Social Security* [2003] UKHL 36 (overruling the Court of Appeal decision in *R v Home Secretary ex p Salem* [1999] 1 AC 450; [1999] QB 805 and High Court in *R (Paulo) v Secretary of State for the Home Department and Secretary of State for Social Security* [2001] EWHC Admin 480).

134 See paras 3.149–3.151.

2.102   A person with leave to enter or remain in the UK who applies for it to be extended or varied before it expires is treated as having leave on the same terms (and carrying the same entitlement to benefits) until the application is decided by the Home Office. This rule previously derived from the Variation of Leave Order,[135] known by its acronym 'VOLO', although the rule is now contained in IA 1971.[136] Evidence that a relevant application has been made could be provided in the form of a letter from an immigration representative. A letter of acknowledgement from the Home Office or dated receipt from the Home Office should also be acceptable.

2.103   If leave has expired without an application being made to vary or extend and before the grant of HP/DLR/ELR the person was an asylum-seeker with dependent children, the person will continue to be classified as an asylum-seeker and so entitled to asylum support while they have dependent children under 18 living with them in the UK.

2.104   If leave has expired without an application being made to vary or extend and the person is not a former asylum-seeker, he or she is excluded from entitlement to benefits. Such persons may be entitled to help under the community care provisions explained in chapter 6. If they have children, they may be entitled to assistance under Nationality, Immigration and Asylum Act 2002 Sch 3 and the Withholding and Withdrawal of Support (Travel Assistance and Temporary Accommodation) Regulations 2002[137] (see appendix A).

Review of entitlement to non-contributory benefits

2.105   Asylum-seekers entitled to 1996 transitional protection (see paras 2.12–2.16) receiving non-contributory benefits (AA, DLA, CA, SDA and CB) will cease to be entitled to those benefits if the award of benefit is reviewed, superseded or if an award made for a specific period expires.[138] Those left destitute by such loss of benefit should apply to NASS or the local authority for asylum support (see chapter 3).

135 See para 1.24.
136 IA 1971 s3A, as amended by IAA 1999 s3. Section 3A replaced the Variation of Leave Order (VOLO) 1976 SI No 1572 for all cases where an application to vary leave was made on or after 2 October 2000. See Immigration (Variation of Leave) (Amendment) Order 2000 SI No 2445.
137 SI 2002 No 3078.
138 SS(IA)CA Regs reg 12(10); *R (B) v Chief Adjudication Officer* [2001] UKHL 35, [2001] 4 All ER 41; *M (a minor) v Secretary of State for Social Security* [2001] *Times*, 6 July 2001, HL; *R v Chief Adjudication Officer ex p B* [1999] 1 WLR 1695; *Yildiz v Secretary of State for Social Security* [2001] CA 28/02/01, unreported.

Becoming entitled to benefit

Administration, claims and payments

2.106   Asylum-seekers become entitled to benefits following a grant of refugee status, or a grant of humanitarian protection (HP) or discretionary leave to remain (DLR) (formerly known as exceptional leave
to remain (ELR)). Other PSICs may become entitled to benefits if
granted HP, DLR or indefinite leave to remain (ILR).

2.107   Upon the grant of status, it will frequently be necessary to make
multiple claims for benefit. Advisers should check through the
benefits the claimant may be entitled to. Where there is a possibility
of backdating, urgent action is required (see paras 2.136–2.147
below). Consideration should be given to:

  – claiming IS or income-based JSA or SPC, and (in the case of
    refugees) claiming backdated awards of IS or SPC (apply on the
    appropriate claim form to the local social security (DWP) office for
    IS and SPC or jobcentre for income-based JSA);
  – claiming HB and CTB, and (in the case of refugees) claiming back-
    dated awards of those benefits (apply on the appropriate claim
    form to the local authority (borough or district council); it is also
    possible to claim on forms supplied with claim packs for IS and
    JSA);
  – claiming tax credits – WTC and CTC (apply on the appropriate
    claim form to the Inland Revenue Tax Credit Office);
  – claiming a crisis loan or interim support where there are delays in
    the administration of other claims (apply to the local social secur-
    ity (DWP) office);
  – claiming CB where there are children (apply on the appropriate
    claim form to the Child Benefit Centre, Newcastle upon Tyne);
  – claiming DLA and CA where there is a disabled claimant (apply on
    the appropriate claim forms to the local Disability Benefits Office
    of the DWP);
  – making separate claims for each non-dependant adult in the
    household;
  – claiming a community care grant where there are costs to be met
    of setting up home (apply to the local social security (DWP) office).

2.108   It is to be noted that the assessment of claims for income-based JSA
and IS made after 6 April 2004 no longer cover the needs of children.
All personal allowances and premiums in respect of children are abolished for new claims from that date and, instead, claims need to be
made for CB and CTC. Those with existing claims at 6 April 2004 will

have the element for children transferred over to CTC in due course. Adults still need to claim IS or income-based JSA for themselves.

2.109   For who can be included in the claim, see mixed households at paras 2.84–2.97.

The end of NASS or interim support

2.110   Asylum support or interim support entitlement ends when an asylum claim is 'determined' for the purposes of IAA 1999 s94(3). A claim is determined at the end of the 'prescribed period'. The prescribed period is 28 days, which starts either:

- on the date the applicant is notified of the decision, which is two days after posting if the decision is sent by first class post; or
- on the date the appeal is disposed of.

This means asylum-seekers will only receive interim or asylum support for 28 days after notification of a decision on the asylum claim. A favourable decision may arise as a result of an appeal but, in practice, the Home Office will not terminate asylum support until 28 days after it issues its own decision following the appeal. During the 28-day period, the former asylum-seeker will need to sort out any benefit claim and make alternative housing arrangements. The 28-day period is not long enough to process an IS or HB claim in most cases. In London, processing an application for a national insurance number (NINO) (which is treated as a prerequisite of an IS or HB claim) can take several weeks. In order to advise those faced with this difficulty, advisers will need to be familiar with the evidence and NINO requirements (see paras 2.115–2.126), rules about interim or other urgent payments (see para 2.131) and should consider urgent applications for judicial review (see para 2.131). If all else fails, community care help should be sought in cases involving children[139] or adults with needs arising from age, ill-health, pregnancy, etc (see chapter 6).

2.111   If a household has been receiving asylum support from NASS, the asylum-seeker should be issued with a termination of support letter when a final decision is made on the asylum claim. Form NASS 35, which should be issued by NASS when support stops, gives details of the Home Office decision, the names of household members and the period and value of asylum support. It contains a photograph of the main applicant for support. Adult dependants will receive a shorter letter giving details of support received.

139 Children Act 1989 s17.

2.112   Where an asylum-seeker is granted HP, DLR or ILR on appeal, it will not be possible to claim benefit until the Home Office has issued formal letters notifying the grant of status. There are frequently delays in the Home Office issuing such letters. The asylum-seeker's immigration adviser should consider judicial review to compel the Home Office to comply. A common problem is that NASS sends the NASS 35 to the address of the asylum-seeker's NASS accommodation after they have been evicted from it through the termination of NASS support. Persons who are in NASS temporary accommodation pending assessment of their NASS application at the time an asylum decision is made will not be issued with a NASS 35 form at all.

2.113   Persons granted status frequently experience practical difficulties with the initial claim for benefits. Asylum support or interim support ends 28 days after the Home Office notification of the favourable decision. The duty to offer asylum or interim support ceases if the household is excluded because of eligibility for IS.[141] Many asylum-seekers are left with no means of support because of Home Office delays in issuing documents and DWP delays in issuing a national insurance number.[142] The Home Office has completed a successful pilot scheme issuing national insurance numbers along with letters granting status, but there is no timetable for extending this at the time of writing.

Claims for income support and income-based jobseeker's allowance

2.114   To make a valid claim for IS and income-based JSA, the claimant must satisfy 'the evidence requirement' and the 'National Insurance Number (NINO) requirement'.

The evidence requirement

2.115   The evidence requirement means the application form must be completed in full and accompanied by other evidence requested,[143] that is, any of the following that the claimant has:

- pay-slips;
- proof of other income (this will be form NASS 35 provided by

141 Note that a destitute asylum-seeker or dependant of an asylum-seeker can claim asylum or interim support if only part of the household is eligible for social security benefit (see paras 2.86–2.93).

142 Social services help may be available in the case of children or people with community care needs (see para 6.123 onwards).

143 SS(CP) Regs reg 4(1A), (1B).

NASS in the case of an asylum-seeker who has been receiving asylum support from NASS, but note that production of a NASS 35 form is not a pre-requisite for benefit to be assessed, if other evidence is available);
– proof of any savings or payment from an insurance policy;
– proof of service charges or ground rent.

If the form is not properly completed and the evidence requirement is not met, the DWP should contact the claimant allowing one month from the date of the claim to remedy the problem. If the evidence requirement is not met within that period, the claim may be rejected.[144]

2.116   Where asylum-seekers are unable to meet the evidence requirement within the specified period, or at all, they can ask the DWP for an exemption, for an extension of the one-month period, or to get the information on their behalf.

2.117   If a claimant cannot meet the evidence requirement, a request can be made for exemption on any of the following grounds:[145]

– a physical, mental learning or communication difficulty where it is not reasonably practicable for the claimant to find someone else to assist, for example, an isolated asylum-seeker with mental health needs who cannot read or write English;
– the information required does not exist or could not be obtained except with a serious risk of physical or mental harm to the claimant, for example, documents are in the country of origin;
– a third party has the information and it is not reasonably practicable to obtain it.

Where it is decided that the evidence requirement has been met, the regulations[146] state that there is no right of appeal, but the Commissioner has decided otherwise,[147] holding that the exclusion of a right of appeal must be disapplied as being non-compliant with ECHR article 6.

---

144 SS(CP) Regs reg 6(1A) and (4AB).
145 SS(CP) Regs reg 4(1B).
146 SSCS(DA) Regs Sch 2 para 5.
147 CIS/540/2002; at the time of writing, an appeal against this decision to the Court of Appeal is pending. See also CIS/345/2003; another commissioner has upheld the *vires* of the rules in CJSA/69/2001.

National Insurance number requirement[148]

2.118   A claim for benefit should be treated as an application for a NINO; alternatively, an application may be made on form CA5400 at the local DWP office. Application will lead to an 'evidence of identity' interview, to which documentary evidence should be taken. NINO applications are dealt with by a division of the DWP called the Departmental Central Index (DCI).

2.119   To qualify for benefit, the claimant must provide in respect of every person of 16 and over covered by the claim either:

   (a) ...
      (i) a statement of the person's national insurance number, and information or evidence establishing that that number has been allocated to the person; or
      (ii) information or evidence enabling the national insurance number that has been allocated to that person to be ascertained, or
   (b) the person makes an application for a national insurance number to be ascertained which is accompanied by information or evidence enabling such a number to be so allocated.[149]

It will be seen that, under (b), a claimant is able to establish entitlement to benefit without a NINO actually being allocated. The evidence required to obtain a NINO is evidence of identity, for example, birth and marriage certificates, standard acknowledgement letter from the Home Office, passport, national identity card, driving licence, utility bills, tenancy agreement.[150] In practice, originals of documents or notarised copies are required. In addition, the DWP may refuse to accept evidence of immigration status and identity other than a Home Office letter confirming status, for example, not passports with entry stamps. Unreasonable demands should not be made for documents that the claimant is unable to furnish.[151]

2.120   Before a decision on their immigration status, asylum-seekers may have sent the originals of documents proving identity to the Home Office, which is likely to keep them until an asylum decision is made. To obviate this difficulty, claimants can ask the DWP to

---

148 Useful advice on the National Insurance Number requirement is available in a CPAG briefing at http//www.cpag.org.uk/cro/Briefings/0403ninos.htm
149 SSAA 1992 s1(1B).
150 There are two DWP leaflets on applying for a NINO: 'Applying for a National Insurance Number' (leaflet GL31) and 'How to prove your identity for social security' (GL25) (see appendix C).
151 According to the 'Evidence of Identity Guide' issued to staff.

endorse photocopies of original documents when they first visit the local office with these. If the original documents are later lost or sent to another agency, the photocopies should be relied on. The DWP is likely to argue that the IS and DCI (Departmental Central Index) Sections are discrete and the originals must be provided again.

2.121   The requirement to have a NINO (or be applying for one) as a pre-condition of a claim[152] is one of the main causes of delay for asylum-seekers claiming IS or income-based JSA for the first time. To avoid this delay, advisers should consider whether an asylum-seeker can obtain a NINO prior to any claim for benefit. Asylum-seekers who have the right to work but are not eligible for benefit can apply for a NINO if they have a job offer or are registered with an employment agency, although priority is given to processing 'benefits-inspired applications', that is, NINO applications by benefit claimants. (It appears that 'employment inspired applicants' are dealt with by a separate section of the DWP.) The applicant must apply to the DWP for a NINO interview and complete form CA5400.

2.122   Claimants with HP, DLR or ELR are sometimes refused benefits because DWP or local authority decision-makers misinterpret the immigration documents. HP, DLR or ELR may initially be granted for a period of one year, but should not be confused with other forms of limited leave. In such cases, advisers can refer to IAA 1999 s115(9), which describes the categories of PSICs and, in particular, section 115(9)(a), which defines a PSIC as a person who 'requires leave to enter or remain in the United Kingdom but does not have it'.

2.123   After a decision of HP, DLR, ELR or full refugee status, a common problem is an error in the spelling of names or the order of names, which the Home Office may take months to correct.

2.124   There have been a number of cases in which claimants have been refused benefits because they do not have a NINO and refused asylum support because they are no longer asylum-seekers. In such cases, interim payments and social fund payments are also often refused. It may be possible to challenge a refusal of IS by arguing that the claimant is entitled through having applied for a NINO and given all the necessary evidence. Arguably, the DWP should accept the Home Office's confirmation that the Home Secretary is satisfied as to the claimant's identity. In practice, they often do not, but there is scope for judicial review and/or complaints.

2.125   There are frequently problems where a claimant has a spouse who is a person who has no recourse to public funds. The DWP takes the

152 SSAA 1992 s1(1A).

view that any such partner must satisfy the NINO requirement, even if no benefit is going to be paid in respect of that person. It can be very difficult for such a spouse to prove their identity. It is arguable that, because the spouse is not a person 'in respect of whom'[153] benefit is being claimed, the NINO requirement does not apply to them, but the DWP does not accept this argument. Tactically, the claimant must insist that the spouse can only provide documentation that is available and reasonably required.

2.126   Claimants frequently find that their application for a NINO is refused because the DWP states it is not satisfied with the evidence of identity produced, with no reason given. A concurrent claim for benefit may then be refused for failure to meet the NINO requirement. There is no right of appeal against a decision to refuse to issue a NINO, and the only remedy is judicial review. There is a right of appeal against refusal of a benefit claim because of failure to meet the NINO requirement, and the appellant in such an appeal is entitled to raise the issue of whether a refusal to allocate a NINO was correct in fact and law.[154] If the secretary of state fails to explain the reasons for refusal to allocate a NINO in its submission to the tribunal, the tribunal should be asked to require the evidence to be produced.[155]

Claiming other benefits and tax credits

2.127   In the cases of IS and income-based JSA described above, it has been seen that failure to satisfy the 'evidence requirement' and the 'NINO requirement' prevents there being a valid claim. The commencement of any resulting award of benefit depends upon there being a valid claim. Claims for other benefits, however, should be treated as valid from the date a letter of claim is received by the DWP, Inland Revenue or (for HB and CTB) the local authority, although it will be necessary to complete the relevant application form, to satisfy the NINO requirement[156] and to provide required evidence before a decision can be made on the claim and benefit can be paid. Local authorities are advised[157] that they may accept confirmation from the DWP that the

---

153 SSAA 1992 s1(1A).
154 CIS/0345/2003.
155 The DWP and the tribunal should be referred to the findings and observations of the Commissioner in CIS/245/2003.
156 SSAA 1992 s1; Tax Credits (Claims and Notifications) Regs 2002 reg 5(4); HB Regs reg 2B, CTB Regs reg 2B.
157 Circular HB/CTB A28/2003.

NINO requirement has been met for IS, JSA, SPC or IB as satisfying the requirement for HB and CTB, but in the absence of such confirmation they should not sit back and wait for the DWP to make its own decision – they should make their own assessment.

2.128   In the case of tax credits, there is a discretion to disapply the NINO requirement where it is considered that the claimant has a reasonable excuse for making a claim without satisfying it.[158] There is no right of appeal against a decision of the Inland Revenue that the NINO requirement is not met,[159] and the only remedy is judicial review.

Delays in processing the claim where there is an urgent need

2.129   The process of satisfying the NINO requirement is fraught with delays at every stage, which can leave claimants without resources. As well as repeatedly pressing for decisions to be made, the following interim assistance can be considered.

Crisis loans

2.130   A claimant could consider an application[160] to the DWP for a 'crisis loan' from the discretionary social fund while the claim is being processed. There is a limit of £1,000 on such a loan. Such claims are governed by the Social Fund Directions and the Social Fund Guide. Unlike budgeting loans and community care grants, it is not a precondition that the claimant is in receipt of IS or income-based JSA. Crisis loans are available when required to help meet expenses in an emergency, to avoid serious damage or serious risk to the health and safety of the claimant or a member of the household. There is no definition of an emergency and the High Court has ruled that need and priority of an application should be considered before budgetary considerations.[161] It is arguable that asylum-seekers are entitled to crisis loans because they do not fall within the categories of persons from abroad excluded from eligibility. However, it is a requirement of such a loan that the claimant will have the means to repay and so it would be necessary to show that the claimant will be awarded income, for example, cash as part of an interim support or Children Act 1989

---

158 Tax Credits (Claims and Notifications) Regs 2002 reg 5(6).
159 Appeal rights are limited to decisions specified in Tax Credits Act 2002 s14.
160 Form SF400 or SF401.
161 *R v Social Fund Inspector ex p Taylor* [1998] COD 152, QBD.

s17 payment or that he or she will be eligible for benefit in future. If a crisis loan is refused, a revision within 28 days and written reasons for the decision should be requested.

Interim payments[162]

2.131   There is a discretion to make an interim payment of benefit if the claimant is, or may be, entitled to a DWP benefit, but it is not possible for the claim to be dealt with immediately. It is contrary to departmental guidance for the DWP to refuse an interim payment on the basis that the claimant must meet the NINO requirement.[163] Any such refusal can be challenged where all 'the necessary information' has been provided to enable a NINO to be allocated (see para 2.118). There is no right of appeal against refusal of an interim payment: if income is urgently needed a judicial review application should be considered. A formal letter before action under the judicial review protocol to the DWP solicitors will often resolve the matter.

Payments on account of housing benefit

2.132   Private and housing association tenants should ask for a payment on account (or interim payment) if there is a delay in administering the claim.[164] In fact, such payments should be made automatically once all required information and evidence has been provided and if it is not practicable for the authority to process the claim within 14 days. No request is necessary under the regulation but in practice it is usually necessary to ask. Where required information or evidence has not been provided, a payment on account must still be made if the claimant has 'good cause' for not providing it. It is at least arguable that lack of a NINO should not prevent a payment on account where there is no fault on the part of the claimant. Failure to make a payment on account may be challenged by judicial review.

Community care assistance

2.133   A request to the local authority's social services department for a community care assessment may be appropriate as an emergency

---

162   Social Security (Payments on Account, Overpayments and Recovery) Regulations 1988 SI No 664 reg 2.
163   Joint IS/JSA Bulletin, 30/01, which states that interim payments should be considered for persons awaiting allocation of a NINO.
164   HB Regs reg 91(1).

measure if the claimant has a health need or has children (see further chapter 6).

Community care grants

2.134 Asylum-seekers who are granted ELR or refugee status may be eligible for a community care grant payment from the DWP to enable them to set up home. Social Fund Direction 4(a)(v) provides for the payment of a community care grant to help a person 'set up home in the community as part of a planned resettlement programme following a period during which he or she has been without a settled way of life'. Social fund guidance[165] suggests that those who have been 'staying in temporary accommodation provided by the Home Office pending a decision on their application for asylum in this country' may fall within the definition of unsettled way of life.

2.135 Although the provision is aimed at asylum-seekers who have been receiving support from NASS, there is no reason why it should not apply equally to those who were receiving interim support from local authorities. There may also be asylum-seekers who have been living 'an unsettled way of life' while staying with various friends and relatives who should be considered for a grant. The guidance[166] states that the list at para 3070 is not exhaustive.

Back-dated benefit for refugees

2.136 Asylum-seekers who are granted refugee status are entitled to claim arrears of benefit. This provision applies only to those granted refugee status and does not apply to those granted ELR, HP or DLR. However, the Asylum and Immigration (Treatment of Claimants, etc) Act 2004 ss12–13 abolishes the right to backdated benefit, replacing it with a loan scheme (see para 2.147 below). Paragraphs 2.137–2.146 are of relevance to those who claim before the new Act comes into force.

2.137 If an asylum-seeker is recognised as a refugee,[167] he or she is entitled to IS, SPC, WTC, CTC, HB and CTB from the date of the asylum claim.[168] As between IS, SPC, WTC and CTC, which benefit is

---

165 *Social Fund Guidance manual*, para 3070.
166 *Social Fund Guidance manual*, para 3071.
167 See Form ICD.0725, at appendix D below.
168 IS Regs regs 21ZA and 21ZB and SS(IA)CA regs 3, 6 and 7; HB Regs reg 7B; CTB Regs reg 4D; Tax Credit (Immigration) Regs 2003 regs 3(4)–(9) and 4; SPCA 2002 Sch 2 para 42.

claimed will depend on the claimant's circumstances during the period to which the backdated claim relates. It is not possible to claim arrears of income-based JSA, and those who on being granted status claim income-based JSA must make a separate claim for backdated IS.

2.138   The refugee must apply for backdated IS, HB and CTB within 28 days of the date on which he or she (or her/his solicitor) receives notification that the Home Secretary has recognised him/her as a refugee. In the case of WTC, CTC, and SPC, the claim for backdating must be made (to the Inland Revenue for WTC and CTC, to the DWP Pensions Service for SPC) within three months of the notification date.[169] There is no provision to extend these periods even if there would usually be 'good cause for a late claim'. Claims must be made on a claim form (properly completed): a letter will not be sufficient.[170] If the asylum-seeker fails to make a valid claim within the 28 days or three months, he or she will lose the right to backdated benefit. No backdated IS, HB or CTB will be paid for any period before 5 February 1996, and no backdated SPC for any period before 6 October 2003.

2.139   The 28-day time-limit is short and frequently missed in circumstances where status decisions are communicated to applicants' immigration solicitors and they are not able to get in touch with the applicant in time. It is arguable that such a solicitor or advisor, where authorised to do so, may make the claim or notify an intention to make a claim on behalf of the applicant.[171]

2.140   Evidence of means during the period to which the backdating claim relates will be required. For those previously supported by NASS this should be form NASS 35 issued on the termination of NASS support. For those who have been supported by local authorities, the authority should be approached for a statement of the support provided.

2.141   The arrears will be paid at 100 per cent of the IS applicable amount rather than the UCP rate, provided that the asylum claim was recorded on or after 3 April 2000. Therefore, if such a refugee was previously receiving IS at the 90 per cent UCP rate, he or she is entitled to make a backdated claim for the missing 10 per cent.[172] Those who claimed asylum before 3 April 2000 can only claim arrears of IS and

---

169 TC(I) Regs reg 5.
170 SS(CP) Regs reg 4; HB Regs reg 72; CTB Regs reg 62.
171 See 'Acting for the Claimant – backdating of benefit for refugees', *Welfare Rights Bulletin* (June 2003, issue 174) pp 10–11.
172 SS(IA)CA reg 3(5) amending IS reg 21ZB.

income-based JSA at the UCP rate.[173] Arrears of other benefits are paid at the full rate.

2.142   The claim for backdated HB and CTB should be made to the authority in whose area the refugee is living at the time he or she claims the benefit. That authority should then determine HB and CTB for the whole period.[174] Asylum-seekers will only be eligible for backdated HB and CTB if they have had a liability for rent or council tax. There is an exemption from council tax liability for those who are living in accommodation provided under the asylum or interim support duty. The application should be made by requesting backdating in the relevant section of the HB/CTB claim form.

2.143   In assessing back-dated awards of these benefits (IS, CTC, WTC, SPC, HB and CTB), account will be taken of income received in the relevant period under the usual rules. That income includes asylum support[175] and UCP income support paid. In the case of former asylum-seekers with children, it is to be noted that payments made under Children Act 1989 ss17, 23B, 23C or 24A do not fall to be taken into account.[176] For arrears of HB and CTB, account is taken of any HB or CTB paid in the relevant period.[177]

2.144   Lump sums of arrears of benefit paid in this way are disregarded as income and, for a period of 52 weeks, as capital.[178]

2.145   Payment of arrears of CTB will be credited to the claimant's council tax account. If doing so reduces the account to a nil balance, any excess will be paid to the claimant.[179] Similarly, payment of arrears of HB to a council tenant will be credited to the rent account, with any excess paid to the claimant. In the case of HB for a private tenant, the local authority can pay the arrears direct to the landlord where it considers it reasonable to do so. Before making payment, the local authority should find out from the landlord what rent is owing and consult the tenant before making payment direct to the landlord.[180]

2.146   Refugees who try to make claims for backdated payments and are misadvised by benefits officials that they are not entitled, and so fail to

173 Pre-3 April 2000 asylum-seekers are covered by IS reg 21ZA.
174 HB reg 2A as amended by SS(IA)CA reg 6(5).
175 IS Regs reg 21ZB(3); TC(I) Regs reg 3(9).
176 IS Regs Sch 9 para 28, JSA Regs Sch 7 para 29, HB Regs Sch 4 para 26, CTB Regs para 26.
177 HB Regs Sch A1 para 9, CTB Regs Sch A1 para 8.
178 IS Regs Sch 9 para 57, Sch 10 para 49; HB Regs Sch 4 para 61, Sch 5 para 50; CTB Regs Sch 4 para 60, Sch 5 para 50.
179 CTB Regs reg 4D and Sch A1 para 7.
180 HB Regs reg 7B and Sch A1 para 8.

apply within the 28-day time-limit, should apply for an ex-gratia pay-ment. To do so, write to the relevant benefit office, and consider seek-ing to enlist the support of the local MP.

2.147   As indicated above, the government has legislated to abolish back-dated benefit payments to refugees, apparently prompted by a hostile article in *The Sun* newspaper in March 2004. At the time of writing, the Asylum and Immigration (Treatment of Claimants, etc) Act 2004 has been enacted, although no commencement date has been set. Section 2 of the Act abolishes the right to backdated IS, HB and CTB from a date to be set. It is to be noted that the right to backdated SPC, WTC and CTC is not abolished. Section 13 provides for the establish-ment of a system of discretionary loans, and for those loans to be based on an applicant's means and ability to repay, for interest to be charged and for maximum and minimum amounts to be set by the Secretary of State from time to time. The loans are to be repayable by deduction from social security benefits.

Asylum support: eligibility

continued

Introduction and changes to the law

3.1   This chapter explains who is eligible for asylum support under the Immigration and Asylum Act (IAA) 1999. It covers National Asylum Support Service (NASS) procedures, and explains when NASS may refuse, suspend or withdraw support. It then explains how to challenge these NASS decisions and the procedures for appealing to the Asylum Support Adjudicators (ASA). Finally it looks at the end of the asylum process, considering what other help is available for those who are ineligible for NASS support, and IAA 1999 s4 'hard cases' support for failed asylum-seekers.

3.2   Chapter 4 covers service provision for those who are eligible for NASS support, including the type and level of support provided and adequacy (or inadequacy) of accommodation. It also covers asylum-seekers' legal duties while support is provided and the Home Secretary's criminal law powers if those duties are not met.

3.3   When dealing with an asylum support problem, it is important to distinguish between eligibility and access to support (chapter 3) and the adequacy of that support, once it is provided (chapter 4). For best results, advisers should cross-refer to both chapters, particularly in areas such as dispersal.

Overview

3.4   The 'asylum support' scheme was established by IAA 1999 Part VI. Asylum support replaced mainstream welfare provision with a safety-net of basic living expenses and/or housing for asylum-seekers and their dependants. It is administered by NASS which is part of the Immigration and Nationality Directorate (IND).

3.5   The Asylum Support Regulations (AS Regs) 2000,[1] made under powers in IAA 1999 Sch 8, contain the details of the NASS scheme. Various Amendment Regulations have made minor changes to the type and amount of support and to the interpretation of the 1999 Act.

3.6   The 1999 Act was amended by the Nationality, Immigration and Asylum Act (NIAA) 2002 Parts 2 and 3 which made radical changes to *eligibility* for asylum support. Section 55 of that Act excludes childless asylum-seekers from the right to claim NASS support unless they can show they claimed asylum 'as soon as reasonably practicable' or that the refusal of support is breaching their human rights. NIAA 2002

---

1   SI No 704.

also introduced changes to the *provision* of support with a new scheme of accommodation centres (see chapter 4).

3.7   The Asylum and Immigration (Treatment of Claimants, etc) Act 2004 aims to restrict the right of failed asylum-seekers with dependent children to receive asylum support unless they agree to leave the UK. It also makes radical changes to the asylum appeal structure. It received Royal Assent on 22 July 2004 but regulations are needed before the changes to support come into force.

3.8   Decisions about eligibility for asylum support are formally made by the Home Secretary who delegates this power to decision-makers in NASS. They decide whether a destitute asylum-seeker is eligible for 'asylum support' taking into account the Act, the AS Regs and NASS Policy Bulletins. The Bulletins are non-statutory guidance published on the Home Office website.[2] They reflect NASS's interpretation of the law and are referred to where relevant in the text.

3.9   If NASS decides an asylum-seeker is eligible, provision of support is arranged through contracts with the private, public and/or voluntary sectors (see chapter 4).

3.10   'Asylum support' is distinguished here from 'interim support' provided by local authorities (normally social services) under the Asylum Support (Interim Provisions) Regulations 1999[3] which we refer to as the 'Interim Regs'. The 'interim period' during which local authorities had a duty to support some categories of asylum-seekers is due to end on 4 April 2005.[4] Differences between NASS and interim support eligibility are highlighted where relevant and there is an outline in appendix E.

Key features of the asylum support scheme

3.11   The main features of the asylum support scheme are:

- NASS may provide support for an 'asylum-seeker' and any 'dependant' who appears to be destitute or likely to become destitute within 14 days, or 56 days if they are already receiving asylum support.[5]

2   www.ind.homeoffice.gov.uk/default.asp?Pageid=2056.
3   SI No 3056.
4   See Asylum Support (Interim Provisions) (Amendment) Regulations 2004 SI No 566 and open letter from Angela Roye of NASS to Directors of Social Services and Local Authority Chief Executives, 10 February 2004.
5   IAA 1999 s95(1) and AS Regs 2000 reg 7.

- NASS may not provide support unless it is satisfied that the asylum claim was made as soon as reasonably practicable after the person's entry into the UK.[6]

- There is an exception to NIAA 2002 s55(1) if support is necessary to avoid a breach of the asylum-seeker's rights under the European Convention on Human Rights (ECHR) or if the household includes a dependent child under 18 years old.[7]

- The Home Secretary *must* provide support if the asylum-seeker has a dependent child and the household is destitute, since the family is excluded from Children Act 1989 s17 help.[8]

- The terms 'asylum-seeker' and 'dependant' are defined by IAA 1999 s94(1). 'Asylum-seeker' includes a person of 18 or over who has made an asylum claim or a claim under ECHR art 3. NIAA 2002 amends the definition so that the asylum claim must have been made at 'a designated place' to qualify as an asylum-seeker for support purposes.[9] At present NIAA 2002 s44 is not in force but the requirement applies to applications where section 55 arises, so that 'in-country' asylum applicants must have presented themselves at the Asylum Screening Unit (ASU) to qualify for support.[10]

- An unaccompanied asylum-seeker under 18 is not eligible for asylum support but can obtain social services help under Children Act (CA) 1989 ss17 or 20. From ages 18–21 they may transfer to NASS or may be entitled to continue receiving assistance as a child leaving care under CA 1989 as amended.[11]

- When the asylum claim or appeal is decided, a childless asylum-seeker's entitlement to IAA 1999 ss95 or 98 support from NASS ends after a prescribed period. He or she is no longer an asylum-seeker for support purposes but may be entitled to IAA 1999 s4 'hard cases' support.

- An asylum-seeker with a dependent child under 18 continues to be treated as an asylum-seeker for support purposes (and so entitled to support) for as long as he or she and the child are in the UK.[12] The Asylum and Immigration (Treatment of Claimants, etc)

6 NIAA 2002 s55(1).
7 NIAA 2002 s55(5).
8 IAA 1999 s122. But see para 6.71.
9 NIAA 2002 ss18, 44 and 113(1).
10 NIAA 2002 s18.
11 See chapter 6 for duties to asylum-seekers under 18 and care-leavers.
12 IAA 1999 s94(5).

Act 2004 will end this entitlement for failed asylum-seeker families if they are certified by the Home Secretary as having failed to leave the UK voluntarily.

- A person is *destitute* if he or she does not have adequate accommodation or cannot meet other 'essential living needs' for him/her and any dependants during a prescribed period of 14/56 days.[13] The definition of 'asylum-seeker', 'dependant', and 'destitute' is slightly amended by NIAA 2002 s44,[14] but this is not yet in force.

- Emergency accommodation (that is, temporary support) is arranged under IAA 1999 s98, while NASS considers whether an asylum-seeker is eligible for section 95 support.

- 'Support' means accommodation adequate to the household's needs, and/or essential living expenses which are provided in cash.[15]

- In providing support, NASS must have regard to certain factors (the household's actual and potential resources and the cost of provision) and should disregard others (any preference as to the location of accommodation, its nature and its fixtures and fittings) but this does not prevent individual circumstances from being taken into account.[16]

- Support may be suspended or discontinued if the supported person or any dependant has (i) broken the conditions of support, (ii) committed a criminal offence under IAA 1999 Part VI, (iii) made himself 'intentionally destitute', (iv) left the authorised address, or (v) been away from the address without permission for longer than seven consecutive days or 14 days in a six-month period.[17]

- An asylum-seeker may appeal to the Asylum Support Adjudicators (ASA) if their NASS support ends. The ASA currently only consider appeals against the *refusal* or *withdrawal* of asylum support. Judicial review must be used to challenge the *location* or *adequacy* of support or NIAA 2002 s55 decisions or local authority decisions about interim support.

13 IAA 1999 s95(3) and AS Regs 2000 regs 5, 8 and 9.
14 See appendix A.
15 Asylum Support (Repeal) Order 2002 SI No 782 repealed IAA 1999 s96(3) which provided that asylum support could only be paid in cash in exceptional circumstances.
16 AS Regs 2000 regs 12 and 13.
17 AS Regs 2000 reg 20.

- 'Hard cases' support under IAA 1999 s4 may be provided by NASS to failed asylum-seekers who have no outstanding claim for asylum or appeal and who meet strict criteria. They must first satisfy the NIAA 2002 s55 rules.

Initial considerations – should the application be made to a local authority or NASS?

Interim support

3.12   Responsibility for destitute asylum-seekers was initially shared between NASS and local authorities. Local authorities were required to support asylum-seeker households for an 'interim period' and support was governed by the Asylum Support (Interim Provisions) Regulations (Interim Regs) 1999. The period has been extended until 4 April 2005.[18]

3.13   A table in appendix E gives a detailed breakdown of which scheme applies, according to when and where the asylum claim was made. The Home Secretary issued Directions Nos 1–4[19] stating when NASS would assume responsibility for providing support to newly presenting asylum-seekers and when the responsibility would remain with the local authority under the interim arrangements. In brief, NASS began to support destitute asylum-seekers who had claimed asylum 'on arrival' in the UK on or after 3 April 2000. In Scotland and Northern Ireland all asylum-seekers who applied for asylum on or after 3 April 2000 were eligible for NASS support, whether they were 'on-arrival' or 'in-country' applicants. Destitute asylum-seekers who claimed asylum in-country on or after 3 April 2000 continued to be eligible to claim interim support from local authorities only, rather than NASS. Later, in-country applicants were eligible for NASS support, depending on where they were living in England and Wales, and the date of their asylum claim.

3.14   An asylum-seeker who was receiving interim support or who claimed asylum before the relevant dates will remain the responsibility of the local authorities under the Interim Regs 1999 until their original asylum claim is finally determined (or until the interim period ends in April 2005). An asylum-seeker with a dependent child

---

18   Asylum Support (Interim Provisions) Amendment Regulations 2002 SI No 471 and Asylum Support (Interim Provisions) (Amendment) Regulations 2004 SI no 566.

19   See Appendix B.

under 18 continues to be eligible for interim support for as long as they are in the UK and the child is under 18 (unless excluded by NIAA 2002 Sch 3, see para 6.68). An asylum-seeker receiving interim support without a child under 18 who makes a fresh claim under ECHR art 3 after a negative asylum decision or appeal would need to apply to NASS for support.[20]

3.15   New claims for interim support are rare but could be made either:

a) by a person joining a household currently supported under the interim scheme; or

b) by a household which has been self-financing but now needs support and claimed asylum during the relevant period.

3.16   A household with a dependent child which has received interim support cannot transfer to NASS support.[21] A childless asylum-seeker may transfer to NASS support if he or she makes a fresh asylum or ECHR art 3 claim. An asylum-seeker may not transfer their interim support claims between local authorities. So where an asylum-seeker has been receiving interim support from local authority A, he or she cannot make an application for interim support to authority B within 12 months.[22]

Unaccompanied minors[23]

3.17   An asylum-seeker child under 18 who came to the UK without a parent is not eligible for asylum support, but should apply for social services help under the Children Act 1989. If the Home Office disputes the child's given age, an age assessment should be carried out by the local authority. The power to assess is contained in CA 1989 s17 and Sch 2 Part 1, para 3. If there is no documentary evidence of the child's age, there should be a detailed assessment, with an interpreter present, investigating the child's personal and family history as far as possible.[24]

3.18   When the child reaches 18, whether or not he or she is still an asylum-seeker, they may be entitled to continue receiving Children

---

20 See Direction No 4, at Appendix B below.
21 Direction No 4.
22 Interim Regs 1999 reg 7(1)(c).
23 See further chapter 6.
24 See further CA 1989 Sch 2 Part 1, para 7 and guidance in *R (B) v Merton LBC* [2003] EWHC 1689 (Admin); [2003] 4 All ER 280; (2003) 6 CCLR 457 and NASS Policy Bulletin 33.

Act 1989 support until the age of 21.[25] However, they could apply to NASS for support but may be subject to NIAA 2002 s55 (see para 3.21). NASS Policy Bulletin 29 'Transition at Age 18', the Children Leaving Care Act 2000 Regulations and Guidance para 7–11[26] explain how NASS should deal with applications. It should not seek to disperse an asylum-seeker who had been supported under CA 1989 s20 but would take over financial responsibility for support. An 18-year-old former asylum-seeker is entitled to claim mainstream benefits and housing if leave to remain in the UK has been granted. They would be excluded from Children Act 1989 help if removal directions had been issued (see paras 6.68–6.69, below).

Community care needs[27]

3.19   Where a destitute asylum-seeker would be eligible for NASS support but has community care needs, they may ask a local authority to provide a community care assessment[28] and an assessment of their entitlement to accommodation under National Assistance Act (NAA) 1948 s21. The House of Lords in *Westminster CC v NASS*[29] decided that any asylum-seeker who is in need of care and attention, not otherwise available to them, due to old age, mental illness, ill-health, disability, pregnancy or as a nursing mother may be entitled to NAA 1948 s21 accommodation. The local authority may not refuse to help on the basis that NASS support would be available.

Mixed households[30]

3.20   A mixed household is where household members have more than one immigration status and so are eligible for different types of support. Where someone comes to the UK, claims asylum and then joins the household of a partner or parent, then the immigration status and income of each of them is relevant to the eligibility for NASS support. At first NASS approached the problem by comparing the existing resident's income with the ordinary NASS thresholds so that a couple would be reduced to NASS rates of support (70 per cent of income

25   R *(Berhe, Kidane and others) v Hillingdon LBC and Secretary of State for Education and Skills (interested party)* [2003] EWHC 2075 (Admin); (2003) 6 CCLR 471.
26   See Appendix B.
27   See fuller explanation in chapter 6.
28   Under National Health Service and Community Care Act 1990 s47.
29   [2002] UKHL 38; (2002) 5 CCLR 511.
30   See further chapter 2 above at para 2.84.

Table to show which type of support should be applied for where a new arrival joins a household in the UK

Existing household	New asylum-seeker arrival
In receipt of interim support	If 'a dependant' within the meaning of Interim Regs 1999 reg 2(1), he or she must claim interim support and is ineligible for NASS support
In receipt of 'urgent cases' income support as asylum-seeker	If partner or dependent child of claimant, can be added to the income support claim (see chapter 2 above, SSIA Regs 2000[31] regs 2 and 12).
On low income or claiming income support as settled person, eg, British citizen, person with exceptional/indefinite/discretionary leave to remain	May claim NASS support depending on income and expenditure of existing household (see para 3.20). But client may need immigration advice on whether it is appropriate to claim asylum or whether to claim family reunion/leave in line in which case no entitlement, as not an asylum-seeker (see chapter 1 above).
In receipt of NASS support	NASS support if new arrival is 'a dependant' within meaning of AS Regs 2000 reg 2(4). New arrival will then be exempt from NIAA 2002 s55. NASS support if new arrival is asylum-seeker in own right.

support) even if the existing resident was receiving income support or working. The High Court has rejected this approach. *R (NASS) v Asylum Support Adjudicators and (1) Berkadle and (2) Perrera*[32] decided that NASS cannot simply look at all the household's income including income support, compare it with the NASS threshold amount for a couple and pay the husband the difference. Gibbs J found there was no mathematical formula for calculating entitlement. NASS must look at the household's existing obligations (such as fuel debts and work expenses). 'NASS should exercise a sensible discretion within the

31 Social Security (Immigration and Asylum) Consequential Amendments Regulations 2000 SI No 636.
32 [2001] EWHC Admin 881.

scheme to take account of relevant factors so as to ensure that essential needs are met.' So if a husband comes to the UK to join his wife, the wife's income, accommodation and expenses will be taken into account when calculating whether the husband is destitute for the purposes of entitlement to NASS housing and support. NASS Policy Bulletin 11 outlines NASS's approach to mixed households, and Policy Bulletin 4 the approach to the partner's income. In an ASA appeal[33] where a woman on maternity leave was supporting her child and asylum-seeker husband, the adjudicator remitted the appeal to NASS to reconsider because there was no evidence that Gibbs J's guidance had been taken into account by NASS. The same approach should apply when NASS is considering whether a mixed household has adequate accommodation. Policy Bulletin 11 proposes that a mixed household in overcrowded accommodation should seek private rented accommodation and claim housing benefit. It goes on to say that in areas of the country where such accommodation is not available, the household would be entitled to apply to NASS for accommodation if excluded from rehousing as homeless.[34]

Section 55: exclusion from eligibility for NASS support[35]

> I just want to say that section 55 leads people to despair, loneliness, and theft, as what are you supposed to do when you are sleeping rough and do not have the right to work? NASS seems to think I have hidden people able to help me should things go wrong, but I have no-one, nothing, nowhere.[36]

An overview

3.21   The Nationality, Immigration and Asylum Act 2002 s55(1) provides that the Home Secretary (NASS) may not provide or arrange for the provision of support under IAA 1999 ss4,[37] 95 or 98 unless he is satis-

---

33 ASA 02/04/2522.
34 See chapter 5 below at para 5.9.
35 See also appendix H for NIAA 2002 s55 checklist.
36 26-year-old male from Somalia – awaiting a NIAA 2002 s55 decision (Refugee Arrivals Project). Quote from 'The impact of section 55 on the Inter-Agency Partnership and the asylum-seekers it supports', Puryear, Inter-agency Partnership report, February 2004. See also 'Destitution by Design: Section 55 GLA Impact Assessment for London', Greater London Authority, Feb 2004.
37 'Hard cases' support.

fied that the asylum claim was made 'as soon as reasonably practicable after the person's arrival in the UK'. NIAA 2002 s55(5) provides that this does not prevent support being provided to an asylum-seeker with a dependent child. Section 55(5) also requires NASS to provide support or exercise other powers 'to the extent necessary for the purpose of avoiding a breach of the person's [ECHR] rights'. So if an asylum-seeker is left with no food or accommodation after being refused support under NIAA 2002 s55(1), they will be entitled to support under section 55(5) if they can show support is necessary to avoid 'inhuman and degrading treatment' in breach of ECHR art 3. NASS Policy Bulletin 75[38] was introduced as interim guidance after the Court of Appeal's decision in *Limbuela*, pending an appeal to the House of Lords. The new approach transforms NASS's policy so that asylum-seekers should not be excluded from support by section 55 unless NASS is satisfied that they have food, shelter and access to basic amenities. Should the Home Secretary succeed in an appeal to the House of Lords it is possible the policy will change, so we have set out the case law and backgound to this important area.

3.22   When the Home Secretary announced section 55 to Parliament at the Third Reading of the then Nationality, Immigration and Asylum Bill, he indicated that it was aimed at people who had been in the UK for some time and made late 'in-country' asylum claims to avoid removal.

> We need to be reasonable and take into account the trauma that people experience. We need to allow a reasonable period before we presume that people have come into the country for another reason and have been sustaining themselves, then when they can no longer do so, have decided that the asylum system would sustain them, being more generous than the equivalent something-for-something welfare to work system.
>
> We are saying to people, 'If you have been here for some time, by all means tell us how you got here, what your circumstances are, the means of entry and what you have been doing since you reached this country and we will provide you with support.' That is what our proposals provide and I think that is reasonable . . .[39]

3.23   However, after NIAA 2002 s55 was introduced on 8 January 2003, it soon became clear that any asylum-seeker who failed to apply for asylum at the airport was likely to be refused under section 55(1). During 2003, an estimated 9,145 asylum-seekers were refused access to

38 Current version 5.0, issued 24 June 2004, available at www.ind.homeoffice. gov.uk.
39 Hansard, HC Debates Col 199, 5 November 2002.

NASS support, out of 12,105 childless applicants: a refusal rate of over 75 per cent.[40] By September 2003, 1,100 claimants had challenged section 55 decisions by judicial review, resulting in injunctions in over 90 per cent of cases.[41]

Section 55(1): the case law

3.24   In *R (Q and others) v Secretary of State for the Home Department*,[42] the Court of Appeal considered what is 'as soon as reasonably practicable' and gave guidance as to what is a fair procedure for NASS to apply. In making decisions under NIAA 2002 s55(1), NASS must take into account the asylum-seeker's personal circumstances, including their state of mind on arrival. The Court of Appeal decided that the procedures operated by NASS in implementing section 55 were unfair and did not comply with ECHR art 6 but could be improved so as to be compatible with the Human Rights Act 1998. At the end of the judgment is a useful summary of the correct approach both to NIAA 2002 s55(1) and (5) and to decision-making by public authorities. The court set out the section 55(1) approach as follows:

> The test whether an asylum-seeker claimed asylum 'as soon as reasonably practicable' under section 55(1) may be framed in this way: on the premise that the purpose of coming to this country was to claim asylum and having regard both to the practical opportunity for claiming asylum and to the asylum-seeker's personal circumstances, could the asylum-seeker reasonably have been expected to claim asylum earlier than he or she did?[43]

3.25   In *R (S, D and T) v Secretary of State for the Home Department*,[44] D, an Ethiopian man who had arrived by air and claimed asylum the next day was found to have met the 'as soon as reasonably practicable' requirement. Maurice Kay J noted a number of propositions about immigration procedures at airports and the general circumstances of asylum-seekers. The decision was not appealed on NIAA 2002 s55(1) and is useful for an asylum-seeker with a possible challenge to a section 55(1) decision. He recorded the following points:

---

40 Quarterly Home Office Research Development Service statistics on asylum decisions and NASS support are published at www.homeoffice.gov.uk/rds/immigration1.html.

41 *R (Q and others) v Secretary of State for the Home Department* [2003] EWCA Civ 364; [2003] 3 WLR 365; (2003) 6 CCLR 136.

42 [2003] EWCA Civ 364.

43 [2003] EWCA Civ 364 at [119].

44 [2003] EWHC 1941 (Admin); (2004) 7 CCLR 32.

1. Many refugees know little or nothing of asylum procedures, of airport procedures, airlines, etc.
2. Many asylum-seekers are illiterate and rely on oral information.
3. Most asylum-seekers using an agent depend completely on him.
4. It is common for asylum-seekers not to know the details in their travel documents.
5. It is common for immigration officers at airports not to ask questions or to ask the agent.
6. It is common for a person to pass through immigration control with a forged EU passport.
7. Many asylum-seekers do not understand the concept of claiming asylum as soon as reasonably practicable.
8. It is common and quite likely for asylum-seekers not to see posters in airports.

3.26 NASS continued to apply an approach which failed fully to take into account Maurice Kay J's decision and the evidence presented in *S, D and T*.[45] The issues were later reviewed at a permission hearing which looked at the procedure for challenging NIAA 2002 s55 decisions. In *R (Q, D and others) v Secretary of State for the Home Department (Shelter intervener)*[46] Maurice Kay J made it clear that he did not consider that it was necessary for NASS to require asylum-seekers to provide evidence in every case to support the generic issues that were covered in *S, D and T*. He stated that he considered NASS has the power to provide IAA 1999 s98 temporary accommodation after the NIAA 2002 s55 refusal letter has been issued, giving an asylum-seeker a reasonable period of notice before he or she becomes homeless. He did not consider whether it was unlawful to evict without notice as in Operation Platinum cases where asylum-seekers were interviewed, issued with a NIAA 2002 s55 refusal letter and lost support all on the same day. It has been suggested that it is unlawful to evict an asylum-seeker who is already in accommodation without any notice because of a common law right to reasonable notice.[47]

Policy Bulletin 75 and the 72-hour rule

3.27 When introducing the Asylum and Immigration (Treatment of Claimants, etc) Bill, the Home Secretary announced that NASS would operate a presumption that where an asylum-seeker had claimed

45 See Inter-Agency Partnership report footnote 36.
46 [2003] EWHC 2507.
47 See chapter 5 below and *R v Secretary of State for the Environment ex p Shelter and Refugee Council* 23 August 1996 (unreported) and *R v Newham LBC ex p Ojuri (No 5)* [1999] 31 HLR 631.

asylum within 72 hours of arriving in the UK, the claim would be treated as made 'as soon as reasonably practicable', and said that the previous notional period was 24 hours.[48] NASS's revised interpretation of the 'as soon as reasonably practicable' test (and the '72-hour rule') is explained in Policy Bulletin 75, Version 5, Annex F. Any request for reconsideration of a NIAA 2002 s55 decision by NASS should now be considered under the new policy. Policy Bulletin 75 states that 72 hours normally means three working days but the rule should be applied flexibly, for example, if an asylum-seeker arrives on the Friday night before a bank holiday and claims asylum on the following Tuesday this will normally be reasonable. If they claim on Wednesday or Thursday, the decision will depend on the reasons for that delay. The three-day time limit is a guideline which should not be strictly applied as a deadline.

3.28   Some asylum-seekers continue to fall foul of NIAA 2002 s55(1), for example, if they have no evidence of their date of arrival. However, the new interpretation of section 55(5), allowing support to all those who are destitute has reduced the impact of section 55(1). There is an emphasis on credibility in Policy Bulletin 75 (see also *R (Wembo) v Secretary of State for the Home Department*)[49] and it may be important to produce evidence which supports the asylum-seeker's account (see below).

Section 55(5) and the article 3 threshold: the case law

> As regards the types of 'treatment' which fall within the scope of article 3 of the Convention, the Court's case law refers to 'ill-treatment' that attains a minimum level of severity and involves actual bodily injury or intense physical or mental suffering. Where treatment humiliates or debases an individual showing lack of respect for, or diminishing, his or her human dignity or arouses feelings of fear, anguish or inferiority capable of breaking an individual's moral and physical resistance, it may be characterised as degrading and also fall within the prohibition of article 3. The suffering which flows from naturally occurring illness, physical or mental, may be covered by article 3, where it is, or risks being exacerbated by treatment, whether flowing from conditions of detention, expulsion or other measures, for which the authorities can be held responsible.[50]

---

48   See Hansard Col 1594, 17 December 2003. See www.publications.parliament.uk/pa/cm200304/cmhansrd/cm031217/debtext/31217-10.htm.
49   [2004] EWHC (Admin); [2004] All ER (D) 264 (Jan).
50   *Pretty v United Kingdom* (2002) 35 EHRR 1.

3.29   NIAA 2002 s55(5) enables the Home Secretary to provide support, despite a late claim, 'to the extent necessary to prevent a breach of the person's Convention rights' and to provide support where the applicant has a dependent child under 18.

3.30   In *R (Q and others) v Secretary of State for the Home Department*,[51] the Court of Appeal agreed that the refusal of support under NIAA 2002 s55 could amount to 'treatment' under ECHR art 3. But it was not enough that there was 'a real risk' that an asylum-seeker would be reduced to a state of degradation. To breach article 3, the asylum-seeker's condition must be 'verging on' that described above in the *Pretty* case. So when deciding whether there is a breach of article 3, the individual elements of this test need to be separately considered, for example:

- Is there a diminution in the asylum-seeker's human dignity?
- Is he or she experiencing feelings or fear, anguish or inferiority?
- Is the asylum-seeker's physical or mental illness exacerbated by, or at risk of being exacerbated by, sleeping rough, lack of access to sanitary facilities, limited access to food and so on?

3.31   In *R (S, D and T) v Secretary of State for the Home Department*,[52] the next leading case, Maurice Kay J gave a detailed and considered judgment as to what circumstances would constitute a breach of ECHR art 3 in relation to NIAA 2002 s55(5). He found that there is little or no charitable support available so it is inevitable that most asylum-seekers refused section 55 support will be reduced to a state of destitution and 'within a short period of time the demands of article 3 require the relief of damage to human dignity which is caused by a life so destitute that . . . no civilised nation can tolerate it . . .'[53] The Home Secretary did not produce evidence of the existence of charitable support to disprove this. Maurice Kay J's decision was eventually appealed only in relation to T, and not in relation to the claimants S and D. The quoted part of the judge's approach to article 3 was not expressly disapproved by the Court of Appeal and has been followed by the Administrative Court in cases such as *R (Limbuela) v Secretary of State for the Home Department*[54] (see para 3.37 below).

3.32   In *R (T) v Secretary of State for the Home Department*[55] the Court of

---

51 [2003] EWCA Civ 364.

52 [2003] EWHC 1941 (Admin); (2004) 7 CCLR 32.

53 [2003] EWHC 1941 (Admin) at [33].

54 [2004] EWHC 219 (Admin) upheld in *R (Limbuela and others) v Secretary of State for the Home Department* [2004] EWCA Civ 540.

55 [2003] EWCA Civ 1285; (2004) 7 CCLR 53.

Appeal decided that T's rights under ECHR art 3 had not been breached and he did not meet the NIAA 2002 s55(5) threshold because he had shelter and cash for food and access to sanitary facilities, and he was not so unwell as to need immediate treatment. Although he appeared to have a serious mental illness, he had no medical evidence and this was a matter for a community care assessment under National Assistance Act 1948 s21. The court found that the article 3 threshold fell somewhere between T and S. S, a Somali asylum-seeker who was found by Kay J to qualify for support under NIAA 2002 s55(5), had been sleeping rough and begging, had lost weight almost to the point of malnutrition, had a swelling on his neck and had a GP's report about psychological disturbance. The Court of Appeal decided that a case did not have to reach the same level of severity as S's to reach the threshold.

3.33   The court repeated the *Pretty* test as to what will amount to inhuman and degrading treatment, refusing to 'lay down any simple test which can be applied in every case' and finding that each case has to be judged in relation to all the circumstances which are relevant to it. Instead it used the two cases of S and T as illustrations of cases that were on different sides of the line.

3.34   The conclusion from *T*, is that if an asylum-seeker has no cash for food or no shelter or no access to sanitary facilities, he or she may meet the ECHR art 3 threshold. This interpretation of the NIAA 2002 s55(5) test was confirmed by Maurice Kay J in *Q, D and others*.[56]

The post T decisions: when is NIAA 2002 s55(5) satisfied?

3.35   A series of High Court decisions since *T* have struggled to decide exactly where the ECHR art 3 threshold falls – how much does an asylum-seeker have to suffer before they qualify for support? At the time of writing, NASS had appealed in relation to a number of the cases below in *Secretary of State for the Home Department v (1) Limbuela (2) Tesema and (3) Adam (Shelter Intervener)* [2004] EWCA Civ 540. The appeal was rejected by a majority on 21 May 2004. Carnwath LJ found no reason to interfere with the Administrative Court's decisions (see below) that without support the asylum-seekers would have reached, or would very quickly reach a condition which breached article 3, applying the *Pretty* test. Jacob LJ agreed but was also influenced by evidence submitted by Shelter (intervening). He noted that

---

56   *R (Q, D and others) v Secretary of State for the Home Department* [2003] EWHC 2507 (Admin).

if the appeals were allowed, then 666 other asylum-seekers whose cases were pending might be left without support, increasing the risk of denial of food and shelter by charities which could not cope. Laws LJ, dissenting, found that none of the individual cases exhibited exceptional features so as to require support under section 55(5). NASS has appealed to the House of Lords but in the meantime accepts that support must be provided under section 55(5) unless it is satisfied that the asylum-seeker has an alternative source of suport (Policy Bulletin 75).

Factual background

3.36   In *R (Zardasht) v Secretary of State for the Home Department*,[57] Z had spent four nights in early September sleeping in a park and two nights sleeping in a church. He had intermittent access to food but had obtained some daytime food from the Refugee Council. There was no evidence of health problems. NASS produced a detailed witness statement about day centres and voluntary organisations which it claimed could offer food and other assistance to asylum-seekers. Z had little evidence other than his original witness statement outlining his general circumstances. Newman J rejected the application. He found that there must be sufficiently detailed and persuasive evidence to clearly show that the applicant has not had shelter and/or food and/or sanitary facilities and (where relevant) was ill and that in fact there has been such an adverse effect on physical and/or mental health that the *Pretty* threshold has been crossed.

3.37   In *R (Limbuela) v Secretary of State for the Home Department*,[58] L, a 23-year-old Angolan man, had spent two nights in July sleeping rough in a park in Croydon without food, was humiliated by begging for money and had pain in his stomach and testicles. His solicitor presented evidence that there was no accommodation available to asylum-seekers in L's position and Collins J granted his application, deciding that the court must consider the position of the claimant if he were made homeless in the winter months when the hearing took place. He acknowledged that the decision in *Zardasht* may have been justified by the lack of evidence in that case, but he adopted a different approach to ECHR art 3, stressing that persuasive proof of destitution, particularly during the winter months should be enough to meet the threshold. The claimant or his representative would need to show

57 [2004] EWHC 91 (Admin).
58 [2004] EWHC 219 (Admin).

the court they had taken reasonable steps to try to obtain charitable support.

> But if he shows that he has taken reasonable steps and that no assistance is available except by begging and hoping, then the fact that he will have to sleep rough, he has no money, he has no proper access to food or other facilities, will be likely to suffice to establish his case.

3.38   In *R (Tesema) v Secretary of State for the Home Department*,[59] T, a 26-year-old Ethiopian man, had medical evidence that he was suffering from a depressed mood and that he had scars consistent with his account of torture. He had pain above his knee and an undiagnosed ear or hearing problem. He would be street homeless if the claim was unsuccessful, but had not yet been forced to sleep rough. His solicitor presented evidence that there was no accommodation for him and that Ethiopian community organisations had been contacted and were unable to help. Agreeing with the reasoning in Limbuela, Gibbs J allowed the application, deciding that a correct interpretation of T led to the conclusion that to force a person to sleep in the open without basic shelter is normally inhuman and degrading treatment which fell within the Pretty test (set out above at para 3.29). He emphasised that this was particularly unlawful where the person had no financial support, was present in the UK as an asylum applicant rather than as a citizen, and during the winter months. He found there was no real possibility of T finding any accommodation.

3.39   In *R (Adam) v Secretary of State for the Home Department*,[60] A, a 27-year-old Sudanese man, had slept rough in a car park near the Refugee Council for a month from 16 October. He had medical evidence saying he had back pain, gastritis, scars consistent with his account of ill-treatment in detention and depression. Charles J accepted the application, finding common ground between *Zardasht* and *Limbuela* in the need for evidence of the lack of charitable support and the conditions of the individual asylum-seeker. He accepted the evidence that A had slept rough for a month, had no money and had eaten only one meal a day. He found that where the claimant showed there was a lack of charitable assistance, NASS must identify a particular organisation which could offer help to a particular claimant and he decided that it was unlikely that A would secure accommodation.

---

59   [2004] EWHC 295 (Admin).
60   [2004] EWHC 354 (Admin).

Challenging NIAA 2002 s55 decisions: procedure

3.40　　NASS Policy Bulletin 75: Section 55 (Late Claims) 2002 Act Guidance,[61] gives an outline of NASS's policy and practice. The section 55 screening procedures are explained in more detail in para 3.138 below. NASS currently only carries out a level 2 screening interview where a single adult is subject to NIAA 2002 s55(1), that is, has not claimed asylum as soon as reasonably practicable after arrival.[62] Asylum-seekers should be provided with a copy of the screening notes after the level 1 interview. NASS will now issue a section 55 decision letter and/or a letter allowing access to emergency accommodation based on information gathered at the level 1 interview. NASS has suggested that ECHR art 3 issues are considered in the level 1 screening interview since the applicant is questioned about their health *and* cannot be granted support to avoid a breach of article 3 under section 55(1), for example, because they are claiming subsistence-only support while staying with friends. Initial NIAA 2002 s55 refusal letters usually concentrate on section 55(1) issues, with no enquiries or consideration of the effect on the applicant, for example, of eviction from their accommodation in January. At present the method of asking for section 55(5) issues to be considered or of responding to errors in the section 55(1) decision is to post or fax a letter to the NASS Eligibility and Assessment Team (NEAT).[62]

3.41　　The former procedure was to send representations to the Resticted Access to NASS Support (RANS) Team. This now forms part of the new NEAT Unit. There remains a small number of cases where NASS may refuse support under NIAA 2002 s55(1) or (5) and representations will be needed.[63]

3.42　　Representations should include the asylum-seeker's full name, country of origin, date of birth and Home Office reference number. They should deal with errors in the section 55(1) decision if that is to be challenged. They should then explain how the client meets the ECHR art 3 threshold, for example, number of days sleeping on the streets, access to food, any attempts to beg, medical ill-effects, access to toilet/washing facilities, etc.[64]

3.43　　NASS has collected evidence about the availability of health care, food, shelter and other amenities. As explained above, in *R (Zardasht)*

61　Version 5.0, issued 24 June 2004.

62　Fax 020 8633 3820.

63　See Policy Bulletin 75 version 5.0 at www.indd.homeofffice.gov.uk/ind/en/ home/applying/national-asylum-support.htm/.

64　See questionnaire in appendix H for a useful article 3 checklist.

v Secretary of State for the Home Department,[65] Newman J rejected a claim under NIAA 2002 s55(5), partly because of a lack of evidence to show that charitable support was not available. However, in *R (Limbuela and others) v Secretary of State for the Home Department*[66] the lack of charitable support appears to have been accepted.

3.44   Before bringing a judicial review, an asylum-seeker or their representative should make efforts to contact organisations who might be able to help. National organisations such as Shelter and the Inter-Agency Project may be able to provide details of the current availability of food and shelter. A witness statement accompanying a court application will need to include a detailed account of the asylum-seeker's condition, their attempts to obtain help or reasons why they were unable to, their experiences of degradation, supported by third party evidence where possible, for example, a letter from agencies who have seen the asylum-seeker and/or are unable to help. In addition it is desirable to provide general evidence about the local availability of food and shelter, or otherwise. Other relevant evidence of local conditions, for example, the weather forecast from the Met Office website, or local crime reports in relation to assaults on asylum-seekers or rough-sleepers could be provided to NASS. Where general evidence about local conditions has previously been provided to NASS or the Home Office in other cases, that information should be treated as within their knowledge but could be referred to.

3.45   If NASS refuses to reconsider or fails to respond to representations, the remedy is an application for judicial review (on form N461), with a request for urgency (N463) if interim relief is needed, for example, because the client is homeless that night. There is no right of appeal to the Asylum Support Adjudicators. A procedural checklist for solicitors bringing a NIAA 2002 s55 judicial review is in appendix H. In *Q, D and others*[67] the court made it clear that it would not entertain out-of-hours telephone applications unless there were wholly exceptional circumstances. Examples include where the asylum-seeker has serious health problems, or is vulnerable due to age or is a woman who has experienced sexual assault.

3.46   The new NASS procedures for interviewing asylum-seekers in connection with section 55 are set out in Annex G to Policy Bulletin 75. Support should not be withdrawn or refused prior to a level 2

---

65 [2004] EWHC 91 (Admin).
66 [2004] ENHC 219; (2004) 7 CCLR 267.
67 *R (Q, D and others) v Secretary of State for the Home Department* [2003] EWHC 2507 (Admin).

interview. The NEAT will attempt to make a (positive) section 55 decision based on the information on the level 1 Screening Form and NASS 1 application form on the basis of ECHR art 3 and NIAA 2002 s55(5).

3.47   In *R (Q, D and others) v Secretary of State for the Home Department,*[68] Maurice Kay J decided NASS had the power to provide emergency accommodation under section 55(5)(a) and issued this guidance as to the procedure to follow in section 55 cases.[69]

- The Home Secretary (NASS) must establish an adequate and efficient decision-making procedure, applying the law as set down in *Q* and *T*, doing so within a timescale which meets urgent needs and avoiding the need for so many court applications.
- The aim should be for NASS to provide resources to produce decisions on further representations within the timescale previously set by NASS (on the same day if representations are received before 2pm, otherwise by the next day).
- If notified of an immediate judicial review application, NASS should consider and normally grant or continue interim accommodation and support without the need for a court order until the court has considered the permission application or until there is a court order. NASS should decide within 24 hours if it thinks the case is unarguable, in which case the asylum-seeker will have to apply to court for an injunction.
- Asylum-seekers' solicitors should make their representations as detailed as possible, both for NASS and for the court. The court will soon approve and require the use of a new pro-forma N463 application for the case to be considered urgently which was proposed by members of the Housing Law Practitioners Association (HLPA) and the Housing and Immigration Group (HIG).
- Asylum-seekers' solicitors should only make telephone applications in exceptional circumstances.
- The court will not shorten the 21-day time limit for NASS to 'acknowledge service' of the judicial review application.[70]
- Within 14 days of the court granting permission to apply for judicial review, NASS must reach a decision on whether it wishes to settle the case or go ahead with a full hearing. If there is a full hearing, the court will consider whether it should be expedited. Otherwise a draft consent order should be filed at court to settle the case.

68 [2003] EWHC 2507 (Admin).
69 See the court service website at www.courtservice.gov.uk.
70 But see also para 3.49 below.

3.48　The Legal Services Commission (LSC) has since issued its own guidance suggesting that following this decision, detailed representations must be faxed to NASS at least 24 hours before the grant of emergency public funding.

3.49　Collins J, as lead judge in the Administrative Court issued a Practice Statement allowing the Treasury Solicitor an extension, from the normal 21 days, to two months to file their acknowledgement of service, responding to a NIAA 2002 s55 judicial review claim.[71] If no acknowledgement of service is filed within two months, the application will be put before a judge within 14 days to consider whether permission should be granted for the claim to be considered at a full hearing.

NIAA 2002 section 57

3.50　NASS may refuse to consider an application for support if the secretary of state is not satisfied that the information is complete or accurate or that the applicant is co-operating with enquiries. Section 57 introduced this change on 8 January 2003 with the Asylum Support (Amendment) Regulations 2002[72] amending the AS Regs 2000 and the NASS 1 application form so that it includes questions about the applicant's route to the UK and method of entry. If the IND is not satisfied that an asylum-seeker is giving a full account of their route here, NASS may refuse asylum support. NASS Policy Bulletin 79 'Application for support: false or incomplete information 2002 Act guidance' gives more examples. NIAA 2002 s57 is normally applied at the stage where an asylum-seeker has submitted their NASS application form and NASS believes the information is inaccurate or incomplete. As explained in Policy Bulletin 79, NASS should then write to the applicant to give them a chance to explain or offer more information. If they fail to do this, support may be refused. Like section 55, there is no right of appeal to the ASA against a refusal of support. Unlike section 55, there is no exemption where refusing support would breach an asylum-seeker's human rights. This may mean that section 57 is incompatible with the Human Rights Act 1998 and the European Convention on Human Rights. To date, NASS appears to have relied mainly on NIAA 2002 s55, rather than section 57, or used section 57 to supplement section 55, to reject claims where it doubts an asylum-seeker's credibility.

71　Practice Statement (Section 55 of the Nationality, Immigration and Asylum Act 2002) [2004] All ER (D) 217 (Feb).
72　SI No 3110.

Eligibility for support

3.51   Under Immigration and Asylum Act (IAA) 1999 s95(1):

> The Secretary of State may provide, or arrange for the provision of support for –
> (a) asylum-seekers, or
> (b) dependants of asylum-seekers,
> who appear to the Secretary of State to be destitute or to be likely to become destitute within such a period as may be prescribed.

3.52   The provision of support for adult asylum-seekers is expressed as a power rather than a duty in both the Act and the AS Regs 2000. Stanley Burnton J has decided that there is a duty to provide support where the criteria for entitlement are met in *R (Husain) v Asylum Support Adjudicator and Secretary of State for the Home Department*.[73]

3.53   There is a slightly different test of eligibility for emergency accommodation under IAA 1999 s98, which is provided pending a decision on full section 95 asylum support. Emergency accommodation may be provided for:

> (a) asylum-seekers, or
> (b) dependants of asylum-seekers,
> who it appears to the Secretary of State may be destitute.[74]

3.54   An asylum-seeker is eligible for emergency accommodation if the household appears to have an immediate need for housing and support. Therefore, an asylum-seeker who appears likely to become destitute within 14 days, but not immediately, is entitled to asylum support under IAA 1999 s95(1)(b) but not to emergency accommodation under section 98. This would apply where an asylum-seeker is able to stay briefly with friends or community members when he or she arrives in the UK. IAA 1999 s98 support is provided as a stop-gap until there is time to carry out a full assessment, and in every other respect the test of eligibility is the same. IAA 1999 s95(2)–(11) apply to an assessment of the emergency accommodation duty.[75]

3.55   Once the NIAA 2002 s55 requirements have been met, there are three basic steps in assessing whether an applicant is eligible for IAA 1999 s95 asylum support:

> a) is the applicant an 'asylum-seeker' or the 'dependant' of an asylum-seeker?

---

73 [2001] EWHC Admin 582; (2001) *Times* 15 November.
74 IAA 1999 s98(1).
75 IAA 1999 s98(3).

b) is the applicant excluded from support?

c) is the household destitute, that is, without a home or living expenses?

Is the applicant an 'asylum-seeker' or the 'dependant of an asylum-seeker'?

3.56   Only asylum-seekers and their dependants who come within the IAA 1999 s94(1) definition may receive asylum support. Immigrants outside this definition such as visitors and students are not eligible, even if they are completely destitute, because IAA 1999 s115 excludes 'persons subject to immigration control' (PSIC) from social security benefits and most other welfare provision.[76]

3.57   In the context of asylum support, the terms 'asylum-seeker' and 'dependant of an asylum-seeker' have a different meaning from their ordinary immigration law meaning.[77] Here is a brief checklist of who is an asylum-seeker for support purposes:

i) must be 18 or over, and

ii) must have made a claim for asylum as a refugee or human rights claim under ECHR art 3 which has been recorded, and

iii) must be still awaiting the result of the claim or appeal, or

iv) must have dependent child under 18 – even if all asylum claims and appeals have been rejected.

Meaning of 'asylum-seeker'

3.58   An 'asylum-seeker' for asylum support purposes is a person aged 18 or over who has 'made a claim for asylum which has been recorded by the Secretary of State but which has not been determined'.[78] This is to be amended by NIAA 2002 s44 so that an asylum-seeker for support purposes is one who 'has made a claim for asylum at a place designated by the Secretary of State'. Useful decisions on the definition of an 'asylum-seeker' dealing with issues such as when an asylum claim has been recorded or determined can be viewed on the ASA website[79] by searching the index of decisions.

---

76   See para 3.287 and chapter 6 on exclusions from/entitlements to community care help for those outside the asylum-seeker definition.

77   IAA 1999 s94(1).

78   IAA 1999 s94(1).

79   www.asylum-support-adjudicators.org.uk/decisions/.

Unaccompanied asylum-seekers under 18

3.59   A child under 18 who claims asylum in his/her own right is an 'asylum-seeker' for immigration law purposes only. If the child is in the UK without a parent and has an outstanding asylum application as an 'unaccompanied minor' he or she is entitled to housing and support under the Children Act 1989 and not under the IAA 1999 s95 asylum support provisions until he or she reaches the age of 18.[80]

'Designated place' (claims in person)

3.60   Asylum-seekers who fail to claim asylum at the port of entry are now required to make their initial asylum application in person at a place designated by the Home Secretary for immigration purposes unless there are exceptional circumstances such as compelling medical evidence which shows the applicant is unfit to attend. Currently 'designated places' include the Asylum Screening Units (ASU) at Croydon, Liverpool and Solihull. This has presented difficulties for those wishing to apply for asylum who lack the money to travel and who previously would have applied by post. A man who arrived by lorry in Plymouth issued judicial review proceedings arguing the policy was a breach of his ECHR arts 3 and 8 rights because he could not afford to travel to the ASU.[81] The Home Secretary permitted a woman who was eight and a half months pregnant, to apply other than at a designated place.[82] Although NIAA 2002 s44 has not yet amended the definition of asylum-seeker to require asylum-seekers to apply at a designated place for support purposes, the requirement applies to asylum-seekers who are subject to NIAA 2002 s55 or Sch 3.[83] NIAA 2002 s113(1) also amends the definition of asylum claim to mean a claim which is made at a designated place. In practice therefore, it appears that an in-country asylum-seeker must generally have made the asylum claim in person at the ASU, or made the claim by post and then presented there to be eligible for NASS support.

---

80 See chapter 6 at para 6.128.
81 R (Musilkare) v Secretary of State for the Home Department CO/2059/2003 unreported.
82 R (Assoua) v Secretary of State for the Home Department CO/1712/2003 unreported.
83 NIAA 2002 s18.

'Claim for asylum'[84]

3.61   A claim for asylum for support purposes is defined by IAA 1999 s94(1) as either 'a claim that it would be contrary to the UK's obligations under the Refugee Convention, or under article 3 of the Human Rights Convention for that person to be removed from or required to leave the United Kingdom'. An asylum-seeker whose ordinary claim for refugee status under the Refugee Convention is refused may be able to make a free-standing claim under ECHR art 3 or may raise article 3 arguments in the appeal.[85]

Fresh claims

3.62   It is possible to make an ECHR art 3 claim or a second asylum claim which re-triggers entitlement to asylum support only in limited circumstances. In *R v Secretary of State for the Home Department ex p Onibiyo*,[86] the Court of Appeal decided that the fresh claim must be sufficiently different from the earlier claim so that there is a realistic prospect of success. In deciding whether a 'fresh' claim has been made, only certain evidence will be considered (see Immigration Rules HC 395 para 346). If the original decision on the asylum claim was made before the Human Rights Act 1998 came into force on 2 October 2000, it may be possible to make a second claim on human rights grounds. In *R (Nigatu) v Secretary of State for the Home Department*,[86a] 9 July 2004, Collins J found that a purportedly fresh asylum claim did not automatically trigger continuing asylum support as the Home Secretary should first decide whether or not the claim was in fact a fresh claim. However, NASS had been wrong to refuse to continue suport in N's case as the situation (involving fresh medical evidence) was overwhelmingly likely to involve a fresh claim.

3.63   The Home Secretary's position is that 'until the conditions set out in paragraph 346 of HC 395 apply, there is no fresh claim and this approach is endorsed in an ASA decision.[87] L had applied for asylum on 30 January 2002 and been refused on 23 March 2002, with an immigration adjudicator dismissing the appeal on 13 November 2002. An application for permission to appeal to the Immigration Appeal Tribunal was refused. L's immigration solicitors had submit-

---

84   A claim for asylum includes an appeal.
85   See chapter 1.
86   [1996] QB 768, CA.
86a   [2004] EWHC 1806 (Admin).
87   ASA 03/12/7421.

ted a fresh claim for asylum dated 22 October 2003 on the basis of new evidence. The Chief Asylum Support Adjudicator referred to *R v Immigration Appellate Authority ex p Secretary of State for the Home Department*[88] in which Lightman J held that the Home Secretary alone has the authority to decide what is or is not a fresh application, subject only to a challenge in judicial review proceedings on *Wednesbury* grounds. Lightman J held that until the Home Secretary made a decision to treat further representations as a fresh application, the only remedy available to an appellant lies in an application in judicial review proceedings for orders requiring him to consider and determine the application.

3.64 Where an ordinary asylum or other immigration application has been refused and an ECHR art 3 claim is being made (which allows a claim for asylum support), it is important that it is made at the earliest possible opportunity.[89] As part of the current procedure for appealing against a refusal of asylum, the asylum-seeker must state any additional ECHR grounds for wishing to stay in the UK.

3.65 ECHR points should be raised at the asylum appeal. The Human Rights Act (HRA) 1998 and Convention do not preclude an asylum-seeker from making a fresh article 3 claim after the appeal. However, in the absence of any new circumstances, the Home Office could simply refuse such a claim and rely on IAA 1999 s74(7) to refuse an appeal. There may be exceptional circumstances which would require consideration of a fresh article 3 claim after an unsuccessful appeal, for example, if the political situation in the country of origin changed radically or if the applicant had suddenly developed a life-threatening medical condition.

Meaning of 'recorded'

3.66 The ECHR art 3 or fresh asylum claim must be a claim which has been 'recorded' by the Home Secretary (IND), but not decided, to trigger an asylum support duty.[90] The Home Secretary may decide not to 'record' a fresh claim if it does not disclose new evidence meeting the *Onibiyo* test (see para 3.63).

3.67 The burden of proof of showing a claim has been made is on the asylum-seeker.[91] The meaning of recorded has not yet been decided

---

88 [1998] Imm AR 52, IAT.
89 See chapter 1, para 1.48.
90 IAA 1999 s94(1).
91 ASA 00/11/0111.

by the courts in this context. ASA decisions[92] suggest that evidence that an ECHR art 3 claim has been received by the Immigration and Nationality Directorate (IND) for example, a copy of a solicitor's letter received by the IND and a recorded delivery slip would normally satisfy the requirement. These cases were decided before the introduction of NIAA 2002 s55 or the requirement to apply for asylum at a designated place (see para 3.60). NASS now requires an asylum-seeker firstly to receive confirmation from the Home Office that it is considering a fresh claim, and secondly to present at an Asylum Screening Unit to obtain a NIAA 2002 s55 or NEAT confirmation letter before he or she is eligible for support (see para 3.40 onwards).

3.68   In the social security context a Commissioner has held there is 'no specified way in which a claim should be recorded'.[93] A response from the Home Office requesting the appellant's address was treated as proof that a claim had been recorded.[94] A request to the IND for a copy of the asylum-seeker's file under Data Protection Act 1998 s7 may be another way of obtaining the necessary evidence.[95]

Meaning of 'determined' – when entitlement ends

3.69   Entitlement to support ends on the 'date of determination'. This is not simply the date on which the asylum decision is made or received, but is prescribed for the purposes of IAA 1999 s94(3) by the AS Regs 2000 reg 2(2), as amended. The aim is to allow a 'grace period' for the successful or unsuccessful asylum-seeker to make other arrangements and move out of the NASS accommodation.

3.70   In a household without dependent children under 18, an asylum-seeker stops being an 'asylum-seeker' for support purposes 28 days after the Home Secretary notifies the asylum claimant of a favourable asylum decision, or 21 days after notification of a refusal. If there is an appeal, the period ends 28 days after any final appeal is disposed of.[96] An appeal is usually disposed of when any time limit for a further appeal has expired. An appeal was allowed where NASS had ended support during the prescribed period.[97] The asylum appeal had been

---

92   Such as ASA 02/04/0262, 02/03/2220, 02/01/1684 and 01/01/0168.
93   CIS/4439/98.
94   ASA 02/08/4047.
95   See para 3.154 below.
96   AS Regs 2000 reg 2(2) as amended by Asylum Support Amendment Regulations 2002 SI No 472 and see Asylum Support (Interim Provisions) (Amendment) Regulations 2002 SI No 471.
97   ASA 03/01/5489.

Table to show when IAA 1999 s98/95 asylum support entitlement ends

	Leave to remain granted	Asylum refused
IND decision	28 days after IND notifies of decision (plus 2 days if posted by 1st class post)	21 days after IND notifies of decision (plus 2 days if posted by 1st class post)
Appeal decision	10 working days after appeal decision is 'promulgated' [check the appeal decision to find this date – it means the date the appeal is issued, not necessarily the date of the hearing] plus 28 days (plus 2 days if posted by 1st class post)	10 working days after date appeal decision is 'promulgated', plus 21 days (plus 2 days if posted by 1st class post)

successful but support was withdrawn incorrectly before the expiry of the time limit during which the Home Secretary could appeal. A late appeal will trigger entitlement to support while a decision is being awaited on permission to appeal out of time. In *R (Erdogan) v Secretary of State for the Home Department*,[98] the Court of Appeal decided that the asylum claim was finally determined even if a decision on an application to appeal out of time was pending. There was no entitlement to support unless the tribunal agreed to consider a late appeal.

3.71   If the decision has been sent to the asylum-seeker or his/her representative by post, it is assumed it has been received on the second day after the day it was posted.[99] This applies even if it has been posted to the asylum-seeker's representative but not received by the asylum-seeker. Since asylum support stops 21/28 days later unless there is an appeal, it is important for representatives to pass on notification promptly. The adjudicator found that IAA 1999 s94(9) was not satisfied where the asylum decision had been sent to an incorrect address, and so asylum support should continue until the asylum decision had been properly notified.[100]

98 [2004] EWCA Civ 1087.
99 IAA 1999 s94(9).
100 ASA 02/03/2349.

3.72   If an asylum-seeker has a dependent child under 18, he or she continues to be treated as an 'asylum-seeker' for as long as the child is
under 18 and they both remain in the UK.[101] The meaning of dependent child is explained below. So 'failed' asylum-seeker households
with dependent children are entitled to asylum support, rather than
help under Children Act 1989 s17, for as long as the family is in the
UK.[102] If an asylum-seeker has been refused asylum and has either
failed to appeal or appealed unsuccessfully, he or she will stop being
treated as an asylum-seeker for support purposes if the child leaves
the UK or reaches 18. He or she will otherwise only cease to be an
asylum-seeker for support purposes if asylum or exceptional leave to
enter or remain in the UK is granted, in which case the 28-day prescribed period applies (see previous para).

Meaning of 'dependant'

3.73   'Dependant' in relation to an asylum-seeker or supported person is
defined for asylum support purposes by IAA 1999 s94 and AS Regs
2000 reg 2(4). The categories are listed below. The dependant's own
immigration status is not relevant, for example, an asylum-seeker may
claim asylum support for his wife, even if her asylum claim has been
rejected. So coming within the 'dependant' definition is a means of
accessing support for some PSIC who would otherwise be excluded.

3.74   The definition of dependant can be crucial, for example, in cases
where family members arrive in the UK separately. If a family member is not treated as a dependant he or she could be dispersed to a
different part of the UK from other relatives claiming NASS support.
This happened where a disabled man refused dispersal accommodation in Leeds because his brother was living in Kent.[103] NASS may be
asked to house different family members together even if they have
separate claims.[104]

Interim support

3.75   The definition of dependant was differently drafted in the Interim
Regs 1999, to allow for a wider category of dependants in cases where

---

101 IAA 1999 s94(5).
102 Note that this will change when the Asylum and Immigration (Treatment of
      Claimants, etc) Act 2004 adds such households to those excluded from support
      for failing to leave the UK voluntarily. Regulations are needed.
103 ASA 00/06/0018.
104 See ASA 02/08/4016 for a case where two unaccompanied brothers were
      housed together.

the local authority is supporting the family under the interim scheme.[105] Where additional family members arrive to join an applicant receiving interim support, they would be expected to apply for interim support as part of that household if they were eligible.[106] There may be limited circumstances in which they could choose arrangements making them eligible for NASS asylum support instead of interim support, for example, an adult disabled family member might arrive in the UK, claim asylum and form a separate household from the household in receipt of interim support.

Whose dependant?

3.76 The claim for asylum support may be made either by the asylum-seeker or by any dependant.[107] 'Dependant' is defined by AS Regs 2000 reg 2(4) as the dependant of 'an asylum-seeker, the supported person or an applicant for asylum support'. Where the applicant for support is a dependant of the asylum-seeker, his or her dependants must also be dependants of the asylum-seeker to fall within the AS Regs 2000 reg 2(4) definition. (Unlike the position under the Interim Regs 1999, a dependant of a dependant does not otherwise come within the definition). Assume asylum-seeker A is in detention and his 17-year-old daughter, B makes a claim for support as the dependant of A. Daughter B cannot claim support for her own daughter, C unless the grandchild C comes within the definition of a dependant of A. C could be a dependant of A, for example, if she had lived in his household since birth or was a dependant on his asylum claim (see below).

Categories of dependants

3.77 The categories of dependants are:

Husband or wife

3.78 The regulations use the term 'spouse' which is limited to a 'married couple', defined as 'a man and woman who are married to each other and are members of the same household'.[108]

3.79 A husband or wife, unlike a partner in an unmarried couple, would be treated as a dependant even if the couple had not been living

---

105 Interim Regs 1999 reg 2(1).
106 AS Regs 2000 reg 4(4)(a) and see mixed households para 3.20 above.
107 AS Regs 2000 reg 3(1).
108 AS Regs 2000 reg 2(1).

together before they applied for support together. In cases where a husband or wife arrives in the UK after a spouse who is receiving asylum support, a new application for support could be made. Both husband and wife may have made an asylum claim in their own right, in which case NASS may require some evidence of the marriage. If the spouse is treated as a dependant for the purposes of the husband's or the wife's asylum claim, then the evidence accepted by the IND should be accepted by NASS.

Dependent child under 18

3.80   The child must be under 18 on the date of the application for asylum support or on the date when he or she joined a supported household. He or she will qualify as a dependant if:

- he or she is a child of the applicant, or of the applicant's spouse, and dependent on the applicant; or
- he or she is a member of the close family of the applicant, or the applicant's spouse, provided the child has been living as part of the applicant's household since birth or for six of the 12 months before this application for support.

3.81   It appears that a child who has been adopted, whether formally or informally, should come within the definition of 'close family'. Dependant includes any child, related or unrelated, who has been living as part of the household for six months in the year preceding the claim for support provided they are under 18 at the date they ask to be included in the claim. In ASA 04/05/8109 this included a nephew of the asylum-seeker. Where a couple is unmarried, it could be argued that the child of a dependent partner is a member of the asylum-seeker's close family. The argument that an unborn child was 'a dependant' of her pregnant mother was rejected by the adjudicator.[109]

Disabled family member over 18

3.82   The family member will qualify as a dependant if he or she is 'in need of care and attention from the applicant or a member of his household by reason of a disability', and:

- he or she is a child of the applicant or of the applicant's spouse and dependent on the applicant; or
- he or she is a member of the close family of the applicant or the applicant's spouse provided he or she has been living as part of the applicant's household since birth or for six of the 12 months before this application for support.

109 ASA 03/02/5731.

3.83   Therefore, an adult who has a disability or mental health condition may be treated as part of the household, despite the fact that he or she is over 18.[110] The term 'in need of care and attention' comes from National Assistance Act 1948 s21(1)(a) and is explained in chapter 6 at para 6.58 below.

Unmarried couples

3.84   An unmarried couple means a heterosexual couple who can show they have been living together for two of the three years before the application for support or before the joint application if they arrived in the UK separately. 'Unmarried couple' is defined as 'a man and woman who though not married to each other, are living together as if married' so a member of a same-sex couple is excluded from NASS's definition of dependant unless he or she is a dependant for the purposes of the asylum claim (see below). In an ASA appeal[111] a gay man had refused to travel to a dispersal area because his partner, with whom he had come to the UK, was subject to NIAA 2002 s55 and so was not to be accommodated with him. The adjudicator remitted the decision back to NASS to 'reconsider the appellant's case in conjunction with that of his partner, apparently on the basis that there was a reasonable excuse for the failure to travel.[112]

3.85   There have now been several asylum claims in which the Home Office has granted refugee status or exceptional leave to enter or remain on the basis of persecution on the ground of sexuality. The exclusion of same-sex couples therefore appears irrational and open to a judicial review with HRA 1998 arguments under the European Convention of Human Rights (ECHR) articles 8 and 14 (breach of right to respect for family life and discrimination on the grounds of sexual orientation).

3.86   Some unmarried partners with long-term relationships may not satisfy the 'two out of the last three years' rule, for example, where they have been separated in civil war or while fleeing from their country of origin. If an unmarried heterosexual partner is not treated as a dependant then NASS's decision to refuse them support as a dependant could be challenged by an appeal to the ASA. It could be argued that the AS Regs 2000 must be read so as to be compatible with article 8 (right to respect for home and family life) and article 14 (discrimination on the basis of unmarried status) of the ECHR.

110 AS Regs 2000 reg 2(1).
111 ASA 03/06/6653.
112 AS Regs 2000 reg 2(1).

Supported as a dependent child before the IAA 1999 came into force

3.87   Anyone who is living as part of the applicant's household and was receiving assistance from a local authority under Children Act 1989 s17 immediately before 6 December 1999 (the date when the Interim Regs 1999 came into force), will qualify as a dependant. This category ensured that children whose parents were receiving social services' help because they were under 18, could be supported as dependants rather than adult children being required to make separate claims for support in their own right.[113]

Treated as a dependant by the IND

3.88   Anyone who has made a claim for leave to enter or remain in the UK, or for variation of any such leave, which is being considered on the basis that he or she is dependent on the asylum-seeker, will automatically be treated as a dependant of the asylum-seeker for asylum support purposes.[114] This can be demonstrated by the applicant's immigration documents. If the asylum-seeker has an Application Registration Card (ARC), the number of their dependant(s) will appear on the back of the card, but a dependant over the age of 5 will have their own card which records the ARC reference of the main asylum applicant. If the asylum-seeker has a Home Office standard acknowledgement letter (SAL), the photographs and details of dependants will normally appear on the back of the SAL. This category extends to dependants for the purposes of the immigration claim even if they would otherwise be excluded from qualifying as dependants for support purposes, for example, same-sex partners. Note that where a family member is applying for leave in line with an asylum-seeker who has been granted refugee status, he or she is not a dependant of an asylum-seeker.[115]

'The relevant time'

3.89   Whether the family member is 'a dependant' should be judged at 'the relevant time', which is the date of the application for asylum support. Where another family member arrives in the UK or joins the supported household after arrival, the relevant time is the date of joining a person who is already a supported person.[116]

113 AS Regs 2000 reg 2(4)(g).
114 AS Regs 2000 reg 2(4)(i).
115 ASA 03/08/6919.
116 AS Regs 2000 reg 2(6).

Challenging the classes of dependant

3.90 The limits in AS Regs 2000 reg 2(5) on who can be classed as a dependant lead to practical problems and possible breaches of ECHR art 8 for extended asylum-seeker families. For example, it seems to exclude a dependent sibling of the asylum-seeker's partner if he or she has not been living with the household for the previous six months. There is a solution to these difficulties when the family member qualifies as a 'dependant' because he or she is treated as a dependant for the purposes of the asylum claim.[117] However, this may not assist if family members have arrived in the UK at different times and/or if there is more than one claim for asylum.

3.91 The effects of AS Regs 2000 reg 2 can be seen where asylum-seekers have appealed to the Asylum Support Adjudicators after support has been terminated. In some cases it is possible to circumvent the limitations of the definition of dependant by showing that there was a 'reasonable excuse' for their failure to travel because of the dependence on family members. One appeal[118] concerned an Afghan asylum-seeker who wanted to be treated as part of the same household as his three nephews aged between 23 and 29. NASS had withdrawn support under AS Regs 2000 reg 20(1) on the grounds that the uncle had breached the conditions subject to which support was provided, that is, he had failed to travel to Hull. One of the nephews was in Kent, suffering from depression and anxiety, the other two had previously been dispersed to Wolverhampton. The appellant argued successfully that he had a 'reasonable excuse' for refusing to be dispersed alone. The adjudicator decided that he had a family duty and a cultural duty to care for and support his nephews who spoke no English, and noted that all of them had been in the UK for less than three weeks at the date of NASS's decision.

3.92 NASS Policy Bulletin 30 states at paragraph 8.22 '. . . as a general rule an asylum-seeker would have to demonstrate that there exists close personal ties between themselves and a relative, before a decision could be made to place him/her in a particular area simply because that family member lives there'. Policy Bulletin 31, para 4 considers the effect of ECHR art 8, 'the person's individual circumstances and the nature of the relationship with that relative should always be carefully taken into account. But in the absence of exceptional circumstances dispersal will generally be appropriate'. The

117 AS Regs 2000 reg 2(4)(i).
118 ASA 00/11/0110.

adjudicator[119] has found that NASS had not considered this discretion properly, allowing the appeal of a frail elderly man and his wife who were dependent on a daughter in London for help with shopping and housework.

3.93   Where a family member is not treated as a dependant, the first option is to negotiate with NASS for the household to be supported or accommodated together, even though NASS may process two separate applications. If that fails and the asylum-seeker refuses to be dispersed to a part of the UK away from the family member or leaves accommodation to be near a family member, and if NASS then withdraws support under AS Regs 2000 reg 20(1), there may be an appeal to the ASA, provided the appellant has no dependent children (see further para 3.174 on dispersal). If the householders are accommodated separately in different parts of the UK, a judicial review of the adequacy of the accommodation offered could be considered relying on the HRA 1998 and ECHR, arguing that dispersal is a breach of article 8.

Who can apply for support?

3.94   The person applying for support may be either the asylum-seeker or their dependant. The explanatory notes to the Immigration and Asylum Act (IAA) 1999 (at para 270) give the example of a dependant claiming support if the asylum-seeker is in detention. There are a number of other circumstances where the dependants may need to claim or continue to receive support while temporarily or even permanently separated from the asylum-seeker. A dependent wife can claim support for herself and her dependent children after a relationship breakdown, although she should be advised of the implications for her immigration status.

The destitution test

3.95   An applicant will be destitute either if he or she does not have access to 'adequate accommodation' or if he or she cannot meet the 'essential living needs' of him/herself and any dependant(s).[120] So an asylum-seeker may be living with friends and simply need help with living expenses, or he or she may have enough money to cover living

119 ASA 01/08/0714.
120 IAA 1999 s95(3).

expenses but need help with housing. The prescribed matters which NASS must consider in assessing destitution are contained in AS Regs 2000 regs 5–9. Note that local authorities must apply their own destitution test in interim support cases.[121]

3.96   The steps in the NASS assessment process are as follows:[122]

a) What income and assets are available to the applicant during the prescribed period?

b) Can the applicant meet the essential living needs of the asylum-seeker and any dependant(s)?

c) Does the applicant have adequate accommodation for him or herself and any dependants?

d) Can the applicant meet essential living needs and secure adequate accommodation until after the end of the prescribed period?

a) What income and assets are available to the applicant?[123]

3.97   Asylum support provided by NASS, including emergency accommodation provided under IAA 1999 s98 must be ignored in assessing resources.

3.98   Any income, support or assets which the asylum support applicant, the supported person or any dependant has or 'might reasonably be expected to have' in the prescribed period must be taken into account. The prescribed period is 14 days for new applications and 56 days for those already receiving support. (For interim support purposes, the period is always 14 days). It includes assets outside the UK if they are available or might reasonably be expected to become available.[124] In an appeal to the ASA[125] the appellant had a home in Sri Lanka which he was reluctant to sell. A community organisation was paying his £750 per month rent in the UK, but not his living expenses. The Chief Asylum Support Adjudicator analysed the destitution test, concluding that the family should be supported for three months to allow him time to take steps to sell the house.

3.99   It is difficult to see how notional help from friends and family can

---

121 See appendix E.
122 Note that the definition is slightly changed by NIAA 2002 ss19 and 44 so that a person and his dependants are destitute 'if they do not have and cannot obtain both adequate accommodation, and food and other essential items' but there is no indication of when the amendment will be implemented.
123 AS Regs 2000 reg 6.
124 AS Regs 2000 reg 6(4).
125 ASA 02/08/4018.

be assessed in practice and there is no specific provision for this in the regulations. The explanatory notes to the IAA 1999 (para 282) suggest that this includes resources to which an asylum-seeker might be expected to have access, for example, from friends and family in the UK. The Home Office Consultation paper[126] said this applies to cases where support is being provided by friends and relatives or other sources. The intention seems to be to take account of support that family and friends are willing and can reasonably afford to provide. This should be distinguished from the emergency support which family or friends cannot really afford, but may offer on a humanitarian basis to prevent physical or mental injury. The schedule to the regulations asks applicants to provide information about any support that friends or relatives are giving at the time of the application, as well as any financial support that friends or relatives can give.

3.100   A Zimbabwean asylum-seeker who was released from Oakington successfully appealed against NASS's decision that she was not destitute because she had £100 in travellers' cheques.[127] The adjudicator accepted evidence that the money was not available to her – she could not cash the cheques because her passport was held by the Immigration Service and she had no money to contact them and retrieve it.

3.101   In a case where NASS refused support to a Zimbabwean woman who had spent £109 on warm clothes, the Chief Asylum Support Adjudicator 'was prepared to accept that a sum of £50 for warm clothing should have been taken into account in assessing the appellant's available means'.[128] In that case the appellant was successful because this left her with less than the £267.68 then allowed by NASS for 14 days' food and accommodation.

Resources which must be taken into account

3.102   Only those assets listed in AS Regs 2000 reg 6(5) can be taken into account:

(i)   cash;
(ii) savings;
(iii) investments;
(iv) land;
(v)   cars or other vehicles; and
(vi) goods held for the purposes of a trade or other business.

---

126 NASS 'Consultation Document on the Main Regulations under Part VI of the Immigration and Asylum Act 1999' November 1999, para 21.
127 ASA 00/09/0065.
128 ASA 00/05/0010.

3.103 The NASS 1 application form requires the person claiming support to notify NASS of all the household's assets and then explain why they are not 'available' to him/her, for example, assets which are abroad. An asylum-seeker is eligible for support while he or she takes steps to recover property not currently available. Where assets are realised the Home Secretary may recover sums paid in support.[129]

Resources which are not taken into account

3.104 NASS will not take into account jewellery, personal clothing, medical items, and bedding.[130] The claimant is expected to inform NASS if the value of jewellery owned by the household is more than £1,000 in total. Jewellery includes watches. Jewellery is not an asset for the purposes of AS Regs 2000 reg 6(5). If jewellery is sold for cash, it would then become an asset and the supported person would have a duty to report it to NASS as a change of circumstances within AS Regs 2000 reg 15(2)(b). The guidance notes on the asylum support application form, which are attached to the regulations, explain this.

b) Can the applicant meet essential living needs?

3.105 NASS Policy Bulletin 4 contains a table showing the thresholds NASS expects will meet an asylum-seeker's essential living needs. Policy Bulletin 65 shows thresholds for those who have or gain access to some income or capital and covers the practical arrangements, for example, for making a weekly contribution to NASS while continuing to be supported in NASS accommodation. NASS will only decide that the household is destitute if its resources or income fall below the threshold. It appears that NASS continues to apply the thresholds fairly rigidly, refusing support where the household has resources slightly above the threshold. *R (Secretary of State for the Home Department) v ASA and (1) Berkadle (2) Perera*[131] confirms that in each case the income, living expenses and housing costs must be examined individually. Where an asylum-seeker was working on a low income so could not afford to pay for subsistence and accommodation, the adjudicator found that the thresholds had been applied too rigidly, failing to take into account accommodation costs and allowed his appeal.[132] The rates in Policy Bulletin 4 are currently based on £16.50 per person per night in Bed and Breakfast. There is no authority in the Act or the

129 AS Regs 2000 reg 17.
130 See As Regs 2000 Sch, note.
131 [2001] EWHC Admin 811 and see para 3.20 above.
132 ASA 02/04/2341.

Threshold table to show amounts NASS considers will meet a new applicant's essential living needs for the next 14 days

Type of Applicant	Subsistence-only applicant		Applicant claiming housing and subsistence	
	Assets	Weekly income	Assets	Weekly income
Single person aged 25 or over	£76.52	£38.26	£292.12	£146.06
Single person aged 18 to 24	£60.56	£30.28	£276.16	£138.08
Couple	£120.06	£60.03	£551.26	£275.63
Mixed household couple (excludes interim and income support cases)	£145.78	£72.89	£576.98	£288.49
Lone parent	£76.52	£38.26	£292.12	£146.06
Child aged 16 and 17	£65.80	£32.90	£281.40	£140.07
Child aged under 16	£77.00	£38.50	£292.60	£146.30

regulations for applying fixed thresholds. There are clear arguments that each case should be looked at on its merits, for example, a newly arrived asylum-seeker in London would normally need more than the ordinary NASS threshold amounts to secure accommodation and subsistence for 14 days since he or she would need to pay higher housing costs. Bed and Breakfast at that rate might not be available or suitable for some asylum-seeker families, in which case the local cost of rent and deposits/rent in advance should be taken into account. Evidence of the cost of housing (such as local reference rents) and essential living needs should be provided at ASA appeals to support these arguments.

3.106   The table above shows the amounts NASS consider will meet a new applicant's essential living needs for 14 days.[133]

133 See NASS Policy Bulletin 4, Version 1.2, issued 3 September 2003.

3.107   There are no items specified which NASS must take into account to decide whether living needs are met. A number of items may not be taken into account by virtue of IAA 1999 s95(7) and AS Regs 2000 reg 9:

a) the cost of faxes;
b) computers and the cost of computer facilities:
c) the cost of photocopying;
d) travel expenses;[134]
e) toys and other recreational items;
f) entertainment expenses.

3.108   There are arguments that additional support should be provided to cover some of these excluded expenses, perhaps under IAA 1999 s96(1). The cost of faxes, copying and travel may all be incidental to and necessary for a supported person's claim for asylum or appeal. The Consultation Paper[135] stated that 'Legal expenses associated with the asylum-seekers' asylum claim may be provided through the Legal Aid Scheme'. However, Legal Services Commission (LSC) funding only covers the expense of reasonable travel to a solicitor's office as a legal help disbursement if it can be demonstrated there is no local solicitor available.[136] Thresholds at which asylum support entitlement is calculated are less than 70 per cent of income support levels. It may be difficult for an asylum-seeker who is working on a low income, just below asylum support threshold, to finance travel to his or her legal representative. In many parts of the UK there is a shortage of immigration lawyers, exacerbated by the 2004 changes to LSC funding of asylum and immigration work. The CLS direct website[137] will provide details of immigration solicitors within a radius but it would be necessary to phone them to check whether they were currently taking on new asylum cases. If the cost of travel to an immigration solicitor is not available, it may be possible to use ECHR arguments either in relation to NASS or the LSC.

3.109   It has been suggested that the exclusion of toys from the assessment of essential living needs may constitute a breach of article 31 of the UN Convention on the Rights of the Child, which recognises the child's rights to rest and leisure '. . . to engage in play and recreational activities appropriate to the age of the child . . .'

---

134 Except for the initial journey to the address where support is provided.
135 See NASS 'Consultation Document on the Main Regulations under Part VI of the Immigration and Asylum Act 1999' November 1999, para 14, note 5
136 LSC Contract Specification on Disbursements rule 2.13.
137 www.clsdirect.org.uk. Tel 0845 345 4345

3.110   In considering whether a person's clothing needs are met, his personal preference as to clothing is excluded. A distinction is then drawn between 'his personal preference as to clothing' and 'his individual circumstances'.[138] It could be argued that individual circumstances include clothing required by cultural and religious norms or that warm clothing is needed by reference to the current weather.

3.111   If NASS decides that an applicant is destitute, either because he or she cannot meet his or her essential living needs or has inadequate accommodation, the question of income and assets will be considered to decide what level and kind of support should be provided.[139]

c) Does the applicant have 'adequate accommodation' for the household?

3.112   For the purposes of this section, a person is destitute if–

(a) he does not have adequate accommodation or any means of obtaining it (whether or not his essential living needs are met).[140]

3.113   An applicant is destitute if he or she is homeless, that is, if he or she has no accommodation at all or no means of obtaining any adequate accommodation.[141] This means adequate accommodation for both the applicant and any dependant(s).[142]

3.114   The statutory test of whether the asylum-seeker has 'adequate accommodation' when NASS is assessing whether or not the household is eligible for support under IAA 1999 s95(6) is slightly different from the question of whether the accommodation which NASS provides for the household it is supporting is adequate under IAA 1999 s97. The meaning of 'adequate accommodation' in the context of housing provided by NASS is discussed in chapter 4. The Court of Appeal has decided there is little difference between the meaning of 'suitable accommodation' in homelessness law and 'adequate accommodation' in the IAA 1999, see *R (A) v NASS and Waltham Forest LBC*.[143] In the case of an asylum-seeker, adequacy must be tested by reference to the actual needs of the homeless family, but the context is important.

---

138 AS Regs 2000 reg 9(2).
139 AS Regs 2000 reg 12 and see para 4.17 below.
140 IAA 1999 s95(3).
141 IAA 1999 s95(3).
142 IAA 1999 s95(4) and AS Regs 2000 reg 8(3)(f).
143 [2003] EWCA Civ 1473; (2003) 6 CCLR 538.

The meaning of 'adequate accommodation'

3.115   The approach to assessing whether asylum-seekers have adequate accommodation is similar to the test of homelessness in Housing Act 1996 ss175–177.[144] The main difference is that an asylum-seeker is not treated as destitute because of 'no enforceable right to occupy' the accommodation.[145] A homeless applicant who has an eviction order to take effect within 28 days is 'threatened with homelessness' and entitled to assistance. An applicant for asylum support may have to wait until 14 days before the eviction order before he or she is awarded support because that is the prescribed period under AS Regs 2000 reg 7(a).

3.116   The IAA 1999 provides that asylum-seekers should have 'no-choice' about their accommodation, but the regulations reflect the test of 'accommodation which is reasonable to continue to occupy' (as developed in homelessness law). Both the IAA 1999 and the AS Regs 2000 borrow from the structure and terminology of Housing Act 1996 Part VII.

3.117   To decide whether accommodation is adequate, NASS must have regard to prescribed matters and may not have regard to matters listed at IAA 1999 s95(6) or to other prescribed matters. The AS Regs 2000 include factors which must be taken into account. So far the Home Secretary has not made regulations with prescribed factors which may not be taken into account.

Factors which may not be considered

3.118   There are four specified factors which should not be taken into consideration by NASS in deciding whether an asylum-seeker's accommodation is adequate under IAA 1999 s95(6):

(a) there is no enforceable right to occupy the accommodation;
(b) all or part of the accommodation is shared;
(c) the accommodation is temporary;
(d) the location of the accommodation.

3.119   These factors will need to be interpreted broadly to make sense of the provisions, for example, if an applicant has no enforceable right to occupy accommodation under IAA 1999 s95(6)(a), he or she may not be able to secure entry to it, which is a relevant matter under AS Regs 2000 reg 8(d). The government gave various assurances when the matter was debated:

144 See chapter 5.
145 IAA 1999 s95(6).

We would not ignore real or serious overcrowding or the fact that a large number of people were relying on very limited shared sanitary or cooking facilities . . . Some accommodation would be overcrowded even if it were in single person occupancy because there is not enough room for a large family . . . If there were overcrowding, it would be a relevant consideration because the accommodation would not then be adequate. On a slightly different point, some accommodation in Birmingham might well be adequate but it might not be suitable if it were unsafe if it were in an area where there had been racial attacks. Those are the kind of factors we would wish to take into account.[146]

3.120   Since the Asylum and Immigration Appeals Act 1993, an asylum-seeker eligible to apply for housing as homeless is not homeless if 'he has any accommodation in the United Kingdom, however temporary available for his occupation'. This definition was incorporated into Housing Act 1996 s186. The Court of Appeal in *Lismane v Hammersmith and Fulham LBC*[147] decided that an asylum-seeker who was living in accommodation in an appalling state of repair was homeless despite the 'however temporary' test. It may be useful to refer to *Lismane* should a similar question arise in relation to adequacy of an asylum-seeker's accommodation given the wording of IAA 1999 s95(6)(a). Most of the ASA cases where NASS has withdrawn support deciding that the asylum-seeker has adequate accommodation are due to the asylum-seeker's income from employment. An income of £82 per week for a childless adult was not considered enough to obtain adequate accommodation.[148] The adjudicator allowed an appeal where NASS had refused to support an asylum-seeker who was living in one room with her husband and a six-week-old child, paying £65 per week rent from income of £130 per week.[149]

Factors which must be considered[150]

3.121   The AS Regs 2000 require the Home Secretary to take the following matters into account in deciding whether anyone in the household applying for asylum support is destitute because he or she does not have adequate accommodation:

146 Lord Williams of Mostyn, Hansard, HL Debates, cols 1159–1160, 20 October 1999.
147 (1999) 31 HLR 427 and see para 5.24.
148 See ASA 02/04/2752.
149 ASA 02/09/4414.
150 AS Regs 2000 reg 8(3).

a) whether it would be reasonable for the person to continue to occupy the accommodation;
b) whether the accommodation is affordable;
c) whether it is emergency accommodation provided as IAA 1999 s98 temporary support while a claim of support is being considered;
d) whether the person can secure entry to the accommodation;
e) where the accommodation is a vehicle or caravan, whether the applicant has a place where it can be parked and lived in;
f) whether the accommodation is available for occupation by the person's dependants together with him;
g) whether it is probable that the person's continued occupation of the accommodation will lead to domestic violence against him or any of his dependants.

3.122   The housing needs of both the applicant and any dependant(s) should be considered.[151] Where the family is living separately but wants to live as one household, it can be argued that the applicant is destitute because he or she does not have adequate accommodation for all those who come within the definition of dependant (see para 3.90).

3.123   The 'reasonable to continue to occupy' consideration is qualified by AS Regs 2000 reg 7(4): '. . . regard may be had to the general circumstances prevailing in relation to housing in the district of the local housing authority where the accommodation is'. These concepts are taken from homelessness legislation.[152] This allows NASS to consider the asylum-seeker's housing situation in the light of the local housing situation. For example, NASS could not rely on AS Regs 2000 reg 7(4) to decide that it is reasonable for an asylum-seeker to continue to occupy a Bed and Breakfast hotel, in an area where there is a plentiful supply of empty council housing.

3.124   To decide whether the accommodation is affordable, NASS must have regard to income or assets which are available or might be expected to be available, the cost of the accommodation and the applicant's other reasonable living expenses.[153] Affordability is a concept used by Housing Act 1996 s177(3), and the Homelessness Code of Guidance para 6.23.[154] In general, the factors referred to in the AS Regs 2000 are the same and so homelessness case law will again be useful.

---

151 IAA 1999 s95(4) and AS Regs 2000 reg 3(f).
152 Housing Act (HA) 1996 ss175(3) and 177(2).
153 AS Regs 2000 reg 5.
154 Homelessness Code of Guidance for Local Authorities, Department of Health, July 2002.

3.125   Accommodation provided under the IAA 1999 s98 emergency accommodation duty is not taken into account in assessing whether or not an applicant has adequate accommodation.

3.126   Other factors which NASS may take into account when it considers whether accommodation is reasonable to continue to occupy are listed in the notes which form a schedule to the AS Regs 2000 and NASS 1 application form.[155] These are racial harassment or attacks, physical violence, sexual abuse or sexual harassment or harassment because of the asylum-seeker's religion.

3.127   Domestic violence means violence or threats of violence which are likely to be carried out from a close family member or someone who was formerly a close family member. Although the homelessness provisions[156] refer to domestic violence from an associated person, this definition in practice may not be very different from 'close family member'. The remainder of the definition in AS Regs 2000 is in the same terms, so homelessness case law may help interpret the provision.

3.128   If an asylum-seeker claims subsistence-only support from NASS, he or she will be expected to show that the accommodation is adequate. It must not be NASS accommodation occupied by another asylum-seeker (see Policy Bulletin 24). An asylum-seeker would not normally be permitted to live in 'expensive accommodation and claim subsistence only support from NASS while paying for the unaffordable accommodation from other resources.[157] He or she will not be permitted to stay in the emergency accommodation provided under IAA 1999 s98, for example, to avoid dispersal, as the accommodation is normally terminated two days after the dispersal date for childless asylum-seekers and five days after for families.

d) Can the applicant meet essential living needs and secure adequate accommodation for the prescribed period?

3.129   Support may be provided for asylum-seekers or their dependants who 'appear to the Secretary of State to be destitute or to be likely to become destitute'[158] within a specified period. Two different periods are prescribed by the regulations, depending on whether the applicant is making a new claim or is already in receipt of support.

155   See www.ind.homeoffice.gov.uk/ind/en/home/applying/national-asylum-support.html/.

156   HA 1996 ss177–178.

157   See ASA 02/08/4018.

158   IAA 1999 s95(1).

New applications

3.130 The prescribed period is '14 days beginning with the day on which the question falls to be determined' in relation to an application for support where the asylum-seeker is not already receiving support at the time of assessment.[159]

3.131 There have been a number of asylum support appeals in cases where the asylum-seeker has arrived in the UK with savings over NASS's limits, and asylum support has been refused. Where the application for asylum support is for living expenses only, NASS will refuse support if the asylum-seeker's assets exceed the relevant asylum support amount for 14 days' living expenses. Where the application is for accommodation and living expenses, there are fixed amounts depending on the household size which are set out in Policy Bulletins 4 and 65.

3.132 Where an asylum-seeker arrives in the UK with savings and spends some of the money, the ASA approach has generally been to allow only small amounts to be spent on clothing, particularly in cases where the appellant is unable to produce receipts. A 37-year-old Iranian woman who arrived in the UK with her seven-year-old daughter and without luggage was refused asylum support for living expenses because she had £258.34. In her written appeal she explained she had spent £223 on buying basic clothes for herself and her child.[160] The Adjudicator decided that £40 for the mother and £30 for the daughter would have been realistic for basic clothing. Since the asylum support she would have received for essential living needs for 14 days was £126.28, he found that she was not destitute at the date of the application and dismissed her appeal. The appellant was unrepresented and it appears that no evidence was presented, for example, about the difficulties which a newly arrived asylum-seeker might have in obtaining cheap replacement clothes in London.

Supported households

3.133 In a case where the applicant is already receiving asylum support but there is a change of circumstances such as an additional family member joining the household or a partner getting a job, the relevant period is '56 days beginning with the day on which that question falls to be determined'.[161]

---

159 AS Regs 2000 reg 7(a).
160 ASA 00/10/0070.
161 AS Regs 2000 reg 7(b).

3.134   The assessment of destitution is an ongoing assessment while support is provided to the 'supported person(s)'. The supported person has a duty to report changes of circumstances such as income or assets becoming available. AS Regs 2000 reg 15 lists the relevant changes of circumstances.

3.135   NASS should only withdraw support if an asylum-seeker has sufficient resources to support him or herself and his or her dependants for more than eight weeks from the date on which destitution is reconsidered by NASS. The capital and income thresholds for supported households and arrangements for contributing to NASS support are outlined in Policy Bulletin 65. A supported asylum-seeker could obtain very short-term employment or receive a small lottery win without loss of accommodation and support. AS Regs 2000 reg 10 allows an asylum-seeker who has an income or is working to make contributions to their support.

NASS procedures

3.136   NASS's procedures are contained partly in the AS Regs 2000, and partly in internal guidance, some of which is published as NASS Policy Bulletins. These can be accessed from NASS's page on the IND website.[162]

Voluntary sector agents for NASS

3.137   NASS funds voluntary organisations, known collectively as the Inter-Agency Partnership (IAP) to carry out some of its functions as agent for NASS:

a) 'reception assistance' which involves managing IAA 1999 s98 emergency accommodation on NASS's behalf and assisting clients to apply to NASS for support by completing the NASS 1 application form.

b) 'One Stop Service' front-line advice and assistance to asylum-seekers who are receiving IAA 1999 s95 support (normally those who have been dispersed).

---

162 www.ind.homeoffice.gov.uk/ind/en/home/applying/national-asylum-support.html/.

Section 55 and screening procedures

3.138 The Home Office requires each asylum applicant and their spouse to participate in the screening process. The aim of screening is to establish identity, nationality, route to the UK and previous travel history. The procedures for screening and authorising access to emergency accommodation are explained in a letter from NASS to the IAP dated 9 February 2004 (see NASS Policy Bulletin 75, Version 5, Annex E).

Port applicants

3.139 If an asylum-seeker claims asylum at the port of entry on arrival in the UK, he or she should be issued with form IS96 endorsed with 'applied on arrival' as evidence of this. If there is not time to carry out a level one screening interview and issue an application registration card (ARC) on arrival, the IS96 should be presented to the Refugee Arrivals Project (or other voluntary organisation acting for NASS) to allow access to emergency accommodation for one night. Such cases should not require a NIAA 2002 s55 decision since the asylum-seeker is treated as having applied for asylum 'as soon as reasonably practicable'.

'In-country' applicants

3.140 'In-country' applicants, including families who are exempt from NIAA 2002 s55, must obtain a 'section 55 letter' by completing a level one screening interview to access emergency accommodation. The asylum screening procedures are explained in chapter 1 (see para 1.67). As a result of NIAA 2002 s55, they are closely linked to the procedures for accessing NASS support but significant changes to the procedure were made after the Court of Appeal decision in *Limbuela* (see para 3.40 onwards). Screening interviews are carried out at places 'designated' by the Home Secretary for the recording of an asylum claim, currently the Asylum Screening Units in Croydon, Liverpool and Solihull. Childless 'in-countr'y applicants who are claiming asylum support may be asked to participate in a level two screening interview to access NASS support. Level three interviews deal with 'third country' issues and credibility. Level four interviews are normally conducted if it is considered that an immigration or criminal offence has occurred. The applicant and officer should sign the screening form at the end of each screening interview. Although it is the Home Office's policy to provide the applicant with a copy of the screening interview notes, this sometimes does not happen.

Level one interview

3.141   At this interview, the asylum-seeker's fingerprints are taken and he or she is asked basic questions about nationality, identity, and route to the UK. An application registration card (ARC) is normally issued at this stage. If an asylum-seeker can provide a travel document and/or there are no doubts as to the claimed identity, nationality and route to the UK, no further interview would be needed unless there is a claim for asylum support which is subject to NIAA 2002 s55.

Level two interview

3.142   The interviewer asks a number of questions about identity, the arrangements for travel and route to the UK. It is used to decide whether an asylum-seeker has applied for asylum as soon as reasonably practicable under NIAA 2002 s55(1) where support cannot be allowed under section 55(5).

Application for asylum support

3.143   The procedure for applying for support is to complete an application form NASS 1. Copies of the form and guidance notes are available by telephoning or writing to NASS. The form can now be downloaded from the NASS website.[163] There are 17 pages of notes explaining to the applicant how the form should be completed. These form a schedule to the AS Regs 2000. The form should be faxed to NASS followed by a hard copy, supporting documents and four photographs in the post.

3.144   NASS has arranged for voluntary organisations known as the One Stop Service to assist asylum-seekers with completing the NASS 1 form and provide an interpreter if necessary.[164] Applicants may complete the form themselves or with help, for example, from a community organisation or advice worker. One photograph should be signed by any adviser who helps with the completion of the form. Legal Help funded by the Community Legal Service (CLS) is not normally available for form-filling. It may be reasonable to assist a client with NASS 1 form if an issue of law arises, for example, whether they should apply for NASS or National Assistance Act 1948 s21 support. Legal Help is available for advice about legal rights in relation to NASS sup-

---

163 www.ind.homeoffice.gov.uk/ind/en/home/applying/national-asylum-support.html/.

164 See appendix F for list of One Stop Service organisations.

port, for example, whether the client is eligible, under the contract for housing, immigration, community care, welfare benefits, or 'tolerance', depending on the type of problem.[165]

Asylum-seekers awaiting a NASS decision

3.145 Newly-arrived and newly-presenting asylum-seekers and their dependants who are in need of support are entitled to help from the voluntary sector reception assistants who assess eligibility for, and arrange temporary support in the form of emergency accommodation under IAA 1999 s98 while the application to NASS is being considered.[166]

3.146 Voluntary sector organisations are being funded by NASS under IAA 1999 Part VI to provide reception services and emergency accommodation to destitute asylum-seekers while the asylum claim is being assessed. The reception assistants are an integral part of the network of the one stop services which also provide support and advice to asylum-seekers who are receiving IAA 1999 s95 support.

3.147 Where special needs are identified, the applicant should be referred to a local authority (social services department) for an assessment of community care needs. Where the applicant claims to be under 18, though this is disputed by the Home Office, he or she should be referred to a social services department for an age assessment (see further chapter 6). The reception assistant is expected to refer the asylum-seeker to the Medical Foundation for the Care of Victims of Torture where appropriate.

IAA 1999 s98 'emergency accommodation' while awaiting a NASS decision[167]

3.148 NASS initially stated that it aimed to make a decision within two working days of receiving the NASS 1 form but this target has not been met. Despite improvements and a reduction in the backlog, there are delays in processing the forms. Some applicants, such as those needing special accommodation or women who cannot be dispersed due to pregnancy may stay in IAA 1999 s98 emergency accommodation for months while awaiting an offer of IAA 1999 s95 support. The reception assistants help asylum-seekers access emergency accommodation, which they manage on behalf of NASS (the Refugee

---

165 See further paras 1.157 and 3.189.
166 See list in appendix F.
167 See NASS Policy Bulletin 73.

Council is winding down its emergency accommodation in London and no longer admits new applicants).[168]

Procedure for 'disbenefited' asylum-seekers

3.149   A 'disbenefited' asylum-seeker is one whose asylum claim was refused on or after 25 September 2000 and who was previously in receipt of income support, and normally housing as a homeless person. There is a memo of understanding between the Home Office and local authorities (the Local Government Association) outlining the arrangements.[169]

3.150   NASS's arrangements for disbenefited asylum-seekers, including emergency provision are explained in NASS Policy Bulletins 51–53. Disbenefited former asylum-seekers who live with a child under 18 or are 'vulnerable' under homelessness law[170] should approach their local authority. If they were housed as homeless in another area, they should contact the authority to which they originally applied as homeless. The authority acts as an agent for NASS, assisting with completion of the form and assessing the adequacy of the household's existing accommodation. The local authority should provide emergency subsistence for three weeks while NASS considers the application. NASS will normally allow the family to remain at their existing address if the accommodation is adequate, affordable and within three miles of a post office (to allow the collection of support arranged by Sodexho with the ARC as evidence of identity).

3.151   Other disbenefited former asylum-seekers (who are entitled to support until their asylum appeal is determined), such as childless 'non-vulnerable' adults may ask the local authority for a NASS 1 form or contact NASS to obtain a form by post. If they need emergency accommodation or help claiming subsistence only support, they should contact the Refugee Arrivals Project (RAP) in London or the local One Stop Service. Note that emergency accommodation for disbenefited asylum-seekers is normally outside London.

---

168 See further para 4.7 onwards.
169 The administrative procedures are described in a 'Disbenefited Process Summary' produced by NASS.
170 See chapter 5, para 5.35.

NASS decision to provide or refuse IAA 1999 s95 support[171]

3.152   If NASS writes to say that it is not willing to accept an application under NIAA 2002 ss55 or 57 (see para 3.21), the remedy is a request for reconsideration followed by judicial review. Applicants may now receive help from the One Stop Service with completing a NASS 1 before being granted a positive section 55 decision.

3.153   When NASS has processed the NASS 1 application form, it writes to the applicant with a decision to provide or refuse support, or a request for more information. If NASS decides to provide support to an asylum-seeker under IAA 1999 s95, a support package is sent to the applicant enclosing a letter with details of the travel arrangements and the location of the accommodation, for example, 'Yorkshire' – it may be weeks or months before an offer of IAA 1999 s95 (dispersal) support is offered. This is a result of serious difficulties in providing suitable (language cluster, size, etc) dispersal accommodation for NASS supported asylum-seekers. The support package should contain the NASS agreement with conditions of support. It should also contain details of emergency payments, normally paid at any general post office via the ARC at the rate of £30 per household member. The support letter will explain the amounts of weekly support entitlement and explain amounts and periods of emergency support. Once arrangements have been made with the local post office, an asylum-seeker must attend with their ARC identity card to obtain cash there each week. NASS monitors the collection of support so that an investigation is triggered, for example, into whether the asylum-seeker has left their accommodation or is working if receipts are not cashed regularly. The arrangement also enables NASS to end support promptly when an asylum-seeker receives a decision on the asylum claim.

Access to information from NASS

3.154   An asylum-seeker is entitled to a copy of their Home Office file, including full records of their NASS claim under Data Protection Act 1998 s7 within 40 days of making the request with signed authorisation and the £10 fee made payable to Accounting Officer, Home

---

171 NASS's procedures are described in detail in 'Dealing with Post Allocation Queries', internal guidance which has been copied to Citizen's Advice and ILPA.

Office and sent to the Subject Access Bureau,[172] quoting the applicant's Home Office reference number. If the file is not produced within 40 days, a complaint may be made to the Data Protection Information Commissioner[173] who will investigate.

Complaints about NASS

3.155   NASS's service has improved in many respects, but its weaknesses are recorded in reports such as 'Distant Voices: CAB clients' experience of continuing problems with the National Asylum Support Service'.[174] As yet there is no formal complaints procedure and in many respects NASS is unaccountable, at least to the main users of its service: asylum-seekers. Here are some possible ways of making a complaint:

- Write to the Director of NASS, relevant Section Head or Assistant Director.
- Use the IND complaints procedure (see www.ind.homeoffice. gov.uk) which gives the NASS phone number for comments or complaints as 08456 021 739. Complain about NASS service or staff conduct by writing to the IND at PO Box 1384, Croydon CR9 3YJ; fax 020 8760 4310 or e-mail ind.cu@homeoffice.gsi.gov.uk.
- Ask the local MP to write to the Home Secretary.
- Make a complaint to the Parliamentary Ombudsman.[175]

3.156   At a policy level, complaints could be made through the National Asylum Support Forum at which national bodies such as Shelter, Citizen's Advice, the Refugee Council and ILPA are represented (see appendix G), or an MP could be contacted to ask a Parliamentary Question.

A warning note

3.157   The procedures for assessing eligibility have serious implications for the asylum-seeker's asylum claim as well as for eligibility for support and the type of support provided. NIAA 2002 increased the role of immigration control in the provision of NASS asylum support. If the Home Secretary is not satisfied that the applicant has provided

---

172   IND, Lunar House, 40 Wellesley Road, Croydon CR9 2BY; tel 0870 606 7766; fax 020 8760 3017.

173   See appendix G for address.   .

174   Dunstan, NACAB, October 2002, available at www.citizensadvice.org.uk.

175   See appendix G.

complete or accurate information or is co-operating with enquiries, NASS may refuse to consider an application, and there is no right of appeal.[176] Any information given to NASS may be passed on to a wide range of agencies from the police, government departments and local authorities, to private landlords and the post office. There is a risk of prosecution in cases of failure to provide accurate information or notify relevant changes of circumstances.[177] NASS has wide powers to require information. AS Regs 2000 reg 4(5) allows the Home Secretary to make further enquiries of the applicant about any matter connected with the application.

Failure to co-operate with enquiries

3.158   NIAA 2002 s57 allows NASS to refuse to consider an application for support where an asylum-seeker fails to co-operate with enquiries made by the immigration authorities or NASS.[178] Prior to NIAA 2002 s57, applications for support were sometimes rejected on the ground that the application had not been validly completed, which was a breach of a condition of support. An applicant could then appeal to the Asylum Support Adjudicators (ASA) against this decision. The remedy if an application is rejected under section 57 is judicial review. NIAA 2002 s57 allows NASS to refuse support where an asylum-seeker's account of their travel arrangements to the UK is not found to be credible. (Level 1 and 2 screening notes have been copied in triplicate: one copy is intended for NASS, one for the Asylum Casework Directorate (ACD) and one for the asylum-seeker). These changes make it desirable for an asylum-seeker's asylum support adviser to liaise with their immigration adviser to ensure that information provided to the IND is consistent. If an asylum-seeker finds errors in the screening notes, they should discuss with their immigration solicitor whether they are significant enough to be notified to the IND.

Offences

3.159   There is a risk of prosecution in cases of failure to provide accurate information or notify relevant changes of circumstances.[179] There have been few prosecutions to date as NASS has concentrated on

---

176 NIAA 2002 s57, see para 3.50 above.
177 See also paras 4.140.
178 See NASS Policy Bulletin 79.
179 See also para 4.140–4.160.

using the provision to end support. In an ASA appeal,[180] an asylum-seeker had been sentenced to 17 months in prison after pleading guilty to defrauding NASS of £63,567 and later had his support withdrawn. At the ASA hearing, he said he had pleaded guilty on his QC's advice in exchange for the Crown Prosecution Service (CPS) withdrawing charges of funding terrorist activity in the UK. He explained he had opened a bank account with £10,000 belonging to his brother, a businessman while continuing to claim NASS support, but he had no access to the money. However, he admitted to receiving NASS payments of £3–5,000 relating to asylum-seekers who were no longer in the UK. The adjudicator rejected his appeal on the basis that he had pleaded guilty to the offence before the Magistrates, produced no evidence of Counsel's advice, no credible evidence that the money belonged to his brother or what had become of it. There was also evidence that his brother had provided financial assistance when required in the past so the adjudicator rejected his argument that the family's ECHR art 3 rights would be breached by a lack of support.

Refusal, suspension or termination of support and challenges

General considerations

3.160   There are some general considerations which apply when NASS support is refused or withdrawn (see also para 3.287 below). NASS Policy Bulletin 12 explains that the procedure NASS should follow when refusing support is to send the applicant a refusal letter and a reasons letter, together with a notice of appeal form and explanatory letter. If this procedure is not followed, an applicant may have a valid ground for requesting an extension of the three-day time limit for submitting an appeal to the ASA. In practice, asylum-seekers discover their support is terminated in a variety of ways, such as when the Post Office refuses to cash their receipt book or when an accommodation-provider asks them to leave. The first step in such cases is to phone the 'Termination of Support' section at NASS to establish the reason why support has stopped and fax them any relevant evidence. If support is not reinstated, or if there is no response, an appeal to the ASA is likely to result in NASS re-examining the case and possibly with-

---

180   ASA 03/04/6328.

drawing their decision. Rights of appeal to the ASA and procedures for appealing are explained below at para 3.246.

3.161 The leading case on the withdrawal of support from asylum-seekers was decided under National Assistance Act (NAA) 1948 s21 but provides useful general guidance on the approach which NASS (or a local authority) should take before deciding to end support where there is an allegation of breach of conditions or other fault on the part of the asylum-seeker. The question of withdrawing NAA 1948 s21 help from a 'disruptive' asylum-seeker was considered in *R v Kensington and Chelsea RLBC ex p Kujtim.*[181]

3.162 The Court of Appeal decided that, firstly a fair and thorough investigation must be carried out, taking account of the asylum-seeker's current needs before ending assistance. This investigation should allow the asylum-seeker to respond to the allegations. Second, a refusal to comply with requirements of support must be 'persistent and unequivocal'. Third, the case needed to be reconsidered if the asylum-seeker had mended his ways and wished to comply with conditions of support.

Refusal or withdrawal of support

3.163 NASS support may be *refused* or *withdrawn* for the following reasons:

a) the supported person is not or ceases to be 'an asylum-seeker' or dependant of 'an asylum-seeker' under IAA 1999 s94(1);[182]

b) there is a change of circumstances so that the supported household is no longer destitute (for example, due to income over the NASS threshold becoming available).This includes where NASS considers that the asylum-seeker is not destitute because he or she is 'in need of care and attention' and so the local authority is responsible for residential accommodation under NAA 1948 s21;[183]

c) the asylum-seeker or dependant is excluded from support under AS Regs 2000 reg 7;

d) there is a relevant change of circumstances under AS Regs 2000 reg 15;

e) the asylum-seeker is in breach of conditions of support under AS Regs 2000 reg 19.

f) the asylum-seeker is excluded from support by NIAA 2002 Schedule 3 for example, as an EEA national.

181 [1999] 4 All ER 161; (1999) 2 CCLR 340, CA and see para 6.35.
182 See para 3.59 onwards and 3.164.
183 But see para 6.75.

(a) Not an 'asylum-seeker'

3.164 If asylum support is refused on this ground, the Asylum Support Adjudicators (ASA) must first consider whether the appellant is an asylum-seeker (or dependant). If they conclude he or she is not, they have no jurisdiction. The procedure for dealing with jurisdiction only is referred to in ASA 03/01/5461 and ASA 02/08/4215. In ASA 02/03/2052, despite clear flaws in the NASS decision letter, there was no jurisdiction because a wife had applied for leave in line with her husband who had indefinite leave to remain, but there was no evidence of a separate asylum claim. In ASA 02/03/2053, a claim had been made which referred to a fear of persecution but did not specifically refer to ECHR art 3. The adjudicator found that the statement disclosed an article 3 claim so the appellant was 'an asylum-seeker' for support purposes.

(b) and (d) Change of circumstances

3.165 NASS has discretion to refuse to consider a new application for support if it has previously been suspended or withdrawn under AS Reg 2000 reg 20 and there is no material change of circumstances. There is no right of appeal against this decision so the remedy would be judicial review. In exercising this discretion, as a public authority interpreting the AS Regs 2000, NASS must take Human Rights Act 1998 and Convention considerations into account. A material change of circumstances is one of those listed at AS Regs 2000 reg 15. A common example is where an asylum-seeker whose support stops after he or she fails to travel to a dispersal area, arranges to stay with a friend and applies for subsistence-only support, notifying NASS of a change of circumstances. It has also been argued that a change of circumstances includes the situation where an asylum-seeker's address has changed after the termination of support because he or she has left the NASS accommodation. If NASS has ended support and there has been no appeal or an unsuccessful appeal, NASS need not consider a further application 'unless the Secretary of State considers there are exceptional circumstances which justify it being entertained'.

(c) and (f) Exclusion from support

3.166 An asylum-seeker must be refused IAA 1999 s98 or s95 asylum support under AS Regs 2000 reg 7 if the whole household is eligible to claim means-tested social security benefits or local authority support under the Interim Regs 1999. The relevant social security benefits are income support, income-based jobseeker's allowance, housing benefit and council tax benefit since these are the benefits to which transitional protection applies. The exclusion applies even if a local authority has refused, suspended or terminated interim support unless refusal is due to ineligibility rather than, say, intentional destitution (see para 3.222 below). An applicant is also excluded if at the time of the asylum support application, NASS decides he or she does not come within the definition of 'asylum-seeker' or 'dependant of an asylum-seeker'. These definitions are explained above. NASS has also decided that asylum-seekers were excluded from support by virtue of NIAA 2002 Schedule 3 when their countries of origin joined the European Union. The effect of Schedule 3 and its exceptions are described in chapter 6. The ASA have considered whether there was a potential breach of the article 3 and article 8 rights when support was withdrawn from 'A8' nationals and found that in some cases there was and the cases should be remitted to NASS for reconsideration (see for example ASA 04/04/7885, 7894. The new benefit and housing rights of 'A8' or accession nationals are described in chapter 2 and 5.

Exclusion of some family members

3.167　An asylum-seeker can claim asylum support even if one or more dependants are eligible for means-tested social security benefits. If an asylum-seeker is in receipt of social security benefits and is joined by dependants for social security purposes, the benefits can be increased. If a non-asylum-seeker is in receipt of benefits, for example a husband with discretionary leave to remain in the UK, he cannot include his wife and children in his income support claim if she arrives in the UK and claims asylum for herself and her children. She could apply for asylum support and his benefits would be taken into account as resources (see para 3.20). Therefore, an application will not necessarily be excluded on the ground that some, but not all, of the household are eligible for means-tested benefits. This enables an asylum-seeker to claim asylum support including housing for the whole family including family members who are already in the UK receiving benefits.

Suspension or discontinuance of support[184]

3.168　In *R (Secretary of State for the Home Department) v Chief Asylum Support Adjudicator*,[185] Ms Manzana had misrepresented to NASS that

184　AS Regs 2000 reg 20.
185　[2003] EWHC 269 Admin.

she claimed asylum on arrival. When NASS discovered this, they wrote to advise her she was excluded from asylum support and support was terminated under AS Regs 2000 reg 21(3) because she was entitled to interim support from a local authority. At the ASA hearing, NASS substituted their previous decision, submitting that she had fraudulently obtained support through the use of forged documents and that as she was never entitled to support (being an 'in-country' applicant), they could cease to provide support without the need to make a decision. The adjudicator allowed her appeal, deciding that since support was in payment, it could only be withdrawn under AS Regs 2000 reg 20. Toulson J rejected the ASA approach, deciding that NASS may cease to support an applicant if it discovers that he or she never met the qualifying criteria. It was not necessary for a decision to be made under AS Regs 2000 reg 20.

3.169   Asylum support may be *suspended* or *discontinued* if any one of the following apply:[186]

a) suspected breach of asylum support condition without reasonable excuse;

b) suspected offence in relation to obtaining support;

c) intentional destitution;

d) one or more of supported household not living at authorised address;

e) unauthorised absence from authorised address for seven consecutive nights or 14 nights in a six-month period.

(a) Suspected breach of conditions

3.170   IAA 1999 provides for support to be provided subject to conditions, which must be set out in writing and given to the supported person.[187] Support may be suspended or withdrawn where there are reasonable grounds to suspect that the supported person or any dependant has failed to comply with any condition subject to which support is provided. Support can only be withdrawn under IAA 1999 s20(1)(a) if the suspected breach is 'without reasonable excuse', which has allowed the ASA some discretion to require NASS to continue support where an asylum-seeker has a valid reason for their behaviour. An asylum-seeker may be able to challenge a decision by NASS to withdraw support for breach of conditions if he or she was not provided with a

---

186 AS Regs 2000 reg 20(1).
187 IAA 1999 s95(9)–(11).

written copy of the conditions and/or they were not translated or interpreted. If this is in dispute, the representative could ask NASS to produce a copy of any conditions signed by the applicant. The ASA have recognised the importance of conditions being properly notified to the supported person before NASS can withdraw support for a breach of conditions (see para 3.172).

3.171   It is a condition of NASS support that an asylum-seeker lives at 'the authorised address'. Where an asylum-seeker ceases to live at that accommodation, NASS may rely on 'suspected breach of conditions' AS Regs 2000 reg 20(a), as well as AS Regs 2000 reg 20(d) and (e) as a reason for withdrawing support.

Understanding the conditions

3.172   The conditions of support include the duty to notify a change of circumstances as specified by AS Regs 2000 reg 15. Failure to do so is also a criminal offence under IAA 1999 ss105(d) and 106(c).[188] When NASS decides to provide IAA 1999 s95 support, it provides the asylum-seeker with a pack containing the NASS agreement with conditions of support. The agreement is often provided at the same time as a lot of other information in English, such as leaflets about local services and access to healthcare. It is not necessarily interpreted to the supported household. The ASA have taken a strict approach to an asylum-seeker's responsibility to ensure the agreement is interpreted to them and that they understand it, particularly in cases where applicants have worked and claimed NASS support. In ASA 01/06/0434, an appeal was dismissed because it was the asylum-seeker's duty to ensure he obtained assistance in getting documents translated and the fact that he had failed to do so and misunderstood did not amount to a reasonable excuse for breaching the conditions of support. Similarly in ASA 02/07/3728, the adjudicator found the onus was on the appellant to understand the NASS agreement and all its conditions. In some cases it may be possible to challenge this approach, arguing that a traumatised asylum-seeker who has recently arrived in the UK, has a reasonable excuse for not being able to understand the NASS agreement or identify which parts are important. Obviously this will depend on other factors such as his or her level of education, the availability of translation and interpreting facilities in the dispersal area and the seriousness of the alleged breach of conditions.

188 See para 4.155.

Judicial review or ASA appeal

3.173   Much of the ASA workload to date involves cases where NASS has withdrawn support on the ground that the asylum-seeker has breached conditions without reasonable excuse. The breach of the condition that support is provided subject to the requirement to live at, or travel to, a specified address is a common reason for the withdrawal of support. There have been a number of appeals by childless asylum-seekers[189] who have refused to be dispersed out of London or have left accommodation due to racial harassment. Such appeals have been an indirect way of challenging the adequacy of accommodation after support has been withdrawn by NASS. A childless asylum-seeker may exercise the right to appeal to the ASA against withdrawal of support and also bring a judicial review of the decision that the accommodation is adequate. There is a different legal test for each remedy so it would be possible to succeed in an ASA appeal but not in a judicial review and vice versa. The disadvantage of using an ASA appeal as an indirect challenge to the adequacy of accommodation, rather than judicial review, is that if the appeal (and any subsequent judicial review of the adequacy of accommodation or the ASA decision) is unsuccessful, NASS has discretion not to consider a further application for support unless there has been a material change of circumstances (see para 3.241 below and NASS Policy Bulletin 17, paras 4.20–4.27). An asylum-seeker could move to the dispersal area and challenge the adequacy of accommodation while bringing a judicial review. Alternatively, if a judicial review and interim relief are applied for urgently when the decision is made to disperse but before support is withdrawn, an asylum-seeker may be able to postpone the decision about whether to move until after the outcome of the judicial review. If the review were unsuccessful, he or she could accept the accommodation. See also the paragraph below on ASA practice of suspending support pending dispersal.

Dispersal: breach of conditions by failure to travel

3.174   This section covers the law and practice where support has been terminated after an asylum-seeker fails to travel to a dispersal area, in

---

189   Households with a child have no right to bring an ASA appeal in these circumstances because NASS states that accommodation in the dispersal area is left open to them so support has not been discontinued, see para 3.175.

particular ASA decisions. It should be read in conjunction with the chapter 4 section on adequacy of accommodation which outlines High Court dispersal decisions which are argued on the basis that the accommodation is not adequate.[190] Since the test of adequacy is different from the test of 'reasonable excuse for failure to travel', there is a higher rate of success in indirect challenges to dispersal through the ASA appeal mechanism.

3.175   Where an asylum-seeker with a dependent child refuses to travel to a dispersal area, the remedy is judicial review since there is no right of appeal to the ASA, following *R (Secretary of State for the Home Department) v Chief Asylum Support Adjudicator and Ahmet Dogan (interested party)*.[190a] NASS approaches such cases by ending the IAA 1999 s98 emergency accommodation, arguing there is no right of appeal to the ASA because IAA 1999 s95 support is available in the dispersal area and so has not terminated.

Practical and legal steps

3.176   Appeals in dispersal cases are a category in the index of decisions on the ASA website. They can be found under the heading 'Failure to Travel' or by carrying out a keyword search for 'dispersal'. There have been a number of successful ASA appeals where the adjudicator has decided that an asylum-seeker had a reasonable excuse not to travel to a dispersal area, and where NASS has therefore then decided to accommodate the household in London. There have been a few successful judicial reviews of dispersal decisions by NASS, that is, decisions that accommodation in a dispersal area appears to the Secretary of State to be adequate accommodation under IAA 1999 s96(1). There have also been some judicial reviews where permission to apply for judicial review has been granted and the case has then been reconsidered by NASS before a full hearing or has resolved itself in other ways.

3.177   There may be an advantage to an asylum-seeker appealing to the ASA against dispersal since if they find there is no reasonable excuse not to travel, it has become the ASA practice to suspend support pending compliance with the NASS instructions to travel, instead of dismissing the appeal. In *R (Lik Cani) v Asylum Support Adjudicators and Secretary of State for the Home Department (interested party)*[191] the

190   From para 4.19.
190a   [2003] EWCA Civ 1673.
191   CO/4768/2002 unreported.

appellant applied for judicial review because the adjudicator had dismissed the appeal outright. The judicial review was settled by setting aside the ASA decision by consent and remitting the case back to the ASA for re-hearing.

Dispersal procedure

3.178   NASS Policy Bulletin 17: Failure to Travel[192] explains the procedure in dispersal cases. Normally the asylum-seeker is in IAA 1999 s98 emergency accommodation when he or she receives the NASS decision letter, support package and notice of dispersal. He or she should be given a week's notice of dispersal and may be asked to move to a 'pre-dispersal' unit a day or two before the travel date. If the asylum-seeker fails to leave, he or she is allowed 24 hours to explain the reasons to NASS, after which NASS should send a 'withdrawal of support' decision letter. Emergency accommodation normally ends on the fifth working day after that letter was served for asylum-seekers with a child under 18, and the third working day for childless adults. If the letter is posted, the date of service is two working days after the date of postage. A childless adult may appeal to the ASA within three days of the date of service. There is no right of appeal for families (see para 3.175). Families and childless adults are given a second chance to travel if they had a reasonable excuse not to travel, for example, they were sick on the day of the journey, misunderstood or otherwise missed the opportunity to travel and are willing to be dispersed as soon as it can be rearranged. If the Policy Bulletin 17 procedure has not been followed in any significant respect, there is a good chance of success at an ASA appeal, but this will normally just provide a short respite before a further dispersal.

Challenging dispersal on procedural grounds

3.179   The ASA have allowed dispersal appeals where NASS has not followed its own procedures or complied with public law standards of fairness:

- There was a reasonable excuse not to travel where arrangements and a warning of the consequence of failure to travel were not properly communicated in ASA 01/04/0269.
- An Albanian single mother who was illiterate and had two children under 5 years old, one of whom was sick, had not understood the dispersal requirement or had an opportunity to have it translated in ASA 00/09/0046.

192 Currently Version 1.1.

Dispersal criteria

3.180 Dispersal may be challenged if NASS has failed to take into account its own criteria for providing accommodation in dispersal areas. NASS Policy Bulletin 31 outlines NASS's approach to dispersal, reinforcing the IAA 1999 s97 presumption that NASS accommodation is 'temporary' and that it is desirable to provide it in areas where there is low demand, that is, outside London and the south-east. The Policy Bulletin provides a checklist of factors which NASS should take into account. NASS decisions usually list the factors which it is meant to consider, so they appear to have complied with the public law requirement of taking individual and relevant circumstances into account in each case. If NASS has carried out a 'group dispersal' or the decision letter withdrawing support is clearly standardised, this is a potential ground for judicial review, but unlikely to be enough on its own.

Factors in Policy Bulletin 31

Medical treatment

3.181 The Policy Bulletin and NASS's medical adviser simply consider the availability of medical treatment in the dispersal area. The ASA have taken a broader approach, deciding that the disruption to the medical treatment that a supported person is receiving would constitute a reasonable excuse for failing to travel in cases such as:

- Asylum-seeker had serious physical injuries which were being treated in London.[193]
- Medical appointments justifying deferring of dispersal.[194]
- An elderly Polish Roma couple with multiple physical health needs depended on their extensive family network for support. Relying on *Secretary of State for the Home Department v Abdi*[195] the Chief Asylum Support Adjudicator found dispersal would be an ECHR art 8 breach. Although dispersal was a legitimate aim, it was not necessary or proportionate in the circumstances of the case.[196]
- Evidence of continuity of care from GP and Croatian speaking therapist over lengthy period. The adjudicator saw this as an exceptional case and distinguished it from similar cases. She was

193 ASA 01/01/0166.
194 ASA 01/06/0365.
195 Imm AR 148, CA.
196 ASA 00/11/0095. See appendix B.

influenced by evidence of 'severe signs of psychological distress' with 'overwhelming' anxiety and fear. Ms [X] described the appellant as [being] 'on the edge of total collapse' and refers twice in her letter to the appellant's suicidal ideation'.[197]

- HIV positive couple receiving treatment in Liverpool.[198] The appeal was strengthened by the fact that the appellant was already in a dispersal area.[199]

3.182   There have been various cases where a combination of medical needs and family support has provided a reasonable excuse not to travel.

- A couple with health needs successfully argued they needed to remain close to their adult children for practical support.[200]
- There was a need for psychiatric and family support.[201]

3.183   Often medical treatment may result simply in a decision to defer dispersal until an assessment, investigation or course of treatment is completed. In ASA 02/07/4305, the adjudicator decided it was reasonable to defer dispersal pending an ultrasound investigation where an asylum-seeker had gynaecological problems.

Special needs

3.184   Chapter 6 explains when asylum-seekers with special needs will be the responsibility of a local authority and when they will be supported by NASS.

- It was a reasonable excuse for a disabled appellant to breach their conditions where the accommodation offered was inadequate.[202]
- Where an asylum-seeker with two disabled children had failed to travel to dispersal accommodation, the Court of Appeal decided that it would be reasonable for NASS to place the family in lower standard accommodation in London while it looked for other accommodation.[203]

---

197   ASA 02/09/4292.

198   ASA 03/07/6831.

199   See also para 4.44 on *R (Muwangusi) v Secretary of State for the Home Department* [2003] EWHC 813 (Admin).

200   ASA 01/08/0714.

201   ASA 01/11/1307.

202   ASA 01/05/0314.

203   *R (A) v (1) NASS and (2) Waltham Forest LBC* [2003] EWCA Civ 1473; (2003) 6 CCLR 538; January 2004 *Legal Action* 20, see also paras 4.26 and 4.49.

Family ties

3.185 NASS must consider whether dispersal will interfere with the household's right to respect for private, home and family life under ECHR art 8.

- In ASA 01/06/0368 an asylum-seeker was divorced from her husband (who had leave to remain in the UK) but her children had daily contact with him. She argued that dispersal would interfere with the children's article 8 rights. The ASA decided the relevant question was whether the father could afford contact:

    ... provided that the father is able to visit the children at weekends, during school holidays, and bank holidays, there is no interference with the family life of the children. If however, his earnings are so limited that he would effectively be prevented from visiting his children then there may be an interference under article 8 ...

- In *R (Blackwood) v Secretary of State for the Home Department,*[204] an asylum-seeker who had lived in London for 12 years relied on ECHR art 8 to show that dispersal accommodation was not adequate.

Education

3.186 If a child of the household has attended the same school for 12 months, the family should not normally be dispersed.[205] The ASA have taken article 2 of the First Protocol into consideration in cases where asylum-seekers have argued they wished to complete courses of further or higher education.[206]

- Where an asylum-seeker in Manchester who was studying a postgraduate degree in dentistry had evidence this was the only available course in the north, the case was remitted to NASS for reconsideration.[207]
- Where an asylum-seeker wanted to complete their HND course in IT and Business, the adjudicator dismissed the appeal, noting that article 2 applies mainly to primary and secondary education, but recommending that dispersal be postponed for six weeks until the course had completed.[208]

204 [2003] EWHC 97 Admin.
205 See Policy Bulletins 31 and 53 and ASA 02/04/2460.
206 ASA 00/11/0132 and ASA 02/02/2002.
207 ASA 03/04/6367.
208 ASA 02/05/2924.

Religion

3.187   There have been a number of ASA cases considering whether difficulties in practising religion in a dispersal area amount to a reasonable excuse not to travel and/or a breach of ECHR art 9, which protects the right to hold or adhere to religious beliefs and manifest them in worship.[209]

- In ASA 02/04/2665 a Congolese asylum-seeker gave as one of the reasons for failing to travel that he needed to attend a catholic church which was French-speaking. The ASA found that the most important feature of participating in mass was physical attendance at the service. The decision was upheld by the administrative court in *R (Djamba Kazema) v Asylum Support Adjudicators and Secretary of State for the Home Department (interested party)*, which noted that the words of the mass recurred each week.[210] The ASA approach is to reject the argument that the first language of the asylum-seeker should be spoken, provided there is a place of worship within a reasonable travelling distance of the dispersal accommodation.[211]

Employment

3.188   An asylum-seeker or a member of their household might be working in the south-east and claiming a top-up of NASS support. This could justify failure to travel. Note that on 23 July 2002 the 'right to work concession' was withdrawn[212] and since then it has only been possible for an asylum-seeker to apply for the right to work in exceptional circumstances such as if they have been waiting 12 months for an initial asylum decision.[213]

Availability of legal advice

3.189   This will not normally justify a failure to travel since NASS's stock response is to refer to the availability of travel expenses to solicitors from the Legal Services Commission where there is no local solicitor. The LSC Manual Volume 2, para 2D-029 rule 2.13 states that travel costs can be claimed by the solicitor for the client as a disbursement in immigration, mental health, education, community care or public

---

209 See appendix A and note the immigration decision in *R (Ullah) v Special Adjudicator* [2004] UKHL 27.

210 CO/2674/02.

211 See also ASA 02/03/2056, ASA 03/09/4413.

212 See para 1.152.

213 See para 1.152.

law cases if they have a contract in that area. To qualify, the cheapest return fare must exceed £5 and only the difference between £5 and the fare will be paid, except in an immigration case where the client is supported by NASS (when the full fare may be paid). The client should be informed in advance that the fare will be paid. The purpose of the interview must be to take instructions. The solicitor must show 'there is no other local contractor in the category of law concerned who is able to take the case, or the client's problem is so specialised that it is appropriate for [them] to deal with the case notwithstanding the existence of other local contractors'.

Language

3.190　NASS's policy is to *consider* dispersal to language-based cluster areas. A list of these can be obtained from NASS or the One Stop Service organisations.[214] Occasionally NASS has mistakenly dispersed to an incorrect area. Failure to consider this criterion could be a reasonable excuse not to travel until NASS offers dispersal to the relevant area.

Other factors

Torture survivors

3.191　NASS's stated policy in Policy Bulletin 19: 'The Medical Foundation for Care of Victims of Torture' is not to disperse those who 'have been accepted for treatment' by the Medical Foundation.[215] It is not enough for the asylum-seeker simply to be on a waiting list for treatment, awaiting assessment, or to have a report from the Foundation. If a torture survivor is receiving treatment analogous to Medical Foundation treatment, such as intensive counselling after sexual assault, it could be argued that this is a 'reasonable excuse' for failure to travel. In *R (Wanjugi) v Secretary of State for the Home Department*[216] an asylum-seeker who was receiving counselling for post-traumatic stress disorder unsuccessfully argued that W's case should be treated in the same way as those covered by the Medical Foundation exception. Elias J refused to extend the Policy Bulletin 19 exception to cases where asylum-seekers had illnesses similar to those suffered by some of the patients treated by the Foundation. He decided that the policy was linked to the particular nature of the institution and the kind of treatment that it provided. However, medical evidence provided by W did justify reconsideration of NASS's decision to disperse her.

214　See appendix F.
215　See ASA 02/08/4050.
216　[2003] EWHC 3116 (Admin). See a fuller account of decision at para 4.42.

3.192   The adjudicator found a reasonable excuse where an asylum-seeker was receiving counselling due to psychological problems following torture, rape and beatings. There was also a GP's letter stating dispersal should be postponed due to abdominal pain.[217]

3.193   Where an asylum-seeker is awaiting Medical Foundation assessment at the time of dispersal, it is NASS's policy to consider deferring dispersal pending the assessment. Policy Bulletin 19 gives details of NASS's arrangements for paying travel expenses of a supported asylum-seeker to attend a Medical Foundation assessment. In some cases NASS may go ahead with the dispersal, but offer travel expenses to the appointment. A dependant's travel expenses are not covered. If a dependant is in need of assessment and a decision is made to disperse, a refusal to agree to cover travel expenses might constitute a 'reasonable excuse' not to travel for ASA purposes.

3.194   ASA appeals were remitted to allow another decision to disperse after NASS provided an undertaking to pay appellants' travel expenses to Medical Foundation and hospital appointments.[218]

HIV treatment

3.195   NASS's policy of dispersing asylum-seekers with HIV to parts of the UK where it states that HIV treatment is available has been found to be lawful (but see also chapter 4, para 4.43). Where a woman was receiving anti-retroviral therapy and treatment for depression, the ASA found she had a reasonable excuse not to travel because NASS had not made the necessary arrangements for the transfer of her treatment.[219] They decided her dispersal should be deferred until this had been done.

3.196   The ASA's approach is to consider the availability of HIV services in the dispersal area and the effect of disruption. The adjudicator has found that it was not enough to say that suitable medical and support services existed in the dispersal area where NASS's medical adviser had entirely failed to consider any harm the appellant might suffer as a result of dispersal . . . 'there must be evidence that these services can be provided in such a way as to compensate for the problems arising out of the disruption to services provided in London'.[220]

3.197   An appeal against dispersal was also allowed in a case where medical evidence was lodged to show dispersal would be detrimental to

217 ASA 01/06/0365.
218 ASA 02/02/1907.
219 ASA 03/04/6333.
220 ASA 03/07/6850.

the appellant's health.[221] The High Court's decision in *Muwangusi*[222] was considered but the adjudicator did not find NASS's decision to disperse was proportionate. The ongoing medical care could not be replicated outside London without detriment to the appellant's health.

Pregnancy

3.198 NASS Policy Bulletin 61 contains guidance on the dispersal of pregnant women. It states that during the final weeks of pregnancy, NASS should attempt to limit the journey time to 4 hours. Where a woman in a late stage of pregnancy refused dispersal to Stockton-on-Tees, a journey of 10 hours 40 minutes, the appeal was successful.[223]

Dispersal from dispersal area

3.199 Where an asylum-seeker is already living in a dispersal area and wishes to remain there, it is NASS's policy not to disperse, see para 2.3 of Policy Bulletin 31 as referred to in ASA 02/08/4233 where the decision to disperse from Glasgow was overturned. In ASA 02/08/4239 a young asylum-seeker had appealed against dispersal from Birmingham. The adjudicator noted that Immigration and Asylum Act (IAA) 1999 s97(1)(b) requires NASS to take into account the desirability of providing accommodation in areas where there is a ready supply of accommodation.[224]

Unsuitable accommodation

3.200 Where an appellant argued it was unreasonable to expect her to share a room with her mother and her one-month-old baby the adjudicator remitted the appeal.[225]

Transfer of medical treatment

3.201 There was a reasonable excuse for an asylum-seeker with mental health problems not to travel until she knew how to access psychiatric support in the dispersal area and that it would be promptly available.[226]

---

221 ASA 03/09/7003.
222 *R (Muwangusi) v Secretary of State for the Home Department* [2003] EWHC 813 (Admin).
223 ASA 02/02/1840.
224 See also ASA 03/04/6367.
225 ASA 02/07/3729.
226 ASA 02/04/2574.

Breach of conditions by leaving NASS accommodation

Racial harassment

3.202   The question of racial harassment has generally arisen where asylum-seekers have breached conditions of support by leaving NASS accommodation in a dispersal area and refusing to return.[227] There have been a number of reported incidents of racial harassment in dispersal areas but individualised evidence is usually necessary to challenge NASS's decisions in this area. The High Court has confirmed that the general policy of providing accommodation within an inner city estate is not unlawful, provided there is a general system of providing police protection, social support and programmes designed to improve community relations.[228]

3.203   NASS's approach to complaints of racial harassment and its investigation procedures are outlined in Policy Bulletin 81. Policy Bulletin 73 confirms that where an asylum-seeker has left accommodation due to racial or other harassment, he or she may be admitted to emergency accommodation in exceptional circumstances. Asylum-seekers face a relatively high standard of proof in demonstrating they have 'a reasonable excuse' for leaving NASS accommodation due to harassment. Both NASS and the ASA have adopted a strict approach to evidence in such cases. It is not uncommon for asylum-seekers to leave accommodation with little or no evidence of recorded incidents because of lack of interpreting facilities in organisations such as the police in dispersal areas.

3.204   The following steps are recommended where asylum-seekers are experiencing racial or other harassment in their accommodation or have left accommodation:

1) Every incident should be reported to the police. If the police appear not to have recorded the incident as racially motivated or at all, a report should be made even if the incident occurred some time in the past. If necessary an informal police complaint should be made to ensure there is a record if the police refuse to record an incident properly.

2) The asylum-seeker should report and seek advice about incidents at any relevant official agency, for example, local race equality council, Citizen's Advice Bureau or advice centre, local authority,

---

227 See also para 3.227 onwards on leaving authorised accommodation. AS Regs 2000 reg 20(1) (d) and (e).

228 *R (Gezer) v Secretary of State for the Home Department* [2003] EWHC 860 (Admin) and see para 4.38.

community organisations. He or she could also contact the local councillor or MP.

3) The asylum-seeker should keep a diary of incidents and report incidents to the accommodation provider, to NASS and to the local One Stop Service.[229]

4) The asylum-seeker should attend the GP with any household member whose health is adversely affected and ask the doctor to make a record.

5) Evidence should be collected of whether there is a history of incidents in the area, for example, through local newspaper reports, by word of mouth in refugee and minority communities, by searching the Home Office website of recorded crime, or by contacting the Commission for Racial Equality, local race equality council or similar bodies.

ASA decisions on racial harassment

3.205   The ASA have approached the question by emphasising the relevance of the effect of the harassment on the individual or household. In ASA 00/08/0036, a case where an asylum-seeker had suffered serious racial harassment, the factual background included:

- verbal abuse of the appellant who also had an egg and banana skin thrown at him;
- a British National Party demonstration outside the accommodation followed by the assault of two asylum-seekers nearby after which the appellant had acted as interpreter for one of the victims;
- the robbery and assault of an asylum-seeker occupying the same accommodation;
- local and national media coverage;
- offers of support by the police and service provider.

3.206   The adjudicator decided 'in looking at questions of reasonableness I should be concerned not with the general efforts made to combat racial harassment but with how the situation affects this appellant in particular'. She followed *R v Brent LBC ex p McManus*,[230] a judicial review by a family who were found to be intentionally homeless after fleeing the psychological effects of sectarian violence in Northern Ireland. In McManus the High Court decided the correct approach was to investigate the individual circumstances, including medical evidence and that the council was wrong simply to take account of the prevailing situation of violence in Belfast.

229 See appendix F.
230 (1993) 25 HLR 643.

3.207   Looking at the asylum-seeker's circumstances, the adjudicator decided 'in this case the appellant did have reasonable excuse . . . very real fear of risk of attack'. She went on to set out an approach to racial harassment which has been followed in other ASA appeals, stating:

> no matter how ethnically and culturally mixed the local population may be, there is unlikely to be any area of the UK in which freedom from racial harassment can be guaranteed. In reaching a decision I have therefore had regard to the nature, degree, frequency, persistence and organisation of the harassment involved and its immediacy to the appellant.

3.208   ASA 00/09/0044 concerned a torture survivor who had left accommodation after racist abuse, which he did not understand at the time, and incidents of racial harassment affecting other occupiers. The adjudicator stated ' . . . there exists sufficient protection against racial harassment in this country in the form of a system of criminal law which makes violent attacks by persecutors punishable and a reasonable willingness to enforce that law on the part of law enforcement agencies . . . I am satisfied that the police have provided protection to the appellant when called upon to do so'. In ASA 03/06/6684 an appeal was allowed where a Roma family from Romania returned to London from accommodation in Cleveland where they were experiencing racial harassment and slept in a park. The adjudicator found that NASS had not complied with the Policy Bulletin 18 (now 81) procedures for investigating racist incidents and that the withdrawal of support interfered with their ECHR article 8 and article 3 rights.

3.209   NASS has at times suspended dispersal to parts of the country where there is a high incidence of racial harassment of asylum-seekers.[231] On police advice, it suspended dispersal to Glasgow after the murder of an asylum-seeker on the Sighthill estate. The conclusion from the ASA decisions is that there must be convincing evidence of the asylum-seeker's circumstances and/or of the local situation for an appeal to succeed. This is consistent with the approach in *R (Thiab) v NASS*[232] where an asylum-seeker left Sighthill with his family after the murder and presented at emergency accommodation in London. Four months later, when his judicial review was heard, the family had been dispersed back to Glasgow where steps had been taken to tackle the harassment. He failed in challenging the decision since the family

---

231 See Hansard, HL, Written Answers Col 68, 16 December 2002.
232 [2002] EWHC 905 (Admin).

had not experienced further racially-motivated incidents, he was in part-time work and community relations had improved.[233]

Domestic violence

3.210 NASS Policy Bulletin 70 explains NASS's procedures for investigating domestic violence and allowing access to emergency accommodation where someone has left domestic violence. It covers domestic violence from 'associated persons' so is not limited to domestic violence from a partner within the home. As with racial harassment, it is advisable that evidence is collected about any incidents by reporting them to the police, GP, or local One Stop Service and keeping a diary. An asylum-seeker or dependant who is considering leaving domestic violence should obtain independent legal advice about whether it will have any effect on her immigration status. Domestic violence cases have not generated many ASA appeals, which is consistent with NASS's comment in Policy Bulletin 70, that only a small number of cases of domestic violence are reported.

Inadequate accommodation

3.211 There were a series of appeals after asylum-seekers staged a protest about conditions in a Liverpool hostel and walked out after their complaints were overruled. Their support was withdrawn after they refused to comply with a NASS warning that it was a condition of support that they return to the accommodation. One of the appeals was successful on the ground that the warning letter had been sent to the incorrect address.[234] In another appeal the adjudicator found a breach of ECHR art 3: 'I am satisfied on the evidence before me that the requirement to take meals only at the rigidly enforced times, the non-existing facilities for the preparation of food if meals were missed, with the resultant effects on the health and well-being of the appellant, a possible heart patient, represents a violation of article 3'. The adjudicator concluded that the appellant had reasonable excuse not to return until the result of NASS's investigations had been notified to him and his grievances addressed.

3.212 Where an asylum-seeker was forbidden from having any visitors at his accommodation and photographed by the hostel manager without his consent, the adjudicator decided this might constitute an

233 See also para 4.39.
234 ASA 00/11/0102.
235 ASA 00/12/0135.

interference with his privacy in breach of article 8 and remitted the case back to NASS for further consideration.[235]

Other breaches of conditions

Working cases

3.213   There have been a number of (largely unsuccessful) appeals where support has been stopped due to an asylum-seeker's failure to notify NASS that he or she is working. NASS's usual reasons for withdrawal of support in working cases are both 'breach of conditions' and 'suspected offence'. Relevant ASA decisions are explained below at para 3.220.

Nuisance

3.214   H's support was terminated on the grounds of nuisance, which was a breach of his occupancy agreement after he allegedly caused a disturbance including making threats to kill in the residential home where he was accommodated. He was unsuccessful at his ASA appeal, at which he was unrepresented but then brought a successful judicial review of the decision. In *R (Husain) v Asylum Support Adjudicator*,[236] Stanley Burnton J found that a single incident of assault in the common parts could not constitute 'use of the demised premises' since the 'demised premises' did not include the whole building.

3.215   An asylum-seeker had been arrested while trying to set fire to himself after allegedly setting fire to his NASS hostel in ASA 01/01/0107. The adjudicator found that these actions gave rise to questions about the appellant's mental health and remitted the case back to NASS for further consideration with a direction that a psychiatric report should be provided. Relying on *R v Kensington and Chelsea RLBC ex p Kujtim*,[237] she found that conduct will need to be shown to be persistent and unreasonable in all the circumstances.

3.216   An asylum-seeker who was evicted due to nuisance claimed subsistence only support and appealed against the withdrawal of accommodation. The adjudicator found that the eviction was brought upon him by his own conduct and the withdrawal of support did not interfere with his rights under article 3 because he still had subsistence.[238]

---

236 [2001] EWHC Admin 582; (2001) *Times* 15 November.
237 [1999] 4 All ER 161; 32 HLR 579; (1999) 2 CCLR 340, CA. See para 3.161.
238 ASA 02/12/5284.

(b) Suspected criminal offence under IAA 1999 Part VI

3.217   Support may be withdrawn where NASS has reasonable grounds to suspect that the supported person or any dependant has committed an offence under IAA 1999 Part VI. These offences are discussed in more detail at para 4.147. The relevant offences are:

– where false or dishonest representations were made to obtain support; or
– where an applicant has caused delay or obstruction of asylum support functions.

3.218   'Representations' include an omission, such as a failure to notify a change of circumstances. The relevant changes of circumstances are listed in AS Regs 2000 reg 15 (see para 4.146). The ASA have decided that although the standard of proof for failing to disclose a material fact is a civil balance of probability, it requires a high degree of probability bearing in mind the seriousness of the consequences.[239] The burden of proof is on NASS. The circumstances surrounding the completion of the NASS 1 application form must be looked at.

3.219   The ASA considered an appeal against refusal of support where a minor had given an incorrect name and date of birth, which were recorded on her SAL1.[240] The appeal was dismissed because as a minor she was not entitled to support. The adjudicator commented that if NASS had been aware of her true name and age when she applied for support, support could have been refused on the ground that she had committed an offence under IAA 1999 s105(1)(a). 'The offence in question would have been making a statement or representation which the appellant knew to be false in a material particular with a view to obtaining support for herself.'

Working cases

3.220   NASS's investigation teams have discovered a number of cases of asylum-seekers working while claiming support by carrying out investigations at particular workplaces and employment agencies in dispersal areas. In Plymouth a number of supported asylum-seekers, whose support was cut off after it was discovered they were working in factories, appealed arguing that they thought they were acting lawfully since they had permission to work, had applied for a national insurance number and were paying tax and national insurance. They

239 ASA 00/06/0012.
240 ASA 00/09/0061.

said they had not understood that they were breaching their conditions of support and committing a criminal offence by not reporting the employment.

3.221   In some cases asylum-seekers have stopped working or did not have Home Office permission to work. The ASA has generally dismissed appeals in working cases and as yet there have been no judicial reviews to test their approach. In many of the cases during 2002–3, the asylum-seeker had IND permission to work. The concession was withdrawn by the Home Secretary on 23 July 2002 but still applies in exceptional cases.[241] Some working cases may involve asylum-seekers with no lawful permission to work, arguing that withdrawal of support would interfere with their rights under ECHR art 3.

- An appeal was allowed where an asylum-seeker had reported his employment to the accommodation provider and was unaware of the requirement to report it to NASS.[242]
- An appeal was remitted to NASS where the appellant was on a low income, often below the NASS threshold, and his pregnant wife gave evidence she might miscarry if support was terminated.[243]
- An appeal was allowed where the appellant with a dependent wife and son had stopped work due to an injury and it was argued that withdrawal of support would breach ECHR arts 3 and 8, following *Husain*.[244]
- An appeal failed where an asylum-seeker working as a pizza chef who was found by NASS to own a range of IT and stereo equipment, argued that he had not reported the job to NASS because it was insecure and he was waiting to see if it lasted.[245]

(c) Intentional destitution

3.222   An applicant is 'intentionally destitute' if he or she is 'destitute as a result of an act or omission deliberately done by him or any dependant of his without reasonable excuse while in the United Kingdom'. There have been few ASA appeals under this heading and a category search of intentional destitution on the ASA website currently shows just one decision. It is arguable that NASS can only make a decision

---

241 See para 1.152 and 3.188.
242 ASA 01/10/0928.
243 ASA 02/05/2939.
244 ASA 02/05/3005. *R (Husain) v Asylum Support Adjudicator* [2001] EWHC Admin 582; (2001) *Times* 15 November.
245 ASA 02/04/2475.

of intentional destitution where an applicant is already receiving support because the wording of AS Regs 2000 reg 20 limits it to 'suspension or discontinuation of support'.

3.223   IND guidance to the Interim Regs 1999 dated 19 November 1999 suggested that an asylum-seeker will be 'intentionally destitute' if [he] has 'deliberately squandered his resources'.

3.224   An Iranian asylum-seeker has won an appeal against a NASS decision that he was intentionally destitute. He had arrived in the UK with £979.96, which he had borrowed to get here, and then he had sent the money back to his sick father. The ASA applied social security case law[246] and decided that 'to reach a finding of intentional destitution, it must be shown that the appellant knew of the rules which he is alleged to have circumvented'. The appellant was not intentionally destitute because he had not received a clear warning from NASS about the consequences of any future disposal of funds. See also paras 3.166 and 3.170 above.

3.225   The Court of Appeal granted permission to apply for judicial review of a decision that an asylum-seeker was intentionally destitute under the Interim Regs 1999, in a case where he had left his accommodation before the IAA 1999 came into force (*R (Fetiti) v Islington LBC*)[247] It was argued that a finding of intentional destitution might cause indefinite destitution and so violate Mr Fetiti's ECHR rights (articles 3, 6, 8 and 14).

3.226   If NASS or the ASA find that an asylum-seeker comes within the 'intentional destitution' definition, the question of whether it is necessary to provide support to avoid a breach of ECHR art 3 needs to be considered.[248] If one of the supported persons is under 18, a local authority may have duties to the family under the Children Act 1989. If the applicant is 'in need of care or attention' for a reason that does not arise solely out of the physical effects of destitution, for example, where there are also other factors such as age, disability, illness, mental illness or pregnancy, he or she may be entitled to help under National Assistance Act 1948 s21.

246 CIS 124/90.
247 C/00/2748, 19 October 2000 (unreported).
248 See para 3.259.

(d) and (e) Temporary or permanent absence from the 'authorised address'[249]

3.227   Asylum support may cease if any member of the household moves or is temporarily away from his or her address without permission. This requirement underlines the monitoring role of NASS as part of the Home Office's IND. An asylum-seeker who moves house is also required to inform the Home Office or the port of entry for immigration purposes and IND records will be amended to show the new address. Many of the ASA decisions on failure to travel are also relevant to AS Regs 2000 reg 20(1)(d) and (e) (see dispersal at para 3.174 onwards).

3.228   If a supported person leaves his or her accommodation for longer than seven days consecutively or 14 days in total during a six-month period without permission, support can be withdrawn. The minimum period is 'seven days *and nights*'.[250]

3.229   It is a condition of NASS support that an asylum-seeker lives at 'the authorised address'. Where an asylum-seeker ceases to live at that accommodation, NASS is likely to rely on 'suspected breach of conditions' in AS Regs 2000 reg 20(a) as well as reg 20(d) and (e) as a reason for withdrawing support, so the case law on this may be relevant (see para 3.17 onwards).

- An appeal was allowed where the asylum-seeker had informed the Home Office but not NASS of the change of address.[251]
- An appeal was remitted for medical evidence where an asylum-seeker argued his absence from the authorised address was due to isolation aggravating the mental and physical effects of torture.[252]
- An appeal was allowed where an asylum-seeker who had been beaten up and hospitalised for 13 days temporarily moved in with a friend to convalesce.[253]

3.230   Although there is no reference to 'reasonable excuse' for leaving accommodation in AS Regs 2000 reg 20(1)(d) and (e), the ASA have implied one, finding that since NASS has a discretion when deciding whether or not to terminate support in those paragraphs, the approach should be analogous to the 'reasonable excuse' approach to

---

249   AS Regs 2000 reg 20(1)(d) and (e).
250   See ASA 02/04/2570.
251   ASA 02/08/3979.
252   ASA 02/12/5224.
253   ASA 02/06/3555.

AS Regs 2000 reg 20(1)(a).[254] 'It is equally open to an appellant under subparagraph (d) or (e) as under paragraph (a) to seek to discharge the burden of proof upon him by showing that his actions were reasonable in the circumstances.'

3.231　　There have been a number of appeals against decisions to discontinue support where asylum-seekers have left accommodation because of racial harassment and/or because they believed the accommodation was inadequate (see para 3.202). In one of the series of appeals arising from a walk-out of asylum-seekers from a Liverpool hostel (referred to at para 3.211), the Chief Asylum Support Adjudicator found the regime at the hostel was so harsh and rigid that it amounted to inhumane and degrading treatment within the meaning of ECHR art 3 and the asylum-seeker 'had reasonable excuse not to return to the authorised address'.

3.232　　IAA 1999 s125 gives a power to obtain a warrant to enter the supported household's home using reasonable force. A warrant may be granted where there is a reasonable belief that one or more of the supported household is not living in accommodation provided by NASS (see further para 4.148).

3.233　　Whether the asylum-seeker is staying in accommodation that they found, or in accommodation organised by NASS, and claiming subsistence only support, the accommodation is referred to as the 'authorised address'. The supported person is required to notify NASS if the household moves to a new address even if it is provided by friends or family. NASS may visit the authorised address to check that the supported household is living there and may terminate support, both under this ground and on grounds of breach of conditions, if it believes they are not.

3.234　　Since asylum-seeker households are dispersed around the UK, it is not unlikely that they will need to be absent from accommodation at some point, for example, to visit friends or legal representatives in other parts of the country. The asylum-seeker may write to NASS to request permission to be absent, to avoid a breach of AS Regs 2000 reg 20(1)(a) and (e). The regulation does not specify that permission must be obtained in advance, although supported persons should be advised to do so. Where necessary, there is an argument that permission should be granted retrospectively, for example, if the asylum-seeker needed to travel urgently to visit a sick relative.

254 ASA 00/11/0100.

Asylum decisions and end of support entitlement

3.235   An asylum-seeker is only entitled to support for as long as he or she comes within the definition of asylum-seeker in IAA 1999 s94(1) explained at the start of this chapter. Entitlement to support ends if the asylum-seeker withdraws the asylum claim or if the claim is refused and there is no outstanding appeal. Entitlement also ends if there is a favourable decision on the asylum claim.

3.236   The asylum-seeker and any dependant(s) who are refused or granted full refugee status or exceptional leave to enter/remain in the UK become ineligible for support at the end of a prescribed period.[255]

3.237   In the case of a favourable decision this allows very limited time for a supported person to transfer to mainstream welfare support, for example, to apply as homeless or obtain income support. Tactics for addressing these issues are discussed at paras 2.106–2.136.

3.238   If an asylum-seeker is granted indefinite leave after being recognised as a refugee he or she can claim backdated child benefit and tax credits. He or she may be able to claim housing benefit, income support and council tax benefit but this right is due to be abolished and replaced by an integration loan.[256] A valid backdating claim must be made within 28 days of receiving the status decision or entitlement is lost, except that there is a three-month time limit in the case of tax credits and child benefit.

3.239   Where an asylum-seeker is refused asylum, he or she remains 'an asylum-seeker' eligible for IAA 1999 Part VI asylum support as long as the household includes a dependent child under 18 (see para 3.72 above). If there is no dependent child, community care provision or IAA 1999 s4 'hard cases' support may be available as a last resort (see para 3.291).

Effect of withdrawal of support

3.240   There is no prescribed notice period for withdrawal of NASS support except that entitlement continues for the 21/28-day grace period explained above at para 3.69. Any notice to quit may be limited to seven days.[257]

---

255 See para 3.69.

256 Asylum and Immigration (Treatment of Claimants, etc) Act 2004 ss12 and 13 will be introduced by order.

257 AS Regs 2000 reg 22.

New applications after withdrawal of support[258]

3.241 Where an award of asylum support has been suspended or discontinued under AS Regs 2000 reg 20, no further application will be considered unless:

- there has been a material change of circumstances of the kind which the asylum-seeker would have to report if he or she were receiving support, for example, arrival of a new household member (see para 4.146);
- NASS considers there are exceptional circumstances.

3.242 NASS may allow a fresh application but then decide that an applicant is not eligible for support.[259]

3.243 There have been some unsuccessful ASA appeals where the asylum-seeker has arrived in the UK with savings over the limit for support. In such cases the ASA have suggested that there will be a change of circumstances, justifying a further claim for support, when the savings have reduced to below the destitution threshold.

Notices to quit and security of tenure

3.244 Where a supported person is living in accommodation provided by NASS, there are special rules about notices to quit and eviction. These are described in more detail in para 5.149.

Challenging refusal or withdrawal of support

3.245 Where support has been refused or withdrawn, the first step is to establish the reason, the second to check whether NASS has followed its own procedures and guidance and the third to decide on whether the remedy is an ASA appeal, judicial review or both. The tables on pp188 and 189 are a quick guide to some of the common reasons why support is refused and the appropriate responses.

Appeals to the Asylum Support Adjudicators

3.246 A unique appeals system has been developed to review NASS decisions to refuse or withdraw support. IAA 1999 ss102–104 and Sch 10, as amended by NIAA 2002, provides for the appointment of Asylum

258 AS Regs 2000 reg 21(3).
259 AS Regs 2000 reg 21(3).

Table to show NASS refusals and possible responses for a childless adult asylum-seeker

NASS decision	Response
NIAA 2002 s55 refusal.	1. Fax letter to NEAT Unit of NASS requesting reconsideration of the decision with medical evidence and details of the client's current condition and any human rights arguments. 2. If no reply in 24 hours and asylum-seeker has no shelter or food, consider judicial review application and injunction (requiring NASS to provide emergency accommodation until judicial review hearing).
Refusal/withdrawal of support on grounds that applicant is not 'an asylum-seeker' under IAA 1999 s94(1).	1. If applicant has outstanding asylum claim or appeal, appeal to ASA within three days* of notification of NASS decision, OR 2. If applicant has lost asylum claim or appeal, consider claim for IAA 1999 s4 'hard cases' support or application to local authority for community care help under NAA 1948 s21.
Refusal/withdrawal of support on grounds that applicant is a failed asylum-seeker subject to removal directions and has failed to leave the UK (NIAA 2002 Sch 3).[260]	Check whether removal directions were issued by IND, and if so whether they were withdrawn, eg, because there is outstanding asylum appeal or judicial review. If so, appeal to ASA within three days of NASS decision.*
Refusal/withdrawal of support on grounds that applicant is not destitute.	Appeal to ASA within three days of notification of NASS decision* with evidence of income, expenditure and local housing costs.
Refusal/withdrawal of support on grounds that applicant has refused to travel to accommodation in dispersal area or left accommodation.	1. Appeal to ASA within three days of notification of NASS decision* 2. Consider judicial review of decision that accommodation in dispersal area is adequate. 3. Consider application for injunction. 4. If asylum-seeker has adequate accommodation with friend or relative, he or she could notify NASS of a change of circumstances and claim subsistence only support.
Refusal/withdrawal of support under AS Regs 2000 reg 20 on grounds that applicant has breached conditions/ committed an offence/is intentionally destitute.	Appeal to ASA within three days of notification of NASS decision.* * The time period may be extended in the interests of justice, see para 3.267.

260 As of 4 February 2004, NASS reported to Refugee Action that it had not refused support to any household under this ground.

Table to show NASS refusals and possible responses for an adult asylum-seeker with a dependent child

NASS decision	Response
NIAA 2002 s55 decision.	An asylum-seeker with a dependent child is exempt from NIAA 2002 s55(1) as long as child is under 18 and part of their household. Section 55 decision should be letter confirming this and allowing them access to emergency accommodation.
Refusal/withdrawal of support on grounds that applicant is a failed asylum-seeker subject to removal directions and has failed to leave the UK (NIAA 2002 Sch 3).	Check whether removal directions were issued by IND, and if so whether they were withdrawn. If so, appeal to ASA within three days of NASS decision.*
Refusal/withdrawal of support on grounds that asylum-seeker has failed to return to their country of origin/leave the UK voluntarily (NIAA 2002 Sch 3).[261]	Check whether correct procedure has been followed by the IND in certifying the asylum-seeker's failure to leave. Consider ASA appeal if there is a procedural error and/or if there are human rights or other reasons preventing the family from returning.
Refusal/withdrawal of support on grounds that applicant is not destitute.	Appeal to ASA within three days of notification of NASS decision* with evidence of income, expenditure and local housing costs for whole household.
Refusal/withdrawal of emergency support after applicant refused to travel to accommodation in dispersal area. Decision to offer continuing accommodation in dispersal area.	1. There is no right of appeal to ASA. 2. Consider judicial review of decision that accommodation in dispersal area is adequate and application for injunction. 3. If family has adequate accommodation with friend or relative, they could notify NASS of a change of circumstances and claim subsistence only support.
Refusal/withdrawal of support under AS Regs 2000 reg 20 on grounds that applicant has breached conditions/committed an offence/is intentionally destitute.	Appeal to ASA within three days of notification of NASS decision.* Argue that refusal/withdrawal of support will interfere with household's rights under ECHR art 3 if family would be left without food and shelter.

* The time period may be extended in the interests of justice, see para 3.267.

261 This is the Class 5 amendment to be inserted by Asylum and Immigration (Treatment of Claimants, etc) Act 2004 s9.

Support Adjudicators (ASA) and sets out their jurisdiction. The tribunal is formally known as 'the Asylum Support Adjudicators' and an appeal is heard by 'an adjudicator'. They are currently funded and appointed by the Home Office and supervised by the Council on Tribunals. The ASA website contains a range of information including notice of appeal forms, ASA decisions and an explanation of how the tribunal works at its office in Croydon where oral hearings are held.[262]

3.247   The detailed rules governing appeals are contained in the Asylum Support (Appeals) Procedure Rules 2000 ('the Appeals Rules').[263] The Rules were amended by the Asylum Support Appeals (Procedure) Amendment Rules 2003[264] on 11 August 2003 to extend the time limits for appealing and processing appeals.

3.248   Currently the ASA are appointed and financed by the Home Secretary. The Legatt review of tribunals recommended that the ASA should be transferred to the Lord Chancellor's Department (now Department for Constitutional Affairs) and it was announced on 11 March 2003 that a unified tribunal service would be established between 2005–2008. The Home Secretary has agreed to the transfer in principle.

Jurisdiction

3.249   The ASA jurisdiction is limited to appeals against a decision by NASS to refuse or withdraw support, not against the type, level or adequacy of support. Challenges of local authority decisions in relation to interim support, are excluded and must be challenged by judicial review. This leaves many decisions outside the remit of the ASA. In such cases judicial review will be the appropriate remedy. NIAA 2002 restricted access to the ASA by specifying that there was no right of appeal where support was refused under sections 55 or s57 of that Act.

3.250   An applicant has a right of appeal to the ASA by virtue of IAA 1999 s103 either:

(a) If, on an application for support under s95 [NASS] decides that an applicant does not qualify for support under that section . . . or
(b) If [NASS] decides to stop providing support for a person under section 95 before that support would otherwise have come to an end . . .

---

262 www.asylum-support-adjudicators.org.uk.
263 SI No 541.
264 SI No 1735.

3.251   The extent of an asylum-seeker's right of appeal under IAA 1999 s103 was considered in *R (Secretary of State for the Home Department) v Chief Asylum Support Adjudicator and Ahmet Dogan (interested party)*.[265] NASS had introduced the policy that where a family fails to travel to a dispersal area, the offer of accommodation there would be left open and emergency accommodation would be terminated. The Court of Appeal found that in such cases there was no right of appeal because this was really an appeal about the location of support, not an appeal about 'stoppage' of support. The right of appeal was limited to 'non-qualification' and 'stoppage' appeals until the NIAA 2002 amendment came into force (see following para below). D had argued unsuccessfully that since NASS had accepted a duty to support, the termination of support at his temporary accommodation constituted a 'stoppage' of support, not merely a termination of IAA 1999 s98 emergency accommodation. At the time of publication, D was petitioning the House of Lords for permission to appeal because of the public importance of the decision for other asylum-seekers.

Future changes to the jurisdiction

3.252   NIAA 2002 extends the jurisdiction of the ASA but the amendments are not yet in force.[266] The amendments allow for an appeal against a decision that the person is not qualified to receive the support under IAA 1999 s95 or under NIAA 2002 s17 ('non-qualification appeals') and for an appeal against the location of support ('location appeals'). These amendments are related to potential appeals by asylum-seekers when a system of accommodation centres is in place. A new right of appeal is to be introduced by Asylum and Immigration (Treatment of Claimants, etc) Act 2004 s9 for failed asylum-seeker families refused support on grounds they have failed to voluntarily leave the UK. Section 10 introduces a right of appeal in relation to IAA 1994 s4 hard cases decisions (see para 3.296).

ASA powers

3.253   During the appeal, the ASA powers include:

a) extending the time limit for entering the appeal,
b) making directions as to further evidence to be produced by NASS or the appellant,
c) summonsing witnesses.

---

265 [2003] EWCA Civ 1673.
266 See appendix A.

3.254   In *R (Secretary of State for the Home Department) v Chief Asylum Support Adjudicator,*[267] Toulson J found that the ASA have an inherent power to adjourn an appeal in the interests of justice. He also found that the ASA could refuse to accept a request by NASS to substitute the decision appealed against with a fresh decision which raised new issues if this would cause prejudice to the appellant. NASS's remedy was to withdraw the decision and make a fresh decision allowing the asylum-seeker a fresh right of appeal.

Possible outcomes of an ASA appeal

3.255   When considering an appeal an adjudicator may:

a) remit the appeal to NASS for further investigation and a fresh decision (IAA 1999 s103(3)(a));

b) allow the appeal unconditionally, substituting their decision for NASS's decision (s103(3)(b));

c) allow the appeal conditionally, suspending the payment of support until the appellant has complied with a specific condition (s103(3)(b));

d) dismiss the appeal (s103(3)(c)).

3.256   It is common for NASS to review and withdraw a decision after an appeal has been issued, resulting in a high withdrawal rate of appeals.

Backdating of support

3.257   Where an appeal has been successful, backdated support may be awarded in exceptional circumstances. In *R (Secretary of State for the Home Department) v Asylum Support Adjudicators and (1) Berkadle (2) Perera,*[268] Gibbs J decided that NASS support could only be backdated by relying on NASS's power to provide support in other ways 'in exceptional circumstances' in IAA 1999 s96(2). An adjudicator was entitled to rely on that section and use their power to substitute a decision to decide to backdate support. In ASA 02/04/2462 NASS had delayed by 18 months in processing the application for support. The adjudicator decided to order backdated support on grounds of exceptional circumstances.

3.258   NASS is currently reviewing its policy on backdating. Backdated support will normally be paid where the delay is due to fault on the part of NASS. An alternative would be to consider an ombudsman complaint (see para 3.155).

---

267 [2003] EWHC 269 Admin.
268 [2001] EWHC Admin 881.

Human rights issues

3.259   *R (Husain) v Asylum Support Adjudicators and Secretary of State for the Home Department (interested party)*[269] was the first full judicial review of an ASA decision and it established various useful principles. It was argued firstly that the ASA was not an independent tribunal as required by the ECHR art 6 right to a fair hearing because adjudicators were appointed and funded by the Home Office. Stanley Burnton J decided that asylum support was a 'civil right' within the meaning of ECHR art 6. He found that appellants' rights to a fair hearing were satisfied by the current arrangements, applying the test of what an informed observer would think about the process. He went on to find that the *withdrawal* of support may interfere with an asylum-seeker's right to freedom from inhuman and degrading treatment under ECHR art 3.

3.260   This approach to ECHR art 3 and asylum support has been extended in the cases which deal with asylum-seekers affected by NIAA 2002 s55.[270] In *R (Q and others) v Secretary of State for the Home Department*[271] the Court of Appeal found there was no real difference between a refusal of support and a withdrawal of support. Either could constitute 'treatment' which might interfere with an asylum-seeker's ECHR art 3 rights.

3.261   Human Rights Act 1998 s3(1), means that courts must interpret regulations and guidance so that they are 'human rights compliant'. So even if an adjudicator decides that NASS has withdrawn or terminated support correctly within the strict terms of the AS Regs 2000, he or she must interpret the regulations so they are compatible with the Human Rights Act 1998 and Convention. In ASA 01/03/0229 an asylum-seeker father had breached conditions of support by repeatedly failing to travel to dispersal addresses. The adjudicator allowed the appeal because he decided that ending support would interfere with the 6-month-old baby's rights under ECHR art 8.

The appeal process

3.262   The table on p194 gives a guide to the possible timescale in which an appeal may be considered. The ASA target is to list cases on the 4th day following 'consideration day' which allows a more realistic

---

269 [2001] EWHC Admin 582; (2001) *Times* 15 November.
270 See para 3.30 onwards for a fuller discussion.
271 [2003] EWCA Civ 364; [2003] 3 WLR 365; (2003) 6 CCLR 136.

Table to show summary of the appeal procedure ('day' means working day)[272]

Day 1	**Date of NASS decision** NASS posts decision letter refusing or withdrawing support with details of how to appeal. Letter is treated as served (received) two days after posting unless hand-delivered.
Day 3–5	**Appeal deadline** Appellant should fax valid, signed appeal notice to be received by the ASA within three working days of the date decision served by NASS, that is within five days of the NASS decision letter. If the appeal is late, explain reasons and ask for it to be considered out of time.
Day 3–7	**ASA fax appeal to NASS** The ASA must fax the appeal to NASS on the day it is received or within two working days.
Day 4–9	**NASS faxes appeal bundle to ASA and appellant** NASS must either withdraw decision or fax an appeal bundle to the ASA within two days. NASS should also fax or post the appeal bundle to the appellant or their representative (this doesn't always take place).
Day 4–10	**Consideration Day** The day after receiving the appeal bundle, the ASA must consider whether to order an oral hearing. If the appeal is to be decided on the papers, the adjudicator must make a decision within five days. If the appellant has requested an oral hearing, it should take place within five days.
Day 9–15	**Appeal hearing** The appellant may attend in person or may be represented by whoever they choose. The ASA arrange an interpreter. The adjudicator may allow or dismiss the appeal or substitute their decision for NASS's decision. The decision must be announced at the hearing.
Day 5–17	**Reasons statement** The ASA must send a full statement of the reasons for their decision to the appellant and to NASS no later than three days after their determination.

---

272 Asylum Support Appeals Procedure Rules 2000 SI No 541 as amended by Asylum Support Appeals (Procedure) Amendment Rules 2003 SI No 1735.

preparation period. The preamble to the Appeals Rules 2000[273] states that they are made 'having regard to the desirability of securing, so far as is reasonably practicable, that appeals are brought and disposed of with the minimum delay'. The appeals procedure is designed as a fast-track procedure, with an ASA decision or 'reasons statement' provided within 12 working days of the ASA receiving the appeal if an oral hearing is requested, and nine in cases considered on the papers. The speed is necessary because the ASA have no power to order temporary support until an appeal is decided so an appellant may be without subsistence or housing until the appeal decision. In some cases it may be possible to obtain interim relief by issuing judicial review proceedings, for example, in dispersal cases where it is argued that accommodation is not adequate.

Completing the appeal notice

3.263   There is a simple form to complete which is attached as a schedule to the Appeals Rules (as amended).[274] Under para 3(1) of these Rules, the form must be completed in full and in English. The NASS reference number must be included and the grounds of appeal. Under para 3(2) it must be signed by the applicant or his or her representative. The appellant should provide an address where he or she can be sure of receiving correspondence about the appeal – not the NASS address if eviction is imminent.

3.264   The ASA have reported that as many as 38 per cent of appeals are rejected as invalid, either because the appeal is out of time or because the notice of appeal has not been properly completed. Where an asylum-seeker who was in detention completed the notice in good English, stating that he would provide the grounds of appeal at the hearing, the adjudicator found the appeal was invalid.[275]

3.265   The appellant needs to indicate on the appeal notice whether he or she wants an oral hearing. An oral hearing will mean the appeal takes longer than if it is decided on the papers but allows the appellant to attend the hearing and give evidence. An appellant may decide to submit written evidence such as medical reports and submissions from their legal adviser instead of attending the hearing. After the notice is filed, the ASA often issue directions which have to be complied with in a short timescale, for example, requesting further evidence. If the

273 SI 2000 No 541.
274 See appendix A or ASA website: www.asylum-service-adjudicators.org.uk.
275 ASA 02/05/3018.

notice of appeal is completed to state that a legal representative is representing the appellant, the representative will then be responsible for the progress of the appeal, including compliance with these directions.

Time limits

3.266   The notice of appeal must be received by the adjudicator not later than three days after the day the NASS decision is served on the applicant. The date of service is prescribed as the second day after the decision is posted. So an asylum-seeker has five days from the date of the decision within which to fax their appeal to the ASA.

3.267   The adjudicator may extend the time limit if he or she considers it is in the interests of justice to do so *and* if the appellant or his or her representative was prevented from appealing in time 'by circumstances beyond his control'. Reasons for entering a late appeal should be included on the appeal form, for example, illness, difficulties obtaining interpretation/legal advice, non-receipt of the letter. The adjudicator extended the time limit in a case where the asylum-seeker was not informed of the right of appeal.[276]

Next steps

3.268   The adjudicator must fax the notice of appeal to NASS on the date of receipt of the appeal or the following day. NASS may decide to withdraw its decision after receiving the appeal.

3.269   NASS must send the appeal bundle by fax or by hand to the adjudicator no later than two days after the adjudicator received notice of the appeal. It must be sent back to the adjudicator by fax or by hand and to the appellant or his or her representative by first class post or fax on the same day.

3.270   The day after NASS sends the appeal bundle to the adjudicator is 'consideration day'. On that day the adjudicator must decide whether there should be an oral hearing. If the appeal is to be decided without a hearing it should be decided on consideration day or as soon as possible thereafter and not later than five days after consideration day.

3.271   There must be an oral hearing if the appellant has requested one in the notice of appeal or if the adjudicator considers it necessary to dispose of the appeal justly. Where an appellant arrived late at a hearing only to discover that it had taken place in his absence, because of the inadequate travel arrangements made by NASS, the adjudicator

276 ASA 00/07/0030.

relied on Appeals Rules 2000 r19 and ordered a fresh hearing. The adjudicator must give notice of an oral hearing to the appellant and to NASS. If the appellant wants to provide additional evidence after entering the notice of appeal he or she must send it to both the adjudicator and NASS.

3.272 If neither NASS nor the appellant attends the oral hearing, the appeal can be considered in their absence provided a notice of the date, time and place of hearing has been served.

The hearing

3.273 Hearings are relatively informal and a decision is provided at the end with reasons statements to follow. Interpreters are provided by the ASA. Hearings are generally inquisitorial, partly due to the frequent lack of representation. There are some simple rules governing evidence.[277] The adjudicator may take into account matters which he or she considers relevant even if they arose after the date of the NASS decision. Evidence may be given by witnesses on oath. The appellant and Home Secretary are entitled to receive and consider copies of any documents if they have not received them in advance. The appeal hearing will usually be a public hearing and it should be recorded. The appellant may ask the adjudicator to exercise his/her power to exclude members of the public from a hearing.

3.274 The adjudicator must inform the appellant or his/her representative of the decision at the end of the hearing. If neither party is present the adjudicator should send his or her decision to the appellant on the same day, with a 'reasons statement' not later than three days after the appeal.

3.275 The possible decisions open to an adjudicator are listed above at para 3.255.

3.276 If an appeal is dismissed a further application for support will only be considered if there is a material change of circumstances.[278]

3.277 If an appeal is dismissed, the appellant may be able to bring judicial review proceedings of the ASA decision arguing ordinary administrative law principles, for example, if the ASA have not applied the law correctly, or if NASS's procedures have not been followed.

---

277 AS Regs 2000 reg 10.
278 IAA 1999 s103(3).

Practical aspects of ASA appeals

Representation and public funding

3.278   Some appellants have had difficulty in attending or failed to attend hearings because of NASS delays in paying travel costs in advance. The majority of appellants continue to be unrepresented because of the lack of public funding, the short time limits and the complexity of asylum support law. NASS is normally represented by a Home Office Presenting Officer (HOPO), or occasionally by a solicitor and/or counsel. ASA appeals are outside the scope of a Community Legal Service (CLS) public funding for representation certificate.

3.279   Legal help under a CLS contract for housing, immigration, welfare benefits or 'tolerance' can be used to advise and assist appellants. This could cover drafting a written appeal and corresponding with the ASA, obtaining further evidence, obtaining counsel's advice. The adviser could attend the hearing as a 'Mackenzie friend' under the Legal Help scheme and claim travel, waiting and assisting at the hearing. The guidance in the Legal Services Commission (LSC) manual, Volume 2, Part E, Appendix B paras 25–29 allows for this in cases where the need can be demonstrated due to the difficulty of the case, its importance to the client or the inability of the client to act on their own without legal assistance, for example, learning or other relevant disability, language difficulties.

3.280   In this case, the adviser should not be on the record as the appellant's representative and it would be desirable for the adjudicator to be asked at the hearing to record that the adviser is there in the capacity of Mackenzie friend. As described above, a serious obstacle to asylum-seekers wishing to exercise their appeal rights or attend an oral hearing is that there is no statutory provision for emergency or other support while the appeal is being decided. It may be possible to apply separately for interim relief by judicial review.[279]

3.281   It is arguable that the absence of public funding for representation or controlled legal representation is a breach of an appellant's rights under ECHR art 6, particularly in a complex case which requires representation. To date there has been no attempt to judicially review the exclusion from scope of ASA appeals. In theory it might be possible to obtain 'exceptional public funding' under Access to Justice Act 1999 s6(8)(b) on the ground of 'overwhelming importance to the

---

279   See para 3.32 above on Maurice Kay J's comments in *R (S, D and T) v Secretary of State for the Home Department* [2003] EWHC 1941 (Admin); (2004) 7 CCLR 32.

client', and possibly 'significant wider public interest' but the application process makes it almost impossible for funding to be obtained in time.[280]

Travel expenses

3.282 NASS is responsible for sending a travel warrant to the address the appellant gives on the appeal form to enable travel to the ASA appeal. A failure to facilitate travel has been accepted as a good reason to order an adjournment of an appeal.[281] In the same case, the Chief Asylum Support Adjudicator ordered a rehearing of the appeal before a different adjudicator where inadequate travel arrangements had been made by NASS. The hearing had gone ahead without the appellant and had been dismissed. Although there was no express provision to order a rehearing, the adjudicator considered that she had a duty to interpret Appeal Rules 2000 r19(2) so that it was compatible with the ECHR art 6 right to a fair hearing. The appellant later won his appeal.

Resources

3.283 Apart from the legislation, previous ASA decisions and NASS Policy Bulletins are the most useful resources to rely on at an appeal. All ASA decisions are held on the website under the reference number. They can also be searched under specific categories, under keywords and under the name of the adjudicator. Appeals which appear likely to be legally complex cases are usually decided by the Chief or Deputy Chief Asylum Support Adjudicator. Another way of finding decisions in a specific subject area on the Internet is to use a search engine, to search within results, for example, by typing in the ASA website address and then adding the words which you would like to search, eg, 'dispersal and HIV' to find all decisions involving the dispersal and HIV. This is also a means of finding decisions in which specific cases have been referred to, for example, by adding 'Husain'.

---

280 Such applications should be submitted on the usual CLS forms to the Head Office, LSC Policy and Legal Department, 85 Gray's Inn Road, London WC1X 8TX with a covering letter explaining that the application is for exceptional funding. Search the LSC website (www.legalservices.gov.uk) for Focus articles explaining the criteria.

281 ASA 00/11/016.

Judicial review

3.284   To challenge an ASA decision or to challenge a NASS decision about the type or level of support, the appropriate remedy is judicial review. The most appropriate defendant will be 'the Asylum Support Adjudicators' in a judicial review of an ASA decision, although the Chief Asylum Support Adjudicator has been named as defendant. The 'Secretary of State for the Home Department' will generally be an interested party unless he or she is the defendant. The Home Secretary is the defendant in a challenge to a NASS decision about service provision. In either case, a letter before action should be sent to NASS and court documents served on the Treasury Solicitor[282] (in Scotland, the Home Secretary is represented by the Scottish office). NASS's procedure for dealing with judicial review applications is set out in Policy Bulletin 47. CLS public funding for representation is available. Cases are likely to involve European Convention on Human Rights arguments, be of exceptional importance to the client, and/or be of public interest making it easier to obtain public funding if the prospects of success are low.

3.285   Any local authority decisions about support may only be challenged by judicial review. NASS *eligibility* decisions which can be challenged by judicial review (instead of an ASA appeal) include:

- NIAA 2002 ss55 or 57 decisions refusing access to NASS support under IAA 1999 ss4, 98 or 95.
- Decision that applicant is not 'an asylum-seeker', and/or that the Home Office has not recorded an asylum or ECHR art 3 claim (this may also arise in an ASA appeal where there is a question about whether or not the ASA has jurisdiction).
- Decision refusing IAA 1999 s4 'hard cases' support (but see para 3.252 above).

3.286   Judicial review may be brought on the usual administrative law grounds:

- Procedural irregularity, for example, if NASS's own procedures have not been followed.
- Illegality, for example, if NASS has not correctly interpreted the IAA 1999 and AS Regs 2000 or case law.
- Irrationality, for example, if NASS has failed to properly take into account all the relevant facts and reached a perverse decision.
- Breach of the Human Rights Act 1998 and ECHR, for example,

---

282 See appendix G for details.

where NASS's decision interferes with ECHR art 3 right to freedom from inhuman and degrading treatment (as in NIAA 2002 s55 cases), or where there is a serious breach of an asylum-seekers ECHR art 8 rights to respect for family, home and private life and correspondence which cannot be justified.

Remedies where applicants are ineligible for asylum support under IAA 1999 Part VI

3.287   NIAA 2002 s54 and Sch 3 have broad exclusions from NASS support, IAA 1999 s4 'hard cases' support or community care/Children Act 1989 support. Those who are not excluded by NIAA 2002 Sch 3 may be eligible for help under Children Act 1989 s17. If they have a need related to age, disability, illness or pregnancy, that is, not solely in need due to lack of accommodation and income, they may be eligible for help under National Assistance Act 1948 s21 (see further chapter 6).

3.288   In the light of the judicial statements made in cases such as *R v Secretary of State for Social Security ex p B*,[283] *R v Hammersmith and Fulham LBC ex p M*,[284] *R v Kensington and Chelsea RLBC ex p Kujtim*,[285] and *R v Wandsworth LBC ex p O*[286] and the NIAA 2002 s55 cases (see para 3.21 above) it may be possible for an asylum-seeker or former asylum-seeker who is left completely destitute by NASS or by the local authority to challenge the decision on human rights' grounds even if there is no right to an ASA appeal or ordinary basis for judicial review (see further chapter 6). In *R (H and D) v Secretary of State for the Home Department*,[286a] two asylum-seekers who had become European nationals on 1 May 2004, were granted permission to judicially review NASS's decision to withdraw support on the basis that they were excluded by NIAA 2002 Sch 3. NASS had written to all EU accession nationals, ending support on 30 April, with less than four weeks' notice and instructed local authorities who were supporting households under the interim scheme to do the same. The asylum-seekers, who were settled in the UK with school-age children, argued that the lack of notice was procedurally unfair and that the potential breach of their ECHR art 8 rights to respect for family life was discriminatory

283   [1997] 1WLR 275, CA.

284   (1998) 30 HLR 10; (1997) 1 CCLR 85, CA.

285   [1999] 4 All ER 161; (1999) 2 CCLR 340, CA.

286   [2000] 1 WLR 2539; [2000] 4 All ER 590; (2000) 3 CCLR 237, CA.

286a   CO/2106/04 and CO2096/04, 4 May 2004.

under article 14. NASS then agreed to carry out assessments of all those affected by the decision and instructed local authorities to do the same. Similar arguments about procedural fairness may be useful in other cases where support is withdrawn without proper notice.

Childless adults

3.289   If an asylum-seeker or former asylum-seeker stops receiving NASS asylum support (or local authority Interim Regs 1999 support), he or she may be entitled to help under community care provisions if he or she is not subject to removal directions or if destitution could lead to a risk of a breach of human rights. A request for a community care assessment may be appropriate if there is a need for care and attention arising to some extent from age, disability, pregnancy, mental health or other reason which is not solely due to the physical or anticipated physical effects of destitution.[287] If he or she is a failed asylum-seeker with no outstanding asylum claim, there may be entitlement under the IAA 1999 s4 'hard cases' scheme.

Households with children

3.290   IAA 1999 s122 excludes households from Children Act 1989 help if there are no other Children Act needs or if support is being offered or arranged. This is explained below at para 6.123 onwards. Where a person is 'subject to immigration control' and the household contains children under 18 years old, the family may be eligible for Children Act 1989 s17 help if NASS refuses or withdraws support (see para 6.12)

IAA 1999 s4 – 'hard cases' support

3.291   IAA 1999 s4 gives the secretary of state power to support those whose asylum claims and appeals have been rejected. When IAA 1999 s4 was first introduced it was intended that accommodation would be provided by the voluntary sector, but in the absence of volunteers, it is now provided by NASS. IAA 1999 s4 was amended by NIAA 2002 s49 so that the Home Secretary 'may provide, or arrange for the provision of facilities for the accommodation' of a former asylum-seeker whose claim for asylum was rejected and for their dependant(s)'.

3.292   Unlike the power to provide section 95 support under Part VI of

287 This is explained more fully in chapter 6.

the 1999 Act, it is not limited to those who come within the section 94(1) definition of an asylum-seeker. NASS currently administers a scheme known as S4 or 'hard cases' support, which is provided to failed asylum-seekers who meet strict criteria, set out in NASS Policy Bulletin 71.[288] NIAA 2002 s55 applies to S4 cases so to be eligible to apply, an applicant must have originally applied for asylum 'as soon as reasonably practicable' under NIAA 2002 s55(1) or the refusal of support must breach their ECHR rights under section 55(5). Where a hard cases applicant applied for asylum before the introduction of NIAA 2002 s55 on 8 January 2003, he or she may need to attend the ASU and complete the screening process if section 55(1) applies, that is, if he or she applied for asylum in-country. The Refugee Council has produced a useful guide to the scheme.[289] Provision is normally in the form of board and lodging outside London with no cash payments.

3.293 It has been notoriously difficult for ex-asylum-seekers to find out about the existence of hard cases support or how to apply for it and there have been delays in processing applications. All these points were made in *R (Salih and Rahmani) v Secretary of State for the Home Department*.[290] Stanley Burnton J found that although it is defined as a discretion, eligibility for S4 Hard Cases support is in practice treated as a right. He decided that the Home Office's stated policy of not informing asylum-seekers of this statutory right was unlawful. He also found that NASS had failed to justify delays in decision-making, in S's case of eight weeks and in R's case of three weeks. NASS has since agreed to review the criteria for Hard Cases support and publish a Policy Bulletin (Policy Bulletin 71).

3.294 The criteria for eligibility are that:

- the applicant no longer falls within the definition of asylum-seeker and his or her asylum claim has been refused;
- the applicant has received support from NASS or local authority support under the Interim Regs 1999;
- the applicant appears to be destitute;
- the applicant cannot get support from another source such as friends, family or a local authority under community care provisions.

3.295 In addition an applicant who is eligible under these criteria will not

288 See appendix B. See also para 4.127 onwards.
289 Available at www.refugeecouncil.org.uk.
290 [2003] EWHC 2273 (Admin).

usually receive support unless either they agree to leave the UK or it is physically impracticable for them to travel to any other country, for example, due to pregnancy, or they have been granted permission to apply for judicial review or have a meritorious application for permission outstanding or unless there are other exceptional circumstances.

3.296   The scheme is administered by the S4 (Hard Cases) Section of NASS[291] and procedure for applying is to write by fax or send a completed form available from that section. Asylum-seekers who qualify for S4 support may be expected to attend monthly reviews. If there is insufficient evidence that they have taken steps to leave the country, 'hard cases support will be terminated'. If support is not provided or is refused, the remedy is a judicial review at the time of writing but the Asylum and Immigration (Treatment of Claimants, etc) Act 2004 s10 introduces a right of appeal to the ASA in relation to refusal and withdrawal of support. A commencement order is needed before this becomes law, amending IAA 1999 s103 (see Appendix A).

3.297   There have been attempts to extend S4 support, arguing that it should apply to those who are unable to travel back to countries such as Somalia and Eritrea, because there are no safe travel routes or there is civil war. Evidence produced by Amnesty or the UNHCR may be used to illustrate the current situation in particular countries and support such a claim. The UNHCR produced position reports on 26 January 2004 outlining problems and expressing opposition to removals to Eritrea, southern Somalia, Angola, the Ivory Coast and Zimbabwe because of the situation in those countries. The Home Office suspended forced removals to Zimbabwe on 15 January 2002.[292] Enquiries could also be made of the Home Office, directly or by an MP's written or oral question as to the numbers of asylum-seekers who have been removed to a specific country to demonstrate that voluntary return is not feasible. However, the Administrative Court has upheld NASS's decision to refuse support to a failed Zimbabwean asylum-seeker in *R (Guveya) v NASS*.[293] This decison is likely to be appealed.

---

291 See appendix B for form and F for contact details.
292 Hansard HL, Written Answers Col 101, 4 November 2003.
293 CO/959/04. 30 July 2004.

Asylum support: service provision

continued

Introduction

4.1 This chapter explains service provision for asylum-seekers who are eligible for asylum support under Immigration and Asylum Act (IAA) 1999 Part VI ss95–98, including accommodation and cash payments.[1] Other forms of provision that a supported person is entitled to, such as healthcare and education, are included. Remedies for inadequate service provision are discussed towards the end of the chapter, but specific challenges relating to each topic are referred to throughout the text. Finally, the responsibilities of the asylum-seeker or dependant while they are supported, and NASS's powers if those responsibilities are not met, are outlined.

Overview of NASS and local authority provision

4.2 IAA 1999 Part VI contains a simple framework for the kind of support which may be provided to destitute asylum-seekers by the Home Secretary, whose powers are exercised by the National Asylum Support Service (NASS). The Asylum Support Regulations (AS Regs) 2000[2] contain more detailed rules about support. NASS Policy Bulletins, which are published on the Home Office website,[3] contain internal guidance about how NASS interprets and implements the law. Interim support, which is provided by local authorities, is governed by Part VI, and by the Asylum and Immigration (Interim Provisions) Regulations (Interim Regs), as amended.[4] The interim scheme is due to end on 4 April 2005.[5] Although the first part of this chapter applies mainly to the NASS scheme, significant differences between the schemes are highlighted. Asylum-seekers' responsibilities and criminal offences are generally applicable to both schemes.

Changes in the law

4.3 The Nationality, Immigration and Asylum Act 2002 provides for significant changes to NASS support. Part 2 of the Act is entitled 'Accommodation Centres' and Part 3 is entitled 'Other Support and Assistance'. At the time of writing, only a few of the changes are in

---

1 Chapter 3 explains who is *eligible* for and how to challenge a refusal of support.
2 SI No 704 (see Appendix A), made under IAA 1999 s95(12) and Sch 8.
3 www.ind.homeoffice.gov.uk.
4 See para 3.12 and see Appendix E for an outline of the interim scheme.
5 Asylum Support (Interim Provisions) (Amendment) Regulations 2004 SI No 566.

force and there is no date for the main support reforms, such as accommodation centres, to be implemented, but they are outlined in the relevant parts of this chapter.[6] In the White Paper which preceded the Act, *Secure borders, safe haven: integration with diversity in modern Britain*,[7] the Home Secretary described an asylum-seeker's progress through the system as three streamlined steps:

– induction;
– accommodation;
– removal or integration.

4.4   He envisaged that an asylum-seeker would arrive in the UK, claim asylum and then be briefed about procedures in an induction centre. Then, the household would be transferred to an accommodation centre, outside London and the south-east, and outside mainstream British society. If the asylum claim were successful, he or she could move out of the accommodation and be integrated into society. If the asylum claim is unsuccessful he or she would be transferred to a removal centre and removed from the UK without having established roots in society. Central to this process is a scheme of accommodation centres at which supported asylum-seeker households would live and be educated, as set out at NIAA 2002 Part 2. The plan to introduce the centres on a trial basis has been significantly delayed by planning objections, leaving the existing system of housing and support intact at the time of publication. This chapter explains how the centres will work if and when Part 2 comes into force.

Key features

4.5   The key features of asylum support provision are:

- NASS provides three main forms of support under IAA 1999: section 98 temporary support (emergency accommodation), section 95 full NASS support and section 4 'Hard Cases' support. Local authorities may provide interim support under section 98 or section 95.
- There are two new forms of support under NIAA 2002: section 17 support in an accommodation centre and section 24 'provisional

---

6   See Nationality, Immigration and Asylum Act 2002 (Commencement No 6) Order 2003 SI No 3156 and later commencement orders for list of provisions which are in force.

7   www.homeoffice.gov.uk or www.official-documents.co.uk/documents/cm53/5387/cm5387.htm.

assistance' while NASS considers support in an accommodation centre, but these accommodation centre provisions are not yet in force.[8]

- When an asylum-seeker applies for support, and has no means of obtaining accommodation, he or she will receive 'temporary support' for the household under IAA 1999 s98 in emergency accommodation while the application for full section 95 support is considered.

- Section 98 accommodation may be provided at an induction centre. An asylum-seeker may be required to live at or near an induction centre for up to 14 days after he or she claims asylum.[9]

- Support is provided in the form of 'essential living needs and/or adequate accommodation' as provided by IAA 1999 s96(1). NIAA 2002 s45 redefines 'essential living needs' as 'food and other essential items' but is not yet in force. Section 96(1) also provides for the cost of travel to bail hearings and limited expenses connected to the asylum claim, such as travel to IND interviews and appeal hearings, but not travel to solicitors.

- NASS support is provided in the form of cash, at rates fixed by the AS Regs as amended. It is paid by a local post office on production of the asylum-seeker's Application Registration Card (ARC).

- The rates and methods of payment of interim support are not fixed, but are decided by each local authority.

- The section 95 power to provide support must be met by having regard to 'the desirability, in general, of providing accommodation in areas in which there is a ready supply of accommodation'. The policy is to disperse asylum-seekers around the UK to 'cluster' areas.[10]

- NASS does not own or directly manage accommodation. If an asylum-seeker is eligible for support, NASS makes arrangements for accommodation and/or living expenses through contracts with public, private and/or voluntary sector suppliers.

- Section 96(1) allows for accommodation and living expenses to be provided separately. An asylum-seeker may apply to NASS for 'subsistence-only' support if they have accommodation with friends or relatives. The provision has been used by asylum-

---

8 See Nationality, Immigration and Asylum Act 2002 (Commencement No 6) Order 2003 SI No 3156 and later commencement orders for list of provisions which are in force.

9 NIAA 2002 s70.

10 This will not apply to decisions to accommodate in an accommodation centre, see para 4.70 below.

seekers to avoid dispersal, but the right would be ended by NIAA 2002 s43.[11] The subsistence-only option is not available to child-less adult asylum-seekers receiving interim support from local authorities.[12]

- The whole household's income and assets are taken into account in assessing the level of support. Therefore, an asylum-seeker with other resources, for example, working part-time, may receive a lower rate of support or may contribute to their support.[13]

- Where an adult asylum-seeker (usually childless) has been refused asylum and has exhausted their appeal rights, he or she may be entitled to IAA 1999 s4 'hard cases' support administered by NASS if strict criteria are met.[14]

- Both section 98 emergency accommodation and section 4 hard cases support are usually board and lodging with no cash pay-ments. Section 4 hard cases accommodation is usually outside London. An asylum-seeker supported under section 98 or section 4 is not generally eligible for various passported benefits which are linked to section 95 support, such as maternity payments.

- Where the standard of support is being challenged, the remedy is usually an application for judicial review, not an appeal to the Asylum Support Adjudicators (ASA). The ASA may only hear appeals at present where support has been refused or withdrawn.[15]

Forms of support

4.6   The first step in dealing with any problem about support provision is to identify which form of support is being provided. An asylum-seeker supported by NASS or a local authority may be receiving sec-tion 98 temporary support, or section 95 asylum support while the asylum claim is pending, and then NASS section 4 hard cases support as a failed asylum-seeker. If/when NIAA 2002 Part 2 comes into force, he or she may be receiving section 17 support in an accommo-dation centre or section 24 provisional assistance. If an asylum-seeker is being supported while bringing a judicial review under section 55, the type of support will usually be section 98 emergency accommodation.

---

11 See para 4.81, but it is not yet in force.
12 Interim Reg 5(1).
13 See also the section on mixed households at para 3.20.
14 See para 3.291 and 4.27.
15 See para 3.246.

Section 98 temporary support

4.7   The Home Secretary may provide section 98 temporary support, which is generally referred to as 'emergency accommodation' (EA), under IAA 1999 only until a decision is reached on eligibility for full asylum support under section 95.[16] Local authorities have a duty to provide section 98 support in cases covered by the interim period.[17]

4.8   Temporary support may be provided for:

(a) asylum-seekers, or
(b) dependants of asylum-seekers,
who it appears to the Secretary of State may be destitute.[18]

4.9   There is little case law interpreting section 98. The remedy for a refusal to provide section 98 support would be judicial review. The schedule to the AS Regs provides that emergency accommodation could be provided for up to three months in a case where an applicant has assets such as property abroad, but needs time to realise them.[19]

Access to and management of emergency accommodation

4.10   Policy Bulletin 73 describes NASS's procedures for admittance and readmittance to emergency accommodation. Any asylum-seeker wishing to access emergency accommodation is subject to NASS's 'section 55' procedures.[20] In practice, this may mean that an asylum-seeker who makes an asylum or ECHR article 3 claim 'in-country' must make it at an Asylum Screening Unit or 'designated place'[21] to obtain the necessary documentation in order to access emergency accommodation. An asylum-seeker with a dependent child under 18 will need to provide evidence either that he or she applied for asylum at the port or a letter from NASS to confirm that they are exempt from NIAA 2002 s55. A childless adult asylum-seeker must provide evidence that he or she claimed at the port of arrival or a 'NEAT decision letter' to show that NASS has agreed to allow access to emergency acommodation. Or, they will need an injunction ordering the Home Secretary to provide support until a judicial review application is considered. Overnight accommodation may be provided to vulnerable applicants before the screening interview.

16   See para 3.54 for IAA 1999 s98 eligibility.
17   IAA 1999 s99, as amended by NIAA 2002 s56.
18   IAA 1999 s98(1).
19   AS Regs Sch, Note 8.
20   The effect of section 55 is explained at para 3.21 onwards.
21   NIAA 2002 s18 and see para 3.60.

4.11   NASS funds voluntary organisations, known collectively as the Inter-Agency Partnership (IAP) to carry out some of its functions as agent for NASS. The IAP provides 'reception assistance', which involves managing section 98 emergency accommodation on NASS's behalf and assisting clients to apply to NASS for support by completing the NASS 1 application form. A list of the organisations is provided in Appendix F. The Refugee Council has stopped providing section 98 accommodation to new applicants in London but carries out other functions such as helping asylum-seekers to access emergency accommodation.

Standards in emergency accommodation

4.12   There is no definition of what qualifies as section 98 'temporary support' in the IAA 1999. The explanatory notes to the Act suggest it 'may take any form'.[22] The standard of section 95 support must be 'adequate',[23] but there is no mention in the Act of adequacy in relation to section 98. If emergency accommodation is very poor quality accommodation or if insufficient food or subsistence is provided, the following could be considered:

a) a complaint to the accommodation provider or voluntary organisation managing the accommodation, followed by a complaint to NASS;[24]

b) a request for an inspection by the local council's environmental health officer. As with accommodation provided under the full support duty, there are no specific requirements for adequate standards in emergency accommodation, but ordinary environmental health law provisions apply (explained at para 5.157 onwards). A complaint to the local authority's environmental health officer if the accommodation is 'prejudicial to health' or 'unfit for human habitation' may compel repairs by the landlord, particularly if backed by the threat of enforcement action;

c) if the accommodation is extremely unsuitable for the household and/or the above approaches fail, a judicial review of NASS's decision to accommodate in that accommodation, or of its delay in processing a section 95 claim to transfer the household to more adequate accommodation could be considered. In some circum-

---

22 IAA 1999 Explanatory notes para 307; see www.legislation.hmso.gov.uk/acts/en/1999en33.htm

23 IAA 1999 s96.

24 See para 3.155 onwards concerning complaints about NASS.

stances, it may be possible to bring a judicial review of NASS's decision to provide inadequate temporary support based on ECHR articles 3 or 8;[25]

d) the European Union minimum reception standards cover health, education, accommodation and freedom of movement of asylum-seekers and come into force in February 2005.[26]

Delays and access to other support while in emergency accommodation

4.13   When the IAA 1999 was passed, the Home Secretary indicated that emergency accommodation would be for a couple of days while the NASS application is processed. In practice, a NASS application is not processed in the two days referred to in the guidance notes to NASS 1 application form. Asylum-seekers may wait weeks and even months in their pre-dispersal emergency accommodation with no cash for basic needs such as travel and communications and a delayed ability to settle and fulfil a normal life. In some cases, a final asylum decision is received and appeal disposed of while an asylum-seeker is still in the emergency accommodation. It may be possible to speed up a decision by writing to NASS to threaten judicial review or issuing proceedings, although some asylum-seekers may prefer to delay the date of dispersal.

Eviction from emergency accommodation

4.14   There is no formal notice period for an asylum-seeker who has been asked to leave EA. Usually, EA is provided in a hostel or bed and breakfast accommodation where there is no security of tenure and so a short period of 'reasonable notice' may be given. If an asylum-seeker is present in the accommodation at the time of eviction, refusing to leave, it is an offence under the Criminal Law Act 1977 s6 to use or threaten violence to secure entry to the emergency accommodation if the occupier is present and is opposed to the entry. Therefore, an offence could be committed, for example, if the accommodation-provider had to break into premises to physically remove an asylum-seeker against his/her will, without a court order.[27]

4.15   If asylum support has been refused, and an applicant has appealed to the Asylum Support Adjudicators (ASA), he or she is not usually entitled to section 98 support pending the appeal. It may be possible

25   See para 4.130 for challenges.
26   EU Directive 2003/9/EC27/1/03. See appendix C.
27   See para 5.149.

to obtain 'interim relief' by judicial review, for example, in a dispersal case where there is both a High Court challenge about the adequacy of the accommodation and an ASA appeal. Social Services provision could be considered if the appellant has community care needs or a dependent child.[28] In exceptional circumstances, asylum-seekers will be allowed access to emergency accommodation after their section 95 support has been withdrawn, for example, where they have left accommodation due to domestic violence, racial or other forms of harassment and their complaints are being investigated.[29]

Induction centres

4.16   Asylum-seekers may be subject to a residence condition requiring them to live at or near an induction centre for up to 14 days after they claim asylum.[30] At present, there are induction centres at Ashford and Dover (managed by Migrant Helpline) and in Leeds (to be managed by Leeds City Council) and Manchester. Like accommodation centres, they are politically sensitive and a number of proposed centres have been dropped at the planning stage.[31] Accommodation at or near an induction centre is provided by NASS under the section 98 temporary support duty. The induction centre process should include briefing asylum-seekers on the immigration and NASS processes, health screening and referral of asylum-seekers with special needs to a local authority for a community care assessment.

Type and level of section 95 support

4.17   Once NASS decides that a household is eligible for section 95 support, that is, 'destitute', it should arrange for the applicant to be offered full asylum support under section 95. Section 96 sets out the 'ways in which support may be provided'. NASS will only provide:

a)   accommodation adequate for the household's needs;
b)   essential living needs;
c)   expenses connected to the asylum claim;
d)   expenses of attending bail hearings;
e)   other forms of support if there are exceptional circumstances.

28   See paras 3.287 and chapter 6.
29   See Policy Bulletins 81, 70 and 73.
30   NIAA 2002 s70.
31   See www.ind.homeoffice.gov.uk for the latest information on induction centres.

4.18 Before deciding what form of support to provide or to continue to provide, NASS must take certain matters into account and ignore others.[32] The applicant's resources *must* be taken into account in deciding the kind and level of support.[33] The supported person's compliance with any conditions subject to which support is provided *may* be taken into account.[34] Because this is a discretionary consideration, ECHR issues would be relevant.[35]

Adequate accommodation under section 95

Background

> Accommodation will be offered on a no-choice basis just as it may be in respect of UK residents who present themselves as homeless, usually where accommodation is more readily available outside London and the south-east. That does not mean that asylum-seekers will be placed in isolated or derelict accommodation.[36]

4.19 Shelter's report, *Far from home,*[37] highlighted the inadequacies of accommodation provided under the IAA 1999. Of 154 properties occupied at that time by asylum-seeker households, the majority were not safe from fire.

4.20 In the first edition of this book we referred to reports that asylum-seekers in Liverpool were being housed in two crumbling tower-blocks abandoned by the council as unfit for its own tenants. Complaints by asylum-seekers about overcrowding, poor management and harassment of those who complained, supported by a local campaign eventually compelled the Home Office to announce an independent inquiry into Landmark Liverpool Ltd. The inquiry found many of the complaints could not be proven because asylum-seekers in Landmark accommodation were reluctant to give evidence. It made general recommendations, which included:

- NASS should make evidence of social housing management skills compulsory for companies seeking a contract with NASS;
- NASS should revise performance standards for its contractors;

---

32 IAA 1999 s97(1), (2) and (4).
33 AS Reg 12.
34 AS Reg 19.
35 See para 4.131.
36 Ministerial statement, second reading of the IAA 1999, HC Debates, col 45, 22 February 1999.
37 *Far from home: the housing of asylum-seekers in private rented accommodation,* Garvie (January 2001, Shelter publications).

–   there should be a new complaints procedure protecting an asylum-
    seeker's confidentiality.

4.21   The Home Office refused to publish the report of the inquiry but
stated that it accepted the recommendations. At the same time, the
Home Office announced that an internal review of NASS had concluded that some of its functions should be regionalised to 12 offices,
which would initially deal with housing contract management, fraud
investigation, outreach functions and reports by asylum-seekers of
anti-social behaviour and racial harassment.

Overview

4.22   Where NASS decides that an asylum-seeker is destitute, it may provide accommodation which appears 'to be adequate for the needs of
the supported person and his dependants (if any)'.[38] Section 97 then
sets out the factors which must and may not be taken into account in
providing housing.[39] The supported person's 'preference' as to the
type and location of his/her accommodation must not be taken into
account, but his/her 'individual circumstances' must be taken into
account:

> The legislation does not allow us to take asylum-seekers' preferences
> as to location of accommodation into consideration. But if there is
> a particular reason . . . why an individual, or one of his dependants
> needs to be placed in a certain area, for example for ease of access to
> a specialised hospital to meet specific health needs, that will be taken
> into consideration by the directorate before reaching a decision.
>   . . . We shall have regard to any special needs, not least the safety,
> welfare and protection of children. Obviously, we shall apply our
> minds to the maintenance of public health and work closely with
> local authorities, health authorities and public bodies to ensure
> that proper account is taken of these matters . . . As part of the
> arrangements we are making for the provision of accommodation
> and support, we shall be ensuring that the necessary translation
> services are made available . . . With regard to education, it is the
> government's clear aim to ensure that all children of school age have
> proper access to the educational system that the Secretary of State
> would operate the dispersal policy with regard 'to any special needs,
> not least the safety, welfare and protection of children'.[40]

4.23   Accommodation may be provided on a self-contained, bed and breakfast, full or half-board basis, in a hostel, flat or house without regard to

---

38   IAA 1999 s96(1)(a).
39   See paras 4.27–4.29.
40   Lord Williams of Mostyn, *Hansard*, HL Debates, col 1163, 20 October 1999.

the asylum-seeker's 'preference'. In practice, since individual circumstances, such as the asylum-seeker's health needs are relevant, the question of 'preference' has limited relevance.[41] NASS must take into account circumstances such as the location of other family members, education, medical and other social welfare needs when reaching a decision about where to accommodate a supported household.[42] Detailed questions about the household's needs are asked in the NASS 1 application form, which forms part of the AS Regs. The headings of the Schedule to the regulations[43] are: 'Ethnic Group and Religion, Health, Disability, Dietary needs, Any other information'. NASS claims that it takes these factors into account as relevant considerations in determining the nature and location of accommodation. For example, under 'Ethnic Group and Religion' the note begins 'You should tell us your ethnic group and religion because it will help us to identify a suitable area for any accommodation we may give you'.

The standard of section 95 accommodation – adequate or suitable?

4.24   There is limited guidance on the standard of accommodation which should be provided to supported persons. Both the IAA 1999 and the AS Regs use the word 'adequate' rather than 'suitable', reflecting the 'no-choice' policy. However, ministers have repeatedly suggested that the 'no-choice' approach to the housing of asylum-seekers is the same as the 'one offer' approach to the housing of homeless families, for example:

> We have tried broadly to replicate the arrangements for people who are homeless but lawfully resident here whereby people have the one offer of accommodation and no more.[44]

4.25   Offers of inadequate accommodation to asylum-seekers may be challenged on grounds similar to those used to challenge offers of unsuitable accommodation to homeless persons. The Home Office gave this ministerial reply to a parliamentary question:

> The accommodation provider will have a contract with the National Asylum Support Service. They will ensure that the accommodation is 'suitable' in that it will be of an adequate standard; the relevant

41   See para 4.28 below.
42   As set out in Policy Bulletin 31.
43   At Note 11.
44   Home Secretary Jack Straw giving evidence to the Special Standing Committee considering the Immigration and Asylum Bill, 25 March 1999.

standard. The relevant standards are the same applied by local authorities when re-housing any homeless residents.[45]

4.26   The Court of Appeal has found there was no material difference between the meaning of 'adequate' accommodation for asylum-seekers under IAA 1999 and 'suitable' accommodation in the context of National Assistance Act (NAA) 1948 s21 or in the homelessness provisions.[46] The court found there was no justification for providing a different standard of provision for disabled children as compared with disabled adults under NAA 1948 21. To do so could be discriminatory under ECHR article 14. It explained that any difference in the test of adequacy lies in the context, and the context of asylum support is that the accommodation is intended to be temporary accommodation to prevent destitution. The court found that article 8 was engaged due to the effect of the housing conditions on the physical and psychological integrity of the family, but the breach was justified because of the financial cost and effect on other families (on the council waiting list) if Mrs A's family was suitably housed.

Section 95 accommodation – irrelevant factors

4.27   In exercising its power to provide accommodation, NASS may not have regard to, 'any preference that the supported person or his dependants (if any) may have as to the locality in which the accommodation is to be provided'.[47]

4.28   Section 97 provides for regulations to prescribe factors which must or may not be taken into account. The AS Regs reg 13(2) exclude from consideration any preference as to the 'nature of accommodation' to be provided and as to 'the nature and standard of fixtures and fittings'. But the regulation continues:

> . . . this shall not be taken to prevent the person's individual circumstances as they relate to accommodation needs being taken into account.

The government has drawn a distinction between preference and individual circumstances stating:

> . . . it is not required to have regard to preferences but we can have regard to circumstances. So we can look at the background circumstances of a group of asylum-seekers to disperse all those

---

45   HC Written Answers, Vol 348, col 593, 20 April 2000.
46   *R (A) v (1) NASS and (2) Waltham Forest LBC* [2003] EWCA Civ 1473.
47   IAA 1999 s97(2).

with a common ethnic, linguistic or territorial origin to a place common to all of them. That is looking at the circumstances and not preferences.[48]

This approach is reflected in Policy Bulletin 31 and clearly requires NASS to take into account the location of other family members, education, medical and other social welfare needs when deciding on accommodation provision. However, provided NASS can show the considerations have been *taken into account*, its decisions will be difficult to challenge (see dispersal decisions below).

Section 95 accommodation – relevant factors

When exercising his power under section 95 to provide accommodation, the Secretary of State must have regard under s97(1) to:
- the fact that the accommodation is to be temporary pending determination of the asylum-seeker's claim;
- the desirability, in general, of providing accommodation in areas where there is a ready supply of accommodation; and
- such other matters as may be prescribed.

To date, no matters have been prescribed. Although the Home Office has dramatically speeded up asylum decision-making and cleared much of its backlog, many asylum-seekers are in NASS accommodation for years rather than months and the notion that section 95 accommodation is 'temporary' remains a policy aspiration. During the passage of the IAA 1999, the Home Secretary gave a 'two plus four' assurance, indicating that asylum decisions would be made within two months of the claim, and appeals processed within four months. During 2003, 80 per cent of initial decisions were decided within two months, but only 43 per cent of appeals were decided with six months.[49]

4.29   Thus, asylum-seekers who are challenging the adequacy of support under section 97(1)(a) could present evidence of any delay in their own case and general evidence to demonstrate that the provision is not temporary, particularly for some categories of applicant, to argue that the length of time in the accommodation is relevant to the standard of accommodation.

---

48 HL Debates, cols 1200–1201, 20 October 1999.
49 Home Office Asylum Statistics: 4th Quarter 2003; www.homeoffice.gov.uk/rds/immigration1.html.

Policy Bulletin factors

4.30   NASS's approach to deciding where and how to accommodate is contained in Policy Bulletin 31: *Dispersal Guidelines*. See para 3.181 onwards for the factors listed in Policy Bulletin 31 and their interpretation. There are other Policy Bulletins dealing with particular needs which are also relevant, such as Bulletin 19 on the Medical Foundation, Bulletin 29 on Transition at 18, and Bulletin 63 on Education. In order for NASS to have lawfully reached a decision that accommodation in a dispersal area is adequate, it should have properly considered the guidance in its bulletins.

Health

4.31   Accommodation that does not meet the supported household's physical or mental health needs, or with disrepair, which makes it a significant risk to health, may fall outside the definition of 'adequate'. Shared accommodation may be inadequate if sharing would adversely affect health or interfere with the family's right to respect for family life under ECHR article 8. Accommodation may be inadequate if the supported person needs to be near friends, family or members of the same refugee community for practical or emotional support.

Access to immigration advice/interpreters

4.32   This is unlikely to succeed as a ground for judicial review provided that the Legal Services Commission (LSC) remains willing to fund travel to an immigration solicitor as a disbursement.[50]

One year in school[51]

As a matter of policy, where an asylum seeker has dependent children of school age (including of an age to attend pre-school classes or nursery school) and has attended a particular school for at least 12 months, dispersal will not normally be appropriate. Cases that fall outside this criteria should be examined on their own merits and will depend on the effect of the disruption that would be caused to the dependent minor children if the family were to be dispersed.[52]

4.33   Dispersal may also be delayed where a child's GCSE exams are imminent.[53]

---

50   *LSC guidance, General Civil Contract (solicitors)*, rule 2.13 para 10 on disbursements, in the contracting section of www.legalservices.gov.uk and see para 3.189.

51   See also disbenefited cases at para 4.52.

52   Policy Bulletin 63: Education, para 4.

53   Policy Bulletin 63, para 5.

4.34   In *R (Agolli) v Secretary of State for the Home Department*,[54] NASS had offered dispersal accommodation to an asylum-seeker whose children had been in school for less than a year and he had refused it. He reapplied for support and accommodation later, after the children had been in school for two years and brought a judicial review of the dispersal decision under the 'one year in school policy'. Jackson J rejected the application, deciding an asylum-seeker could not 'manipulate the system' by declining to be dispersed until the children fell within the policy. However, it was a relevant factor in his decision that NASS undertook not to disperse the family until after the end of the school term.

Settled in one area

4.35   Where a household has lived in a particular area for over a year, there is support from parliamentary statements that they should not be dispersed, particularly if the children are settled in school:

> If people have waited for some time for the processing of a claim – whether it is genuine or unfounded; the circumstances of the transfer from their country are often traumatic, – and have settled in an area, I, my honourable friend the under-secretary and the officials in the department have no interest in gratuitously disrupting reasonably settled lives.[55]

The first dispersal judicial review was brought by a Turkish Kurdish family who argued that they should be accommodated in London where they received medical treatment and support from the Kurdish community.[56] The case is often cited by NASS and others to show that dispersal cannot easily be challenged, but note should be taken of its particular facts. Mr Altun was a depressed, failed asylum-seeker who had exhausted all his appeal rights. He had lived in London for about eight years but the judicial review and NASS application were made in the name of his wife who had only recently arrived in the UK with the children and claimed asylum. So it was difficult to demonstrate that they were settled in London or that there was no justification for dispersal under ECHR article 8 in those circumstances.

4.36   *R (Blackwood) v Secretary of State for the Home Department*[57]

54 [2002] EWHC 1250 (Admin).

55 Home Secretary Jack Straw MP, *Hansard*, HC Debates, col 985, 9 November 1999.

56 *R (Altun) v Secretary of State for the Home Department* [2001] EWHC Admin 296; August 2001 *Legal Action* 24.

57 [2003] EWHC 97 Admin.

concerned a 22-year-old Jamaican woman who had lived in London since the age of ten without regularising her immigration status and then made an application to the Home Office that to remove her from the UK would interfere with her rights under ECHR article 3. She had applied to NASS for support for her and her baby, including rent on her council tenancy. When NASS decided to disperse her outside London, away from family, friends and her support network, she brought a successful judicial review of the decision. Collins J found that article 8 was engaged because the adverse effect on her health, increasing her dependence on social and mental healthcare services would directly affect her and her child's psychological well-being. Respect for private and family life under article 8 included physical and psychological integrity.

Racial or other harassment/domestic violence

4.37   NASS's approach to harassment is contained in Policy Bulletin 81, a recent Policy Bulletin on Racial Incidents, replacing Policy Bulletin 18 and confirming that NASS applies the definition of a racist incident established by the Stephen Lawrence Inquiry report as 'any incident which is perceived to be racist by the victim or any other person'.[58] Policy Bulletin 70 covers domestic violence and Policy Bulletin 73 covers re-admittance to emergency accommodation for households fleeing violence and harassment. Tactics for dealing with cases where asylum-seekers have experienced racial harassment are explored at para 3.202 onwards.

4.38   In *R (Gezer) v Secretary of State for the Home Department*,[59] NASS had housed a Turkish Kurdish asylum-seeker who was a torture survivor in an area in Glasgow where another Kurdish asylum-seeker had been murdered a month earlier. He was placed in emergency accommodation by the police after experiencing serious racial harassment including his 13-year-old son being threatened with a knife. NASS cut off his support because he had left his accommodation. After he applied for judicial review, NASS agreed to reinstate support, pay backdated support and provide alternative accommodation. The court was left to consider a claim for damages for breach of ECHR articles 3. Mr Justice Moses rejected the damages claim on the basis that the treatment the family was subjected to was not treatment by the government or their agents and so the dispersal decision itself

---

58   See further Home Office Code of Practice on reporting and recording racist incidents at www.homeoffice.gov.uk/crimpol/police/racerelations/index.html

59   [2003] EWHC 860.

could not be classed as inhuman and degrading treatment within the meaning of article 3. He found that the level of protection provided by the police up to the time of the incident had been adequate. In the absence of a specific danger, NASS was entitled as a matter of policy to provide accommodation within an inner-city area, provided there was a general system for providing police protection, social support and programmes designed to improve community relations.

4.39   The case of *R (Thiab) v NASS*[60] concerned an asylum-seeker who left the Sighthill estate with his family after the Glasgow murder referred to above and brought a judicial review of NASS's decision not to admit them to emergency accommodation, in particular of its failure to follow the guidance in Policy Bulletin 18 now 81). There was evidence of 100 racially motivated incidents reported by asylum-seekers prior to the murder. While the judicial review was still pending, the claimant was offered different accommodation in Glasgow and had to return there, later finding a part-time job. Some steps had been taken by the police and community to improve the situation at Sighthill and the family did not report any further harassment after their return. The court found there was undisputed evidence that community relations had significantly improved in the area. There was also limited evidence that the family had complained about the original harassment. The Administrative Court decided that the application was academic by the time it reached a full hearing, some seven months later and dismissed the application.[61]

Specialist medical needs/Medical Foundation treatment

4.40   The availability of specialist support from organisations such as the Medical Foundation for the Care of Victims of Torture should be taken into account when decisions are taken about where asylum-seekers should be accommodated. This is documented in Policy Bulletin 19 as well as in correspondence between the Medical Foundation and the Home Office and in the parliamentary debates on the IAA 1999:

> I pay tribute to the very fine work of the Medical Foundation for the Care of Victims of Torture. Where it is clear that someone needs specialised services which cannot be delivered other than through a body of that sort, and the location of that body does not fit in with our normal cluster arrangements, we shall consider the possibility of finding accommodation adjacent to those services . . .[62]

60   [2002] EWHC 905.
61   See also para 3.209.
62   Lord Williams of Mostyn, *Hansard*, HC Debates, col 1112, 21 July 1999.

4.41   The asylum-seeker will need to show that he or she is receiving treatment from the Medical Foundation, not merely awaiting an assessment, see Policy Bulletin 19.

4.42   In *R (Wanjugu) v Secretary of State for the Home Department*,[63] W, a woman with mental health needs, who was referred to local counselling because there was a nine-month waiting list for the Medical Foundation, brought a judicial review of her dispersal, arguing that the policy should be applied to her because she was receiving treatment analogous to that provided by the Foundation. Mr Justice Elias rejected this argument, finding that the services offered by the Foundation (which are described in Policy Bulletin 19) were linked to the particular nature of the institution and the treatment it provided. He was reluctant to extend the policy simply because W suffered from a serious illness of the same kind as some of those treated by the Foundation. However, the court found that NASS needed to reconsider its decision to disperse W because of new medical evidence she had produced. It remains possible to argue that accommodation in a dispersal area is not adequate accommodation if an asylum-seeker is receiving highly specialised treatment elsewhere, which is analogous to that provided by the Foundation, or under the 'health' consideration which is contained in Policy Bulletin 31.[64]

HIV status[65]

> We have not selected particular areas for those with HIV infection. Instead when asylum-seekers make an application for asylum they are invited to indicate whether they have any special needs. Consideration is given on a case-by-case basis to those needs both in terms of the accommodation and support package and the proximity to any medical treatment which may be required.[66]

4.43   The All-party Parliamentary Group on AIDS published a report: *Migration and HIV: improving lives in Britain, an inquiry into the impact of the UK nationality and immigration system on people living with HIV*[67] following an inquiry, which heard evidence on the effect of dispersal on people living with HIV and AIDS. It made various recommendations including:

---

63   [2003] EWHC 3116 (Admin).
64   See health para above and para 3.181.
65   See also para 3.195.
66   Barbara Roche MP, Under-Secretary of State for the Home Office, in response to a parliamentary question, *Hansard*, HC Debates, col 378, 17 April 2000.
67   July 2003, see www.appg-aids.org.uk.

- a person with HIV should not be dispersed if dispersal is going to severely impact upon their health;
- when a decision on dispersal is made by NASS regarding a person known to be living with HIV, all such decisions should necessarily take into account expert medical and professional advice. Any decision by NASS to overrule specialist advice should be justified;
- NASS should only continue to disperse people living with HIV to areas where HIV clinical expertise and capacity is available to treat the manifold needs of migrants and asylum-seekers, in particular, to places with a multiplicity of cultural and language services, mental healthcare services for trauma victims and HIV support services and networks;
- when an asylum-seeker with HIV is dispersed, he or she should be given sufficient notice – at least seven working days. The government should ensure that an organised process of referral and handover of care is in place.

4.44 It has been NASS's practice to disperse to areas of the country where HIV and AIDS treatment is available, making their decisions difficult to challenge unless there are additional factors such as a high level of mental health needs. In *R (Muwangusi) v Secretary of State for the Home Department*[68] a woman with full-blown AIDS who had been in London for a short period but was obtaining appropriate medical and psychological support was unsuccessful in her judicial review of a dispersal to Leeds. Mr Justice Goldring found that medical treatment was available in Leeds, and that NASS's decision was rational. He decided that although her article 8 rights could be engaged, it was proportionate for NASS to disperse in the circumstances of the case.

4.45 There has been some success in challenging decisions that dispersal accommodation is adequate where it can be shown that the effect of disruption to medical or other service provision is so severe that it cannot be justified.[69]

4.46 To challenge dispersal, asylum-seekers with AIDS or HIV would need clear medical evidence that appropriate treatment was not available in the dispersal area or that dispersal would be detrimental to their health for other reasons. NASS should be asked to produce evidence of HIV services in the area to which the household is being dispersed. Where the claimant is in need of care and attention due to their medical condition, a request to social services for a community

68 [2003] EWHC 813.
69 See *R (M) v SSHD* at para 4.47 below.

care assessment and provision of accommodation under NAA 1948 s21 should be considered (see chapter 6).

Child's welfare/disruption in services

4.47   There appears to be a greater chance of success in judicial review where it can be shown that dispersal will interfere with the welfare of the child. A torture survivor with AIDS, whose medical needs were being met in London, successfully challenged his dispersal to Middlesbrough.[70] While the court rejected the father's argument about inadequate HIV services in the dispersal area, it accepted that NASS had failed to take into account the evidence of the needs of his son, S, which included letters from his school and social services. S had settled in school in London despite his trauma after having observed some of his father's torture and was then racially harassed in Middlesbrough. Richards J held:

> The question was whether the disruption to the services being provided would be liable to have such deleterious consequences for the asylum-seeker that dispersal was inappropriate . . . There was no evidence . . . that the available services in Middlesbrough could be provided in such a way as to compensate for the problems arising out of the disruption to the services provided in London . . .

Family life under article 8

4.48   In *R (Hetoja) v Secretary of State for the Home Department*,[71] a Kosovan grandmother was living in Leicester with her son and providing considerable childcare for her grandson with whom she lived as an extended family. She challenged her dispersal to Barnsley, arguing this would interfere with her article 8 rights by separating her from her son and grandson, and NASS compromised, agreeing to house her in Leicester in a hostel. The court then rejected her claim that the hostel accommodation breached her article 8 rights because visitors were not allowed and so she could not care for her grandson adequately. It decided that while NASS must consider the claimant's personal circumstances, article 8 did not require the provision of particular accommodation. See also *R (Blackwood) v SSHD* (at para 4.36 above).

---

70   *R (M) v Secretary of State for the Home Department* [2002] EWHC Admin 1924; November 2002 *Legal Action* 25.

71   [2002] EWHC 2146 (Admin); (2002) 24 October, unreported.

Special cases

Adequate accommodation for those with special needs[72]

4.49   In *R (A) v (1) NASS and (2) Waltham Forest LBC*,[73] Mrs A lived with her husband and two disabled teenage children in a flat which did not meet their special needs, including the need for wheelchair access. The bedrooms were upstairs and the toilets were downstairs. The Court of Appeal decided that the family's needs for suitable accommodation had to be balanced against the context of NASS's duty to provide adequate accommodation for destitute asylum-seekers in an area where there was a scarcity of accommodation. The court described NASS's duties in finding adequate accommodation as including:

– to make arrangements with a local authority under IAA 1999 s99;
– to request one or more local authorities to assist under IAA 1999 s100 and to ensure they complied with the request;
– to make its own enquiries of registered social landlords (RSLs) or estate agents.

4.50   Although local authorities did not have the primary responsibility for accommodating the disabled children of asylum-seekers, their responsibilities included:

– to co-operate in giving NASS such assistance as is reasonable in the circumstances;
– generally to look outside its own stock, but there are circumstances where it should use its own stock, for example, where the accommodation is extremely inadequate.

Former unaccompanied minors

4.51   It is NASS's policy not to disperse a young person of 18 who has been supported by a local authority as a 'looked after' child under Children Act 1989 s20.[74]

'Disbenefited' cases[75]

4.52   Where asylum-seekers who are in receipt of social security benefits and/or housing as homeless receive a negative decision on their

72   See also para 6.78.
73   [2003] EWCA Civ 1473.
74   See Policy Bulletin 31. Guidance on the transfer arrangements is contained in Policy Bulletin 29: Transition at Age 18; but see also para 3.17 and 6.132.
75   See also para 3.149.

asylum claim on or after 25 September 2000, they are referred to as 'disbenefited' asylum-seekers. If they have an outstanding appeal or have a child under 18, they are entitled to NASS support. NASS Policy Bulletins 51–53 explain provision in disbenefited cases and give instructions to local authorities who act as agents for NASS in providing support to disbenefited families. It is NASS's policy to consider not dispersing families in this category if they have a dependent child who has been in the same school in the area where they live for three consecutive school terms. A childless asylum-seeker will need to demonstrate 'exceptional compelling or compassionate reasons' for remaining in the area where they are settled.

4.53   When the IAA 1999 was being debated, the Home Secretary made a parliamentary concession that families who were settled should not be dispersed.[76] Barbara Roche MP later announced the policy on disbenefited asylum-seekers:

> Any asylum-seeker who is in receipt of social security benefits and whose asylum claim is recorded as refused on or after 25 September 2000 and who would otherwise be destitute may seek support from the National Asylum Support Service (NASS) . . . Asylum-seekers who are no longer entitled to social security benefits after 25 September and who apply for a full support package from NASS are likely to be offered accommodation outside the south-east. However, NASS will give due consideration to cases where there are exceptional compelling or compassionate reasons why an asylum-seeker should be allowed to remain in the area in which he was living at the time the social security benefits were stopped. In cases where families have children who attended a particular school for at least 12 months, we will give consideration to enabling those asylum-seeker families to remain in their existing accommodation so that the education of those families is not unduly disrupted . . .[77]

4.54   It is arguable that asylum-seekers who have settled in an area over a long period, forming family and social ties, should not be dispersed, both on the basis of individual circumstances, ECHR considerations and the discriminatory nature of such a policy. Evidence to support the argument could include medical and psychological needs, family and community ties, language needs, religious worship, and the effect on any children who have been at school for periods of less than a year or who are settled at nursery school. If the dispersal interferes with article 8 or other qualified Convention rights, NASS would need to demonstrate that the policy is proportionate and legitimate.

---

76 See para 4.32 and *Hansard*, HC Debates, cols 983–985, 9 November 1999.
77 *Hansard*, HC Debates, col 766W, 26 January 2001.

Challenges and complaints in dispersal cases/where accommodation is inadequate

4.55   Challenges to dispersal are explained in detail in chapter 3. If an asylum-seeker refuses to travel to accommodation in a dispersal area, NASS may withdraw support. The remedy will then be an appeal to the Asylum Support Adjudicators (ASA). If such an appeal is unsuccessful, any new application for support may be rejected unless there has been a change of circumstances. Another method of challenging dispersal directly is to apply for judicial review on the basis that the accommodation is not 'adequate'. Only a few days' notice is usually given of a requirement to travel to the dispersal area, leaving little time to collect evidence and consider the merits of applying for permission for judicial review and an injunction. Asylum-seekers should be clearly warned of the possible consequences of failure to travel. In some cases, it may be advisable for them to move briefly to the dispersal area until the court has considered whether to grant permission to apply for judicial review.

4.56   IAA 1999 s97(1) sets out the presumption in favour of dispersing asylum-seekers around the UK. An asylum-seeker can challenge dispersal if accommodation has been offered without taking into account individual circumstances and/or if the accommodation offered is not adequate for the household within the meaning of section 96(1)(a). Although NASS cannot take into account 'preferences' as to locality,[78] it should take personal circumstances into account. Therefore, to bring a judicial review of dispersal, an asylum-seeker would argue provision in a dispersal area is not 'adequate accommodation' claiming that the decision does not adequately take account of their personal circumstances or of the ECHR.

4.57   Sometimes, an ASA appeal may be an indirect way of challenging dispersal, for example, an appeal against the withdrawal of support by an asylum-seeker who left accommodation after being racially harassed in Town X and wishes to be housed elsewhere. Although ASA decisions are not binding on the Administrative Court, they are a relevant consideration for NASS in deciding what kind of support to provide, and have influenced NASS policy and decision-making.

---

78   IAA 1999 s97.

Effect of refusing an offer of accommodation

4.58 In cases where an asylum-seeker has refused an initial offer of accommodation, support can be refused[79] or withdrawn on the ground of
breach of conditions. NASS may refuse to entertain a new application
for support unless there is a change of circumstances.[80]

Accommodation centres[81]

4.59 NIAA 2002 s16, which came into force on 7 November 2002, gave the
Home Secretary power to establish accommodation centres, with a
hearing centre nearby at which asylum appeals could be heard. The
rest of NIAA 2002 Part 2, which is not in force at the time of publication, covers eligibility for support in an accommodation centre and
service provision in the centres. One of the objections to Part 2 in
parliament was that it gives wide powers to make regulations without
parliamentary scrutiny. These include provisions governing the procedures for applying for and receiving support in a centre, for restricting the 'destitution test', for prescribing classes of dependant, for age
assessment, and for withdrawing or refusing support. The centres
may be managed privately or by a local authority, but will not be managed directly by the Home Office.[82]

4.60 There was detailed debate about accommodation centres when
NIAA 2002 Part 2 passed through parliament, particularly in the
House of Lords, so it may be useful to refer to *Hansard* if any dispute
arises about the type of provision offered in a centre, as a guide to
interpreting what type of provision should be made.[83] There is also
some background information in the White Paper, *Secure Borders,
Save Haven: Integration with Diversity in Modern Britain.*[84] Regular
updates on the progress of induction and accommodation centres are
published on the Home Office website.[85] At present, the government
is planning centres at two sites, which have been heavily opposed, and
has reached the late stages of planning challenges:

– the Defence Storage and Distribution Centre (DSDC), Bicester,
  Oxfordshire;

79 AS Reg 19.
80 See paras 3.241 and 4.146.
81 NIAA 2002 Part 2.
82 NIAA 2002 s38.
83 See *Hansard*, HL Debates, 9 and 10 July 2002.
84 At paras 4.28–4.41; www.official-documents.co.uk/documents/cm53/5387/
   cm5387.htm.
85 www.ind.homeoffice.gov.uk.

– RAF Newton, Nottinghamshire.

It is also looking for a suitable location for a third site on which to trial a smaller centre for up to 400 residents.

4.61 An attempt to challenge the decision of the Office of the Deputy Prime Minister (ODPM) to overrule planning objections to the Bicester accommodation centre was unsuccessful in *R (Cherwell District Council) v First Secretary of State and Secretary of State for the Home Department (Interested party).*[86] Collins J found that because the development was to be carried out on behalf of the Crown, it attracted Crown immunity and so the development did not require planning permission and could go ahead despite being rejected by the planning inspector.

Eligibility for an accommodation centre

4.62 NIAA 2002 ss18 and 19 slightly amend the definition of 'asylum-seeker' and 'destitution' for the purposes of support in an accommodation centre. To be eligible for support under Part 2, an asylum-seeker must have applied for support in person at a designated place, usually an asylum screening unit.[87] His/her claim for asylum must have been recorded by the Home Secretary and 'not been determined'.[88] Section 19 provides that an asylum-seeker is destitute if he or she does not have and cannot obtain both adequate accommodation and food and other essential items for him/herself and any dependant(s).

Temporary provision

4.63 Section 24 allows NASS to make temporary provision while considering whether an asylum-seeker is eligible for accommodation in an accommodation centre under section 17.

Length of stay

4.64 The maximum stay in an accommodation centre is six months,[89] though this can be extended by another three months if the Home Secretary 'thinks it appropriate in relation to a person because of the circumstances of his case', for example, because an asylum decision is imminent. At this stage, an asylum-seeker may either choose to

86 [2004] EWHC 724 (Admin).
87 See para 3.60.
88 See para 3.66 onwards.
89 NIAA 2002 s25.

remain in the centre or move out to ordinary section 95 accommodation in a dispersal area.

Residence requirements

4.65   Residence in an accommodation centre will be subject to reporting
and residence restrictions. Regulations may be made allowing for
conditions which require a person not to be absent during specified
hours, for example, overnight. Support may be ended if the condition
is breached.[90] The government minister gave assurances in the
House of Lords debate on accommodation centres that support would
not be withdrawn unreasonably or disproportionately and that decisions would be in line with the way in which NASS support is currently withdrawn or terminated under AS Reg 20.[91]

4.66   The accommodation centre conditions are in addition to an
asylum-seeker's 'asylum conditions'. IA 1971 Sch 2 para 21(2C) allows
for regulations to require residence in particular accommodation and
prohibiting a person's absence from the accommodation. Although
an asylum-seeker is not 'detained' at a centre, if he or she leaves without authorisation, he or she may lose support and may risk formal
detention. During the passage of the IAA 1999, the House of Lords
Committee on delegated legislation considered the legality of a
requirement for asylum-seekers to reside in accommodation and
possible ways in which such a requirement breached the ECHR.[92]

Facilities

4.67   NIAA 2002 s29(1) provides that facilities 'may' include:

a) food and other essential items;
b) money (described in parliament as 'a small cash allowance'; the
amount may be specified in regulations);[93]
c) transport to asylum interviews and appeals;
d) transport to and from the centre;
e) assistance with expenses due to voluntary work 'or other activities';
f) education and training (a resident's child is excluded from mainstream education or a local authority nursery unless the child has
a statement of special educational needs.[94] The Home Secretary
announced that education would be subject to regular OFSTED

---

90 NIAA 2002 s30.
91 *Hansard*, 10 July 2002, HL Debates, col 732 onwards.
92 www.publications.parliament.uk/pa/ld199899/ldselect/lddreg/110/11001/htm.
93 NIAA 2002 s29(2).
94 NIAA 2002 s36.

inspections and tailored to the individual needs of the child);[95]

g) health facilities;

h) facilities for religious observance;

i) anything which the Home Secretary considers should be provided for the purpose of providing a resident with a proper occupation and for the purpose of maintaining good order;

j) anything which the Home Secretary thinks ought to be provided for a person because of his exceptional circumstances.

The Home Office website materials on accommodation centres suggest that interpreting and transport facilities will be provided. Access to legal advice before any appointment with the Home Office is provided for in NIAA 2002 s29(3) and (4).[96]

Standards of accommodation and security of tenure

4.68 The centre resident will not have a tenancy, but will have an excluded licence, which is subject to conditions.[97] There is no 'adequacy' requirement and it would seem that ordinary residential environmental health standards may not apply. The remedy for poor quality accommodation would be to complain first through the centre's complaints procedure, then to NASS and/or the Accommodation Advisory Group (see below) and from there to the local MP, and if necessary to the office of the Parliamentary Ombudsman.[98]

Inspection and monitoring

4.69 The Home Secretary must appoint an Accommodation Advisory Group, which may visit the centre at any time. It should be made up of organisations with an interest in and experience of asylum-seekers' needs including local organisations such as faith groups. There is also a duty to appoint a Monitor of Accommodation Centres, who must report annually to the Home Secretary who is required to lay the report before parliament. The Monitor must consider various matters including 'whether in the case of any accommodation centre, its location prevents a need of its residents from being met'.[99] The role of the Monitor is to check the running of centres, in particular, the quality and 'effectiveness' of accommodation and other facilities provided there, including the treatment of residents.

---

95 NIAA 2002 amends the Education Act 1996 s13, 14 and 19 and the School Standards and Framework Act 1998 s86(1) and (2) and s110.

96 See also *Hansard*, HC Debates, col 163, 5 November 2002.

97 NIAA 2002 s32(5), amending Protection from Eviction Act 1977 s3A.

98 See Appendix G for address.

99 NIAA 2002 s34.

Challenges and complaints about accommodation centres

Challenging an offer of support in an accommodation centre

4.70   NIAA 2002 s26 provides for the withdrawal of support if an asylum-seeker refuses to travel to an accommodation centre. It seems likely that regulations will be introduced providing that NASS may withdraw or refuse accommodation centre support on the same basis as section 95 support.[100] NIAA 2002 s52 would extend the jurisdiction of the Asylum Support Adjudicators to include a 'location appeal' (by amending IAA 1999 s103) but there is no right of appeal as such against a decision to accommodate an asylum-seeker in an accommodation centre. Unlike section 95 accommodation, there is no statutory requirement that the accommodation is adequate. Another obstacle to challenging an accommodation centre offer is NIAA 2002 s51 – 'choice of form of support'. This provides that in deciding what form of support to offer an asylum-seeker, NASS may take into account 'administrative or other matters which do not concern the person's personal circumstances, regard one of those matters as conclusive, and apply different criteria to different persons for administrative reasons'. If the provision comes into force, it seems to allow a very wide scope to NASS to arrange mass dispersals of a group of asylum-seekers to an accommodation centre without taking into account their individual circumstances at all. It also applies to other forms of support. This would still leave a potential judicial review challenge on the basis that accommodation in a centre was in breach of an asylum-seeker's ECHR rights under articles 3 or 8.

Essential living needs

4.71   The phrase 'essential living needs' in IAA 1999 s95(1) was considered by the Administrative Court in *R (Ouji) v Secretary of State for the Home Department*,[101] a case which considered whether NASS or social services were responsible for providing extra support to a disabled child. Collins J held:

> What was being considered within the phrase 'essential living need' were those needs which had to be met for a person to live in a reasonable fashion. Those needs included sufficient food, nourishment, clothing and warmth so as to prevent that person

100 See para 3.163 onwards.
101 [2002] EWHC 1839 (Admin).

falling into illness. They were the kinds of needs that people in general had so as to prevent that person falling into illness.

Level of support

> The proposed provision is set at 70 per cent of the equivalent income support because the asylum support system is intended to be on a short-term basis, a safety net arrangement, and it should be possible to live on these amounts for short periods only.[102]

4.72 Where the household has no other income, the levels for maximum asylum support were set by the AS Regs at approximately 70 per cent of income support levels (excluding premiums) and 100 per cent of the income support level for a child at the time the IAA 1999 came into force. Because premiums for age and disability and parenthood are not included, the NASS support levels are often considerably lower than 70 per cent of the income support level for an equivalent household.

4.73 The rates are contained in a table in the schedule to the AS Regs. Unlike the annual uprating of income support, there is no statutory provision for a periodical review, although there was a government commitment 'to make regular annual reviews of the level at which support is provided to asylum-seekers'.[103] The rates have been increased in response to lobbying and court decisions, most recently by the Asylum Support (Amendment) Regulations 2004.[104]

4.74 There are no fixed rates for households receiving local authority support under the Asylum Support (Interim Provisions) Regulations 1999,[105] which may be paid at different rates according to the council's discretion.

4.75 Apart from the planned temporary nature of support, the explanation given for setting asylum support at a lower level than income support was that asylum-seekers would not have overheads such as the need to replace household items or utility bills.[106]

> The accommodation will contain domestic utensils and equipment necessary for a decent level of existence including linen, pots and pans, cutlery, crockery and so forth. In addition, council tax will be paid and the utilities – gas, electricity and water – will be paid also.[107]

---

102 Home Secretary Jack Straw MP, *Hansard*, Vol 333 col 475, 15 June 1999.

103 Lord Williams of Mostyn, *Hansard*, HL Debates, col 1164, 20 October 1999.

104 SI No 763; see Appendix A for amended version of AS Regs.

105 SI No 3056.

106 *Asylum-seekers' Support: an information document setting out proposals for the new support scheme*, Home Office, March 1999, para 4.19.

107 Lord Williams of Mostyn, *Hansard*, HL Debates, col 251, 29 June 1999.

Table showing weekly support levels[109]

Qualifying couple (married/unmarried, both must be 16 or over, one over 18)	£61.11
Lone parent aged 18 or over	£38.96
Single person aged 25 or over	£38.96
Single person aged at least 18 but under 25	£30.84
Dependent child aged 16–17* (except a member of a qualifying couple)	£33.50
Dependent child aged under 16	£42.27
Pregnant woman or child aged 2–3	extra £3
child under 1	extra £5

* Amount decreases from first Monday in September after 18th birthday.

If a supported household is not being provided with the above, it may be possible to challenge the level of support provided (see below). Where accommodation is provided under the section 95 duty by NASS or a local authority, it is the landlord and not the asylum-seeker who is liable for council tax.[108]

4.76   When specifying these levels of support, AS Reg 10 states that asylum support may be expected to be provided at these levels *as a general rule*. This allows NASS scope for greater or lesser amounts to be provided where appropriate. The government suggested that regulations would be made under the IAA 1999 to specify the circumstances in which the Home Secretary could make payments to meet special needs, for example, where a medical condition gives rise to special needs.[110] Similarly, IAA 1999 Sch 8 allows for regulations to provide for particular items falling outside the definition of 'essential living needs'. There are no such regulations to date – the AS Regs do not expressly make any such provision. NASS has introduced a one-off maternity payment of £300.[111] The section 96(1)(b) provision for

108 See para 5.167.
109 Asylum Support (Amendment) Regulations 2003 SI No 241.
110 IAA 1999 Sch 8 paras 3 and 4, and explanatory notes para 281.
111 NASS Policy Bulletin 37.

essential living needs would allow NASS to make payment at an appropriate level, for example, a higher payment may be appropriate if an asylum-seeker can produce evidence of a need for additional clothing or a special diet due to a medical condition. Asylum-seekers with health needs could argue for support to be provided at a higher level.

Challenges to the levels of support

4.77   There have been various attempts to challenge the level of local authority interim support and NASS support respectively:

- In *R (Gjini) v Islington LBC*,[112] a lone parent with one child challenged the reduction of her weekly income to a total of £42. In addition, her utility bills and some travel expenses were paid and her son received free school meals, and a school clothing grant of £35 every six months. The council argued that the total was equivalent to 72 per cent of income support. The Administrative Court found that a policy of paying interim support at the rate of 72 per cent was irrational and unlawful, although a fixed daily rate of £5 for single adults and £3 per person for families was lawful. The Court of Appeal then dismissed the appeal and decided the 72 per cent policy was lawful.

- In *R (Satu) v Hackney LBC*,[113] a lone parent brought a judicial review claiming that her low level of support was irrational and in breach of ECHR article 8. She received £78.64 for an adult and two children and had to pay utility bills, whereas a similar household supported by NASS received £89 per week with utility bills paid. The High Court refused her application. The decision was upheld by the Court of Appeal, which rejected the argument that the Interim Regs were ultra vires and dismissed her appeal.[114] The court found that, to succeed she would need to have shown that taking all the relevant matters, including the cost of providing support, the rate paid was not a rate that could have appeared to the local authority to meet the claimant's essential living needs.

4.78   In *R (T and another) v Secretary of State for Health and Secretary of State for the Home Department*,[115] the Child Poverty Action Group (CPAG)

112 [2003] EWCA Civ 558; EWHC 205 (Admin).
113 [2002] EWHC 952 (Admin); [2002] All ER (D) 86.
114 *R (Satu) v Hackney LBC* [2002] EWCA Civ 1843; [2002] All ER (D) 86; [2002] All ER (D) 178.
115 [2002] EWHC 1887 (Admin).

supported a (successful) challenge to the levels of support paid by NASS to nursing mothers as well as an (unsuccessful) challenge of the Department of Health's refusal to provide asylum-seekers with milk tokens. T, who was HIV positive, did not want to risk breast-feeding her new baby because there was a risk of transmission and she could not afford powdered milk from her NASS support. The case led to an increase in weekly support rates for pregnant mothers and children under five years old.[116]

Subsistence-only support

4.79   An asylum-seeker who is able to live in accommodation provided by friends or relatives may claim cash-only support while living at an authorised address. The provision has been used by asylum-seekers whose support is cut off and who have lost ASA appeals, often in dispersal cases. They may reapply for 'subsistence-only' support, notifying NASS there has been a change of circumstances. NASS carries out periodic inspections to check that asylum-seekers are actually living at their given address. NASS has refused to provide section 98 temporary support to those who are claiming cash only. Where an asylum-seeker has faced a long delay while their claim for cash-only support is processed, he or she could bring a judicial review of the delay.

4.80   There are problems in making an initial claim for subsistence-only support for a childless adult asylum-seeker who has not applied for asylum 'as soon as reasonably practicable' under NIAA 2002 s55(1).[117] He or she will need to show that refusal of support will be inhuman and degrading treatment to meet the section 55(5) test. If friends or relatives can provide shelter, this is likely to be more difficult.

4.81   This right to claim subsistence-only support may be ended in part or in full by NIAA 2002 s43, if the Home Secretary introduces an order. This requires an affirmative resolution by parliament and so would have to be debated.[118] An asylum-seeker offered accommodation in an accommodation centre under NIAA 2002 Part 2 would not be able to reject it and claim subsistence-only support.

Excluded items

4.82   Support may be given 'by providing what appear to the Secretary of State to be essential living needs of the supported person and his

116 See para 4.102 below.
117 See para 3.21.
118 *Hansard*, HC WA 259, 9 June 2003.

dependants'.[119] These are prescribed by AS Reg 9(4)[120] and exclude the cost of faxes, computer facilities, photocopying, travel (except to bail hearings, Home Office interviews/appeals and the initial journey to NASS accommodation), toys and entertainment expenses. The exclusion of toys for children was controversial. The purpose of including toys on the list appears to be to indicate that in the Home Secretary's view they are not an essential living need for the provision of public funds. However, it has been suggested that the exclusion may breach UN Convention on the Rights of the Child article 31. The exclusions were more significant when an asylum-seeker received voucher support and only £10 cash per week.

Expenses connected with the asylum claim or bail hearings[121]

4.83   The supported person may be provided with expenses other than legal expenses, which are incurred in connection with the asylum claim. The provision covers the cost of travel to interviews at the Home Office or port of entry, and to appeal hearings. It also covers travel to appointments at the Medical Foundation for a medical assessment connected to the claim[122] and arguably should cover other similar medical appointments. The NASS Travel Section processes payments.

4.84   The IAA 1999 explanatory notes at para 300[123] suggest that it includes the cost of preparing and copying documents. AS Reg 9(4)(c) specifically excludes photocopying costs from the assessment of an asylum-seeker's essential living needs when considering whether he or she is destitute. The LSC will usually finance the cost of travel to an immigration solicitor as a Legal Help disbursement.[124] The asylum-seeker and his/her dependants should receive travel costs to enable them to attend bail hearings of either an asylum-seeker or dependant who is detained under any provision of the Immigration Acts.[125] This is aimed at enabling the whole supported household to travel back to the dispersal area after a court hearing.[126]

119 IAA 1999 s96(1)(b).
120 See para 4.71 and appendix A.
121 IAA 1999 s96(1)(c)–(e).
122 NASS Policy Bulletin 19.
123 www.legislation.hmso.gov.uk/acts/en/1999en33.htm.
124 See paras 3.189 and 4.32 and LSC Manual Volume 2, paras 2D–029, rule 2.13.
125 IAA 1999 s96(1)(d) and (e).
126 See also NASS Policy Bulletin 26: Oakington.

Extra payments in exceptional circumstances

4.85   If an asylum-seeker needs an occasional or regular additional payment, for example, to cover a special diet, NASS may provide support in other ways if it considers that the circumstances of a particular case are exceptional.[127]

4.86   In *R (T and another) v Secretary of State for Health and Secretary of State for the Home Department*,[128] T, an HIV-positive mother applied for a judicial review of the Department of Health's exclusion of asylum-seeker nursing mothers from the right to receive milk tokens. In the alternative, she challenged NASS's failure to exercise its powers under IAA 1999 s96(2) to provide an extra payment to cover the cost of baby milk. The court rejected the claim against the Department of Health, but allowed her application in relation to NASS. It decided that NASS should have considered that the risk of the mother transmitting HIV to her child through breastfeeding, if she were unable to buy formula milk from her low income, could amount to an exceptional circumstance.[129]

4.87   Although section 96(2) provides for a discretion rather than a duty, it could be read in conjunction with the HRA 1998 to extend the limited provision provided by the IAA 1999 and AS Regs. It should allow more extensive provision in the form of cash or by other means, for example, where a supported person has a physical disability or HIV positive status if this gives rise to additional costs.[130]

Payment problems and procedures[131]

Additional support for special needs

4.88   If an asylum-seeker or dependant wants to claim a one-off or regular additional payment on the ground of exceptional circumstances under section 96(1), a letter outlining the need should be sent to Team Four, Post Allocation Casework Unit, NASS,[132] with a supporting letter from his/her doctor and/or social services.

---

127 IAA 1999 s96(2).
128 [2002] EWHC 1887 (Admin).
129 See also, November 2002 *Legal Action* 12 and 35.
130 Disabled asylum-seekers are excluded from eligibility for disability living allowance, which enables other disabled people to cover extra costs: IAA 1999 s115(1)(d).
131 See also Appendix F about contacting NASS and para 3.155 about complaints.
132 Voyager House, 30 Wellesley Road, Croydon, CR0 2AD, fax 020 8633 0213.

Payment of support

4.89 When the NASS scheme was introduced, support was provided in vouchers which could be exchanged at specified shops, supposedly to deter 'abusive' asylum claims. After a national campaign against the stigmatising effect of the scheme, IAA 1999 s96(3), which provided that support could only be paid in cash in exceptional circumstances was repealed,[133] so that asylum support can now be provided in cash. The standard amounts of cash support are listed in the table on p236.

4.90 The Home Office entered a contract for the provision of vouchers (now cash) with a company called Sodexho Pass International which has experience of operating similar schemes in other parts of Europe. During 2002/3 there was an 'ARC replacement exercise' in which every asylum-seeker and dependant over 3 years old was issued with an identity card known as 'Application Registration Card' or ARC. The procedure for claiming NASS subsistence is now to attend a specified local post office and produce the ARC card. The post office then pays the weekly cash amount unless it has instructions from NASS to terminate payment.

Action if payment is not received

4.91 If an asylum-seeker does not receive an expected payment, whether an emergency payment by post, a dispersal travel package, or the regular cash payment at the post office, the procedure is to phone the NASS hotline 'Support Discontinuation and Voucher Enquiries'.[134] The NASS telephonist should 'log' the call and notify the relevant section of NASS. A written acknowledgement of this call should be received by post. In cases where there is no apparent justification for cessation or non-payment of support, emergency vouchers should be sent too the household until the problem is resolved.[135]

Lost or stolen ARC or payments

4.92 The asylum-seeker should report the loss or theft of an ARC to the police and Home Office as soon as possible and then phone the Sodexho helpline.[136] NASS should then arrange emergency support tokens until the Immigration Service has notified them that the ARC

133 Asylum Support (Repeal) Order 2002 SI No 782.
134 Tel: 0845 6000914.
135 See also para 3.155 for complaints about NASS and Appendix F for details of how to contact NASS.
136 Tel: 0845 842 4444.

has been replaced. The Immigration Service usually takes about four weeks to replace the ARC. They will invite the asylum-seeker to attend the nearest reporting centre or local enforcement office for a finger-print check and replacement ARC. The ARC holder should keep receipts for any related journeys of three miles or more to claim a refund from NASS.

4.93   Where emergency vouchers or 'support notifications' have been stolen, the asylum-seeker should notify the police, and then NASS by fax.[137]

Setting the level of support

4.94   The Home Secretary may decide that an asylum-seeker is destitute due to inadequate resources or accommodation even though the household has some income or assets. In deciding what kind and level of support to offer, AS reg 12 repeats the list of relevant factors at AS reg 6(4). Any income, assets or support for the applicant or his/her dependant(s) may be taken into account in deciding what kind of sup-port should be offered and at what level. Support provided under IAA 1999 is excluded but other resources are relevant, whether in or out-side the UK, if they might reasonably be expected to be available to the household.

Contributions to support

4.95   Where an asylum-seeker has resources, the Home Secretary can:
   – set the asylum support at a level to reflect the resources; or
   – set the asylum support at the standard level but require the supported person to make payments to NASS in the form of 'con-tributions'.[138]

4.96   AS reg 12 should be read in conjunction with reg 16. Prompt payment of contributions may be made a condition of continued asylum sup-port.[139] Policy Bulletin 65 explains the arrangements for an asylum-seeker with income or capital to make weekly payments to NASS as a contribution to their support.

Overpayments

4.97   Where asylum support has been overpaid due to an error by NASS, the IAA 1999 allows for the Home Secretary to recover the overpay-

137 Tel: 020 8633 0721.
138 AS Reg 16.
139 IAA 1999 s95(9) and AS reg 16(4).

ment as a debt by bringing an action against the asylum-seeker in the County Court.[140] It can also be recovered by deductions from the asylum support.[141] These provisions don't apply to the local authority interim scheme.

4.98   Section 114 limits recovery to an overpayment that is the result of 'an error on the part of the Secretary of State'. Where overpayment is due to a criminal misrepresentation by the applicant or a third party, recovery may be ordered by the court, even if there is no finding of fraud.[142] It could be argued that the overpayment provisions do not apply in a case where the overpayment is due to an innocent error on the part of the applicant and/or where there are no court proceedings.

Backdating and delays in processing claims for section 95 support

4.99   NASS has indicated that a payment should be made under IAA 1999 s96(2) as an exceptional payment where a delay in payment is caused by NASS, but is currently reviewing the question of backpayments. If NASS fails to respond to complaints, a complaint and request for compensation could be made to the Parliamentary Ombudsman.[143]

4.100   An asylum-seeker who had waited several weeks with no income after claiming NASS support, obtained permission to apply for judicial review of the delay in processing his claim for section 95 support and an injunction ordering NASS to provide subsistence and accommodation under section 98.[144] Evidence was presented of NASS delays and maladministration in other cases but NASS processed the section 95 application so the case was settled.

Other forms of support and welfare provision

Six-monthly lump sum[145]

4.101   After six months of receiving section 95 support, an asylum-seeker may claim a cash payment of £50, for each supported person. It is up to each household to make a claim, as the payment is not awarded

---

140 IAA 1999 s114 or AS Reg 17.
141 AS Reg 18.
142 IAA 1999 s112.
143 See para 3.155.
144 *R (Koch) v NASS* CO/735/01 Admin; January 2002 *Legal Action* 26.
145 AS reg 11; note that at the time of writing, NASS was ending this entitlement from June 2004.

automatically. The claim may be made every six months for as long as support is being received and a claim is made. A family with a dependent child under 18 will be eligible for it for as long as they are in the UK receiving support, even after an unsuccessful appeal. NASS may refuse to make the payment if it believes the supported person is responsible without reasonable excuse for the delay in 'the determination of his claim for asylum'.[146] The procedure is to post or fax a letter containing the NASS reference, date of asylum claim, names and dates of birth of each household member and address, signed by the asylum-seeker to the NASS Liaison Team.[147]

Provision for pregnant and nursing mothers

4.102   NASS Policy Bulletin 61: 'Pregnancy' provides guidance which includes the circumstances where NASS will delay dispersal due to pregnancy,[148] details of parts of the UK where there are services for pregnant women with HIV, and details of the maternity grant.

4.103   A supported person may claim a one-off maternity payment of £300 for themselves or their dependant if they are receiving section 95 support.[149] The claim should be made four weeks before the birth or two weeks after, with medical evidence of the expected week of confinement or an official copy of the birth certificate from the local register of births. A difficulty arises because where women are too pregnant to travel long distances they may remain in emergency accommodation on section 98 support until the child is born. An emergency payment of only £50 is paid to women who are receiving section 98 rather than section 95 support, which may be challengeable if they are not able to transfer to section 95 support shortly afterwards and claim the full grant.

4.104   A pregnant woman or woman with a child aged one to three years is entitled to an extra £3 or £5 during the first year after birth.[150] It is not paid automatically. To receive this payment, the asylum-seeker must write to NASS with evidence of the pregnancy/birth of the child, which is a change of circumstances, to ensure the provision of increased weekly support. The procedure is described in Policy Bulletin 78: 'Additional Payments to Pregnant Women and Children Aged under 3'.

---

146 AS reg 11(6).
147 Waterside Court, 471 Kirkstall Road, Leeds, LS4 2QB; fax: 0113 386 5700.
148 See para 3.198.
149 NASS Policy Bulletin 37.
150 Asylum Support (Amendment) Regulations 2003 SI No 241.

4.105   Local authorities have duties to pregnant and nursing mothers under NAA 1948 s21(1)(a).[151] The duty to provide accommodation to a pregnant or nursing mother under section 21(1)(a) will be useful where an asylum-seeker has been refused or is excluded from NASS support, for example, due to NIAA 2002 s55(1) or because her asylum claim and appeal have been refused.

4.106   A pregnant woman, or a woman with a child under one year old is entitled to an exemption certificate entitling her to free prescriptions and exemption from dental charges by applying to the Prescription Pricing Authority.[152]

4.107   NASS guidance states that it would avoid dispersing a woman in the last few weeks of pregnancy or who has medical evidence of a risk of miscarriage, in particular, where the journey would last more than four hours.[153]

Funeral costs[154]

4.108   NASS's policy is not to pay for the funeral costs of an asylum-seeker who dies while receiving NASS support on the ground that there is no power to provide for them, because they are no longer an asylum-seeker within the meaning of IAA 1999 s94(1). If a close relative of the deceased is in receipt of income support, jobseeker's allowance, housing benefit, council tax benefit or tax credits, he or she may be eligible for a social fund payment towards funeral costs.[155] If the dependant of a supported person dies, an application for a funeral payment could be applied for on the basis of exceptional circumstances under section 96(2). Otherwise, the local council's Environmental Health Department or NHS may be responsible for cremation costs.

Education and leisure[156]

4.109   AS Reg 14 makes provision for 'services' to asylum-seekers in the form of education, including English language classes and 'developmental

151   See para 6.60.
152   www.ppa.org.uk
153   Policy Bulletin 61.
154   See NASS Policy Bulletin 59.
155   Social Fund Maternity and Funeral Expenses (General) Regulations 1987 SI No 481, as amended by Social Fund Maternity and Funeral Expenses (General) Amendment Regulations 2001 SI No 3023.
156   See also para 4.67 about education provision for residents of accommodation centres who are excluded from some of the rights described below.

activities' such as sport but only 'for the purpose of maintaining good order' among supported persons. Policy Bulletin 63: Education gives an overview of education facilities for supported households, for example, pre-school children of asylum-seekers may be entitled to nursery provision from the age of three.

4.110   Asylum-seeker children of school age are entitled to primary and secondary education under Education Act 1996 s16, which places a duty on local education authorities to secure adequate places in primary and secondary schools for children residing temporarily or permanently in their area. The duty covers education appropriate to the age, aptitude, abilities and any special educational needs they may have up to the age of 16. There are two Codes of Practice on school admissions. The School Admissions Code[157] Annex B states: 'All children of compulsory school age in the UK have a right of access to education'. It goes on to refer to the children of asylum-seekers and unaccompanied asylum-seeking children as included in this right, subject to the provisions about accommodation centres.[158] The School Admissions Appeal Code[159] explains the procedures for appealing against a refusal of a school to admit a pupil but makes no reference to immigration or asylum-seeker status.

4.111   The Special Education Needs Code of Practice[160] sets out detailed procedures for the identification of special educational needs and the provisions that should be made to meet those needs. Responsible bodies, such as local education authorities, schools, government-funded nursery providers and associated agencies such as social services and health trusts have a statutory duty to have regard to the code.

4.112   Asylum-seeker parents have a duty to ensure their children receive full-time education whether by attendance at school or otherwise[161] and may face prosecution if they fail to do this. The Education Act 1996 requires local education authorities and governors of maintained schools to admit a child to the school of their parents' choice, subject to resource considerations. Parents can appeal to the relevant Admissions Authority if refused a school place. The appeal right in relation to infant classes (reception, Year 1 and Year 2) is restricted by the Education (Infant Class Sizes) (England) Regulations 1998,[162]

157 DfES/0031/2003.
158 See para 4.67 above.
159 DfES/0030/2003.
160 DfES/581/2001.
161 Education Act 1997 s7.
162 SI No 1973.

which limit the maximum number of children in a class to 30. In some parts of the country, and particularly in London, there is a shortage of school places. This problem commonly affects the children of asylum-seekers who move into an authority area between admission rounds. Local education authorities have a duty under Education Act 1996 s19 to make suitable educational provision available to a pupil who is out of school due to illness, exclusion or otherwise. Judicial review could be considered where a local education authority fails to provide either an adequate school place for an asylum-seeker child or alternative interim provision under section 19.

4.113 Local education authorities must provide free school meals to children of asylum-seekers receiving asylum support under IAA 1999 Part VI, which should include those supported by local authorities under the interim scheme.[163] Grants for school uniforms and travel passes are discretionary, but the authority should consider the exercise of its discretion fairly and taking into account the asylum-seeker child's rights under ECHR article 8 and article 14 (freedom from discrimination). Where an authority refuses assistance, reasons should be given. A local authority would also need to consider its discretion to make provision under Children Act 1989 s17 or Local Government Act 2000 s2. In making a decision, the authority would also need to take into account its general duty to promote equality of opportunity and good race relations between different racial groups,[164] which might be adversely affected if asylum-seeker pupils were stigmatised by the inability to purchase school uniform worn by British pupils. This is explained in more detail under challenges at para 4.134 below.

Further and higher education

4.114 Asylum-seekers are not eligible for Student Support, Access Funds or Hardship Loans. The Learning and Skills Council funds tuition fees on further education courses for asylum-seekers on NASS or interim support, as well as refugees and former asylum-seekers with exceptional leave to remain or discretionary leave who are in receipt of income support or JSA.[165] The college or school will require evidence of immigration status and income. Asylum-seekers aged 16–18 and people with ELR, HP or DL who do not meet the three-year residence requirement are entitled to the Learner Support Fund.

4.115 Asylum-seekers will be expected to pay university tuition fees at

163 IAA 1999 Sch 14 para 117 amended Education Act 1996 s512(3).
164 Race Relations Act 1976 s71, as amended.
165 www.lsc.gov.uk/news docs/Funding Guidance-FE.pdf

the same rate as an overseas student. People with refugee status are assessed as a home student from the date when indefinite leave is granted. People with exceptional or discretionary leave and EEA nationals or their dependants must have resided in the UK for three years preceding the course before they will be treated as a home student.[166]

Voluntary work

4.116   Asylum-seekers are entitled to do voluntary work even if they do not have permission to carry out paid work without permission from the Home Office or NASS, provided the activities are genuinely voluntary and not job substitution.[167] Policy Bulletin 72 explains NASS's position on volunteering and that it is not NASS's role to approve, or refuse to approve, any such activities. There is no clear guidance on how NASS should treat income from volunteering but it should be argued that genuine volunteer expenses for travel and meal allowances have no effect on NASS support. Asylum-seekers in accommodation centres may be required to carry out 'purposeful' voluntary work activities.

Healthcare and costs

4.117   There is a wealth of information about healthcare resources, reports about refugee health issues, and more detailed information about accessing health provision and specialist help on the internet, including the Department of Health, whose website contains guidance about entitlement to free healthcare.[168]

Free health care

Overseas visitors exempt from charges:
No charge shall be made in respect of any services forming part of the health services forming part of the health service provided for an overseas visitor, being a person, or the spouse of a person – who has been accepted as a refugee in the United Kingdom, or who has made a formal application for leave to stay as a refugee in the United Kingdom . . .[169]

---

166   Education (Fees and Awards) Regulations 1997 SI No 1972 and Education (Student Support) (No 2) Regulations 2002 SI No 195.

167   See para 1.152 for the limitations on the right to paid work.

168   See Appendix G.

169   National Health Service (Charges to Overseas Visitors) Regulations 1989 SI No 306, and see Health Service Circular HSC 1999/018 *Overseas visitors' eligibility to receive free primary care.*

4.118 Although asylum-seekers and their dependants remain entitled to free NHS care until their asylum claim or appeal has been decided,[170] these regulations have been amended to allow charges to be made potentially limiting access to hospital treatment for some failed asylum-seekers and other migrants.[171] At the time of writing there were proposals to extend these restrictions to primary care such as GP treatment. The amended regulations may be challengeable if the discretion to charge is not properly exercised taking ECHR considerations into account.

4.119 A failed asylum-seeker who has been in the UK for less than 12 months is liable to be charged for hospital treatment, but is entitled to emergency or immediately necessary healthcare.[172] There is an exception where the patient is already receiving a course of treatment. Emergency services provided at walk-in centres remain free of charge. A failed asylum-seeker is entitled if they are the spouse or a child of a person with leave to remain in the UK.[173] A failed asylum-seeker who has been lawfully resident in the UK for 12 months or more remains entitled to free treatment. EEA nationals and their family members are entitled to free healthcare without providing an E111 form. In addition, there are some reciprocal agreements between countries which entitle their citizens to free medical care if they are lawfully present in the UK, for example, citizens of the Council of Europe Social Charter countries.[174] Full-time students on a course of longer than six months are also exempt.

4.120 Accident and emergency treatment at walk-in centres is not covered by the exemption, so that migrants who are excluded from other services may receive emergency treatment there. The Department of Health has published its interpretation of the amendment regulations.[175]

4.121 The Court of Appeal has decided that an NHS Trust had the discretion to require payment in advance or an acceptable guarantee of payment from an overseas visitor for NHS treatment where a Nigerian man came to the UK for a kidney transplant which was not emergency treatment.[176]

---

170 See HC11 leaflet; www.dh.gov.uk
171 National Health Service (Charges to Overseas Visitors) (Amendment) Regulations 2004 SI No 614.
172 Ibid.
173 Ibid, reg 4(4).
174 See Appendix C.
175 www.dh.gov.uk
176 *R v Hammersmith Hospitals NHS Trust ex p Reffell* (2001) 4 CCLR 159, CA.

4.122   National Health Service Act 1977 s29 requires each Primary Care Trust (PCT) to make arrangements for the provision of medical services for all persons in its area who may wish to take advantage of the arrangements. Some asylum-seekers receive treatment under a personal medical services scheme, which is a pilot scheme for providing healthcare to asylum-seekers.

4.123   Some asylum-seekers are being asked for payment or refused healthcare, perhaps due to publicity about these changes. There are a number of cases where asylum-seeker trying to register with a GP have been asked to produce an ARC card and refused registration, or asked for payment for hospital treatment, if they do not have one. Evidence that the patient has made an asylum claim and the date of the claim should satisfy the amended regulations. This could include an immigration solicitor's letter, a Home Office letter, an old SAL1 or SAL2 or some other evidence of a past asylum claim.

Problems registering with a GP/getting treatment

4.124   If an asylum-seeker cannot find a GP to register with, telephone NHS Direct[177] (who can access interpreters via Language Line) for information about local services. The local Primary Care Trust (PCT) should have details of languages spoken by GPs and local interpreting provision. If local lists are closed, the PCT's registration department should arrange temporary allocation to a local practice for three months. The PCT has power to allocate an asylum-seeker to a GP. A GP is required to provide emergency treatment or immediate necessary treatment for a maximum of 14 days or the duration of the treatment, and so could be requested to provide an asylum-seeker with treatment as 'a temporary patient' who is not registered on their list. For basic emergency treatment, the local Walk-In Centre should help. Asylum-seekers supported by NASS can receive assistance from the One-Stop Service with accessing health care.[178] If a GP refuses to allow an asylum-seeker to register, a complaint could be made to the PCT. If the PCT fails to resolve problems in obtaining medical treatment, a complaint could be made to the Health Service Ombudsman.[179]

Free prescriptions and other charges

4.125   If a household is in receipt of asylum support, certain health benefits

---

177   Tel: 0845 4647.

178   See Appendix F.

179   See www.ombudsman.org.uk

are passported.[180] The supported person should be provided by NASS with an HC2 certificate, which allows free prescriptions, fares to and from hospital, dental treatment, sight tests, wigs and fabric supports. Vouchers for the cost of glasses or contact lenses and travel costs to and from hospital may also be available. Where prescriptions have already been paid for, a refund can be claimed within three months on form FP57, available in chemists. The HC2 lasts for six months (or 12 months for patients with HIV/AIDS). An application for a replacement then needs to be made to NASS.[181]

4.126 Where an asylum-seeker is not in receipt of NASS support, for example, because he or she has been refused support under section 55 or has lost an appeal, he or she can apply on form HC1 for an exemption from charges based on low income but will need a postal address and it may take a few weeks for the application to be processed. There is a fast-tracking system for asylum-seekers applying for an HC2. Envelopes with the relevant address or other details may be obtained from the Health Benefits Division help desk[182] or by writing to Prologistics at the Department of Health.[183] The HC1 form is available at chemists, hospitals and surgeries, Benefits Offices or from the Prescription Pricing Authority which also arranges for exemptions for mothers who are pregnant or have a child under one year old.[184]

Section 4 hard cases support[185]

4.127 IAA 1999 s4, as amended by NIAA 2002 s49 gives the Home Secretary the power to provide or arrange for the provision of facilities for the accommodation of a failed asylum-seeker and any dependant as well as an asylum-seeker with temporary admission or who has been released on bail from detention. When a claim for asylum is made, an immigration officer or the Home Office considers whether to detain the applicant or grant temporary admission. Asylum-seekers detained at Oakington are supported under section 4.[186]

180 AS Regs Sch.
181 Post Allocation Casework Unit, Casework Team 2, Voyager House, 30 Wellesley Rd, Croydon, CR9 2AA; fax: 020 8633 0213.
182 Tel: 0191 203 5555.
183 PO Box 777, London, SE1 6XN.
184 www.ppa.org.uk
185 See para 3.291 for eligibility and application procedure.
186 See further para 1.90.

4.128   Section 4 hard cases support is provided to asylum-seekers whose claim for asylum and appeal has been refused and who meet the eligibility criteria.[187] At present, a failed asylum-seeker with a dependent child under 18 would continue to be treated as an asylum-seeker entitled to section 95 support, provided that the child was born before the claim was finally determined. A failed asylum-seeker who has a child after the asylum claim is finally determined may be entitled to NAA 1948 s21 support as a nursing mother or support under Children Act 1989 s17 (provided they are not excluded by Sch 3, for example, if removal directions have been issued and see para 6.7).

4.129   There are no statutory requirements governing the adequacy or type of section 4 support and so the opportunities for challenging poor housing and food are limited, as with section 98 support. The Home Office's policy is that section 4 support is board and lodging outside London and that asylum-seekers claiming section 4 support must move from their current NASS or other accommodation.[188] An asylum-seeker wishing to challenge the quality of accommodation and food provided under section 4 would need to bring a judicial review of the decision to provide support in that way, relying on ECHR article 8 and possibly article 3. If the housing conditions were damaging to health, a complaint could be made to the local authority's environmental health department which could take enforcement action.[189] Note that Asylum and Immigration (Treatment of Claimants, etc) Act 2004 s10 allows for regulations to be introduced making IAA 1999 s4 support conditional on the supported adult's participation in community activities. It also allows for an ASA appeal on refusal or withdrawal of support.

Challenges and complaints about inadequate service provision

4.130   The first step is a letter to NASS or the local authority asking them to reconsider their decision or take relevant steps. The various methods for contacting and/or complaining about NASS are described from para 3.155 and in appendix F. If either NASS or a local authority fails to provide adequate accommodation or support, the remedy is judicial review. The limited statutory provisions governing the quality of

187 See appendix B and Policy Bulletin 71.
188 See *R (Salih and Rahmani) v SSHD* [2003] EWHC 2273 (Admin).
189 See para 5.157.

service provision make it more difficult to successfully challenge low standard provision. Despite this, the quality of provision for asylum-seekers has been improved by a combination of complaints, policy work and judicial review proceedings. Success has involved the collection of detailed evidence, reference to NASS and local authorities' published procedures, and arguments based on legal provisions outside the immediate asylum support field, backed up by the ordinary public law rules and requirement of fairness.

Human Rights Act considerations[190]

4.131　As public bodies, NASS or a local authority, including where they are using an agent to providing support on their behalf, must take into account the Human Rights Act (HRA) 1998 and European Convention on Human Rights when making decisions about NASS support. The provisions must also be taken into account by the courts and the ASA when interpreting the AS Regs and the Interim Regs. Complaints about inadequate service provision and requests to make alternative provision should include reference to relevant ECHR articles, with a request to the provider to take those articles into consideration when making a decision.

4.132　　Throughout this chapter we have referred to articles 3 (freedom from inhuman and degrading treatment) and 8 (right to respect for private and family life, home and correspondence, which is qualified to allow interference where this is necessary in a democratic society, for example, on economic grounds). The Court of Appeal has accepted that article 8 could be engaged if a property were in an extremely poor state of repair.[191]

4.133　　Other relevant ECHR articles include article 9, the right to freedom of thought, conscience and religion. The First Protocol contains article 1, which provides for the protection of property and the right to the peaceful enjoyment of possessions, and article 2 provides the right to education. All the ECHR rights must be interpreted in accordance with article 14 which prohibits discrimination, including discrimination on the ground of 'other status', which could include asylum-seeker status. HRA 1998 s8 also provides for a free-standing damages claim where there have been serious breaches of human rights (see *R (Kanidagli) v Secretary of State for the Home Department*[191a] and para

---

190　See *European Human Rights Law*, Starmer (LAG, 1999) for an in-depth explanation of the Human Rights Act and Convention.

191　*Lee v Leeds CC* [2002] 34 HLR 367.

191a　[2004] EWHC 1585 (Admin).

6.173).The Administrative Court has considered a case where a local authority was accommodating a disabled claimant and her carer in wholly inappropriate accommodation which was not adapted to meet her needs, decided there was a breach of article 8, but not of article 3, and awarded damages.[192]

Race Relations (Amendment) Act 2000[193]

4.134   The Race Relations (Amendment) Act 2000 gave public bodies such as local authorities a general duty, when carrying out their functions, to promote equality of opportunity and good relations between persons of different racial groups.[194] In addition, regulations reverse the burden of proof, placing it on the defendant in race discrimination damages claims and claims involving racial harassment.[195] Race discrimination within the meaning of the 1976 Act includes discrimination on grounds of colour, race, nationality, ethnic or national origin. The Home Office is subject to these provisions but there is an exception in relation to its immigration functions where discrimination is expressly authorised on grounds of ethnic or national origin. It is arguable that the provision of support by NASS is not an immigration function.

4.135   An individual asylum-seeker could bring a judicial review of a public authority if it considered the duty had not been complied with in a specific case or include such a complaint in other judicial review proceedings. A possible example might be if a local authority refused to exercise its discretion to provide school clothing grants to asylum-seeker children in a context where those children where clearly stigmatised and distinct from British children. In addition, the Commission for Racial Equality has power under the Act to serve a 28-day compliance notice where it considers a specific duty has not been complied with and to bring County Court proceedings within three months.

4.136   As yet, there is no authority on the use of the provisions in the context of asylum-seekers but there may be factual situations in which they are relevant and providers of support should be asked to take them into consideration.

---

192 *R (Bernard) v Enfield LBC* [2002] EWHC Admin 2282.

193 www.homeoffice.gov.uk/comrace/race/raceact/amendact.html.

194 Race Relations Act 1976 s71, as amended by Race Relations (Amendment) Act 2000.

195 Race Relations Act 1976 (Amendment) Regulations 2003 SI No 1626.

Problems with accommodation

4.137   Problems with the standard of NASS accommodation and harassment or similar complaints are discussed in chapter 5 at para 5.153 onwards. Policy Bulletin 81 gives details of the steps which should be taken where an asylum-seeker wants to complain about racial or other forms of harassment.[196] Where accommodation is damaging to the health of the household or unfit for human habitation, a complaint should first be made to the local authority's environmental health officer. If they refuse to act, an asylum-seeker could threaten judicial review to compel them to take action or bring proceedings in their own name in the magistrates' court under Environmental Protection Act 1990 s82.[197]

Judicial review

4.138   The ASA do not have jurisdiction to hear appeals about the adequacy of accommodation or the kind and level of support provided. If a supported household is provided with accommodation which is not adequate, an application for judicial review should be made of the decision by the Home Secretary (ie, by NASS decision-makers) to provide the accommodation, on the basis that he or she has failed to take into account relevant circumstances or has acted unlawfully. NASS will be represented in any such action by the Treasury Solicitor, who should be notified of any hearing.[198]

4.139   A supported person may wish to bring a challenge on the basis that the level or kind of support is inappropriate, for example, that support should be provided in cash rather than in kind due to exceptional circumstances or that more vouchers are needed because of special needs such as a diabetic diet. Again, judicial review would be the appropriate remedy.

Asylum-seekers' responsibilities and NASS's powers

4.140   NASS's provision of support under IAA 1999 is linked to the Home Office's immigration control functions by powers contained in Part VI of the Act. Support is provided subject to conditions and asylum-

---

196 See also para 3.202.
197 See chapter 5.
198 See NASS Policy Bulletin 47, Treasury Solicitor, 25 Queen Anne's Gate, London SW1; tel: 020 7210 3000; fax: 020 7210 3433.

seekers may be prosecuted if they fail to report a relevant change of circumstances.[199] NASS has wide powers to obtain and exchange information, and to enter premises. The effect of these provisions is that a
supported asylum-seeker and members of his/her household have a
duty to fully disclose to NASS any information affecting their entitlement to support. A number of criminal offences aim to deter fraud
and misrepresentation by asylum-seekers or those who seek to profit
from them. To-date, there have been few prosecutions but support is
often withdrawn by NASS on the ground of a suspected criminal
offence under IAA 1999 Part VI , for example, if the asylum-seeker is
claiming support while failing to declare that he or she is working.

Asylum-seekers' responsibilities

Conditions of support[200]

4.141   Support is provided subject to written conditions.[201] The extent to
which the household has complied with any conditions is specified as
a factor that may be taken into account in deciding the level or kind of
support to be provided.[202] A breach of conditions also allows support
to be withdrawn.[203] An example of this is that the NASS agreement
provides that travel to accommodation in the dispersal areas is a
condition of support. If an asylum-seeker fails to travel, NASS may
terminate support on the basis that conditions have been breached.
The qualification that conditions have been breached 'without reasonable excuse' applies explicitly in cases of suspension or termination of support due to breach of conditions. The question of when
support should be withdrawn due to a breach of conditions is discussed in detail in chapter 3.

4.142   The leading case on withdrawing support after an asylum-seeker
has breached conditions is *R v Kensington and Chelsea RBC ex p
Kujtim.*[204] Although this related to support provided under NAA 1948
s21, its guidance has been widely applied and approved in later NASS
and local authority interim support court decisions. It was held that
section 21 accommodation for destitute asylum-seekers should only
be withdrawn after a thorough investigation. The Court of Appeal

199 As listed at para 4.146.
200 AS Reg 19, see also para 3.170.
201 IAA 1999 s95(9) and (1).
202 AS Reg 19(1)(b).
203 AS Reg 19(1)(a), and see para 3.170.
204 [1999] 4 All ER 161; (1999) 2 CCLR 340, CA.

also indicated that a discharge of duty could only occur after a persistent refusal to comply with requirements and a warning letter. It is arguable that NASS should take these considerations into account when exercising its discretion to reduce the level of support or change the form of support.

Complying with conditions of support

4.143   A written copy of the asylum support conditions should be provided to the supported person by NASS or the local authority responsible for support and a copy could be requested if it is alleged that conditions have been breached.[205] It is reasonable for that authority to arrange for conditions to be translated into the asylum-seeker's first language or interpreted where possible, particularly for newly-arrived households. ASA decisions have generally supported this approach, depending on the circumstances. However, the Chief Asylum Support Adjudicator has found that it is an asylum-seeker's duty to ensure he or she gets assistance in getting such documents translated and this approach has not yet been challenged by judicial review.[206]

4.144   In relation to accommodation, conditions are likely to be in the form of a licence agreement. In relation to living expenses, the conditions will be based on the duty to notify change of circumstances, for example, if the asylum-seeker gets income from a job or moves house.

Notifying NASS of change of circumstances

4.145   The supported person or a dependant must notify NASS by letter or fax, without delay, of any relevant change of circumstances.[207] There are 18 relevant changes listed in AS Reg 15(2), which range from pregnancy to death.[208] If a person (not simply the applicant) does not notify relevant changes, he or she faces suspension or termination of support and/or prosecution.

4.146   In summary, the relevant changes of circumstances in relation to the supported person or a dependant are:
 – a new dependant arrives in the UK;
 – new assets/income;
 – gaining/losing employment;
 – marriage/divorce/cohabitation/separation;
 – name change;

205 IAA 1999 s95(9)–(11).
206 ASA/01/06/0434.
207 See Appendix F concerning contacting NASS.
208 See Appendix A.

- pregnancy/childbirth;
- leaving school;
- sharing accommodation with someone new;
- moving house/leaving accommodation;
- hospital/prison admission;
- leaving the UK;
- death.

There is a power to make further inquiries and request further information from the supported person or his/her dependants if NASS considers that it affects the future provision of asylum support.[209]

NASS's powers

Exchange of information about asylum-seekers

4.147   Information held by the police, the National Criminal Intelligence Service, the national crime squad, or Customs and Excise may be supplied to the Home Office for use in the provision of support to asylum-seekers.[210] Similarly, the Home Office can pass on information to those agencies.[211] The Home Secretary's aim is to obtain information from other agencies, including contractors, to identify and prosecute those who use the asylum support scheme for the purposes of fraud.[212]

Warrants under IAA 1999 s125

4.148   The Home Secretary has the power to obtain a warrant to enter accommodation which NASS has provided to a supported household. The warrant can be executed 'at any reasonable time . . . using reasonable force'. A justice of the peace may grant a warrant to a person authorised in writing by the Home Secretary, if satisfied that there is reason to believe that:

a) the supported person or any dependants of his for whom the accommodation is provided is not resident in it;
b) the accommodation is being used for any purpose other than the accommodation of the asylum-seeker or any dependants of his; or
c) any person other than the supported person and his dependants (if any) is residing in the accommodation.

209 AS Reg 15(3).
210 IAA 1999 s20.
211 IAA 1999 s21.
212 Mike O'Brien, Under Secretary of State for the Home Department, *Hansard*, HC Debates, col 499, 16 June 1999.

Information from property owners[213]

4.149　The power to obtain a warrant to forcibly enter asylum-seekers' homes is supplemented by a power to obtain information about where supported persons live. Section 126 enables the Home Secretary to obtain information from friends, relatives or others providing accommodation to asylum-seekers who are receiving cash-only support from NASS. Information may be required from any person appearing to the Home Secretary to have any interest or be involved in any way in the management or control of the accommodation.

4.150　　The Home Secretary can demand 'such information with respect to the premises and the persons occupying them as he may specify'. The only limitation is that information obtained may only be used in the exercise of his functions under IAA 1999 Part VI (the support provisions), as opposed to in the asylum and immigration decision-making process.

Information from postal services[214]

4.151　The Home Secretary may track down persons who have moved while receiving asylum support by requiring postal services to give details of any forwarding address. The terms of the power are that the information is:

a) for use in the prevention, detection, investigation or prosecution of criminal offences under this Part;
b) for use in checking the accuracy of information relating to support provided under this Part;
c) for any other purpose relating to the provision of support to asylum-seekers.

Unlike section 126, there is no limit on the use of the information obtained, provided it is obtained for one of the above purposes. So such information could be passed on to those responsible for deciding the asylum claim.

Information from financial institutions[215]

4.152　The Home Secretary may require a financial institution such as a bank or building society to supply information (such as bank statements)

213　IAA 1999 s126.
214　IAA 1999 s127.
215　NIAA 2002 s135.

about a person if NASS reasonably suspects that the person has committed an offence[216] by making false or dishonest representations to obtain asylum support.

Criminal offences

4.153   A series of criminal offences which relate to the provision of asylum support was established by IAA 1999 ss105–108. Prosecution is in the magistrates' court. The most serious offence has a maximum sentence of seven years' imprisonment.

4.154   It is not merely the asylum-seeker or applicant for support who is liable to prosecution. Any person or body corporate, such as a private landlord or housing association, may be found guilty of the offence. This renders an asylum-seeker's representative, friend, relative or housing provider potentially liable if he or she fails to pass on information. In the case of a body corporate, it will be liable if an offence has been committed with the consent or connivance of an officer (director, manager, secretary or similar) or due to his/her neglect. Both the relevant officer and the organisation may be prosecuted and sentenced.[217]

False or dishonest representations[218]

4.155   The first two offences in Part VI cover misrepresentations or failure to notify a change of circumstances. The wording reflects the misrepresentation provisions governing homeless and housing register applicants.[219] There is no express requirement in the IAA 1999 to explain to every applicant his/her duties and potential liability in ordinary language, as required by the Housing Act 1996. The ASA considered the effect of section 105(1) in an ASA appeal where support had been withdrawn after a young asylum-seeker gave incorrect information about her age and identity. The adjudicator decided that no offence had been committed under section 105(1)(a), because there had been no warning.[220]

4.156   A distinction is drawn between false and dishonest representations.

– 'False representations'[221] are where the aim is 'obtaining support for himself or any other person'. The offence is triable in the mag-

---

216 Under IAA 1999 s105(1)(a)(b) or (c) or s106(1)(a), (b) or (c).
217 IAA 1999 s109.
218 IAA 1999 ss105 and 106.
219 Housing Act 1996 ss171 and 124.
220 ASA/00/09/0061.

istrates' court, with a sentence of up to three months and/or a fine of up to scale 5 (currently £2,000). Perhaps the most notable of the new offences is section 105(c), which makes it an offence not to notify a relevant change of circumstance 'when required to do so'. AS Reg 15 imposes an onerous requirement to notify specified changes of circumstances 'without delay' (see paras 4.91 and 4.92). Asylum-seekers should be informed of these when they claim support. If there are any prosecutions under this clause, one possible defence may be that the relevant circumstances and the duty to notify were not explained to the supported person in his/her first language.

– 'Dishonest representations'[222] are where the aim is 'obtaining any benefit or other payment or advantage for himself or any other person' and the conduct must be dishonest. The sentence if tried in the magistrates' court is up to six months' imprisonment and/or the statutory maximum fine. In the case of more serious offences it can be tried in the Crown Court with imprisonment of up to seven years and/or a fine.

The section 106 'dishonest misrepresentations' offence is aimed at serious and calculated fraud 'such as where someone makes a plan to extract as much from the Home Office as possible by deception'.[223]

4.157　　In the case of either IAA 1999 s105 or s106, the person may be guilty of an offence under any one of four heads:

– making a statement or representation knowing it is false;
– producing or arranging for the production of false documents or information;
– failing to notify a change of relevant circumstances when required to do so in accordance with any provision made by or under Part VI (this is qualified by 'without reasonable excuse' in the case of false representations only);
– knowingly causing another person's failure to notify a change of relevant circumstances (without reasonable excuse in the case of s105).

Delay or obstruction

4.158　　Section 107 introduces a vague and broad offence of 'delay or obstruction without reasonable excuse', which is punishable in the magis-

221　IAA 1999 s105.
222　IAA 1999 s106.

trates' court by a fine of up to scale 3 (£1,000). Any person may be guilty of this if he or she:

a) intentionally delays or obstructs a person exercising functions conferred by or under this Part; or

b) refuses or neglects to answer a question, give any information or produce any document when required to do so in accordance with any provision made by or under this Part.

There is considerable scope for prosecuting asylum-seekers and their associates under this provision. The broad framing of the provision may indicate an aim of deterrence rather than conviction.

Failure of sponsor to maintain

4.159   Section 108 introduces the offence of a refusal or neglect of a sponsor to maintain his/her spouse or dependent relative. The failure must result in asylum support being provided and there is a defence of 'reasonable excuse' or being on strike. Sponsorship is discussed at para 1.24. The provision is aimed at cases where someone obtains leave to enter the UK on the basis of sponsorship and subsequently claims asylum. The sentence is up to three months' imprisonment and/or a fine up to level 4 (£1,500).

Challenges and complaints

4.160   The Home Office's powers may breach various articles of the ECHR, both in relation to the supported person and those who accommodate him/her including friends, relatives or voluntary sector organisations. However, as yet, there have been no challenges to these parts of the Act, for example, on the basis that they are incompatible with ECHR article 8, or article 1 of Protocol 1. The provision for issuing a warrant to enter property allows the grant of a warrant in a very wide range of circumstances and would appear challengeable if abused. Where an asylum-seeker believes any such power has been used unfairly, the Home Office's complaints procedure could be used followed by a complaint to an MP, and/or the Parliamentary Ombudsman.[224]

---

223 IAA 1999, explanatory notes, para 322.
224 See para 3.155.

Housing rights

continued

Introduction

5.1 This chapter deals with the limited rights of asylum-seekers in relation to accommodation under the Housing Act (HA) 1996 and other
'mainstream' housing legislation. The legislation making specific
accommodation provision for asylum-seekers is dealt with in chapter
4, and accommodation provision under community care law is dealt
with in chapter 6. Broadly, the Immigration and Asylum Act (IAA)
1999 excludes asylum-seekers and other persons subject to immigration control (PSIC) from entitlement to assistance as homeless persons under HA 1996 Part VII, and to the allocation of social housing
under HA 1996 Part VI. With very limited exceptions, those who
claimed asylum in the UK from 3 April 2000 are not entitled to assistance under the HA 1996, until a favourable decision is made on their
application.

5.2 However, entitlement remains for limited categories of asylum-
seekers. There is transitional protection for some asylum-seekers,
and there is a restoration of entitlement to those granted refugee
status or leave to remain. This chapter therefore considers the
entitlement to housing assistance for those with asylum decisions
pending, and those who are the subject of favourable decisions.
The IAA 1999 also removes from asylum-seekers rights of security of tenure and to protection from eviction where they are housed
under the Act.

5.3 This chapter begins with an examination of the elements of statutory provision for the homeless with particular reference to the rights
of asylum-seekers. The allocation of accommodation is then similarly treated. There is an analysis of the effects upon accommodation
rights of changes in immigration status. The chapter concludes with
a description of remedies available to asylum-seekers for poor housing conditions and harassment and a note on liability for council tax.

Homelessness and allocation under the HA 1996

5.4 The HA 1996 makes provision for securing accommodation for homeless people (Part VII) and for allocating long-term social housing to
people (Part VI).[1] Part VII[2] places duties on local authorities to assess

---

1 For a full treatment of these statutory provisions and their associated case-law,
see *Homelessness & Allocations*, Arden & Hunter (revised 6th edn, LAG, 2003).
2 In force 27 January 1997.

certain homeless applicants, and to secure accommodation for applicants meeting qualifying criteria for a limited period. Part VI[3] establishes a framework within which local authorities must allocate tenancies of their own housing stock and that of registered social landlords (including most housing associations).

5.5   The HA 1996 contains a series of restrictions on the rights of persons from abroad, including asylum-seekers. Sections of the IAA 1999 contain a parallel series of wider restrictions, and repeal the corresponding sections in the HA 1996. However, at the time of writing, the repeal has not yet been implemented, and the respective provisions have to be read together.

5.6   For those advising asylum-seekers, most problems concern two areas – whether people qualify for assistance and accommodation and, in relation to the homeless, the nature of the assistance that is provided.

Homelessness: does the local authority have a duty to assist?

5.7   Duties under Part VII are triggered when a person applies to a housing authority and the housing authority has reason to believe that he or she 'may be' homeless or threatened with homelessness.[4]

5.8   In respect of such a person, the housing authority is required to 'make such inquiries as are necessary to satisfy themselves' whether or not the person is *eligible, homeless, in priority need*, and *intentionally homeless*; the authority may also inquire about whether he or she has any *local connection*. Whether any duty is owed by the authority to the person depends on the outcome of these inquiries.

Eligibility

5.9   Eligibility is restricted on the ground of immigration status, and in the case of asylum-seekers and their dependants, additionally on the ground of accommodation available. The restrictions leave two groups of asylum-seekers eligible:

–   those given 'transitional protection' from the previous statutory scheme – a group that will diminish in time;

3   In force 1 April 1997.
4   HA 1996 s183.

- those eligible because of their nationality.

In addition, there are those who acquire eligibility through a favourable decision being made on their asylum application.

Ineligibility through immigration status

5.10 The restrictions on the ground of immigration status operate by making a general exclusion from eligibility, and then 're-including' people falling in specified classes.

5.11 An applicant who is a person from abroad is ineligible if he or she is a person subject to immigration control within the meaning of the Asylum and Immigration Act (AIA) 1996 unless he or she falls within one of certain categories specifically accorded eligibility.[5] People who are not subject to immigration control may nonetheless be ineligible if they are subject to, and do not satisfy, the habitual residence test.

5.12 By AIA 1996 s13(2), a person is subject to immigration control if he or she is a person who under the Immigration Act (IA) 1971 requires leave to enter or remain in the UK (whether or not such leave has been given). By IA 1971 ss2 and 3, all people require leave to enter or remain except:

- British citizens;
- Commonwealth citizens with right of abode;
- citizens of the Republic of Ireland;
- citizens of European Economic Area (EEA) states who are 'workers', self-employed or providing services[6] and their family members.

5.13 It should be noted that this is a wider category than the definition of 'persons subject to immigration control' who are excluded from entitlement to benefits and other welfare provision by IAA 1999 s115: the category includes all those requiring leave to enter or remain, whether or not they are subject to a condition requiring that they have no recourse to public funds.

5.14 The categories specifically accorded eligibility are Classes A to I in Homelessness (England) Regulations 2000 reg 3:[7]

Class A: Persons recorded as being refugees.

---

5 HA 1996 s185(2).
6 IA 1988 s7(1); see paras 1.19–1.20. These provisions parallel those applicable to social security benefits which are discussed in detail at paras 2.31–2.53.
7 SI No 701; see Appendix A. The same regulations are applied to Wales by the Homelessness (Wales) Regs 2000 SI No 1079.

Class B: Persons with humanitarian protection/discretionary leave to remain (HP/DLR/ELR) whose leave does not exclude them from recourse to public funds.

Class C: Persons with a current leave to enter or remain which is not subject to any limitation or condition and who are habitually resident in the Common Travel Area, other than sponsored immigrants who have been here for less than five years and whose sponsor is still alive.[8]

Class D: Persons who left Montserrat after 1 November 1995 because of the volcanic eruption.

Class E: Persons who are habitually resident in the Common Travel Area and who are either (i) lawfully present and a national of a state which has ratified the European Convention on Social and Medical Assistance (ECSMA) or the Council of Europe Social Charter (CESC), or (ii) who continue to be owed a duty that arose prior to 3 April 2000, under HA 1985 Part III (old homelessness scheme) or HA 1996 Part VII (new homelessness scheme) and who are nationals of a state which is a signatory to ECSMA or CESC. See the table in Appendix C for the states which are covered. The scope of this class may be limited – see para 5.16 below.

Class F: Asylum-seekers whose claims have been recorded by the Home Secretary as having been made on arrival (other than on re-entry) and which have not been recorded as having been decided (other than on appeal) or abandoned.

Class G: Persons who have been recorded by the Home Secretary as having claimed asylum within three months of an upheaval declaration[9] and whose claims have not been recorded as having been decided (other than on appeal) or abandoned.

Class H: Asylum-seekers who made a 'relevant claim' for asylum on or before 4 February 1996 and who were, on 4 February 1996, entitled to housing benefit under Housing Benefit (General) Regulations 1987 reg 7A (the regulation that deals with persons from abroad). A 'relevant claim' for asylum is one:
a) on which no initial decision has been recorded and which is not recorded as abandoned, or

8   In *R (Jamaali) v Haringey LBC*, it was held that family members joining a person granted refugee status under the family reunion provisions were not required to meet maintenance conditions and so were not 'sponsored'.

9   See paras 2.60–2.61.

10 Homelessness (England) Regs 2000 reg 3(2).

b) on which there has been an initial refusal decision made before 5 February 1996, but there is an appeal still pending made either before 5 February 1996 or within the relevant time limits.[10]

Class I: Persons receiving income-based jobseekers' allowance (income-based JSA) or income support (IS) (except those with limited leave to enter or remain subject to a condition that they have no recourse to public funds but who receive benefit because of a temporary interruption in the receipt of funds from abroad).

5.15 'Asylum-seekers' in Classes F, G and H above are only eligible if, additionally, they are 18 or over, and have their asylum claim recorded by the Home Secretary as being made before 3 April 2000, and that claim must not have been determined.[11] Those with asylum claims made on or after 3 April 2000 fall within the scope of National Asylum Support Service (NASS) assistance.

5.16 Considering the categories 're-included' in relation to asylum-seekers, it is to be noted that asylum-seekers may be rendered eligible under Classes F, G and H, but also under Classes E and I. However, in the case of Class E, asylum-seekers can only qualify under the subsisting homelessness duty limb (reg 3(3)(e)(ii)) since asylum-seekers have been found not to be 'lawfully present'.[12] It is to be noted also that the homelessness eligibility of asylum-seekers ends with the first decision on the asylum application: unlike asylum support, it is not extended during an appeal or by there being dependent children in the household. Furthermore, doubt has been cast on whether these regulations are effective in re-including categories of asylum-seekers: IAA 1999 s117(4) prevents people who are subject to immigration control under IAA 1999 s115 being re-included in this way. People may be taken out of the scope of section 115 for particular purposes by regulations made under section 115(3) and (4), but the Homelessness (England) Regulations 2000 are not made under these subsections; they are made under powers given to the Home Secretary by

11 Homelessness (England) Regs 2000 reg 2; in this context 'determined' should probably be taken to have the same meaning as 'decided' in relation to social security benefits, as laid down by the Court of Appeal in *R (Anufrijeva) v Secretary of State for the Home Department and Secretary of State for Social Security* [2003] UKHL 36: ie, that the Secretary of State has recorded a decision on the application and that decision has been notified to the applicant. See para 2.92.

12 *Kaya v Haringey LBC* [2001] EWCA Civ 677; [2002] HLR 1, CA; *Szoma v Secretary of State for the Department of Work and Pensions* [2003] EWCA Civ 1131; there is a possibility that this finding will be reversed, since the *Szoma* case is the subject of an appeal to the House of Lords.

13 This was argued in the county court in *Kaya v Haringey LBC* [2001] EWCA Civ

HA 1996 s185(2). Thus, it is arguable that the regulations are ultra vires.[13]

5.17 Those not subject to immigration control may nonetheless be ineligible if they do not have the 'right to reside' and satisfy the 'habitual residence test'. As noted above, certain people are not subject to immigration control:

a) British citizens;
b) Commonwealth citizens with right of abode;
c) citizens of the Republic of Ireland;
d) citizens of EEA states.

Of these, people falling within a), b) and c) all have the 'right to reside' but are ineligible unless:[14]

- they are 'habitually resident' in the Common Travel Area (the UK, Channel Islands, Isle of Man and Republic of Ireland); or
- they are receiving IS or income-based JSA; or
- they left Montserrat after 1 November 1995 because of the volcanic eruption.

For the meaning of 'right to reside' see paras 2.76–2.81 and for the meaning of 'habitually resident' see paras 2.68–2.75.

5.18 So far as citizens of EEA states are concerned, those are eligible who are within the categories of 'workers' or former 'workers', or those who have the 'right to reside' unqualified by a condition that they support themselves, or who are self-employed or providing services, plus the 'family members' of these groups.[15] See paras 2.34–2.42 for the meaning of these categories. Citizens of the eight eastern European states acceded to the EEA on 1 May 2004 ('A8 nationals') must additionally register for work under a Home Office scheme, and will be eligible only so long as they remain in employment for which they are registered. After 12 months of continuous registered employment, such A8 nationals will acquire the same rights as other EEA nationals, and cease to be required to register their employment.

---

677 but the Court of Appeal did not consider the issue.

14 HA 1996 s185(3) and Homelessness (England) Regs 2000 reg 4, as amended by Allocation of Housing and Homelessness (Amendment) (England) Regulations 2004 SI No 1235 reg 3. Note that the requirement of having a 'right to reside' in this context, in addition to satisfying the 'habitual residence test', was imposed on 1 May 2004, and does not affect an application for assistance as a homeless person made before that date. See Appendix A.

15 HA 1996 s185(3) and Homelessness (England) Regs 2000 reg 4.

16 HA 1996 s186(1).

For A8 nationals, eligibility will cease if they cease to be employed during the period they are required to register (see paras 2.44–2.45).

5.19   EEA nationals (including A8 nationals) who do not fall within these categories, that is, those who are 'not economically active' (people of working age who are neither working nor seeking work, and retired people) only have a right to reside if they are not an unreasonable burden on the social assistance system of the UK: in most cases this will mean they are prevented from having access to social housing. For the position of EEA nationals who are work-seekers, see para 2.42, and for that of A8 nationals who are work-seekers, see para 2.44.

Ineligibility through accommodation being available

5.20   There is a further hurdle placed in the path of asylum-seekers who surmount the eligibility criteria based on immigration status, above.

5.21   By HA 1996 s186, an asylum-seeker or a dependant of an asylum-seeker who is otherwise eligible is to be considered ineligible for assistance if he or she has any accommodation in the UK, however temporary, available for his/her occupation.[16] This applies only to asylum-seekers, and persons within classes A to E and I above are not affected unless they are asylum-seekers.

5.22   Under section 186, a person is an asylum-seeker from the point when his/her claim for asylum is recorded by the Home Secretary until the point where the claim is recorded by the Home Secretary as having been finally determined or abandoned and that decision is notified to the asylum-seeker.[17]

5.23   A dependant is a spouse, or a child of the asylum-seeker under 18 years, who does not him/herself have right of abode or indefinite leave to remain in the UK.[18] A person is a dependant of an asylum-seeker from the point he or she is recorded by the Home Secretary as being a dependant until the point when the Home Secretary records that he or she is no longer a dependant, or the point when the claim for asylum of the asylum-seeker whose dependant he or she is recorded as has finally been determined or abandoned and that decision is notified to the asylum-seeker.[19]

5.24   The impact of section 186 is limited by the effect of HA 1996 s175(3). In *Lismane v Hammersmith and Fulham LBC,*[20] the Court of

17   HA 1996 s186(2); see also para 2.99 for the meaning of these terms.
18   HA 1996 s186(4).
19   HA 1996 s186(3). See also para 2.99.
20   (1999) 31 HLR 427.
21   IAA 1999 s117(5) repeals HA 1996 s186, but has not yet come into force. IAA

Appeal held that an asylum-seeker who occupied temporary accommodation, which was clearly unsuitable for her needs, would qualify for housing assistance notwithstanding the provisions of HA 1996 s186(1) – a determination of her eligibility did not exclude the application of section 175(3), which required a consideration of whether the accommodation was such that it was reasonable for her to continue to occupy it.

5.25   Furthermore, it appears that HA 1996 s186 will be repealed.[21] If the government does decide to repeal section 186, whether the occupation of some form of accommodation is a bar to assistance will, for eligible asylum-seekers as for other applicants, depend on the test of homelessness under section 175 (see paras 5.30–5.34 below).

Assessing eligibility

5.26   The above rules are complex and confusing: there follows a 12-step guide to establish if an asylum-seeker is eligible for assistance as a homeless person (see table opposite). References in italics are to the detailed provisions above. The table applies to asylum-seekers who are subject to immigration control. For those not subject to immigration control, see paras 5.17–5.19 above.

Ineligible applicants

5.27   Asylum-seekers who are homeless but ineligible under the above provisions should seek assistance with accommodation from NASS (see chapter 3) or from the local authority social services department under community care legislation (see chapter 6).

5.28   The local authority's duties to provide appropriate advice and assistance to secure accommodation for applicants who are intentionally homeless or not in priority need[22] do not apply to applicants who are ineligible.

5.29   A person who is ineligible to apply may nonetheless be accommodated if there is another member of the household (or another person with whom he or she may reasonably be expected to live) who is eligible to apply. To qualify for assistance the eligible person will have to be homeless without regard to the accommodation needs of ineligible

---

1999 (Commencement No 3) Order 2000 SI No 464 implements IAA 1999 Part VI with the exception of s117(5).

22   HA 1996 ss190 and 192.

23   HA 1996 s175.

Assessing eligibility for assistance as a homeless person

	Yes	No
1 Is the asylum-seeker getting IS or income-based JSA? (*see para 5.14, Class I*)	Go on to 12	Go on to 2
2 Has the claim for asylum been determined? (*see para 5.21*)	Go on to 3	Go on to 8
3 Has it been determined by a grant of refugee status? (*see para 5.14, Class A*)	Eligible	Go on to 4
4 Has it been determined by a grant of HP/DLR/ELR (with no condition preventing recourse to public funds attached)? (*see para 5.14, Class B*)	Eligible	Go on to 5
5 Has it been refused and no appeal lodged?	Ineligible	Go on to 6
6 Has it been refused, an appeal lodged, and the appeal refused?	Ineligible	Go on to 7
7 Is it a claim which was refused before 5 February 1996 and in which an appeal was lodged within the time limits which is still pending? (*see para 5.14, Class H*)	Go on to 12	Ineligible
8 The person has a pending asylum application: was it made before 5 February 1996? (*see para 5.14, Class H*)	Go on to 12	Go on to 9
9 Was the asylum application made by a person from Sierra Leone or the Congo (formerly Zaire) within three months of 1 July 1997 (Sierra Leone) or 16 May 1997 (Congo)? (*see para 5.14, Class G*)	Go on to 12	Go on to 10
10 Was the asylum application made on arrival? (*see para 5.14, Class F*)	Go on to 11	Ineligible
11 Was the asylum application made before 3 April 2000? (*see para 5.15*)	Go on to 12	Ineligible
12 Does the asylum-seeker have any accommodation, however temporary, available for his/her occupation and which it is reasonable for him/her to continue to occupy? (*see paras 5.20–5.25*)	Ineligible	Eligible

household members (see para 5.32 below) and in priority need without reliance upon ineligible household members (see paras 5.37–5.39 below). However, where the eligible person does so qualify, the duty upon the local authority is to secure accommodation for the eligible applicant and anyone who can reasonably be expected to live with him/her – including household members who are themselves ineligible (see para 5.54 below).

Homelessness

5.30   After considering eligibility, the local authority should consider whether an applicant is homeless or threatened with homelessness. To be considered homeless[23] a person must have no accommodation available for his/her occupation in the UK or elsewhere which he or she is entitled to occupy because:

a) he or she has a legal interest (including ownership, a lease or a tenancy); or
b) he or she has a licence; or
c) he or she has a right to occupy under a court order; or
d) a statute or rule of law states that he or she can occupy or prevents another person from recovering possession from him/her.

5.31   A person may also be homeless because:

e) his/her home is a boat, caravan or similar and he or she has nowhere to moor or park it; or
f) although he or she has accommodation under a) to d) above, he or she cannot secure entry to it; or
g) although he or she has accommodation under a) to d) above, it would not be reasonable for him/her to continue to occupy it.

A person is threatened with homelessness if it is likely that he will become homeless within 28 days.

5.32   Particular issues need to be considered in deciding whether asylum-seekers are homeless or threatened with homelessness:

– The standard of homelessness is in effect made more stringent for asylum-seekers and their dependants by HA 1996 s186 (discussed at paras 5.21–5.25), excluding from assistance any person who has 'any accommodation however temporary available for his occupation'. Strictly, this requirement would exclude asylum-seekers

24 *Begum v Tower Hamlets LBC* (2000) 32 HLR 445.

from eligibility rather than result in their being considered 'not homeless'.

- The definition of homelessness refers to the availability of accommodation in the UK 'or elsewhere': in practice, asylum-seekers with pending applications or appeals will not be considered to have accommodation available in the country they have fled from, although this may be an issue if they have entered the UK from a third country where they have accommodation. If a person cannot afford to travel to the accommodation which it would otherwise be reasonable for him/her to continue to occupy, then that factor would make it unreasonable to occupy the accommodation.[24]

- Accommodation will only be considered to be available for occupation if it is available for occupation by the applicant and any other person who usually resides with him/her as a family member or any other person who might reasonably be expected to reside with him/her. However (and this has particular importance for asylum-seekers who are joined in the UK by, or who are themselves joining, other family members), it should be noted that any ineligible person is to be disregarded in deciding whether an applicant is homeless or threatened with homelessness.[25] Thus, to qualify as homeless, an applicant must be without accommodation for him/herself and eligible members; the accommodation needs of ineligible persons are ignored in deciding whether the eligible applicant has accommodation available for occupation. For example, accommodation will not 'cease to be available' to an applicant in circumstances where he or she has a right to occupy it but is not permitted (say, under the terms of the tenancy agreement) to have living with him/her family members who themselves are ineligible for assistance. Similarly, it will not be unreasonable for an applicant to continue to occupy accommodation if it is suitable for single occupation but too small for him/her to live in with family members who themselves are ineligible for assistance. Similar rules apply to proving priority need – see para 5.35 below. However, where the eligible applicant does so qualify as homeless and in priority need, the duty upon the local authority is to secure accommodation for the eligible applicant and anyone who can reasonably be expected to live with her/him – including household members who are themselves ineligible (see para 5.54 below).

25   HA 1996 s185(4).
26   SI No 704; see Appendix A.

5.33   Where an applicant is not homeless under these rules, but being joined in the accommodation by an ineligible spouse, partner or dependants results in the accommodation becoming inadequate (for example, overcrowded), then the household will be eligible for accommodation under the asylum support provisions. Assistance is provided depending on whether the existing accommodation is 'adequate', applying IAA 1999 ss95–96 and Asylum Support Regulations 2000 (AS Regs) reg 8.[26]

5.34   A particular problem arises for those granted refugee status or ELR, HP or DLR if their NASS accommodation remains available for them after the decision is made on their application. In some cases, NASS accommodation in dispersal areas – especially hard-to-let public sector properties in areas of low housing demand – may not be terminated with the grant of leave to remain. Families who leave such accommodation and, for example, apply as homeless to London authorities, are likely to be found not to be homeless (or, if the accommodation then ceases to be available, intentionally homeless – see paras 5.44–5.48 below). For such families the only recourse (apart from return) will be, in exceptional cases, to argue that the dispersed accommodation was not reasonable for the family to continue to occupy.

Priority need

5.35   Only those applicants with a priority need for accommodation fall within the local authority's duty to secure accommodation. The following have a priority need for accommodation:[27]

a) a pregnant woman or a person with whom she resides or might reasonably be expected to reside;

b) a person with whom dependent children reside or might reasonably be expected to reside;

c) a person who is vulnerable as a result of old age, mental illness, handicap or physical disability or other special reason, or with whom such a person resides or might reasonably be expected to reside;

d) a person who is homeless or threatened with homelessness as a result of an emergency such as flood, fire or other disaster;

27 HA 1996 s189; Homeless Persons (Priority Need) (Wales) Order 2001 SI 2001 No 607 (W30) (in force, 1 March 2001); Homelessness (Priority Need for Accommodation) (England) Order 2002 SI 2002 No 2051 (in force 31 July 2002).

28 Homelessness Code of Guidance for Local Authorities (England) (DoH/ODPM,

e) in England only:
  i) a person who is 16 or 17 years old, and who is not a 'relevant child' for the purposes of local authority duties under Children Act 1989 s23A (certain 16–17 year olds formerly looked after by a local authority), or owed duties under CA 1989 s20 (16–17 year olds currently looked after by a local authority);
  ii) a person who is 18–20 years old and has been in care (as defined by Children Act 1989 s24(2), as amended), or 21 years and over who has become vulnerable as a result of being in care;
  iii) a person who is vulnerable as a result of ceasing to occupy accommodation by reason of violence from another person, or threats of violence from another person which are likely to be carried out;
  iv) a person who is vulnerable as a result of having been a member of the armed forces;
  v) a person who is vulnerable as a result of having been in custody (by way of either sentence, or committal, or remand);
f) in Wales only:
  i) a person who is 16 or 17 years old;
  ii) a person who is 18–20 years old and who either is at particular risk of sexual or financial exploitation, or has been in care at any time;
  iii) a person who has been subject to domestic violence, or is at risk of domestic violence, either now or if he or she returns home;
  iv) a person who formerly served in the armed forces and has been homeless since leaving those forces;
  v) a person who is a former prisoner who has been homeless since leaving custody and has a local connection with the local authority.

5.36 Particular issues need to be considered in deciding whether asylum-seekers have a priority need. It is to be noted that the Code of Guidance[28] makes specific reference to the possibility that former asylum-seekers may be vulnerable as a result of persecution in their country of origin and severe hardship in their efforts to reach the UK.

5.37 As with the test of homelessness, an applicant is not entitled to rely on persons who are ineligible for housing assistance to establish

July 2002) para 8.33.
29 HA 1996 s185(4) and see *R (Morris) v Westminster City Council* (2003) 13

a priority need.[29] Thus, an eligible applicant who has living with him a pregnant wife or dependent children who are themselves ineligible cannot rely on their residence with him to give him a priority need for accommodation. (In the example of the pregnant wife, once the child is born in the UK the father would be in priority need, since the child would not be ineligible.[30]) Similarly, an applicant who lives with and cares for an elderly or disabled person who is him/herself ineligible for housing assistance will not thereby acquire priority need.[31]

5.38   Where an applicant is not in priority need under these rules, but being joined in the accommodation by an ineligible spouse, partner or dependants results in the accommodation becoming inadequate (for example, overcrowded), then the household will be eligible for accommodation under the asylum support provisions. Assistance is provided depending on whether the existing accommodation is 'adequate', applying AS Regs reg 8.[32]

5.39   Asylum-seekers who have no dependent children or no eligible dependent children may themselves qualify as being in priority need in their own right. Many asylum-seekers will satisfy the test of being vulnerable as a result of old age, mental illness, handicap or physical disability or other special reason. A person is 'vulnerable' when he is, when 'homeless, less able to fend for himself than an ordinary homeless person so that injury or detriment to him will result when a less vulnerable man would be able to cope without harmful effects'.[33] It is to be construed in a housing context, and thus means less able to fend for oneself in funding and keeping accommodation.[34] While lack of English[35] or lack of money will not by itself amount to vulnerability, a combination of factors is capable of amounting to 'other special reason'.[36] Asylum-seekers who fall short of 'mental illness or handicap or physical disability' are nonetheless likely to exhibit a variety of

October, unreported.

30 See para 1.94.

31 At the time of writing, an application for a declaration that these provisions are incompatible with ECHR article 14 is pending in the High Court in the case of *R (Morris) v Westminster City Council* [2003] EWHC 2266 (Admin).

32 See Appendix A.

33 *R v Camden LBC ex p Pereira* (1999) 31 HLR 317, CA.

34 *R v Kensington and Chelsea RLBC ex p Kihara* (1996) 29 HLR 147, CA; *R v Bath CC ex p Sangermano* (1984) 17 HLR 94; *R v Lambeth LBC ex p Carroll* (1987) 20 HLR 142.

35 *R v Bath CC ex p Sangermano* (1984) 17 HLR 94.

36 *R v Kensington and Chelsea RLBC ex p Kihara* (1996) 29 HLR 147, CA.

37 See Homelessness Code of Guidance for Local Authorities (England)

factors which would be relevant to 'other special reason', such as post-traumatic stress disorder, the effects of torture and detention, and the loss of family members.[37]

5.40   Dependent children cannot make an application as homeless in their own right,[38] but their birth or presence in the household may give rise to priority need, where one of the adults in the household is eligible.

5.41   Asylum-seekers who are 16 or 17 years old and (in England) are either 'relevant children' or are currently in care will have their accommodation needs met by the local authority under the Children Act (CA) 1989 (see paras 6.123–6.153) or under the Children (Leaving Care) Act 2000 (see paras 6.132–6.153). Care leavers who are 18 to 20 will have priority need in Wales and – if vulnerable as a result – in England – see para 5.35 (e)(ii) and (f)(ii) above. This will include those asylum-seekers who arrived as unaccompanied minors, are granted leave to remain and have until now been looked after by the local authority (see para 6.132).

5.42   Again, where the eligible homeless applicant is in priority need, the duty upon the local authority is to secure accommodation for the eligible applicant and anyone who can reasonably be expected to live with her/him – including household members who are themselves ineligible (see para 5.54 below).

5.43   If an applicant is homeless or threatened with homelessness, but not in priority need, only limited duties are owed to her/him (see para 5.57 below).

Intentional homelessness

5.44   A person becomes intentionally homeless if he or she deliberately does or fails to do anything in consequence of which he or she ceases to occupy accommodation which is available for his/her occupation and which it would have been reasonable for him/her to continue to occupy.[39] The act or omission will not be considered 'deliberate' if the person was unaware of any relevant fact and acted or failed to act in good faith.[40]

5.45   In relation to asylum-seeker applicants it should be noted that a

(DoH/ODPM, July 2002), para 8.33.

38   *R v Oldham MBC ex p Garlick* [1993] AC 509, 25 HLR 319, HL.

39   HA 1996 s191(1).

40   HA 1996 s191(2).

41   HA 1996 s175(1).

person may be intentionally homeless by leaving accommodation abroad,[41] although in practice local authorities are unlikely to conclude that an asylum-seeker is intentionally homeless for leaving accommodation in the country he or she is fleeing from, while an asylum application is pending.

5.46   Findings of intentional homelessness are likely to be more common where asylum-seekers have left accommodation in areas they have been dispersed to, either before or after a decision on their asylum application. It should be noted that the test of whether or not such a person is intentionally homeless is different from the test of 'intentional destitution' that would be applied if the person were to re-apply to NASS or for local authority interim support: 'intentional homelessness' refers only to the act or omission of the applicant, while 'intentional destitution' may arise from the act or omission of any dependant.[42]

5.47   Applicants who are in priority need but intentionally homeless are owed only limited duties[43] (see para 5.57).

5.48   Applicants found intentionally homeless but not in priority need are entitled only to 'appropriate' advice and assistance.

Local connection

5.49   The local connection provisions are considered below (see paras 5.69–5.80).

Homelessness: what are the duties owed?

Temporary accommodation pending decision

5.50   A person who applies as homeless to a local authority may be entitled to temporary accommodation while the authority enquires into his/her case. By HA 1996 s188(1):

> If the local housing authority have reason to believe that an applicant may be homeless, eligible for assistance and have a priority need, they shall secure that accommodation is available for his occupation pending a decision as to the duty (if any) owed . . .

---

42   HA 1996 s191; AS Regs reg 20(2); Asylum Support (Interim Provisions) Regs 1999 SI No 3056 reg 7(2); see paras 3.112–3.116.

43   HA 1996 s190.

44   HA 1996 ss205(1), 206(1); *R v Ealing LBC ex p Surdonja* (1999) 31 HLR 686. See

5.51   Such accommodation must be suitable[44] for the applicant and anyone else who can reasonably be expected to live with the applicant (including 'ineligible persons' – see para 5.54 below). The extent to which particular temporary accommodation must suit an applicant's needs will vary according to how long it is occupied.[45] Bed and breakfast accommodation is commonly used despite guidance that it should only be considered as a 'last resort' and that it is unsuitable for families with children.[46] The particular circumstances of asylum-seekers may render such accommodation unsuitable even in the short-term, but compelling evidence would be required to challenge such a decision.[47] The practice of local authorities to simply allocate whatever accommodation is available on the day an applicant becomes homeless, without regard to individual needs, is unlawful.[48]

5.52   The authority may not refer the applicant to another authority for accommodation under this section, but may nonetheless itself find temporary accommodation for the applicant outside its own area.

The 'full housing duty'

5.53   If the authority is satisfied that an applicant is homeless, eligible, in priority need and not intentionally homeless then a duty arises to ensure that accommodation is available to the applicant.[49]

5.54   The duty is to secure that accommodation is available for the applicant and anyone else who usually resides with the applicant as a family member, or anyone else who can reasonably be expected to live with the applicant.[50] 'Anyone else' here includes persons subject to immigration control who would fail the eligibility requirement in HA 1996 s185: once an applicant is owed the housing duty, that duty extends to securing accommodation for the whole of his/her household whether or not they are eligible. The accommodation will be temporary accommodation, since such accommodation cannot be let on a secure or assured tenancy. However, in many local authority areas, an offer of permanent accommodation under HA 1996 Part VI

also para 5.59 onwards.

45 *R v Exeter CC ex p Gliddon* (1984) 14 HLR 103.

46 DoE/DoH Code of Guidance on Housing Act 1996 Parts 6 and 7, para 20.2; see para 5.59 onwards.

47 *R v Newham LBC ex p Sacupima* [2001] 33 HLR 1 and 18.

48 *R v Newham LBC ex p Sacupima* [2001] 33 HLR 1 and 18.

49 HA 1996 s193(2).

50 HA 1996 s176.

51 HA 1996 s193(3) and (5)–(8).

will follow, depending on supply and the local allocation policy – see paras 5.83–5.100 below.

5.55   The duty continues until terminated by one of a series of specified events[51] whereby the temporary accommodation secured is refused, or intentionally lost, or the applicant ceases to occupy it, or the applicant accepts or refuses to accept Part VI accommodation, or in certain circumstances the applicant accepts an offer of an assured shorthold tenancy. The duty also ends if the applicant ceases to be eligible.

5.56   The accommodation secured must be 'suitable' – see paras 5.59–5.68 below.

Other housing duties

5.57   If an applicant is homeless and in priority need, but found intentionally homeless, the authority has a duty under HA 1996 s190(2) to:[52]

(a) secure that accommodation is available for his occupation for such period as they consider will give him a reasonable opportunity of securing accommodation for his occupation; and
(b) provide him with such advice and assistance as they consider appropriate in the circumstances in any attempts he may make to secure that accommodation becomes available for his occupation.

The provision of advice and assistance must follow an assessment of housing need.[53] It is common for local authorities to allow a 28-day period in all cases, but it is arguable that all cases should be considered individually according to need; for instance, an asylum-seeker family with children in London would arguably require a longer period to afford the 'reasonable opportunity'. Accommodation secured under section 190(2)(a) must be 'suitable' (see paras 5.59–5.68 below).

5.58   If an applicant is homeless (whether or not intentionally), but not in priority need, the authority owes the 'advice and assistance' duty described in section 190(2)(b).[54] It should be noted that NASS guidance[55] states that such applicants will be expected to take advantage of such advice and assistance, and to take reasonable steps to find alternative accommodation, before they will be entitled to the provision of accommodation by NASS. Local authorities have a power (not a duty)

---

52 HA 1996 s190.
53 HA 1996 s192(4).
54 HA 1996 ss190(3) and 192.
55 NASS Policy Bulletin 11.
56 Homelessness Code of Guidance for Local Authorities (England) HMSO July

to secure accommodation for such applicants who are not intentionally homeless. There is guidance[56] on when this power should be exercised, but no duty on local authorities to give written decisions or reasons for decisions not to exercise the power, and no right of review of such a decision.

Suitability of accommodation

5.59   Accommodation secured by the local authority must be suitable[57] for the applicant and anyone else who usually resides with the applicant as a family member, or anyone else who can reasonably be expected to live with the applicant.[58] Again, 'anyone else' here includes persons who would fail the eligibility requirement in HA 1996 s185.

5.60   In determining what is suitable, the authority must have regard to HA 1996 Parts IX, X and XI (slum clearance, overcrowding and houses in multiple occupation).[59] Lord Hoffmann in *Awua v Brent LBC*[60] observed that:

> ... [t]his points to suitability being primarily a matter of space and arrangement, though no doubt other matters (such as whether the occupant can afford the rent) may also be material.

In *R v Newham LBC ex p Sacupima*,[61] the Court of Appeal held that the location of accommodation was relevant to its suitability. The use of privately-owned or managed bed and breakfast accommodation will not be considered suitable for families including dependent children or pregnant women for more than a six-week period, or if any other accommodation is available.[62] In this context, 'bed and breakfast accommodation' means accommodation where more than one household shares toilet, washing or cooking facilities.[63]

5.61   The obligation to secure accommodation that is suitable is a continuing one, but there will need to be a change of circumstances to

---

2002, chapter 14.

57   HA 1996 ss193 and 206.

58   HA 1996 s176.

59   HA 1996 s210.

60   [1996] 1 AC 55; (1996) 27 HLR 453.

61   (2001) 33 HLR 18.

62   Homelessness (Suitability of Accommodation) (England) Order 2003 SI No 3326; in force 1 April 2004.

63   Homelessness (Suitability of Accommodation) (England) Order 2003 para 2.

64   *R (Zaher) v Westminster City Council* [2003] EWHC 101 (Admin), 28 January,

trigger a duty on the housing authority to reconsider the suitability of accommodation already provided.[64]

5.62   The circumstances of asylum-seekers may give rise to special consideration in relation to suitability. For example, the courts have quashed suitability decisions where an asylum-seeker refused a basement estate flat which reminded her of a prison where she had been tortured,[65] and where an asylum-seeker refused an offer where she would be in contact with Turkish and Kurdish communities in circumstances where she had a genuine terror of such contact and where her daughter's mental health would be damaged by acceptance.[66]

5.63   So far as is reasonably practicable, authorities must accommodate the homeless person within their own district.[67] Authorities should have regard to the importance of housing homeless people as close as possible to where they previously lived so that they can keep the same schools, doctors, social workers, etc.[68] These requirements are modified in the case of asylum-seekers.

Suitability of accommodation for asylum-seekers

5.64   In addition to the above factors, local authorities are directed to consider particular factors in relation to asylum-seekers when considering suitability of accommodation.[69] The authority:

   (a) shall also have regard to the fact that the accommodation is to be temporary pending determination of the applicant's claim for asylum; and
   (b) shall not have regard to any preference that the applicant, or any person who might reasonably be expected to reside with him, may have as to the locality in which the accommodation is to be secured.

5.65   HA 1996 s210(1A) has the effect that the accommodation must be suitable as temporary accommodation. The decision in *Lismane v Hammersmith and Fulham LBC*[70] would, however, still apply to this accommodation (see para 5.24 above). Section 210(1A) excludes mere

---

   unreported.
65 *R v Brent LBC ex p Omar* (1991) 23 HLR 446.
66 *R v Haringey LBC ex p Karaman* (1997) 29 HLR 366.
67 HA 1996 s208.
68 Code of Guidance paras 21.15–2.19.; see also *R (Yumsak) v Enfield LBC* [2002] EWHC 280 6/2/2002.
69 HA 1996 s210(1A), as amended by Homelessness (Asylum-seekers) (Interim Period) (England) Order 1999 SI No 3126; see Appendix A.
70 (1999) 31 HLR 427.
71 HA 1996 s208(1); it is submitted that s208(1A) should not apply in such cases.

accommodation preferences from consideration. It does not, however, permit the housing authority to disregard real welfare considerations which relate to the location of accommodation, for example, its proximity to medical assistance, social support and the like.

5.66 It is arguable that where the applicant is an eligible person who is not an asylum-seeker and he or she is to be housed with family or household members who are asylum-seekers, the authority in considering the provision of accommodation should not apply the restrictions on suitability applicable to asylum-seeker applications (section 210 as amended) and should secure accommodation in its district so far as is reasonably practicable.[71] This issue has yet to be decided by the courts.

5.67 The requirement upon local authorities to house homeless people within their area where practicable (see para 5.63 above) is modified in the case of asylum-seekers: the requirement is removed where another housing authority has agreed in writing that the first authority can secure accommodation for all or an agreed number of asylum-seekers in its area.[72] Nonetheless, the requirements as to suitability (as modified in the case of asylum-seekers) still apply.

5.68 If there is no agreement in writing with another housing authority, authorities can still house asylum-seeker applicants outside their area, but will need to be satisfied that it was not reasonably practicable to house them within the area.[73]

Referral of the housing duty through 'local connection' to another authority

Referral of persons who are not asylum-seekers

5.69 In the case of homeless applicants who are not asylum-seekers, where a person is owed the full housing duty, the authority can transfer the duty to house to another housing authority, by 'referring' the case.[74] The 'conditions for referral' are given in HA 1996 s198(2):

(2) The conditions for referral of the case to another authority are met if:
    (a) neither the applicant nor any person who might reasonably be expected to reside with him has a local connection with the district of the authority to whom his application was made;

---

72 HA 1996 s208(1A).
73 HA 1996 s208.
74 HA 1996 s198(1).
75 *R v Eastleigh BC ex p Betts* [1983] 2 AC 613; (1983) 10 HLR 97, HL.

    (b) the applicant or a person who might reasonably be expected to reside with him has a local connection with the district of that other authority; and

    (c) neither the applicant nor any person who might reasonably be expected to reside with him will run the risk of domestic violence in that other district.

(2A) But the conditions of referral mentioned at subsection (2) are not met if:

    (a) the applicant or any person who might reasonably be expected to reside with him has suffered violence (other than domestic violence) in the district of the other authority; and

    (b) it is probable that the return to that district of the victim will lead to further violence of a similar kind against him.

5.70   The term 'local connection' is defined in HA 1996 s199 and the duties on referring and target authorities are set out more fully in HA 1996 s200.

5.71   Asylum-seekers who are granted refugee status or HP, DLR or ELR are likely to be particularly affected by the 'local connection' provisions. Typically, a person has been dispersed under NASS asylum support or local authority interim support, and that accommodation is terminated upon the change of immigration status, whereupon the person applies to a London local authority. If accepted as owed the full housing duty by the London authority, that person would stand to be referred back to the dispersal area authority for housing if he or she could not establish that he or she or anyone who could reasonably be expected to reside with him/her:

a) had a local connection with the London borough in question, and

b) where there is no such connection, had no local connection with the area of the authority to which he or she had been dispersed.

In either case, local connection is defined by HA1996 s199: a person has a local connection with an authority area if he or she meets one of four criteria:

– he or she is or was in the past usually resident in it, and his/her residence is or was of his/her own choice;

– he or she is employed in it;

– he or she has family associations;

– there are special circumstances.

5.72   These criteria are developed in the Code of Guidance chapter 16, and the Local Authority Association Joint Local Connection Agreement contains guidelines for resolving disputes between local authorities as to where homeless persons have local connections. The criteria and the guidance are not to be applied rigidly however, so that the ordinary meaning of the term 'local connection' is lost.[75] The material time for considering whether the local connection conditions are satisfied is the date of decision, or the date of review (even if the applicant has acquired or lost local connection in the meantime).[76]

5.73   In the typical case of people granted refugee status or HP, DLR or ELR, referred to above, it should be noted that 'normal residence' must be of choice, and accommodation provided under the dispersal provisions of the IAA 1999 or the referral provisions of the HA 1996 is not capable of being regarded as of the asylum-seeker's choice.[77] So decided the House of Lords in *Al-Ameri v Kensington & Chelsea RLBC; Osmani v Harrow LBC*: in both cases, the applicants had left dispersed NASS accommodation in Glasgow and applied to the defendant authorities. The authorities accepted housing duties but sought to refer them to Glasgow City Council. The House of Lords held that there could not be residence of choice in circumstances where by IAA 1999 s97(2), NASS was forbidden to have regard to the preferences of the applicants. Guidance to local authorities suggests that 'normal residence' will be established by residence for six months of the last 12 months, and that 'family associations' will exist where there are parents, adult children, brothers or sisters residing for at least five years in the area in question. The criterion of 'other special circumstance' leaves open a wide range of considerations that may give rise to a local connection. However, the government has to reverse the effect of the decision in *Al Ameri*. At the time of writing the Asylum and Immigration (Treatment of Claimants, etc) Act 2004 has been enacted but no commencement date has been set. Section 11 of the Act amends s199 of the Housing Act 1996 to provide that a person will have a local connection with the district of a housing authority if s/he was (at any time) provided with accommodation in that district under s95 of IAA 1999. The effect of this will be that applicants will stand to be referred back to their dispersal area for housing unless they can establish a local connection in the area of the authority to which they apply. For those who were dispersed to Scotland and apply to authorities in England and Wales, s11 will have the effect of removing the full housing duty under s193, and replacing it with a discretion to provide accommodation for

---

76 *Mohamed v Hammersmith & Fulham LBC* [2001] UKHL 57.

77 *Al-Ameri v Kensington & Chelsea RLBC; Osmani v Harrow LBC* [2004] UKHL 4; [2004] 1104; the case concerned NASS dispersal accommodation, but the same is likely to apply to asylum-seekers referred under s198(4A) and (4B). See also *Sarac v Camden LBC*, April 2002 *Legal Action* 28, Central London County Court.

78 See paras 4.17–4.54.

a period giving the applicant a reasonable opportunity of finding accommodation, plus advice and assistance in doing so. It would thus be open to such applicants to re-apply in Scotland.

Referral of asylum-seekers

5.74   In the case of homeless applicants who are asylum-seekers, the position is modified. Provision for asylum-seekers under NASS asylum support and local authority interim support includes machinery for the dispersal of applicants to accommodation outside London and the south east.[78] Parallel provision has been made for applicants as homeless under the HA 1996 by extending the referral conditions in section 198. The conditions for referral made it difficult for housing authorities to refer persons from abroad elsewhere, even when such persons had no connection with the housing authority's area. The reason for this was that such persons would also often not have a local connection with any other housing authority. Such persons had to remain the responsibility of the housing authority to whom they applied and this was perceived as imposing a disproportionate burden on housing authorities in London and those near ports of entry to the UK.[79] Accordingly, section 198 was amended.[80]

5.75   These amendments make it possible to refer asylum-seekers to other housing authorities:

- irrespective of whether the asylum-seeker or any person residing with her/him has a local connection with the area of any local authority; and
- irrespective of any preference that the asylum-seeker or a person residing with him/her might express.

5.76   The only conditions for referral in the case of asylum-seekers are that the two housing authorities concerned have agreed in writing that a referral should take place and neither the asylum-seeker nor any person who might reasonably be expected to reside with him/her runs the risk of domestic or other violence[81] in the district of the other authority.

5.77   In deciding whether or not to refer, the housing authority concerned will be expected to act rationally in a public law sense. That

79   *R v Hillingdon LBC ex p Streeting* [1980] 1 WLR 1425 at 1429.

80   IAA 1999 s169(2) and Sch 15 para 13, and Homelessness (Asylum-seekers) (Interim Period) (England) Order 1999 SI No 3126, amending s198 by adding s198(4A) and (4B).

81   Defined in HA 1996 s177, as amended by Homelessness Act 2002 s10.

82   See guidance on Homelessness (Asylum-seekers) (Interim Period) (England)

probably means that it would have to have regard at least to relevant considerations such as a need for local medical treatment or reliance upon support from locally-resident family members that might make it unreasonable to refer the asylum-seeker to another authority.[82]

5.78 The authority to which an asylum-seeker is referred would also have to act rationally in that sense and would also be under the duty to provide 'suitable accommodation' under sections 206 and 210, as amended (see paras 5.59–5.68 above).

5.79 It should be noted that the referral provisions apply only to applicants owed the full housing duty, and not to applicants in temporary accommodation pending a decision.[83] Accommodation provided under HA 1996 s188 must be provided by the housing authority itself, although it can nevertheless be outside the housing authority's own district.

5.80 It is to be noted that the amendments to section 198 described in this section stand to be repealed when IAA 1999 s117(5) comes into force and, in practice, the group of asylum-seekers currently affected by them is small.

Homelessness: applications and decisions

Applications

5.81 A homeless person may apply to any local housing authority (borough councils in cities, and district councils elsewhere). A person does not have to apply to the authority where he or she is or was last living; however, upon a decision being made on the application, an authority may refer the applicant to another authority for housing – see paras 5.69–5.73 above. Authorities will not in practice accept applications where an applicant has an application pending with another authority.

Order 1999 SI No 3126 issued by the DETR on 22 November 1999 under HA 1996 s182. The following guidance issued to local authorities is relevant to the implementation of these provisions: 'Guidance Note to Local Authorities in England and Wales – Interim Arrangements for Asylum-seeker Support' (Local Government Association); letter from Home Office Immigration and Nationality Directorate to all chief executives of local authorities in England and Wales concerning IAA 1999 and Asylum Support (Interim Provisions) Regs 1999, dated 19 November 1999.

83 See guidance issued by the DETR dated 22 November 1999 to the Homelessness (Asylum-seekers) (Interim Period) (England) Order 1999 SI No 3126.

84 HA 1996 s184.

Decisions

5.82   Authorities must make inquiries and on their completion notify the applicant in writing of their decision, with reasons for any adverse finding.[84] The decision letter must advise the applicant of his/her right to request a review and of the time limit for doing so.[85] These requirements apply to decisions about homelessness, eligibility, priority need, intentional homelessness and local connection, but they do not apply to a decision that an offer of accommodation is suitable. For remedies available in the case of an adverse homelessness decision, see paras 5.102–5.105 below.

Allocation

What is allocation?

5.83   HA 1996 Part VI governs the 'allocation' of housing accommodation by local housing authorities.

5.84   A housing authority 'allocates' accommodation when it selects a person to be a secure or introductory tenant of council accommodation; nominates a person to be a secure or introductory tenant of other accommodation (for example, owned by a body that can grant a secure or introductory tenancy, such as a housing action trust); or nominates a person to be an assured tenant of a registered social landlord.[86] Note, however, that the grant of a tenancy by a local authority (but not the nomination of a person to be an assured tenant of a registered social landlord), which is made in order to provide accommodation under the asylum support provisions of IAA 1999 is not an allocation under HA 1996 Part VI.[87] Allocation includes a transfer made at the request of an existing tenant. For the granting of tenancies or other rights of occupation in local authority housing stock falling outside the scope of allocation under HA 1996 Part VI, see paras 5.109–5.112 below.

5.85   The allocation of accommodation must take place in accordance with rules as to priorities and procedure devised by the housing authority and set out in its 'allocation scheme'.[88] The schemes are

85   HA 1996 s184(5).
86   HA 1996 s159.
87   HA 1985 Sch 1 para 4A, as amended by IAA 1999 Sch 14 para 81.
88   HA 1996 s167.
89   HA 1996 s166(3).

usually 'points based'. The authority must consider applications made to it.[89] Since 31 January 2003, authorities are no longer under a duty to keep a housing register, but all persons on the housing register at that date are considered to have applied for accommodation.[90]

Eligible persons

5.86 A housing authority may only allocate accommodation to 'eligible persons'.[91] Most asylum-seekers are not eligible persons and so cannot obtain public sector accommodation unless and until they are granted refugee status or HP, DLR or ELR in the UK. Eligible persons are not excluded by the presence of ineligible persons in the household.[92]

5.87 An applicant may be ineligible either through the direct provisions of HA 1996 s160A, or by regulations made thereunder, or by the exercise of powers given to local authorities under that section to treat persons as ineligible. These powers enable local authorities to decide that an applicant is ineligible on the ground that he or she is guilty of unacceptable behaviour making them unsuitable to be a tenant.[93] The inclusion or exclusion of persons from abroad for the purposes of allocation of public housing is regulated along similar lines to the scheme for homeless people described at paras 5.9–5.25 above. There is a general exclusion of all persons subject to immigration control, modified by the 're-inclusion' of people falling within classes specified in regulation. The general exclusion does not apply to transfer applicants.[94]

5.88 Persons subject to immigration control within the meaning of the AIA 1996 can only be eligible persons if they come within a prescribed class[95] and they are not excluded from entitlement to Housing Benefit by IAA 1999 s115.[96] Persons who are not subject to immigration control may nonetheless be ineligible if they are subject to, and do not satisfy, the habitual residence test.[97] Where a local authority

---

90 Homelessness Act 2002 s14(3).
91 HA 1996 s160A.
92 But see para 5.100.
93 HA 1996 s160A(7).
94 HA 1996 s160A(6).
95 HA 1996 s160A(1), (3).
96 HA 1996 s160A(4).
97 See paras 2.67–2.80.
98 HA 1996 s160A(9), (10)

decides that an applicant is ineligible, it must give notice of its decision in writing and with reasons.[98]

5.89   By AIA 1996 s13(2), a person is subject to immigration control if he or she is a person who under the IA 1971 requires leave to enter or remain in the UK (whether or not such leave has been given). By IA 1971 ss2 and 3, all persons require leave to enter or remain except:

a) British citizens;
b) Commonwealth citizens with right of abode;
c) citizens of the Republic of Ireland;
d) citizens of EEA states who are workers, self-employed or providing services[99] and their family members.

5.90   It should be noted that this is a wider category than the definition of 'persons subject to immigration control' who are excluded from entitlement to benefits and other welfare provision by IAA 1999 s115. The category includes all those requiring leave to enter or remain, whether or not they are subject to a condition requiring that they have no recourse to public funds.

5.91   The classes specifically accorded eligibility (by Allocation of Housing (England) Regulations 2002 reg 4)[100] are:

Class A: Persons recorded as being refugees.

Class B: Persons with HP, DLR or ELR whose leave does not exclude them from recourse to public funds.

Class C: Persons with current leave to enter or remain which is not subject to any limitation or condition (that is, those with settled status) and who are habitually resident in the Common Travel Area, other than sponsored immigrants who have been here for less than five years and whose sponsor is still alive.

Class D: Persons who are habitually resident in the Common Travel Area and who are either:
(i) lawfully present and a national of a state which has ratified the ECSMA or the CESC, or
(ii) who continue to be owed a duty that arose prior to 3 April 2000, under HA 1985 Part III (old homelessness scheme) or HA 1996 Part VII (new homelessness scheme) and who are nationals of a state which is a signatory to ECSMA or CESC (see para 2.62 for the states covered).

99 See paras 1.19–1.20 and 2.30–2.37.
100 SI 2002 No 3264; see Appendix A. The same rules are applied to Wales by the Allocation of Housing (Wales) Regulations 2003 SI No 239 (W36).
101 HA 1996 s160A(4).

5.92 It should be noted that, in contrast to the homelessness provisions, no specific class of asylum-seekers was 're-included', and thus all asylum-seekers are excluded from eligibility for the allocation of public housing, unless they fall within the subsisting homelessness duty limb of Class D (reg 4(e)(ii)) since asylum-seekers have been found not to be 'lawfully present' (see para 5.16 above). As and when the new regulations are made, they may not accord eligibility to any person excluded from entitlement to Housing Benefit.[101]

5.93 As with the homelessness provisions a person who is *not* subject to immigration control may nonetheless be ineligible if he or she does not have the 'right to reside' and/or is not 'habitually resident'.[102] It has been noted at para 5.85 that certain persons are not subject to immigration control. Of these, people falling within a), b) and c) have a right to reside in the Common Travel Area (the UK, Channel Islands, Isle of Man and Republic of Ireland) but are ineligible unless[103] they are 'habitually resident' there. As to persons falling within d), EEA citizens who are workers, self-employed or providing services do not require habitual residence to be eligible; other EEA citizens must both have a right to reside and be habitually resident to be eligible.

5.94 For the meaning of 'right to reside', see paras 2.77–2.80 and of 'habitually resident' see paras 2.69–2.75. For the special rules applicable to nationals of east European states joining the European Union on 1 May 2004 ('A8 nationals') see paras 2.43–2.44.

5.95 Children born in the UK are not 'persons subject to immigration control': they do not require leave to enter or remain, and so are not excluded from eligibility. There is nothing in HA 1996 Part VI to exclude children from applying for housing, although local authority allocation schemes may exclude them.

5.96 Where a joint application for housing is made by two or more persons, and one of those persons is ineligible, then all applicants will be

---

102 HA 1996 s160A(5); Allocation of Housing (England) Regulations 2002 SI No 3264; (for Wales, the Allocation of Housing (Wales) Regulations 2003 SI No 239 (W36); Allocation of Housing and Homelessness (Amendment) (England) Regulations 2004 SI No 1235. Note that the requirement of having a 'right to reside' in this context in addition to satisfying the 'habitual residence test' was imposed on 1 May 2004, and does not affect an application for an allocation of accommodation made before that date: ibid, reg 4.

103 Allocation of Housing (England) Regulations 2002 SI No 3264 reg 5, as amended by Allocation of Housing and Homelessness (Amendment) (England) Regulations 2004 SI No 1235 reg 2.

104 HA 1996 s160A(1)(c).

treated as ineligible,[104] but there is nothing to prevent eligible applicants applying on their own, and including ineligible persons in their household for re-housing purposes.

5.97   It has been noted above that persons who are excluded from entitlement to housing benefit by IAA 1999 s115 are ineligible, and that the secretary of state may not make regulations to 're-include' classes of persons not entitled to housing benefit. IAA 1999 s115 makes all persons subject to immigration control ineligible for Housing Benefit unless re-included by regulation, and the classes re-included are specified by the Social Security (Immigration and Asylum) Consequential Amendments Regs 2000. At present, this additional criterion for eligibility adds nothing. There is no class of person excluded by section 115 or re-included by these regulations which is not excluded by Housing Act 1996 s160A or reincluded by Allocation of Housing (England) Regulations 2002 reg 4.

5.98   Housing authorities exercising allocation functions are required to have regard to guidance issued by the Home Secretary.[105] The ODPM Code of Guidance on Allocation of Accommodation contains helpful guidance as to the meaning of eligibility for allocation purposes at chapter 4, and useful notes on identifying eligible and ineligible persons in the Annexes.

5.99   The table[106] opposite assists to establish whether a person is eligible for allocation. The classes of applicant specified in the table are eligible if they meet the conditions of eligibility.

5.100   Once a person has been accepted as eligible, the local authority's allocation scheme will apply to determine whether and when accommodation is offered, and what that accommodation will be. In assessing the needs of applicants, for example, in relation to household size, local authorities have a wide discretion: they are not required to have regard to whether household members are eligible or ineligible, and most do not in practice do so. The rules concerning who is or is not an eligible person do not apply to household members of a registered applicant when the authority is considering the applicant's needs.[107]

105 HA 1996 s169.

106 Based on a table appearing in the ODPM Code of Guidance on the Allocation of Accommodation (November 2002).

107 *R v Tower Hamlets LBC ex p Kimvono* (2000) 5 December, QBD; February 2001 *Legal Action* 27.

108 SI No 71.

Eligibility for allocation

Class of applicant	Conditions of eligibility	Verification
Existing tenant of public sector property (ie, transfer applicant)	None	
British citizen	Must be habitually resident in the Common Travel Area	Passport
EEA citizen	Must have a right to reside in the UK and be habitually resident in the Common Travel Area unless the applicant is a worker	Passport or national identity card
Person subject to immigration control granted refugee status	None	Passport or Home Office letter
Person subject to immigration control granted HP, DLR or ELR	HP, DLR or ELR must not be subject to a condition preventing recourse to public funds	Passport or Home Office letter
Person subject to immigration control granted indefinite leave to remain	Must be habitually resident in Common Travel Area, and, if granted ILR on a sponsorship undertaking, five years has passed, or the sponsor is dead	Passport or Home Office letter
Person subject to immigration control who is a citizen of a country that has ratified ECSMA or ESC	Must be lawfully present in the UK and must be habitually resident in the Common Travel Area	Passport

Remedies in homelessness and allocation cases

Challenging homelessness decisions

5.101   Detailed provisions about the review of homelessness decisions and appeal to the county court are set out in HA 1996 ss202–204, and the Allocation of Housing and Homelessness (Review Procedures) Regulations 1999.[108] A brief summary is given here.

5.102   The applicant has a right to request a review of decisions made by local authorities concerning[109] eligibility; whether duties to secure accommodation, advise and assist[110] are owed, and what those duties are; whether the applicant is to be referred to another authority; and whether or not accommodation is suitable.

5.103   The review must be requested within 21 days of the decision. The review must be carried out by a more senior officer and be completed within 56 days of the request. The applicant must be notified of the decision on review. If the decision on review is adverse, the applicant has a right of appeal on a point of law to the county court.[111] The applicant has 21 days from the review decision (or from the expiry of the 56 days if no decision is made within that time) to lodge the appeal.[112] If the local authority refuses to continue the provision of temporary accommodation pending hearing of the appeal, the applicant can appeal to the county court against that decision also.[113]

5.104   Not all decisions made on homelessness applications carry a right to review and appeal. Most importantly, decisions about the provision of temporary accommodation pending assessment[114] and pending review [115] carry no right to review or appeal. Such decisions may be challenged by way of judicial review.

5.105   Where there is a right to a statutory review of a suitability decision, an applicant may both accept an offer of accommodation and seek a review of its suitability.[116] Where an applicant wishes to challenge an

---

109   HA 1996 s202.

110   That is, duties under HA 1996 ss190–193 and 195–197.

111   HA 1996 s204(1).

112   HA 1996 s204; the court has a discretion, on application, to consider appeals made outside the 21-day limit where there is good reason for the delay: s204(2A).

113   HA 1996 s204A.

114   Under HA 1996 s188(1).

115   Under HA 1996 s202.

116   HA 1996 s202(1A).

117   HA 1996 s167(4A)(d).

offer, it will therefore usually be prudent to accept it and seek a review, rather than refuse it, since if an offer is refused and the review is unsuccessful, the applicant is likely to receive a decision that the authority has discharged its duty by making the offer, and be left with no accommodation at all.

Challenging allocation decisions

5.106 There is a statutory right to review of a decision of a housing authority as to whether or not a person is eligible: authorities must include in their allocation schemes a right to request a review, and a right of the applicant to be informed of the review decision and the grounds for it.[117] The local authority must publish the allocation scheme itself,[118] and applicants are entitled to be given information about assessments, likelihood of being re-housed and the length of time they are likely to have to wait.[119]

5.107 There is a similar right to request a review of a decision that accommodation allocated under HA 1996 Part VI is suitable,[120] so as to discharge a local authority's obligations under Part VII towards a homeless applicant.

5.108 There is no right of appeal to the County Court against a review decision: it may only be challenged by an application for judicial review. Other decisions of local authorities in relation to allocation, including the lawfulness or otherwise of allocation schemes, may only be challenged by judicial review.

The use of social housing as accommodation for asylum-seekers

5.109 It has been seen that HA 1996 Parts VI and VII as routes into social housing are blocked for most asylum-seekers and people from abroad. This does not mean, however, that local authorities cannot use their own housing stock to accommodate such persons. The requirement that all lettings be through HA 1996 Part VI is confined to allocation by local authorities of secure or introductory tenancies, nomination by local authorities to registered social landlords for

---

118 HA 1996 s168.
119 HA 1996 s167(4A)(a).
120 HA 1996 s202(1)(f), as amended by Homelessness Act 2002 s8(2)(a).
121 The classes of occupation exempt from security are defined by HA 1985 Sch 1.

letting on assured tenancies, and transfers requested by tenants. It does not embrace:

a) the grant of or nomination to a tenancy or licence by a local authority which is exempt from security;[121]

b) the nomination of a person to a tenancy or licence which is exempt from assured status.[122]

5.110 Lettings under a) which are exempt from security include a tenancy or licence granted to provide accommodation under IAA 1999 Part VI,[123] that is, accommodation for asylum-seekers through NASS or under the Interim Regs. There is parallel provision exempting tenancies or licences granted by registered social landlords from assured status.[124] Local authorities may thus either nominate asylum-seekers to registered social landlords, or lease accommodation from a registered social landlord to provide temporary accommodation.[125] Both NASS[126] and local authorities[127] may require registered social landlords to provide 'reasonable assistance' in providing accommodation under IAA 1999 Part VI. Similarly, a county council (social services authority) may require such assistance from a district council (housing authority) in its area.[128] Neither the exemption from security of accommodation for asylum-seekers nor the powers to require assistance extend to accommodation provided for other persons subject to immigration control. Leasing from housing associations or private landlords may, however, be used to accommodate such persons.

5.111 These provisions are complemented by IAA 1999 s118, which requires that housing authorities avoid 'so far as practicable' granting tenancies or licences to persons subject to immigration control as defined by IA 1971 ss2 and 3 (see para 5.89 above), unless they do so to provide accommodation for asylum-seekers under IAA 1999 s95 or for

---

122 The classes of occupation exempt from assured status are defined by HA 1988 Sch 1.

123 HA 1985 Sch 1 para 4A, as amended by IAA 1999 Sch 14 para 81.

124 HA 1988 Sch 1 para 12A, as inserted by IAA 1999 Sch 14 para 88. The reference to 'private landlord' in para 12A includes RSLs.

125 HA 1985 Sch 1 para 6.

126 IAA 1999 s100; see also *R (A) v NASS and Waltham Forest LBC* [2003] EWCA Civ 1473; (2003) 6 CCLR 538.

127 IAA 1999 Sch 9 para 11, and Asylum Support (Interim Provisions) Regs 1999 SI No 3056 reg 10.

128 IAA 1999 Sch 9 para 11, and Asylum Support (Interim Provisions) Regs 1999 SI No 3056 reg 10.

129 IAA 1999 s118(1)(a) and Persons Subject to Immigration Control (Housing

persons falling within classes specified by the Home Secretary. The classes specified[129] are the same as those applied to allocation under HA 1996 Part VI (see para 5.91 above) with the addition of classes comprising:

- those owed a duty under National Assistance Act (NAA) 1948 s21 (see paras 6.88–6.105);
- those owed a duty under CA 1989 s17 (see paras 6.123–6.153);
- those owed housing duties under homelessness legislation (see paras 5.7–5.58);
- those entitled to assistance under the interim provisions (see paras 3.12–3.16);
- students in accommodation provided under arrangements between colleges and local authorities.

5.112　Interpreting IAA 1999 ss100 and 118, the court[130] has said that 'reasonable assistance' will require the local authority to look first outside its own housing stock, but to use its own stock where an applicant's present accommodation is so inadequate as to make it unreasonable not to use their own stock.

Succession and assignment

5.113　Successions to and assignments of tenancies are unaffected by immigration status. The rules which exclude asylum-seekers from housing allocation do not apply to successions and assignments. In local authority housing stock, successions and assignments are excluded from the scope of allocation under Part VI[131] and, in that they do not involve the 'grant' of rights of occupation by a local authority, are not embraced by the restrictions in IAA 1999 s118, above.

Effects of changes in immigration status

5.114　This section describes the consequences for the provision of assistance under HA 1996 Parts VI and VII and for other housing rights of

Authority Accommodation and Homelessness) Order 2000 SI No 706.
130　*R (A) v NASS and Waltham Forest LBC* [2003] EWCA Civ 1473; (2003) 6 CCLR 538, per Waller LJ.
131　HA 1996 s160.
132　Asylum Support (Interim Provisions) Regs 1999 SI No 3056 reg 2(6), as

changes in the status of asylum-seekers. The following changes of status are considered:

- the grant of refugee status or HP, DLR or ELR;
- the refusal of an asylum application or an appeal;
- the asylum-seeker and others reaching 18 years of age.

Grant of refugee status or HP, DLR or ELR

5.115   A successful asylum application will conclude with a decision by the Home Secretary or at the conclusion of an appeal to grant the applicant refugee status or HP, DLR or ELR (see paras 1.107–1.131).

5.116   People who have refugee status or HP, DLR or ELR are eligible to apply for assistance under HA 1996 Parts VI and VII.

5.117   Where the person is in accommodation provided by NASS or under local authority interim support at the point when such a decision is made, the provision of accommodation will cease 28 days from the date of notification of the Home Secretary's decision or, where an appeal has been made, from the appeal decision.

5.118   The power to provide assistance under the Asylum Support and Interim Regs schemes ends 28 days after the determination of the claim for asylum.[132] Where the person and his/her dependants are in NASS accommodation, they will be expected to leave the accommodation at the end of the 28-day period. Where the person is in accommodation provided under the Interim Regs, the local authority must cease assistance at the end of the 28-day period.[133] In the latter case, it may be that, if the local authority has a duty under the HA 1996 to secure accommodation for the person, it will decide to maintain him/her in the present accommodation under that duty, in place of its duty under the Interim Regs.[134]

5.119   Where the household of the person whose asylum claim has been determined includes persons with their own asylum claims which remain pending, then the continuation of accommodation under the asylum support scheme for the latter will depend upon whether the

amended by the Asylum Support (Interim Provisions) (Amendment) Regs 2002 SI 471 reg 4; Asylum Support Regulations 2000 SI No 704 reg 2(2), as amended by the Asylum Support (Amendment) regs 2002 SI No 472 reg 3.

133   Asylum Support (Interim Provisions) Regs 1999 SI No 3056 reg 8(1); see appendix A.

134   It is unlikely, however, that they are under any duty to do so; see *Sharp v Brent LBC* (2003) 14 April, unreported.

135   NAA 1948 s21.

former is entitled to accommodation for the whole household under the homelessness provisions (see paras 5.37 and 5.54 above).

5.120   Where the asylum-seeker whose claim is determined is supported with accommodation by the local authority under community care legislation (usually NAA 1948 s21 or CA 1989 s17), then, unless the asylum-seeker requires residential care, the social services department is likely to take steps to terminate that support and transfer responsibility to the housing department. However, there is no requirement to end support within 28 days as is the case with asylum support. The local authority should not terminate support until satisfied that, as the case may be, the applicant's needs are otherwise being met[135] or that the child is no longer a child in need.[136] The change of circumstances occasioned by a grant of refugee status or HP, DLR or ELR in such circumstances should give rise to a formal review of the community care or CA 1989 assessment and revision of the care plan before any changes are made to service provision. Precipitate termination of community care services in such cases could be challenged by judicial review.

5.121   Where an asylum-seeker is granted refugee status or HP, DLR or ELR and he or she has been staying with relatives (with or without provision for essential living needs by NASS or the local authority), he or she remains entitled to occupy that accommodation until his/her licence to do so is terminated by the tenant or owner, for example, by the owner/relative giving them a letter asking them to leave the accommodation by a certain date.

5.122   Where an asylum-seeker is granted refugee status or ELR, HP or DLR and he or she has a tenancy, he or she should at once claim housing benefit. Those granted refugee status will be entitled to apply for arrears of housing benefit if they claim within 28 days.[137]

5.123   The asylum-seeker, upon notification of a grant of refugee status or HP, DLR or ELR, should at once apply to the local authority to register for public sector housing. As soon as he or she is informed that his/her accommodation provided by NASS or the local authority is to be terminated, he or she should apply to the local housing authority for assistance under HA 1996 Part VII as a homeless person.

5.124   Asylum-seekers granted refugee status or HP, DLR or ELR should not leave their accommodation provided by NASS or the local

---

136 CA 1989 s17.

137 See paras 2.136–2.147. The government proposes to remove this entitlement to backdated benefit.

138 HA 1996 s188.

authority or by relatives until it is terminated. If they do, they risk being found not to be homeless or to be intentionally homeless upon their applying for accommodation as homeless persons. This is particularly likely to occur where asylum-seekers who have been dispersed are granted status and thereupon return to London and apply to local authorities as homeless persons.

5.125   A person granted refugee status or HP, DLR or ELR whose accommodation has been terminated by NASS or the local authority or by relatives will be 'threatened with homelessness' as soon as he or she is within 28 days of the date when he or she has to leave the accommodation, and 'homeless' on the day he or she does have to leave. Such an applicant will be eligible for assistance. If he or she is in priority need, the local authority will have a duty to secure interim accommodation for him/her and anyone who can reasonably be expected to live with him/her,[138] pending the conclusion of inquiries (see paras 5.50–5.52 above).

5.126   If the applicant cannot satisfy the authority that he or she may be in priority need, there is no duty to secure interim accommodation. However, the authority is still under a duty to make inquiries into the applicant's circumstances and to make a decision on the application.[139] If it is decided that the applicant does not have a priority need, the authority must assess the person's housing need and provide appropriate advice and assistance in the applicant's attempts to secure accommodation him/herself. In practice, this usually means advice and information about private sector housing and may include a scheme for providing deposits and rent in advance. Before any decision is made on the application, the authority has a duty to make advice and information available.[140] Such a person, even though not eligible for accommodation as a homeless person, should nonetheless make a housing list application. He or she will also be eligible for housing benefit.

5.127   On the conclusion of inquiries, the local authority will make decisions upon whether the applicant is homeless, eligible for assistance, in priority need, intentionally homeless and about local connection, and depending on those decisions, duties to secure accommodation may follow: see paras 5.7–5.58 above.

5.128   A common practical problem arises when a decision is made by the Home Secretary or on appeal granting refugee status or HP,

139 HA 1996 s184.
140 HA 1996 s179(1).
141 HA 1996 s160A(9), (10).

DLR or ELR, but the decision is not formally communicated to the applicant. Typically, the consequence is that asylum support accommodation is terminated, but on approaching the local authority, the applicant is told that he or she will not be assisted until he or she can produce the standard documentation (form ICD.0725 – previously GEN23 – for refugee cases, or Home Office letter granting HP, DLR or ELR for a specified period or ILR – see paras 1.103–1.131). The remedies for the applicant are by way of judicial review, either of the failure of the Home Office or appellate authority to issue a decision, or of the local authority for breach of its duty under HA 1996 ss184 and 188. The second option will be preferable in most cases: the threshold is a low one – it is only necessary to give the local authority 'reason to believe' that the applicant 'may' be eligible for assistance. There will, however, be cases where there has been a successful appeal but the applicant does not become eligible until the Home Office makes a fresh decision or issues documentation, where the first option should be taken. Parallel problems arise in claiming benefits (see paras 2.110–2.135), and housing authorities frequently refuse to assist applicants unless they can show proof of benefit entitlement or of the allocation of a national insurance (NI) number. Given the time taken to process benefit claims and NI number applications, such requirements arguably place the threshold under HA 1996 s188 too high. It should be recalled that people with refugee status or HP, DLR or ELR are not subject to the habitual residence test.

Refusal of an asylum application or an appeal

5.129 An unsuccessful asylum application concludes with a refusal decision by the Home Secretary, or a refusal on appeal. In a few cases, such a refusal of an asylum application is subsequently superseded by a decision to grant HP, DLR or ELR, in which case the consequences of refusal discussed below are also superseded.

5.130 Applicants who are subject to such a refusal are not entitled to assistance under HA 1996 Part VI (allocation) or Part VII (homelessness), unless:

- they fall within Class E (habitually resident citizens of states who are signatories or ratifiers of two European treaties (see above, paras 5.14 and 5.16 (homelessness) and 5.91 (allocation)); or
- they fall within Class I for homelessness only (receiving IS or means-tested JSA (see above, para 5.14).

5.131   Those who as a result of refusal cease to be eligible persons under HA 1996 Part VI must be advised in writing with reasons of any decision that they are ineligible.[141] The effect of refusal on rights to remain in different categories of accommodation is considered below.

Where the person is in accommodation provided under the asylum or interim support schemes

5.132   Where the person is in accommodation provided by NASS or under the Interim Regs at the point when such a decision is made, the provision of accommodation will end 21 days from the date of the Home Secretary's decision or, where an appeal has been made, from the appeal decision.[142] The accommodation provider will be told to issue a seven-day notice to quit.[143] There is one exception which applies to an applicant who has either:

– been refused and has not appealed; or
– has exhausted his/her appeal rights; or
– has withdrawn his/her claim for asylum

and whose household includes a dependent child under 18 years of age.

5.133   In such cases, accommodation will only cease if leave to remain is granted, or if the child reaches 18, leaves the household, ceases to be dependent, or leaves the UK.[144] Thus, accommodation for households with dependent children continues under the asylum support scheme notwithstanding that the asylum application has failed.

5.134   Unsuccessful asylum-seekers without dependent children required to leave asylum support accommodation will be made homeless. If their need for accommodation has arisen solely because of destitution or because of the physical effects or anticipated physical effects of destitution, they will be excluded from assistance with accommodation under NAA 1948 s21, and their only prospect of government assistance is under the hardship provisions of the asylum support scheme (see paras 4.127 onwards). Conversely, those who have a need for accommodation which does not arise solely because of destitution or its physical effects, should at once apply to the

---

142   Asylum Support (Interim Provisions) Regs 1999 SI No 3056 reg 2(6), as amended by the Asylum Support (Interim Provisions) (Amendment) Regs 2002 SI 471 reg 4; Asylum Support Regulations 2000 SI No 704 reg 2(2), as amended by the Asylum Support (Amendment) Regs 2002 SI No 472 reg 3.

143   NASS Policy Bulletin 22.

144   IAA 1999 s94(5) and (6).

145   HA 1996 s193(6)(a).

social services department for assistance (see paras 6.31–6.37 and 6.88–6.105).

Where the person refused is in accommodation secured under HA 1996 Part VII

5.135 When an asylum-seeker who is being provided with assistance under HA 1996 Part VII as a homeless person has his/her application for asylum refused by the Home Secretary, the local authority ceases to be under a duty to provide that assistance (except for Class E cases – see paras 5.14 and 5.16 above).[145] Note that, unlike accommodation under the asylum support scheme, Part VII assistance does not continue until the determination of an appeal, and does not continue if the household contains dependent children.

5.136 Where a person continues to be assisted by the local authority, having originally been provided with assistance under the old homelessness scheme[146] before AIA 1996 s9(2) came into force (19 August 1996),[147] the exclusion of ineligible persons does not apply, and the local authority's duty continues.[148] This is because the duty to secure accommodation for the unintentionally homeless in priority need under HA 1985 Part III[149] was not time limited. Thus, an applicant to a local authority originally assisted to secure accommodation under HA 1985, who subsequently loses that accommodation and whose circumstances have otherwise not changed will be entitled to continuing assistance under the HA 1985 provisions.

5.137 Whether or not the termination of the duty under the homelessness provisions results in loss of accommodation, and whether this is sooner or later, will depend on the accommodation the person has. Such accommodation may be temporary and excluded from any security of tenure, or it may be a tenancy attracting a degree of security (see paras 5.146–5.152 below).

5.138 Where the person is in temporary accommodation provided by a local authority, he or she will be entitled to reasonable notice.[150] According to the Code of Guidance, the period 'should not, reasonably, be less than the period usually given to someone who is found to

---

146 HA 1985 Part III.
147 Now repealed by IAA 1999 s169(1), (3), Sch 14 paras 108, 110–112, Sch 16.
148 *R v Hackney LBC ex p K* (1998) 30 HLR 760.
149 HA 1985 s65(2) (now repealed).
150 *R v Secretary of State for the Environment ex p Shelter* [1997] COD 49, QBD.
151 Para 12.38.

be intentionally homeless':[151] that is, 'such period as they [the local authority] consider will give him a reasonable opportunity of securing accommodation for his occupation'.[152] Arguably, in the case of refused asylum-seekers, given that they will not be entitled to housing benefit, that period should be longer than the 28 days used as a 'rule of thumb' by most local authorities.

Where the person whose asylum application is refused has a tenancy

5.139   Where the person has an assured tenancy (shorthold or otherwise) or a secure tenancy, ordinary housing law applies. Changes in immigration status do not affect security of tenure.[153] The person will be entitled to remain until a possession order is obtained and lawfully executed. The fact that refused asylum-seekers cease to be entitled to housing benefit and so may be unable to pay the rent does not alter this position. See paras 5.146–5.152 below.

5.140   A tenant who has lost housing benefit as a result of a refusal of his/her asylum application is likely to face possession proceedings on the ground of rent arrears. If the tenancy is secure, or if it is assured (but not if it is a shorthold tenancy and not if possession is sought on HA 1988 Sch 2 ground 8), a possession order will only be made if the judge considers it reasonable to do so. A possession order may be avoided by arguing that there is an obligation on social services to assist[154] and an application for such assistance has been made, or that in a case where an asylum appeal is pending, a successful appeal resulting in the grant of refugee status would mean an entitlement to arrears of housing benefit, and that the court should not decide the possession proceedings until the outcome of the appeal is known.

Asylum support where other accommodation lost

5.141   Where a person who has been accommodated outside the asylum support scheme loses that accommodation or it becomes inadequate or impractical to continue to occupy, he or she can apply for accommodation under the asylum support scheme.

5.142   Where the person has no dependent child in his/her household, support will continue to be available until a decision is made on the asylum application without an appeal; or until a decision is made on

152 HA 1996 s190(2)(a); *R v Newham LBC ex p Ojuri (No 5)* (1999) 31 HLR 631.
153 *Akinbolu v Hackney LBC* (1997) 29 HLR 259.
154 See paras 6.29–6.51.

appeal, or until the asylum application is withdrawn. An application for support can be made while support is available.

5.143   Where the person has a dependent child, support will only cease to be available if leave to remain is granted, or if the child reaches 18, leaves the household, ceases to be dependent, or leaves the UK.[155] An application for support can be made while support is available.

5.144   See paras 3.12–3.16 for whether the application is made to NASS or to the local authority under the interim scheme.

The asylum-seeker and others reaching 18 years of age

5.145   Unaccompanied asylum-seekers aged under 18 are the responsibility of the social services department. When they reach 18, responsibility for accommodating them may change (see paras 6.165–6.167). They may in limited cases be eligible in their own right for assistance as homeless persons.

Recovery of possession, protection from eviction and harassment

Security of tenure

5.146   The ordinary law relating to the recovery of possession of land applies to tenants who are asylum-seekers or other persons subject to immigration control, just as it applies to other tenants.[156] Changes in a person's immigration status do not affect the rights of such tenants in relation to security of tenure and protection from eviction. This applies to those tenants who acquired their tenancy through arrangements made before 6 December 1999 or who have acquired their tenancy since that date otherwise than through arrangements made by NASS or the local authority.

5.147   However, where accommodation is provided to accommodate asylum-seekers, security of tenure is restricted. A tenancy or licence granted by a local authority to provide accommodation under IAA 1999 Part VI (that is, to provide NASS asylum support or local authority interim support) is not a secure tenancy or licence under the HA

---

155 IAA 1999 s94(5) and (6).
156 *Akinbolu v Hackney LBC* (1997) 29 HLR 259.
157 HA 1985 Sch 1 para 4A, as amended by IAA 1999 s169(1) and Sch 14 para 81.

1985.[157] Similarly, a tenancy or licence granted by a private landlord or housing association to provide accommodation under IAA 1999 Part VI is not an assured tenancy under the HA 1988.[158] Any tenancy or licence granted in order to provide accommodation under IAA 1999 Part VI is an excluded tenancy or licence under the Protection from Eviction Act 1977.[159] In consequence, there is no requirement for a landlord to obtain a court order to recover possession or to provide a minimum of four weeks' notice to quit. These provisions may be in breach of the HRA 1998 and ECHR on the ground that they discriminate between different classes of occupier on the basis of asylum-seeker status.[160]

5.148   It is to be noted that these restrictions do not apply in the following circumstances:

- where the tenancy or licence was granted before the tenant or licensee made their claim for asylum;
- where the tenancy or licence was initially self-funded by the asylum-seeker (with or without housing benefit) and subsequently the rent was subsidised by NASS or the local authority;
- where the tenant or licensee is not an asylum-seeker or dependant of an asylum-seeker;
- where the tenancy or licence has been granted as part of provision made under CA 1989 s17 or NAA 1948 s21.

In this last case, it may not be easy to establish under what statutory provisions a local authority is providing accommodation. Where a request for assessment has been made under National Health Service and Community Care Act (NHSCCA) 1990 s47 to establish whether a person has a need for services, for example, under CA 1989 s17 or NAA 1948 s21, the local authority has power to make emergency provision under NHSCCA 1990 s47(5), but may instead provide accommodation by arrangement with and on behalf of NASS.

Recovery of possession of accommodation provided under the asylum support scheme

5.149   A procedure is specified for terminating accommodation provided by NASS. It does not apply to the termination of accommodation by local

158 HA 1988 Sch 1 para 12A, as amended by IAA 1999 s169(1) and Sch 14 para 88.
159 Protection from Eviction Act 1977 s3A(7A), as inserted by IAA 1999 s169(1) and Sch 14 para 73.
160 *Larkos v Cyprus* (1999) 7 BHRC 244.
161 IAA 1999 s95 and Sch 8 para 9; AS Regs, reg 22(1)

authorities under interim support. This applies where a person 'has' a tenancy or licence 'as a result of asylum support'.[161] This is not a clear formulation but arguably should be restricted to those cases where a tenancy or licence has been granted in order to provide accommodation under IAA 1999 Part VI, and not extended to cases where asylum support has met the cost of accommodation.

5.150   The procedure provides for a Notice to Quit to be served where one or more of the following conditions apply:

- asylum support is withdrawn under AS Regs reg 20 (see appendix A);
- the asylum claim or appeal has been determined;
- the supported person is no longer destitute;
- the supported person is to be moved to other accommodation.

The notice to quit must be in writing and the notice period must be not less than seven days, except in the case of determination of an asylum claim or appeal, where it must be not less than 21 days. Where the decision is posted, the 21 days runs from the second day after the IND posted the decision on the asylum claim.[162] Notwithstanding these provisions, a period of less than seven days is allowed if 'the circumstances of the case are such that the notice period is justified'.[163]

5.151   In cases where at least seven days or at least 21 days is allowed, how long should the notice period be? It was held to be arguable in *R v Newham LBC ex p Ojuri*,[164] that a housing authority was under a public duty to act reasonably in terminating temporary accommodation provided to a homeless person with dependent children under Housing Act 1996 s188. In the circumstances of that case, the High Court decided that a 28-day period was reasonable. In *R v Secretary of State for the Environment ex p Shelter and Refugee Council*,[165] it was decided that local authorities were under a public law duty to act reasonably in evicting asylum-seekers from accommodation in cases where the statutory duty to provide accommodation had been withdrawn. Subject to consideration of individual cases, the court suggested that at least 28 days was generally appropriate.

5.152   If it is found that NASS is allowing a notice period of less than seven days, representatives may wish to consider ECHR arguments

162 AS Regs reg 22(3).
163 AS Regs reg 22(4).
164 (1999) 31 HLR 631.
165 [1997] COD 49.
166 [1944] 1 KB 298.

in relation to respect for private and family life, peaceful enjoyment of possessions, discrimination, etc (articles 8 and 14, and article 1 of the First Protocol). There is also an old domestic authority for the proposition that having to cope in a foreign country should be taken into account. In *Ministry of Health v Belotti*,[166] Lord Green said:

> They find themselves removed to this country and provision made for them by the government under a licence of this kind, and it must surely be the implied intention of the parties that, if they were turned out by the ministry, they should be given such an opportunity as strangers in the land might require, to enable them to find other accommodation. That consideration ought to be taken into account in deciding what time is to be allowed to such licensees as those in this case to comply with the notice determining their licences.

A short notice period is probably only lawful in limited cases, for example, where the basis of the decision is that the supported household has adequate accommodation otherwise available.

Harassment and domestic violence[167]

5.153   Much of the statutory protection from harassment afforded to tenants and licensees has been taken away from asylum-seekers. Such tenancies and licences are excluded from the protection under Protection from Eviction Act (PFEA) 1977 s3, which requires landlords to apply for a court order to permit them to recover possession.[168] However, while such tenancies or licences continue, the tenants/licensees are 'residential occupiers' and so have the protection of PFEA 1977 s1. Under section 1, it is an offence for any person unlawfully to deprive the occupier of occupation, or to commit acts of harassment with intent to gain possession or to obstruct the occupier's exercise of their rights and remedies.[169] The protection under section 1 for tenancies and licences excluded under section 3A ends when the right to occupy ends, for example, by the expiry of a notice to quit, a fixed term or a notice of termination of licence. Breaches of section 1 should be referred to the Tenancy Relations Service of the local authority: there is no direct remedy available to the individual, though if a Tenancy

---

167 See also NASS Policy Bulletins on Domestic Violence (No 70) and on Racial Harassment (unnumbered).
168 Protection from Eviction Act 1977 s3A, as amended by IAA 1999 s169(1) and Sch 14 para 73.
169 Protection from Eviction Act 1977 s1.
170 NASS Policy Bulletin 81.

Relations Service unlawfully fails to act, it may be subject to judicial review.

5.154   Asylum-seekers suffering harassment may also complain to the accommodation provider under its complaints procedure, or direct to NASS, or to the police. The contract between NASS and the accommodation provider requires the latter to have a complaints procedure to deal with allegations of harassment, in the same way as complaints about sub-standard accommodation (see para 5.158 below). The supported person can contact NASS directly if he or she has been harassed by the housing provider.

5.155   NASS's policy guidance[170] states that its role in investigating racial harassment is to establish whether it is appropriate to provide alternative accommodation because there is a significant risk of violence occurring if the person were to remain. It goes on to say that 'the responsibility for tackling harassment lies with the police and the relevant local authority'. The guidance lists the various legal remedies, which asylum-seekers who are suffering racial harassment can pursue. NASS's approach has been to consider whether there is an immediate and significant risk to the household.

5.156   If a supported person needs to leave NASS accommodation due to domestic violence or racial or other harassment, he or she should make an immediate complaint to the housing provider. Internal instructions specifically provide for consideration of a move in such circumstances. If NASS does not provide alternative accommodation, judicial review (of the decision not to provide adequate accommodation) would be the appropriate remedy. There have been a number of appeals to the Asylum Support Adjudicators where NASS has terminated support in cases of racial harassment on the ground that the asylum-seeker has breached a condition of support by failing to travel back to the accommodation from which he or she fled. These are discussed at paras 3.168 onwards.

Housing conditions[171]

5.157   Many asylum-seekers are housed in sub-standard accommodation.[172] The contractual basis of accommodation provision by NASS is an

171 See further *Repairs: tenants' rights*, Appendices, Luba & Knafler (3rd edn, LAG, 1999).

172 See *Far from home: the housing of asylum-seekers in private rented accommodation*, Garvie (Shelter Publications, January 2001). .

173 Housing providers are asked by the Home Office to sign the Official Secrets

'occupancy agreement', which the supported person should have been asked to sign when he or she moved into the accommodation provided on behalf of NASS by a contractor. It should contain details of the landlord's obligations to maintain and manage the property. It may contain an express contractual duty to maintain the accommodation or carry out repairs.

5.158   The housing provider will also have entered a contract with NASS which should contain terms about the condition of the property.[173] Contractors who are providing accommodation on behalf of NASS are expected, as a term of their contract, to have an internal complaints procedure to enable the supported person(s) to make a complaint about harassment or about the service provided, for example, where utilities are not provided, furniture is missing, or the property is in disrepair. The housing provider should respond to the complaint within seven days and record the outcome in a logbook. If the supported person is not satisfied, it is the function of the landlord to make a referral to the nearest one-stop service for advice and advocacy, and from there to NASS. The terms of such agreements between NASS and the housing provider may be enforceable by the asylum-seeker who is accommodated despite his/her not being a party to the agreement. A term will be so enforceable under Contracts (Rights of Third Parties) Act 1999 s1 if it purports to confer a benefit on the asylum-seeker.

5.159   IAA 1999 s96 provides for accommodation 'appearing to the Secretary of State to be adequate' for the needs of the supported person and any dependants. 'Adequate' suggests that the accommodation should be in basic repair and (in a non-technical sense) fit for human habitation with basic facilities such as adequate space, and with water, heating, sanitation and cooking facilities in proper working order. It is part of NASS's role to inspect accommodation to ensure contracts are being fulfilled.[174] Commentators have pointed out the difficulty of the Home Office carrying out a function more suited to the local authority housing and environmental health departments with local knowledge of landlords. NASS has a contract with the Property Advisors to the Civil Estate to inspect properties to ensure that the physical standard of accommodation provided complies with the terms of the contract. This programme of inspections is supplemented by NASS's Performance Monitoring Inspections Team. Its role is 'to ensure that accom-

Act and may not disclose the location of properties let through the NASS scheme.

174 Bob Eagle, Director of NASS, 25 March 1999 in his submissions to the Special Standing Committee on the Immigration and Asylum Bill.

175 [1954] 2 QB 127.

modation providers are complying with the contract requirements for effective housing management and access to support services'.

5.160   The courts seem likely to treat an occupation agreement entered into under IAA 1999 as a licence to occupy accommodation rather than a tenancy. Landlord and Tenant Act 1985 s11 implies an obligation upon the landlord to repair into a tenancy but not into a licence.

5.161   This does not mean that property owners have no legal duties to asylum-seeker occupiers. Licensors of dwellings may have retained sufficient control of the dwelling to be liable to the occupiers in negligence for personal injury or property damage, or to justify an implied term as to repair or fitness for purpose, depending on the circumstances of the case. In *Greene v Chelsea BC*,[175] the council exercised statutory powers to requisition housing accommodation. Those powers made it impossible to grant occupiers a tenancy, only a licence. When one occupier was injured after a ceiling collapsed, the council was held liable in negligence. It had been informed about the bulging ceiling but had failed to repair it. The case is significant because landlords do not usually owe a duty of care in negligence to licensees.

5.162   It has been held to be an implied term, on the facts and in a case relating to business premises, that the premises would be fit for their purposes.[176]

5.163   Even if a county court action is available, there are difficulties for an asylum-seeker in bringing it, because he or she will not generally have any security of tenure. An award of compensation could temporarily remove eligibility for support because the household would have some money. Unless an emergency injunction is available, another problem is that occupation of the accommodation is intended to be short-term. An asylum-seeker may prefer to use the speedier Environmental Protection Act 1990 procedures.

Accommodation which is prejudicial to health

5.164   If an asylum-seeker is placed in accommodation which is 'prejudicial to health', in a poor state of repair, lacking adequate amenities or means of escape from fire, a request could be made to the local authority's environmental health officer (EHO) to inspect with a view to taking action under Environmental Protection Act 1990 s80 if the accommodation appears to be prejudicial to health or a nuisance. The EHO should also act if the accommodation is 'unfit' under the HA

---

176   *Wetter Electric Ltd v Welsh Development Agency* [1983] 1 QB 796, slightly doubted in *Morris-Thomas v Petticoat Lane Rentals* (1986) 53 P & CR 238.

177   See further *Repairs: tenants' rights*, Appendices, Luba & Knafler (3rd edn, LAG,

1985, which covers overcrowding, inadequate fire escapes and serious disrepair. If the landlord refuses to do repairs after the local authority has served a notice, the authority can take enforcement action, doing the works itself and recouping the cost from the landlord. If the EHO will not act promptly or at all, an asylum-seeker could consider a judicial review of the EHO's decision. The EHO will not take action where the landlord is the same local authority.

5.165   In cases where the EHO will not act, the asylum-seeker can take individual action under Environmental Protection Act 1990 s82, by serving a 21-day standard notice[177] at the landlord's registered office, supported by evidence of the prejudice to health. If the landlord does not do the necessary repair works to 'abate the nuisance' within 21 days, the asylum-seeker can start a fast-track procedure to prosecute the landlord in the magistrates' court. Community Legal Service Legal Help funding will be needed for an independent EHO's report to support the action. This may be justified by demonstrating that the local authority EHO will not intervene.

5.166   Many asylum-seekers are housed by private sector landlords. If an asylum-seeker is considering action to enforce repairs, advice should be given about the risk of the landlord responding with possession proceedings to which there may be no defence if there is only a licence agreement or an assured shorthold tenancy. Furthermore, asylum-seekers do not have protection from harassment and illegal eviction under the Protection from Eviction Act 1977[178]– see para 5.146 above.

Asylum-seekers and council tax

5.167   Asylum-seekers occupying accommodation provided by NASS or by local authorities under the Interim Provisions are not liable for council tax. The reason for this is that liability for council tax falls upon owners rather than occupiers in certain categories of dwelling prescribed by the Council Tax (Liability for Owners) Regulations 1992 reg 2.[178a] These regulations were amended with effect from 3 April 2000 by the Council Tax (Liability for Owners) (Amendment) Regula-

        1999).
178 Accommodation provided under IAA 1999 Part VI is an excluded tenancy or licence under Protection from Eviction Act 1977 s3A, as amended by IAA 1999 s169(1) and Sch 14 para 73.
178a SI No 551.
179   SI No 537, reg 2.

tions 2000[179] to add a new category comprising a dwelling provided to an asylum-seeker under, or under arrangements made under, IAA 1999 s95. Specific provision is not made for Interim Provisions cases,[180] but the government has stated that those on interim support do not have to pay council tax.[181]

5.168 Liability remains in certain cases:

a) Asylum-seekers who have arranged their own accommodation (although they will not be liable if staying in someone else's household, or in hostel or HMO accommodation). Such asylum-seekers will often be those who have lost entitlement to state benefits, and who thus cease to receive council tax benefit in their own accommodation. A liability for council tax in such cases is not specified as eligible for support, but is arguably an essential living need,[182] and representations should be made to NASS or the local authority as appropriate.

b) Asylum-seekers supported under National Assistance Act 1948 s21 or other community care statutes. The liability for council tax in such cases should be brought to the attention of the social services department, with a request that provision be reviewed to take account of it.

c) Council tax due for periods prior to 3 April 2000, for those supported by social services departments at that time. Arguably, such a liability should have been included in the provision made by social services at that time, but in practice such asylum-seekers' best prospect is to make representations to the local authority to write off the debt.[183] Should enforcement procedures reach the stage of committal, a request can be made to the magistrates' court that the tax should be remitted on the ground that failure to pay is not blameworthy and the asylum-seeker cannot pay.[184]

5.169 Councils can obtain liability orders in the magistrates' court against asylum-seekers, notwithstanding their inability to pay.[185]

---

180 Interim Provisions Regulations are made pursuant to IAA 1999 ss94 and 166, and are not themselves arrangements under s95.

181 Angela Eagle MP in the debate on the Nationality, Immigration and Asylum Bill in Standing Committee E on 14 May 2002.

182 As described in AS Regs reg 10 and Interim Regs reg 5(1)(b).

183 Guidance is given to local authorities in writing off debts in Practice Note 9 (issued by the Office of the Deputy Prime Minister).

184 Council Tax (Administration and Enforcement) Regulations 1992 SI No 613 reg 48(2), as amended.

185 *R v Hackney LBC ex parte Adebiri* (1997) 31 July QBD.

Community care services for asylum-seekers

continued

Introduction

6.1 All asylum-seekers and many (but by no means all) persons subject to immigration control (PSIC) are eligible for free medical care from the NHS.[1] The community care regime gives rise to two basic issues in the immigration context:

 – In the case of asylum-seekers: is NASS or a local authority responsible for the provision of basic accommodation and support?
 – In the case of PSIC, to what extent are they ineligible for community care services?

6.2 Between 24 July 1996, when the Asylum and Immigration Act (AIA) 1996 excluded asylum-seekers who failed to claim asylum on arrival and other PSIC from income support and related state benefits, and the coming into force of the Immigration and Asylum Act (IAA) 1999 on 6 December 1999 (local authority interim support) and 3 April 2000 (NASS support), community care services provided by local authorities constituted the only source of accommodation and subsistence for destitute asylum-seekers and other PSIC. A central purpose of the IAA 1999 was to establish a system for providing support to all asylum-seekers (but not to other PSIC) and, correspondingly, to withdraw both access to state benefits and community care services from asylum-seekers. Accordingly, the IAA 1999 set up the National Asylum Support Service (NASS) to provide centrally-administered asylum support. Until the NASS scheme could be fully implemented, the IAA 1999 provided (as it continues to provide) for support to be given essentially to earlier-claiming asylum-seekers by local authorities under the Interim Regs.[2] At the same time, the IAA 1999 created a series of exclusions, which made PSIC ineligible for almost all state welfare benefits and for many local authority community care services. The exclusions from community care service were far from comprehensive. However, Nationality, Immigration and Asylum Act (NIAA) 2002 s54 and Sch 3 introduced significantly broader community care exclusions and the Asylum and Immigration (Treatment of Claimants, etc) Act 2004 threatens to continue that process. On the other hand, the extension of the EEA to include many eastern European countries potentially increases eligibility for community care services (see paras 2.42 onwards).

---

1 National Health Service (Charges to Overseas Visitors) Regulations 1989 SI No 306 as amended. See further para 4.117 onwards.
2 Asylum Support (Interim Provisions) Regulations 1999 SI No 3056.

6.3   This chapter comprises an overview of the way in which the community care scheme now fits in with the asylum support scheme, with a summary of who is excluded from community care services and who is included. There follows a detailed examination of:

  – the meaning of 'community care services';
  – the machinery of assessment;
  – exclusions affecting PSIC; and
  – the nature of services available.

In each case, services under the National Health Service and Community Care Act (NHSCCA) 1990 and services under the Children Act (CA) 1989 are considered separately.

6.4   This chapter concludes with an examination of problems arising upon changes of immigration or other status, and an outline of the remedies available.

Overview

Community care services

6.5   Community care services comprise a range of means of providing for the needs of people through the social services departments of local authorities and, in some cases, through health authorities. Needs which can be met include needs for accommodation, subsistence, and support services. In practice, local authorities use their powers and duties under the community care statutes (particularly National Assistance Act (NAA) 1948 s21 and the CA 1989) to provide accommodation and subsistence for all destitute individuals who are not excluded from eligibility. However, in general, while some community care statutes such as the NAA 1948 can give rise to individual rights (subject to assessment of need), other statutes, such as the CA 1989, usually give rise to general duties and powers to promote the welfare of people in their area and define ways in which local authorities may meet those responsibilities. Whether or not an individual has recourse to the courts when a local authority fails to make provision will usually depend on whether the authority has complied with its responsibilities in a public law sense.

6.6   IAA 1999 Part VI and NIAA 2002 s54 and Sch 3 have excluded asylum-seekers and others from community care services to a considerable extent, but important areas remain where eligibility for assistance is available. In particular, it should be noted that the exclusions referred to below never exclude any asylum-seeker or PSIC from services under Mental Health Act (MHA) 1983 s117 which remain fully available irrespective of immigration status.

Who is excluded?

6.7   Healthy, able-bodied asylum-seeking adults with children receive accommodation and essential living needs from NASS under IAA 1999 s95 and the Asylum Support Regulations 2000 (AS Regs)[3] or from local authorities under the Interim Regs.[4] This applies even if the children are disabled or otherwise have special needs. Eligibility for asylum support continues even after a refusal of the asylum claim, because IAA 1999 s94(5) defines a person whose household contains a dependent child under 18 as remaining an asylum-seeker for asylum support purposes for as long as he or she remains in the UK, notwithstanding the failure of his asylum claim. When in force, however, Immigration and Asylum (Treatment of Claimants, etc) Act 2004 s9 will allow the Home Secretary to certify that such families have not taken reasonable steps to leave the UK voluntarily, in which case the adults but not the children will be excluded from support under CA 1989, NAA 1948 and other community care services. Up until that point, if entitlement to asylum support ends for some other reason, the family is, in principle, eligible for support under CA 1989 (see paras 6.124–6.127).

6.8   Healthy, able-bodied, destitute adult asylum-seekers without dependent children also receive support from NASS under IAA 1999 s95 and the AS Regs or from local authorities under the Interim Regs. This provision continues until a final decision is made upon their application for asylum (including by way of appeal). After that, accommodation may be available in limited cases under the IAA 1999 s4 hard cases scheme (see paras 3.291–3.297) but there is no community care safety net. If entitlement to asylum support ends for some other reason, there is no community care safety net.

6.9   Asylum-seekers who require services on reaching the age of 18 after having been in local authority care, and who are healthy and able-bodied, receive NASS support but with some local authority input (see paras 6.132–6.152).

6.10   Adults who are citizens of other EEA countries, or who have been granted refugee status by other EEA countries, or who are failed

---

3   SI No 704.

4   Asylum Support (Interim Provisions) Regulations 1999 SI No 3056.

asylum-seekers who have failed to co-operate with removal directions or who are present in the UK in breach of the immigration laws, are excluded from almost all community care services by NIAA 2002 s54 and Sch 3, except to the extent that European Community law or the ECHR requires provision to be made (see paras 6.63–6.74).

Who is included?

6.11   Unaccompanied asylum-seeking children are exclusively the responsibility of local authorities under CA 1989 Part III (see para 6.128) and are not covered by NASS or the Interim Regs.

6.12   In the case of families with dependent children, if services under NASS or the Interim Regs are suspended or discontinued for any reason (for example, because it is decided that the adults became 'intentionally destitute') then the children become eligible for assistance under CA 1989 Part III – and under CA 1989 s17 that can and usually should include assistance for the whole family (see paras 6.124–6.127).

6.13   Adult asylum-seekers and other PSIC who have a need for services, which derives at least in part from a cause other than simple lack of accommodation and subsistence (such as pregnancy, old age, physical or mental illness, or disability) are eligible for support under the community care regime, including accommodation and basic living requirements under NAA 1948 s21, as well as domiciliary help and other services under the usual community care provisions (see paras 6.106–6.120). They should apply to the social services department of the local authority, and not to NASS.[5] If such adults have children then NASS will be financially responsible for the children.[6]

6.14   An asylum-seeker who has been detained for treatment under Mental Health Act (MHA) 1983 s3 is entitled to services including accommodation, subsistence and support under MHA 1983 s117 whether or not his/her current needs arise through destitution alone (see paras 6.120–6.122).

6.15   Adult asylum-seekers who have (as children) been in local authority care are entitled to support on leaving care while they remain asylum-seekers (see paras 6.132–6.153). In practice, however, since such children will also be eligible for asylum support when they reach 18, NASS will take over financial responsibility at least.[7] Eligibility ceases

---

5   *R (Westminster) v NASS* [2002] UKHL 38; (2002) 5 CCLR 511.
6   *R (O) v Haringey LBC* [2004] EWCA Civ 535; (2004) 7 CCLR 310.
7   See Children (Leaving Care) Act 2000 Regulations and Guidance, paras 2.7–2.11.

by virtue of NIAA 2002 s54 and Sch 3, after the asylum claim has been refused (see para 6.153). If the former children are disabled then they will continue to be entirely a local authority responsibility, under NAA 1948 s21.

Assessments and remedies

6.16   Access to community care services is through an 'assessment of need' followed by a 'care plan' (see paras 6.29–6.51).

6.17   If a local authority fails or refuses to complete an assessment of need or a care plan in respect of a child or adult then, unless the person concerned is plainly ineligible for assistance, the most appropriate remedy is likely to be judicial review proceedings to ensure that the local authority carries out its duty. If the assessment of need or care plan is unsatisfactory, the appropriate remedy will be either pursuing a formal complaint through the local authority complaints procedures to obtain a different decision or judicial review to correct errors of law, including failures to comply with the assessment procedures set out in relevant statutory guidance (see further paras 6.39–6.50). In practice, the judicial review avenue is chosen when the case is urgent, or there is an important point of law in issue.

What are community care services?

6.18   Community care services are defined[8] as those services which a local authority may provide or arrange to be provided under:
  – NAA 1948 Part III;
  – Health Services and Public Health Act (HSPHA) 1968 s45 (a range of services for the elderly including home help, meals and social work support);
  – National Health Service Act (NHSA) 1977 s21 and Sch 8 (a range of services for the social care and aftercare of the ill including home helps and laundry but not accommodation); and
  – MHA 1983 s117 (aftercare services for mentally-ill persons discharged from detention in hospital can include accommodation, board where required, social work assistance and, in effect, anything that is needed).

6.19   Services provided under NAA 1948 Part III include residential accommodation under NAA 1948 s21 (accommodation and, where

---

8   NHSCCA 1990 s46(3).

needed, board and other welfare services provided in connection with the accommodation). Additionally, a wide range of other services for disabled people can be provided under NAA 1948 s29 and also Chronically Sick and Disabled Persons Act (CSDPA) 1970 s2.[9] These services include social work assistance, recreational facilities in the home (such as radios, televisions, telephones, etc), the provision of disability-related training, suitable employment, domiciliary care (for example, help with dressing, washing, toileting, housework, shopping, cooking, etc), home adaptations and meals.

6.20   Services under CA 1989 Part III (a very wide range of services, which can include accommodation, cash, and assistance in kind) are not 'community care services' as defined by statute.[10] Nonetheless, many services for children under Part III are analogous to adult services under the NHSCCA 1990 and many of the procedures are very similar, so they are generally considered to be part of 'community care' in a broader sense.

6.21   Furthermore, support or other community care-type provision might be available under Local Government Act (LGA) 2000 s2.[11]

Which local authority to approach?

6.22   Most community care services are administered by the social services department of a unitary local authority. In the case of non-unitary authorities, the social services department will be part of the county council. Some services (under MHA 1983 s117 and the NHSA 1977) also involve health authorities in responsibility for service provision.

6.23   Sometimes, social services authorities are driven, usually by shortage of resources, to dispute with social services authorities in other areas which authority is responsible for a particular individual in need of services. So far as concerns most community care services, the authority responsible is usually the authority in whose area the individual is 'ordinarily resident'. A person will be ordinarily resident in an area if he or she can show a regular habitual and lawful mode of life in a particular place, the continuity of which has persisted despite any temporary absences.[12] There is no statutory definition of the term

---

9   Services under CSDPA 1970 s2 qualify as 'community care services' because they are provided under NAA 1948 s29 (which is within NAA 1948 Part III): *R v Kirklees MBC ex p Daykin* (1998) 1 CCLR 512.

10   NHSCCA 1990 s46(3).

11   *R (J) v Enfield LBC* (2002) 5 CCLR 434.

12   *Shah v Barnet LBC* [1983] 2 AC 309.

'ordinarily resident' but there is central government guidance at LAC(93)7.[13]

6.24 Importantly for asylum-seekers, ordinary residence will not be acquired where residence has not been voluntarily adopted (for example, because NASS has required them to live at a particular location), or where there has been no settled purpose in living in a particular residence.[14] Many asylum-seekers will, accordingly, not acquire ordinary residence in any local authority area. But where they do it is important to note that once provided with accommodation under NAA 1948 s21 (see paras 6.88–6.105), the person remains ordinarily resident in the area of the authority where he or she was living before that accommodation was provided.[15] In the case of *R (Mani) v Lambeth LBC*,[16] the court held that the relevant date for considering whether an asylum-seeker was ordinarily resident in a particular local authority area was the date he made his application (not the date judicial review proceedings were issued) and that an asylum-seeker living in temporary accommodation in Eurotower for six months had become ordinarily resident in that area.

6.25 In the case of provision under CA 1989 s17, however, (see paras 6.123–6.153), the duty is owed by an authority to children who are physically present 'within their area', whether or not the children are ordinarily resident in the area.[17]

6.26 For example, where authority A provides accommodation to an asylum-seeker in the area of authority B: if the asylum-seeker is an adult who was ordinarily resident in the area of authority A, he or she remains the responsibility of authority A if he or she loses the accommodation; if he or she is an adult asylum-seeker who had not established ordinary residence in area A, he or she will become the responsibility of authority B upon losing this accommodation; if he or she is an unaccompanied minor, he or she will become the responsibility of authority B if he or she loses his/her accommodation.[18]

---

13 See www.dh.gov.uk.

14 *Al-Ameri v Kensington & Chelsea RLBC* [2004] UKHL 4.

15 NAA 1948 s24(5).

16 [2002] EWHC 735 (Admin); (2002) 5 CCLR 486.

17 *R (Stewart) v Wandsworth, Lambeth and Hammersmith & Fulham LBC* (2001) 4 CCLR 466; *R(M) v Barking and Dagenham LBC* [2002] EWHC 2663 Admin, (2003) 6 CCLR 87.

18 The rules about ordinary residence are different in cases of provision under MHA 1984 s117. The relevant health authority is the health authority of the discharging hospital but the relevant social services authority is the authority for the area in which the person resides or where he or she is sent on discharge: see s117(3).

6.27   In relation to the provision of accommodation under NAA 1948 s21 (see paras 6.88–6.105), a local authority's duty to provide accommodation extends to those who are ordinarily resident in its area, but also to those who are not ordinarily resident in any area but are in its area when the need arises, and to those (whether or not ordinarily resident anywhere) who are in urgent need.[19] In addition, the authority has power to provide for a person who is ordinarily resident in the area of another authority if that authority agrees.[20]

6.28   Disputes between authorities about ordinary residence in relation to NAA 1948 s21 are generally settled by referral to the secretary of state,[21] but they can be settled by the courts.[22] Under no circumstances should authorities fail to assess or meet needs merely because there is a dispute about financial responsibility: the 'authority of the moment' should take the necessary steps, subject to the determination of financial responsibility later on: see LAC(93)7. Furthermore, ordinary residence is not generally relevant in deciding which local authority should conduct an assessment. The need for assessment is triggered by an application by a person to an authority or by that authority becoming aware that an individual may have a need for community care services, which the authority has a power to provide. The authority cannot refuse to assess because a person is not ordinarily resident in its area.[23]

Assessing applicants for community care services

6.29   In order to make decisions about whether or not to provide community care services, local authorities follow a set procedure for conducting an assessment and preparing a care plan. A person seeking such services triggers this procedure by requesting the authority to carry out an assessment of need and complete a care plan. The assessment of need identifies what needs the local authority considers the applicant has (including needs – 'unmet needs' – which the authority has no present intention of meeting). The care plan then sets out what needs the local authority has decided to meet and its plan for meeting them.

19 NAA 1948 s24(3); Approvals and Directions LAC(93)10.
20 NAA 1948 s24(4).
21 NAA 1948 s32(3).
22 *R v Kent CC ex p Salisbury and Pierre* (2000) 3 CCLR 38.
23 *R v Berkshire CC ex p P* (1998) 1 CCLR 141, QBD.

6.30 In urgent cases, the local authority may make emergency provision for a person's needs pending the outcome of the assessment process.[24]

Assessment for services under the NHSCCA 1990

6.31 When a local authority is aware that a person may be in need of a community care service which it has a power to provide, it has a duty to carry out an assessment and a duty to make a decision on the basis of the assessment as to whether the person needs the provision of services.[25] The failure of a local authority to complete an assessment or a care plan can be the subject of a formal complaint but, at least in urgent cases, is generally challenged by way of judicial review proceedings. In such cases, in practice, the matter is invariably resolved speedily, at or around the stage of applying for permission.

6.32 The threshold test for assessment (whether there 'may be' a need for services) is very low and the consequent duty to assess is absolute (in other words, does not depend on whether resources are available to carry out assessments, or on whether the local authority would be likely to provide relevant services).[26] Accordingly, it would be difficult for a local authority to justify delay in completing an assessment for any reasons other than professional reasons inherent in the assessment process itself.[27]

6.33 If, during an assessment of need, it appears to the local authority that the person concerned is disabled, the local authority is required to make a decision as to the services the person requires under the Disabled Persons (Services, Consultation and Representation) Act 1986 s4, without his/her requesting the authority to do so.[28] This simply means that the local authority has to assess the person's needs for services under CSDPA 1970 s2. Furthermore, the local authority must inform him/her that it will be carrying out this assessment and of his/her rights under that Act, one of which is the right to have account taken of the ability of any carer to continue to provide care on a regular basis.[29]

---

24 NHSCCA 1990 s47(5); *R (AA) v Lambeth LBC* (2002) 5 CCLR 36.
25 NHSCCA 1990 s47.
26 *R v Bristol CC ex p Penfold* (1998) 1 CCLR 315.
27 *R v Kirklees MBC ex p Daykin* (1998) 1 CCLR 512.
28 NHSCCA 1990 s47(2).
29 Disabled Persons (Services, Consultation and Representation) Act 1986 s8.

6.34   Carers who provide substantial amounts of care are entitled to participate in assessments and to request an assessment of their own ability to provide care without assistance, under the Disabled Persons (Services, Consultation and Representation) Act 1986 and also under the Carers (Recognition and Services) Act 1995. There is guidance at LAC(96)7. Under the Carers and Disabled Children Act 2000, carers are entitled to assessments of their ability to care and local authorities are given the power to provide services to carers to help them provide care.

6.35   If at any time during an assessment, it appears to the local authority that the person concerned might need health services or housing services, the local authority must notify the relevant health authority or local housing authority and invite them to assist, as far as is reasonable in the circumstances, in completing the assessment. In making any decision as to the provision of services, the local authority must take into account any services that are likely to be made available by that health authority or the local housing authority.[30] Conversely, of course, the local authority would have to take into account the fact that services might not be likely to be forthcoming from the health authority or local housing authority, which could increase the needs that the social services authority would have to consider meeting. For example, if a disabled person has a need for housing that is not likely to be met by the housing department, and if as a result the person has unmet community care needs, including a need for suitable accommodation, then the local authority has at least to consider exercising its community care powers to meet such needs and may be under a duty to do so.[31]

6.36   Assessments under MHA 1983 s117 are multidisciplinary assessments involving both the social services authority and also the health authority.[32]

6.37   Assessments sometimes only address domiciliary as opposed to residential accommodation needs but this is unlawful:

30 NHSCCA 1990 s47(4).

31 *R v Tower Hamlets LBC ex p Bradford* (1998) 1 CCLR 294; *R v Wigan MBC ex p Tammadge* (1998) 1 CCLR 581; *R v Lambeth LBC ex p K* (2000) 3 CCLR 141; *R v Bristol CC ex p Penfold* (1998) 1 CCLR 315; *R v Kensington and Chelsea RLBC ex p Kujtim* (1999) 2 CCLR 340; *R (Batantu) v Islington LBC* (2001) 4 CCLR 445; *R (Wahid) v Tower Hamlets LBC* (2001) 5 CCLR 239.

32 HC(90)23/LASSL(90)11 (setting out 'the care programme approach' (CPA)), *Effective Care and Co-ordination in Mental Health Services* issued under the relatively new *National Service Framework for Mental Health* (HSC(1999)223; LAC(1999)34) (for patients discharged after a treatment section).

An assessment is something that is directed at the particular person who presents with an apparent need. One cannot be said to have been carried out unless the authority concerned has fully explored that need in relation to services it has the power to supply. In some cases the exercise will be very simple; in others more complex.[33]

Assessment for services under the CA 1989

6.38 It is implicit in Children Act 1989 s17 and explicit in Sch 2 para 1 (the duty to identify the extent to which there are children in need within the area) that local authorities are required to assess the needs of children who might be 'children in need' for the purposes of the CA 1989.[34]

Assessment procedures: adults

6.39 In exercising their social services functions, local authorities are regulated by directions and guidance issued by central government. There are no directions specific to NHSCCA 1990 assessments.[35] Local Authority Social Services Act (LASSA) 1970 s7 provides that local authorities shall, in the exercise of their social services functions, including the exercise of any discretion conferred by any relevant legislation, act under the general guidance of the secretary of state. 'Social services functions'[36] include the assessment procedures and the provision of all community care services, and services under CA 1989 Part III. Guidance issued under LASSA 1970 s7 is known generally as 'statutory guidance' or 'mandatory guidance'. Circulars issued to local authorities almost always clearly state whether they have been issued under LASSA 1970 s7.

6.40 Guidance issued under LASSA 1970 s7 must be followed in substance. The duty under section 7 to 'act under' this type of guidance requires local authorities to follow the path charted by the guidance, with liberty to deviate from it where the local authority judges on admissible grounds that there is good reason to do so, but without the freedom to take a substantially different course.[37]

6.41 Much guidance that the practitioner comes across is not issued

---

33 *R v Bristol CC ex p Penfold* (1997) 1 CCLR 315.
34 *R (W, A, G) v Lambeth and Barnet LBC* [2003] UKHL 57.
35 The secretary of state has power to issue directions under NHSCCA 1990 s47(4) but has not yet done so.
36 Defined in LASSA 1970 Sch 1.
37 *R v Islington LBC ex p Rixon* (1998) 1 CCLR 119.

under LASSA 1970 s7, by the secretary of state, but is 'departmental guidance' or 'practice guidance', issued by the relevant civil service department.[38] The local authority must have regard to this guidance[39] but can act differently if it has good reason. However, it cannot act contrary to the guidance simply because it does not agree with it. That would, in effect, be to disregard it.[40]

6.42   Until relatively recently, the main general guidance issued by the secretary of state under LASSA 1970 s7 so far as concerns community care services has been the circular *Community care in the next decade and beyond*.[41] This is commonly referred to as the 'Policy Guidance'. The Policy Guidance has now been substantially supplemented by guidance called *Fair Access to Care Services* (FACS). Since the decision in *R v Islington LBC ex p Rixon*,[42] local authorities and other practitioners have operated on the basis that the Policy Guidance and FACS apply to assessments under NHSCCA 1990 s47 by virtue of LASSA 1970 s7. In a recent case it was held that since NHSCCA 1990 s47(4) expressly provides that – subject to any directions made by the secretary of state – authorities are free to carry out assessments in such manner and in such form as they consider appropriate, such guidance is not substantially binding by virtue of LASSA 1970 s7.[43] This decision would appear, however, to fail to take into account the effect of LASSA 1970 Sch 1, as amended after the enactment of NHSCCA 1990, and is probably wrong.

6.43   The Policy Guidance on assessment procedures includes the following (summarised here):

a) the individual service user and, usually with his/her agreement, any carers, should be involved throughout the assessment and care management process and should feel that the process is aimed at meeting his/her wishes;[44]

b) the local authority is required to publish readily accessible information about care services, criteria and policies to enable users and carers to exercise choice and participate properly;[45]

---

38 See *Care management and assessment: a practitioner's guide* (HMSO, 1991); *Care management and assessment: a manager's guide* (HMSO, 1991); *Empowerment, assessment, care management and the skilled worker* (HMSO, 1993).

39 *R v Islington LBC ex p Rixon* (1998) 1 CCLR 119.

40 *R v North Derbyshire HA ex p Fisher* (1998) 1 CCLR 150.

41 HMSO, November 1990.

42 (1998) 1 CCLR 119.

43 *R (B and H) v Hackney LBC* [2003] EWHC 1654.

44 Policy Guidance para 3.16.

45 Policy Guidance para 3.18.

c) the assessment and care management process should take into account particular risk factors for service users, carers and the community generally: abilities and attitudes; health (especially remediable conditions or chronic conditions requiring continuing healthcare) and accommodation and social subordinates;[46]

d) once needs have been assessed, the services to be provided or arranged and the objectives of any intervention should be agreed in the form of a care plan which, so far as possible, should preserve or restore normal living;[47]

e) the aim should be to secure the most cost-effective package of services that meets the user's care needs, taking account of the user's and carer's own preferences. Where agreement between all the parties is not possible, the points of difference should be recorded;[48]

f) decisions on service provision should include clear agreement about what is going to be done, by whom and by when;[49]

g) it is necessary to assess the needs of carers and the ability of carers to continue to cope;[50]

h) care needs should be reviewed at regular intervals and should be reviewed if it is clear that community care needs have changed;[51]

Further and more detailed guidance is contained in the *Managers' Guide Care*[52] and the *Practitioners' Guide*.[53]

6.44   FACS in essence prescribes the eligibility criteria that local authorities should adopt to determine who is eligible for community care services and contains further procedural guidelines (FACS is set out in full in appendix B).

Assessment procedures: children

6.45   The procedure for conducting children assessments is also derived from guidance. The relevant guidance is again issued under LASSA 1970 s7 (see para 6.42) and is thus substantially binding. There are

---

46 Policy Guidance para 3.19.
47 Policy Guidance para 3.24.
48 Policy Guidance para 3.25.
49 Policy Guidance para 3.26.
50 Policy Guidance paras 3.27–3.29.
51 Policy Guidance para 3.51.
52 *Management and assessment: managers' guide* (HMSO, 1991).
53 *Care management and assessment: a practitioners' guide* (HMSO, 1991).

two main sources of guidance: the *Children Act 1989 Regulations and Guidance* (CA 1989 RG) (six volumes) and the *Framework for the Assessment of Children in Need* (FACN) (sometimes referred to as the 'lilac book').

6.46   Volume 2 of the CA 1989 RG contains the following relevant provisions summarised here:

a) The definition of 'need' in section 17(10) of the Act is deliberately wide to reinforce the emphasis on preventative support and services to families. The child's needs will include physical, emotional and educational needs according to his/her age, sex, race, religion, culture and language and the capacity of the current carer to meet those needs. CA 1989 requires each authority to decide its own level and scale of services appropriate to the children in need within its area, however, a local authority cannot lawfully substitute any other definition of 'need', for example, by confining services to children at risk of significant harm.[54]

b) In assessing individual need, authorities must assess the existing strengths and skills of the families concerned and help them overcome identified difficulties and enhance strengths. Sometimes the needs will be found to be intrinsic to the child; at other times, however, it may be that parenting skills and resources are depleted.[55]

c) Good practice requires that the assessment of need should be undertaken in an open way and should involve those caring for the child, the child and other significant persons. Families with a child in need, whether the need results from family difficulties or the child's circumstances, have the right to receive sympathetic support and sensitive intervention.[56]

d) In making an assessment, the local authority should take account of the particular needs of the child, that is, in relation to health, development, disability, education, religious persuasion, racial origin, cultural and linguistic background, etc.[57]

e) Assessment must identify and find a way to provide as helpful a guide as is possible to the child's needs.[58] Once the need has been identified, a plan for the best service provision will be required.[59]

---

54   Para 2.4.
55   Para 2.5.
56   Para 2.7.
57   Para 2.8.
58   Para 2.9.
59   Para 2.10.

6.47 Volume 3 contains further provisions relevant to assessments:

a) Assessments must cover the child's needs, the parent's abilities, the wishes and views of the child, and all factors relevant to the welfare of the individual child.[60]

b) There is no prescribed format for a child care plan, but there should be such a plan recorded in writing, containing the child's and his/her family's social history and a number of key elements including the child's identified needs, how those needs might be met, the timescale, the proposed services, a contingency plan, details of the roles all relevant persons are to play, the extent to which the wishes and views of the child, his/her parents and anyone else with a sufficient interest in the child have been obtained and acted upon and explanations of why wishes or views have been discounted, dates for reviews and so forth.[61]

6.48 The FACN contains very detailed provisions for the holistic assessment of children in need, together with recommended assessment pro formas. It also makes it clear that a decision should be made whether – and if so, how – to assess, within one working day, an initial assessment (as defined) should be completed within five working days, while a comprehensive assessment (as defined) should be completed within 30 working days.

6.49 Assistance under CA 1989 s17 may be provided unconditionally or subject to conditions as to the repayment of the assistance or of its value (in whole or in part).[62] Before giving any assistance, or imposing any conditions, the local authority has to have regard to the means of the child and his/her parents.[63] Charges cannot be made to persons in receipt of income support or family credit (now replaced by working families tax credit).

6.50 For the particular problems that arise in relation to assessing children's ages, see para 6.131 below.

Where a need is identified, does a local authority have to meet it?

6.51 Local authorities have a duty to provide some community care services and a discretion as to whether to provide others. A duty can exist in relation to services under CSDPA 1970 s2 and NAA 1948 s21. Once

60 Paras 2.21–2.22; see also paras 2.56–2.57.
61 Para 2.62.
62 CA 1989 s17(7).
63 CA 1989 s17(8).

a local authority has decided that a person needs services under these statutes, it has a duty to take steps to provide the services needed, irrespective of the authority's resources situation, albeit that the authority will retain a discretion as to how to best and most cost-effectively meet the assessed need. Where, however, provision is discretionary, or under a general duty, the authority must consider whether or not to meet the need. In deciding whether or not a need exists, the local authority must apply the language of the relevant statute, but in doing so may have regard to its 'eligibility criteria'. Eligibility criteria is a system of placing individuals in a hierarchy of categories (or 'bands') according to levels of risk of harm if services are not provided. Eligibility criteria used to vary widely from one local authority to another but now, as a result of FACS (see paras 6.42–6.44 above), can be expected to be virtually identical and to closely reflect the criteria in FACS.

Exclusion of PSIC and others from community care services

6.52   The IAA 1999 and the NIAA 2002 exclude certain persons subject to immigration control (PSIC) (see para 2.6 for the meaning of PSIC) and other persons from abroad from certain community care services. Not all PSIC are excluded, and the exclusion operates only in relation to certain services.

6.53   If a person is clearly excluded by IAA 1999 or the NIAA 2002, there is no duty on the local authority to complete a formal assessment, since the duty to complete an assessment and care plan only arises in relation to a person for whom a local authority might have the power to provide or arrange for the provision of community care services.[64] However, where – as is usually the case – it is not clear whether a person is excluded, at least some form of assessment, for example at least of the person's immigration status, would appear to be required. Furthermore, where exclusion is conditional on it being unnecessary to make provision in order to avoid a breach of ECHR rights, under the NIAA 2002, for example, it would appear that some form of assessment is required, in order to enable the local authority to ascertain whether or not it has the power to provide services, having regard to immigration status, care needs and ECHR rights. In such cases, where for example it transpires that the applicant is ineligible, assess-

64   NHSCCA 1990 s47.

ments can be expected to be relatively brief but nonetheless would have to be essentially fair, rational and properly reasoned.

Community care services excluded by IAA 1999

6.54 The exclusions in the IAA 1999 are at sections 116–117 and operate only in relation to three kinds of services:
- NAA 1948 s21 (residential accommodation);
- Health Services and Public Health Act (HSPHA) 1968 s45 (a range of services (described at para 6.100) for the elderly); and
- National Health Service Act (NHSA) 1977 Sch 8 para 2 (a range of services (described at para 6.110) for the social care and aftercare of the ill).

Thus there is no exclusion in relation to services under the following:
- NAA 1948 s29, including services under CSDPA 1970 s2 (a wide range of non-residential services for the disabled (described at para 6.114);
- MHA 1983 s117 (a very wide range of services (described at para 6.120) including accommodation for the aftercare of mentally-ill persons discharged from detention).

6.55 In the case of each of the three types of community care services where the exclusion operates, the exclusion from eligibility applies only to:
- PSIC as defined by IAA 1999 s115; who are also
- persons whose need for the service in question has arisen solely because they are destitute, or because of the physical effects or anticipated physical effects of their destitution.

6.56 The definition of 'PSIC' in IAA 1999 s115 has the effect of 're-including', as eligible for housing and state benefits, classes of people prescribed in regulations, who would otherwise be ineligible under section 115. However, in relation to community care services, no such regulations have been made, and thus all PSIC stand to be excluded. Accordingly, a person is excluded if he or she is not a national of a European Economic Area state and if he or she:
a) requires leave to enter or remain in the UK but does not have it; or
b) has leave to enter or remain in the UK, which is subject to a condition that he or she does not have recourse to public funds; or
c) has leave to enter or remain in the UK given as a result of the maintenance undertaking (a written undertaking given by another person in pursuance of the immigration rules, to be responsible for that person's maintenance and accommodation); or

d) has leave to enter or remain in the UK pending the conclusion of an appeal.

6.57   As mentioned above, a person is only excluded if, in addition to being a person to whom IAA 1999 s115 applies, his/her need for assistance has arisen solely because he or she is destitute, or because of the physical effects, or anticipated physical effects, of his/her being destitute.

6.58   The statutory criteria for residential accommodation under NAA 1948 s21 include needing 'care and attention . . . not otherwise available' by reason of 'age, illness, disability or any other circumstances'. Before the IAA 1999, the courts held that destitution and the other difficulties that faced many asylum-seekers at that time could be 'any other circumstances', giving rise to a threat of illness and therefore a need for 'care and attention'.[65] It was, accordingly, established that for all practical purposes destitution gave rise to a need for residential accommodation under NAA 1948 s21, and the same consideration would appear to apply to other community care services.

6.59   IAA 1999 ss116–117 ensure that people falling within section 115 may not be provided with community care services under NAA 1948 s21, HSPHA 1968 s45 or NHSA 1977 Sch 8 para 2 if their need arises solely because of destitution or because of the physical effects, or anticipated physical effects of destitution. However, destitution can still be a component, even the major component, of the need for community care services. The person is only excluded if destitution is the sole element in the need. Accordingly, the courts have held that the following were eligible, or potentially eligible for residential accommodation:

– a man who required medical treatment for cancer[66] and a woman disabled by cancer;[67]
– a woman with chronic and relapsing depression with psychotic features during episodes of relapse;[68]
– men and women with HIV;[69]

---

65 *R v Westminster CC ex p M, P, A & X* (1998) 1 CCLR 85.

66 *R v Wandsworth LBC ex p O* [2000] 1 WLR 2539; (2000) 3 CCLR 237.

67 *R (Westminster) v NASS* (2002) 5 CCLR 511.

68 *R v Wandsworth LBC ex p O* [2000] 1 WLR 2539; (2000) 3 CCLR 237.

69 *R (J) v Enfield LBC* [2002] EWHC 432; (2003) 5 CCLR 434; *R (Mani and others) v Lambeth and others* [2002] EWHC 735; (2002) 5 CCLR 486; *R (H) v Kingston upon Thames* [2002] EWHC 3158 (Admin); (2003) 6 CCLR 240; *R (B and H) v Hackney LBC* [2003] EWHC 1654; *R (M) v Slough BC* [2004] EWHC 1109 (subject to appeal).

- a woman vulnerable as the result of historic but long-standing and severe domestic violence;[70]
- a man with severe ankylosing spondylitis (leaving him with no movement in his neck and only slight movement in his spine);[71]
- a man disabled by thoracic spinal injury and a man disabled by the effects of polio, neither of whom were able to stand without crutches and calipers or perform everyday tasks without a wheelchair and special adaptations;[72]
- a man whose right leg was half the length of his left leg as the result of congenital disability;[73]

6.60   Other obvious examples would include persons suffering from mental illness, old and frail persons, expectant and nursing mothers (specifically referred to in NAA 1948 s21(1)(aa)), persons recovering from drug or alcohol dependency and persons recovering from significant illness or accident.

6.61   This is the effect of the decision of the Court of Appeal in *R v Wandsworth LBC ex p O*,[74] the leading case on the interpretation of these provisions:

> In what circumstances, then, is it to be said that destitution is the sole cause of need? The local authorities contend that the approach should be this. First ask if the applicant has (a) somewhere to live ('adequate accommodation') and (b) means of support (the means to 'meet his other essential living needs') [see section 95(3) of the Act of 1999]. Assuming the answer is 'no' to each of those questions, ask next whether, but for those answers, he would need section 21 assistance. If not, he does not qualify. In other words, it is only if an applicant would still need assistance even without being destitute that he is entitled to it.
>
> The applicants contend for an altogether different approach. They submit that if an applicant's need for care and attention is to any material extent made more acute by some circumstance other than mere lack of accommodation and funds, then, despite being subject to immigration control, he qualifies for assistance. Other relevant circumstances include, of course, age, illness and disability, all of which are expressly mentioned in section 21(1) itself. If, for example, an immigrant, as well as being destitute, is old, ill or

---

70 *R (Khan) v Oxfordshire CC* (2003) 5 CCLR 611 (reversed on the facts but not as to the principle in the Court of Appeal at [2004] EWCA Civ 309).

71 *R (Mani and others) v Lambeth and others* [2002] EWHC 735; (2002) 5 CCLR 486.

72 *R (Murua and Gichura) v Croydon LBC* (2002) 5 CCLR 51.

73 *R (Mani and others) v Lambeth and others* [2002] EWHC 735; (2002) 5 CCLR 486 and in the Court of Appeal at [2003] EWCA Civ 836; (2003) 6 CCLR 376.

74 [2000] 1 WLR 2539; (2000) 3 CCLR 237.

disabled, he is likely to be yet more vulnerable and less well able to survive than if he were merely destitute.

Given that both contended-for constructions are tenable, I have not the least hesitation in preferring the latter. The word 'solely' in the new section is a strong one and its purpose there seems to me evident. Assistance under the Act of 1948 is, it need hardly be emphasised, the last refuge of the destitute. If there are to be immigrant beggars on our streets, then let them at least not be old, ill or disabled (per Simon Brown LJ).

This decision has been followed in subsequent cases.[75]

6.62   It should be noted that people who have needs that do not arise solely from destitution, and who therefore potentially qualify for these community care services, include not only asylum-seekers, but all other PSIC, including applicants for humanitarian protection or discretionary leave to remain, people lawfully here with leave and people unlawfully here (as was the case in fact in *ex p O*) and whether or not they are pursuing some form of immigration appeal. The principal aim of NIAA 2002 Sch 3 was to further restrict eligibility for community care services among such persons.

Community care services excluded by NIAA 2002

6.63   The exclusions under NIAA 2002 s54 and Sch 3 relate to the following community care and other services described below at paras 6.88–6.114, 6.153:[76]

- NAA 1948 ss21 and 29 (note that now NAA 1948 s29 is excluded, for the first time, so too is CSDPA 1970 s2 because services under section 2 are performed in the exercise of functions under NAA 1948 s29);[77]
- NHSA 1977 s21 and Sch 8;
- CA 1989 ss17, 23C, 24A, 24B;
- LGA 2000 s2.

There continues to be no exclusion as far as concerns MHA 1983 s117 (a very wide range of services, including accommodation and board, for the aftercare of mentally ill persons discharged from detention).

6.64   While IAA 1999 excludes PSIC by imposing more restrictive

75 *R (Westminster) v NASS* [2002] UKHL 38; (2002) 5 CCLR 511; *R (Mani) v Lambeth LBC* (2003) 5 CCLR 376.

76 See NIAA 2002 Sch 3 para 1.

77 Services under CSDPA 1970 s2 qualify as 'community care services' because they are provided under NAA 1948 s29 (which is within NAA 1948 Part III).

eligibility criteria, NIAA 2002 simply excludes defined categories of persons altogether[78] unless the person is also:

- a British citizen;
- a child;
- included by virtue of regulations;

or unless it is necessary to provide a service in order to avoid a breach of the person's ECHR rights, or his/her rights under EEA Treaties.[79]

6.65   Accordingly, for example, provision can be made for the children of ineligible adults (such as accommodation and support under CA 1989) but cannot also be made for their parents, unless required by the ECHR or EEA Treaties.

6.66   It is true that, on the face of it, the ECHR can require the state to accommodate children with parents[80] and to support the destitute.[81] Having taken these potential obligations into account, however, the Court of Appeal held that the ECHR does not require any support to be provided to a destitute adult in the UK, even where necessary to enable the adult to enjoy family life with his/her child, if there is no Convention reason the adult cannot travel to his/her country of origin.[82] If the child becomes destitute, or is handed over to foster carers while his/her parent lives as a destitute person, *K* instructs us that all resulting unhappiness is attributable solely to the choices made by the parent. This remains the case even though, as in *K* the adult is lawfully present in the UK and pursuing an immigration application, which he or she is entitled to pursue 'in-country' and which, if successful, would lead to a right to remain and an entitlement to benefits.

6.67   It will be necessary to provide community care services to avoid a breach of a person's rights under EEA Treaties when a person is a member of an EEA country and is a worker, self-employed or providing services for a family member (see para 2.31).[83]

6.68   The categories of persons excluded by NIAA 2002 Sch 3 are as follows:

- persons granted refugee status by another EEA State and their dependants;[84]

---

78 See NIAA 2002 Sch 3 para 2.
79 NIAA 2002 Sch 3 para 3.
80 *R (J) v Enfield LBC* [2002] EWHC 432; (2003) 5 CCLR 434.
81 *R (Q) v SSHD* [2003] EWCA Civ 364; [2003] 3 WLR 365.
82 *R (K) v Lambeth LBC* [2003] EWCA Civ 1150.
83 Regulation EC/1612/68 and *Lebon* [1987] ECR 2811 and *R v IAT ex p Antonissen* [1991] 2 CMLR 373.
84 NIAA 2002 Sch 3 para 4.

- nationals of other EEA States and their dependants;[85]
- former asylum-seekers who have failed to co-operate with removal directions and their dependants (see para 1.143);[86]
- persons in the UK in breach of the immigration laws within the meaning of NIAA 2002 s11 who are not asylum-seekers.[87]

6.69　A person is in the UK in breach of the immigration laws within the meaning of NIAA 2002 s11 if;

- he or she is present in the UK;
- does not have the right of abode;
- does not have a currently valid leave to enter or remain;
- is not entitled to remain in the UK without leave as an EEA citizen or his/her dependant; and
- is not exempted from the need to have leave (certain crew members, diplomats, forces personnel). It should be noted, however, that NIAA 2002 s11 applies Immigration Act 1971 s11, with the result that a person who has an extant 'temporary admission' into the UK and who has not otherwise entered the UK (for example, unlawfully or with leave) is not in the UK in breach of the immigration laws – and so a person who claims asylum on arrival, for example, and who is granted temporary admission, is not unlawfully in the UK for so long as that temporary admission lasts.

6.70　The scope of 'dependant' is defined by Withholding and Withdrawal of Support (Travel Assistance and Temporary Accommodation) Regulations 2002 reg 2(2). It is notable, however, that a person married to an EEA national as the result of a marriage of convenience is still his/her dependant for these purposes.[88]

6.71　Asylum and Immigration (Treatment of Claimants, etc) Act 2004 s9 creates a further class of excluded persons by inserting into NIAA 2002 Sch 3 class 5, which excludes failed asylum-seekers with dependant children who have failed without reasonable excuse to take reasonable steps to leave the UK voluntarily, according to the secretary of state's certificate.

6.72　By virtue of NIAA 2002 Sch 3 paras 8, 9 and 10, the secretary of state has made the Withholding and Withdrawal of Support (Travel Assistance and Temporary Accommodation) Regulations (WWS(TATA)R) 2002. Furthermore, by virtue of NIAA 2002 Sch 3 para 2 and

---

85　NIAA 2002 Sch 3 para 5.
86　NIAA 2002 Sch 3 para 6.
87　NIAA 2002 Sch 3 para 7.
88　*R (K) v Lambeth LBC* [2003] EWCA Civ 1150.

WWS(TATA)R 2002 reg 4, the secretary of state has issued guidance, to which local authorities must have regard, called *Nationality, Immigration and Asylum Act 2002 section 54 and Schedule 3 and the Withholding and Withdrawal of Support (Travel Assistance and Temporary Accommodation) Regulations 2002: Guidance to Local Authorities and Housing Authorities* (the NIAA 2002 Guidance).[89]

6.73   WWS(TATA)R 2002 reg 3(1) empowers local authorities to make travel arrangements enabling EEA refugees and EEA nationals[90] to leave the UK to travel to the relevant EEA State. Providing the person in question has a dependant child with him/her, WWS(TATA)R 2002 reg 3(2) empowers local authorities to accommodate him/her, with his/her child, pending the implementation of such travel arrangements (at least until such time as he or she fails to co-operate with the travel arrangements – see reg 5).

6.74   The WWS(TATA)R 2002 do not empower local authorities to make travel arrangements enabling former asylum-seekers who have not failed to co-operate with removal directions or persons unlawfully present in the UK[91] to travel to their countries of origin. Regulation 3(3) does, however, empower local authorities to accommodate persons unlawfully present in the UK who have not failed to co-operate with removal directions, providing such persons have a dependant child. In *R (M) v Islington LBC*,[92] the local authority decided that, in the light of the NIAA 2002 Guidance, it could only lawfully provide such accommodation for a very short period of ten days or so, and could then provide assistance with travel to the family's country of origin, but not other assistance, under CA 1989 s17 on the basis that this was in the children's best interests. The court quashed this decision holding that local authorities have power under WWS(TATA)R 2002 to provide accommodation up until the unlawfully present adult fails to comply with removal directions. In considering how to exercise this power, regard had to be given to the ECHR, with reference to which it would be difficult not to see an offer of travel with an alternative of no accommodation (made not for social reasons but as an attempt to enforce immigration control other than by issuing removal directions) as an unjustifiable interference with article 8 rights. In *R (G) v Lambeth LBC*[92a] the court then held that in

89   www.asylumsupport.info/withholdingand withdrawing.htm.
90   The categories of persons excluded by NIAA 2002 Sch 3 paras 4 and 5.
91   The categories of persons excluded by NIAA 2002 Sch 3 paras 6 and 7.
92   [2003] EWCA Civ 235.
92a [2004] EWHC 1524.

the case of families unlawfully present in the UK, local authorities had no power to arrange for their removal under CA 1989 s17 or LGA 2000 s2 but had to accommodate them under WWS(TATA)R 2002 until the family obtained their own funding, until they ceased to need accommodation or until the secretary of state made removal directions which the family failed to comply with.

The local authority/NASS divide

6.75   Where persons are not asylum-seekers, or failed asylum-seekers, no question of NASS support arises and the individuals in question either will or will not qualify for local authority help, depending on the extent to which they are excluded by IAA 1999 and NIAA 2002. In the case of individual asylum-seekers, or families of asylum-seekers, however, NASS and local authorities have potentially overlapping responsibilities so far as concerns the provision of accommodation and basic support (albeit that only local authorities have the power to provide more specialised forms of care).

6.76   Adult asylum-seekers who are healthy and able-bodied and who do not have children are the responsibility of NASS.[93]

6.77   When such persons cease to be asylum-seekers they may qualify for accommodation under IAA 1999 s4 (see para 3.291) but will not qualify for support under NAA 1948, because their need will arise solely on account of destitution (see paras 6.58–6.61), or for accommodation under WWS(TATA)R 2002 (because they do not have a child).

6.78   Adult asylum-seekers who are healthy and able-bodied and who do have children are, together with their children, the responsibility of NASS,[94] irrespective of whether the children are healthy and able-bodied.[95] Only the local authority has the power to provide specialised care going beyond accommodation and support to disabled children, but NASS still has the duty to provide accommodation and basic support that meets the needs of disabled children, however complex, for example, adapted accommodation and special diets.[96]

6.79   In a case where NASS is not under a duty to support such families under IAA 1999 s122, for example, because they are 'intentionally destitute' or have failed to comply with conditions attached to sup-

93   R *(Westminster) v NASS* [2002] UKHL 38; (2002) 5 CCLR 511.

94   Because of IAA 1999 s122.

95   *R(A) v NASS (1) and Waltham Forest LBC (2)* [2003] EWCA Civ 1473; (2003) 6 CCLR 538.

96   Although NASS can seek local authority assistance under IAA 1999 s100.

port,[97] the families become a local authority responsibility under CA 1989 ss17 and 20.

6.80   Currently, such families do not cease to be asylum-seekers for the purposes of asylum support, even after the final adverse determination of their asylum claim.[98] When Asylum and Immigration (Treatment of Claimants, etc) Act 2004 s9 is brought into force by order, adding a new class 5 to NIAA 2002 Sch 3, such persons will cease to be asylum-seekers once the secretary of state certifies that they have failed to take reasonable steps to return to their countries of origin. At that point, the family as a whole will be excluded from NASS support and the adults, but not the children, will be excluded from local authority support, except to the extent that the lack of support will give rise to a breach of ECHR or EEA Treaty rights. By analogy with *K*,[99] however, it may be difficult for the failed asylum-seeker to derive any assistance from the ECHR if there is no convention or Refugee Convention reason why he or she cannot return to his/her country of origin (see para 6.66 above). There will be a right of appeal to the Asylum Support Adjudicators.

6.81   Adult asylum-seekers who do not have children but who need special care, or whose need for ordinary support is materially exacerbated by old age, illness, disability or some other factor going beyond the physical, or anticipated physical, effects of destitution, are a local authority responsibility under NAA 1948 s21.[100]

6.82   When such persons cease to be asylum-seekers (see chapter 3) they may qualify for accommodation under IAA 1999 s4 but will also continue to qualify for local authority support under NAA 1948 s21 unless and until they fail to co-operate with removal directions.[101] There are, however, two provisos:

> 1) if such failed asylum-seekers are also unlawfully present in the UK within the meaning of NIAA 2002 s11, they may be excluded from assistance under NAA 1948 s21 by NIAA 2002 Sch 3 para 7: this is an issue which may have to be resolved by the court.
> 2) no case has as yet explored whether in the case of failed but disabled asylum-seekers NASS is responsible for support under IAA 1999 s4 or whether local authorities remain liable under NAA 1948 s21 and the question would not appear to be straightforward.

---

97 See Asylum Support Regulations 2000 reg 20.

98 See IAA 1999 s94(5).

99 *R (K) v Lambeth LBC* [2003] EWCA Civ 1150.

100 *R (Mani) v Lambeth LBC* [2003] EWCA Civ 836; (2003) 6 CCLR 376.

101 See NIAA 2002 Sch 3 para 6.

6.83   In a case where adult asylum-seekers are a local authority responsibility under NAA 1948 s21, NASS is financially responsible for the children.[102]

6.84   When such families cease to be asylum-seekers, their circumstances are likely to become difficult to unravel, but logically the provisions set out in para 6.82 above can be expected to apply to them.

6.85   Unaccompanied children, whether or not they are asylum-seekers, are exclusively the responsibility of local authorities, under CA 1989 s20 (asylum support is only available to asylum-seekers aged 18 and over).[103]

6.86   Adult asylum-seekers who have (as children) been in local authority care are entitled to support on leaving care and there is no exclusion of persons from abroad from the children leaving care machinery in CA 1989 (see paras 6.132–6.153). In practice, however, since such children will also be eligible for asylum support when they reach 18, NASS will take over financial responsibility at least[104] although the local authority's duty to maintain a pathway plan and personal adviser and the local authority's overarching welfare duty remains. If the former children are disabled, etc, then they will continue to be entirely a local authority responsibility, under NAA 1948 s21.

6.87   When such persons (who are now adults) cease also be asylum-seekers their eligibility for assistance under the children leaving care machinery of CA 1989 also ceases, by virtue of NIAA 2002 s54 and Sch 3. As failed asylum-seeker adults, they are entitled to no more than other failed asylum-seeker adults (which is nothing, other than possibly hard cases support under IAA 1999 s4).

The nature and extent of community care services

Services under the NHSCCA 1990 subject to exclusions

Residential accommodation under NAA 1948 s21

6.88   Asylum-seekers and other PSIC who have needs, which derive at least in part from causes other than destitution or the physical effects of destitution (for example, because they are elderly, handicapped, disabled, physically or mentally ill, or pregnant, or because they are a

---

102 *R (O) v Haringey* [2004] EWCA Civ 535.

103 IAA 1999 s94(1).

104 See Children (Leaving Care) Act 2000 Regulations and Guidance chapter 2 paras 7–11.

nursing mother),[105] will be entitled to have their needs for accommodation and subsistence met by the local authority social services department under NAA 1948 s21.

6.89 Local authorities have powers to provide residential accommodation under NAA 1948 s21, and those powers are converted into duties by, and in the circumstances set out in, the approvals and directions made under section 21 by the Secretary of State for Social Services.[106] PSIC are excluded from these services in the circumstances described above (see paras 6.54–6.58 and 6.63–6.68).

6.90 Most commonly, the duty arises under the combination of NAA 1948 s21(1)(a) and the direction at para 2(1)(b) of the approvals and directions, in respect of 'persons aged 18 or over who by reason of age, illness, disability or any other circumstances are in need of care and attention not otherwise available to them' and who are ordinarily resident in the local authority area or who have no settled residence or are in urgent need. The structure of these provisions warrants careful note, as the duty is to provide 'residential accommodation' to those – not, as may be expected, in need of accommodation, but to those – in need of care and attention not otherwise available to them. In particular circumstances, an authority may be under a duty to provide accommodation to a person who, at the point of assessment, has accommodation available. In *R (Wahid) v Tower Hamlets LBC*,[107] Hale LJ stated that the 'natural and ordinary meaning' of the expression 'in need of care and attention' in this context was 'looking after': this can obviously include feeding the starving, as with the destitute asylum-seekers'. She provided the following introduction to NAA 1948 s21:

> Some basic points may deserve emphasis given the recent expansion of litigation in this field. Under section 21(1)(a) of the National Assistance Act 1948, local social services authorities have a duty to make arrangements for providing residential accommodation for people over 18 (who are ordinarily resident in their area or in urgent need) where three inter-related conditions are fulfilled:
> 1) the person is in need of care and attention;
> 2) that need arises by reason of age, illness, disability or any other circumstances; and
> 3) that care and attention is not available to him otherwise than by the provision of residential accommodation under this particular power.

105 See NAA 1948 s21(1)(aa).
106 See appendix B.
107 (2002) 5 CCLR 239.

Three further points are also relevant:

1) it is for the local social services authority to assess whether or not these conditions are fulfilled and, if so, how the need is to be met, subject to the scrutiny of the court on the ordinary principles of judicial review;

2) section 21 does not permit the local social services authority to make provision which may or must be made by them or any other authority under an enactment other than Part III of the 1948 Act (see s21(8)); but

3) having identified a need to be met by the provision of residential accommodation under section 21, the authority have a positive duty to meet it which can be enforced in judicial review proceedings

. . . 'residential accommodation' can mean ordinary housing without the provision of any ancillary services'.

6.91   Care and attention can be 'otherwise available' to a person if they have family members who can provide them with support and/or care or if there are charitable or other avenues of voluntary support. Emergency support provided, for example, by community members on a short-term basis in order to help a desperate person ought not to preclude eligibility: see by analogy *R v Ealing LBC ex p Sidhu*.[109]

6.92   Where residential accommodation is provided, there is a duty to meet needs for food and other welfare services, where required.[110] No assistance can be given, however, in the form of cash.[111]

6.93   The case of *R v Westminster City Council ex p M, P, A & X*[112] established that destitute asylum-seekers, in danger of suffering illness as the result of their inability to obtain shelter and food, were in need of care and attention for the purposes of these provisions. Later cases established that a person could still need care and attention (and thus give rise to a duty to provide accommodation) because of destitution even though he or she was able to meet some needs (for example, accommodation but not food)[113] or was entitled to work but not able to find work.[114]

6.94   The rationale of the court's approach to provision under NAA 1948 s21 appears to have been adopted in IAA 1999, which provides

---

109 (1981) 2 HLR 41.

110 NAA 1948 s21(5) and Approvals and Directions para 4.

111 *R v Secretary of State for Health ex p M and K* (1998) 1 CCLR 495.

112 (1997) 1 CCLR 85.

113 *R v Newham LBC ex p Gorenkin* (1998) 1 CCLR 309.

114 *R v Newham LBC ex p Plastin* (1998) 1 CCLR 304; see further *R v Southwark LBC ex p Hong Cui* (1999) 2 CCLR 86.

that a person is destitute either if he or she does not have adequate accommodation or any means of obtaining it (whether or not his/her other essential needs are met), or if he or she has adequate accommodation or the means of obtaining it, but cannot meet other essential living needs.[115]

6.95   For the duty under NAA 1948 s21 to arise in relation to a PSIC (see para 2.61), the need for care and attention must not arise solely because of destitution or the physical effects of destitution.[116] There would, therefore, have to be another element present, of the kind mentioned in section 21, that is, age, illness, disability, pregnancy, nursing or some other circumstance giving rise to a need for care and attention. Cases in which the court has found 'destitution plus' to be present include the following:

- a woman disabled by cancer;[117]
- men and women with HIV,[118]
- a woman vulnerable as the result of historic but long-standing and severe domestic violence;[119]
- a man with severe ankylosing spondylitis (leaving him with no movement in his neck and only slight movement in his spine);[120]
- a man whose right leg was half the length of his left leg as the result of congenital disability.[121]

6.96   Other obvious examples would include persons suffering from mental illness, old and frail persons, expectant and nursing mothers (specifically referred to in NAA 1948 s21(1)(aa)), persons recovering from drug or alcohol dependency and persons suffering from significant illness or accident.

6.97   The approvals and directions set out a number of types of cases where there is a duty or power to provide residential accommodation. Local authorities will also have published eligibility criteria, under

---

115 IAA 1999 s95(3).

116 NAA 1948 s21(1A), introduced by IAA 1999 s116.

117 *R (Westminster) v NASS* [2002] UKHL 38; (2002) 5 CCLR 511.

118 *R (J) v Enfield LBC* [2002] EWHC 432, (2003) 5 CCLR 434; *R (Mani and others) v Lambeth and others* [2002] EWHC 735, (2002) 5 CCLR 486; *R (H) v Kingston upon Thames* [2002] EWHC 3158 (Admin), (2003) 6 CCLR 240; *R (B and H) v Hackney LBC* [2003] EWHC 1654.

119 *R (Khan) v Oxfordshire CC* (2003) 5 CCLR 611 (reversed on the facts but not as to the principle in the Court of Appeal at [2004] EWCA Civ 309).

120 *R (Mani and others) v Lambeth and others* [2002] EWHC 735; (2002) 5 CCLR 486.

121 *R (Mani and others) v Lambeth and others* [2002] EWHC 735; (2002) 5 CCLR 486 and in the Court of Appeal at [2003] EWCA Civ 836; (2003) 6 CCLR 376.

NHSCCA 1990 s46 and FACS, by reference to which social workers decide whether a 'need' for residential accommodation exists. If the criteria are too stringent, having regard to the statutory framework, judicial review is possible. Once a local authority has assessed a need for residential accommodation as existing, then it must meet the need.[122]

6.98   'Residential accommodation' can be accommodation in an institution, a hostel or an ordinary house or flat.[123] It should be suitable, which in this context requires the local authority to have regard to the welfare of all persons for whom accommodation is provided, and to provide different descriptions of accommodation suited to different descriptions of persons.[124] It must meet whatever needs have been assessed as existing.[125] The authority should strive to meet the assisted person's preferences within its available resources.[126] It has to plan how best to meet the needs assessed and how best to meet preferences in accordance with the provisions of the Policy Guidance and FACS (see para 6.39–6.44).

6.99   Where the assisted person has children, there is no doubt that the local authority has the power to accommodate him/her together with the children, if need be, by using its powers under CA 1989 s17. The local authority would be under a duty to exercise its powers under CA 1989 s17 in this way if not to do so would result in a breach of ECHR article 8.[127] It has been the long-standing practice of local authorities to accommodate assisted persons together with adult family members or carers (for example, an elderly spouse).[128] The court has recently indicated that this practice is legal.[129]

6.100   Where the NAA 1948 (Choice of Accommodation) Directions 1992[130] conditions are met, the assisted person has the right to choose

---

122 *R v Kensington and Chelsea RLBC ex p Kujtim* (1999) 2 CCLR 340; *R (Wahid) v Tower Hamlets LBC* (2002) 5 CCLR 239.

123 *R v Newham LBC ex p Medical Foundation for the Care of Victims of Torture* (1998) 1 CCLR 227; *R v Bristol City Council ex p Penfold* (1998) 1 CCLR 315; *R (Wahid) v Tower Hamlets LBC* (2002) 5 CCLR 239.

124 NAA 1948 s21(2).

125 *R v Avon CC ex p M* (1999) 2 CCLR 185.

126 The Policy Guidance para 3.25.

127 *R (J) v Enfield LBC* (2003) 6 CCLR 434.

128 *R (Khana) v Southwark LBC* (2001) 4 CCLR 267; *R (Batantu) v Islington LBC* (2001) 4 CCLR 445; *R (Wahid) v Tower Hamlets LBC* (2002) 5 CCLR 239 are some cases which refer to this practice.

129 *R (O) v Haringey LBC* [2004] EWCA Civ 535.

130 LAC(92)29. See www.dh.gov.uk.

his/her 'preferred accommodation'. This could apply where, for example, the local authority has located accommodation some distance away, but the asylum-seeker has found cheaper accommodation located near relatives and friends. The conditions summarised here are that:[131]

a) the preferred accommodation appears to the local authority to be suitable in relation to the person's needs as assessed by them;
b) the cost of making arrangements at the preferred accommodation would not require the authority to pay more than it would usually expect to pay having regard to the assessed needs;
c) the preferred accommodation is available;
d) the persons in charge of the preferred accommodation provide it subject to the authority's usual terms and conditions.

If the accommodation would require the authority to pay more than it would usually expect to pay, third parties are permitted to 'top up' the difference.[132]

6.101   It is important to note that, while an authority absolutely must meet assessed needs, the way in which the authority meets those needs is largely a matter for the authority to decide, although it must strive to meet preferences within available resources.[133] This is in stark contrast to the support system under the IAA 1999, wherein it is repeatedly stressed that no regard is to be had to an applicant's preferences.

6.102   Residential accommodation can be provided by the local authority entering into arrangements with the private sector, under NAA 1948 s26. Alternatively, it can be provided by the local authority using accommodation held for that purpose under NAA 1948 s21 itself. The local authority can grant licences of its own housing stock for this purpose.[134]

6.103   It is only in an exceptional case that a local authority is entitled to treat its duty under section 21 as discharged, so that it does not have to offer further accommodation, for example, on account of disruptive behaviour. In *R v Kensington and Chelsea RLBC ex p Kujtim*,[135] the

---

131 Direction 3.
132 Direction 4.
133 Policy Guidance para 3.25.
134 The proscription on local authorities granting tenancies and licences to PSIC imposed by IAA 1999 s118 is lifted for the purposes of NAA 1948 s21 by Persons Subject to Immigration Control (Housing Authority Accommodation and Homelessness) Order 2000 SI No 706 reg 4(1)(a).
135 [1999] 4 All ER 161.

Court of Appeal emphasised that it was essential that local authorities should not reach the conclusion that their duty to provide residential accommodation was discharged unless satisfied that the applicant had unreasonably refused to accept accommodation provided, or that he or she had persistently and unequivocally refused to comply with the local authority's requirements (for example, as to behaviour) so as in effect to reject the accommodation, coupled with a careful consideration of his/her current needs and circumstances (including any change of heart on the part of the applicant).

6.104   A local authority may charge for accommodation provided under section 21. There is a detailed scheme of means testing and regulation.[136] These charging provisions are not usually relevant to asylum-seekers with limited resources.

6.105   NIAA 2002 Sch 3 and s54 absolutely exclude EEA refugees, EEA nationals, former asylum-seekers who have failed to co-operate with removal directions and certain persons unlawfully present in the UK from services under NAA 1948 s45, except where provision is required to avoid a breach of the ECHR or Community Treaties (see paras 6.63–6.68).[137] Other persons from abroad are not excluded. As to which asylum-seekers are eligible for local authority support under NAA 1948 s21 and which are the responsibility of NASS see paras 6.59–6.61, 6.95.

Services for the elderly under HSPHA 1968 s45

6.106   Asylum-seekers and other PSIC who have needs which derive at least in part from causes other than destitution or the physical effects of destitution (for example, because they are elderly, handicapped, disabled, physically or mentally ill) will be eligible for services under HSPHA 1968 s45.

6.107   The services provided under HSPHA 1968 s45 are miscellaneous services, which local authorities are empowered to provide for the elderly, in accordance with approvals and directions made under that section, which are found in Circular LAC 19/71. The services include meals on wheels and recreation, in the home or elsewhere, social work assistance, practical assistance and adaptations in the home and

---

136   See NAA 1948 s22, National Assistance (Assessment of Resources) Regulations 1992 SI No 2977 and Charging for Residential Accommodation Guide (LAC(95)7), as frequently amended.

137   The exclusion will also apply to failed asylum-seekers certified as not taking reasonable steps to leave the UK when Asylum and Immigration (Treatment of Claimants, etc) Act 2004 s9 is brought into force by regulations.

warden services. Almost by definition, it might be thought, a person likely to qualify for this kind of service would not be in need solely by reason of destitution, but also by reason of old age.

6.108   The exclusion of certain PSIC by IAA 1999 will have little impact in relation to services under HSPHA 1968 s45, since there will be few people (if any) with a need for these services for whom destitution is the only cause of that need.

6.109   It will be recollected, however, that NIAA 2002 absolutely excludes EEA refugees, EEA nationals, former asylum-seekers who have failed to co-operate with removal directions and certain persons unlawfully present in the UK from services under HSPHA 1968 s45, except where provision is required to avoid a breach of the ECHR or Community Treaties (see paras 6.63–6.74).[138]

Services for the sick under the NHSA 1977

6.110   The services provided under NHSA 1977 s21 and Sch 8 para 2 relate to services that local authorities may, and in some cases must, provide for the prevention of illness, the care of people suffering from illness and the aftercare of people who have been suffering from illness. Provision is made in accordance with approvals and directions.[139] The kinds of services involved are day centres and similar facilities, social services support, social and recreational facilities. Provision is discretionary.

6.111   Again, almost by definition, it might be thought, a person likely to qualify for these kinds of services would not be in need solely by reason of destitution, but also by reason of past or present illness and, thus, the limited exclusion of PSIC by IAA 1999 described at paras 6.55–6.61 is likely to have little impact.

6.112   It will be recollected, however, that NIAA 2002 absolutely excludes EEA refugees, EEA nationals, former asylum-seekers who have failed to co-operate with removal directions and certain persons unlawfully present in the UK from services under NHSA 1977 s21 and Sch 8 para 2, except where provision is required to avoid a breach of the ECHR or Community Treaties (see paras 6.63–6.74).[140]

---

138 The exclusion will also apply to failed asylum-seekers certified as not taking reasonable steps to leave the UK when Asylum and Immigration (Treatment of Claimants, etc) Act 2004 s9 is brought into force by regulations.

139 LAC(93)10.

140 The exclusion will also apply to failed asylum-seekers certified as not taking reasonable steps to leave the UK when Asylum and Immigration (Treatment of Claimants, etc) Act 2004 s9 is brought into force by regulations.

Services under the NHSCCA 1990 not subject to exclusions under IAA 1999

6.113   There is no exclusion in IAA 1999 of asylum-seekers or other PSIC from services under NAA 1948 s29, CSDPA 1970 s2, LGA 2000 s2 and MHA 1983 s117. Of these sets of provisions, only MHA 1983 s117 and LGA 2000 s2 offer the possibility of the provision of assistance with accommodation and subsistence. There are, however, exclusions under NIAA 2002 in respect of NAA 1948 s29, CSDPA 1970 s2 and LGA 2000 s2.

NAA 1948 s29, CSDPA 1970 s2 and LGA 2000 s2

6.114   These enactments apply only to substantially disabled persons: 'persons aged 18 or over who are blind, deaf or dumb, or who suffer from mental disorder of any description and other persons aged 18 or over who are substantially and permanently handicapped by illness, injury, or congenital deformity or such other disabilities as may be prescribed by the Minister'.[141]

6.115   Services under NAA 1948 s29 are provided in accordance with approvals and directions made under that section[142] and, again, each local authority will have its own published eligibility criteria which, currently, can be expected to mirror the eligibility criteria in FACS (see paras 6.42–6.44). The services provided include social work assistance, different types of day centres, holiday homes, travel, and warden schemes.

6.116   The services available under CSDPA 1970 s2 are set out in the section itself and include practical assistance in the home, various kinds of leisure provision, home adaptations, telephones and meals. The assessment process was considered by the House of Lords in *R v Gloucestershire CC ex p Barry*.[143] The conclusion was that, in assessing needs and whether it was necessary to meet them, local authorities are entitled and obliged to have regard to:

-   current standards of living;
-   the nature and extent of the disability;
-   the extent and manner to which quality of life would be improved; and
-   the cost of providing the service in the context of the resources available to the local authority.

141   NAA 1948 s29(1).
142   LAC(93)10.
143   [1997] AC 584; (1997) 1 CCLR 40.

The relative cost is to be weighed against the relative benefit and the relative need for that benefit, in the light of the local authorities' published community care criteria.

6.117 Additionally, in the case of persons from abroad, the local authority will inevitably have to pay particular attention to the effect on such persons of destitution.

6.118 LGA 2000 s2 empowers local authorities to do anything which they consider likely, among other things, to promote the social well-being of their area.[144] It is expressly provided that local authorities can make provision for individuals, including financial assistance and accommodation.[145] However, this power does not allow local authorities to do something to the extent prohibited or restricted by another enactment.[146] Furthermore, the power must be exercised having regard to the local authority's own strategy[147] and guidance issued by the secretary of state.[148] It appears that the power under LGA 2000 s2 can be used to provide support required by the ECHR, for which there is no clear alternative statutory basis.[149] Otherwise, the nature and purpose of the power fits uneasily with the notion that it can be used to address cases of individual hardship.

6.119 It will be recollected that NIAA 2002 absolutely excludes EEA refugees, EEA nationals, former asylum-seekers who have failed to co-operate with removal directions and certain persons unlawfully present in the UK from services under NAA 1948 s29, CSDPA 1970 s2 and LGA 2000 s2, except where provision is required to avoid a breach of the ECHR or Community Treaties (see paras 6.63–6.74).[150] LGA 2000 s2 is also excluded in respect of asylum-seekers who do not claim asylum as soon as reasonably practicable upon arrival.[151]

MHA 1983 s117

6.120 Asylum-seekers and PSIC who are so mentally ill as to have been compulsorily detained remain eligible for and indeed entitled to

---

144 LGA 2000 s2(1).

145 LGA 2000 s2(2) and (4).

146 LGA 2000 s3; *R (Khan) v Oxfordshire CC* [2004] EWCA Civ 309.

147 LGA 2000 ss2(3) and 4.

148 LGA 2000 s3(5).

149 *R (J) v Enfield LBC* (2002) 5 CCLR 434.

150 The exclusion will also apply to failed asylum-seekers certified as not taking reasonable steps to leave the UK when Asylum and Immigration (Treatment of Claimants, etc) Act 2004 s9 is brought into force by regulations.

151 NIAA 2002 s55.

support irrespective of their immigration status, because there are no immigration exclusions from services under MHA 1983 s117. These services are 'aftercare' services provided for persons who cease to be detained under the treatment provisions of the MHA 1983.[152] They include 'social work, support in helping the ex-patient with problems of employment, accommodation or family relationships, the provision of domiciliary services and the use of day centre and residential facilities'.[153] They also include the provision of residential accommodation and charges cannot be made.[154] Responsibility for the provision of services rests jointly upon the health and social services authorities.

6.121   Essentially, before a mentally-ill person is discharged from detention, there has to be a multidisciplinary assessment of his/her needs around the time of discharge, completed by relevant medical and social services officers.[155]

6.122   So far as concerns all of these services, people subject to immigration control are eligible for assistance on the same basis as British citizens. The only additional factor likely to arise, is that the destitution of people from abroad may result in needs existing that would not otherwise have existed and may increase the needs that fall to be met under the community care scheme if physical or mental damage is to be avoided.

Services for children

6.123   The IAA 1999 marked a new departure by taking the subsistence and accommodation needs of children living with their families who are asylum-seekers outside the scope of the CA 1989,[156] except in highly

---

152 MHA 1983 s117 applies to those detained for treatment under ss3, 37 and 41, but not those detained for assessment under s2 and not to those who become in-patients voluntarily.

153 *Clunis v Camden and Islington HA* (1998) 1 CCLR 215 at 225GH.

154 *R (Stennett) v Manchester CC* [2002] UKHL 34; [2002] 2 AC 1127; (2002) 5 CCLR 500.

155 See *The Care Programme Approach* at HC(90)23/LASSL(90)23 and in *Effective Care and Co-ordination in Mental Health Services,* issued under the relatively new *National Service Framework for Mental Health* at HSC(1999)223; see also LAC(1999)34 *Guidance on the Discharge of Mentally Disordered People and their Continuing Care in the Community; Building Bridges: a Guide to Arrangements for the Inter-Agency Working for Care and Protection of Severely Mentally Ill People* at LASSL(94)4), HSG(94)27; *R v Ealing LBC ex p Fox* [1993] 3 All ER 170; *R v Mental Health Review Tribunal ex p Hall* (1999) 2 CCLR 361.

156 IAA 1999 s122.

residual cases (see para 6.79 above). NIAA 2002 Sch 3 goes further and excludes adults, but not children, from support under CA 1989 s17 if they are EEA refugees, EEA nationals, former asylum-seekers who have failed to co-operate with removal directions and certain categories of persons unlawfully present.[157] Apart from these exclusions, services for children are almost exclusively provided under the CA 1989. An exception is made in respect of children who are disabled,[158] who are eligible for all of the services within CSDPA 1970. Provision for unaccompanied children who claim asylum is made entirely under the CA 1989.

Children in need

6.124   Local authorities have powers and duties under CA 1989 Part III in relation to 'children in need'. A child is defined as a person under 18 years of age.[159] The term 'child in need' is defined in CA 1989 s17(10) as being a child who is:

– unlikely to achieve or maintain, or to have the opportunity of achieving or maintaining, a reasonable standard of health[160] or development,[161] without the provision for him/her of services by the local authority under CA 1989 Part III; or
– likely to suffer significant impairment of health or development, or further impairment, without the provision for him/her of services by the local authority under CA 1989 Part III; or
– disabled: that is a child who is blind, deaf or dumb or who suffers from mental disorder of any kind or who is substantially and permanently handicapped by illness, injury or congenital deformity.

Children of families of asylum-seekers lacking accommodation and the means of support are likely to fall within the scope of this definition.

---

157 The exclusion will also apply to failed asylum-seekers certified as not taking reasonable steps to leave the UK when Asylum and Immigration (Treatment of Claimants, etc) Act 2004 s9 is brought into force by regulations.
158 As defined in NAA 1948 s29.
159 CA 1989 s105(1).
160 'Health' is defined as including physical or mental health.
161 'Development' is defined as including physical, intellectual, emotional, social or behavioural development.

Services for children in need living with their families

6.125   The services provided can include assistance in kind and also cash.[162] All of the services can be provided for the child or, where appropriate, for the child and his/her family.[163] Assistance in kind can include accommodation.[164] Where a child is homeless, the local authority is under a duty to provide assistance to the child,[165] but there is no absolute duty under section 17 to house homeless children together with their families. Rather, local authorities must take such steps as are reasonably practicable to enable a child to live with his/her family where it is necessary to promote and safeguard the child's welfare.[166] It is not unlawful for a local authority to have a general policy of not accommodating children with families, where its experience is that homeless families invariably make do.[167] However, each case must be considered individually and local authorities are subject to judicial review in accordance with ordinary public law principles.[168] Furthermore, ECHR article 8 can require local authorities to accommodate families together.[169] Local authorities can grant tenancies or licences to accommodate families under section 17.[170] Local authorities must make such provision as they consider appropriate in respect of advice, social activities, travel for the purpose of using services, and holidays.[171] This could include assistance with school clothing, books and other study materials, toys, etc.

6.126   Prior to the IAA 1999, local authorities provided destitute asylum-seeker families with accommodation, food and other basic necessities under CA 1989 s17 on a very large scale. The great advantage of the CA 1989 regime is its flexibility. Once the authority has decided to provide assistance, there is no limit to the type of assistance that can be provided or the way in which it can be provided.

---

162 CA 1989 s17(6).

163 CA 1989 s17(3).

164 CA 1989 s17(6).

165 CA 1989 s20.

166 CA 1989 s17(1) and (3).

167 *R (W, A, G) v Lambeth LBC* [2003] UKHL 57.

168 *R (W, A, G) v Lambeth LBC* [2003] UKHL 57.

169 *R (J) v Enfield LBC* (2002) 5 CCLR 434.

170 The proscription on local authorities granting tenancies and licences to PSIC imposed by IAA 1999 s118 is lifted for the purposes of children in need by Persons Subject to Immigration Control (Housing Authority Accommodation and Homelessness) Order 2000 SI No 706 reg 4(1)(b).

171 CA 1989 s17 and Sch 2 Part I para 8.

6.127 However, it is a flexibility that cuts both ways. Assistance under CA 1989 s17 confers no absolute right to services to meet an assessed need, far less to particular accommodation and services. Furthermore, a local authority can discharge its duties in a variety of ways, as it considers appropriate in the circumstances. Thus, it may satisfy a need for accommodation by securing accommodation itself, or by providing assistance to parents to secure accommodation in the private rented sector. The assistance must, however, be effective.[172]

Services for unaccompanied asylum-seeker children

6.128 This covers children under 18 years of age who arrive in the UK, claim asylum and are without close adult family members either accompanying them or already present in the UK and whom they can join. Such children are the responsibility of the social services department of the local authority in whose area they are for the time being, and should on arrival be referred immediately to the social services department for an assessment and for the immediate provision of assistance. Assistance provided ranges from accommodation and food to foster carers, leisure, language help and trauma counselling. Such children should be treated no differently from UK children who have been taken into care except, of course, that they may need extra help.

6.129 Assistance is provided to such children under CA 1989 s20. The authority must provide accommodation to any child in need who appears to require it as a result of there being no one who has parental responsibility for him/her, being lost or abandoned, or the child's carers being prevented for the time being from providing suitable accommodation or care. In addition to providing accommodation, the authority must maintain the child.[173] Provision must, so far as practicable, have regard to the wishes of the child[174] but otherwise local authorities are given a wide discretion as to how they discharge their duty.[175] Where the authority is also providing accommodation for a sibling, the children should be accommodated together.[176] Fostering arrangements with a family of the same refugee community are common.

---

172 *R v Barking & Dagenham LBC ex p Ebuki* (2000) 5 December, QBD.
173 CA 1989 s23(1).
174 CA 1989 s22(4) and (5).
175 CA 1989 s23(2).
176 CA 1989 s23(7).

6.130   Assessment takes place under CA 1989 s17 and Sch 2 Part 1 para 1,[177] and subject to the guidance referred to at paras 6.45–6.50. Provision must be reviewed regularly.[178]

6.131   In these cases, a preliminary issue often arises as to whether applicants are in fact children, or adults. This issue is fraught. It is in the interests of young asylum-seekers to be treated as a child and looked after under CA 1989, because the CA 1989 regime is, in many respects relatively liberal, while children also have advantages in terms of asylum procedures. On the other hand, it is very much in the economic and practical interests of local authorities not to accept young asylum-seekers for long-term care under CA 1989 and it is in the practical interests of the Home Secretary to treat young asylum-seekers as adults whenever possible. The assessment of age is notoriously subjective, age documentation is often regarded with suspicion, it is easily possible to interview genuine children in such a way as to make them appear to have contradicted themselves or to have told untruths thereby casting doubt on the age they claim to be: the whole process is notoriously fallible for a number of reasons. It is possible, and indeed common, to obtain paediatric reports on age: such reports generally have a margin of error of up to two years either way but can reliably establish probable age. NASS Policy Bulletin 33 provides some guidance and the court gave detailed guidance in relation to age assessments in *R (B) v Merton LBC*:[179]

– the social services department of a local authority cannot simply adopt a decision made by the Home Office. It must itself decide whether an applicant is a child in need: that is, whether the applicant is a child and, if so, whether he or she is in need within the meaning of CA 1989 Part III. A local authority may take into account information obtained by the Home Office; but it must make its own decision, and for that purpose must have available to it adequate information;

– except in clear cases, the decision-maker should not decide age solely on the basis of the appearance of the applicant;

– in general, the decision-maker must seek to elicit the general background of the applicant, including family circumstances and history, educational background, and activities during the previous few years. Ethnic and cultural information may also be important. If there is reason to doubt the applicant's statement as to age, the

---

177 *R (W, A, G) v Lambeth and Barnet LBC* [2003] UKHL 57.

178 CA 1989 s26 and Review of Children's Cases Regulations 1991 SI No 895.

179 [2003] EWHC 1689; [2003] 4 All ER 280; (2003) 6 CCLR 457.

decision-maker will have to make an assessment of credibility, and he or she will have to ask questions designed to test credibility;

- if an applicant has previously stated that he or she was over 18, the decision-maker will take that previous statement into account and, in the absence of an acceptable explanation, it may, when considered with the other material available, be decisive;
- the appearance and demeanour of the applicant may justify a provisional view that he or she is indeed a child or an adult;
- where an interpreter is required, it is obviously greatly preferable for him/her to be present during the interview. Using a telephone interpreting service carries with it the risk of misunderstanding, and great care is required to ensure that no mistakes are made;
- the decision-maker must explain to an applicant the purpose of the interview. If the decision-maker forms the view, which must at that stage be a provisional view, that the applicant is lying about his/her age, the applicant must be given the opportunity to address the matters that have led to that view, so that he or she can explain him/herself if possible;
- a local authority is obliged to give adequate reasons for its decision that an applicant claiming to be a child is not a child, and who is therefore refused support under CA 1989 Part III. The consequences of such a decision may be drastic for the applicant, and he or she is entitled to know the basis for it, and to consider, if possible, with legal assistance if it is available to him/her, whether the decision is a lawful one.

6.132 The Children (Leaving Care) Act 2000 amended CA 1989 so as to provide a detailed regime for managing the transition to adulthood of children who have been in public care.

6.133 By CA 1989 Sch 2 para 19A, it is the duty of a local authority looking after a child to 'advise, assist and befriend him with a view to promoting his welfare when they have ceased to look after him'.

6.134 By CA 1989 Sch 2 para 19B, a local authority must assess the needs of 'eligible children' whom it is 'looking after' and prepare a 'pathway plan', addressing what advice, assistance and support it would be appropriate to provide the child with under the other CA 1989 functions (considered below at paras 6.143–6.150), while it is still looking after him/her and after it ceases to look after him/her. The local authority must keep this pathway plan under review.

6.135 By CA 1989 Sch 2 para 19C, a local authority must provide a 'personal adviser' to each eligible child whom it is looking after.

6.136 By virtue of CA 1989 Sch 2 para 19A and the Children Leaving

Care (England) Regulations 2001[180] reg 3, a child is an 'eligible child' for present purposes if he or she is aged 16 or 17 and has been 'looked after' by a local authority for periods totalling at least 13 weeks, beginning on a day after the child reached the age of 14 and ending on a day after the child reached the age of 16 years.

6.137   Up until 7 November 2002, a child was 'looked after' by a local authority if it was provided with accommodation by the local authority in the exercise of *any* social services functions. Accordingly, up until 7 November 2002, a child was a looked after child whether he or she was accommodated by a local authority under CA 1989 ss17 or 20.[181]

6.138   By virtue of amendments made to CA 1989 s22(1) by Adoption and Children Act 2002 s116(2), effective on and from 7 November 2002, children are not 'looked after' children if they are accommodated under, among other things, CA 1989 s17.

6.139   A 'relevant child' is a child who is not being looked after by any local authority but who was an eligible child before he or she last ceased to be looked after and is aged 16 or 17.[182]

6.140   The local authority is required to take reasonable steps to keep in touch with a relevant child and to appoint a personal adviser for him/her, to assess his/her needs and to prepare a pathway plan for him/her (and keep it under review), if it has not already done so.[183]

6.141   By CA 1989 s23B(8), the local authority must safeguard and promote the relevant child's welfare and, unless satisfied that his/her welfare does *not* require it, support him/her by maintaining him/her, or by providing him/her with suitable accommodation or by providing such other support as may be prescribed (that is, under the Children Leaving Care (England) Regulations 2001).

6.142   One must then consider the so-called 'former relevant child'. There are no fewer than two types:

1) a person who has been a relevant child and would be if he or she was still under 18 years;

2) a person who was being looked after when he or she reached 18 and immediately before ceasing to be looked after was an eligible child.[184]

---

180   SI No 2874. See also guidance at wwww.dh.gov.uk.

181   CA 1989 s22(1).

182   CA 1989 s23A, subject to exclusions under Children Leaving Care (England) Regulations 2001 reg 4.

183   CA 1989 s23B.

184   CA 1989 s23C(1).

6.143   So far as concerns former relevant children, local authorities must take reasonable steps to keep in touch with them, they must continue the appointment of a personal adviser and they must keep the pathway plan under review.[185] Furthermore, they must give the former relevant child (broadly speaking, until he or she attains the age of 21 years):

a) the assistance referred to in section 24(B)(1), to the extent that his/her welfare requires it;
b) the assistance referred to in s24(B)(2), to the extent that his/her welfare and education or training needs require it;
c) other assistance, to the extent that his/her welfare requires it.[186]

6.144   Assistance under CA 1989 s24(B)(1) comprises a contribution towards the cost of living near a place of actual or sought-after employment.

6.145   Assistance under CA 1989 s24(B)(2) comprises a contribution towards the cost of living near a place of education or training, or towards the cost of such education or training.

6.146   The 'other assistance' referred to in CA 1989 s23C(4)(c) is only defined to the extent that CA 1989 s23C(5) provides that it may be assistance in kind or, in exceptional circumstances, cash. This language precisely reflects the language found in CA 1989 s17(6), which has essentially been regarded as sufficiently broad to include any service within reason, including the provision of accommodation.[187]

6.147   Finally, there is the 'person qualifying for advice and assistance'. This person is under 21 years, is not currently being looked after but was looked after, at some point when he or she was 16 or 17.[188]

6.148   The local authority is under a duty to contact such persons to the extent it considers appropriate, with a view to discharging its functions under CA 1989 ss24A and 24B.

6.149   There are duties and powers to befriend and advise at CA 1989 s24A(1)–(3) and at (4) there is a power to provide assistance, which may be in kind or, in exceptional circumstances, may be cash or – providing CA 1989 s24B does not apply – accommodation.

6.150   CA 1989 s24B contains a power to provide assistance by contributing to the expense of living near employment, education or training and the associated expenses of education or training (up to the age of 24 years).

185 CA 1989 s23C(2) and (3).
186 CA 1989 s23B(4)–(7).
187 *R (W) v Lambeth LBC* [2002] EWCA Civ 613; (2002) 5 CCLR 203.
188 CA 1989 s24(1).

6.151   The Department of Health has issued guidance under Local Social Services Act 1970 s7 called the *Children (Leaving Care) Act 2000 Regulations and Guidance*, which makes it clear that the provisions of the Children (Leaving Care) Act 2000 apply to unaccompanied asylum-seeking children and that when such children reach 18 NASS will contribute to the cost of their ongoing care (at their current location) up to a pre-set limit and will not disperse them.[189] It would appear that the local authority remains liable for maintaining a personal adviser and pathway plan and continues to have overarching responsibility for the former child's residual welfare needs.

6.152   New Guidance at LAC(2003)13 suggests, contentiously, that local authorities could rationally decide to provide accommodation assistance under section 17, instead of looking after a child under section 20. As from the amendments to the CA 1989 made by the Children and Adoption Act 2002, on 7 November 2002, the result of such a decision would be that the leaving care arrangements would not apply to section 17 children. It is, however, difficult to see how any decision to accommodate children under CA 1989 s17 instead of section 20 could ever be rational or consistent with the statutory scheme. The leaving care arrangements apply to all children accommodated prior to that date, however, whether under section 17 or section 20.[190]

6.153   NIAA 2002 Sch 3 excludes all former looked after children from these leaving care provisions if they are EEA refugees, EEA nationals, former asylum-seekers who have failed to co-operate with removal directions and certain categories of persons unlawfully present, except to the extent necessary to avoid a breach of the ECHR or Community Treaties.[191]

Effects of changes of status

6.154   This section describes the consequences for the provision of services under the community care statutes and the CA 1989 of changes in the status of asylum-seekers. The following changes of status are considered:

189   See chapter 2, paras 7–11.

190   *R (Berhe) v Hillingdon LBC* [2003] EWHC 2075, (2003) 6 CCLR 471; *R (W) v Essex CC* [2003] EWHC 3175. For the relevant *Hansard* debates see HL Debates, col 1384, 23 October 2002.

191   The exclusion will also apply to failed asylum-seekers with children certified as not taking reasonable steps to leave the UK when Asylum and Immigration (Treatment of Claimants, etc) Act 2004 s9 is brought into force by regulations.

- the grant of refugee status or humanitarian protection/discretionary leave to remain;
- the refusal of an asylum application or an appeal;
- the asylum-seeker and others reaching 18 years of age.

The grant of refugee status or humanitarian protection or discretionary leave to remain

6.155   A successful asylum application will conclude with a decision by the Home Secretary or at the conclusion of an appeal to grant the applicant refugee status or humanitarian protection (HP) or discretionary leave to remain (DLR) in the UK (see paras 1.107–1.121).

6.156   People who have refugee status or HP/DLR will be eligible for assistance under Housing Act (HA) 1996 Parts VI and VII. NASS support ends 28 days after the grant of asylum or other leave.[192] The asylum-seeker, upon notification of a grant of refugee status or leave to remain, should at once apply to register on the housing register of the local authority and, upon becoming homeless or threatened with homelessness, apply for assistance under Part VII as a homeless person (see para 5.7 onwards). Such people will also be entitled to work and to state benefits. If not working, they should immediately apply for tax credits, income support or jobseeker's allowance and housing benefit and council tax benefit (including, if granted refugee status, backdated benefits – but see para 2.136), as appropriate.

6.157   Where the asylum-seeker whose claim is determined is supported with accommodation and subsistence by the local authority under community care legislation (usually NAA 1948 s21 or CA 1989 s17), then – unless the asylum-seeker requires residential care leaving aside entirely the question of destitution – the social services department is likely to take steps to terminate that support and transfer responsibility to the housing department, its own benefit department and to the relevant social security body (see para 2.110). However, there is no requirement to end support within 28 days as is the case with asylum support. The local authority should not terminate support until satisfied that, as the case may be, the applicant's needs are otherwise being met[193] or the child is no longer a child in need.[194] The change of circumstances occasioned by a grant of refugee status or HP/DLR should give rise to a formal review of the community care or

---

192 Asylum Support Regs 2000 reg 2(2A).
193 NAA 1948 s21.
194 CA 1989 s17.

CA 1989 assessment and revision of the care plan before any changes are made to service provision. Peremptory termination of community care services in such cases could be challenged by judicial review.

6.158   There is commonly a practical problem when a decision is made by the Home Secretary, or on appeal, granting refugee status or HP/DLR, because the applicant has not yet received documents proving his/her new immigration status. NASS or the social services department may, in such circumstances, terminate assistance, but on approaching the local housing authority or the Benefits Agency, the applicant is told that he or she will not be assisted until he or she can produce the standard documentation (form ICD.0725 or ACD.2151 – previously GEN23 – for refugee cases, or Immigration Status document granting HP/DLR for a specified period (see paras 1.162–1.175) or provide a National Insurance number (see para 2.114 onwards for difficulties in processing benefits claims). The most obvious remedies for the applicant are by way of judicial review, of the failure of the Home Office to issue the necessary status documentation and/or of the local authority social services department for breach of its duties under NAA 1948 s21 or under CA 1989 s17 or under CA 1989 ss24, 24A and 24B.

6.159   Unaccompanied asylum-seeker children who are the subject of positive decisions on their applications will not have their support under the CA 1989 terminated in consequence. Those who are 16 years old or over may qualify for means-tested jobseeker's allowance, tax credits or income support, including arrears if granted refugee status (but see para 2.136). They will be eligible for housing assistance (see para 5.9).

Refusal of an asylum application or an appeal

6.160   An unsuccessful asylum application concludes with a refusal decision by the Home Secretary or a refusal on appeal. Two questions arise:

    1) What will be the effect of such a decision on services already being provided to the applicant?

    2) In what circumstances will such a decision lead to an applicant being entitled to community care services because of the withdrawal of other means of support?

6.161   NIAA 2002 Sch 3 paras 1 and 6 exclude former asylum-seekers from eligibility for services under:

    – NAA 1948 ss21 and 29,

    – CSDPA 1970 s2,

- HSPHA 1968 s45,
- NHSA 1977 s21 and Sch 8,
- CA 1989 ss17, 23C, 24A and 24B,
- LGA 2000 s2

but only if they have also failed to co-operate with removal directions. If they are also unlawfully present in the UK, as well as being a former asylum-seeker, they may be excluded by NIAA 2002 Sch 3 para 7, irrespective of whether they have failed to co-operate with removal directions, although it is arguable that NIAA 2002 Sch 3 para 7 is intended to apply only to persons whose only status is that they are unlawfully present in the UK and not to former asylum-seekers, who may or may not be unlawfully present and whose circumstances appear to be specifically dealt with in NIAA 2002 Sch 3 para 6. Again, the exclusion is subject to any need to make provision to avoid a breach of ECHR or Community Treaty rights.[195]

6.162   Former asylum-seekers may be eligible for hard cases support under IAA 1999 s4 (see paras 3.291–3.297) and will remain entitled to aftercare services including accommodation under MHA 1983 s117 (see para 6.120).

6.163   In the case of unaccompanied asylum-seeker children, negative decisions on their applications will have no effect. The support described above (see paras 6.128–6.152) continues after a negative asylum decision, so long as the child remains under 18 and in the UK.

6.164   As far as concerns adults whose households include dependent children, the position currently is that asylum support will continue following an adverse asylum decision unless the youngest child reaches 18, or the dependent child leaves the household or the UK, or unless leave to remain is granted.[196] However, when Immigration and Asylum (Treatment of Claimants, etc) Act s9 takes effect, the secretary of state will be able to certify that such families have not taken reasonable steps to leave the UK voluntarily, in which case the adults but not the children will be excluded from assistance under CA 1989 (and all the other provisions set out above at para 6.63), except to the extent that provision is required to be made by the ECHR or Community Treaties.

---

195 NIAA 2002 Sch 3 para 3.
196 IAA 1999 s94(5).

The asylum-seeker and others reaching 18 years of age

6.165   Unaccompanied asylum-seekers aged under 18 are excluded from support under the asylum support scheme[197] and are the responsibility of the social services department, which is under a duty to look after them under CA 1989 s20 or may possibly look after them under CA 1989 s17 (see paras 6.123–6.131). Where a child has been looked after under section 20, the local authority remains under a duty under CA 1989 s23A–E and s24A–B to provide assistance where appropriate up to the age of 21 and in some cases beyond (see paras 6.132–6.153 above).

6.166   If an asylum-seeker child (unaccompanied or not), on reaching his/her eighteenth birthday, has had his/her asylum application refused and has exhausted the appeal rights, then he or she will not be entitled to assistance from NASS because he or she will no longer be an asylum-seeker. He or she may be entitled to assistance with accommodation under NAA 1948 s21, if his/her need for assistance arises other than solely because of destitution or the physical effects of destitution (see paras 6.88–6.105 above). He or she will be excluded from continuing care under CA 1989 s23A–E and s24A–B by NIAA 2002 Sch3 para 6, but only if he or she has also failed to co-operate with removal directions. If he or she is also unlawfully present in the UK, as well as being a former asylum-seeker, then he or she may be excluded by NIAA 2002 Sch 3 para 7, irrespective of whether he or she has failed to co-operate with removal directions, although it is arguable that NIAA 2002 Sch 3 para 7 is intended to apply only to persons whose only status is that they are unlawfully present in the UK and not to former asylum-seekers, who may or may not be unlawfully present and whose circumstances appear to be specifically dealt with in NIAA 2002 Sch 3 para 6. Again, the exclusion is subject to any need to make provision to avoid a breach of ECHR or Community Treaty rights.[198] As a last resort, the hard cases scheme at IAA 1999 s4 may be available (see paras 3.291–3.297).

6.167   If an asylum-seeker child (unaccompanied or not), on reaching his/her eighteenth birthday, has a pending asylum application or appeal, then he or she will be eligible for support from NASS. In the case of unaccompanied children, the social services department is advised to arrange for a NASS application to be made two weeks before the child reaches his/her eighteenth birthday, and should pro-

---

197 IAA 1999 s94(1).
198 NIAA 2002 Sch 3 para 3.

vide evidence of destitution, including evidence of support provided under the CA 1989.[199] NASS and local authorities should then share the responsibility of continuing care for such young adults (see para 6.151).

Community care challenges

6.168   In practice, many challenges to a failure by a local authority to carry out an assessment or provide a community care service are likely to be by way of judicial review, on the basis that the local authority has mis-construed its statutory powers or acted irrationally or unfairly. Practitioners in this field will need little reminding of the paramount need to act in a proportionate and non-litigious manner: see, for example, *R (Anufrijeva) v Southwark LBC*[200] and *R v (Cowl) v Plymouth CC*.[201]

6.169   If there is a generalised breakdown of local authority provision, then it is possible to ask the Home Secretary to exercise his/her default powers under LASSA 1970 s7D. It is rare for the existence of default powers to constitute an alternative remedy to judicial review and it is believed that the secretary of state has never exercised such powers in a community care case.

6.170   Otherwise, many decisions can be challenged by way of the complaints procedures, which local authorities are required to set up under LASSA 1970 s7B and the Local Authority Social Services (Complaints Procedure) Order 1990.[202] Complaints ultimately result, if successful, in recommendations being made by the Social Services Complaints Review Panel. Although not binding, local authorities must have good reason for not complying with such recommendations.[203] The complaints procedure is well-suited to cases where there is a dispute about the detail of service provision, that is, whether accommodation is suitable, whether food is suitable, whether enough food or enough suitable clothing has been provided, etc. The complainant can attend the Social Services Complaints Review Panel and present his/her predicament orally to the panel.

6.171   The complaints procedure is suitable where the issue relates to questions of fact and degree. It is not likely to constitute an alternative

199 NASS Policy Bulletin 29.
200 [2003] EWCA Civ 1406.
201 (2002) 5 CCLR 42.
202 SI No 2244.
203 *R v Avon CC ex p M* (1999) 2 CCLR 185.

remedy to judicial review where a discrete issue of law arises,[204] however, a dispute can be suited to the complaints procedure, despite the existence of legal issues. Those advising claimants must always bear well in mind the very strong desirability of avoiding judicial review litigation wherever possible: *R (Cowl) v Plymouth CC.*[205]

6.172   The Local Government Ombudsman (see appendix G for details) has power to intervene in community care cases, although in this context he or she will often not be able to act quickly enough. There can, however, sometimes be considerable advantages in involving the Local Government Ombudsman, as he or she has power to:

- recommend that compensation is paid;
- carry out investigations and ascertain facts that it might be difficult to ascertain in the course of judicial review;
- review local authority procedures in the round;
- in effect force local authorities to change procedures and to report back to demonstrate that change has occurred.[206] The ombudsman can also be brought in if the local authority fails to implement the complaints procedure correctly or promptly.

6.173   In exceptional cases, a failure by a local authority to discharge community care functions can give rise to a claim for damages under ECHR article 3 or 8. Generally, there must be a clear interference with family life or serious damage bordering on inhuman and degrading treatment, which the authority knew or should have known about: *R v Enfield LBC ex p Bernard*[207] and *R (Anufrijeva) v Southwark LBC.*[208]

---

204 *R v Devon CC ex p Baker* [1995] 1 All ER 72; *R v Sutton LBC ex p Tucker* (1998) 1 CCLR 251.

205 (2002) 5 CCLR 42.

206 See, eg, *Investigation into Complaint No 97/A/2959 against Hackney LBC.*

207 [2002] EWHC 2282 (Admin), (2002) 5 CCLR 577.

208 [2003] EWCA Civ 1406, (2003) 6 CCLR 415.

APPENDICES

Extracts from legislation

Legislation is reproduced as amended. The amendments are only
highlighted where the provision is not yet in force.

---

continued

Asylum support

IMMIGRATION AND ASYLUM ACT 1999 s4, Part VI, s167, Schs 8, 14 paras 73, 81, 82, 87, 88, 116, Sch 15 paras 13, 14

> **As amended by Nationality, Immigration and Asylum Act (NIAA) 2002.**
> **Material in square brackets is to be substituted by NIAA 2002, from a date to be appointed, and replaced by the subsequent material in italics. Material reproduced in italics is not yet in force. Previous amendments to the Act, that are in force, have not been highlighted.**

Accommodation

4 (1) The Secretary of State may provide, or arrange for the provision of, facilities for the accommodation of persons–

    (a) temporarily admitted to the United Kingdom under paragraph 21 of Schedule 2 to the 1971 Act;

    (b) released from detention under that paragraph; or

    (c) released on bail from detention under any provision of the Immigration Acts.

  (2) The Secretary of State may provide, or arrange for the provision of, facilities for the accommodation of a person if–

    (a) he was (but is no longer) an asylum-seeker, and

    (b) his claim for asylum was rejected.

  (3) The Secretary of State may provide, or arrange for the provision of, facilities for the accommodation of a dependant of a person for whom facilities may be provided under subsection (2).

  (4) The following expressions have the same meaning in this section as in Part VI of this Act (as defined in section 94)–

    (a) asylum-seeker,

    (b) claim for asylum, and

    (c) dependant.

Part VI
SUPPORT FOR ASYLUM-SEEKERS

INTERPRETATION
Interpretation of Part VI

94 (1) In this Part–

    'adjudicator' has the meaning given in section 102(2);

    ['asylum-seeker' means a person who is not under 18 and has made a claim for asylum which has been recorded by the Secretary of State but which has not yet been determined;]

'asylum-seeker' means a person–

(a) *who is at least 18 years old,*

(b) *who is in the United Kingdom,*

(c) *who has made a claim for asylum at a place designated by the Secretary of State,*

(d) *whose claim has been recorded by the Secretary of State, and*

(e) *whose claim has not been determined;*[1]

'claim for asylum' means a claim that it would be contrary to the United Kingdom's obligations under the Refugee Convention, or under Article 3 of the Human Rights Convention, for the claimant to be removed from, or required to leave, the United Kingdom;

'the Department' means the Department of Health and Social Services for Northern Ireland;

['dependant' in relation to an asylum-seeker or a supported person means a person in the United Kingdom who–

(a) is his spouse;

(b) is the child of his, or of his spouse, who is under 18 and dependent on him; or

(c) falls within such additional category, if any, as may be prescribed.]

'dependant' in relation to an asylum-seeker or a supported person means a person who–

(a) *is in the United Kingdom, and*

(b) *is within a prescribed class;*[2]

'the Executive' means the Northern Ireland Housing Executive;

'housing accommodation' includes flats, lodging houses and hostels;

'local authority' means–

(a) in England and Wales, a county council, a county borough council, a district council, a London borough council, the Common Council of the City of London or the Council of the Isles of Scilly;

(b) in Scotland, a council constituted under section 2 of the Local Government, etc, (Scotland) Act 1994;

'Northern Ireland authority' has the meaning given by section 110(9);

'supported person' means –

(a) an asylum-seeker, or

(b) a dependant of an asylum-seeker,

who has applied for support and for whom support is provided under section 95.

(2) References in this Part to support provided under section 95 include references to support which is provided under arrangements made by the Secretary of State under that section.

[(3) For the purposes of this Part, a claim for asylum is determined at the end of

---

1   Definition of 'asylum-seeker' in subs (1) substituted by words in italics by NIAA 2002, s44(1), (2), from a date to be appointed.

2   Definition of 'dependant' in subs (1) substituted by words in italics by NIAA 2002, s44(1), (3), from a date to be appointed.

such period beginning–

(a) on the day on which the Secretary of State notifies the claimant of his decision on the claim, or

(b) if the claimant has appealed against the Secretary of State's decision, on the day on which the appeal is disposed of,

as may be prescribed.]

(3) A claim for asylum shall be treated as determined for the purposes of subsection (1) at the end of such period as may be prescribed beginning with–

(a) the date on which the Secretary of State notifies the claimant of his decision on the claim, or

(b) if the claimant appeals against the Secretary of State's decision, the date on which the appeal is disposed of.

(3A) A person shall continue to be treated as an asylum-seeker despite paragraph (e) of the definition of 'asylum-seeker' in subsection (1) while–

(a) his household includes a dependant child who is under 18, and

(b) he does not have leave to enter or remain in the United Kingdom.[3]

(4) An appeal is disposed of when it is no longer pending for the purposes of the Immigration Acts or the Special Immigration Appeals Commission Act 1997.

[(5) If an asylum-seeker's household includes a child who is under 18 and a dependant of his, he is to be treated (for the purposes of this Part) as continuing to be an asylum-seeker while–

(a) the child is under 18; and

(b) he and the child remain in the United Kingdom.

(6) Subsection (5) does not apply if, on or after the determination of his claim for asylum, the asylum-seeker is granted leave to enter or remain in the United Kingdom (whether or not as a result of that claim).[4]]

(7) For the purposes of this Part, the Secretary of State may inquire into, and decide, the age of any person.

(8) A notice under subsection (3) must be given in writing.

(9) If such a notice is sent by the Secretary of State by first class post, addressed –

(a) to the asylum-seeker's representative, or

(b) to the asylum-seeker's last known address,

it is to be taken to have been received by the asylum-seeker on the second day after the day on which it was posted.

PROVISION OF SUPPORT
Persons for whom support may be provided

95 (1) The Secretary of State may provide, or arrange for the provision of, support for–

(a) asylum-seekers, or

(b) dependants of asylum-seekers,

---

3   Subs (3) IAA 1999 to be substituted by subss (3), (3A) NIAA 2002, s44(1), (4), from a date to be appointed.

4   Subss 5 and 6 repealed, from a date to be appointed, by NIAA 2002 ss 44 (1), (5), 161, sch 9.

who appear to the Secretary of State to be destitute or to be likely to become destitute within such period as may be prescribed.

[(2) In prescribed circumstances, a person who would otherwise fall within subsection (1) is excluded.

(3) For the purposes of this section, a person is destitute if–

    (a) he does not have adequate accommodation or any means of obtaining it (whether or not his other essential living needs are met); or

    (b) he has adequate accommodation or the means of obtaining it, but cannot meet his other essential living needs.

(4) If a person has dependants, subsection (3) is to be read as if the references to him were references to him and his dependants taken together.

(5) In determining, for the purposes of this section, whether a person's accommodation is adequate, the Secretary of State–

    (a) must have regard to such matters as may be prescribed for the purposes of this paragraph; but

    (b) may not have regard to such matters as may be prescribed for the purposes of this paragraph or to any of the matters mentioned in subsection (6).

(6) Those matters are –

    (a) the fact that the person concerned has no enforceable right to occupy the accommodation;

    (b) the fact that he shares the accommodation, or any part of the accommodation, with one or more other persons;

    (c) the fact that the accommodation is temporary;

    (d) the location of the accommodation.

(7) In determining, for the purposes of this section, whether a person's other essential living needs are met, the Secretary of State –

    (a) must have regard to such matters as may be prescribed for the purposes of this paragraph; but

    (b) may not have regard to such matters as may be prescribed for the purposes of this paragraph.

(8) The Secretary of State may by regulations provide that items or expenses of such a description as may be prescribed are, or are not, to be treated as being an essential living need of a person for the purposes of this Part.]

(2) *Where a person has dependants, he and his dependants are destitute for the purpose of this section if they do not have and cannot obtain both –*

    (a) adequate accommodation, and

    (b) food and other essential items.

(3) *Where a person does not have dependants, he is destitute for the purpose of this section if he does not have and cannot obtain both –*

    (a) adequate accommodation, and

    (b) food and other essential items.

(4) *In determining whether accommodation is adequate for the purposes of subsection (2) or (3) the Secretary of State must have regard to any matter prescribed for the purposes of this subsection.*

(5) *In determining whether accommodation is adequate for the purposes of subsection (2) or (3) the Secretary of State may not have regard to –*

(a) *whether a person has an enforceable right to occupy accommodation,*

(b) *whether a person shares all or part of accommodation,*

(c) *whether accommodation is temporary or permanent,*

(d) *the location of accommodation, or*

(e) *any other matter prescribed for the purposes of this subsection.*

(6) *The Secretary of State may by regulations specify items which are or are not to be treated as essential items for the purposes of subsections (2) and (3).*

(7) *The Secretary of State may by regulations –*

(a) *provide that a person is not to be treated as destitute for the purposes of this Part in specified circumstances;*

(b) *enable or require the Secretary of State in deciding whether a person is destitute to have regard to income which he or a dependant of his might reasonably be expected to have;*

(c) *enable or require the Secretary of State in deciding whether a person is destitute to have regard to support which is or might reasonably be expected to be available to the person or a dependant of his;*

(d) *enable or require the Secretary of State in deciding whether a person is destitute to have regard to assets of a prescribed kind which he or a dependant of his has or might reasonably be expected to have;*

(e) *make provision as to the valuation of assets.*[5]

(9) Support may be provided subject to conditions.

(9A) A condition imposed under subsection (9) may, in particular, relate to –

(a) any matter relating to the use of the support provided, or

(b) compliance with a restriction imposed under paragraph 21 of Schedule 2 to the 1971 Act (temporary admission or release from detention) or paragraph 2 or 5 of Schedule 3 to that Act (restriction pending deportation).

(10) The conditions must be set out in writing.

(11) A copy of the conditions must be given to the supported person.

(12) Schedule 8 gives the Secretary of State power to make regulations supplementing this section.

(13) Schedule 9 makes temporary provision for support in the period before the coming into force of this section.

Ways in which support may be provided

96 (1) Support may be provided under section 95 –

(a) by providing accommodation appearing to the Secretary of State to be adequate for the needs of the supported person and his dependants (if any);

[(b) by providing what appear to the Secretary of State to be essential living needs of the supported person and his dependants (if any);]

(b) *by providing the supported person and his dependants (if any) with food and other essential items;*[6]

(c) to enable the supported person (if he is the asylum-seeker) to meet what appear to the Secretary of State to be expenses (other than legal expenses

---

5 Subs (2)–(8) substituted by subs (2)–(7) NIAA 2002, s44(1), (6) from a date to be appointed.

6 Subs (1) para (b) substituted by NIAA 2002 s45(1) from date to be appointed.

or other expenses of a prescribed description) incurred in connection with his claim for asylum;

(d) or to enable the asylum-seeker and his dependants to attend bail proceedings in connection with his detention under any provision of the Immigration Acts;

(e) to enable the asylum-seeker and his dependants to attend bail proceedings in connection with the detention of a dependant of his under any such provision.

(2) If the Secretary of State considers that the circumstances of a particular case are exceptional, he may provide support under section 95 in such other ways as he considers necessary to enable the supported person and his dependants (if any) to be supported.

[*subs (3)–(6) repealed*]

Supplemental

97 (1) When exercising his power under section 95 to provide accommodation, the Secretary of State must have regard to –

(a) the fact that the accommodation is to be temporary pending determination of the asylum-seeker's claim;

(b) the desirability, in general, of providing accommodation in areas in which there is a ready supply of accommodation; and

(c) such other matters (if any) as may be prescribed.

(2) But he may not have regard to –

(a) any preference that the supported person or his dependants (if any) may have as to the locality in which the accommodation is to be provided; or

(b) such other matters (if any) as may be prescribed.

(3) The Secretary of State may by order repeal all or any of the following –

(a) subsection (1)(a);

(b) subsection (1)(b);

(c) subsection (2)(a).

(4) When exercising his power under section 95 to provide [essential living needs] *food and other essential items*, the Secretary of State –

(a) must have regard to such matters as may be prescribed for the purposes of this paragraph;

(b) may not have regard to such other matters as may be prescribed for the purposes of this paragraph.

(5) In addition, when exercising his power under section 95 to provide [essential living needs] *food and other essential items*, the Secretary of State may limit the overall amount of the expenditure which he incurs in connection with a particular supported person –

(a) to such portion of the income support applicable amount provided under section 124 of the Social Security Contributions and Benefits Act 1992, or

(b) to such portion of any components of that amount,

as he considers appropriate having regard to the temporary nature of the support that he is providing.

(6) For the purposes of subsection (5), any support of a kind falling within section

96(1)(c) is to be treated as if it were the provision of essential [living needs] *items*.[7]

(7) In determining how to provide, or arrange for the provision of, support under section 95, the Secretary of State may disregard any preference which the supported person or his dependants (if any) may have as to the way in which the support is to be given.

SUPPORT AND ASSISTANCE BY LOCAL AUTHORITIES ETC
Provision of support by local authorities

99 (1) A local authority or Northern Ireland authority may provide support for asylum-seekers and their dependants (if any) in accordance with arrangements made by the Secretary of State under section 95 or 98.

(2) Support may be provided by an authority in accordance with arrangements made with the authority or with another person.

(3) Support may be provided by an authority in accordance with arrangements made under section 95 only in one or more of the ways mentioned in section 96(1) and (2).

(4) An authority may incur reasonable expenditure in connection with the preparation of proposals for entering into arrangements under section 95 or 98.

(5) The powers conferred on [an authority] by this section include power to –
   (a) provide services outside their area;
   (b) provide services jointly with one or more [other bodies];
   (c) form a company for the purpose of providing services;
   (d) tender for contracts (whether alone or with any other person).

Local authority and other assistance for Secretary of State

100 (1) This section applies if the Secretary of State asks –
   (a) a local authority,
   (b) a registered social landlord,
   (c) a registered housing association in Scotland or Northern Ireland, or the Executive,
   (d) to assist him to exercise his power under section 95 to provide accommodation.

(2) The person to whom the request is made must co-operate in giving the Secretary of State such assistance in the exercise of that power as is reasonable in the circumstances.

(3) Subsection (2) does not require a registered social landlord to act beyond its powers.

(4) A local authority must supply to the Secretary of State such information about their housing accommodation (whether or not occupied) as he may from time to time request.

(5) The information must be provided in such form and manner as the Secretary of State may direct.

---

7 Words in square brackets in subs (4), (5) and (6) to be replaced with words in italics by NIAA 2002 s45(2)(a)–(c) respectively, from a date to be appointed.

(6) 'Registered social landlord' has the same meaning as in Part I of the Housing Act 1996.

(7) 'Registered housing association' has the same meaning –

    (a) in relation to Scotland, as in the Housing Associations Act 1985; and

    (b) in relation to Northern Ireland, as in Part II of the Housing (Northern Ireland) Order 1992.

Reception zones

101 (1) The Secretary of State may by order designate as reception zones –

    (a) areas in England and Wales consisting of the areas of one or more local authorities;

    (b) areas in Scotland consisting of the areas of one or more local authorities;

    (c) Northern Ireland.

(2) Subsection (3) applies if the Secretary of State considers that –

    (a) a local authority whose area is within a reception zone has suitable housing accommodation within that zone; or

    (b) the Executive has suitable housing accommodation.

(3) The Secretary of State may direct the local authority or the Executive to make available such of the accommodation as may be specified in the direction for a period so specified –

    (a) to him for the purpose of providing support under section 95; or

    (b) to a person with whom the Secretary of State has made arrangements under section 95.

(4) A period specified in a direction under subsection (3) –

    (a) begins on a date so specified; and

    (b) must not exceed five years.

(5) A direction under subsection (3) is enforceable, on an application made on behalf of the Secretary of State, by injunction or in Scotland an order under section 45(b) of the Court of Session Act 1988.

(6) The Secretary of State's power to give a direction under subsection (3) in respect of a particular reception zone must be exercised by reference to criteria specified for the purposes of this subsection in the order designating that zone.

(7) The Secretary of State may not give a direction under subsection (3) in respect of a local authority in Scotland unless the Scottish Ministers have confirmed to him that the criteria specified in the designation order concerned are in their opinion met in relation to that authority.

(8) Housing accommodation is suitable for the purposes of subsection (2) if it –

    (a) is unoccupied;

    (b) would be likely to remain unoccupied for the foreseeable future if not made available; and

    (c) is appropriate for the accommodation of persons supported under this Part or capable of being made so with minor work.

(9) If housing accommodation for which a direction under this section is, for the time being, in force –

    (a) is not appropriate for the accommodation of persons supported under this Part, but

(b) is capable of being made so with minor work,

the direction may require the body to whom it is given to secure that that work is done without delay.

(10) The Secretary of State must make regulations with respect to the general management of any housing accommodation for which a direction under subsection (3) is, for the time being, in force.

(11) Regulations under subsection (10) must include provision –

(a) as to the method to be used in determining the amount of rent or other charges to be payable in relation to the accommodation;

(b) as to the times at which payments of rent or other charges are to be made;

(c) as to the responsibility for maintenance of, and repairs to, the accommodation;

(d) enabling the accommodation to be inspected, in such circumstances as may be prescribed, by the body to which the direction was given;

(e) with respect to the condition in which the accommodation is to be returned when the direction ceases to have effect.

(12) Regulations under subsection (10) may, in particular, include provision –

(a) for the cost, or part of the cost, of minor work required by a direction under this section to be met by the Secretary of State in prescribed circumstances;

(b) as to the maximum amount of expenditure which a body may be required to incur as a result of a direction under this section.

(13) The Secretary of State must by regulations make provision ('the dispute resolution procedure') for resolving disputes arising in connection with the operation of any regulations made under subsection (10).

(14) Regulations under subsection (13) must include provision –

(a) requiring a dispute to be resolved in accordance with the dispute resolution procedure;

(b) requiring the parties to a dispute to comply with obligations imposed on them by the procedure; and

(c) for the decision of the person resolving a dispute in accordance with the procedure to be final and binding on the parties.

(15) Before–

(a) designating a reception zone in Great Britain,

(b) determining the criteria to be included in the order designating the zone, or

(c) making regulations under subsection (13),

the Secretary of State must consult such local authorities, local authority associations and other persons as he thinks appropriate.

(16) Before –

(a) designating Northern Ireland as a reception zone, or

(b) determining the criteria to be included in the order designating Northern Ireland,

the Secretary of State must consult the Executive and such other persons as he thinks appropriate.

(17) Before making regulations under subsection (10) which extend only to Northern Ireland, the Secretary of State must consult the Executive and such other persons as he thinks appropriate.

(18) Before making any other regulations under subsection (10), the Secretary of State must consult –

(a) such local authorities, local authority associations and other persons as he thinks appropriate; and

(b) if the regulations extend to Northern Ireland, the Executive.

Asylum Support Adjudicators

102 (1) There are to be adjudicators to hear appeals under this Part.

(2) A person appointed as an adjudicator under this Part is to be known as an Asylum Support Adjudicator (but is referred to in this Part as 'an adjudicator').

(3) Schedule 10 makes further provision with respect to adjudicators.

Appeals

[103(1) If, on an application for support under section 95, the Secretary of State decides that the applicant does not qualify for support under that section, the applicant may appeal to an adjudicator.

(2) If the Secretary of State decides to stop providing support for a person under section 95 before that support would otherwise have come to an end, that person may appeal to an adjudicator.

(2A) *If the Secretary of State decides not to provide accommodation for a person under section 4, or not to continue to provide accommodation for a person under section 4, the person may appeal to an adjudicator.*

(3) On an appeal under this section, the adjudicator may –

(a) require the Secretary of State to reconsider the matter;

(b) substitute his decision for the decision appealed against; or

(c) dismiss the appeal.

(4) The adjudicator must give his reasons in writing.

(5) The decision of the adjudicator is final.

(6) If an appeal is dismissed, no further application by the appellant for support under section *4 or* 95 is to be entertained unless the Secretary of State is satisfied that there has been a material change in the circumstances.

(7) The Secretary of State may by regulations provide for decisions as to where support provided under section *4 or* 95 is to be provided to be appealable to an adjudicator under this Part.

(8) Regulations under subsection (7) may provide for any provision of this section to have effect, in relation to an appeal brought by virtue of the regulations, subject to such modifications as may be prescribed.

(9) The Secretary of State may pay any reasonable travelling expenses incurred by an appellant in connection with attendance at any place for the purposes of an appeal under this section.]⁸

> 8 Section 103 substituted by ss103, 103A and 103B (in italics) by NIAA s53, from a date to be appointed. Subsection (1)(a)–(c) has been further substituted by Asylum and Immigration (Treatment of Claimants etc) Act 2004. The 2004 Act also inserts subsection 2A and the words in italics in subss (6) and (7) from a date to be appointed.

(1) *This section applies where a person has applied for support under all or any of the following provisions –*

 (a) *section 4,*

 (b) *section 95, and*

 (c) *section 17 of the Nationality, Immigration and Asylum Act 2002.*

(2) *The person may appeal to an adjudicator against a decision that the person is not qualified to receive the support for which he has applied.*

(3) *The person may also appeal to an adjudicator against a decision to stop providing support under a provision mentioned in subsection (1).*

(4) *But subsection (3) does not apply –*

 (a) *to a decision to stop providing support under one of the provisions mentioned in subsection (1) if it is to be replaced immediately by support under the other provision, or*

 (b) *to a decision taken on the ground that the person is no longer an asylum-seeker or the dependant of an asylum-seeker.*

(5) *On an appeal under this section an adjudicator may–*

 (a) *require the Secretary of State to reconsider a matter;*

 (b) *substitute his decision for the decision against which the appeal is brought;*

 (c) *dismiss the appeal.*

(6) *An adjudicator must give his reasons in writing.*

(7) *If an appeal under this section is dismissed the Secretary of State shall not consider any further application by the appellant for support under a provision mentioned in subsection (1)(a) or (b) unless the Secretary of State thinks there has been a material change in circumstances.*

(8) *An appeal under this section may not be brought or continued by a person who is outside the United Kingdom.*

Appeals: location of support under section 4 or 95

103A(1) *The Secretary of State may by regulations provide for a decision as to where support provided under section 4 or 95 is to be provided to be appealable to an adjudicator under this Part.*

 (2) *Regulations under this section may provide for a provision of section 103 to have effect in relation to an appeal under the regulations with specified modifications.*[9]

Appeals: travelling expenses

103B *The Secretary of State may pay reasonable travelling expenses incurred by an appellant in connection with attendance for the purposes of an appeal under or by virtue of section 103 or 103A.*[10]

Secretary of State's rules

104 (1) The Secretary of State may make rules regulating –

 (a) the bringing of appeals under this Part; and

 (b) the practice and procedure of the adjudicators.

 9 Substituted together with ss103 and 103B for s130 by NIAA s53 from a date to be appointed. The words '4 or' in 103A(1) and the title are to be inserted by AI(TC)etc)A 2004 from a date to be appointed.

 10 Substituted together with ss103 and 103A for s130 by NIAA s53 from a date to be appointed.

(2) The rules may, in particular, make provision–
- (a) for the period within which an appeal must be brought;
- (b) as to the burden of proof on an appeal;
- (c) as to the giving and admissibility of evidence;
- (d) for summoning witnesses;
- (e) for an appeal to be heard in the absence of the appellant;
- (f) for determining an appeal without a hearing;
- (g) requiring reports of decisions of adjudicators to be published;
- (h) conferring such ancillary powers on adjudicators as the Secretary of State considers necessary for the proper discharge of their functions.

(3) In making the rules, the Secretary of State must have regard to the desirability of securing, so far as is reasonably practicable, that appeals are brought and disposed of with the minimum of delay.

OFFENCES
False representations

105 (1) A person is guilty of an offence if, with a view to obtaining support for himself or any other person under any provision made by or under this Part, he –
- (a) makes a statement or representation which he knows is false in a material particular;
- (b) produces or gives to a person exercising functions under this Part, or knowingly causes or allows to be produced or given to such a person, any document or information which he knows is false in a material particular;
- (c) fails, without reasonable excuse, to notify a change of circumstances when required to do so in accordance with any provision made by or under this Part; or
- (d) without reasonable excuse, knowingly causes another person to fail to notify a change of circumstances which that other person was required to notify in accordance with any provision made by or under this Part.

(2) A person guilty of an offence under this section is liable on summary conviction to imprisonment for a term not exceeding [three months] *51 weeks*[11] or to a fine not exceeding level 5 on the standard scale, or to both.

Dishonest representations

106 (1) A person is guilty of an offence if, with a view to obtaining any benefit or other payment or advantage under this Part for himself or any other person, he dishonestly –
- (a) makes a statement or representation which is false in a material particular;
- (b) produces or gives to a person exercising functions under this Part, or causes or allows to be produced or given to such a person, any document or information which is false in a material particular;
- (c) fails to notify a change of circumstances when required to do so in accordance with any provision made by or under this Part; or
- (d) causes another person to fail to notify a change of circumstances which

11 Words in square brackets repealed, and substituted with words in italics, from a date to be appointed by Criminal Justice Act 2003 s 280(2), (3), Sch 26, para 53(1), (2).

that other person was required to notify in accordance with any provision made by or under this Part.

(2) A person guilty of an offence under this section is liable –

   (a) on summary conviction, to imprisonment for a term not exceeding six months or to a fine not exceeding the statutory maximum, or to both; or

   (b) on conviction on indictment, to imprisonment for a term not exceeding seven years or to a fine, or to both.

(3) In the application of this section to Scotland, in subsection (1) for 'dishonestly' substitute 'knowingly'.

Delay or obstruction

107 (1) A person is guilty of an offence if, without reasonable excuse, he –

   (a) intentionally delays or obstructs a person exercising functions conferred by or under this Part; or

   (b) refuses or neglects to answer a question, give any information or produce a document when required to do so in accordance with any provision made by or under this Part.

(2) A person guilty of an offence under subsection (1) is liable on summary conviction to a fine not exceeding level 3 on the standard scale.

Failure of sponsor to maintain

108 (1) A person is guilty of an offence if, during any period in respect of which he has given a written undertaking in pursuance of the immigration rules to be responsible for the maintenance and accommodation of another person –

   (a) he persistently refuses or neglects, without reasonable excuse, to maintain that person in accordance with the undertaking; and

   (b) in consequence of his refusal or neglect, support under any provision made by or under this Part is provided for or in respect of that person.

(2) A person guilty of an offence under this section is liable on summary conviction to imprisonment for a term not exceeding [3 months] *51 weeks*[12] or to a fine not exceeding level 4 on the standard scale, or to both.

(3) For the purposes of this section, a person is not to be taken to have refused or neglected to maintain another person by reason only of anything done or omitted in furtherance of a trade dispute.

Supplemental

109 (1) If an offence under section 105, 106, 107 or 108 committed by a body corporate is proved –

   (a) to have been committed with the consent or connivance of an officer, or

   (b) to be attributable to neglect on his part,

   the officer as well as the body corporate is guilty of the offence and liable to be proceeded against and punished accordingly.

(2) 'Officer', in relation to a body corporate, means a director, manager, secretary or other similar officer of the body, or a person purporting to act in such a capacity.

---

12 Words in square brackets repealed, and substituted with words in italics, from a date to be appointed by Criminal Justice Act 2003 s 280(2), (3), Sch 26, para 53(1), (2).

(3) If the affairs of a body corporate are managed by its members, subsection (1) applies in relation to the acts and defaults of a member in connection with his functions of management as if he were a director of the body corporate.

(4) If an offence under section 105, 106, 107 or 108 committed by a partnership in Scotland is proved –

(a) to have been committed with the consent or connivance of a partner, or

(b) to be attributable to neglect on his part,

the partner as well as the partnership is guilty of the offence and liable to be proceeded against and punished accordingly.

(5) 'Partner' includes a person purporting to act as a partner.

EXPENDITURE
Payments to local authorities

110 (1) The Secretary of State may from time to time pay to any local authority or Northern Ireland authority such sums as he considers appropriate in respect of expenditure incurred, or to be incurred, by the authority in connection with –

(a) persons who are, or have been, asylum-seekers; and

(b) their dependants.

(2) The Secretary of State may from time to time pay to any –

(a) local authority,

(b) local authority association, or

(c) Northern Ireland authority,

such sums as he considers appropriate in respect of services provided by the authority or association in connection with the discharge of functions under this Part.

(3) The Secretary of State may make payments to any local authority towards the discharge of any liability of supported persons or their dependants in respect of council tax payable to that authority.

(4) The Secretary of State must pay to a body to which a direction under section 101(3) is given such sums as he considers represent the reasonable costs to that body of complying with the direction.

(5) The Secretary of State must pay to a directed body sums determined to be payable in relation to accommodation made available by that body under section 101(3)(a).

(6) The Secretary of State may pay to a directed body sums determined to be payable in relation to accommodation made available by that body under section 101(3)(b).

(7) In subsections (5) and (6) –

'determined' means determined in accordance with regulations made by virtue of subsection (11)(a) of section 101, and

'directed body' means a body to which a direction under subsection (3) of section 101 is given.

(8) Payments under subsection (1), (2) or (3) may be made on such terms, and subject to such conditions, as the Secretary of State may determine.

(9) 'Northern Ireland authority' means–

(a) the Executive; or

(b) a Health and Social Services Board established under Article 16 of the Health and Personal Social Services (Northern Ireland) Order 1972; or

(c) a Health and Social Services trust established under the Health and Personal Social Services (Northern Ireland) Order 1991.

Grants to voluntary organisations

111 (1) The Secretary of State may make grants of such amounts as he thinks appropriate to voluntary organisations in connection with –

(a) the provision by them of support (of whatever nature) to persons who are, or have been, asylum-seekers and to their dependants; and

(b) connected matters.

(2) Grants may be made on such terms, and subject to such conditions, as the Secretary of State may determine.

Recovery of expenditure on support: misrepresentation etc

112 (1) This section applies if, on an application made by the Secretary of State, the court determines that –

(a) a person ('A') has misrepresented or failed to disclose a material fact (whether fraudulently or otherwise); and

(b) as a consequence of the misrepresentation or failure, support has been provided under section 95 or 98 (whether or not to A).

(2) If the support was provided by the Secretary of State, the court may order A to pay to the Secretary of State an amount representing the monetary value of the support which would not have been provided but for A's misrepresentation or failure.

(3) If the support was provided by another person ('B') in accordance with arrangements made with the Secretary of State under section 95 or 98, the court may order A to pay to the Secretary of State an amount representing the payment to B which would not have been made but for A's misrepresentation or failure.

(4) 'Court' means a county court or, in Scotland, the sheriff.

Recovery of expenditure on support from sponsor

113 (1) This section applies if –

(a) a person ('the sponsor') has given a written undertaking in pursuance of the immigration rules to be responsible for the maintenance and accommodation of another person; and

(b) during any period in relation to which the undertaking applies, support under section 95 is provided to or in respect of that other person.

(2) The Secretary of State may make a complaint against the sponsor to a magistrates' court for an order under this section.

(3) The court –

(a) must have regard to all the circumstances (and in particular to the sponsor's income);and

(b) may order him to pay to the Secretary of State such sum (weekly or otherwise) as it considers appropriate.

(4) But such a sum is not to include any amount attributable otherwise than to support provided under section 95.

(5) In determining –

(a) whether to order any payments to be made in respect of support provided under section 95 for any period before the complaint was made, or

(b) the amount of any such payments

the court must disregard any amount by which the sponsor's current income exceeds his income during that period.

(6) An order under this section is enforceable as a magistrates' court maintenance order within the meaning of section 150(1) of the Magistrates' Courts Act 1980.

(7) In the application of this section to Scotland –

(a) omit subsection (6);

(b) for references to a complaint substitute references to an application; and

(c) for references to a magistrates' court substitute references to the sheriff.

(8) In the application of this section to Northern Ireland, for references to a magistrates' court substitute references to a court of summary jurisdiction and for subsection (6) substitute –

'(6) An order under this section is an order to which Article 98(11) of the Magistrates' Courts (Northern Ireland) Order 1981 applies.'

Overpayments

114 (1) Subsection (2) applies if, as a result of an error on the part of the Secretary of State, support has been provided to a person under section 95 or 98.

(2) The Secretary of State may recover from a person who is, or has been, a supported person an amount representing the monetary value of support provided to him as a result of the error.

(3) An amount recoverable under subsection (2) may be recovered as if it were a debt due to the Secretary of State.

(4) The Secretary of State may by regulations make provision for other methods of recovery, including deductions from support provided under section 95.

EXCLUSIONS
Exclusion from benefits

115 (1) No person is entitled to income-based jobseeker's allowance under the Jobseekers Act 1995 or to state pension credit under the State Pension Credit Act 2002 or to –

(a) attendance allowance,

(b) severe disablement allowance,

(c) carer's allowance,

(d) disability living allowance

(e) income support

(f) [*repealed*]

(g) [*repealed*]

(h) a social fund payment,

(i) child benefit,

     (j) housing benefit, or

     (k) council tax benefit,

under the Social Security Contributions and Benefits Act 1992 while he is a person to whom this section applies.

(2) No person in Northern Ireland is entitled to –

     (a) income-based jobseeker's allowance under the Jobseekers (Northern Ireland) Order 1995, or

     (b) any of the benefits mentioned in paragraphs (a) to (j) of subsection (1),

under the Social Security Contributions and Benefits (Northern Ireland) Act 1992 while he is a person to whom this section applies.

(3) This section applies to a person subject to immigration control unless he falls within such category or description, or satisfies such conditions, as may be prescribed.

(4) Regulations under subsection (3) may provide for a person to be treated for prescribed purposes only as not being a person to whom this section applies.

(5) In relation to child benefit, 'prescribed' means prescribed by regulations made by the Treasury.

(6) In relation to the matters mentioned in subsection (2) (except so far as it relates to child benefit), 'prescribed' means prescribed by regulations made by the Department.

(7) Section 175(3) to (5) of the Social Security Contributions and Benefits Act 1992 (supplemental powers in relation to regulations) applies to regulations made by the Secretary of State or the Treasury under subsection (3) as it applies to regulations made under that Act.

(8) Sections 133(2), 171(2) and 172(4) of the Social Security Contributions and Benefits (Northern Ireland) Act 1992 apply to regulations made by the Department under subsection (3) as they apply to regulations made by the Department under that Act.

(9) 'A person subject to immigration control' means a person who is not a national of an EEA State and who –

     (a) requires leave to enter or remain in the United Kingdom but does not have it;

     (b) has leave to enter or remain in the United Kingdom which is subject to a condition that he does not have recourse to public funds;

     (c) has leave to enter or remain in the United Kingdom given as a result of a maintenance undertaking; or

     (d) has leave to enter or remain in the United Kingdom only as a result of paragraph 17 of Schedule 4.

(10) 'Maintenance undertaking', in relation to any person, means a written undertaking given by another person in pursuance of the immigration rules to be responsible for that person's maintenance and accommodation.

Amendment of section 21 of the National Assistance Act 1948

116   In section 21 of the National Assistance Act 1948 (duty of local authorities to provide accommodation), after subsection (1), insert –

        '(1A) A person to whom section 115 of the Immigration and Asylum Act 1999 (exclusion from benefits) applies may not be provided with residential accommodation under subsection (1)(a) if his need for care and attention has arisen solely –

(a) because he is destitute; or

(b) because of the physical effects, or anticipated physical effects, of his being destitute.

(1B) Subsections (3) and (5) to (8) of section 95 of the Immigration and Asylum Act 1999, and paragraph 2 of Schedule 8 to that Act, apply for the purposes of subsection (1A) as they apply for the purposes of that section, but for the references in subsections (5) and (7) of that section and in that paragraph to the Secretary of State substitute references to a local authority.'

Other restrictions on assistance: England and Wales

117 (1) In section 45 of the Health Services and Public Health Act 1968 (promotion by local authorities of the welfare of old people), after subsection (4), insert –

'(4A) No arrangements under this section may be given effect to in relation to a person to whom section 115 of the Immigration and Asylum Act 1999 (exclusion from benefits) applies solely –

(a) because he is destitute; or

(b) because of the physical effects, or anticipated physical effects, of his being destitute.

(4B) Subsections (3) and (5) to (8) of section 95 of the Immigration and Asylum Act 1999, and paragraph 2 of Schedule 8 to that Act, apply for the purposes of subsection (4A) as they apply for the purposes of that section, but for the references in subsections (5) and (7) of that section and in that paragraph to the Secretary of State substitute references to a local authority.'

(2) In paragraph 2 of schedule 8 to the National Health Service Act 1977 (arrangements by local authorities for the prevention of illness and for care and aftercare), after sub-paragraph (2), insert –

'(2A) No arrangements under this paragraph may be given effect to in relation to a person to whom section 115 of the Immigration and Asylum Act 1999 (exclusion from benefits) applies solely –

(a) because he is destitute; or

(b) because of the physical effects, or anticipated physical effects, of his being destitute.

(2B) Subsections (3) and (5) to (8) of section 95 of the Immigration and Asylum Act 1999, and paragraph 2 of Schedule 8 to that Act, apply for the purposes of subsection (2A) as they apply for the purposes of that section, but for the references in subsections (5) and (7) of that section and in that paragraph to the Secretary of State substitute references to a local social services authority.'

(3)–(4) [*Repealed*].

(5) In the 1996 Act, omit section 186 (asylum-seekers and their dependants).

(6) In section 187(1) of the 1996 Act (provision of information by Secretary of State), in paragraph (a), for 'or has become an asylum-seeker, or a dependant of an asylum-seeker' substitute 'a person to whom section 115 of the Immi-

gration and Asylum Act 1999 (exclusion from benefits) applies'.

Housing authority accommodation

118 (1) Each housing authority must secure that, so far as practicable, a tenancy of, or licence to occupy, housing accommodation provided under the accommodation provisions is not granted to a person subject to immigration control unless –
   (a) he is of a class specified in an order made by the Secretary of State; or
   (b) the tenancy of, or licence to occupy, such accommodation is granted in accordance with arrangements made under section 95.

(2) 'Housing authority' means –
   (a) in relation to England and Wales, a local housing authority within the meaning of the Housing Act 1985;
   (b) in relation to Scotland, a local authority within the meaning of the Housing (Scotland) Act 1987; and
   (c) in relation to Northern Ireland, the Executive.

(3) 'Accommodation provisions' means–
   (a) in relation to England and Wales, Part II of the Housing Act 1985;
   (b) in relation to Scotland, Part I of the Housing (Scotland) Act 1987;
   (c) in relation to Northern Ireland, Part II of the Housing (Northern Ireland) Order 1981.

(4) 'Licence to occupy', in relation to Scotland, means a permission or right to occupy.

(5) 'Tenancy', in relation to England and Wales, has the same meaning as in the Housing Act 1985.

(6) 'Person subject to immigration control' means a person who under the 1971 Act requires leave to enter or remain in the United Kingdom (whether or not such leave has been given).

(7) This section does not apply in relation to any allocation of housing to which Part VI of the Housing Act 1996 (allocation of housing accommodation) applies.

Homelessness: Scotland and Northern Ireland

119 (1) A person subject to immigration control –
   (a) is not eligible for accommodation or assistance under the homelessness provisions, and
   (b) is to be disregarded in determining for the purposes of those provisions, whether another person–
      (i) is homeless or is threatened with homelessness, or
      (ii) has a priority need for accommodation,
   unless he is of a class specified in an order made by the Secretary of State.

(2) An order under subsection (1) may not be made so as to include in a specified class any person to whom section 115 applies.

(3) 'The homelessness provisions' means –
   (a) in relation to Scotland, Part II of the Housing (Scotland) Act 1987; and
   (b) in relation to Northern Ireland, Part II of the Housing (Northern Ireland) Order 1988.

(4) 'Person subject to immigration control' has the same meaning as in section 118.

Other restrictions on assistance: Scotland

120 (1) In section 12 of the Social Work (Scotland) Act 1968 (general social welfare services of local authorities), after subsection (2) insert –

'(2A) A person to whom section 115 of the Immigration and Asylum Act 1999 (exclusion from benefits) applies is not to receive assistance under subsection (1) of this section (whether by way of residential accommodation or otherwise) if his need for assistance has arisen solely –

(a) because he is destitute; or

(b) because of the physical effects, or anticipated physical effects, of his being destitute.

(2B) Subsections (3) and (5) to (8) of section 95 of the Immigration and Asylum Act 1999, and paragraph 2 of Schedule 8 to that Act, apply for the purposes of subsection (2A) as they apply for the purposes of that section, but for the references in subsections (5) and (7) of that section and in that paragraph to the Secretary of State substitute references to a local authority.'

(2) In section 13A of that Act (provision of residential accommodation with nursing), after subsection (3) insert –

'(4) No arrangements under subsection (1) above may be given effect to in relation to a person to whom section 115 of the Immigration and Asylum Act 1999 (exclusion from benefits) applies solely–

(a) because he is destitute; or

(b) because of the physical effects, or anticipated physical effects, of his being destitute.

(5) Subsections (3) and (5) to (8) of section 95 of the Immigration and Asylum Act 1999, and paragraph 2 of Schedule 8 to that Act, apply for the purposes of subsection (4) above as they apply for the purposes of that section, but for the references in subsections (5) and (7) of that section and in that paragraph to the Secretary of State substitute references to a local authority.'

(3) In section 13B of that Act (provision of care and after-care), after subsection (2) insert –

'(3) No arrangements under subsection (1) above may be given effect to in relation to a person to whom section 115 of the Immigration and Asylum Act 1999 (exclusion from benefits) applies solely–

(a) because he is destitute; or

(b) because of the physical effects, or anticipated physical effects, of his being destitute.

(4) Subsections (3) and (5) to (8) of section 95 of the Immigration and Asylum Act 1999, and paragraph 2 of Schedule 8 to that Act, apply for the purposes of subsection (3) above as they apply for the purposes of that section, but for the references in subsections (5) and (7) of that section and in that paragraph to the Secretary of State sub-

stitute references to a local authority.'
[(4) In section 7 of the Mental Health (Scotland) Act 1984 (functions of local authorities), after subsection (2) insert –

'(3)   No arrangements under paragraph (a) or (c) of subsection (1) above may be given effect to in relation to a person to whom section 115 of the Immigration and Asylum Act 1999 (exclusion from benefits) applies solely–
(a) because he is destitute; or
(b) because of the physical effects, or anticipated physical effects, of his being destitute.

(4)   Subsections (3) and (5) to (8) of section 95 of the Immigration and Asylum Act 1999, and paragraph 2 of Schedule 8 to that Act, apply for the purposes of subsection (3) above as they apply for the purposes of that section, but for the references in subsection (5) and (7) of that section and in that paragraph to the Secretary of State substitute references to a local authority.'

(5) In section 8 of that Act (provision of after-care services), after subsection (3) insert –

'(4)   After care services may not be provided under subsection (1) above in respect of any person to whom section 115 of the Immigration and Asylum Act 1999 (exclusion from benefits) applies solely–
(a) because he is destitute; or
(b) because of the physical effects, or anticipated physical effects, of his being destitute.

(5)   Subsections (3) and (5) to (8) of section 95 of the Immigration and Asylum Act 1999, and paragraph 2 of Schedule 8 to that Act, apply for the purposes of subsection (4) above as they apply for the purposes of that section, but for the references in subsection (5) and (7) of that section and in that paragraph to the Secretary of State substitute references to a local authority.']^13

(6) In the Asylum and Immigration Appeals Act 1993, omit sections 4 and 5 and Schedule 1 (provisions relating to housing of asylum-seekers).

Other restrictions on assistance: Northern Ireland

121 (1) In Article 7 of the Health and Personal Social Services (Northern Ireland) Order 1972 (prevention of illness, care and after-care), after paragraph (2) insert –

'(3)   No arrangements made under paragraph (1) may be given effect to in relation to a person to whom section 115 of the Immigration and Asylum Act 1999 applies solely–
(a) because he is destitute; or
(b) because of the physical effects, or anticipated physical effects, of his being destitute.

(3A)   Subsections (3) and (5) to (8) of section 95 of the Immigration and

13 Subs (4),(5) repealed by the Mental Health (Care and Treatment) (Scotland) Act 2003 s331(2) from a date to be appointed.

Asylum Act 1999, and paragraph 2 of Schedule 8 to that Act, apply for the purposes of paragraph (3) as they apply for the purposes of that section, but for the references in subsections (5) and (7) of that section and in paragraph 2 of that Schedule to the Secretary of State substitute references to the Department.'

(2) In Article 15 of that Order (general social welfare), after paragraph (5) insert –

'(6)   Assistance may not be provided under paragraph (1) in respect of any person to whom section 155 of the Immigration and Asylum Act 1999 applies if his need for assistance has arisen solely–

(a) because he is destitute, or

(b) because of the physical effects, or anticipated physical effects, of his being destitute.

(7)   Subsections (3) to (8) of section 95 of the Immigration and Asylum Act 1999, and paragraph 2 of Schedule 8 to that Act, apply for the purposes of paragraph (6) as they apply for the purposes of that section, but for references to the Secretary of State in subsections (5) and (7) of that section and in paragraph 2 of that Schedule substitute references to the Department.'

(3) In the Asylum and Immigration Appeals Act 1993, omit sections 4 and 5 and Schedule 1 (provisions relating to housing of asylum-seekers).

[Support for children] *Family with children*

[122(1) In this section 'eligible person' means a person who appears to the Secretary of State to be a person for whom support may be provided under section 95.

(2) Subsections (3) and (4) apply if an application for support under section 95 has been made by an eligible person whose household includes a dependant under the age of 18 ('the child').

(3) If it appears to the Secretary of State that adequate accommodation is not being provided for the child, he must exercise his powers under section 95 by offering, and if his offer is accepted by providing or arranging for the provision of, adequate accommodation for the child as part of the eligible person's household.

(4) If it appears to the Secretary of State that essential living needs of the child are not being met, he must exercise his powers under section 95 by offering, and if his offer is accepted by providing or arranging for the provision of, essential living needs for the child as part of the eligible person's household.

(5) No local authority may provide assistance under any of the child welfare provisions in respect of a dependant under the age of 18, or any member of his family, at any time when –

(a) the Secretary of State is complying with this section in relation to him; or

(b) there are reasonable grounds for believing that–

(i) the person concerned is a person for whom support may be provided under section 95; and

(ii) the Secretary of State would be required to comply with this section if that person had made an application under section 95.

(6) 'Assistance' means the provision of accommodation or of any essential living needs.

(7) 'The child welfare provisions' means–
   (a) section 17 of the Children Act 1989 (local authority support for children and their families);
   (b) section 22 of the Children (Scotland) Act 1995 (equivalent provision for Scotland); and
   (c) Article 18 of the Children (Northern Ireland) Order 1995 (equivalent provision for Northern Ireland).
(8) Subsection (9) applies if accommodation provided in the discharge of the duty imposed by subsection (3) has been withdrawn.
(9) Only the relevant authority may provide assistance under any of the child welfare provisions in respect of the child concerned.
(10) 'Relevant authority' means –
   (a) in relation to Northern Ireland, the authority within whose area the withdrawn accommodation was provided;
   (b) in any other case, the local authority within whose area the withdrawn accommodation was provided.
(11) In such circumstances as may be prescribed, subsection (5) does not apply.]¹⁴

(1) This section applies where a person ('the asylum-seeker') applies for support under section 95 of this Act or section 17 of the Nationality, Immigration and Asylum Act 2002 (accommodation centres) if –
   (a) the Secretary of State thinks that the asylum-seeker is eligible for support under either or both of those sections, and
   (b) the asylum-seeker's household includes a dependant child who is under 18.
(2) The Secretary of State must offer the provision of support for the child, as part of the asylum-seeker's household, under one of the sections mentioned in subsection (1).
(3) A local authority (or, in Northern Ireland, an authority) may not provide assistance for a child if –
   (a) the Secretary of State is providing support for the child in accordance with an offer under subsection (2),
   (b) an offer by the Secretary of State under subsection (2) remains open in respect of the child.
   (c) the Secretary of State has agreed that he would make an offer in respect of the child under subsection (2) if an application were made as described in subsection (1).
(4) In subsection (3) 'assistance' means assistance under –
   (a) section 17 of the Children Act 1989 (c 41) (local authority support),
   (b) section 22 of the Children (Scotland) Act 1995 (c 36) (similar provision for Scotland), or
   (c) Article 18 of the Children (Northern Ireland) Order 1995 (SI 1995/755 (NI 2)) (similar provision for Northern Ireland).
(5) The Secretary of State may by order disapply subsection (3) in specified circumstances.
(6) Where subsection (3) ceases to apply to a child because the Secretary of State stops

---

14 s122 substituted by new s122, in italics, by NIAA 2002 s47, from a day to be appointed.

providing support, no local authority may provide assistance for the child except the authority for the area within which the support was provided.

Back-dating of benefits where person recorded as refugee[14a]

123 (1) This section applies if –

 (a) a person is recorded by the Secretary of State as a refugee within the meaning of the Refugee Convention; and

 (b) before the refugee was so recorded, he or his dependant was a person to whom section 115 applied.

 (2) Regulations may provide that a person mentioned in subsection (1)(b) may, within a prescribed period, claim the whole, or any prescribed proportion, of any benefit to which he would have been entitled had the refugee been so recorded when he made his claim for asylum.

 (3) Subsections (5) and (6) apply if the refugee has resided in the areas of two or more local authorities and he or his dependant makes a claim under the regulations in relation to housing benefit.

 (4) Subsections (5) and (6) also apply if the refugee has resided in the areas of two or more local authorities in Great Britain and he or his dependant makes a claim under the regulations in relation to council tax benefit.

 (5) The claim must be investigated and determined, and any benefit awarded must be paid or allowed, by such one of those authorities as may be prescribed by the regulations ('the prescribed authority').

 (6) The regulations may make provision requiring a local authority who are not the prescribed authority to supply that authority with such information as they may reasonably require in connection with the exercise of their functions under the regulations.

 (7) The regulations may make provision in relation to a person who has received support under this Part *or Part 2 of the Nationality, Immigration and Asylum Act 2002 (accommodation centres)*[15] or who is a dependant of such a person –

 (a) for the determination, or for criteria for the calculation, of the value of that support; and

 (b) for the sum which he would be entitled to claim under the regulations to be reduced by the whole, or any prescribed proportion, of that valuation.

 (8) The reductions permitted by subsection (7) must not exceed the amount of the valuation.

 (9) 'Regulations' means –

 (a) in relation to jobseeker's allowance under the Jobseekers Act 1995, regulations made by the Secretary of State under that Act or the Social Security Administration Act 1992;

 (b) in relation to jobseeker's allowance under the Jobseekers (Northern Ireland) Order 1995, regulations made by the Department under that Order or the Social Security Administration (Northern Ireland) Act 1992;

 (ba) in relation to child benefit (and guardian's allowance), regulations made

---

14a   Section 123 repealed by Asylum and Immigration (Treatment of Claimants etc) Act 2004 s12, from a date to be appointed.

15   Words in italics inserted by NIAA 2002 s52, from a date to be appointed.

by the Treasury;

(c) in relation to a benefit (apart from a child benefit and guardian's allowance) under the Social Security Contributions and Benefits Act 1992 or state pension credit, regulations made by the Secretary of State under that Act, the Social Security Administration Act 1992 or the State Pension Credit Act 2002;

(d) in relation to a benefit (apart from a child benefit and guardian's allowance) from under the Social Security Contributions and Benefits (Northern Ireland) Act 1992, regulations made by the Department under that Act or the Social Security Administration (Northern Ireland) Act 1992.

MISCELLANEOUS
Secretary of State to be corporation sole for purposes of Part VI

124 (1) For the purpose of exercising his functions under this Part, the Secretary of State is a corporation sole.

(2) Any instrument in connection with the acquisition, management or disposal of property, real or personal, heritable or moveable, by the Secretary of State under this Part may be executed on his behalf by a person authorised by him for that purpose.

(3) Any instrument purporting to have been so executed on behalf of the Secretary of State is to be treated, until the contrary is proved, to have been so executed on his behalf.

Entry of premises

125 (1) This section applies in relation to premises in which accommodation has been provided under section 95 or 98 for a supported person.

(2) If, on an application made by a person authorised in writing by the Secretary of State, a justice of the peace is satisfied that there is reason to believe that –

(a) the supported person or any dependants of his for whom the accommodation is provided is not resident in it,

(b) the accommodation is being used for any purpose other than the accommodation of the asylum-seeker or any dependant of his, or

(c) any person other than the supported person and his dependants (if any) is residing in the accommodation,

he may grant a warrant to enter the premises to the person making the application.

(3) A warrant granted under subsection (2) may be executed –

(a) at any reasonable time;

(b) using reasonable force.

(4) In the application of subsection (2) to Scotland, read the reference to a justice of the peace as a reference to the sheriff or a justice of the peace.

Information from property owners

126 (1) The power conferred by this section is to be exercised with a view to obtaining information about premises in which accommodation is or has been provided for supported persons.

(2) The Secretary of State may require any person appearing to him –
   (a) to have any interest in, or
   (b) to be involved in any way in the management or control of,
   such premises, or any building which includes such premises, to provide him with such information with respect to the premises and the persons occupying them as he may specify.

(3) A person who is required to provide information under this section must do so in accordance with such requirements as may be prescribed.

(4) Information provided to the Secretary of State under this section may be used by him only in the exercise of his functions under this Part.

Requirement to supply information about redirection of post

127 (1) The Secretary of State may require any person conveying postal packets to supply redirection information to the Secretary of State–
   (a) for use in the prevention, detection, investigation or prosecution of criminal offences under this Part;
   (b) for use in checking the accuracy of information relating to support provided under this Part; or
   (c) for any other purpose relating to the provision of support to asylum-seekers.

(2) The information must be supplied in such manner and form, and in accordance with such requirements, as may be prescribed.

(3) The Secretary of State must make payments of such amount as he considers reasonable in respect of the supply of information under this section.

(4) 'Postal packet' has the same meaning as in the Post Office Act 1953.

(5) 'Redirection information' means information relating to arrangements made with any person conveying postal packets for the delivery of postal packets to addresses other than those indicated by senders on the packets.

Interpretation

167 (1) In this Act –
   'the 1971 Act' means the Immigration Act 1971;
   'adjudicator' (except in Part VI) means an adjudicator appointed under section 57;
   'Chief Adjudicator' means the person appointed as Chief Adjudicator under section 57(2);
   'claim for asylum' (except in Parts V and VI and section 141) means a claim that it would be contrary to the United Kingdom's obligations under the Refugee Convention for the claimant to be removed from, or required to leave, the United Kingdom;
   'the Commission' means the Special Immigration Appeals Commission;
   'country' includes any territory;
   'EEA State' means a State which is a Contracting Party to the Agreement on the European Economic Area signed at Oporto on 2nd May 1992 as it has effect for the time being;
   'the Human Rights Convention' means the Convention for the Protection of Human Rights and Fundamental Freedoms, agreed by the Council of

Europe at Rome on 4th November 1950 as it has effect for the time being in relation to the United Kingdom;

'the Immigration Acts' has the meaning given by section 158 of the Nationality, Immigration and Asylum Act 2002;

'prescribed' means prescribed by regulations made by the Secretary of State;

'the Refugee Convention' means the Convention relating to the Status of Refugees done at Geneva on 28 July 1951 and the Protocol to the Convention;

'voluntary organisations' means bodies (other than public or local authorities) whose activities are not carried on for profit.

(2) The following expressions have the same meaning as in the 1971 Act –

'certificate of entitlement';

'entry clearance';

'illegal entrant';

'immigration officer';

'immigration rules';

'port';

'United Kingdom passport';

'work permit'

SCHEDULE 8 – PROVISION OF SUPPORT: REGULATIONS

General regulation-making power

1   The Secretary of State may by regulations make such further provision with respect to the powers conferred on him by section 95 as he considers appropriate.

[Determining whether a person is destitute

2 (1) The regulations may provide, in connection with determining whether a person is destitute, for the Secretary of State to take into account, except in such circumstances (if any) as may be prescribed –

(a) income which the person concerned, or any dependant of his, has or might reasonably be expected to have, and

(b) support which is, or assets of a prescribed kind which are, or might reasonably be expected to be, available to him or to any dependant of his,

otherwise than by way of support provided under section 95.

(2) The regulations may provide that in such circumstances (if any) as may be prescribed, a person is not to be treated as destitute for the purposes of section 95.][16]

Prescribed levels of support

3   The regulations may make provision –

(a) as to the circumstances in which the Secretary of State may, as a general rule, be expected to provide support in accordance with prescribed levels or of a prescribed kind;

(b) as to the circumstances in which the Secretary of State may, as a general

---

16   Para 2 repealed by NIAA 2002 ss45(3), 161, Sch 9, from a date to be appointed.

rule, be expected to provide support otherwise than in accordance with the prescribed levels.

Provision of items and services

4   The regulations may make provision for prescribed items or services to be provided or made available to persons receiving support under section 95 for such purposes and in such circumstances as may be prescribed.

Support and assets to be taken into account

5   The regulations may make provision requiring the Secretary of State, except in such circumstances (if any) as may be prescribed, to take into account, when deciding the level or kind of support to be provided –

(a) income which the person concerned, or any dependant of his, has or might reasonably be expected to have, and

(b) support which is, or assets of a prescribed kind which are, or might reasonably be expected to be, available to him or to any dependant of his,

otherwise than by way of support provided under section 95.

[Valuation of assets

6   The regulations may make provision as to the valuation of assets.][17]

Breach of conditions

7   The regulations may make provision for the Secretary of State to take into account, when deciding –

(a) whether to provide, or to continue to provide, support under section 95, or

(b) the level or kind of support to be provided,

the extent to which any condition on which support is being, or has previously been, provided has been complied with.

Suspension or discontinuation of support

8 (1) The regulations may make provision for the suspension or discontinuance of support under section 95 in prescribed circumstances (including circumstances in which the Secretary of State would otherwise be under a duty to provide support).

(2) The circumstances which may be prescribed include the cessation of residence –

(a) in accommodation provided under section 95; or

(b) at an address notified to the Secretary of State in accordance with the regulations.

Notice to quit

9 (1) The regulations may provide that if –

(a) as a result of support provided under section 95, a person has a tenancy or a licence to occupy accommodation,

(b) one or more of the conditions mentioned in sub-paragraph (2) are satisfied, and

17 Para 6 repealed by NIAA 2002 ss45(3), 161, Sch 9, from a date to be appointed.

(c) he is given such notice to quit as may be prescribed by the regulations, his tenancy or licence is to be treated as ending with the period specified in that notice, regardless of when it could otherwise be brought to an end.

(2) The conditions are that –

(a) the support provided under section 95 is suspended or discontinued as a result of any provision of a kind mentioned in paragraph 8;

(b) the relevant claim for asylum has been determined;

(c) the supported person has ceased to be destitute;

(d) he is to be moved to other accommodation.

Contributions to support

10 The regulations may make provision requiring a supported person to make payments to the Secretary of State, in prescribed circumstances, by way of contributions to the cost of the provision of that support.

Recovery of sums by Secretary of State

11 (1) The regulations may provide for the recovery by the Secretary of State of sums representing the whole or part of the monetary value of support provided to a person under section 95 where it appears to the Secretary of State –

(a) that that person had, at the time when he applied for support, assets of any kind in the United Kingdom or elsewhere which were not capable of being realised; but

(b) that those assets have subsequently become, and remain, capable of being realised.

(2) An amount recoverable under regulations made by virtue of sub-paragraph (1) may be recovered –

(a) as if it were a debt due to the Secretary of State; or

(b) by such other method of recovery, including by deduction from support provided under section 95 as may be prescribed.

Procedure

12 The regulations may make provision with respect to procedural requirements including, in particular, provision as to –

(a) the procedure to be followed in making an application for support;

(b) the information which must be provided by the applicant;

(c) the circumstances in which an application may not be entertained;

(d) the making of further enquiries by the Secretary of State;

(e) the circumstances in which, and person by whom, a change of circumstances of a prescribed description must be notified to the Secretary of State.

SCHEDULE 14 – CONSEQUENTIAL AMENDMENTS
The Protection from Eviction Act 1977

73   In section 3A of the Protection from Eviction Act 1977 (excluded tenancies and licences), after subsection (7), insert –

'(7A) A tenancy or licence is excluded if it is granted in order to provide accommodation under Part VI of the Immigration and Asylum Act 1999.'

The Housing (Northern Ireland) Order 1983 SI 1983 No 1118 (NI 15)

78   In Schedule 2 to the Housing (Northern Ireland) Order 1983 (tenancies which are not secure tenancies), after paragraph 3, insert –

'Accommodation for asylum-seekers

3A(1) A tenancy is not a secure tenancy if it is granted in order to provide accommodation under Part VI of the Immigration and Asylum Act 1999.

(2) A tenancy mentioned in sub-paragraph (1) becomes a secure tenancy if the landlord notifies the tenant that it is to be regarded as a secure tenancy.'

The Rent (Scotland) Act 1984

79   In section 23A of the Rent (Scotland) Act 1984 (excluded tenancies and occupancy rights), after subsection (5) insert –

'5A   Nothing in section 23 of this Act applies to a tenancy or right of occupancy if it is granted in order to provide accommodation under Part VI of the Immigration and Asylum Act 1999.

The Housing Act 1985

81   In Schedule 1 to the Housing Act 1985 (tenancies which cannot be secure tenancies), after paragraph 4, insert –

'Accommodation for asylum-seekers

4A(1) A tenancy is not a secure tenancy if it is granted in order to provide accommodation under Part VI of the Immigration and Asylum Act 1999.

(2) A tenancy mentioned in sub-paragraph (1) becomes a secure tenancy if the landlord notifies the tenant that it is to be regarded as a secure tenancy.'

The Housing (Scotland) Act 1987

82   In Schedule 2 to the Housing (Scotland) Act 1975 (tenancies which cannot be secure tenancies), after paragraph 5, insert –

'5A(1) A tenancy is not a secure tenancy if it is granted in order to provide accommodation under Part VI of the Immigration and Asylum Act 1999.

(2) A tenancy mentioned in sub-paragraph (1) becomes a secure tenancy if the landlord notifies the tenant that it is to be regarded as a secure tenancy.'

The Housing (Scotland) Act 1988

87   In Schedule 4 to the Housing (Scotland) Act 1988 (tenancies which cannot be

assured tenancies), after paragraph 11A, insert –

'Accommodation for asylum-seekers

11B(1) A tenancy granted under arrangements for the provision of support for asylum-seekers or dependants of asylum-seekers made under Part VI of the Immigration and Asylum Act 1999.

The Housing Act 1988

88   In Schedule 1 to the Housing Act 1988 (tenancies which are not assured tenancies), after paragraph 12, insert –

'Accommodation for asylum-seekers

12A(1) A tenancy granted by a private landlord under arrangements for the provision of support for asylum-seekers or dependants of asylum-seekers made under Part VI of the Immigration and Asylum Act 1999.

(2) 'Private landlord' means a landlord who is not within section 80(1) of the Housing Act 1985.'

The Housing Act 1996

116   In section 183(2) of the Housing Act 1996 (interpretation of expressions related to assistance), in the definition of 'eligible for assistance', omit 'or section 186 (asylum seekers and their dependants)'.

SCHEDULE 15 – TRANSITIONAL PROVISIONS AND SAVINGS
DUTIES UNDER NATIONAL ASSISTANCE ACT 1948

Assistance under Part VII of the Housing Act 1996

13 (1) The Secretary of State may by order provide for any provision of Part VII of the Housing Act 1996 (homelessness) to have effect in relation to section 185(2) persons, during the interim period, with such modifications as may be specified in the order.

(2) An order under this paragraph may, in particular, include provision –

(a) for the referral of section 185(2) persons by one local housing authority to another by agreement between the authorities;

(b) as to the suitability of accommodation for such persons;

(c) as to out-of-area placements of such persons.

(3) 'Interim period' means the period beginning with the passing of this Act and ending on the coming into force of the repeal of section 186 of the Act of 1996 (asylum-seekers and their dependants) by this Act (as to which see section 117(5)).

(4) 'Local housing authority' has the same meaning as in the Act of 1996.

(5) 'Section 185(2) person' means a person who –

(a) is eligible for housing assistance under Part VII of the Act of 1996 as a result of regulations made under section 185(2) of that Act; and

(b) is not made ineligible by section 186 (or any other provision) of that Act.

(6) The fact that an order may be made under this paragraph only in respect of the interim period does not prevent it from containing provisions of a kind authorised under section 166(3)(a) which are to have continuing effect after the end of that period.

Provision of support

14 (1) The Secretary of State may, by directions given to a local authority to whom Schedule 9 applies, require the authority to treat the interim period fixed for the purposes of that Schedule as coming to an end –

(a) for specified purposes,

(b) in relation to a specified area or locality, or

(c) in relation to persons of a specified description,

on such earlier day as may be specified.

(2) The Secretary of State may, by directions given to an authority to whom an amended provision applies, provide for specified descriptions of person to be treated –

(a) for specified purposes, or

(b) in relation to a specified area or locality,

as being persons to whom section 115 applies during such period as may be specified.

(3) Directions given under this paragraph may –

(a) make such consequential, supplemental or transitional provision as the Secretary of State considers appropriate; and

(b) make different provision for different cases or descriptions of case.

(4) 'Specified' means specified in the directions.

(5) 'Amended provision' means any provision amended by –

(a) section 116;

(b) section 117(1) or (2);

(c) section 120; or

(d) section 121.

NATIONALITY, IMMIGRATION AND ASYLUM ACT 2002 Parts 2 and 3 (extracts), Sch 3

> For the most part, Part 2 of NIAA 2002 is not yet in force. Those sections that are in force are in roman. All sections not yet in force are in italics.

PART 2
Accommodation Centres

ESTABLISHMENT
Establishment of centres

16 (1) The Secretary of State may arrange for the provision of premises for the accommodation of persons in accordance with this Part.

(2) A set of premises provided under this section is referred to in this Act as an 'accommodation centre'.

(3) The Secretary of State may arrange for –

   (a) the provision of facilities at or near an accommodation centre for sittings of adjudicators appointed for the purpose of Part 5 in accordance with a determination of the Lord Chancellor under paragraph 2 of Schedule 4;

   (b) the provision of facilities at an accommodation centre for the taking of steps in connection with the determination of claims for asylum (within the meaning of section 18(3)).[19]

USE OF CENTRES
Support for destitute asylum-seeker

17 *(1) The Secretary of State may arrange for the provision of accommodation for a person in an accommodation centre if –*

   (a) the person is an asylum-seeker or the dependant of an asylum-seeker, and

   (b) the Secretary of State thinks that the person is destitute or is likely to become destitute within a prescribed period.

(2) The Secretary of State may make regulations about procedure to be followed in respect of the provision of accommodation under this section.

(3) The regulations may, in particular, make provision –

   (a) specifying procedure to be followed in applying for accommodation in an accommodation centre;

   (b) providing for an application to be combined with an application under or in respect of another enactment;

   (c) requiring an applicant to provide information;

   (d) specifying circumstances in which an application may not be considered (which provision may, in particular, provide for an application not to be considered where the Secretary of State is not satisfied that the information provided is complete or accurate or that the applicant is co-operating with enquiries under

19 In force.

paragraph *(e)*);

(e) *about the making of enquiries by the Secretary of State;*

(f) *requiring a person to notify the Secretary of State of a change in circumstances.*

(4) *Sections 18 to 20 define the following expressions for the purpose of this Part –*

(a) *asylum-seeker,*

(b) *dependant, and*

(c) *destitute.*

Asylum-seeker: definition

18(1) *For the purposes of this Part a person is an 'asylum-seeker' if –*

(a) *he is at least 18 years old,*

(b) *he is in the United Kingdom,*

(c) *a claim for asylum has been made by him at a place designated by the Secretary of State,*

(d) *the Secretary of State has recorded the claim, and*

(e) *the claim has not been determined.*

(2) *A person shall continue to be treated as an asylum-seeker despite subsection (1)(e) while –*

(a) *his household includes a dependent child who is under 18, and*

(b) *he does not have leave to enter or remain in the United Kingdom.*

(3) *A claim for asylum is a claim by a person that to remove him from or require him to leave the United Kingdom would be contrary to the United Kingdom's obligations under –*

(a) *the Convention relating to the Status of Refugees done at Geneva on 28th July 1951 and its Protocol, or*

(b) *Article 3 of the Convention for the Protection of Human Rights and Fundamental Freedoms agreed by the Council of Europe at Rome on 4th November 1950*

Destitution: definition

19(1) *Where a person has dependants, he and his dependants are destitute for the purpose of this Part if they do not have and cannot obtain both –*

(a) *adequate accommodation, and*

(b) *food and other essential items.*

(2) *Where a person does not have dependants, he is destitute for the purpose of this Part if he does not have and cannot obtain both –*

(a) *adequate accommodation, and*

(b) *food and other essential items.*

(3) *In determining whether accommodation is adequate for the purposes of subsection (1) or (2) the Secretary of State must have regard to any matter prescribed for the purposes of this subsection.*

(4) *In determining whether accommodation is adequate for the purposes of subsection (1) or (2) the Secretary of State may not have regard to –*

(a) *whether a person has an enforceable right to occupy accommodation,*

(b) *whether a person shares all or part of accommodation,*

(c) *whether accommodation is temporary or permanent,*

(d) *the location of accommodation, or*

(e) *any other matter prescribed for the purposes of this subsection.*

(5) *The Secretary of State may by regulations specify items which are or are not to be treated as essential items for the purposes of subsections (1) and (2).*

(6) *The Secretary of State may by regulations –*

    (a) *provide that a person is not to be treated as destitute for the purposes of this Part in specified circumstances;*

    (b) *enable or require the Secretary of State in deciding whether a person is destitute to have regard to income which he or a dependant of his might reasonably be expected to have;*

    (c) *enable or require the Secretary of State in deciding whether a person is destitute to have regard to support which is or might reasonably be expected to be available to the person or a dependant of his;*

    (d) *enable or require the Secretary of State in deciding whether a person is destitute to have regard to assets of a prescribed kind which he or a dependant of his has or might reasonably be expected to have;*

    (e) *make provision as to the valuation of assets.*

Dependant: definition

20   *For the purposes of this Part a person is a 'dependant' of an asylum-seeker if (and only if) that person –*

    (a) *is in the United Kingdom, and*

    (b) *is within a prescribed class.*

Sections 17 to 20: supplementary

21 (1) *This section applies for the purposes of sections 17 to 20.*

  (2) *The Secretary of State may inquire into and decide a person's age.*

  (3) *A claim for asylum shall be treated as determined at the end of such period as may be prescribed beginning with –*

    (a) *or the date on which the Secretary of State notifies the claimant of his decision on the claim, (b) if the claimant appeals against the Secretary of State's decision, the date on which the appeal is disposed of.*

  (4) *A notice under subsection (3)(a) –*

    (a) *must be in writing, and*

    (b) *if sent by first class post to the claimant's last known address or to the claimant's representative, shall be treated as being received by the claimant on the second day after the day of posting.*

  (5) *An appeal is disposed of when it is no longer pending for the purpose of –*

    (a) *Part 5 of this Act, or*

    (b) *the Special Immigration Appeals Commission Act 1997.*

Immigration and Asylum Act 1999 s95

22   *The Secretary of State may provide support under section 95 of the Immigration and Asylum Act 1999 (c 33) (destitute asylum-seeker) by arranging for the provision of accommodation in an accommodation centre.*

Person subject to United Kingdom entrance control

23(1) A residence restriction may include a requirement to reside at an accommodation centre.

(2) In subsection (1) 'residence restriction' means a restriction imposed under –

(a) paragraph 21 of Schedule 2 to the Immigration Act 1971 (temporary admission or release from detention), or

(b) paragraph 2(5) of Schedule 3 to that Act (control pending deportation).

(3) Where a person is required to reside in an accommodation centre by virtue of subsection (1) the Secretary of State must arrange for the provision of accommodation for the person in an accommodation centre.

(4) But if the person is required to leave an accommodation centre by virtue of section 26 or 30 he shall be treated as having broken the residence restriction referred to in subsection (1).

(5) The Secretary of State may provide support under section 4 of the Immigration and Asylum Act 1999 (persons subject to entrance control) (including that section as amended by section 49 of this Act) by arranging for the provision of accommodation in an accommodation centre.

Provisional assistance

24(1) If the Secretary of State thinks that a person may be eligible for the provision of accommodation in an accommodation centre under section 17, he may arrange for the provision for the person, pending a decision about eligibility, of –

(a) accommodation in an accommodation centre, or

(b) other support or assistance (of any kind).

(2) Section 99 of the Immigration and Asylum Act 1999 (provision of support by local authority) shall have effect in relation to the provision of support for persons under subsection (1) above as it has effect in relation to the provision of support for asylum-seekers under sections 95 and 98 of that Act.

Length of stay

25 (1) The Secretary of State may not arrange for the provision of accommodation for a person in an accommodation centre if he has been a resident of an accommodation centre for a continuous period of six months.

(2) But –

(a) subsection (1) may be disapplied in respect of a person, generally or to a specified extent, by agreement between the Secretary of State and the person, and

(b) if the Secretary of State thinks it appropriate in relation to a person because of the circumstances of his case, the Secretary of State may direct that subsection (1) shall have effect in relation to the person as if the period specified in that subsection were the period of nine months.

(3) Section 51 is subject to this section.

(4) The Secretary of State may by order amend subsection (1) or (2)(b) so as to substitute a shorter period for a period specified.

Withdrawal of support

26 (1) The Secretary of State may stop providing support for a person under section 17 or 24 if –

(*a*) the Secretary of State suspects that the person or a dependant of his has committed an offence by virtue of section 35, or

(*b*) the person or a dependant of his has failed to comply with directions of the Secretary of State as to the time or manner of travel to accommodation provided under section 17 or 24.

(2) The Secretary of State may by regulations specify other circumstances in which he may stop providing support for a person under section 17 or 24.

(3) In determining whether or not to provide a person with support or assistance under section 17 or 24 of this Act or section 4, 95 or 98 of the Immigration and Asylum Act 1999 (asylum-seeker) the Secretary of State may take into account the fact that –

(*a*) he has withdrawn support from the person by virtue of this section or section 30(4) or (5), or

(*b*) circumstances exist which would have enabled the Secretary of State to withdraw support from the person by virtue of this section had he been receiving support.

(4) This section is without prejudice to section 103 of the Immigration and Asylum Act 1999 (appeal against refusal to support).

OPERATION OF CENTRES
Resident of centre

27 A reference in this Part to a resident of an accommodation centre is a reference to a person for whom accommodation in the centre is provided –

(*a*) under section 17,

(*b*) by virtue of section 22,

(*c*) by virtue of section 23, or

(*d*) under section 24.

Manager of centre

28 A reference in this Part to the manager of an accommodation centre is a reference to a person who agrees with the Secretary of State to be wholly or partly responsible for the management of the centre.

Facilities

29(1) The Secretary of State may arrange for the following to be provided to a resident of an accommodation centre –

(*a*) food and other essential items;

(*b*) money;

(*c*) assistance with transport for the purpose of proceedings under the Immigration Acts or in connection with a claim for asylum;

(*d*) transport to and from the centre;

(*e*) assistance with expenses incurred in connection with carrying out voluntary work or other activities;

(*f*) education and training;

(*g*) facilities relating to health;

(*h*) facilities for religious observance;

(*i*) anything which the Secretary of State thinks ought to be provided for the purpose of providing a resident with proper occupation and for the purpose of maintaining good order;

(j) anything which the Secretary of State thinks ought to be provided for a person because of his exceptional circumstances.

(2) The Secretary of State may make regulations specifying the amount or maximum amount of money to be provided under subsection (1)(b).

(3) The Secretary of State may arrange for the provision of facilities in an accommodation centre for the use of a person in providing legal advice to a resident of the centre.

(4) The Secretary of State shall take reasonable steps to ensure that a resident of an accommodation centre has an opportunity to obtain legal advice before any appointment made by an immigration officer or an official of the Secretary of State for the purpose of obtaining information from the resident to be used in determining his claim for asylum.

(5) The Secretary of State may by order amend subsection (1) so as to add a reference to facilities which may be provided.

Conditions of residence

30(1) The Secretary of State may make regulations about conditions to be observed by residents of an accommodation centre.

(2) Regulations under subsection (1) may, in particular, enable a condition to be imposed in accordance with the regulations by –

(a) the Secretary of State, or

(b) the manager of an accommodation centre.

(3) A condition imposed by virtue of this section may, in particular –

(a) require a person not to be absent from the centre during specified hours without the permission of the Secretary of State or the manager;

(b) require a person to report to an immigration officer or the Secretary of State.

(4) If a resident of an accommodation centre breaches a condition imposed by virtue of this section, the Secretary of State may –

(a) require the resident and any dependant of his to leave the centre;

(b) authorise the manager of the centre to require the resident and any dependant of his to leave the centre.

(5) If a dependant of a resident of an accommodation centre breaches a condition imposed by virtue of this section, the Secretary of State may –

(a) require the resident and any dependant of his to leave the centre;

(b) authorise the manager of the centre to require the resident and any dependant of his to leave the centre.

(6) Regulations under this section must include provision for ensuring that a person subject to a condition is notified of the condition in writing.

(7) A condition imposed by virtue of this section is in addition to any restriction imposed under paragraph 21 of Schedule 2 to the Immigration Act 1971 (c 77) (control of entry to United Kingdom) or under paragraph 2(5) of Schedule 3 to that Act (control pending deportation).

(8) A reference in this Part to a condition of residence is a reference to a condition imposed by virtue of this section.

Financial contribution by resident

31 (1) A condition of residence may, in particular, require a resident of an accommodation centre to make payments to –

    (a) the Secretary of State, or

    (b) the manager of the centre.

  (2) The Secretary of State may make regulations enabling him to recover sums representing the whole or part of the value of accommodation and other facilities provided to a resident of an accommodation centre if –

    (a) accommodation is provided for the resident in response to an application by him for support,

    (b) when the application was made the applicant had assets which were not capable of being realised, and

    (c) the assets have become realisable.

  (3) In subsection (2) 'assets' includes assets outside the United Kingdom.

  (4) An amount recoverable by virtue of regulations made under subsection (2) may be recovered –

    (a) as a debt due to the Secretary of State;

    (b) by another prescribed method (which may include the imposition or variation of a residence condition).

Tenure

32 (1) A resident of an accommodation centre shall not be treated as acquiring a tenancy of or other interest in any part of the centre (whether by virtue of an agreement between the resident and another person or otherwise).

  (2) Subsection (3) applies where –

    (a) the Secretary of State decides to stop arranging for the provision of accommodation in an accommodation centre for a resident of the centre, or

    (b) a resident of an accommodation centre is required to leave the centre in accordance with section 30.

  (3) Where this subsection applies –

    (a) the Secretary of State or the manager of the centre may recover possession of the premises occupied by the resident, and

    (b) the right under paragraph (a) shall be enforceable in accordance with procedure prescribed by regulations made by the Secretary of State.

  (4) Any licence which a resident of an accommodation centre has to occupy premises in the centre shall be an excluded licence for the purposes of the Protection from Eviction Act 1977.

  (5) The following shall be inserted after section 3A(7A) of the Protection from Eviction Act 1977 (disapplication of section 3: Part VI of Immigration and Asylum Act 1999 c 33)) –

    '(7B) Section 32 of the Nationality, Immigration and Asylum Act 2002 (accommodation centre: tenure) provides for a resident's licence to occupy an accommodation centre to be an excluded licence.'

  (6) The following shall be inserted after section 23A(5A) of the Rent (Scotland) Act 1984 (c 58) (excluded tenancies and occupancy rights) –

    '(5B) Nothing in section 23 of this Act applies to a resident's occupancy of an accommodation centre provided under section 16 or 24(1)(b) of the Nationality, Immigration and Asylum Act 2002 ('resident' being construed in accordance with section 27 of that Act).'

(7) In this section a reference to an accommodation centre includes a reference to premises in which accommodation is provided under section 24(1)(b).

Advisory Groups

33 (1) The Secretary of State shall appoint a group (to be known as an Accommodation Centre Advisory Group) for each accommodation centre.

(2) The Secretary of State may by regulations –

(a) confer functions on Advisory Groups;

(b) make provision about the constitution and proceedings of Advisory Groups.

(3) Regulations under subsection (2)(a) must, in particular, provide for members of an accommodation centre's Advisory Group –

(a) to visit the centre;

(b) to hear complaints made by residents of the centre;

(c) to report to the Secretary of State.

(4) The manager of an accommodation centre must permit a member of the centre's Advisory Group on request –

(a) to visit the centre at any time;

(b) to visit any resident of the centre at any time, provided that the resident consents.

(5) A member of an Advisory Group shall hold and vacate office in accordance with the terms of his appointment (which may include provision about retirement, resignation or dismissal).

(6) The Secretary of State may –

(a) defray expenses of members of an Advisory Group;

(b) make facilities available to members of an Advisory Group.

GENERAL

The Monitor of Accommodation Centres

34 (1) The Secretary of State shall appoint a person as Monitor of Accommodation Centres.

(2) The Monitor shall monitor the operation of this Part of this Act and shall, in particular, consider –

(a) the quality and effectiveness of accommodation and other facilities provided in accommodation centres,

(b) the nature and enforcement of conditions of residence,

(c) the treatment of residents, and

(d) whether, in the case of any accommodation centre, its location prevents a need of its residents from being met.

(3) In exercising his functions the Monitor shall consult –

(a) the Secretary of State, and

(b) such other persons as he considers appropriate.

(4) The Monitor shall report to the Secretary of State about the matters considered by the Monitor in the course of the exercise of his functions –

(a) at least once in each calendar year, and

(b) on such occasions as the Secretary of State may request.

(5) Where the Secretary of State receives a report under subsection (4)(a) he shall lay a copy before Parliament as soon as is reasonably practicable.

(6) The Monitor shall hold and vacate office in accordance with the terms of his appointment (which may include provision about retirement, resignation or dismissal).

(7) The Secretary of State may –

(a) pay fees and allowances to the Monitor;

(b) defray expenses of the Monitor;

(c) make staff and other facilities available to the Monitor.

(8) The Secretary of State may appoint more than one person to act jointly as Monitor (in which case they shall divide or share functions in accordance with the terms of their appointment and, subject to that, by agreement between them).

(9) A person who is employed within a government department may not be appointed as Monitor of Accommodation Centres.

Ancillary provisions

35(1) The following provisions of the Immigration and Asylum Act 1999 shall apply for the purposes of this Part as they apply for the purposes of Part VI of that Act (support for asylum-seeker) –

(a) section 105 (false representation),

(b) section 106 (dishonest representation),

(c) section 107 (delay or obstruction),

(d) section 108 (failure of sponsor to maintain),

(e) section 109 (offence committed by body),

(f) section 112 (recovery of expenditure),

(g) section 113 (recovery of expenditure from sponsor),

(h) section 124 (corporation sole), and

(i) section 127 (redirection of post).

(2) In the application of section 112 a reference to something done under section 95 or 98 of that Act shall be treated as a reference to something done under section 17 or 24 of this Act.

(3) In the application of section 113 a reference to section 95 of that Act shall be treated as a reference to section 17 of this Act.

Education: general

36(1) For the purposes of section 13 of the Education Act 1996 (general responsibility of local education authority) a resident of an accommodation centre shall not be treated as part of the population of a local education authority's area.

(2) A child who is a resident of an accommodation centre may not be admitted to a maintained school or a maintained nursery (subject to section 37).

(3) But subsection (2) does not prevent a child's admission to a school which is –

(a) a community special school or a foundation special school, and

(b) named in a statement in respect of the child under section 324 of the Education Act 1996 (special educational needs).

(4) In subsections (2) and (3) –

    (a) 'maintained school' means a maintained school within the meaning of section 20(7) of the School Standards and Framework Act 1998 (definition), and

    (b) 'maintained nursery' means a facility for nursery education, within the meaning of section 117 of that Act, provided by a local education authority.

(5) The following shall not apply in relation to a child who is a resident of an accommodation centre (subject to section 37) –

    (a) section 86(1) and (2) of the School Standards and Framework Act 1998 (parental preference),

    (b) section 94 of that Act (appeal),

    (c) section 19 of the Education Act 1996 (education out of school),

    (d) section 316(2) and (3) of that Act (child with special educational needs to be educated in mainstream school), and

    (e) paragraphs 3 and 8 of Schedule 27 to that Act (special education needs: making of statement: parental preference).

(6) The power of the Special Educational Needs Tribunal under section 326(3) of the Education Act 1996 (appeal against content of statement) is subject to subsection (2) above.

(7) A person exercising a function under this Act or the Education Act 1996 shall (subject to section 37) secure that a child who is a resident of an accommodation centre and who has special educational needs shall be educated by way of facilities provided under section 29(1)(f) of this Act unless that is incompatible with –

    (a) his receiving the special educational provision which his learning difficulty calls for,

    (b) the provision of efficient education for other children who are residents of the centre, or

    (c) the efficient use of resources.

(8) A person may rely on subsection (7)(b) only where there is no action –

    (a) which could reasonably be taken by that person or by another person who exercises functions, or could exercise functions, in respect of the accommodation centre concerned, and

    (b) as a result of which subsection (7)(b) would not apply.

(9) An accommodation centre is not a school within the meaning of section 4 of the Education Act 1996 (definition); but –

    (a) the School Inspections Act 1996 shall apply to educational facilities provided at an accommodation centre as if the centre were a school (for which purpose a reference to the appropriate authority shall be taken as a reference to the person (or persons) responsible for the provision of education at the accommodation centre),

    (b) section 329A of the Education Act 1996 (review or assessment of educational needs at request of responsible body) shall have effect as if –

        (i) accommodation centre were a relevant school for the purposes of that section,

        (ii) a child for whom education is provided at an accommodation centre under section 29(1)(f) were a registered pupil at the centre, and

        (iii) a reference in section 329A to the responsible body in relation to an accom-

modation centre were a reference to any person providing education at the centre under section 29(1)(f), and

(c) section 140 of the Learning and Skills Act 2000 (learning difficulties: assessment of post-16 needs) shall have effect as if an accommodation centre were a school.

(10) Subsections (1), (2) and (5) shall not apply in relation to an accommodation centre if education is not provided for children who are residents of the centre under section 29(1)(f).

(11) An expression used in this section and in the Education Act 1996 shall have the same meaning in this section as in that Act.

Education: special cases

37 (1) This section applies to a child if a person who provides education to residents of an accommodation centre recommends in writing to the local education authority for the area in which the centre is that this section should apply to the child on the grounds that his special circumstances call for provision that can only or best be arranged by the authority.

(2) A local education authority may –

(a) arrange for the provision of education for a child to whom this section applies;

(b) disapply a provision of section 36 in respect of a child to whom this section applies.

(3) In determining whether to exercise a power under subsection (2) in respect of a child a local education authority shall have regard to any relevant guidance issued by the Secretary of State.

(4) The governing body of a maintained school shall comply with a requirement of the local education authority to admit to the school a child to whom this section applies.

(5) Subsection (4) shall not apply where compliance with a requirement would prejudice measures taken for the purpose of complying with a duty arising under section 1(6) of the School Standards and Framework Act 1998 (limit on infant class size).

(6) A local education authority may not impose a requirement under subsection (4) in respect of a school unless the authority has consulted the school in accordance with regulations made by the Secretary of State.

(7) In the case of a maintained school for which the local education authority are the admission authority, the authority may not arrange for the admission of a child to whom this section applies unless the authority has notified the school in accordance with regulations made by the Secretary of State.

(8) In this section –

(a) 'maintained school' means a maintained school within the meaning of section 20(7) of the School Standards and Framework Act 1998 (definition), and

(b) an expression which is also used in the Education Act 1996 shall have the same meaning as it has in that Act.

Local authority

38 (1) A local authority may in accordance with arrangements made by the Secretary of State –

(a) assist in arranging for the provision of an accommodation centre;

(b) make premises available for an accommodation centre;

(c) provide services in connection with an accommodation centre.

(2) In particular, a local authority may –

(a) incur reasonable expenditure;

(b) provide services outside its area;

(c) provide services jointly with another body;

(d) form a company;

(e) tender for or enter into a contract;

(f) do anything (including anything listed in paragraphs (a) to (e)) for a preparatory purpose.

(3) In this section 'local authority' means –

(a) a local authority within the meaning of section 94 of the Immigration and Asylum Act 1999, and

(b) a Northern Ireland authority within the meaning of section 110 of that Act and an Education and Library Board established under Article 3 of the Education and Libraries (Northern Ireland) Order 1986 (SI 1986/ 594 (NI 3)).[20]

'Prescribed': orders and regulations

39(1) *In this Part 'prescribed' means prescribed by the Secretary of State by order or regulations.*

(2) *An order or regulations under this Part may –*

(a) *make provision which applies generally or only in specified cases or circumstances (which may be determined wholly or partly by reference to location);*

(b) *make different provision for different cases or circumstances;*

(c) *include consequential, transitional or incidental provision.*

(3) *An order or regulations under this Part must be made by statutory instrument.*

(4) *An order or regulations under any of the following provisions of this Part shall be subject to annulment in pursuance of a resolution of either House of Parliament –*

(a) *section 17,*

(b) *section 19,*

(c) *section 20,*

(d) *section 21,*

(e) *section 26,*

(f) *section 29,*

(g) *section 31,*

(h) *section 32,*

(i) *section 33,*

(j) *section 37,*

(k) *section 40, and*

(l) *section 41.*

(5) *An order under section 25 or regulations under section 30 may not be made unless a draft has been laid before and approved by resolution of each House of Parliament.*

20 In force.

Scotland

40 (1) The Secretary of State may not make arrangements under section 16 for the provision of premises in Scotland unless he has consulted the Scottish Ministers.[21]

(2) *The Secretary of State may by order make provision in relation to the education of residents of accommodation centres in Scotland.*

(3) *An order under subsection (2) may, in particular –*

(a) *apply, disapply or modify the effect of an enactment (which may include a provision made by or under an Act of the Scottish Parliament);*

(b) *make provision having an effect similar to the effect of a provision of section 36 or 37.*

Northern Ireland

41 (1) The Secretary of State may not make arrangements under section 16 for the provision of premises in Northern Ireland unless he has consulted the First Minister and the deputy First Minister.[22]

(2) *The Secretary of State may by order make provision in relation to the education of residents of accommodation centres in Northern Ireland.*

(3) *An order under subsection (2) may, in particular –*

(a) *apply, disapply or modify the effect of an enactment (which may include a provision made by or under Northern Ireland legislation);*

(b) *make provision having an effect similar to the effect of a provision of section 36 or 37.*

Wales

42 The Secretary of State may not make arrangements under section 16 for the provision of premises in Wales unless he has consulted the National Assembly for Wales.[23]

PART 3

OTHER SUPPORT AND ASSISTANCE

Asylum-seeker: form of support

43 (1) The Secretary of State may make an order restricting the application of section 96(1)(b) of the Immigration and Asylum Act 1999 (support for asylum-seeker: essential living needs) –

(a) in all circumstances, to cases in which support is being provided under section 96(1)(a) (accommodation), or

(b) in specified circumstances only, to cases in which support is being provided under section 96(1)(a).

(2) An order under subsection (1)(b) may, in particular, make provision by reference to –

21 Subsection (1) in force.
22 Subsection (1) in force.
23 In force.

   (a) location;
   (b) the date of an application.
(3) An order under subsection (1) may include transitional provision.
(4) An order under subsection (1) –
   (a) must be made by statutory instrument, and
   (b) may not be made unless a draft has been laid before and approved by
        resolution of each House of Parliament.[24]

Young asylum-seeker

48   The following provisions of the Immigration and Asylum Act 1999 shall have
     effect as if the definition of asylum-seeker in section 94(1) of that Act did not
     exclude persons who are under 18 –
   (a) section 110 (local authority expenditure on asylum-seekers), and
   (b) section 111 (grants to voluntary organisations).[25]

Choice of form of support

51 *(1) The Secretary of State may refuse to provide support for a person under a provision*
   specified in subsection (2) on the grounds that an offer has been made to the person
   of support under another provision specified in that subsection.
   (2) The provisions are –
   (a) sections 17 and 24 of this Act,
   (b) section 4 of the Immigration and Asylum Act 1999 (accommodation for person
       temporarily admitted or released from detention), and
   (c) sections 95 and 98 of that Act (support for destitute asylum-seeker).
   (3) In deciding under which of the provisions listed in subsection (2) to offer support to
   a person the Secretary of State may –
   (a) have regard to administrative or other matters which do not concern the per-
       son's personal circumstances;
   (b) regard one of those matters as conclusive;
   (c) apply different criteria to different persons for administrative reasons (which
       may include the importance of testing the operation of a particular provision).

Withholding and withdrawal of support

54   Schedule 3 (which makes provision for support to be withheld or withdrawn
     in certain circumstances) shall have effect.[26]

Late claim for asylum: refusal of support

55 (1) The Secretary of State may not provide or arrange for the provision of support
   to a person under a provision mentioned in subsection (2) if –
   (a) the person makes a claim for asylum which is recorded by the Secretary of
        State, and
   (b) the Secretary of State is not satisfied that the claim was made as soon
        as reasonably practicable after the person's arrival in the United King-
        dom.

24 In force.
25 In force.
26 In force.

(2) The provisions are –
  (a) sections 4, 95 and 98 of the Immigration and Asylum Act 1999 (support for asylum-seeker), and
  (b) sections 17 and 24 of this Act (accommodation centre).
(3) An authority may not provide or arrange for the provision of support to a person under a provision mentioned in subsection (4) if –
  (a) the person has made a claim for asylum, and
  (b) the Secretary of State is not satisfied that the claim was made as soon as reasonably practicable after the person's arrival in the United Kingdom.
(4) The provisions are –
  (a) section 29(1)(b) of the Housing (Scotland) Act 1987 (accommodation pending review),
  (b) section 188(3) or 204(4) of the Housing Act 1996) (accommodation pending review or appeal), and
  (c) section 2 of the Local Government Act 2000 (promotion of well-being).
(5) This section shall not prevent –
  (a) the exercise of a power by the Secretary of State to the extent necessary for the purpose of avoiding a breach of a person's Convention rights (within the meaning of the Human Rights Act 1998),
  (b) the provision of support under section 95 of the Immigration and Asylum Act 1999 or section 17 of this Act in accordance with section 122 of that Act (children), or
  (c) the provision of support under section 98 of the Immigration and Asylum Act 1999 or section 24 of this Act (provisional support) to a person under the age of 18 and the household of which he forms part.
(6) An authority which proposes to provide or arrange for the provision of support to a person under a provision mentioned in subsection (4) –
  (a) must inform the Secretary of State if the authority believes that the person has made a claim for asylum,
  (b) must act in accordance with any guidance issued by the Secretary of State to determine whether subsection (3) applies, and
  (c) shall not be prohibited from providing or arranging for the provision of support if the authority has complied with paragraph (a) and (b) and concluded that subsection (3) does not apply.
(7) The Secretary of State may by order –
  (a) add, remove or amend an entry in the list in subsection (4);
  (b) provide for subsection (3) not to have effect in specified cases or circumstances.
(8) An order under subsection (7) –
  (a) may include transitional, consequential or incidental provision,
  (b) must be made by statutory instrument, and
  (c) may not be made unless a draft has been laid before and approved by resolution of each House of Parliament.
(9) For the purposes of this section 'claim for asylum' has the same meaning as in section 18.
(10) A decision of the Secretary of State that this section prevents him from pro-

viding or arranging for the provision of support to a person is not a decision that the person does not qualify for support for the purpose of section 103 of the Immigration and Asylum Act 1999 (appeals).

(11) This section does not prevent a person's compliance with a residence restriction imposed in reliance on section 70 (induction).[27]

Voluntary departure from United Kingdom

58 (1) A person is a 'voluntary leaver' for the purposes of this section if –

   (a) he is not a British citizen or an EEA national,

   (b) he leaves the United Kingdom for a place where he hopes to take up permanent residence (his 'new place of residence'), and

   (c) the Secretary of State thinks that it is in the person's interest to leave the United Kingdom and that the person wishes to leave.

(2) The Secretary of State may make arrangements to –

   (a) assist voluntary leavers;

   (b) assist individuals to decide whether to become voluntary leavers.

(3) The Secretary of State may, in particular, make payments (whether to voluntary leavers or to organisations providing services for them) which relate to –

   (a) travelling and other expenses incurred by or on behalf of a voluntary leaver, or a member of his family or household, in leaving the United Kingdom;

   (b) expenses incurred by or on behalf of a voluntary leaver, or a member of his family or household, on or shortly after arrival in his new place of residence;

   (c) the provision of services designed to assist a voluntary leaver, or a member of his family or household, to settle in his new place of residence;

   (d) expenses in connection with a journey undertaken by a person (with or without his family or household) to prepare for, or to assess the possibility of, his becoming a voluntary leaver.

(4) In subsection (1)(a) 'EEA national' means a national of a State which is a contracting party to the Agreement on the European Economic Area signed at Oporto on 2 May 1992 (as it has effect from time to time).

(5) The following provisions of the Immigration Act 1971 shall cease to have effect –

   (a) section 29 (contributions to expenses of persons returning abroad), and

   (b) section 31(d) (expenses).[28]

International projects

59 (1) The Secretary of State may participate in a project which is designed to –

   (a) reduce migration,

   (b) assist or ensure the return of migrants,

   (c) facilitate co-operation between States in matters relating to migration'

   (d) conduct or consider research about migration, or

   (e) arrange or assist the settlement of migrants (whether in the United Kingdom or elsewhere).

27 In force.
28 In force.

(2) In particular, the Secretary of State may –

    (a) provide financial support to an international organisation which arranges or participates in a project of a kind described in subsection (1);

    (b) provide financial support to an organisation in the United Kingdom or another country which arranges or participates in a project of that kind;

    (c) provide or arrange for the provision of financial or other assistance to a migrant who participates in a project of that kind;

    (d) participate in financial or other arrangements which are agreed between Her Majesty's Government and the government of one or more other countries and which are or form part of a project of that kind.

(3) In this section –

    (a) 'migrant' means a person who leaves the country where he lives hoping to settle in another country (whether or not he is a refugee within the meaning of any international Convention), and

    (b) 'migration' shall be construed accordingly.

(4) Subsection (1) does not –

    (a) confer a power to remove a person from the United Kingdom, or

    (b) affect a person's right to enter or remain in the United Kingdom.[29]

Northern Ireland authorities

60(1) *In section 110(9) of the Immigration and Asylum Act 1999 (support: payment to local authority: Northern Ireland authority) after paragraph (b) there shall be added –*

    '; or

    (c) a Health and Social Services trust established under the Health and Personal Social Services (Northern Ireland) Order 1991 (SI 1991/194 (NI 1).'

  (2) *In section 94(1) of that Act (support: interpretation) after the definition of 'local authority' there shall be inserted –*

    "Northern Ireland authority' has the meaning given by section 110(9).'

SCHEDULE 3 – WITHHOLDING AND WITHDRAWAL OF SUPPORT
SECTION 54

Ineligibility for support

1(1) *A person to whom this paragraph applies shall not be eligible for support or assistance under –*

    (a) section 21 or 29 of the National Assistance Act 1948 (local authority: accommodation and welfare),

    (b) section 45 of the Health Services and Public Health Act 1968 (local authority: welfare of elderly),

    (c) section 12 or 13A of the Social Work (Scotland) Act 1968 (social welfare services),

    (d) Article 7 or 15 of the Health and Personal Social Services (Northern Ireland) Order 1972 (SI 1972/1265 (NI 14)) (prevention of illness, social welfare),

---

29 In force.

(e) *section 21 of and Schedule 8 to the National Health Service Act 1977 (social services),*

(f) *section 29(1)(b) of the Housing (Scotland) Act 1987 (interim duty to accommodate in case of apparent priority need where review of a local authority decision has been requested),*

(g) *section 17, 23C, 24A or 24B of the Children Act 1989 (welfare and other powers which can be exercised in relation to adults),*

(h) *Article 18, 35 or 36 of the Children (Northern Ireland) Order 1995 (welfare and other powers which can be exercised in relation to adults),*

(i) *sections 22, 29 and 30 of the Children (Scotland) Act 1995 (provisions analogous to those mentioned in paragraph (g)),*

(j) *section 188(3) or 204(4) of the Housing Act 1996 (accommodation pending review or appeal),*

(k) *section 2 of the Local Government Act 2000 (promotion of well-being),*

(l) *a provision of the Immigration and Asylum Act 1999, or*

(m) *a provision of this Act.*

(2) *A power or duty under a provision referred to in sub-paragraph (1) may not be exercised or performed in respect of a person to whom this paragraph applies (whether or not the person has previously been in receipt of support or assistance under the provision).*

(3) *An approval or directions given under or in relation to a provision referred to in sub-paragraph (1) shall be taken to be subject to sub-paragraph (2).*

Exceptions

2(1) *Paragraph 1 does not prevent the provision of support or assistance –*

(a) *to a British citizen, or*

(b) *to a child, or*

(c) *under or by virtue of regulations made under paragraph 8, 9 or 10 below, or*

(d) *in a case in respect of which, and to the extent to which, regulations made by the Secretary of State disapply paragraph 1, or*

(e) *in circumstances in respect of which, and to the extent to which, regulations made by the Secretary of State disapply paragraph 1.*

(2) *Regulations under sub-paragraph (1)(d) may confer a discretion on the Secretary of State.*

(3) *Regulations under sub-paragraph (1)(e) may, in particular, disapply paragraph 1 to the provision of support or assistance by a local authority to a person where the authority –*

(a) *has taken steps in accordance with guidance issued by the Secretary of State to determine whether paragraph 1 would (but for the regulations) apply to the person, and*

(b) *has concluded on the basis of those steps that there is no reason to believe that paragraph 1 would apply.*

(4) *Regulations under sub-paragraph (1)(d) or (e) may confer a discretion on an authority.*

(5) *A local authority which is considering whether to give support or assistance to a person under a provision listed in paragraph 1(1) shall act in accordance with*

any relevant guidance issued by the Secretary of State under sub-paragraph (3)(a).

(6) A reference in this Schedule to a person to whom paragraph 1 applies includes a reference to a person in respect of whom that paragraph is disapplied to a limited extent by regulations under sub-paragraph (1)(d) or (e), except in a case for which the regulations provide otherwise.

3 Paragraph 1 does not prevent the exercise of a power or the performance of a duty if, and to the extent that, its exercise or performance is necessary for the purpose of avoiding a breach of –

(a) a person's Convention rights, or

(b) a person's rights under the Community Treaties.

First class of ineligible person: refugee status abroad

4(1) Paragraph 1 applies to a person if he –

(a) has refugee status abroad, or

(b) is the dependant of a person who is in the United Kingdom and who has refugee status abroad.

(2) For the purposes of this paragraph a person has refugee status abroad if –

(a) he does not have the nationality of an EEA State, and

(b) the government of an EEA State other than the United Kingdom has determined that he is entitled to protection as a refugee under the Refugee Convention.

Second class of ineligible person: citizen of other EEA State

5 Paragraph 1 applies to a person if he –

(a) has the nationality of an EEA State other than the United Kingdom, or

(b) is the dependant of a person who has the nationality of an EEA State other than the United Kingdom.

Third class of ineligible person: failed asylum-seeker

6(1) Paragraph 1 applies to a person if –

(a) he was (but is no longer) an asylum-seeker, and

(b) he fails to cooperate with removal directions issued in respect of him.

(2) Paragraph 1 also applies to a dependant of a person to whom that paragraph applies by virtue of sub-paragraph (1).

Fourth class of ineligible person: person unlawfully in United Kingdom

7 Paragraph 1 applies to a person if –

(a) he is in the United Kingdom in breach of the immigration laws within the meaning of section 11, and

(b) he is not an asylum-seeker.

Fifth class of ineligible person: failed asylum-seeker with family[30]

7A(1) Paragraph 1 applies to a person if–

(a) he –

(i) is treated as an asylum-seeker for the purposes of Part VI of the Immigration and Asylum Act 1999 (support) by virtue only of section 94(3A)

---

30 To be inserted by an order under the Asylum and Immigration (Treatment of Claimants, etc) Act 2004.

(failed asylum-seeker with dependent child), or

(ii) *is treated as an asylum-seeker for the purposes of Part 2 of this Act by virtue only of section 18(2),*

(b) *the Secretary of State has certified that in his opinion the person has failed without reasonable excuse to take reasonable steps—*

(i) *to leave the United Kingdom voluntarily, or*

(ii) *to place himself in a position in which he is able to leave the United Kingdom voluntarily,*

(c) *the person has received a copy of the Secretary of State's certificate, and*

(d) *the period of 14 days, beginning with the date on which the person receives the copy of the certificate, has elapsed.*

(2) *Paragraph 1 also applies to a dependant of a person to whom that paragraph applies by virtue of sub-paragraph (1).*

(3) *For the purpose of sub-paragraph (1)(d) if the Secretary of State sends a copy of a certificate by first class post to a person's last known address, the person shall be treated as receiving the copy on the second day after the day on which it was posted.*

(4) *The Secretary of State may by regulations vary the period specified in sub-paragraph (1)(d).*

Travel assistance

8   *The Secretary of State may make regulations providing for arrangements to be made enabling a person to whom paragraph 1 applies by virtue of paragraph 4 or 5 to leave the United Kingdom.*

Temporary accommodation

9(1) *The Secretary of State may make regulations providing for arrangements to be made for the accommodation of a person to whom paragraph 1 applies pending the implementation of arrangements made by virtue of paragraph 8.*

(2) *Arrangements for a person by virtue of this paragraph –*

(a) *may be made only if the person has with him a dependent child, and*

(b) *may include arrangements for a dependent child.*

10(1) *The Secretary of State may make regulations providing for arrangements to be made for the accommodation of a person if –*

(a) *paragraph 1 applies to him by virtue of paragraph 7, and*

(b) *he has not failed to cooperate with removal directions issued in respect of him.*

(2) *Arrangements for a person by virtue of this paragraph –*

(a) *may be made only if the person has with him a dependent child, and*

(b) *may include arrangements for a dependent child.*

Assistance and accommodation: general

11   *Regulations under paragraph 8, 9 or 10 may –*

(a) *provide for the making of arrangements under a provision referred to in paragraph 1(1) or otherwise;*

(b) *confer a function (which may include the exercise of a discretion) on the Secretary of State, a local authority or another person;*

(c) *provide that arrangements must be made in a specified manner or in accor-*

dance with specified principles;

(d) provide that arrangements may not be made in a specified manner;

(e) require a local authority or another person to have regard to guidance issued by the Secretary of State in making arrangements;

(f) require a local authority or another person to comply with a direction of the Secretary of State in making arrangements.

12(1) Regulations may, in particular, provide that if a person refuses an offer of arrangements under paragraph 8 or fails to implement or cooperate with arrangements made for him under that paragraph –

(a) new arrangements may be made for him under paragraph 8, but

(b) new arrangements may not be made for him under paragraph 9.

(2) Regulations by virtue of this paragraph may include exceptions in the case of a person who –

(a) has a reason of a kind specified in the regulations for failing to implement or cooperate with arrangements made under paragraph 8, and

(b) satisfies any requirements of the regulations for proof of the reason.

Offences

13(1) A person who leaves the United Kingdom in accordance with arrangements made under paragraph 8 commits an offence if he –

(a) returns to the United Kingdom, and

(b) requests that arrangements be made for him by virtue of paragraph 8, 9 or 10.

(2) A person commits an offence if he –

(a) requests that arrangements be made for him by virtue of paragraph 8, 9 or 10, and

(b) fails to mention a previous request by him for the making of arrangements under any of those paragraphs.

(3) A person who is guilty of an offence under this paragraph shall be liable on summary conviction to imprisonment for a term not exceeding six months.

Information

14 (1) If it appears to a local authority that paragraph 1 applies or may apply to a person in the authority's area by virtue of paragraph 6, 7 or 7a[31], the authority must inform the Secretary of State.

(2) A local authority shall act in accordance with any relevant guidance issued by the Secretary of State for the purpose of determining whether paragraph 1 applies or may apply to a person in the authority's area by virtue of paragraph 6 or 7.

Power to amend Schedule

15 The Secretary of State may by order amend this Schedule so as –

(a) to provide for paragraph 1 to apply or not to apply to a class of person;

(b) to add or remove a provision to or from the list in paragraph 1(1);

(c) to add, amend or remove a limitation of or exception to paragraph 1.

---

31 To be inserted by an order under the Asylum and Immigration (Treatment of Claimants, etc) Act 2004.

Orders and regulations

16(1) An order or regulations under this Schedule must be made by statutory instrument.

(2) An order or regulations under this Schedule may –

(a) make provision which applies generally or only in specified cases or circumstances or only for specified purposes;

(b) make different provision for different cases, circumstances or purposes;

(c) make transitional provision;

(d) make consequential provision (which may include provision amending a provision made by or under this or another Act).

(3) An order under this Schedule, regulations under paragraph 2(1)(d) or (e) or other regulations which include consequential provision amending an enactment shall not be made unless a draft has been laid before and approved by resolution of each House of Parliament.

(4) Regulations under this Schedule to which sub-paragraph (3) does not apply shall be subject to annulment in pursuance of a resolution of either House of Parliament.

Interpretation

17(1) In this Schedule –

'asylum-seeker' means a person–

(a) who is at least 18 years old,

(b) who has made a claim for asylum (within the meaning of section 18(3)), and

(c) whose claim has been recorded by the Secretary of State but not determined,

'Convention rights' has the same meaning as in the Human Rights Act 1998,

'child' means a person under the age of eighteen,

'dependant' and 'dependent' shall have such meanings as may be prescribed by regulations made by the Secretary of State,

'EEA State' means a State which is a contracting party to the Agreement on the European Economic Area signed at Oporto on 2nd May 1992 (as it has effect from time to time),

'local authority' –

(a) in relation to England and Wales, has the same meaning as in section 129(3),

(b) in relation to Scotland, has the same meaning as in section 129(4), and

(c) in relation to Northern Ireland, means a health service body within the meaning of section 133(4)(d) and the Northern Ireland Housing Executive (for which purpose a reference to the authority's area shall be taken as a reference to Northern Ireland),

'the Refugee Convention' means the Convention relating to the status of Refugees done at Geneva on 28th July 1951 and its Protocol, and

'removal directions' means directions under Schedule 2 to the Immigration Act 1971 (c 77) (control of entry, etc) under Schedule 3 to that Act (deportation) or under section 10 of the Immigration and Asylum Act 1999 (c 33) (removal of person unlawfully in United Kingdom).

(2) For the purpose of the definition of 'asylum-seeker' in sub-paragraph (1) a claim is determined if –

 (a) the Secretary of State has notified the claimant of his decision,

 (b) no appeal against the decision can be brought (disregarding the possibility of an appeal out of time with permission), and

 (c) any appeal which has already been brought has been disposed of.

(3) For the purpose of sub-paragraph (2)(c) an appeal is disposed of when it is no longer pending for the purpose of –

 (a) Part 5 of this Act, or

 (b) the Special Immigration Appeals Commission Act 1997.

(4) The giving of directions in respect of a person under a provision of the Immigration Acts is not the provision of assistance to him for the purposes of this Schedule.

ASYLUM AND IMMIGRATION (TREATMENT OF CLAIMANTS, ETC) ACT 2004

Integration loan for refugees

13 (1) The Secretary of State may make regulations enabling him to make loans to refugees.

(2) A person is a refugee for the purpose of subsection (1) if the Secretary of State has—

(a) recorded him as a refugee within the meaning of the Convention relating to the Status of Refugees done at Geneva on 28 July 1951, and

(b) granted him indefinite leave to enter or remain in the United Kingdom (within the meaning of section 33(1) of the Immigration Act 1971 (c 77)).

(3) Regulations under subsection (1)—

(a) shall specify matters which the Secretary of State shall, in addition to other matters appearing to him to be relevant, take into account in determining whether or not to make a loan (and those matters may, in particular, relate to—

(i   a person's income or assets,

(ii) a person's likely ability to repay a loan, or

(iii) the length of time since a person was recorded as a refugee),

(b) shall enable the Secretary of State to specify (and vary from time to time) a minimum and a maximum amount of a loan,

(c) shall prevent a person from receiving a loan if—

(i) he is under the age of 18,

(ii) he is insolvent, within a meaning given by the regulations, or

(iii) he has received a loan under the regulations,

(d) shall make provision about repayment of a loan (and may, in particular, make provision—

(i)   about interest;

(ii) for repayment by deduction from a social security benefit or similar payment due to the person to whom the loan is made),

(e) shall enable the Secretary of State to attach conditions to a loan (which may include conditions about the use of the loan),

(f) shall make provision about—

(i)   the making of an application for a loan, and

(ii) the information, which may include information about the intended use of a loan, to be provided in or with an application,

(g) may make provision about steps to be taken by the Secretary of State in establishing an applicant's likely ability to repay a loan,

(h) may make provision for a loan to be made jointly to more than one refugee, and

(i) may confer a discretion on the Secretary of State.

(4) Regulations under this section—

(a) shall be made by statutory instrument, and

(b) may not be made unless a draft has been laid before and approved by resolution of each House of Parliament.[32]

---

32 not yet in force.

ASYLUM SUPPORT (INTERIM PROVISIONS) REGULATIONS 1999 SI No 3056

Citation, commencement and extent

1 (1) These Regulations may be cited as the Asylum Support (Interim Provisions) Regulations 1999 and shall come into force on 6th December 1999.

(2) These Regulations do not extend to Scotland or Northern Ireland.

Interpretation

2 (1) In these Regulations –

'assisted person' means an asylum-seeker, or a dependant of an asylum-seeker, who has applied for support and for whom support is provided;

'dependant', in relation to an asylum-seeker, an assisted person or a person claiming support, means a person in the United Kingdom who –

(a) is his spouse;

(b) is a child of his, or of his spouse, who is under 18 and dependent on him;

(c) is under 18 and is a member of his, or his spouse's, close family;

(d) is under 18 and had been living as part of his household:
   (i) for at least six of the 12 months before the day on which his claim for support was made; or
   (ii) since birth;

(e) is in need of care and attention from him or a member of his household by reason of a disability and would fall within sub-paragraph (c) or (d) but for the fact that he is not under 18;

(f) had been living with him as a member of an unmarried couple for at least two of the three years before the day on which his claim for support was made;

(g) is a person living as part of his household who was receiving assistance from a local authority under section 17 of the Children Act 1989 immediately before the beginning of the interim period;

(h) has made a claim for leave to enter or remain in the United Kingdom, or for variation of any such leave, which is being considered on the basis that he is dependent on the asylum-seeker; or

(i) in relation to an assisted person or a person claiming support who is himself a dependant of an asylum-seeker, is the asylum-seeker;

'eligible persons' means asylum-seekers or their dependants who appear to be destitute or to be likely to become destitute within 14 days;

'local authority' means –

(a) in England, a county council, a metropolitan district council, a district council with the functions of a county council, a London borough council, the Common Council of the City of London or the Council of the Isles of Scilly;

(b) in Wales, a county council or a county borough council.

(2) Any reference in these Regulations to support is to support under these Regulations.

(3) Any reference in these Regulations to assistance under section 21 of the

National Assistance Act 1948 is to assistance, the need for which has arisen solely –

(a) because of destitution; or

(b) because of the physical effects, or anticipated physical effects, of destitution.

(4) Any reference in these Regulations to assistance under section 17 of the Children Act 1989 is to the provision of accommodation or of any essential living needs.

(5) The interim period begins on the day on which these Regulations come into force and ends on 4 April 2005.

(6) The period prescribed under section 94(3) of the Immigration and Asylum Act 1999 (day on which a claim for asylum is determined) for the purposes of Part VI of that Act is 28 days where paragraph (7) below applies, and 21 days in any other case.

(7) This paragraph applies where:

(a) the Secretary of State notifies the claimant that his decision is to accept the asylum claim;

(b) the Secretary of State notifies the claimant that his decision is to reject the asylum claim but at the same time notifies him that he is giving him limited leave to enter or remain in the United Kingdom; or

(c) an appeal by the claimant against the Secretary of State's decision has been disposed of by being allowed.

Requirement to provide support

3 (1) Subject to regulations 7 and 8 –

(a) the local authority concerned, or

(b) the local authority to whom responsibility for providing support is transferred under regulation 9,

must provide support during the interim period to eligible persons.

(2) The question whether a person is an eligible person is to be determined by the local authority concerned.

(3) For the purposes of these Regulations, the local authority concerned are the local authority to whom a claim for support is made, except where a claim for support is transferred by a local authority in accordance with regulation 9, in which case the local authority concerned are the local authority to whom the claim is transferred.

Temporary support

4 (1) This regulation applies to support to be provided before it has been determined whether a person is an eligible person ('temporary support').

(2) Temporary support is to be provided to a person claiming support –

(a) by the local authority to whom the claim is made until such time (if any) as the claim is transferred under regulation 9;

(b) where the claim is so transferred, by the local authority to whom the claim is transferred.

(3) Temporary support must appear to the local authority by whom it is provided to be adequate for the needs of the person claiming support and his dependants (if any).

Provision of support

5 (1) Subject to paragraph (2), support is to be provided by providing –

    (a) accommodation appearing to the local authority by whom it is provided to be adequate for the needs of the assisted person and his dependants (if any) ('accommodation'); and

    (b) what appear to the local authority by whom it is provided to be essential living needs of the assisted person and his dependants (if any) ('essential living needs').

(2) Where an assisted person's household includes a child who is under 18 and a dependant of his, support is to be provided –

    (a) in accordance with paragraph (1);

    (b) by providing accommodation; or

    (c) by providing essential living needs.

(3) Support is to be provided to enable the assisted person (if he is the asylum-seeker) to meet reasonable travel expenses incurred in attending –

    (a) a hearing of an appeal on his claim for asylum; or

    (b) an interview in connection with his claim for asylum which has been requested by the Secretary of State.

(4) Where the circumstances of a particular case are exceptional, support is to be provided in such other ways as are necessary to enable the assisted person and his dependants (if any) to be supported.

(5) *Revoked.*

(6) A local authority may provide support subject to conditions.

(7) Such conditions are to be set out in writing.

(8) A copy of the conditions is to be given to the assisted person.

Matters to which the local authority are to have regard

6 (1) In providing support, the local authority are to have regard to –

    (a) income which the assisted person has, or his dependants (if any) have, or might reasonably be expected to have;

    (b) support which is, or assets which are, or might reasonably be expected to be, available to the assisted person, or to his dependants (if any);

    (c) the welfare of the assisted person and his dependants (if any); and

    (d) the cost of providing support.

(2) In providing accommodation under these Regulations, the local authority are not to have regard to any preference that the assisted person or his dependants (if any) may have as to –

    (a) the locality in which the accommodation is to be provided;

    (b) the nature of the accommodation to be provided; or

    (c) the nature and standard of fixtures and fittings in that accommodation.

Refusal of support

7 (1) Unless this paragraph does not apply, support must be refused in the following circumstances –

    (a) where the person claiming support has intentionally made himself and his dependants (if any) destitute;

(b) where the person claiming support has made a claim for support to another local authority, except where the claim is one to which regulation 9 applies;

(c) where the claim for support is made by a person to a local authority other than one to whom, in the previous 12 months, he has made a claim for assistance under section 21 of the National Assistance Act 1948 or under section 17 of the Children Act 1989;

(d) where the person claiming support –
   (i) is an asylum-seeker within the meaning of paragraph (3A)(a) or (aa) of regulation 70 of the Income Support (General) Regulations 1987 who has not ceased to be an asylum-seeker by virtue of sub-paragraph (b) of that paragraph;
   (ii) is a person who became an asylum-seeker under paragraph (3A)(a) of regulation 70 of the Income Support (General) Regulations 1987 and who has not ceased to be an asylum-seeker by virtue of sub-paragraph (b) of that paragraph, as saved by regulation 12(1) of the Social Security (Persons from Abroad) Miscellaneous Amendments Regulations 1996;
   (iii) is not a person from abroad within the meaning of sub-paragraph (a) of regulation 21(3) of the Income Support (General) Regulations 1987 by virtue of the exclusions specified in that sub-paragraph;

(e) where neither the person claiming support nor any of his dependants is an asylum-seeker or has made a claim for leave to enter or remain in the United Kingdom, or for variation of any such leave, which is being considered on the basis that he is dependent on an asylum-seeker.

(2) For the purposes of paragraph (1)(a), a person has intentionally made himself destitute if he appears to be, or likely within 14 days to become, destitute as a result of an act or omission deliberately done or made by him or any dependant of his without reasonable excuse while in the United Kingdom.

(3) Paragraph (1) does not apply where the local authority concerned did not know, or could not with reasonable diligence have known, of any circumstance set out in that paragraph.

Suspension and discontinuation of support

8 (1) Support for the assisted person and his dependants (if any) must be discontinued as soon as the local authority by whom it is provided become aware of any circumstance which, if they had known of it when the claim was made, would have led to the claim being refused in accordance with regulation 7(1).

(2) Support may be suspended or discontinued –
   (a) where the assisted person, or any dependant of his, fails without reasonable excuse to comply with any condition subject to which the support is provided;
   (b) where the assisted person, or any dependant of his, leaves accommodation provided as part of such support for more than seven consecutive days without reasonable excuse.

Transfer of a claim for support or responsibility for providing support by a local authority

9   A local authority may transfer a claim for support made to them, or responsibility for providing support, to another local authority on such terms as may be agreed between the two authorities.

Assistance to those providing support

10   Reasonable assistance to a local authority providing support is to be given by –
   (a) any district council for an area any part of which lies within the area of the local authority providing support, and
   (b) any registered social landlord, within the meaning of Part I of the Housing Act 1996, which manages any house or other property which is in the area of the local authority providing support,

who is requested to provide such assistance by the local authority providing support.

Transitional provision

11   Where an asylum-seeker or a dependant of an asylum-seeker is receiving assistance from a local authority under section 21 of the National Assistance Act 1948 or under section 17 of the Children Act 1989 immediately before the beginning of the interim period, he is to be taken to have been accepted for support by the local authority providing such assistance.

Entitlement to claim support

12   A person entitled to support under these Regulations is not entitled to assistance under section 17 of the Children Act 1989.

ASYLUM SUPPORT APPEALS (PROCEDURE) RULES 2000
SI No 541

GENERAL
Title and commencement

1   These Rules may be cited as the Asylum Support Appeals (Procedure) Rules 2000 and shall come into force on 3rd April 2000.

Interpretation

2 (1) In these Rules –

'the Act' means the Immigration and Asylum Act 1999;

'adjudication' means a decision of an adjudicator made in accordance with section 103(3) of the Act;

'appeal bundle' means a bundle prepared by the Secretary of State containing copies of the following documents –

(a) the form on which the appellant made a claim for support under section 95 of the Act, if the appeal is made under section 103(1) of the Act;

(b) any supporting documentation attached to that form;

(c) the decision letter; and

(d) other material relied on by the Secretary of State in reaching his decision;

'appellant' means a person who appeals under section 103 of the Act against a decision of the Secretary of State;

'bank holiday' means a day that is specified in, or appointed under, the Banking and Financial Dealings Act 1971;

'consideration day' has the meaning given to it by rule 4(4);

'decision letter' means a letter from the Secretary of State giving notice of a decision that gives rise to a right to appeal under section 103;

'excluded day' means a Saturday, a Sunday, a bank holiday, Christmas Day or Good Friday;

'member of the adjudicators' staff' means a person appointed by the Secretary of State under paragraph 5(1) of Schedule 10 to the Act;

'notice of appeal' has the meaning given to it by rule 3(1); and

'party' includes the appellant and the Secretary of State.

(2) Any reference in these Rules:

(a) to an adjudicator, in relation to the sending, giving or receiving of notices or other documents, whether by an adjudicator or a party to the appeal, includes a reference to a member of the adjudicators' staff;

(b) to an adjudicator, in relation to the receiving of a notice of appeal by him, includes a reference to the offices occupied by the adjudicators;

(c) to the appellant, in relation to the sending or giving of notices or other documents by the adjudicator or the Secretary of State, is also a reference to his representative, if he has one; and

(d) to a representative is to be construed in accordance with rule 15.

(3) For the purposes of these Rules, an appeal is determined when an adjudicator gives his adjudication.

PROCEDURE BEFORE DETERMINATION OF APPEAL
Notice of appeal
3 (1) A person who wishes to appeal under section 103 of the Act must give notice to an adjudicator by completing in full, and in English, the form for the time being issued by the Secretary of State for the purpose ('notice of appeal'); and any form so issued is to be in the form shown in the Schedule to these Rules or a form to like effect.

(2) The notice of appeal must be signed by the appellant or his representative.

(3) Subject to paragraph (4), the notice of appeal must be received by the adjudicator not later than 3 days after the day on which the appellant received the decision letter.

(4) The adjudicator may extend the time limit for receiving the notice of appeal (either before or after its expiry) if –
  (a) he considers that it is in the interests of justice to do so; and
  (b) he is satisfied that:
    (i) the appellant; or
    (ii) his representative (if he has one);
was prevented from complying with the time limit by circumstances beyond his control.

Procedure after receiving notice of appeal
4 (1) On the day that the adjudicator receives notice of appeal or, if not reasonably practicable, as soon as possible on the following day , he must send a copy of the notice of appeal or, if not reasonably practicable, as soon as possible on the following day, and any supporting documents, to the Secretary of State by fax.

(2) Two days after the day on which the adjudicator receives notice of appeal, the Secretary of State must send the appeal bundle to the adjudicator by fax or by hand and to the appellant by first class post or by fax.

(3) On consideration day, the adjudicator must –
  (a) decide in accordance with rule 5 whether there should be an oral hearing;
  (b) set the date for determining the appeal in accordance with rule 6;
  (c) if there is to be an oral hearing, give notice to the Secretary of State and the appellant, in accordance with rule 7, of the date on which it is to be held.

(4) 'Consideration day' means the day after the day on which the Secretary of State sends the appeal bundle to the adjudicator in accordance with paragraph (2).

Whether there should be an oral hearing
5 (1) The adjudicator must decide to hold an oral hearing –
  (a) where the appellant has requested an oral hearing in his notice of appeal; or
  (b) if the adjudicator considers that it is necessary for the appeal to be disposed of justly.

(2) In all other cases, the appeal may be determined without an oral hearing.

Date for determination of appeal
6 (1) If there is to be an oral hearing, the hearing must be held and the appeal determined not later than 5 days after consideration day.

(2) In all other cases, the appeal must be determined on consideration day, or as soon as possible thereafter, but in any event not later than 5 days after consideration day.

Notification of date of oral hearing

7   If there is to be an oral hearing, the adjudicator must send a notice to the appellant and to the Secretary of State informing them of the date, time and place of the hearing.

Further evidence provided before the determination of the appeal

8 (1) Where the appellant sends to the adjudicator evidence to which this paragraph applies, the appellant must at the same time send a copy of such evidence to the Secretary of State.

(2) Paragraph (1) applies to evidence which is sent after the appellant has sent notice of appeal to the adjudicator but before the appeal has been determined.

(3) Where the Secretary of State sends to the adjudicator evidence to which this paragraph applies, the Secretary of State must at the same time send a copy of such evidence to the appellant.

(4) Paragraph (3) applies to evidence which is sent after the Secretary of State has sent the appeal bundle to the adjudicator but before the appeal has been determined.

DETERMINATION OF APPEAL
Hearing of appeal in absence of either party

9 (1) If an appellant has indicated in his notice of appeal that he does not want to attend, or be represented at, an oral hearing, the hearing may proceed in his absence.

(2) Where –
   (a) an appellant has indicated in his notice of appeal that he wants to attend, or be represented at, an oral hearing;
   (b) he has been notified of the date, time and place of the hearing in accordance with rule 7; and
   (c) neither he nor his representative (if he has one) attends the hearing;
   the hearing may proceed in his absence.

(3) Where neither the Secretary of State nor his representative (if he has one) attends the hearing, it may proceed in his absence.

Evidence

10 (1) Paragraph (2) applies to all appeals.

(2) The adjudicator may take into account any matters which he considers to be relevant to the appeal (including matters arising after the date on which the decision appealed against was taken).

(3) Paragraphs (4) to (6) apply to oral hearings only.

(4) No person may be compelled to give any evidence or produce any document which he could not be compelled to give or produce on the trial of an action.

(5) The adjudicator may require any witness to give evidence on oath or affirmation, and for that purpose an oath or affirmation in due form may be administered.

(6) When the adjudicator takes into consideration documentary evidence at an oral hearing, a party present at the hearing is to be given an opportunity of inspecting and considering that evidence and taking copies if copies have not been provided previously to that party in accordance with these Rules.

Record of proceedings

11 A record of the proceedings at an oral hearing before the adjudicator is to be made.

Exclusion of public

12 (1) Subject to the provisions of this rule, oral hearings are to take place in public.

(2) Subject to the provisions of paragraph (3), the adjudicator may exclude a member of the public or members of the public generally from a hearing or from part of a hearing if, and to the extent that, he considers it necessary to do so in the public interest.

(3) But nothing in this rule is to prevent a member of the Council on Tribunals, a member of the Scottish Committee of that Council, the Chief Asylum Support Adjudicator or the Deputy Chief Asylum Support Adjudicator, in their capacity as such, from attending an oral hearing.

Adjudication

13 (1) Where an oral hearing is held –

(a) the adjudicator must inform all persons present of his adjudication at the conclusion of the hearing;

(b) if neither the appellant nor his representative (if he has one) is present at the conclusion of the hearing, the adjudicator must send notice of his adjudication on the same day to the appellant;

(c) if the Secretary of State is not present at the conclusion of the hearing, the adjudicator must send notice of his adjudication on the same day to the Secretary of State; and

(d) not later than 3 days after the day on which the appeal is determined, the adjudicator must send a reasons statement to the appellant and the Secretary of State.

(2) Where there is no oral hearing, the adjudicator must on the day that the appeal is determined –

(a) send notice of his adjudication to the appellant and the Secretary of State; and

(b) send a reasons statement to them.

(3) An adjudication takes effect from the day on which it is made.

(4) A 'reasons statement' is a written statement giving reasons for the adjudication.

MISCELLANEOUS
Directions

14 The adjudicator may give directions on any matter arising in connection with an appeal if he considers it necessary or desirable to do so in the interests of justice.

Representation

15   A party to the appeal may be represented by any other person.

Withdrawal of decision

16 (1) Where the Secretary of State withdraws the decision which is appealed against, he must give notice to the adjudicator and the appellant forthwith.

(2) Where the appellant withdraws his appeal, he must give notice to the adjudicator and the Secretary of State forthwith.

(3) Where paragraph (1) or (2) applies, the appeal is to be treated for all purposes as at an end.

Notices

17   In the absence of express provision, any notice or other document required or authorised by these Rules to be sent or given by any party may be sent by first class post, by fax or by hand.

Time

18 (1) Subject to paragraph (2), for the purposes of these Rules, a notice or other document is to be taken to have been received on the day on which it was in fact received.

(2) Where a notice or other document is sent by first class post by the Secretary of State or by the adjudicator, it is to be taken to have been received 2 days after the day on which it was sent, unless the contrary is proven.

(3) Where reference is made in these Rules to a specified number of days after an event, the number of days is to be calculated from the expiry of the day on which the event occurred.

(4) Where these Rules provide that an act is to be done or to be taken to have been done –

(a) not later than a specified number of days after an event; or

(b) a specified number of days after an event;

(c) and that number of days expires on an excluded day, the act is to be taken to have been done as required if done on the next working day;

(d) includes an excluded day, that day is to be discounted.

(5) Where these Rules provide that an act is to be done or to be taken to have been done on a certain day and that day is an excluded day, the act is to be taken to have been done as required if done on the next working day.

Irregularities

19 (1) Any irregularity resulting from failure to comply with these Rules before the adjudicator has determined the appeal is not by itself to render the proceedings void.

(2) But the adjudicator must, if he considers that either party may have been prejudiced, take such steps as he thinks fit to remove or reduce the prejudice.

SCHEDULE – NOTICE OF APPEAL[32]

[Please see Guidance Note at the end of this document for further information on completing this form]

Section one
Give your personal details

Full Name:

Date of Birth:

Nationality:

Your NASS reference number:

Section two
Give an address in the United Kingdom where the Asylum Support Adjudicators can write to you:

Give a daytime fax or telephone number in the UK (if you have one) where the Asylum Support Adjudicators can contact you:

Section three
Give the date of the decision letter against which you are appealing:

Please attach a copy of that decision letter to this form

Section four

I want my appeal determined on the papers	Yes/No
I want an oral hearing of my appeal	Yes/No
I want to attend the hearing of my appeal	Yes/No
If you want to attend the hearing, will you need an interpreter	Yes/No

If so, in what language?

Are you to be represented in this appeal?	Yes/No

If so you must give full details of your representative: name and address, and telephone and fax numbers if available, together with any reference number the representative has given your case.

Will your representative attend any oral hearing of your appeal?   Yes/No

---

32 Substituted by SI 2003 No 1735. In force 11 August 2003, except in relation to decision letters received by appellants before that date.

Section five

You must complete this section. Failure to do so may result in your appeal being treated as invalid.

What are the grounds of your appeal?

What matters in the decision letter do you disagree with?

Signed:

[Appellant/Representative]

Date:

Guidance Note

If you have further information which you would like the Adjudicators to take into account when making a decision about your appeal, you should send this together with copies of any documents with this form.

Please ensure that you complete all sections as fully as possible.

If you have requested an oral hearing, it is in your interests to attend.

You must include your grounds of appeal at section five or your appeal may be treated as invalid.

The Migrant Helpline may be able to help you in completing this form.[33] You can contact them at:

Migrant Helpline
45 Friends Road
Croydon
Surrey CRO 1ED
Telephone Number: (020) 8774 0002

There may be a local office near you.

Return this form to:
Asylum Support Adjudicator
Christopher Wren House
113 High Street
Croydon CRO 1GQ

You may also return this form by Fax. The ASA's fax number is (020) 8688 6075.

The ASA freephone number for appellants who wish to discuss any aspect of the appeal process is 0800 389 7913.

Further information about the ASA is available on www.asylum-support-adjudicators.org.uk

---

33 The Migrant Helpline do not currently offer assistance with completion of appeal forms.

ASYLUM SUPPORT REGULATIONS 2000 SI No 704

GENERAL
Citation and commencement

1   These Regulations may be cited as the Asylum Support Regulations 2000 and shall come into force on 3rd April 2000.

Interpretation

2 (1) In these Regulations –

'the Act' means the Immigration and Asylum Act 1999;

'asylum support' means support provided under section 95 of the Act;

'dependant' has the meaning given by paragraphs (4) and (5);

'the interim Regulations' means the Asylum Support (Interim Provisions) Regulations 1999;

'married couple' means a man and woman who are married to each other and are members of the same household; and

'unmarried couple' means a man and woman who, though not married to each other, are living together as if married.

(2) The period prescribed under section 94(3) of the Act (day on which a claim for asylum is determined) for the purposes of Part VI of the Act is 28 days where paragraph (2A) applies, and 21 days in any other case.

(2A) This paragraph applies where:

(a) the Secretary of State notifies the claimant that his decision is to accept the asylum claim;

(b) the Secretary of State notifies the claimant that his decision is to reject the asylum claim but at the same time notifies him that he is giving him limited leave to enter or remain in the United Kingdom; or

(c) an appeal by the claimant against the Secretary of State's decision has been disposed of by being allowed.

(3) Paragraph (2) does not apply in relation to a case to which the interim Regulations apply (for which case, provision corresponding to paragraph (2) is made by regulation 2(6) of those Regulations).

(4) In these Regulations 'dependant', in relation to an asylum-seeker, a supported person or an applicant for asylum support, means, subject to paragraph (5), a person in the United Kingdom ('the relevant person') who –

(a) is his spouse;

(b) is a child of his or of his spouse, is dependant on him and is, or was at the relevant time, under 18;

(c) is a member of his or his spouse's close family and is, or was at the relevant time, under 18;

(d) had been living as part of his household –

(i)   for at least six of the twelve months before the relevant time, or

(ii) since birth,

and is, or was at the relevant time, under 18;

(e) is in need of care and attention from him or a member of his household by reason of a disability and would fall within sub-paragraph (c) or (d) but for the fact that he is not, and was not at the relevant time, under 18;

(f)   had been living with him as a member of an unmarried couple for at least two of the three years before the relevant time;

(g)   is living as part of his household and was, immediately before 6th December 1999 (the date when the interim Regulations came into force), receiving assistance from a local authority under section 17 of the Children Act 1989;

(h)   is living as part of his household and was, immediately before the coming into force of these Regulations, receiving assistance from a local authority under –

(i)   section 22 of the Children (Scotland) Act 1995; or

(ii)   Article 18 of the Children (Northern Ireland) Order 1995; or

(i)   has made a claim for leave to enter or remain in the United Kingdom, or for variation of any such leave, which is being considered on the basis that he is dependant on the asylum-seeker;

and in relation to a supported person, or an applicant for asylum support, who is himself a dependant of an asylum-seeker, also includes the asylum-seeker if in the United Kingdom.

(5)   Where a supported person or applicant for asylum support is himself a dependant of an asylum-seeker, a person who would otherwise be a dependant of the supported person, or of the applicant, for the purposes of these Regulations is not such a dependant unless he is also a dependant of the asylum-seeker or is the asylum-seeker.

(6)   In paragraph (4), 'the relevant time', in relation to the relevant person, means –

(a)   the time when an application for asylum support for him was made in accordance with regulation 3(3); or

(b)   if he has joined a person who is already a supported person in the United Kingdom and sub-paragraph (a) does not apply, the time when he joined that person in the United Kingdom.

(7)   Where a person, by falling within a particular category in relation to an asylum-seeker or supported person, is by virtue of this regulation a dependant of the asylum-seeker or supported person for the purposes of these Regulations, that category is also a prescribed category for the purposes of paragraph (c) of the definition of 'dependant' in section 94(1) of the Act and, accordingly, the person is a dependant of the asylum-seeker or supported person for the purposes of Part VI of the Act.

(8)   Paragraph (7) does not apply to a person who is already a dependant of the asylum-seeker or supported person for the purposes of Part VI of the Act because he falls within either of the categories mentioned in paragraphs (a) and (b) of the definition of 'dependant' in section 94(1) of the Act.

(9)   Paragraph (7) does not apply for the purposes of any reference to a 'dependant' in Schedule 9 to the Act.

INITIAL APPLICATION FOR SUPPORT

Initial application for support: individual and group applications

3 (1) Either of the following –

   (a) an asylum-seeker, or

   (b) a dependant of an asylum-seeker,

   may apply to the Secretary of State for asylum support.

   (2) An application under this regulation may be –

   (a) for asylum support for the applicant alone; or

   (b) for asylum support for the applicant and one or more dependants of his.

   (3) The application must be made by completing in full and in English the form for the time being issued by the Secretary of State for the purpose; and any form so issued shall be the form shown in the Schedule to these Regulations or a form to the like effect.

   (4) The application may not be entertained by the Secretary of State–

   (a) where it is made otherwise than in accordance with paragraph (3); or

   (b) where the Secretary of State is not satisfied that the information provided is complete or accurate or that the applicant is co-operating with enquiries made under paragraph (5).

   (5) The Secretary of State may make further enquiries of the applicant about any matter connected with the application.

   (6) Paragraphs (3) and (4) do not apply where a person is already a supported person and asylum support is sought for a dependant of his for whom such support is not already provided (for which case, provision is made by regulation 15).

Persons excluded from support

4 (1) The following circumstances are prescribed for the purposes of subsection (2) of section 95 of the Act as circumstances where a person who would otherwise fall within subsection (1) of that section is excluded from that subsection (and, accordingly, may not be provided with asylum support).

   (2) A person is so excluded if he is applying for asylum support for himself alone and he falls within paragraph (4) by virtue of any sub-paragraph of that paragraph.

   (3) A person is so excluded if –

   (a) he is applying for asylum support for himself and other persons, or he is included in an application for asylum support made by a person other than himself;

   (b) he falls within paragraph (4) (by virtue of any sub-paragraph of that paragraph); and

   (c) each of the other persons to whom the application relates also falls within paragraph (4) (by virtue of any sub-paragraph of that paragraph).

   (4) A person falls within this paragraph if at the time when the application is determined –

   (a) he is a person to whom interim support applies; or

   (b) he is a person to whom social security benefits apply; or

   (c) he has not made a claim for leave to enter or remain in the United Kingdom, or for variation of any such leave, which is being considered on the basis that he is an asylum-seeker or dependent on an asylum-seeker.

(5) For the purposes of paragraph (4), interim support applies to a person if –

   (a) at the time when the application is determined, he is a person to whom, under the interim Regulations, support under regulation 3 of those Regulations must be provided by a local authority;

   (b) sub-paragraph (a) does not apply, but would do so if the person had been determined by the local authority concerned to be an eligible person; or

   (c) sub-paragraph (a) does not apply, but would do so but for the fact that the person's support under those Regulations was (otherwise than by virtue of regulation 7(1)(d) of those Regulations) refused under regulation 7, or suspended or discontinued under regulation 8, of those Regulations;

and in this paragraph 'local authority', 'local authority concerned' and 'eligible person' have the same meanings as in the interim Regulations.

(6) For the purposes of paragraph (4), a person is a person to whom social security benefits apply if he is –

   (a) a person who by virtue of regulation 2 of the Social Security (Immigration and Asylum) Consequential Amendments Regulations 2000 is not excluded by section 115(1) of the Act from entitlement to –

      (i) income-based jobseeker's allowance under the Jobseekers Act 1995; or

      (ii) income support, housing benefit or council tax benefit under the Social Security Contributions and Benefits Act 1992;

   (b) a person who, by virtue of regulation 2 of the Social Security (Immigration and Asylum) Consequential Amendments Regulations (Northern Ireland) 2000 is not excluded by section 115(2) of the Act from entitlement to –

      (i) income-based jobseeker's allowance under the Jobseekers (Northern Ireland) Order 1995; or

      (ii) income support or housing benefit under the Social Security Contributions and Benefits (Northern Ireland) Act 1992.

(7) A person is not to be regarded as falling within paragraph (2) or (3) if, when asylum support is sought for him, he is a dependant of a person who is already a supported person.

(8) The circumstances prescribed by paragraphs (2) and (3) are also prescribed for the purposes of section 95(2), as applied by section 98(3), of the Act as circumstances where a person who would otherwise fall within subsection (1) of section 98 is excluded from that subsection (and, accordingly, may not be provided with temporary support under section 98).

(9) For the purposes of paragraph (8), paragraphs (2) and (3) shall apply as if any reference to an application for asylum support were a reference to an application for support under section 98 of the Act.

DETERMINING WHETHER PERSONS ARE DESTITUTE
Determination where application relates to more than one person, etc.

5 (1) Subject to paragraph (2), where an application in accordance with regulation 3(3) is for asylum support for the applicant and one or more dependants of his, in applying section 95(1) of the Act the Secretary of State must decide whether the applicant and all those dependants, taken together, are destitute or likely to become destitute within the period prescribed by regulation 7.

(2) Where a person is a supported person, and the question falls to be determined whether asylum support should in future be provided for him and one or more other persons who are his dependants and are –

(a) persons for whom asylum support is also being provided when that question falls to be determined; or

(b) persons for whom the Secretary of State is then considering whether asylum support should be provided,

in applying section 95(1) of the Act the Secretary of State must decide whether the supported person and all those dependants, taken together, are destitute or likely to become destitute within the period prescribed by regulation 7.

Income and assets to be taken into account

6 (1) This regulation applies where it falls to the Secretary of State to determine for the purposes of section 95(1) of the Act whether –

(a) a person applying for asylum support, or such an applicant and any dependants of his, or

(b) a supported person, or such a person and any dependants of his,

is or are destitute or likely to become so within the period prescribed by regulation 7.

(2) In this regulation 'the principal' means the applicant for asylum support (where paragraph (1)(a) applies) or the supported person (where paragraph (1)(b) applies).

(3) The Secretary of State must ignore –

(a) any asylum support, and

(b) any support under section 98 of the Act,

which the principal or any dependant of his is provided with or, where the question is whether destitution is likely within a particular period, might be provided with in that period.

(4) But he must take into account –

(a) any other income which the principal, or any dependant of his, has or might reasonably be expected to have in that period;

(b) any other support which is available to the principal or any dependant of his, or might reasonably be expected to be so available in that period; and

(c) any assets mentioned in paragraph (5) (whether held in the United Kingdom or elsewhere) which are available to the principal or any dependant of his otherwise than by way of asylum support or support under section 98, or might reasonably be expected to be so available in that period.

(5) Those assets are –

(a) cash;

(b) savings;

(c) investments;

(d) land;

(e) cars or other vehicles; and

(f)   goods held for the purpose of a trade or other business.

(6) The Secretary of State must ignore any assets not mentioned in paragraph (5).

Period within which applicant must be likely to become destitute

7   The period prescribed for the purposes of section 95(1) of the Act is –

(a)   where the question whether a person or persons is or are destitute or likely to become so falls to be determined in relation to an application for asylum support and sub-paragraph (b) does not apply, 14 days beginning with the day on which that question falls to be determined;

(b)   where that question falls to be determined in relation to a supported person, or in relation to persons including a supported person, 56 days beginning with the day on which that question falls to be determined.

Adequacy of existing accommodation

8 (1) Subject to paragraph (2), the matters mentioned in paragraph (3) are prescribed for the purposes of subsection (5)(a) of section 95 of the Act as matters to which the Secretary of State must have regard in determining for the purposes of that section whether the accommodation of –

(a)   a person applying for asylum support, or

(b)   a supported person for whom accommodation is not for the time being provided by way of asylum support,

is adequate.

(2) The matters mentioned in paragraph (3)(a) and (d) to (g) are not so prescribed for the purposes of a case where the person indicates to the Secretary of State that he wishes to remain in the accommodation.

(3) The matters referred to in paragraph (1) are –

(a)   whether it would be reasonable for the person to continue to occupy the accommodation;

(b)   whether the accommodation is affordable for him;

(c)   whether the accommodation is provided under section 98 of the Act, or otherwise on an emergency basis, only while the claim for asylum support is being determined;

(d)   whether the person can secure entry to the accommodation;

(e)   where the accommodation consists of a moveable structure, vehicle or vessel designed or adapted for human habitation, whether there is a place where the person is entitled or permitted both to place it and reside in it;

(f)   whether the accommodation is available for occupation by the person's dependants together with him;

(g)   whether it is probable that the person's continued occupation of the accommodation will lead to domestic violence against him or any of his dependants.

(4) In determining whether it would be reasonable for a person to continue to occupy accommodation, regard may be had to the general circumstances prevailing in relation to housing in the district of the local housing authority where the accommodation is.

(5) In determining whether a person's accommodation is affordable for him, the Secretary of State must have regard to –

(a) any income, or any assets mentioned in regulation 6(5) (whether held in the United Kingdom or elsewhere), which is or are available to him or any dependant of his otherwise than by way of asylum support or support under section 98 of the Act, or might reasonably be expected to be so available;

(b) the costs in respect of the accommodation; and

(c) the person's other reasonable living expenses.

(6) In this regulation –

(a) 'domestic violence' means violence from a person who is or has been a close family member, or threats of violence from such a person which are likely to be carried out; and

(b) 'district of the local housing authority' has the meaning given by section 217(3) of the Housing Act 1996.

(7) The reference in paragraph (1) to subsection (5)(a) of section 95 of the Act does not include a reference to that provision as applied by section 98(3) of the Act.

Essential living needs

9 (1) The matter mentioned in paragraph (2) is prescribed for the purposes of subsection (7)(b) of section 95 of the Act as a matter to which the Secretary of State may not have regard in determining for the purposes of that section whether a person's essential living needs (other than accommodation) are met.

(2) That matter is his personal preference as to clothing (but this shall not be taken to prevent the Secretary of State from taking into account his individual circumstances as regards clothing).

(3) None of the items and expenses mentioned in paragraph (4) is to be treated as being an essential living need of a person for the purposes of Part VI of the Act.

(4) Those items and expenses are –

(a) the cost of faxes;

(b) computers and the cost of computer facilities;

(c) the cost of photocopying;

(d) travel expenses, except the expense mentioned in paragraph (5);

(e) toys and other recreational items;

(f) entertainment expenses.

(5) The expense excepted from paragraph (4)(d) is the expense of an initial journey from a place in the United Kingdom to accommodation provided by way of asylum support or (where accommodation is not so provided) to an address in the United Kingdom which has been notified to the Secretary of State as the address where the person intends to live.

(6) Paragraph (3) shall not be taken to affect the question whether any item or expense not mentioned in paragraph (4) or (5) is, or is not, an essential living need.

(7) The reference in paragraph (1) to subsection (7)(b) of section 95 of the Act includes a reference to that provision as applied by section 98(3) of the Act and, accordingly, the reference in paragraph (1) to 'that section' includes a reference to section 98.

PROVISION OF SUPPORT
Kind and levels of support for essential living needs

10(1) *This regulation applies where the Secretary of State has decided that asylum support should be provided in respect of the essential living needs of a person.*

(2) *As a general rule, asylum support in respect of the essential living needs of that person may be expected to be provided weekly in the form of vouchers redeemable for goods, services and cash whose total redemption value, for any week, equals the amount shown in the second column of the following Table opposite the entry in the first column which for the time being describes that person.*

TABLE

Qualifying couple	£61.11
Lone parent aged 18 or over	£38.96
Single person aged 25 or over	£38.96
Single person aged at least 18 but under 25	£30.84
Person aged at least 16 but under 18 (except a member of a qualifying couple)	£33.50
Person aged under 16	£44.27

(3) In paragraph (1) and the provisions of paragraph (2) preceding the Table, 'person' includes 'couple'.

(4) In this regulation –

(a) 'qualifying couple' means a married or unmarried couple at least one of whom is aged 18 or over and neither of whom is aged under 16;

(b) 'lone parent' means a parent who is not a member of a married or unmarried couple;

(c) 'single person' means a person who is not a parent or a member of a qualifying couple; and

(d) 'parent' means a parent of a relevant child, that is to say a child who is aged under 18 and for whom asylum support is provided.

(5) *Where the Secretary of State has decided that accommodation should be provided for a person (or couple) by way of asylum support, and the accommodation is provided in a form which also meets other essential living needs (such as bed and breakfast, or half or full board), the amounts shown in the Table in paragraph (2) shall be treated as reduced accordingly.*

(6) *The redemption value of the vouchers redeemable for cash which the Secretary of State may be expected to include in the asylum support provided for any week in accordance with paragraph (2) may, as a general rule, be expected not to exceed £10 per person (or, as the case may be, £20 per qualifying couple).*

Additional support for pregnant women and children under 3

10A(1) In addition to the cash support which the Secretary of State may be expected to provide weekly as described in regulation 10(2), in the case of any pregnant woman or child aged under 3 for whom the Secretary of State has decided asylum support should be provided, there shall, as a general rule, be added to the cash support for any week the amount shown in the second column of the following table opposite the entry in the first column which for the time being describes that person.

TABLE

Pregnant woman	£3.00
Child aged under 1	£5.00
Child aged at least 1 and under 3	£3.00

(2) In this regulation, pregnant woman means a woman who has provided evidence to satisfy the Secretary of State that she is pregnant.

Additional single payments in respect of essential living needs

11 *(1)* *At the end of each qualifying period, the Secretary of State may as a general rule be expected to provide, or arrange for the provision of, additional support for an eligible person (in respect of his essential living needs) in the form of a single issue of vouchers redeemable for cash whose total redemption value equals £50 or a single cash payment of £50.*

(2) *In paragraph (1) 'eligible person' means a person for whom asylum support has been provided for the whole of the qualifying period.*

(3) *Each of the following is a qualifying period –*

(a) *the period of six months beginning with the day on which asylum support was first provided for the person; and*

(b) *each period of six months beginning with a re-start day.*

(4) *Each of the following is a re-start day –*

(a) *the day after the day on which the period mentioned in paragraph (3)(a) ends; and*

(b) *the day after the day on which a period mentioned in paragraph (3)(b) ends.*

(5) *Paragraph (1) applies only if an application for the additional support is made to the Secretary of State by or on behalf of the eligible person.*

(6) *Where a person is, in the opinion of the Secretary of State, responsible without reasonable excuse for a delay in the determination of his claim for asylum, the Secretary of State may treat any qualifying period as extended by the period of delay.*

Income and assets to be taken into account in providing support

12 (1) This regulation applies where it falls to the Secretary of State to decide the level or kind of asylum support to be provided for –

(a) a person applying for asylum support, or such an applicant and any dependants of his; or

(b) a supported person, or such a person and any dependants of his.

(2) In this regulation 'the principal' means the applicant for asylum support (where paragraph (1)(a) applies) or the supported person (where paragraph (1)(b) applies).

(3) The Secretary of State must take into account –
- (a) any income which the principal or any dependant of his has or might reasonably be expected to have,
- (b) support which is or might reasonably be expected to be available to the principal or any dependant of his, and
- (c) any assets mentioned in regulation 6(5) (whether held in the United Kingdom or elsewhere) which are or might reasonably be expected to be available to the principal or any dependant of his,

otherwise than by way of asylum support.

Accommodation

13 (1) The matters mentioned in paragraph (2) are prescribed for the purposes of subsection (2)(b) of section 97 of the Act as matters to which regard may not be had when exercising the power under section 95 of the Act to provide accommodation for a person.

(2) Those matters are –
- (a) his personal preference as to the nature of the accommodation to be provided; and
- (b) his personal preference as to the nature and standard of fixtures and fittings;

but this shall not be taken to prevent the person's individual circumstances, as they relate to his accommodation needs, being taken into account.

Services

14 (1) The services mentioned in pararaph (2) may be provided or made available by way of asylum support to persons who are otherwise receiving such support, but may be so provided only for the purpose of maintaining good order among such persons.

(2) Those services are –
- (a) education, including English language lessons,
- (b) sporting or other developmental activities.

Change of circumstances

15 (1) If a relevant change of circumstances occurs, the supported person concerned or a dependant of his must, without delay, notify the Secretary of State of that change of circumstances.

(2) A relevant change of circumstances occurs where a supported person or a dependant of his –
- (a) is joined in the United Kingdom by a dependant or, as the case may be, another dependant, of the supported person;
- (b) receives or gains access to any money, or other asset mentioned in regulation 6(5), that has not previously been declared to the Secretary of State;
- (c) becomes employed;
- (d) becomes unemployed;
- (e) changes his name;
- (f) gets married;
- (g) starts living with a person as if married to that person;

(h) gets divorced;

(i) separates from a spouse, or from a person with whom he has been living as if married to that person;

(j) becomes pregnant;

(k) has a child;

(l) leaves school;

(m) starts to share his accommodation with another person;

(n) moves to a different address, or otherwise leaves his accommodation;

(o) goes into hospital;

(p) goes to prison or is otherwise held in custody;

(q) leaves the United Kingdom; or

(r) dies.

(3) If, on being notified of a change of circumstances, the Secretary of State considers that the change may be one –

(a) as a result of which asylum support should be provided for a person for whom it was not provided before, or

(b) as a result of which asylum support should no longer be provided for a person, or

(c) which may otherwise affect the asylum support which should be provided for a person,

he may make further enquiries of the supported person or dependant who gave the notification.

(4) The Secretary of State may, in particular, require that person to provide him with such information as he considers necessary to determine whether, and if so, what, asylum support should be provided for any person.

Contributions

16 (1) This regulation applies where, in deciding the level of asylum support to be provided for a person who is or will be a supported person, the Secretary of State is required to take into account income, support or assets as mentioned in regulation 12(3).

(2) The Secretary of State may –

(a) set the asylum support for that person at a level which does not reflect the income, support or assets; and

(b) require from that person payments by way of contributions towards the cost of the provision for him of asylum support.

(3) A supported person must make to the Secretary of State such payments by way of contributions as the Secretary of State may require under paragraph (2).

(4) Prompt payment of such contributions may be made a condition (under section 95(9) of the Act) subject to which asylum support for that person is provided.

RECOVERY OF SUMS BY SECRETARY OF STATE
Recovery where assets become realisable

17 (1) This regulation applies where it appears to the Secretary of State at any time (the relevant time) –

    (a) that a supported person had, at the time when he applied for asylum support, assets of any kind in the United Kingdom or elsewhere which were not capable of being realised; but

    (b) that those assets have subsequently become, and remain, capable of being realised.

  (2) The Secretary of State may recover from that person a sum not exceeding the recoverable sum.

  (3) Subject to paragraph (5), the recoverable sum is a sum equal to whichever is the less of –

    (a) the monetary value of all the asylum support provided to the person up to the relevant time; and

    (b) the monetary value of the assets concerned.

  (4) As well as being recoverable as mentioned in paragraph 11(2)(a) of Schedule 8 to the Act, an amount recoverable under this regulation may be recovered by deduction from asylum support.

  (5) The recoverable sum shall be treated as reduced by any amount which the Secretary of State has by virtue of this regulation already recovered from the person concerned (whether by deduction or otherwise) with regard to the assets concerned.

Overpayments: method of recovery

18   As well as being recoverable as mentioned in subsection (3) of section 114 of the Act, an amount recoverable under subsection (2) of that section may be recovered by deduction from asylum support.

BREACH OF CONDITIONS AND SUSPENSION AND DISCONTINUATION OF SUPPORT
Breach of conditions: decision whether to provide support

19 (1) When deciding –

    (a) whether to provide, or to continue to provide, asylum support for any person or persons, or

    (b) the level or kind of support to be provided for any person or persons,

the Secretary of State may take into account the extent to which any relevant condition has been complied with.

  (2) A relevant condition is a condition subject to which asylum support for that person or any of those persons is being, or has previously been, provided.

Suspension or discontinuation of support

20 (1) Asylum support for a supported person and his dependants (if any), or for one or more dependants of a supported person, may be suspended or discontinued if –

    (a) the Secretary of State has reasonable grounds to suspect that the supported person or any dependant of his has failed without reasonable excuse to comply with any condition subject to which the asylum support is provided;

(b) the Secretary of State has reasonable grounds to suspect that the supported person or any dependant of his has committed an offence under Part VI of the Act;

(c) the Secretary of State has reasonable grounds to suspect that the supported person has intentionally made himself and his dependants (if any) destitute;

(d) the supported person or any dependant of his for whom asylum support is being provided ceases to reside at the authorised address; or

(e) the supported person or any dependant of his for whom asylum support is being provided is absent from the authorised address –

(i) for more than seven consecutive days and nights, or

(ii) for a total of more than 14 days and nights in any six month period,

without the permission of the Secretary of State.

(2) For the purposes of this regulation, a person has intentionally made himself destitute if he appears to be, or to be likely to become within the period prescribed by regulation 7, destitute as a result of an act or omission deliberately done or made by him or any dependant of his without reasonable excuse while in the United Kingdom.

(3) For the purposes of this regulation, the authorised address is –

(a) the accommodation provided for the supported person and his dependants (if any) by way of asylum support; or

(b) if no accommodation is so provided, the address notified by the supported person to the Secretary of State in his application for asylum support or, where a change of his address has been notified to the Secretary of State under regulation 15, the address for the time being so notified.

Effect of previous suspension or discontinuation

21 (1) Where –

(a) an application for asylum support is made,

(b) the applicant or any other person to whom the application relates has previously had his asylum support suspended or discontinued under regulation 20, and

(c) there has been no material change of circumstances since the suspension or discontinuation,

the application need not be entertained unless the Secretary of State considers that there are exceptional circumstances which justify its being entertained.

(2) A material change of circumstances is one which, if the applicant were a supported person, would have to be notified to the Secretary of State under regulation 15.

(3) This regulation is without prejudice to the power of the Secretary of State to refuse the application even if he has entertained it.

NOTICE TO QUIT

22 (1) If –

(a) as a result of asylum support, a person has a tenancy or licence to occupy accommodation,

(b) one or more of the conditions mentioned in paragraph (2) is satisfied, and

(c) he is given notice to quit in accordance with paragraph (3) or (4),

his tenancy or licence is to be treated as ending with the period specified in that notice, regardless of when it could otherwise be brought to an end.

(2) The conditions are that –

(a) the asylum support is suspended or discontinued as a result of any provision of regulation 20;

(b) the relevant claim for asylum has been determined;

(c) the supported person has ceased to be destitute; or

(d) he is to be moved to other accommodation.

(3) A notice to quit is in accordance with this paragraph if it is in writing and –

(a) in a case where sub-paragraph (a), (c) or (d) of paragraph (2) applies, specifies as the notice period a period of not less than seven days; or

(b) in a case where the Secretary of State has notified his decision on the relevant claim for asylum to the claimant, specifies as the notice period a period at least as long as whichever is the greater of –

(i) seven days; or

(ii) the period beginning with the date of service of the notice to quit and ending with the date of determination of the relevant claim for asylum (found in accordance with section 94(3) of the Act).

(4) A notice to quit is in accordance with this paragraph if –

(a) it is in writing;

(b) it specifies as the notice period a period of less than seven days; and

(c) the circumstances of the case are such that that notice period is justified.

MEANING OF 'DESTITUTE' FOR CERTAIN OTHER PURPOSES

23 (1) In this regulation 'the relevant enactments' means –

(a) section 21(1A) of the National Assistance Act 1948;

(b) section 45(4A) of the Health Services and Public Health Act 1968;

(c) paragraph 2(2A) of Schedule 8 to the National Health Service Act 1977;

(d) sections 12(2A), 13A(4) and 13B(3) of the Social Work (Scotland) Act 1968;

(e) sections 7(3) and 8(4) of the Mental Health (Scotland) Act 1984; and

(f) Articles 7(3) and 15(6) of the Health and Personal Social Services (Northern Ireland) Order 1972.

(2) The following provisions of this regulation apply where it falls to an authority, or the Department, to determine for the purposes of any of the relevant enactments whether a person is destitute.

(3) Paragraphs (3) to (6) of regulation 6 apply as they apply in the case mentioned in paragraph (1) of that regulation, but as if references to the principal were references to the person whose destitution or otherwise is being determined and references to the Secretary of State were references to the authority or (as the case may be) Department.

(4) The matters mentioned in paragraph (3) of regulation 8 (read with paragraphs (4) to (6) of that regulation) are prescribed for the purposes of subsection (5)(a) of section 95 of the Act, as applied for the purposes of any of the relevant enactments, as matters to which regard must be had in determining for the purposes of any of the relevant enactments whether a person's accommodation is adequate.

(5) The matter mentioned in paragraph (2) of regulation 9 is prescribed for the purposes of subsection (7)(b) of section 95 of the Act, as applied for the purposes of any of the relevant enactments, as a matter to which regard may not be had in determining for the purposes of any of the relevant enactments whether a person's essential living needs (other than accommodation) are met.

(6) Paragraphs (3) to (6) of regulation 9 shall apply as if the reference in paragraph (3) to Part VI of the Act included a reference to the relevant enactments.

(7) The references in regulations 8(5) and 9(2) to the Secretary of State shall be construed, for the purposes of this regulation, as references to the authority or (as the case may be) Department.

SCHEDULE
[*not reproduced.*]

WITHHOLDING AND WITHDRAWAL OF SUPPORT (TRAVEL ASSISTANCE AND TEMPORARY ACCOMMODATION) REGULATIONS 2002 SI 2002 No 3078

Citation and commencement

1   These Regulations may be cited as the Withholding and Withdrawal of Support (Travel Assistance and Temporary Accommodation) Regulations 2002 and shall come into force on 8 January 2003.

Interpretation

2 (1) In these Regulations –

'the Act' means the Nationality, Immigration and Asylum Act 2002,

'person with refugee status abroad' means a person to whom paragraph 1 of Schedule 3 to the Act applies by virtue of paragraph 4 of that Schedule,

'EEA national' means a person to whom paragraph 1 of Schedule 3 to the Act applies by virtue of paragraph 5 of that Schedule,

'person unlawfully in the United Kingdom' means a person to whom paragraph 1 of Schedule 3 to the Act applies by virtue of paragraph 7 of that Schedule,

'relevant EEA State' means–

(a) in relation to a person with refugee status abroad, the EEA State the government of which has determined that he, or a person on whom he is dependent, is entitled to protection as a refugee under the Refugee Convention;

(b) in relation to an EEA national, the EEA State of which he, or a person on whom he is dependent, is a national;

'travel arrangements' means arrangements made under regulation 3(1).

(2) In these Regulations and for the purposes of Schedule 3 to the Act, a 'dependant' of a person means a person who at the relevant time –

(a) is his spouse;

(b) is a child of his or of his spouse;

(c) is a member of his or his spouse's close family and is under 18;

(d) has been living as part of his household–

(i)   for at least six of the twelve months before the relevant time, or

(ii) since birth,

(e) is in need of care and attention from him or a member of his household by reason of a disability and would fall under (c) or (d) but for the fact that he is not under 18;

(f) has been living with him as an unmarried couple for at least two of the three years before the relevant time,

and 'dependant' has the corresponding meaning.

(3) In paragraph (2) –

'relevant time' means, in relation to any arrangements made by a local authority in respect of a person, the time when the local authority begins to make those arrangements;

'unmarried couple' means a man and woman who, though not married to each other, are living together as if married.

Power for local authorities to arrange travel and provide accommodation

3 (1) A local authority may make arrangements ('travel arrangements') enabling a person with refugee status abroad or who is an EEA national to leave the United Kingdom to travel to the relevant EEA State.

(2) A local authority may make arrangements for the accommodation of a person in respect of whom travel arrangements have been or are to be made pending the implementation of those arrangements.

(3) A local authority may make arrangements for the accommodation of a person unlawfully in the United Kingdom who has not failed to co-operate with removal directions issued in respect of him.

(4) Arrangements for a person by virtue of paragraph (2) or (3) –

(a) may be made only if the person has with him a dependent child, and

(b) may include arrangements for that child.

Requirements relating to travel and accommodation arrangements

4 (1) Travel arrangements and arrangements for accommodation must be made so as to secure implementation of those arrangements at the lowest practicable cost to the local authority.

(2) Subject to the requirements in paragraph (1), travel arrangements made in respect of a person must be made so that the person leaves the United Kingdom as soon as practicable.

(3) Travel arrangements and arrangements for accommodation may not include cash payments to a person in respect of whom the arrangements are made and must be made in such a way as to prevent the obtaining of services or benefits other than those specified in the arrangements.

(4) A local authority must have regard to guidance issued by the Secretary of State in making travel arrangements and arrangements for accommodation.

Failure to implement travel arrangements

5 Where a person with refugee status abroad or an EEA national refuses an offer of travel arrangements or fails to implement or co-operate with travel arrangements, a local authority may make new travel arrangements for him to travel to the relevant EEA State.

6 (1) Where a person with refugee status abroad or an EEA national in respect of whom travel arrangements have been made by a local authority fails to implement or co-operate with those travel arrangements, neither that local authority nor any other local authority may make arrangements for the accommodation of that person except in accordance with the following provisions of this regulation.

(2) Where paragraph (1) applies to a person because of his failure to travel as arranged, the relevant local authority or another local authority may make further arrangements for the accommodation of that person pending the implementation of revised travel arrangements if, but only if, the local authority considers that –

(a) the failure was for one or both of the reasons set out in paragraph (3) and for no other reason, and

(b) the person took all reasonable steps to travel as arranged,

and the person has provided or taken all reasonable steps to provide the explanations and evidence requested by the local authority as regards the matters referred to in sub-paragraphs (a) and (b).

(3) The reasons referred to in paragraph (2) are –

    (a) that the applicant or a person within his family group was medically unfit to travel as arranged;

    (b) that despite his having taken all reasonable steps to ensure that he travelled as arranged, he was prevented from doing so by failure of a transport service.

(4) Arrangements for accommodation pursuant to this regulation may only be made in accordance with the provisions of these Regulations, including this regulation.

(5) In this regulation –

    (a) 'family group' in relation to a person means that person and those of his dependants who are to travel with him under arrangements made under these Regulations;

    (b) 'transport service' means a public transport service or any transport provided or arranged by the local authority.

Immigration

IMMIGRATION ACT 1971 s11, Sch 2 paras 2, 2A, 8, 16, 21

Construction of references to entry, and other phrases relating to travel

11 (1) A person arriving in the United Kingdom by ship or aircraft shall for purposes of this Act be deemed not to enter the United Kingdom unless and until he disembarks, and on disembarkation at a port shall further be deemed not to enter the United Kingdom so long as he remains in such area (if any) at the port as may be approved for this purpose by an immigration officer; and a person who has not otherwise entered the United Kingdom shall be deemed not to do so as long as he is detained, or temporarily admitted or released while liable to detention, under the powers conferred by Schedule 2 to this Act *or by Part III of the Immigration and Asylum Act 1999*[31] or section 62 of the Nationality, Immigration and Asylum Act 2002 or by section 68 of the Nationality, Immigration and Asylum Act 2002.

(2) In this Act 'disembark' means disembark from a ship or aircraft, and 'embark' means embark in a ship or aircraft; and, except in subsection (1) above,–

(a) references to disembarking in the United Kingdom do not apply to disembarking after a local journey from a place in the United Kingdom or elsewhere in the common travel area; and

(b) references to embarking in the United Kingdom do not apply to embarking for a local journey to a place in the United Kingdom or elsewhere in the common travel area.

(3) Except in so far as the context otherwise requires, references in this Act to arriving in the United Kingdom by ship shall extend to arrival by any floating structure, and 'disembark' shall be construed accordingly; but the provisions of this Act specially relating to members of the crew of a ship shall not by virtue of this provision apply in relation to any floating structure not being a ship.

(4) For purposes of this Act 'common travel area' has the meaning given by section 1(3), and a journey is, in relation to the common travel area, a local journey if but only if it begins and ends in the common travel area and is not made by a ship or aircraft which –

(a) in the case of a journey to a place in the United Kingdom, began its voyage from, or has during its voyage called at, a place not in the common travel area; or

(b) in the case of a journey from a place in the United Kingdom, is due to end its voyage in, or call in the course of its voyage at, a place not in the common travel area.

(5) A person who enters the United Kingdom lawfully by virtue of section 8(1) above, and seeks to remain beyond the time limited by section 8(1), shall be treated for purposes of this Act as seeking to enter the United Kingdom.

---

34 Words in italics inserted by the Immigration and Asylum Act 1999 s169(1), Sch 14 paras 43, 48, from a date to be appointed.

SCHEDULE 2 – ADMINISTRATIVE PROVISIONS AS TO CONTROL ON ENTRY ETC

Examination by immigration officers, and medical examination

2 (1) An immigration officer may examine any persons who have arrived in the United Kingdom by ship [or aircraft] (including transit passengers, members of the crew and others not seeking to enter the United Kingdom) for the purpose of determining–

    (a) whether any of them is or is not [a British citizen]; and

    (b) whether, if he is not, he may or may not enter the United Kingdom without leave; and

    (c) whether, if he may not–

        (i) he has been given leave which is still in force,

        (ii) he should be given leave and for what period or on what conditions (if any), or

        (iii) he should be refused leave.

(2) Any such person, if he is seeking to enter the United Kingdom, may be examined also by a medical inspector or by any qualified person carrying out a test or examination required by a medical inspector.

(3) A person, on being examined under this paragraph by an immigration officer or medical inspector, may be required in writing by him to submit to further examination; but a requirement under this sub-paragraph shall not prevent a person who arrives as a transit passenger, or as a member of the crew of a ship or aircraft, or for the purpose of joining a ship or aircraft as a member of the crew, from leaving by his intended ship or aircraft.

Examination of persons who arrive with continuing leave

2A(1) This paragraph applies to a person who has arrived in the United Kingdom with leave to enter which is in force but which was given to him before his arrival.

(2) He may be examined by an immigration officer for the purpose of establishing–

    (a) whether there has been such a change in the circumstances of his case, since that leave was given, that it should be cancelled;

    (b) whether that leave was obtained as a result of false information given by him or his failure to disclose material facts; or

    (c) whether there are medical grounds on which that leave should be cancelled.

(3) He may also be examined by an immigration officer for the purpose of determining whether it would be conducive to the public good for that leave to be cancelled.

(4) He may also be examined by a medical inspector or by any qualified person carrying out a test or examination required by a medical inspector.

(5) A person examined under this paragraph may be required by the officer or inspector to submit to further examination.

(6) A requirement under sub-paragraph (5) does not prevent a person who arrives–

    (a) as a transit passenger,

(b) as a member of the crew of a ship or aircraft, or

(c) for the purpose of joining a ship or aircraft as a member of the crew,

from leaving by his intended ship or aircraft.

(7) An immigration officer examining a person under this paragraph may by notice suspend his leave to enter until the examination is completed.

(8) An immigration officer may, on the completion of any examination of a person under this paragraph, cancel his leave to enter.

(9) Cancellation of a person's leave under sub-paragraph (8) is to be treated for the purposes of this Act and Part 5 of the Nationality, Immigration and Asylum Act 2002 (immigration and asylum appeals) as if he had been refused leave to enter at a time when he had a current entry clearance.

(10) A requirement imposed under sub-paragraph (5) and a notice given under sub-paragraph (7) must be in writing.

Removal of persons refused leave to enter and illegal entrants

8 (1) Where a person arriving in the United Kingdom is refused leave to enter, an immigration officer may, subject to sub-paragraph (2) below–

(a) give the captain of the ship or aircraft in which he arrives directions requiring the captain to remove him from the United Kingdom in that ship or aircraft; or

(b) give the owners or agents of that ship or aircraft directions requiring them to remove him from the United Kingdom in any ship or aircraft specified or indicated in the directions, being a ship or aircraft of which they are the owners or agents; or

(c) give those owners or agents [...] directions requiring them to make arrangements for his removal from the United Kingdom in any ship or aircraft specified or indicated in the direction to a country or territory so specified being either–

(i) a country of which he is a national or citizen; or

(ii) a country or territory in which he has obtained a passport or other document of identity; or

(iii) a country or territory in which he embarked for the United Kingdom; or

(iv) a country or territory to which there is reason to believe that he will be admitted.

(2) No directions shall be given under this paragraph in respect of anyone after the expiration of two months beginning with the date on which he was refused leave to enter the United Kingdom (ignoring any period during which an appeal by him under the Immigration Acts is pending) except that directions may be given under sub-paragraph (1)(b) or (c) after the end of that period if the immigration officer has within that period given written notice to the owners or agents in question of his intention to give directions to them in respect of that person.

Detention of persons liable to examination or removal

16 (1) A person who may be required to submit to examination under paragraph 2 above may be detained under the authority of an immigration officer pending

his examination and pending a decision to give or refuse him leave to enter.

(1A) A person whose leave to enter has been suspended under paragraph 2A may be detained under the authority of an immigration officer pending–

(a) completion of his examination under that paragraph; and

(b) a decision on whether to cancel his leave to enter.

(2) If there are reasonable grounds for suspecting that a person is someone in respect of whom directions may be given under any of paragraphs 8 to 10A or 12 to 14, that person may be detained under the authority of an immigration officer pending–

(a) a decision whether or not to give such directions;

(b) his removal in pursuance of such directions.

(3) A person on board a ship or aircraft may, under the authority of an immigration officer, be removed from the ship or aircraft for detention under this paragraph; but if an immigration officer so requires the captain of a ship or aircraft shall prevent from disembarking in the United Kingdom any person who has arrived in the United Kingdom in the ship or aircraft and been refused leave to enter, and the captain may for that purpose detain him in custody on board the ship or aircraft.

(4) The captain of a ship or aircraft, if so required by an immigration officer, shall prevent from disembarking in the United Kingdom or before the directions for his removal have been fulfilled any person placed on board the ship or aircraft under paragraph 11 or 15 above, and the captain may for that purpose detain him in custody on board the ship or aircraft.

Temporary admission or release of persons liable to detention

21 (1) A person liable to detention or detained under paragraph 16 above may, under the written authority of an immigration officer, be temporarily admitted to the United Kingdom without being detained or be released from detention; but this shall not prejudice a later exercise of the power to detain him.

(2) So long as a person is at large in the United Kingdom by virtue of this paragraph, he shall be subject to such restrictions as to residence, as to his employment or occupation and as to reporting to the police or an immigration officer as may from time to time be notified to him in writing by an immigration officer.

(2A) The provisions that may be included in restrictions as to residence imposed under sub-paragraph (2) include provisions of such a description as may be prescribed by regulations made by the Secretary of State.

(2B) The regulations may, among other things, provide for the inclusion of provisions–

(a) prohibiting residence in one or more particular areas;

(b) requiring the person concerned to reside in accommodation provided under section 4 of the Immigration and Asylum Act 1999 and prohibiting him from being absent from that accommodation except in accordance with the restrictions imposed on him.

(2C) The regulations may provide that a particular description of provision may be imposed only for prescribed purposes.

(2D) The power to make regulations conferred by this paragraph is exercisable by statutory instrument and includes a power to make different provision for different cases.

(2E) But no regulations under this paragraph are to be made unless a draft of the regulations has been laid before Parliament and approved by a resolution of each House.

(3) Sub-paragraph (4) below applies where a person who is at large in the United Kingdom by virtue of this paragraph is subject to a restriction as to reporting to an immigration officer with a view to the conclusion of his examination under paragraph 2 or 2A above.

(4) If the person fails at any time to comply with that restriction–

   (a) an immigration officer may direct that the person's examination ... shall be treated as concluded at that time; but nothing in paragraph 6 above shall require the notice giving or refusing him leave

   (b) to enter the United Kingdom to be given within twenty-four hours after that time.

NATIONALITY, IMMIGRATION AND ASYLUM ACT 2002 s11

Unlawful presence in United Kingdom

11 (1) This section applies for the construction of a reference to being in the United Kingdom 'in breach of the immigration laws' in section 4(2) or (4) or 50(5) of, or Schedule 1 to, the British Nationality Act 1981.

(2) A person is in the United Kingdom in breach of the immigration laws if (and only if) he–

(a) is in the United Kingdom,

(b) does not have the right of abode in the United Kingdom within the meaning of section 2 of the Immigration Act 1971,

(c) does not have leave to enter or remain in the United Kingdom (whether or not he previously had leave),

(d) is not a qualified person within the meaning of the Immigration (European Economic Area) Regulations 2000 (SI 2000/2326) (person entitled to reside in United Kingdom without leave) (whether or not he was previously a qualified person),

(e) is not a family member of a qualified person within the meaning of those regulations (whether or not he was previously a family member of a qualified person),

(f) is not entitled to enter and remain in the United Kingdom by virtue of section 8(1) of the Immigration Act 1971 (crew) (whether or not he was previously entitled), and

(g) does not have the benefit of an exemption under section 8(2) to (4) of that Act (diplomats, soldiers and other special cases) (whether or not he previously had the benefit of an exemption).

(3) Section 11(1) of the Immigration Act 1971 (person deemed not to be in United Kingdom before disembarkation, while in controlled area or while under immigration control) shall apply for the purposes of this section as it applies for the purposes of that Act.

(4) This section shall be treated as always having had effect except in relation to a person who on the commencement of this section is, or has been at any time since he last entered the United Kingdom–

(a) a qualified person within the meaning of the regulations referred to in subsection (2)(d), or

(b) a family member of a qualified person within the meaning of those regulations.

(5) This section is without prejudice to the generality of–

(a) a reference to being in a place outside the United Kingdom in breach of immigration laws, and

(b) a reference in a provision other than one specified in subsection (1) to being in the United Kingdom in breach of immigration laws.

ASYLUM AND IMMIGRATION ACT 1996

Persons subject to immigration control

Restrictions on employment

8 (1) Subject to subsection (2) below, if any person ('the employer') employs a person subject to immigration control ('the employee') who has attained the age of 16, the employer shall be guilty of an offence if—

(a) the employee has not been granted leave to enter or remain in the United Kingdom; or

(b) the employee's leave is not valid and subsisting, or is subject to a condition precluding him from taking up the employment,

and (in either case) the employee does not satisfy such conditions as may be specified in an order made by the Secretary of State.

(2) It is a defence for a person charged with an offence under this section to prove that before the employment began any relevant requirement of an order of the Secretary of State under subsection (2A) was complied with.

(2A) An order under this subsection may—

(a) require the production to an employer of a document of a specified description;

(b) require the production to an employer of one document of each of a number of specified descriptions;

(c) require an employer to take specified steps to retain, copy or record the content of a document produced to him in accordance with the order;

(d) make provision which applies generally or only in specified circumstances;

(e) make different provision for different circumstances.

(3) The defence afforded by subsection (2) above shall not be available in any case where the employer knew that his employment of the employee would constitute an offence under this section.

(4) A person guilty of an offence under this section shall be liable on summary conviction to a fine not exceeding level 5 on the standard scale.

(5) Where an offence under this section committed by a body corporate is proved to have been committed with the consent or connivance of, or to be attributable to any neglect on the part of—

(a) any director, manager, secretary or other similar officer of the body corporate; or

(b) any person who was purporting to act in any such capacity, he as well as the body corporate shall be guilty of the offence and shall be liable to be proceeded against and punished accordingly.

(6) Where the affairs of a body corporate are managed by its members, subsection (5) above shall apply in relation to the acts and defaults of a member in connection with his functions of management as if he were a director of the body corporate.

(6A) Where an offence under this section is committed by a partnership (other than a limited partnership) each partner shall be guilty of the offence and shall be liable to be proceeded against and punished accordingly.

(6B) Subsection (5) shall have effect in relation to a limited partnership as if—

    (a) a reference to a body corporate were a reference to a limited partnership, and

    (b) a reference to an officer of the body were a reference to a partner.

(7) An order under this section shall be made by statutory instrument which shall be subject to annulment in pursuance of a resolution of either House of Parliament.

(8) In this section—

'contract of employment' means a contract of service or apprenticeship, whether express or implied, and (if it is express) whether it is oral or in writing;

'employ' means employ under a contract of employment and 'employment' shall be construed accordingly.

(9) section 28(1) of the Immigration Act 1971 (c 77) (extended time limit for prosecution) shall apply in relation to an offence under this section.

(10) An offence under this section shall be treated as—

    (a) a relevant offence for the purpose of sections 28B and 28D of that Act (search, entry and arrest), and

    (b) an offence under Part III of that Act (criminal proceedings) for the purposes of sections 28E, 28G and 28H (search after arrest).

IMMIGRATION RULES (HC 395) paras 327–352F

PART 11: ASYLUM
Definition of asylum applicant

327   Under these Rules an asylum applicant is a person who claims that it would be contrary to the United Kingdom's obligations under the United Nations Convention and Protocol relating to the Status of Refugees for him to be removed from or required to leave the United Kingdom. All such cases are referred to in these Rules as asylum applications.

Applications for asylum

328   All asylum applications will be determined by the Secretary of State in accordance with the United Kingdom's obligations under the United Nations Convention and Protocol relating to the Status of Refugees. Every asylum application made by a person at a port or airport in the United Kingdom will be referred by the Immigration Officer for determination by the Secretary of State in accordance with these Rules.

329   Until an asylum application has been determined by the Secretary of State or the Secretary of State has issued a certificate under section 11 or section 12 of the Immigration and Asylum Act 1999, no action will be taken to require the departure of the asylum applicant or his dependants from the United Kingdom.

330   If the Secretary of State decides to grant asylum and the person has not yet been given leave to enter, the Immigration Officer will grant limited leave to enter.

331   If a person seeking leave to enter is refused asylum, the Immigration Officer will consider whether or not he is in a position to decide to give or refuse leave to enter without interviewing the person further. If the Immigration Officer decides that a further interview is not required he may serve the notice giving or refusing leave to enter by post. If the Immigration Officer decides that a further interview is required, he will then resume his examination to determine whether or not to grant the person leave to enter under any other provision of these Rules. If the person fails at any time to comply with a requirement to report to an Immigration Officer for examination, the Immigration Officer may direct that the person's examination shall be treated as concluded at that time. The Immigration Officer will then consider any outstanding applications for entry on the basis of any evidence before him.

332   If a person who has been refused leave to enter applies for asylum and that application is refused, leave to enter will again be refused unless the applicant qualifies for admission under any other provision of these Rules.

333   [*Deleted*]

Grant of asylum

334   An asylum applicant will be granted asylum in the United Kingdom if the Secretary of State is satisfied that:
(i) he is in the United Kingdom or has arrived at a port of entry in the United Kingdom; and
(ii) he is a refugee, as defined by the Convention and Protocol; and

(iii) refusing his application would result in his being required to go (whether immediately or after the time limited by an existing leave to enter or remain) in breach of the Convention and Protocol, to a country in which his life or freedom would be threatened on account of his race, religion, nationality, political opinion or membership of a particular social group.

335   If the Secretary of State decides to grant asylum to a person who has been given leave to enter (whether or not the leave has expired) or to a person who has entered without leave, the Secretary of State will vary the existing leave or grant limited leave to remain.

Refusal of asylum

336   An application which does not meet the criteria set out in paragraph 334 will be refused.

337   [*Deleted*]

338   When a person in the United Kingdom is notified that asylum has been refused he may, if he is liable to removal as an illegal entrant , removal under section 10 of the Immigration and Asylum Act 1999 or to deportation, at the same time be notified of removal directions, served with a notice of intention to make a deportation order, or served with a deportation order, as appropriate.

339   [*Deleted*]

Consideration of cases

340   A failure, without reasonable explanation, to make a prompt and full disclosure of material facts, either orally or in writing, or otherwise to assist the Secretary of State in establishing the facts of the case may lead to refusal of an asylum application. This includes failure to comply with a notice issued by the Secretary of State or an Immigration Officer requiring the applicant to report to a designated place to be fingerprinted, or failure to complete an asylum questionnaire, or failure to comply with a request to attend an interview concerning the application, or failure to comply with a requirement to report to an Immigration Officer for examination.

341   In determining an asylum application the Secretary of State will have regard to matters which may damage an asylum applicant's credibility. Among such matters are:

(i)   that the applicant has failed without reasonable explanation to apply forthwith upon arrival in the United Kingdom, unless the application is founded on events which have taken place since his arrival in the United Kingdom;

(ii) that the application is made after the applicant has been refused leave to enter under the 1971 Act, or has been recommended for deportation by a court empowered by the 1971 Act to do so, or has been notified of the Secretary of State's decision to make a deportation order against him or has been notified of his liability for removal;

(iii) that the applicant has adduced manifestly false evidence in support of his application, or has otherwise made false representations, either orally or in writing;

(iv) that on his arrival in the United Kingdom the applicant was required to produce a passport in accordance with paragraph 11 (i) and either:

(a) failed to do so without providing a reasonable explanation; or

(b) produced a passport which was not in fact valid, and failed to inform the immigration officer of that fact;

(v) that the applicant has otherwise, without reasonable explanation, destroyed, damaged or disposed of any passport, other document, or ticket relevant to his claim;

(vi) that the applicant has undertaken any activities in the United Kingdom before or after lodging his application which are inconsistent with his previous beliefs and behaviour and calculated to create or substantially enhance his claim to refugee status;

(vii) that the applicant has lodged concurrent applications for asylum in the United Kingdom or in another country.

If the Secretary of State concludes for these or any other reasons that an asylum applicant's account is not credible, the application will be refused.

342 The actions of anyone acting as an agent of the asylum applicant may also be taken into account in regard to the matters set out in paragraphs 340 and 341.

343 If there is a part of the country from which the applicant claims to be a refugee in which he would not have a well-founded fear of persecution, and to which it would be reasonable to expect him to go, the application may be refused.

344 Cases will normally be considered on an individual basis but if an applicant is part of a group whose claims are clearly not related to the criteria for refugee status in the Convention and Protocol he may be refused without examination of his individual claim. However, the Secretary of State will have regard to any evidence produced by an individual to show that his claim should be distinguished from those of the rest of the group.

Third country cases

345 (1) In a case where the Secretary of State is satisfied that the conditions set out in either 11(2), or section 12(7) of the Immigration and Asylum Act 1999 are fulfilled, he will normally refuse the asylum application and issue a certificate under section 11 or section 12 of the Immigration and Asylum Act 1999 (as the case may be) without substantive consideration of the applicant's claim to refugee status. The conditions are:

(i) that the applicant is not a national or citizen of the country or territory to which he is to be sent;

(ii) that the applicant's life and liberty would not be threatened in that country by reason of his race, religion, nationality, membership of a particular social group, or political opinion; and

(iii) that the government of that country or territory would not send him to another country or territory otherwise than in accordance with the Convention.

(2) The Secretary of State shall not remove an asylum applicant without substantive consideration of his claim unless:

(i) the asylum applicant has not arrived in the United Kingdom directly from the country in which he claims to fear persecution and has had an opportunity at the border or within the third country or territory to make contact with the authorities of that third country or territory in order to seek their protection; or

(ii) there is other clear evidence of his admissibility to a third country or territory.

Provided that he is satisfied that a case meets these criteria, the Secretary of State is under no obligation to consult the authorities of the third country or territory before the removal of an asylum applicant to that country or territory.

Previously rejected applications

346   When an asylum applicant has previously been refused asylum during his stay in the United Kingdom, the Secretary of State will determine whether any further representations should be treated as a fresh application for asylum. The Secretary of State will treat representations as a fresh application for asylum if the claim advanced in the representations is sufficiently different from the earlier claim that there is a realistic prospect that the conditions set out in paragraph 334 will be satisfied. In considering whether to treat the representations as a fresh claim, the Secretary of State will disregard any material which:

(i)   is not significant; or

(ii) is not credible; or

(iii) was available to the applicant at the time when the previous application was refused or when any appeal was determined.

347   [*Deleted*]

Rights of appeal

348   [*Deleted*]

Dependants

349   A spouse or minor child accompanying a principal applicant may be included in his application for asylum as his dependant. A spouse or minor child may also claim asylum in his own right. If the principal applicant is granted asylum and leave to enter or remain any spouse or minor child will be granted leave to enter or remain for the same duration. The case of any dependant who claims asylum in his own right will be considered individually in accordance with paragraph 334 above. An applicant under this paragraph, including an accompanied child, may be interviewed where he makes a claim as a dependant or in his own right. If the spouse or minor child in question has a claim in his own right, that claim should be made at the earliest opportunity. Any failure to do so will be taken into account and may damage credibility if no reasonable explanation for it is given. Where an asylum application is unsuccessful, at the same time that asylum is refused the applicant may be notified of removal directions or served with a notice of the Secretary of State's intention to deport him, as appropriate. In this paragraph and paragraphs 350–352 a child means a person who is under 18 years of age or who, in the absence of documentary evidence establishing age, appears to be under that age.

Unaccompanied children

350   Unaccompanied children may also apply for asylum and, in view of their potential vulnerability, particular priority and care is to be given to the handling of their cases.

351   A person of any age may qualify for refugee status under the Convention and the criteria in paragraph 334 apply to all cases. However, account should be taken of the applicant's maturity and in assessing the claim of a child more weight should be given to objective indications of risk than to the child's state of mind and understanding of his situation. An asylum application made on behalf of a child should not be refused solely because the child is too young to understand his situation or to have formed a well founded fear of persecution. Close attention should be given to the welfare of the child at all times.

352   An accompanied or unaccompanied child who has claimed asylum in his own right may be interviewed about the substance of his claim or to determine his age and identity. When an interview is necessary it should be conducted in the presence of a parent, guardian, representative or another adult who for the time being takes responsibility for the child and is not an Immigration Officer, an officer of the Secretary of State or a police officer. The interviewer should have particular regard to the possibility that a child will feel inhibited or alarmed. The child should be allowed to express himself in his own way and at his own speed. If he appears tired or distressed, the interview should be stopped.

352A   The requirements to be met by a person seeking leave to enter or remain in the United Kingdom as the spouse of a refugee are that:

(i)   the applicant is married to a person granted asylum in the United Kingdom; and

(ii)   the marriage did not take place after the person granted asylum left the country of his former habitual residence in order to seek asylum; and

(iii) the applicant would not be excluded from protection by virtue of article 1F of the United Nations Convention and Protocol relating to the Status of Refugees if he were to seek asylum in his own right; and

(iv) each of the parties intends to live permanently with the other as his or her spouse and the marriage is subsisting; and

(v)   if seeking leave to enter, the applicant holds a valid United Kingdom entry clearance for entry in this capacity.

352B   Limited leave to enter the United Kingdom as the spouse of a refugee may be granted provided a valid United Kingdom entry clearance for entry in this capacity is produced to the Immigration Officer on arrival. Limited leave to remain in the United Kingdom as the spouse of a refugee may be granted provided the Secretary of State is satisfied that each of the requirements of paragraph 352A (i)–(iii) are met.

352C   Limited leave to enter the United Kingdom as the spouse of a refugee is to be refused if a valid United Kingdom entry clearance for entry in this capacity is not produced to the Immigration Officer on arrival. Limited leave to remain as the spouse of a refugee is to be refused if the Secretary of State is not satisfied that each of the requirements of paragraph 352A (i)–(iii) are met.

352D   The requirements to be met by a person seeking leave to enter or remain in the United Kingdom in order to join or remain with the parent who has been granted asylum in the United Kingdom are that the applicant:

(i)   is the child of a parent who has been granted asylum in the United Kingdom; and

(ii) is under the age of 18, and

(iii) is not leading an independent life, is unmarried, and has not formed an independent family unit; and

(iv) was part of the family unit of the person granted asylum at the time that the person granted asylum left the country of his habitual residence in order to seek asylum; and

(v) would not be excluded from protection by virtue of article 1F of the United Nations Convention and Protocol relating to the Status of Refugees if he were to seek asylum in his own right; and

(vi) if seeking leave to enter, holds a valid United Kingdom entry clearance for entry in this capacity.

352E Limited leave to enter the United Kingdom as the child of a refugee may be granted provided a valid United Kingdom entry clearance for entry in this capacity is produced to the Immigration Officer on arrival. Limited leave to remain in the United Kingdom as the child of a refugee may be granted provided the Secretary of State is satisfied that each of the requirements of paragraph 352D (i)–(v) are met.

352F Limited leave to enter the United Kingdom as the child of a refugee is to be refused if a valid United Kingdom entry clearance for entry in this capacity is not produced to the Immigration Officer on arrival. Limited leave to remain as the child of a refugee is to be refused if the Secretary of State is not satisfied that each of the requirements of paragraph 352D (i)–(v) are met.

Benefits

SOCIAL SECURITY ADMINISTRATION ACT 1992 s1

Part I: Claims for and Payments and General Administration of Benefit

NECESSITY OF CLAIM

Entitlement to benefit dependent on claim

1 (1) Except in such cases as may be prescribed, and subject to the following provisions of this section and to section 3 below, no person shall be entitled to any benefit unless, in addition to any other conditions relating to that benefit being satisfied –

    (a) he makes a claim for it in the manner, and within the time, prescribed in relation to that benefit by regulations under this Part of this Act; or

    (b) he is treated by virtue of such regulations as making a claim for it.

(1A) No person whose entitlement to any benefit depends on his making a claim shall be entitled to the benefit unless subsection (1B) below is satisfied in relation both to the person making the claim and to any other person in respect of whom he is claiming benefit.

(1B) This subsection is satisfied in relation to a person if –

    (a) the claim is accompanied by –

        (i) a statement of the person's national insurance number and information or evidence establishing that that number has been allocated to the person; or

        (ii) information or evidence enabling the national insurance number that has been allocated to the person to be ascertained; or

    (b) the person makes an application for a national insurance number to be allocated to him which is accompanied by information or evidence enabling such a number to be so allocated.

(1C) Regulations may make provision disapplying subsection (1A) above in the case of –

    (a) prescribed benefits;

    (b) prescribed descriptions of persons making claims; or

    (c) prescribed descriptions of persons in respect of whom benefit is claimed, or in other prescribed circumstances.

(2) Where under subsection (1) above a person is required to make a claim or to be treated as making a claim for a benefit in order to be entitled to it –

    (a) if the benefit is a bereavement payment, the person shall not be entitled to it in respect of a death occurring more than 12 months before the date on which the claim is made or treated as made; and

    (b) if the benefit is any other benefit except disablement benefit or reduced earnings allowance, the person shall not be entitled to it in respect of any period more than 12 months before that date,

except as provided by section 3 below.

(3) Where a person purports to make a claim on behalf of another –

    (a) for an attendance allowance by virtue of section 66(1) of the Contributions and Benefits Act; or

(b) for a disability living allowance by virtue of section 72(5) or 73(12) of that Act,

that other shall be regarded for the purposes of this section as making the claim, notwithstanding that it is made without his knowledge or authority.

(4) In this section and section 2 below 'benefit' means –

(a) benefit as defined in section 122 of the Contributions and Benefits Act;

(aa) a jobseeker's allowance;

(ab) state pension credit; and

(b) any income-related benefit.

(5) This section (which corresponds to section 165A of the 1975 Act, as it had effect immediately before this Act came into force) applies to claims made on or after 1 October 1990 or treated by virtue of regulations under that section or this section as having been made on or after that date.

(6) Schedule 1 to this Act shall have effect in relation to other claims.

SOCIAL SECURITY (IMMIGRATION AND ASYLUM) CONSEQUENTIAL AMENDMENTS REGULATIONS 2000
SI No 636 regs 2, 3, 6, 12, Schedule

Persons not excluded from specified benefits under section 115 of the Immigration and Asylum Act 1999

2 (1) For the purposes of entitlement to income-based jobseeker's allowance, income support, a social fund payment, housing benefit or council tax benefit under the Contributions and Benefits Act, or state pension credit under the State Pension Credit Act 2002, as the case may be, a person falling within a category or description of persons specified in Part I of the Schedule is a person to whom section 115 of the Act does not apply.

(2) For the purposes of entitlement to attendance allowance, severe disablement allowance, carer's allowance, disability living allowance, a social fund payment or child benefit under the Contributions and Benefits Act, as the case may be, a person falling within a category or description of persons specified in Part II of the Schedule is a person to whom section 115 of the Act does not apply.

(3) For the purposes of entitlement to child benefit, attendance allowance or disability living allowance under the Contributions and Benefits Act, as the case may be, a person in respect of whom there is an Order in Council made under section 179 of the Social Security Administration Act 1992 giving effect to a reciprocal agreement in respect of one of those benefits, as the case may be, is a person to whom section 115 of the Act does not apply.

(4) For the purposes of entitlement to –

   (a) income support, a social fund payment, housing benefit or council tax benefit under the Contributions and Benefits Act, as the case may be, a person who is entitled to or is receiving benefit by virtue of paragraph (1) or (2) of regulation 12 of the Persons from Abroad Regulations is a person to whom section 115 of the Act does not apply;

   (b) attendance allowance, disability living allowance, carer's allowance, severe disablement allowance, a social fund payment or child benefit under the Contributions and Benefits Act, as the case may be, a person who is entitled to or is receiving benefit by virtue of paragraph (10) of regulation 12 is a person to whom section 115 of the Act does not apply.

   (c) state pension credit under the State Pension Credit Act 2002, a person to whom sub-paragraph (a) would have applied but for the fact that they have attained the qualifying age for the purposes of state pension credit, is a person to whom section 115 of the Act does not apply.

(5) For the purposes of entitlement to income support by virtue of regulation 70 of the Income Support Regulations (urgent cases), to jobseeker's allowance by virtue of regulation 147 of the Jobseeker's Allowance Regulations (urgent cases) or to a social fund payment under the Contributions and Benefits Act, as the case may be, a person to whom regulation 12(3) applies is a person to whom section 115 of the Act does not apply.

(6) For the purposes of entitlement to housing benefit, council tax benefit or a social fund payment under the Contributions and Benefits Act, as the case may be, a person to whom regulation 12(6) applies is a person to whom section 115 of the Act does not apply.

(7) For the purposes of entitlement to state pension credit under the State Pen-

sion Credit Act 2002, a person to whim paragraph (5) would have applied but for the fact that they have attained the qualifying age for the purposes of state pension credit, is a person to whom section 115 of the Act does not apply.

(8) Where paragraph 1 of Part 1 of the Schedule to these Regulations applies in respect of entitlement to state pension credit, the period for which a claimant's state pension credit is to be calculated shall be any period, or the aggregate of any periods, not exceeding 42 days during any one period of leave to which paragraph 1 of Part 1 of the Schedule to these regulations applies.

Amendment of the Income Support Regulations

3 (1) The Income Support Regulations shall be amended in accordance with the following provisions of this regulation.

(2) In regulation 2(1) (interpretation) –

(a) after the definition of 'housing benefit expenditure' there shall be inserted the following definition –

'"Immigration and Asylum Act" means the Immigration and Asylum Act 1999;'

and

(b) the definition of 'immigration authorities' shall be omitted.

(3) In paragraph (3)(a) of regulation 4ZA, for the words 'regulation 70(3)(a)' there shall be substituted the words 'paragraph 1 of Part I of the Schedule to the Social Security (Immigration and Asylum) Consequential Amendments Regulations 2000'.

(4) In regulation 21 (special cases) –

(a) in paragraph (1) for the words 'regulation 21ZA' there shall be substituted the words 'regulation 21ZB';

(b) in paragraph (3) the first definition of 'person from abroad' shall be omitted;

(c) in paragraph (3), after the opening words, there shall be inserted the following definition –

'"partner of a person subject to immigration control' means a person –

(i) who is not subject to immigration control within the meaning of section 115(9) of the Immigration and Asylum Act; or

(ii) to whom section 115 of that Act does not apply by virtue of regulation 2 of the Social Security (Immigration and Asylum) Consequential Amendments Regulations 2000; and

(iii) who is a member of a couple and his partner is subject to immigration control within the meaning of section 115(9) of that Act and section 115 of that Act applies to her for the purposes of exclusion from entitlement to income support;'; and

(d) in paragraph (3) in the second definition of 'person from abroad' the word 'also' shall be omitted.

(5) For regulation 21ZA (treatment of refugees) after the heading there shall be substituted the following regulation –

'21ZB   (1) This paragraph applies to a person who has submitted a claim for asylum on or after 3rd April 2000 and who is notified that he has been recorded by the Secretary of State as a refugee within the definition in Article 1 of the Convention relating to the Status of Refugees done at Geneva on 28th July 1951 as extended by Article 1(2) of the Protocol relating to the Status of Refugees done at New York on 31st January 1967.

(2) Subject to paragraph (3), a person to whom paragraph (1) applies, who claims income support within 28 days of receiving the notification referred to in paragraph (1), shall have his claim for income support determined as if he had been recorded as a refugee on the date when he submitted his claim for asylum.

(3) The amount of support provided under section 95 or 98 of the Immigration and Asylum Act, including support provided by virtue of regulations made under Schedule 9 to that Act, by the Secretary of State in respect of essential living needs of the claimant and his dependants (if any) as specified in regulations made under paragraph 3 of Schedule 8 to the Immigration and Asylum Act shall be deducted from any award of income support due to the claimant by virtue of paragraph (2).'.[35]

(6) In regulation 40 (calculation of income other than earnings) –

(a) at the beginning of paragraph (4) there shall be inserted the words 'Subject to paragraph (5)';

(b) in paragraph (4) for the words following 'paragraph (1)' there shall be substituted the following sub-paragraphs –

'(a) any payment to which regulation 35(2)(a) or 37(2) (payments not earnings) applies; or

(b) in the case of a claimant who is receiving support provided under section 95 or 98 of the Immigration and Asylum Act including support provided by virtue of regulations made under Schedule 9 to that Act, the amount of such support provided in respect of essential living needs of the claimant and his dependants (if any) as is specified in regulations made under paragraph 3 of Schedule 8 to the Immigration and Asylum Act;';

(c) after paragraph (4) there shall be added the following paragraph –

'(5) In the case of a claimant who is the partner of a person subject to immigration control and whose partner is receiving support provided under section 95 or 98 of the Immigration and Asylum Act including support provided by virtue of regulations made under Schedule 9 to that Act, there shall not be included as income to be taken into account under paragraph (1) the amount of support provided in respect of essential living needs of the partner of the claimant and his dependants (if any) as is specified in regulations made under paragraph 3 of Schedule 8 to the Immigration and Asylum Act.'.

(7) In regulation 70 (urgent cases) –

(a) in paragraph (2) for sub-paragraph (a) there shall be substituted the following sub-paragraph –

---

35 Regulation 21ZB of the Income Support (General) Regulations 1987 SI No 1967, is to be repealed, from a date to be appointed, by the Asylum and Immigration (Treatment of Claimants etc.) Act 2004 s 12(2).

'(a) a claimant to whom paragraph (2A) applies (persons not excluded from income support under section 115 of the Immigration and Asylum Act);';

(b) after paragraph (2) there shall be inserted the following paragraph –

'(2A) This paragraph applies to a person not excluded from entitlement to income support under section 115 of the Immigration and Asylum Act by virtue of regulation 2 of the Social Security (Immigration and Asylum) Consequential Amendments Regulations 2000 except for a person to whom paragraphs 3 and 4 of Part I of the Schedule to those Regulations applies.'; and

(c) paragraphs (3), (3A) and (3B) shall be omitted.

(8) In regulation 71 (applicable amounts in urgent cases) –

(a) in paragraph (1)(d), for the words 'paragraph 17' there shall be substituted the words 'paragraph 16A'; and

(b) in paragraph (2), for the words 'paragraph (3)' in each place where they occur, there shall be substituted the words 'paragraph 2A'.

(9) In Schedule 1B (prescribed categories of person) –

(a) after paragraph 18, there shall be inserted the following paragraph –

'18A A person to whom regulation 21ZB (treatment of refugees)[36] applies by virtue of regulation 21ZB(2) from the date his claim for asylum is made until the date the Secretary of State makes a decision on that claim.';

(b) in paragraph 21, for the words 'regulation 70(3)' there shall be substituted the words 'regulation 70(2A)'.

(10) After paragraph 16 of Schedule 7 (applicable amounts in special cases) –

(a) in column (1) there shall be inserted the following paragraph –

'**Partner of a person subject to immigration control**

16A (a) A claimant who is the partner of a person subject to immigration control.

(b) Where regulation 18 (polygamous marriages) applies and the claimant is a person –

(i) who is not subject to immigration control within the meaning of section 115(9) of the Immigration and Asylum Act; or

(ii) to whom section 115 of that Act does not apply by virtue of regulation 2 of the Social Security (Immigration and Asylum) Consequential Amendments Regulations 2000; and

(iii) who is a member of a couple and one or more of his partners is subject to immigration control within the meaning of section 115(9) of that Act and section 115 of that Act applies to her for the purposes of exclusion from entitlement to income support.';

(b) in column (2) there shall be inserted the following paragraph –

'16A(a) The amount applicable in respect of the claimant only under regulation 17(1)(a) plus that in respect of any child or young person who is

36 Regulation 21ZB of the Income Support Regs is to be repealed, from a date to be appointed, by the Asylum and Immigration (Treatment of Claimants etc.) Act 2004 s 12(2).

a member of his family and who is not a person subject to immigration control within the meaning of section 115(9) of the Immigration and Asylum Act, and to whom section 115 of that Act does not apply for the purposes of exclusion from entitlement to income support, any amounts which may be applicable to him under regulation 17(1)(b), (c) or (d) plus the amount applicable to him under. regulation 17(1)(e), (f) and (g) or, as the case may be, regulation 19 or 21

  (b) The amount determined in accordance with that regulation or regulation 19 or 21 in respect of the claimant and any partners of his and any child or young person for whom he or his partner is treated as responsible, who are not subject to immigration control within the meaning of section 115(9) of the Immigration and Asylum Act and to whom section 115 of that Act does not apply for the purposes of exclusion from entitlement to income support.'.

(11) In paragraph 17 of Schedule 7 (applicable amounts in special cases) for the words in column (1) there shall be substituted the words 'person from abroad' and for the words in column (2) there shall be substituted the word 'nil'.

(12) In paragraph 21 of Schedule 9 (treatment of income in kind) –

  (a) in sub-paragraph (1) for the words 'Subject to sub-paragraph (2)' there shall be substituted the words 'Subject to sub-paragraphs (2) and (3)';

  (b) in sub-paragraph (1) after the words 'except where' there shall be added the following words –

'regulation 40(4)(b) (provision of support under section 95 or 98 of the Immigration and Asylum Act including support provided by virtue of regulations made under Schedule 9 to that Act in the calculation of income other than earnings) or';

  (c) after sub-paragraph (2) there shall be added the following sub-paragraph –

   '(3) The first exception under sub-paragraph (1) shall not apply where the claimant is the partner of a person subject to immigration control and whose partner is receiving support provided under section 95 or 98 of the Immigration and Asylum Act including support provided by virtue of regulations made under Schedule 9 to that Act and the income in kind is support provided in respect of essential living needs of the partner of the claimant and his dependants (if any) as is specified in regulations made under paragraph 3 of Schedule 8 to the Immigration and Asylum Act.'

(13) In paragraph 57 of Schedule 9 (disregards in the calculation of income other than earnings) and paragraph 49 of Schedule 10 (capital to be disregarded) for the words 'regulation 21ZA' there shall be substituted the words 'regulation 21ZB'.

Amendment of the Housing Benefit Regulations

6 (1) The Housing Benefit Regulations shall be amended in accordance with the following provisions of this regulation.

  (2) In regulation 2(1) (interpretation) after the definition of 'housing association' there shall be inserted the following definition –

   '"Immigration and Asylum Act" means the Immigration and Asylum Act 1999;'.

(3) In regulation 7A (persons from abroad) –
   (a) paragraphs (2), (3), (4)(a), (b), (c), (d), (e)(iv), (v) and (vi), (f) and (g), (4A), (5)(a), (b) and (c) and (5A) shall be omitted;
   (b) in paragraph (6) the words 'Paragraphs (3)(b) and (4A)' shall be substituted by the words 'Paragraph 1 of Part I of the Schedule to, and regulation 2 as it applies to that paragraph of, the Social Security (Immigration and Asylum) Consequential Amendments Regulations 2000.'; and
   (c) in paragraph (7) the definitions of the 'Common Travel Area' and the 'Convention relating to the Status of Refugees' shall be omitted.
(4) In paragraph (4) of regulation 33 (calculation of income other than earnings) for the words following 'paragraph (1)' there shall be substituted the following sub-paragraphs –
   '(a) any payment to which regulation 28(2) (payments not earnings) applies; or
   (b) in the case of a claimant who is receiving support under section 95 or 98 of the Immigration and Asylum Act including support provided by virtue of regulations made under Schedule 9 to that Act, the amount of such support provided in respect of essential living needs of the claimant and his dependants (if any) as is specified in regulations made under paragraph 3 of Schedule 8 to the Immigration and Asylum Act.'.
(5) In Schedule A1 (treatment of claims for housing benefit by refugees) –
   (a) in paragraph 1(1)(b) for the words following paragraph (ii) there shall be substituted the following words 'his claim for housing benefit shall be treated as having been made on the date specified in sub-paragraph (2)';
   (b) in paragraph 1(2) for heads (a) and (b), there shall be substituted the following words –
   'on the date on which his claim for asylum was recorded by the Secretary of State as having been made.';
   (c) after paragraph 1 there shall be inserted the following paragraph –
   '**Appropriate authority to whom a claim for housing benefit by a refugee shall be made and time for making a claim**
      2A (1) A claim for housing benefit made by a refugee on or after 3rd April 2000 for the relevant period may be made to the appropriate authority for the area in which the dwelling which the claimant occupied as his home was situate and in respect of which he was liable to make payments.
      (2) Where the claimant has occupied more than one dwelling as his home in the relevant period, only one claim for housing benefit shall be made in respect of that period and such a claim shall be made to the authority for the area in which the dwelling occupied by the refugee is situate and in respect of which he was liable to make payments when, after he is notified that he has been recorded by the Secretary of State as a refugee, he makes a claim for housing benefit.

37 Schedule A1 of the Housing Benefit Regs 1987 is to be repealed, from a date to be appointed, by the Asylum and Immigration (Treatment of Claimants etc.) Act 2004 s 12(2)(f).

(3) The appropriate authority to which a claim for housing benefit is made in accordance with this paragraph, shall determine the claimant's entitlement to that benefit for the whole of the relevant period.

(4) A claim for housing benefit to which this paragraph refers, shall be made within 28 days of a claimant receiving notification from the Secretary of State that he has been recorded as a refugee.

(5) Regulation 72(15) of these Regulations (backdating of claims) shall not have effect with respect to claims to which this Schedule applies.'; and

(d) paragraph 2 shall be omitted.

(6) In paragraph 21 of Schedule 4 (treatment of income in kind) after the words 'income in kind' there shall be added the following words –

'except where regulation 33(4)(b) (provision of support under section 95 or 98 of the Immigration and Asylum Act in the calculation of income other than earnings) applies'.

(7) In paragraph 62 of Schedule 4 and paragraph 51 of Schedule 5 for the words 'regulation 21ZA' there shall be substituted the words 'regulation 21ZB'.

Transitional arrangements and savings

12 (1) Paragraph (2) shall apply where, in relation to a claim for income support, a social fund payment, housing benefit or council tax benefit, as the case may be, a person has submitted a claim for asylum on or before 2nd April 2000 and is notified that he has been recorded by the Secretary of State as a refugee within the definition in Article 1 of the Convention relating to the Status of Refugees done at Geneva on 28th July 1951 as extended by Article 1(2) of the Protocol relating to the Status of Refugees done at New York on 31st January 1967.[38]

(2) Where this paragraph applies –

(a) regulation 21ZA of the Income Support Regulations (treatment of refugees) shall continue to have effect as if regulation 3(4)(a), (5) and (9) had not been made;

(b) regulations 4(3C), 6(4D) and 19(8) of the Claims and Payments Regulations shall continue to have effect as if regulation 5 had not been made;

(c) paragraphs 1 and 2 of Schedule A1, paragraph 62 of Schedule 4 and paragraph 51 of Schedule 5 to the Housing Benefit Regulations (treatment of claims for housing benefit by refugees) shall continue to have effect as if regulation 6(5) and (7) had not been made; and

(d) paragraphs 1 and 2 of Schedule A1, paragraph 62 of Schedule 4 and paragraph 51 of Schedule 5 to the Council Tax Benefit Regulations (treatment of claims for council tax benefit by refugees) shall continue to have effect as if regulation 7(5) and (7) had not been made.[39]

(3) Regulation 70 of the Income Support Regulations and regulation 147 of the Jobseeker's Allowance Regulations, as the case may be, shall apply to a person

38 To be repealed, from a date to be appointed, by the Asylum and Immigration (Treatment of Claimants etc.) Act 2004 s 12(3).
39 ibid.

who is an asylum seeker within the meaning of paragraph (4) who has not ceased to be an asylum seeker by virtue of paragraph (5).

(4) An asylum seeker within the meaning of this paragraph is a person who –

    (a) submits on his arrival (other than on his re-entry) in the United Kingdom from a country outside the Common Travel Area a claim for asylum on or before 2nd April 2000 to the Secretary of State that it would be contrary to the United Kingdom's obligations under the Convent for him to be removed or required to leave, the United Kingdom and that claim is recorded by the Secretary of State as having been made before that date; or

    (b) on or before 2nd April 2000 becomes, while present in Great Britain, an asylum seeker when –

        (i) the Secretary of State makes a declaration to the effect that the country of which he is a national is subject to such a fundamental change of circumstances that he would not normally order the return of a person to that country; and

        (ii) he submits, within a period of three months from the date that declaration was made, a claim for asylum to the Secretary of State under the Convention relating to the Status of Refugees, and

        (iii) his claim for asylum under that Convention is recorded by the Secretary of State has having been made; and

    (c) in the case of a claim for jobseeker's allowance, holds a work permit or has written authorisation from the Secretary of state permitting him to work in the United Kingdom.

(5) A person ceases to be an asylum seeker for the purposes of this paragraph when his claim for asylum is recorded by the Secretary of State as having been decided (other than on appeal) or abandoned.

(6) For the purposes of regulation 7A of the housing Benefit Regulations and regulation 4A of the Council Tax Benefit Regulations, a person who is an asylum seeker within the meaning of paragraph (7) who has not ceased to be an asylum seeker by virtue of paragraph (8), is not a person from abroad within the meaning of paragraph (1) of those regulations.

(7) An asylum seeker within the meaning of this paragraph is a person who –

    (a) submits on his arrival (other than on his re-entry) in the United Kingdom from a country outside the Common Travel Area a claim for asylum on or before 2nd April 2000 to the Secretary of State that it would be contrary to the United Kingdom's obligations under the Convention for him to be removed or required to leave, the United Kingdom and that claim is recorded by the Secretary of State has having been made before that date, or

    (b) on or before 2nd April 2000 becomes, while present in Great Britain, an asylum seeker when –

        (i) the Secretary of State makes a declaration to the effect that the country of which he is a national is subject to such a fundamental change of circumstances that he would not normally order the return of a person to that country; and

        (ii) he submits, within a period of three months from the date that declaration was made, a claim for asylum to the Secretary of State under the Convention relating to the Status of Refugees; and

(iii) his claim for asylum under that Convention is recorded by the Secretary of State has having been made.

(8) A person ceases to be an asylum seeker for the purposes of this paragraph when his claim for asylum is recorded by the Secretary of State as having been decided (other than on appeal) or abandoned.

(9) In paragraphs (4) and (7) 'the Common Travel Area' means the United Kingdom, the Channel Islands, the Isle of Man and the Republic of Ireland collectively and 'the Convention' means the Convention relating to the Status of Refugees done at Geneva on 28th July 1951 as extended by Article 2(1) of the Protocol relating to the Status of Refugees done at New York on 31st January 1967.

(10) Where, before the coming into force of these Regulations, a person has claimed benefit to which he is entitled or is receiving benefit by virtue of regulation 12(3) of the Persons from Abroad Regulations or regulation 14B(g) of the Child Benefit (General) Regulations 1976, as the case may be, those provisions shall continue to have effect, for the purposes of entitlement to attendance allowance, disability living allowance, carer's allowance, severe disablement allowance or child benefit, as the case may be, until such time as –

(a) his claim for asylum (if any) is recorded by the Secretary of State as having been decided or abandoned; or

(b) his entitlement to that benefit is revised or superseded under section 9 or 10 of the Social Security Act 1998, if earlier,

as if regulations 8, 9, 10 and 11 and paragraph (2) or paragraph (3), as the case may be, of regulation 13, had not been made.

(11) In the Persons from Abroad Regulations –

(a) in paragraph (1) of regulation 12, after the words 'shall continue to have effect' there shall be inserted the words '(both as regards him and as regards persons who are members of his family at the coming into force of these Regulations)'; and

(b) notwithstanding the amendments and revocations in regulations 3, 6 and 7, regulations 12(1) and (2) of the Persons from Abroad Regulations shall continue to have effect as they had effect before those amendments and revocations came into force.

SCHEDULE – PERSONS NOT EXCLUDED FROM CERTAIN BENEFITS UNDER SECTION 115 OF THE IMMIGRATION AND ASYLUM ACT 1999

Part I: Persons not excluded under section 115 of the Immigration and Asylum Act from entitlement to income-based jobseeker's allowance, income support, a social fund payment, housing benefit or council tax benefit

1   A person who –

(a) has limited leave (as defined in section 33(1) of the Immigration Act 1971) to enter or remain in the United Kingdom which was given in accordance with the immigration rules (as defined in that section) relating to –

(i) there being or there needing to be, no recourse to public funds, or

(ii) there being no charge on public funds,

during that period of limited leave; and

(b) having, during any one period of limited leave (including any such period as extended), supported himself without recourse to public funds, other than any such recourse by reason of the previous application of this sub-paragraph, is temporarily without funds during that period of leave because remittances to him from abroad have been disrupted, provided there is a reasonable expectation that his supply of funds will be resumed.

2   A person who has been given leave to enter or remain in, the United Kingdom by the Secretary of State upon an undertaking by another person or persons pursuant to the immigration rules within the meaning of the Immigration Act 1971, to be responsible for his maintenance and accommodation and who has not been resident in the United Kingdom for a period of at least five years beginning on the date of entry or the date on which the undertaking was given in respect of him, whichever date is the later and the person or persons who gave the undertaking to provide for his maintenance and accommodation has, or as the case may be, have died

3   A person who –
   (a) has been given leave to enter or remain in, the United Kingdom by the Secretary of State upon an undertaking by another person or persons pursuant to the immigration rules within the meaning of the Immigration Act 1971, to be responsible for his maintenance and accommodation; and
   (b) has been resident in the United Kingdom for a period of at least five years beginning on the date of entry or the date on which the undertaking was given in respect of him, whichever date is the later.

4   A person who is a national of a state which has ratified the European Convention on Social and Medical Assistance (done in Paris on 11th December 1953) or a state which has ratified the Council of Europe Social Charter (signed in Turin on 18th October 1961) and who is lawfully present in the United Kingdom.

Part II: Persons not excluded under section 115 of the Immigration and Asylum Act from entitlement to attendance allowance, severe disablement allowance, invalid care allowance, disability living allowance a social fund payment or child benefit

1   A member of a family of a national of a State contracting party to the Agreement on the European Economic Area signed at Oporto on 2nd May 1992 as adjusted by the Protocol signed at Brussels on 17th March 1993.

2   A person who is lawfully working in Great Britain and is a national of a State with which the Community has concluded an agreement under Article 310 of the Treaty of Amsterdam amending the Treaty on European Union, the Treaties establishing the European Communities and certain related Acts providing, in the field of social security, for the equal treatment of workers who are nationals of the signatory State and their families.

3   A person who is a member of a family of, and living with, a person specified in paragraph 2.

4   A person who has been given leave to enter, or remain in, the United Kingdom by the Secretary of State upon an undertaking by another person or persons pursuant to the immigration rules within the meaning of the Immigration Act 1971, to be responsible for his maintenance and accommodation.

TAX CREDITS (IMMIGRATION) REGULATIONS 2003
SI No 653 regs 3–5

Exclusion of persons subject to immigration control from entitlement to tax credits

3 (1) No person is entitled to child tax credit or working tax credit while he is a person subject to immigration control, except in the following Cases, and subject to paragraphs (2) to (9).

Case 1

He is a person who –

(a) has been given leave to enter, or remain in, the United Kingdom by the Secretary of State upon the undertaking of another person or persons, pursuant to the immigration rules, to be responsible for his maintenance and accommodation, and

(b) has been resident in the United Kingdom for a period of at least 5 years commencing on or after the date of his entry into the United Kingdom, or the date on which the undertaking was given in respect of him, whichever is the later.

Case 2

He is a person who –

(a) falls within the terms of paragraph (a) of Case 1, and

(b) has been resident in the United Kingdom for less than the 5 years mentioned in paragraph (b) of Case 1,

but the person giving the undertaking has died or, where the undertaking was given by more than one person, they have all died.

Case 3

He is a person who satisfies the following conditions –

(a) he has limited leave to enter or remain in the United Kingdom;

(b) that leave was subject to a condition that he does not have recourse to public funds, during that period of limited leave;

(c) he has, during so much as has elapsed of that period of limited leave (including that period as extended), supported himself without recourse to public funds, other than any such recourse by reason of the previous satisfaction of these conditions;

(d) he is temporarily without funds during that period of leave because remittances to him from abroad have been disrupted;

(e) there is a reasonable expectation that his supply of funds will be resumed; and

(f) the period (or aggregate of periods) for which this Case applies does not exceed 42 days during any single period of limited leave (including any extension to that period).

Case 4

Where the claim is for working tax credit, he is –

(a) a national of a state which has ratified the European Convention on Social and Medical Assistance (done in Paris on 11th December 1953) or of a state which has ratified the Council of Europe Social Charter (signed in Turin on 18th October 1961), and

(b) lawfully present in the United Kingdom.

The Case so described also applies where –

(a) the claim is for child tax credit,

(b) the award of child tax credit would be made on or after 6th April 2004, and

(c) immediately before the award is made (and as part of the transition of claimants entitled to elements of income support and income-based job-seeker's allowance, to child tax credit) the person is, or will on the making of a claim be, entitled to any of the amounts in relation to income support or income-based jobseeker's allowance which are described in section 1(3)(d) of the Act.

Case 5

Where the claim is for child tax credit, he is –

(a) a person who is lawfully working in the United Kingdom, and

(b) a national of a State with which the Community has concluded an Agreement under Article 310 of the Treaty of Amsterdam amending the Treaty on European Union, the Treaties establishing the European Communities and certain related Acts providing, in the field of social security, for the equal treatment of workers who are nationals of the signatory State and their families.

(2) Where one member of a married couple or unmarried couple is a person subject to immigration control, and the other member is not or is within any of Cases 1 to 5 or regulation 5 –

(a) the calculation of the amount of tax credit under the Act, the Child Tax Credit Regulations and the Working Tax Credit Regulations (including any second adult element or other element in respect of, or determined by reference to, that person),

(b) the method of making (or proceeding with) a joint claim by the couple, and

(c) the method of payment of the tax credit,

shall, subject to paragraph (3), be determined in the same way as if that person were not subject to such control.

(3) Where the other member is within Case 4 or 5 or regulation 5, paragraph (2) shall only apply to the tax credit to which he (in accordance with those provisions) is entitled.

(4) Where a person has submitted a claim for asylum as a refugee and in consequence is a person subject to immigration control, in the first instance he is not entitled to tax credits, subject to paragraphs (5) to (9).

(5) If that person –

(a) is notified that he has been recorded by the Secretary of State as a refugee, and

(b) claims tax credit within 3 months of receiving that notification,

paragraphs (6) to (9) and regulation 4 shall apply to him.

(6) He shall be treated as having claimed tax credits –

(a) on the date when he submitted his claim for asylum, and

(b) on every 6th April (if any) intervening between the date in sub-paragraph (a) and the date of the claim referred to in paragraph (5)(b),

rather than on the date on which he makes the claim referred to in paragraph (5)(b).

(7) Regulations 7 and 8 of the Tax Credits (Claims and Notifications) Regulations 2002 shall not apply to claims treated as made by virtue of paragraph (6).

(8) He shall have his claims for tax credits determined as if he had been recorded as a refugee on the date when he submitted his claim for asylum.

(9) The amount of support provided under –

(a) section 95 or 98 of the Immigration and Asylum Act 1999,

(b) regulations made under Schedule 9 to that Act, by the Secretary of State in respect of essential living needs of the claimant and his dependants (if any), or

(c) regulations made under paragraph 3 of Schedule 8 to that Act,

(after allowing for any deduction for that amount under regulation 21ZB(3) of the Income Support (General) Regulations 1987) shall be deducted from any award of tax credits due to the claimant by virtue of paragraphs (6) and (8).

Modifications of Part 1 of the Act for refugees whose asylum claims have been accepted

4 (1) For the purposes of claims falling within paragraph (2), Part 1 of the Act shall apply subject to the modifications set out in paragraphs (3) to (5).

(2) A claim falls within this paragraph if it is a claim for tax credits which a person is treated as having made by virtue of regulation 3(6), other than a claim which he is treated as having made in the tax year in which he made his claim under regulation 3(5).

(3) Omit sections 14 to 17 (initial decisions, revised decisions and final notices).

(4) In section 18 (decisions after final notices) –

(a) in subsection (1) for 'After giving a notice under section 17' substitute 'In relation to each claim for a tax credit made by a person or persons for the whole or part of a tax year';

(b) omit subsections (2) to (9);

(c) for subsection (10) substitute –

'(10) Before making their decision the Board may by notice –

(a) require the person, or either or both of the persons, by whom the claim is made to provide any information or evidence which the Board consider they may need for making their decision, or

(b) require any person of a prescribed description to provide any information or evidence of a prescribed description which the Board consider they may need for that purpose,

by the date specified in the notice.';

(d) in subsection (11) omit –

(i) 'any revision under subsection (5) or (9) and';

(ii) paragraph (a);

(iii) in paragraph (b), 'in any other case,'.

(5) In section 19 (enquiries) –

(a) in subsection (4), for paragraphs (a) and (b) substitute
'one year after that decision or, if –

(a) the person, or either of the persons, to whom the enquiry relates is required by section 8 of the Taxes Management Act 1970 to make a return, and

(b) the return becomes final on a day more than one year after that decision,

with that day (or, if both of the persons are so required and their returns become final on different days, with the later of those days).;'

(b) in subsection (5) omit paragraph (a) and, in paragraph (b) 'in any other case,';

(c) omit subsection (6).

Transitional relief – claimants moving from income support and income-based jobseeker's allowance to child tax credit

5　In relation to child tax credit, a person is not treated for the purposes of these Regulations as subject to immigration control where –

(a) the award of child tax credit would be made on or after 6 April 2004;

(b) immediately before the award of child tax credit is made, he is, or will on the making of a claim be, entitled to any of the amounts in relation to income support or income-based jobseeker's allowance which are described in section 1(3)(d) of the Act; and

(c) he is a person who, immediately before the award of child tax credit is made –

(i) was receiving or entitled to income support by virtue of regulation 12(1) of the Social Security (Persons From Abroad) Miscellaneous Amendments Regulations 1996, and his claim for asylum has not been recorded by the Secretary of State as having been decided (other than on appeal) or abandoned; or

(ii) was receiving or entitled to income support or income-based jobseeker's allowance by virtue of regulation 12(3) of the Social Security (Immigration and Asylum) Consequential Amendments Regulations 2000, and his claim for asylum has not been so recorded as having been decided (other than on appeal) or abandoned.

Housing

HOUSING ACT 1996 ss179, 183, 185, 186

Duty of local housing authority to provide advisory services

179 (1) Every local housing authority shall secure that advice and information about homelessness, and the prevention of homelessness, is available free of charge to any person in their district.

(2) The authority may give to any person by whom such advice and information is provided on behalf of the authority assistance by way of grant or loan.

(3) A local housing authority may also assist any such person–

    (a) by permitting him to use premises belonging to the authority,

    (b) by making available furniture or other goods, whether by way of gift, loan or otherwise, and

    (c) by making available the services of staff employed by the authority.

APPLICATION FOR ASSISTANCE IN CASE OF HOMELESSNESS OR THREATENED HOMELESSNESS

Application for assistance

183 (1) The following provisions of this Part apply where a person applies to a local housing authority for accommodation, or for assistance in obtaining accommodation, and the authority have reason to believe that he is or may be homeless or threatened with homelessness.

(2) In this Part –

'applicant' means a person making such an application,

'assistance under this Part' means the benefit of any function under the following provisions of this Part relating to accommodation or assistance in obtaining accommodation, and

'eligible for assistance' means not excluded from such assistance by section 185 (persons from abroad not eligible for housing assistance) or [section 186 (asylum seekers and their dependants)].[40]

(3) Nothing in this section or the following provisions of this Part affects a person's entitlement to advice and information under section 179 (duty to provide advisory services).

Persons from abroad not eligible for housing assistance

185 (1) A person is not eligible for assistance under this Part if he is a person from abroad who is ineligible for housing assistance.

(2) A person who is subject to immigration control within the meaning of the Asylum and Immigration Act 1996 is not eligible for housing assistance unless he is of a class prescribed by regulations made by the Secretary of State.

(2A) Regulations may not be made under subsection (2) so as to include in a prescribed class any person to whom section 115 of the Immigration and Asylum Act 1999 (exclusion from benefits) applies.

---

40 Words in square brackets repealed, from a day to be appointed, by the Immigration and Asylum Act 1999 s170(4).

(3) The Secretary of State may make provision by regulations as to other descriptions of persons who are to be treated for the purposes of this Part as persons from abroad who are ineligible for housing assistance.

(4) A person from abroad who is not eligible for housing assistance shall be disregarded in determining for the purposes of this Part whether another person –

   (a) is homeless or threatened with homelessness, or

   (b) has a priority need for accommodation.

Asylum-seekers and their dependants

186 (1) An asylum-seeker, or a dependant of an asylum-seeker who is not by virtue of section 185 a person from abroad who is ineligible for housing assistance, is not eligible for assistance under this Part if he has any accommodation in the United Kingdom, however temporary, available for his occupation.

(2) For the purposes of this section a person who makes a claim for asylum –

   (a) becomes an asylum-seeker at the time when his claim is recorded by the Secretary of State as having been made, and

   (b) ceases to be an asylum-seeker at the time when his claim is recorded by the Secretary of State as having been finally determined or abandoned.

(3) For the purposes of this section a person –

   (a) becomes a dependant of an asylum-seeker at the time when he is recorded by the Secretary of State as being a dependant of the asylum-seeker, and

   (b) ceases to be a dependant of an asylum-seeker at the time when the person whose dependant he is ceases to be an asylum-seeker or, if it is earlier, at the time when he is recorded by the Secretary of State as ceasing to be a dependant of the asylum-seeker.

(4) In relation to an asylum-seeker, 'dependant' means a person –

   (a) who is his spouse or a child of his under the age of eighteen, and

   (b) who has neither a right of abode in the United Kingdom nor indefinite leave under the Immigration Act 1971 to enter or remain in the United Kingdom.

(5) In this section a 'claim for asylum' means a claim made by a person that it would be contrary to the United Kingdom's obligations under the Convention relating to the Status of Refugees done at Geneva on 28th July 1951 and the Protocol to that Convention for him to be removed from, or required to leave, the United Kingdom.][41]

Local connection

199(1)A person has a local connection with the district of a local housing authority if he has a connection with it—

   (a) because he is, or in the past was, normally resident there, and that residence is or was of his own choice,

   (b) because he is employed there,

   (c) because of family associations, or

   (d) because of special circumstances.

---

41 Section 186 repealed by the Immigration and Asylum Act 1999 ss117(5), 169(3), Sch 16 from a day to be appointed.

(2) A person is not employed in a district if he is serving in the regular armed forces of the Crown.

(3) Residence in a district is not of a person's own choice if—

    (a) he becomes resident there because he, or a person who might reasonably be expected to reside with him, is serving in the regular armed forces of the Crown, or

    (b) he, or a person who might reasonably be expected to reside with him, becomes resident there because he is detained under the authority of an Act of Parliament.

(4) In subsections (2) and (3) "regular armed forces of the Crown" means the Royal Navy, the regular forces as defined by section 225 of the Army Act 1955 or the regular air force as defined by section 223 of the Air Force Act 1955.

(5) The Secretary of State may by order specify other circumstances in which—

    (a) a person is not to be treated as employed in a district, or

    (b) residence in a district is not to be treated as of a person's own choice.

(6) A person has a local connection with the district of a local housing authority if he was (at any time) provided with accommodation in that district under section 95 of the Immigration and Asylum Act 1999 (support for asylum seekers).

(7) But subsection (6) does not apply—

    (a) to the provision of accommodation for a person in a district of a local housing authority if he was subsequently provided with accommodation in the district of another local housing authority under section 95 of that Act, or

    (b) to the provision of accommodation in an accommodation centre by virtue of section 22 of the Nationality, Immigration and Asylum Act 2002 (use of accommodation centres for section 95 support).[42]

---

42 Paras (6) and (7) inserted by the Asylum and Immigration (Treatment of Claimants etc) Act 2004 s10, from a date to be appointed.

ASYLUM AND IMMIGRATION ACT 1996 s13

Short title, interpretation, commencement and extent

13 (1) This Act may be cited as the Asylum and Immigration Act 1996.

(2) In this Act 'the 1971 Act' means the Immigration Act 1971;

'the 1993 Act' means the Asylum and Immigration Appeals Act 1993;

'person subject to immigration control' means a person who under the 1971 Act requires leave to enter or remain in the United Kingdom (whether or not such leave has been given).

HOMELESSNESS (ENGLAND) REGULATIONS 2000 SI No 701

Citation, commencement and extent

1 (1) These Regulations may be cited as the Homelessness (England) Regulations 2000 and shall come into force on 3rd April 2000.

(2) These Regulations extend to England only.

Interpretation

2 (1) In these Regulations –

'the 1971 Act' means the Immigration Act 1971;

'the 1995 Act' means the Jobseekers Act 1995;

'the 1996 Act' means the Housing Act 1996;

'asylum-seeker' means a person who is not under 18 and who made a claim for asylum which is recorded by the Secretary of State as having been made before 3rd April 2000 but which has not been determined;

'claim for asylum' means a claim that it would be contrary to the United Kingdom's obligations under the Refugee Convention for the claimant to be removed from, or required to leave, the United Kingdom;

'the Common Travel Area' means the United Kingdom, the Channel Islands, the Isle of Man and the Republic of Ireland collectively;

'the immigration rules' means the rules laid down as mentioned in section 3(2) of the 1971 Act (general provisions for regulation and control);

'limited leave' means leave under the 1971 Act to enter or remain in the United Kingdom which is limited as to duration; and

'the Refugee Convention' means the Convention relating to the Status of Refugees done at Geneva on 28 July 1951, as extended by Article 1(2) of the Protocol relating to the Status of Refugees done at New York on 31st January 1967.

(2) For the purposes of the definition of 'asylum-seeker', a claim for asylum is determined at the end of such period beginning –

(a) on the day on which the Secretary of State notifies the claimant of his decision on the claim; or

(b) if the claimant has appealed against the Secretary of State's decision, on the day on which the appeal is disposed of,

as may be prescribed under section 94(3) of the Immigration and Asylum Act 1999.

(3) For the purposes of regulations 3(1)(i) (Class I) and 4(d) –

(a) 'an income-based jobseeker's allowance' means a jobseeker's allowance, payable under the 1995 Act, entitlement to which is based on the claimant satisfying conditions which include those set out in section 3 of the 1995 Act (the income-based conditions);

(b) 'income support' has the same meaning as in section 124 of the Social Security Contributions and Benefits Act 1992 (income support); and

(c) a person is on an income-based jobseeker's allowance on any day in respect of which an income-based jobseeker's allowance is payable to him and on any day –

(i) in respect of which he satisfies the conditions for entitlement to an income-based jobseeker's allowance but where the allowance is not paid in accordance with section 19 of the 1995 Act (circumstances in which jobseeker's allowance is not payable); or

(ii) which is a waiting day for the purposes of paragraph 4 of Schedule 1 to the 1995 Act (waiting days) and which falls immediately before a day in respect of which an income-based jobseeker's allowance is payable to him or would be payable to him but for section 19 of the 1995 Act.

Classes of persons subject to immigration control who are eligible for housing assistance

3 (1) The following are classes of persons prescribed for the purposes of section 185(2) of the 1996 Act (persons subject to immigration control who are eligible for housing assistance) –

(a) Class A – a person recorded by the Secretary of State as a refugee within the definition in Article 1 of the Refugee Convention;

(b) Class B –a person –

(i) who has been granted by the Secretary of State exceptional leave to enter or remain in the United Kingdom outside the provisions of the immigration rules; and

(ii) whose leave is not subject to a condition requiring him to maintain and accommodate himself, and any person who is dependent on him, without recourse to public funds;

(c) Class C – a person who has current leave to enter or remain in the United Kingdom which is not subject to any limitation or condition and who is habitually resident in the Common Travel Area other than a person –

(i) who has been given leave to enter or remain in the United Kingdom upon an undertaking given by another person (his 'sponsor') in writing in pursuance of the immigration rules to be responsible for his maintenance and accommodation;

(ii) who has been resident in the United Kingdom for less than five years beginning on the date of entry or the date on which the undertaking was given in respect of him, whichever date is the later; and

(iii) whose sponsor or, where there is more than one sponsor, at least one of whose sponsors, is still alive;

(d) Class D – person who left the territory of Montserrat after 1st November 1995 because of the effect on that territory of a volcanic eruption;

(e) Class E – a person who is habitually resident in the Common Travel Area and who –

(i) is a national of a state which has ratified the European Convention on Social and Medical Assistance done at Paris on 11th December 1953 or a state which has ratified the European Social Charter done at Turin on 18th October 1961 and is lawfully present in the United Kingdom; or

(ii) before 3rd April 2000 was owed a duty by a housing authority under Part III of the Housing Act 1985 (housing the homeless) or Part VII of the 1996 Act (homelessness) which is extant, and who is a national of a state which is a signatory to the European Convention on Social and Medical Assistance done at Paris on 11th December 1953 or a state which is a signatory to the European Social Charter done at Turin on 18th October 1961;

(f) Class F – a person who is an asylum-seeker and who made a claim for asylum –

  (i) which is recorded by the Secretary of State as having been made on his arrival (other than on his re-entry) in the United Kingdom from a country outside the Common Travel Area; and

  (ii) which has not been recorded by the Secretary of State as having been either decided (other than on appeal) or abandoned;

(g) Class G – a person who is an asylum-seeker and –

  (i) who was in Great Britain when the Secretary of State made a declaration to the effect that the country of which that person is a national is subject to such a fundamental change in circumstances that he would not normally order the return of a person to that country;

  (ii) who made a claim for asylum which is recorded by the Secretary of State as having been made within a period of three months from the day on which that declaration was made; and

  (iii) whose claim for asylum has not been recorded by the Secretary of State as having been either decided (other than on appeal) or abandoned;

(h) Class H – person who is an asylum-seeker and –

  (i) who made a relevant claim for asylum on or before 4th February 1996; and

  (ii) who was, on 4th February 1996, entitled to benefit under regulation 7A of the Housing Benefit (General) Regulations 1987 (persons from abroad); and

(i) Class I – a person who is on an income-based jobseeker's allowance or in receipt of income support and is eligible for that benefit other than because –

  (i) he has limited leave to enter or remain in the United Kingdom which was given in accordance with the relevant immigration rules; and

  (ii) he is temporarily without funds because remittances to him from abroad have been disrupted.

(2) In paragraph (1)(h)(i) (Class H), a relevant claim for asylum is a claim for asylum which –

  (a) has not been recorded by the Secretary of State as having been either decided (other than on appeal) or abandoned; or

  (b) has been recorded as having been decided (other than on appeal) on or before 4th February 1996 and in respect of which an appeal is pending which–

    (i) was pending on 5th February 1996; or

    (ii) was made within the time limits specified in the rules of procedure made under section 22 of the 1971 Act (procedure).

(3) In paragraph (1)(i)(i) (Class I), 'relevant immigration rules' means the immigration rules relating to –

(a) there being or there needing to be no recourse to public funds; or

(b) there being no charge on public funds.

Descriptions of persons who are to be treated as persons from abroad ineligible for housing assistance

4 (1) The following are descriptions of persons, other than persons who are subject to immigration control, who are to be treated for the purposes of Part 7 of the 1996 Act (homelessness) as persons from abroad who are ineligible for housing assistance –

(a) subject to paragraphs (2) and (3), a person who is not habitually resident in the United Kingdom, the Channel Islands, the Isle of Man or the Republic of Ireland;

(b) a person whose right to reside in the United Kingdom, the Channel Islands, the Isle of Man or the Republic of Ireland is derived solely from Council Directive No 90/364/EEC or Council Directive No 90/365/EEC

(2) The following persons shall not, however, be treated as persons from abroad who are ineligible pursuant to paragraph (1)(a) –

(a) a person who is a worker for the purposes of Council Regulation (EEC) No 1612/68 or (EEC) No 1251/70;

(b) a person who is an accession state worker requiring registration who is treated as a worker for the purpose of the definition of 'qualified person' in regulation 5(1) of the Immigration (European Economic Area) Regulations 2000 pursuant to regulation 5 of the Accession (Immigration and Worker Registration) Regulations 2004;

(c) a person with a right to reside pursuant to the Immigration (European Economic Area) Regulations 2000, which is derived from Council Directive No 68/360/EEC, No 73/148/EEC or No 75/34/EEC;

(d) a person who left the territory of Montserrat after 1st November 1995 because of the effect on that territory of a volcanic eruption.

(3) A person shall not be treated as habitually resident in the United Kingdom, the Channel Islands, the Isle of Man or the Republic of Ireland for the purposes of paragraph (1)(a) if he does not have a right to reside in the United Kingdom, the Channel Islands, the Isle of Man or the Republic of Ireland.[42]

Prescribed period of notice where an authority proposes to cease securing accommodation under section 194

5 For the purposes of section 194(6) of the 1996 Act (notice of ceasing to exercise power to secure accommodation under section 194), the prescribed period is 28 days.

Period prescribed for the purpose of conditions for referral of an application

6 For the purposes of section 198(4)(b) of the 1996 Act (referral of case to another local housing authority), the prescribed period is the aggregate of –

(a) five years; and

---

42 Substituted by SI 2004 No 1235 reg 3 and in force (except in relation to an applicant whose application for an allocation of housing accommodation under Part 6, or assistance under Part 7, of the Housing Act 1996, was made before that date.

(b) the period beginning on the date of the previous application and ending on the date on which the applicant was first placed in pursuance of that application in accommodation in the district of the authority to whom the application is now made.

Revocation

7 The following Regulations are revoked –

(a) the Homelessness Regulations 1996, in so far as they extend to England;

(b) regulations 4 and 5 of the Allocation of Housing and Homelessness (Amendment) Regulations 1997, in so far as they extend to England;

(c) regulation 3 of the Allocation of Housing and Homelessness (Amendment) (No 2) Regulations 1997, in so far as they extend to England; and

(d) regulations 4 and 5 of the Allocation of Housing and Homelessness (Amendment) (England) Regulations 1999.

ALLOCATION OF HOUSING (ENGLAND) REGULATIONS 2002 SI No 3264

Citation, commencement and application

1 (1) These Regulations may be cited as the Allocation of Housing (England) Regulations 2002 and shall come into force on 31st January 2003.

(2) These Regulations apply in England only.

Interpretation

2   In these Regulations–

'the Act' means the Housing Act 1996;

'the Common Travel Area' means the United Kingdom, the Channel Islands, the Isle of Man and the Republic of Ireland collectively; and

'the immigration rules' means the rules laid down as mentioned in section 3(2) of the Immigration Act 1971 (general provisions for regulation and control).

Cases where the provisions of Part 6 of the Act do not apply

3 (1) The provisions of Part 6 of the Act about the allocation of housing accommodation do not apply in the following cases.

(2) They do not apply where a local housing authority secures the provision of suitable alternative accommodation under section 39 of the Land Compensation Act 1973 (duty to rehouse residential occupiers).

(3) They do not apply in relation to the grant of a secure tenancy under sections 554 and 555 of the Housing Act 1985 (grant of tenancy to former owner-occupier or statutory tenant of defective dwelling-house).

Classes prescribed under section 160A(3) who are eligible persons

4   The following are classes of persons subject to immigration control prescribed for the purposes of section 160A(3) of the Act (persons prescribed as eligible for an allocation of housing accommodation by a local housing authority)–

(a) Class A – a person recorded by the Secretary of State as a refugee within the definition in Article 1 of the Convention relating to the Status of Refugees done at Geneva on 28th July 1951 as extended by Article 1(2) of the Protocol relating to the Status of Refugees done at New York on 31st January 1967;

(b) Class B – a person–

(i)   who has been granted by the Secretary of State exceptional leave to enter or remain in the United Kingdom outside the provisions of the immigration rules; and

(ii) whose leave is not subject to a condition requiring him to maintain and accommodate himself, and any person who is dependent on him, without recourse to public funds;

(c) Class C – a person who has current leave to enter or remain in the United Kingdom which is not subject to any limitation or condition and who is habitually resident in the Common Travel Area other than a person–

(i)   who has been given leave to enter or remain in the United Kingdom upon an undertaking given by another person (his 'sponsor') in writing in pursuance of the immigration rules to be responsible for his maintenance and accommodation;

    (ii) who has been resident in the United Kingdom for less than five years beginning on the date of entry or the date on which the undertaking was given in respect of him, whichever date is the later; and

    (iii) whose sponsor or, where there is more than one sponsor, at least one of whose sponsors, is still alive;

  (d) Class D – a person who is habitually resident in the Common Travel Area and who–

    (i) is a national of a state which has ratified the European Convention on Social and Medical Assistance done at Paris on 11th December 1953 or a state which has ratified the European Social Charter done at Turin on 18th October 1961 and is lawfully present in the United Kingdom; or

    (ii) before 3rd April 2000 was owed a duty by a housing authority under Part 3 of the Housing Act 1985 (housing the homeless) or Part 7 of the Act (homelessness) which is extant, and who is a national of a state which is a signatory to the European Convention on Social and Medical Assistance done at Paris on 11th December 1953 or a state which is a signatory to the European Social Charter done at Turin on 18th October 1961.

Classes of persons from abroad who are ineligible for a housing allocation

5 (1) The following are classes of persons from abroad (not being persons subject to immigration control) prescribed for the purposes of section 160A(5) of the Act (persons prescribed as ineligible for an allocation of housing accommodation) –

  (a) Class E – subject to paragraphs (2) and (3), a person who is not habitually resident in the United Kingdom, the Channel Islands, the Isle of Man or the Republic of Ireland;

  (b) Class F – a person whose right to reside in the United Kingdom, the Channel Islands, the Isle of Man or the Republic of Ireland is derived solely from Council Directive No 90/364/EEC or Council Directive No 90/365/EEC .

(2) The following persons shall not, however, be ineligible pursuant to paragraph (1)(a) –

  (a) a person who is a worker for the purposes of Council Regulation (EEC) No 1612/68 or (EEC) No 1251/70;

  (b) a person who is an accession state worker requiring registration who is treated as a worker for the purpose of the definition of 'qualified person' in regulation 5(1) of the Immigration (European Economic Area) Regulations 2000 pursuant to regulation 5 of the Accession (Immigration and Worker Registration) Regulations 2004;

  (c) a person with a right to reside pursuant to the Immigration (European Economic Area) Regulations 2000, which is derived from Council Directive No 68/360/EEC, No 73/148/EEC or No 75/34/EEC;

  (d) a person who left the territory of Montserrat after 1st November 1995 because of the effect on that territory of a volcanic eruption.

(3) A person shall not be treated as habitually resident in the United Kingdom, the Channel Islands, the Isle of Man or the Republic of Ireland for the purposes of paragraph (1) (a) if he does not have a right to reside in the United Kingdom, the Channel Islands, the Isle of Man or the Republic of Ireland.[43]

Revocation

6   The Allocation of Housing (England) Regulations 2000 are revoked.

---

43 Substituted by SI 2004 No 1235 reg 2 and in force (except in relation to an applicant whose application for an allocation of housing accommodation or assistance under the Housing Act 1996 Pts 6, 7, respectively, was made before that date.

Community care

NATIONAL ASSISTANCE ACT 1948 ss21, 24, 29

Duty of local authorities to provide accommodation

21 (1) Subject to and in accordance with the provisions of this Part of this Act, a local authority may with the approval of the Secretary of State, and to such extent as he may direct shall, make arrangements for providing:

    (a) residential accommodation for persons aged eighteen or over who by reason of age, illness, disability or any other circumstances are in need of care and attention which is not otherwise available to them and

    (aa) residential accommodation for expectant and nursing mothers who are in need of care and attention which is not otherwise available to them.

(1A) A person to whom section 115 of the Immigration and Asylum Act 1999 (exclusion from benefits) applies may not be provided with residential accommodation under subsection (1)(a) if his need for care and attention has arisen solely –

    (a) because he is destitute; or

    (b) because of the physical effects, or anticipated physical effects, of his being destitute.

(1B) Subsections (3) and (5) to (8) of section 95 of the Immigration and Asylum Act 1999, and paragraph 2 of Schedule 8 to that Act, apply for the purposes of subsection (1a) as they apply for the purposes of that section, but for the references in subsections (5) and (7) of that section and in that paragraph to the Secretary of State substitute references to a local authority.

(2) In making any such arrangements a local authority shall have regard to the welfare of all persons for whom accommodation is provided, and in particular to the need for providing accommodation of different descriptions suited to different descriptions of such persons as are mentioned in the last foregoing subsection.

(2A) In determining for the purposes of paragraph (a) or (aa) of subsection (1) of this section whether care and attention are otherwise available to a person, a local authority shall disregard so much of the person's capital as does not exceed the capital limit for the purposes of section 22 of this Act.

(2B) For the purposes of subsection (2A) of this section –

    (a) a person's capital shall be calculated in accordance with assessment regulations in the same way as if he were a person for whom accommodation is proposed to be provided as mentioned in subsection (3) of section 22 of this Act and whose ability to pay for the accommodation falls to be assessed for the purposes of that subsection; and

    (b) 'the capital limit for the purposes of section 22 of this Act' means the amount for the time being prescribed in assessment regulations as the amount which a resident's capital (calculated in accordance with such regulations) must not exceed if he is to be assessed as unable to pay for his accommodation at the standard rate;

and in this subsection 'assessment regulations' means regulations made for the purposes of section 22(5) of this Act.

(3) [*Repealed*]

(4) Subject to section 26 of this Act, accommodation provided by a local authority in the exercise of their functions under this section shall be provided in premises managed by the authority or, to such extent as may be determined in accordance with the arrangements under this section, in such premises managed by another local authority as may be agreed between the two authorities and on such terms as to the reimbursement of expenditure incurred by the said other authority, as may be so agreed.

(5) References in this Act to accommodation provided under this Part thereof shall be construed as references to accommodation provided in accordance with this and the five next following sections, and as including references to board and other services, amenities and requisites provided in connection with the accommodation except where in the opinion of the authority managing the premises their provision is unnecessary.

(6) References in this Act to a local authority providing accommodation shall be construed, in any case where a local authority agree with another local authority for the provision of accommodation in premises managed by the said other authority, as references to the first-mentioned local authority.

(7) Without prejudice to the generality of the foregoing provisions of this section, a local authority may –

    (a) provide, in such cases as they may consider appropriate, for the conveyance of persons to and from premises in which accommodation is provided for them under this Part of the Act;

    (b) make arrangements for the provision on the premises in which accommodation is being provided of such other services as appear to the authority to be required.

(8) Nothing in this section shall authorise or require a local authority to make any provision authorised or required to be made (whether by that or by any other authority) by or under any enactment not contained in this Part of this Act, or authorised or required to be provided under the National Health Service Act 1977.

Authority liable for provision of accommodation

24 (1) The local authority empowered under this Part of this Act to provide residential accommodation for any person shall subject to the following provisions of this Part of this Act be the authority in whose area the person is ordinarily resident.

(2) [*Repealed*]

(3) Where a person in the area of a local authority –

    (a) is a person with no settled residence, or

    (b) not being ordinarily resident in the area of the local authority, is in urgent need of residential accommodation under this Part of this Act,

the authority shall have the like power to provide residential accommodation for him as if he were ordinarily resident in their area.

(4) Subject to and in accordance with the arrangements under section twenty-one of this Act, a local authority shall have power, as respects a person ordinarily resident in the area of another local authority, with the consent of that other

local authority to provide residential accommodation for him in any case where the authority would have a duty to provide such accommodation if he were ordinarily resident in their area.

(5) Where a person is provided with residential accommodation under this Part of this Act, he shall be deemed for the purposes of this Act to continue to be ordinarily resident in the area in which he was ordinarily resident immediately before the residential accommodation was provided for him.

(6) For the purposes of the provision of residential accommodation under this Part of this Act, a patient in a hospital vested in the Secretary of State or an NHS trust shall be deemed to be ordinarily resident in the area, if any, in which he was ordinarily resident immediately before he was admitted as a patient to the hospital, whether or not he in fact continues to be ordinarily resident in that area.

(7) In subsection (6) above 'NHS trust' means a National Health Service trust established under Part I of the National Health Service and Community Care Act 1990 or under the National Health Service (Scotland) Act 1978.

Welfare arrangements for blind, deaf, dumb and crippled persons, etc

29 (1) A local authority may, with the approval of the Secretary of State, and to such extent as he may direct in relation to persons ordinarily resident in the area of the local authority shall make arrangements for promoting the welfare of persons to whom this section applies, that is to say persons aged eighteen or over who are blind, deaf or dumb or who suffer from mental disorder of any description, and other persons aged eighteen or over who are substantially and permanently handicapped by illness, injury, or congenital deformity or such other disabilities as may be prescribed by the Minister.

(2) [*Repealed*]

(3) [*Repealed*]

(4) Without prejudice to the generality of the provisions of subsection (1) of this section, arrangements may be made thereunder –

(a) for informing persons to whom arrangements under that subsection relate of the services available for them thereunder;

(b) for giving such persons instruction in their own homes or elsewhere in methods of overcoming the effects of their disabilities;

(c) for providing workshops where such persons may be engaged (whether under a contract of service or otherwise) in suitable work, and hostels where persons engaged in the workshops, and other persons to whom arrangements under subsection (1) of this section relate and for whom work or training is being provided in pursuance of the Disabled Persons (Employment) Act 1944 or the Employment and Training Act 1973 may live;

(d) for providing persons to whom arrangements under subsection (1) of this section relate with suitable work (whether under a contract of service or otherwise) in their own homes or elsewhere;

(e) for helping such persons in disposing of the produce of their work;

(f) for providing such persons with recreational facilities in their own homes or elsewhere;

(g) for compiling and maintaining classified registers of the persons to whom arrangements under subsection (1) of this section relate.

(4A) Where accommodation in a hostel is provided under paragraph (c) of subsection (4) of this section –

    (a) if the hostel is managed by a local authority, section 22 of this Act shall apply as it applies where accommodation is provided under section 21;

    (b) if the accommodation is provided in a hostel managed by a person other than a local authority under arrangements made with that person, subsections (2) to (4A) of section 26 of this Act shall apply as they apply where accommodation is provided under arrangements made by virtue of that section; and

    (c) sections 32 and 43 of this Act shall apply as they apply where accommodation is provided under sections 21 to 26;

and in this subsection references to 'accommodation' include references to board and other services, amenities and requisites provided in connection with the accommodation, except where in the opinion of the authority managing the premises or, in the case mentioned in paragraph (b) above, the authority making the arrangements their provision is unnecessary.

(5) [*Repealed*]

(6) Nothing in the foregoing provisions of this section shall authorise or require –

    (a) the payment of money to persons to whom this section applies, other than persons for whom work is provided under arrangements made by virtue of paragraph (c) or paragraph (d) of subsection (4) of this section or who are engaged in work which they are enabled to perform in consequence of anything done in pursuance of arrangements made under this section; or

    (b) the provision of any accommodation or services required to be provided under the National Health Service Act 1977.

(7) A person engaged in work in a workshop provided under paragraph (c) of subsection (4) of this section, or a person in receipt of a superannuation allowance granted on his retirement from engagement in any such workshop, shall be deemed for the purposes of this Act to continue to be ordinarily resident in the area in which he was ordinarily resident immediately before he was accepted for work in that workshop; and for the purposes of this subsection a course of training in such workshop shall be deemed to be work in that workshop.

HEALTH SERVICES AND PUBLIC HEALTH ACT 1968 s45

Promotion, by local authorities, of the welfare of old people

45 (1) A local authority may with the approval of the Secretary of State, and to such extent as he may direct shall, make arrangements for promoting the welfare of old people.

(2) [*Repealed*]

(3) A local authority may employ as their agent for the purposes of this section any voluntary organisation or any person carrying on, professionally or by way of trade or business, activities which consist of or include the provision of services for old people, being an organisation or person appearing to the authority to be capable of promoting the welfare of old people.

(4) No arrangements under this section shall provide –

(a) for the payment of money to old people except in so far as the arrangements may provide for the remuneration of old people engaged in suitable work in accordance with the arrangements;

(b) for making available any accommodation or services required to be provided under the National Health Service Act 1977.

(4A) No arrangements under this section may be given effect to in relation to a person to whom section 115 of the Immigration and Asylum Act 1999 (exclusion from benefits) applies solely –

(a) because he is destitute; or

(b) because of the physical effects, or anticipated physical effects, of his being destitute.

[(4B) Subsections (3) and (5) to (8) of section 95 of the Immigration and Asylum Act 1999, and paragraph 2 of Schedule 8 to that Act, apply for the purposes of subsection (4A) as they apply for the purposes of that section, but for the references in subsections (5) and (7) of that section and in that paragraph to the Secretary of State substitute references to a local authority.]

(4B) *Section 95(2) to (7) of that Act shall apply for the purposes of subsection (4A) above; and for that purpose a reference to the Secretary of State in section 95(4) or (5) shall be treated as a reference to a local authority.*[36]

(5) The National Assistance Act 1948 shall have effect as if the following references included a reference to this section, that is to say, –

(a) the reference in section 32, to section 29 of that Act;

(b) the references in sections 35, 45, 52, to Part III of that Act;

(c) the references in sections 56 and 59, to that Act.

(6) [*Repealed*]

(7) [*Repealed*]

(8) [*Repealed*]

(9) The Health Visiting and Social Work (Training) Act 1962 shall have effect in relation to functions of local authorities under this section as it does in relation to functions of local authorities under Part III of the National Assistance Act 1948.

---

36 Subsection 4B, in square brackets, to be substituted by material in italics, from a date to be appointed, by the Nationality, Immigration and Asylum Act 2002 s162(1).

(10) [*Repealed*]

(11) In this section 'local authority' (except where used in the expression 'public or local authority') means the council of a county, other than a metropolitan county, or of a county borough, metropolitan district or London borough, or the Common Council of the City of London, and 'voluntary organisation' means a body the activities of which are carried on otherwise than for profit bur does not include any public or local authority.

---

37 Section 2B, in square brackets, is substituted by the words in italics, from a date to be appointed, by the Nationality, Immigration and Asylum Act 2002 s162(1).

LOCAL AUTHORITY SOCIAL SERVICES ACT 1970 ss7, 7A

Local authorities to exercise social services functions under guidance of Secretary of State

7 (1) Local authorities shall, in the exercise of their social services functions, including the exercise of any discretion conferred by any relevant enactment, act under the general guidance of the Secretary of State.

Directions by the Secretary of State as to exercise of social services functions

7A(1) Without prejudice to section 7 of this Act, every local authority shall exercise their social services functions in accordance with such directions as may be given to them under this section by the Secretary of State.

(2) Directions under this section –

(a) shall be given in writing; and

(b) may be given to a particular authority, or to authorities of a particular class, or to authorities generally.

CHRONICALLY SICK AND DISABLED PERSONS ACT 1970 s2

Provision of welfare services

2 (1) Where a local authority having functions under s29 National Assistance Act 1948 are satisfied in the case of any person to whom that section applies who is ordinarily resident in their area that it is necessary in order to meet the needs of that person for that authority to make arrangements for all or any of the following matters, namely –

(a) the provision of practical assistance for that person in his home;

(b) the provision for that person of, or assistance to that person in obtaining, wireless, television, library or similar recreational facilities;

(c) the provision for that person of lectures, games, outings or other recreational facilities outside his home or assistance to that person in taking advantage of educational facilities available to him;

(d) the provision for that person of facilities for, or assistance in, travelling to and from his home for the purpose of participating in any services provided under arrangements made by the authority under the said section 29 or, with the approval of the authority, in any services provided otherwise than as aforesaid which are similar to services which could be provided under such arrangements;

(e) the provision of assistance for that person in arranging for the carrying out of any works of adaptation in his home or the provision of any additional facilities designed to secure his greater safety, comfort or convenience;

(f) facilitating the taking of holidays by that person, whether at holiday homes or otherwise and whether provided under arrangements made by the authority or otherwise;

(g) the provision of meals for that person whether in his home or elsewhere;

(h) the provision for that person of, or assistance to that person in obtaining, a telephone and any special equipment necessary to enable him to use a telephone,

then, subject to the provisions of section 7(1) of the Local Authority Social Services Act 1970 (which requires local authorities in the exercise of certain functions, including functions under the said section 29, to act under the general guidance of the Secretary of State) and to the provisions of section 7A of that Act (which requires local authorities to exercise their social services functions in accordance with directions given by the Secretary of State) it shall be the duty of that Authority to make those arrangements in exercise of their functions under the said section 29.

NATIONAL HEALTH SERVICE ACT 1977 s21, Sch 8 paras 1–4

CO-OPERATION AND ASSISTANCE
Local social services authorities

21 (1) Subject to paragraphs (d) and (e) of section 3(1) above, the services described in Schedule 8 to this Act in relation to –

   (a) care of mothers,

   (b) prevention, care and after care,

   (c) home help and laundry facilities,

are functions exercisable by local social services authorities, and that Schedule has effect accordingly.

(2) A local social services authority who provide premises, furniture or equipment for any of the purposes of this Act may permit the use of the premises, furniture or equipment –

   (a) by any other social services authority, or

   (b) by any of the bodies constituted under this Act, or

   (c) by a local education authority.

This permission may be on such terms (including terms with respect to the services of any staff employed by the authority giving permission) as may be agreed.

(3) A local social services authority may provide (or improve or furnish) residential accommodation –

   (a) for officers employed by them for the purposes of any of their functions as a local social services authority, or

   (b) for officers employed by a voluntary organisation for the purposes of any services provided under this section and Schedule 8.

SCHEDULE 8: LOCAL SERVICES AUTHORITIES
Care of mothers and young children

1 (1) A local social services authority may, with the Secretary of State's approval, and to such extent as he may direct shall, make arrangements for the care of expectant and nursing mothers (other than for the provision of residential accommodation for them).

Prevention, care and after-care

2 (1) A local social services authority may, with the Secretary of State's approval, and to such extent as he may direct shall, make arrangements for the purpose of the prevention of illness and for the care of persons suffering from illness and for the after-care of persons who have been suffering and in particular for –

   (a) [*Repealed*]

   (b) the provision for persons whose care is undertaken with a view to preventing them from becoming ill, persons suffering from illness and persons who have been so suffering, of centres or other facilities for training them or keeping them suitably occupied and the equipment and maintenance of such centres;

(c) the provision, for the benefit of such persons as are mentioned in paragraph (b) above, of ancillary or supplemental services; and

(d) for the exercise of the functions of the Authority in respect of persons suffering from mental disorder who are received into the guardianship under Part II or III of the Mental Health Act 1983 (whether the guardianship of the local social services authority or of other persons).

Such an authority shall neither have the power nor be subject to a duty to make under this paragraph arrangements to provide facilities for any of the purposes mentioned in section 15(1) of the Disabled Persons (Employment) Act 1944.

(2) No arrangements under this paragraph shall provide for the payment of money to persons for whose benefit they are made except –

(a) in so far as they may provide for the remuneration of such persons engaged in suitable work in accordance with the arrangements, of such amounts as the local social services authority think fit in respect of their occasional personal expenses where it appears to that authority that no such payment would otherwise be made.

(2A) No arrangements under this paragraph may be given effect to in relation to a person to whom section 115 of the Immigration and Asylum Act 1999 (exclusion from benefits) applies solely –

(a) because he is destitute; or

(b) because of the physical effects, or anticipated physical effects, of his being destitute.

[(2B) Subsections (3) and (5) to (8) of section 95 of the Immigration and Asylum Act 1999, and paragraph 2 of Schedule 8 to that Act, apply for the purposes of subsection (2A) as they apply for the purposes of that section, but for the references in subsections (5) and (7) of that section and in that paragraph to the Secretary of State substitute references to a local social services authority.]

(2B) Section 95(2) to (7) of that Act shall apply for the purposes of sub-paragraph (2A) above; and for that purpose a reference to the Secretary of State in section 5(4) or (5) shall be treated as a references to a local social services authority.[37]

(3) The Secretary of State may make regulations as to the conduct of premises in which, in pursuance of arrangements made under this paragraph, are provided for persons whose care is undertaken with a view to preventing them from becoming sufferers from mental disorder within the meaning of that Act of 1983 or who are, or have been, so suffering, facilities for training them or keeping them suitably occupied.

(4A) This paragraph does not apply in relation to persons under the age of 18.

(4AA) No authority is authorised or may be required under this paragraph to provide residential accommodation for any person.

Home help and laundry facilities

3 (1) It is the duty of every local social services authority to provide on such a scale as is adequate for the needs of their area, or to arrange for the provision on such a scale as is so adequate, of home help for households where such help is required owing to the presence of a person who is suffering from illness, lying-in, an expectant mother, aged, handicapped as a result of having suffered from illness or by congenital deformity,and every such authority

has power to provide or arrange for the provision of laundry facilities for households for which home help is being, or can be, provided under this sub-paragraph.

Research

4   Without prejudice to any powers conferred on them by any other Act, a local social services authority may conduct or assist other persons in conducting research into matters relating to the functions of local social services authorities under this schedule.

MENTAL HEALTH ACT 1983 s117

After-care

117 (1) This section applies to persons who are detained under section 3 above, or admitted to a hospital in pursuance of a hospital order made under section 37 above, or transferred to a hospital in pursuance of a hospital direction made under section 45A above or a transfer direction made under section 47 or 48 above, and then cease to be detained and (whether or not immediately after so ceasing) leave hospital.

(2) It shall be the duty of the Primary Care Trust or Health Authority and of the local social services authority to provide, in co-operation with relevant voluntary agencies, after-care services for any person to whom this section applies until such time as the Primary Care Trust or Health Authority and the local social services authority are satisfied that the person concerned is no longer in need of such services but they shall not be so satisfied in the case of a patient who is subject to after-care under supervision at any time while he so remains subject.

(2A) It shall be the duty of the Primary Care Trust or Health Authority to secure that at all times while a patient is subject to after-care under supervision –

(a) a person who is a registered medical practitioner approved for the purposes of section 12 above by the Secretary of State as having special experience in the diagnosis or treatment of mental disorder is in charge of the medical treatment provided for the patient as part of the after-care services provided for him under this section; and

(b) a person professionally concerned with any of the after-care services so provided is supervising him with a view to securing that he receives the after-care services so provided.

(2B) Section 32 above shall apply for the purposes of this section as it applies for the purposes of Part II of this Act.

(3) In this section 'the Primary Care Trust or Health Authority' means the Primary Care Trust or Health Authority and 'the local social services authority' means the local social services authority for the area in which the person concerned is resident or to which he is sent on discharge by the hospital in which he was detained.

CHILDREN ACT 1989 ss17, 20, 22–24B, Sch 2 paras 19A–19C

PART III: LOCAL AUTHORITY SUPPORT FOR CHILDREN AND FAMILIES
Provision of services for children in need, their families and others

17 (1) It shall be the general duty of every local authority (in addition to the other duties imposed upon them by this Part) –

    (a) to safeguard and promote the welfare of children within their area who are in need; and

    (b) so far as is consistent with that duty to promote the upbringing of such children by their families,

by providing a range and level of services appropriate to those children's needs.

(2) For the purpose principally of facilitating the discharge of their general duty under this section, every local authority shall have the specific duties and powers set out in Part I of Schedule 2.

(3) Any service provided by an authority in the exercise of functions conferred on them by this section may be provided for the family of a particular child in need or for any member of his family, if it is provided with a view to safeguarding or promoting the child's welfare.

(4) The Secretary of State may by order amend any provision of Part I of Schedule 2 or add any further duty or power to those for the tune being mentioned there.

(5) Every local authority –

    (a) shall facilitate the provision by others (including in particular voluntary organisations) of services which the authority have power to provide by virtue of this section, or section 18, 20, 23, 23B to 23D, 24A or 24B; and

    (b) may make such arrangements as they see fit for any person to act on their behalf in the provision of any such service.

(6) The services provided by a local authority in the exercise of functions conferred on them by this section may include providing accommodation and giving assistance in kind or, in exceptional circumstances, in cash.

(7) Assistance may be unconditional or subject to conditions as to the repayment of the assistance or of its value (in whole or in part).

(8) Before giving any assistance or imposing any conditions, a local authority shall have regard to the means of the child concerned and of each of his parents.

(9) No person shall be liable to make any repayment of assistance or of its value at any time when he is in receipt of income support under Part VII of the Social Security Contributions and Benefits Act 1992, of any element of child tax credit other than the family element, of working tax credit or of an income-based jobseeker's allowance.

(10) For the purposes of this Part a child shall be taken to be in need if –

    (a) he is unlikely to achieve or maintain, or to have the opportunity of achieving or maintaining, a reasonable standard of health or development without the provision for him of services by a local authority under this Part;

(b) his health or development is likely to be significantly impaired, or further impaired, without the provision for him of such services; or

(c) he is disabled,

and 'family', in relation to such a child, includes any person who has parental responsibility for the child and any other person with whom he has been living.

(11) For the purposes of this Part, a child is disabled if he is blind, deaf or dumb or suffers from mental disorder of any kind or is substantially and permanently handicapped by illness, injury or congenital deformity or such other disability as may be prescribed; and in this Part –

'development' means physical, intellectual, emotional, social or behavioural development; and

'health' means physical or mental health.

(12) The Treasury may by regulations prescribe circumstances in which a person is to be treated for the purposes of this Part (or for such of those purposes as are prescribed) as in receipt of any element of child tax credit other than the family element or of working tax credit.

PROVISION OF ACCOMMODATION FOR CHILDREN
Provision of accommodation for children: general

20 (1) Every local authority shall provide accommodation for any child in need within their area who appears to them to require accommodation as a result of –

(a) there being no person who has parental responsibility for him;

(b) his being lost or having been abandoned; or

(c) the person who has been caring for him being prevented (whether or not permanently, and for whatever reason) from providing him with suitable accommodation or care.

(2) Where a local authority provide accommodation under subsection (1) for a child who is ordinarily resident in the area of another local authority, that other local authority may take over the provision of accommodation for the child within –

(a) three months of being notified in writing that the child is being provided with accommodation; or

(b) such other longer period as may be prescribed.

(3) Every local authority shall provide accommodation for any child in need within their area who has reached the age of sixteen and whose welfare the authority consider is likely to be seriously prejudiced if they do not provide him with accommodation.

(4) A local authority may provide accommodation for any child within their area (even though a person who has parental responsibility for him is able to provide him with accommodation) if they consider that to do so would safeguard or promote the child's welfare.

(5) A local authority may provide accommodation for any person who has reached the age of sixteen but is under twenty-one in any community home which takes children who have reached the age of sixteen if they consider that to do so would safeguard or promote his welfare.

(6) Before providing accommodation under this section, a local authority shall, so far as is reasonably practicable and consistent with the child's welfare –
   (a) ascertain the child's wishes regarding the provision of accommodation; and
   (b) give due consideration (having regard to his age and understanding) to such wishes of the child as they have been able to ascertain.

(7) A local authority may not provide accommodation under this section for any child if any person who –
   (a) has parental responsibility for him; and
   (b) is willing and able to –
      (i) provide accommodation for him; or
      (ii) arrange for accommodation to be provided for him,
   objects.

(8) Any person who has parental responsibility for a child may at any time remove the child from accommodation provided by or on behalf of the local authority under this section.

(9) Subsections (7) and (8) do not apply while any person –
   (a) in whose favour a residence order is in force with respect to the child; [or]³⁸
   *(aa) who is a special guardian of the child; or*³⁹
   (b) who has care of the child by virtue of an order made in the exercise of the High Court's inherent jurisdiction with respect to children,
   agrees to the child being looked after in accommodation provided by or on behalf of the local authority.

(10) Where there is more than one such person as is mentioned in subsection (9), all of them must agree.

(11) Subsections (7) and (8) do not apply where a child who has reached the age of sixteen agrees to being provided with accommodation under this section.

DUTIES OF LOCAL AUTHORITIES IN RELATION TO CHILDREN LOOKED AFTER BY THEM
General duty of local authority in relation to children looked after by them

22 (1) In this Act, any reference to a child who is looked after by a local authority is a reference to a child who is –
   (a) in their care; or
   (b) provided with accommodation by the authority in the exercise of any functions (in particular those under this Act) which are social services functions within the meaning of the Local Authority Social Services Act 1970, apart from functions under sections 17, 23B and 24B.

(2) In subsection (1) 'accommodation' means accommodation which is provided for a continuous period of more than 24 hours.

(3) It shall be the duty of a local authority looking after any child –

---

38 Word in square brackets to be repealed, from a date to be appointed. See below.
39 Paragraph (aa) to be added, from a date to be appointed, by the Adoption and Children Act 2002 s139(1), Sch 3 paras 54, 59.

   (a) to safeguard and promote his welfare; and

   (b) to make such use of services available for children cared for by their own parents as appears to the authority reasonable in his case.

(4) Before making any decision with respect to a child whom they are looking after, or proposing to look after, a local authority shall, so far as is reasonably practicable, ascertain the wishes and feelings of –

   (a) the child;

   (b) his parents;

   (c) any person who is not a parent of his but who has parental responsibility for him; and

   (d) any other person whose wishes and feelings the authority consider to be relevant,

regarding the matter to be decided.

(5) In making any such decision a local authority shall give due consideration –

   (a) having regard to his age and understanding, to such wishes and feelings of the child as they have been able to ascertain;

   (b) to such wishes and feelings of any person mentioned in subsection (4)(b) to (d) as they have been able to ascertain; and

   (c) to the child's religious persuasion, racial origin and cultural and linguistic background.

(6) If it appears to a local authority that it is necessary, for the purpose of protecting members of the public from serious injury, to exercise their powers with respect to a child whom they are looking after in a manner which may not be consistent with their duties under this section, they may do so.

(7) If the Secretary of State considers it necessary, for the purpose of protecting members of the public from serious injury, to give directions to a local authority with respect to the exercise of their powers with respect to a child whom they are looking after, he may give such directions to the authority.

(8) Where any such directions are given to an authority they shall comply with them even though doing so is inconsistent with their duties under this section.

Provision of accommodation and maintenance by local authority for children whom they are looking after

23 (1) It shall be the duty of any local authority looking after a child –

   (a) when he is in their care, to provide accommodation for him; and

   (b) to maintain him in other respects apart from providing accommodation for him.

(2) A local authority shall provide accommodation and maintenance for any child whom they are looking after by –

   (a) placing him (subject to subsection (5) and any regulations made by the Secretary of State) with –

      (i)   a family;

      (ii) a relative of his; or

      (iii) any other suitable person,

on such terms as to payment by the authority and otherwise as the authority may determine;

(aa) maintaining him in an appropriate children's home; or

(f) making such other arrangements as –

    (i) seem appropriate to them; and

    (ii) comply with any regulations made by the Secretary of State.

(2A) Where under subsection (2)(aa) a local authority maintains a child in a home provided, equipped and maintained by the Secretary of State under section 82(5), it shall do so on such terms as the Secretary of State may from time to time determine.

(3) Any person with whom a child has been placed under subsection (2)(a) is referred to in this Act as a local authority foster parent unless he falls within subsection (4).

(4) A person falls within this subsection if he is –

    (a) a parent of the child;

    (b) a person who is not a parent of the child but who has parental responsibility for him; or

    (c) where the child is in care and there was a residence order in force with respect to him immediately before the care order was made, a person in whose favour the residence order was made.

(5) Where a child is in the care of a local authority, the authority may only allow him to live with a person who falls within subsection (4) in accordance with regulations made by the Secretary of State.

(5A) For the purposes of subsection (5) a child shall be regarded as living with a person if he stays with that person for a continuous period of more than 24 hours.

(6) Subject to any regulations made by the Secretary of State for the purposes of this subsection, any local authority looking after a child shall make arrangements to enable him to live with –

    (a) a person falling within subsection (4); or

    (b) a relative, friend or other person connected with him,

unless that would not be reasonably practicable or consistent with his welfare.

(7) Where a local authority provide accommodation for a child whom they are looking after, they shall, subject to the provisions of this Part and so far as is reasonably practicable and consistent with his welfare, secure that –

    (a) the accommodation is near his home; and

    (b) where the authority are also providing accommodation for a sibling of his, they are accommodated together.

(8) Where a local authority provide accommodation for a child whom they are looking after and who is disabled, they shall, so far as is reasonably practicable, secure that the accommodation is not unsuitable to his particular needs.

(9) Part II of Schedule 2 shall have effect for the purposes of making further provision as to children looked after by local authorities and in particular as to the regulations that may be made under subsections (2)(a) and (f) and (5).

(10) In this Act –

'appropriate children's home' means a children's home in respect of which a person is registered under Part II of the Care Standards Act 2000; and

'children's home' has the same meaning as in that Act.

The responsible authority and relevant children

23A(1) The responsible local authority shall have the functions set out in section 23B in respect of a relevant child.

(2) In subsection (1) 'relevant child' means (subject to subsection (3)) a child who –

(a) is not being looked after by any local authority;

(b) was, before last ceasing to be looked after, an eligible child for the purposes of paragraph 19B of Schedule 2; and

(c) is aged sixteen or seventeen.

(3) The Secretary of State may prescribe –

(a) additional categories of relevant children; and

(b) categories of children who are not to be relevant children despite falling within subsection (2).

(4) In subsection (1) the 'responsible local authority' is the one which last looked after the child.

(5) If under subsection (3)(a) the Secretary of State prescribes a category of relevant children which includes children who do not fall within subsection (2)(b) (for example, because they were being looked after by a local authority in Scotland), he may in the regulations also provide for which local authority is to be the responsible local authority for those children.

Additional functions of the responsible authority in respect of relevant children

23B(1) It is the duty of each local authority to take reasonable steps to keep in touch with a relevant child for whom they are the responsible authority, whether he is within their area or not.

(2) It is the duty of each local authority to appoint a personal adviser for each relevant child (if they have not already done so under paragraph 19C of Schedule 2).

(3) It is the duty of each local authority, in relation to any relevant child who does not already have a pathway plan prepared for the purposes of paragraph 19B of Schedule 2 –

(a) to carry out an assessment of his needs with a view to determining what advice, assistance and support it would be appropriate for them to provide him under this Part; and

(b) to prepare a pathway plan for him.

(4) The local authority may carry out such an assessment at the same time as any assessment of his needs is made under any enactment referred to in sub-paragraphs (a) to (c) of paragraph 3 of Schedule 2, or under any other enactment.

(5) The Secretary of State may by regulations make provision as to assessments for the purposes of subsection (3).

(6) The regulations may in particular make provision about –

(a) who is to be consulted in relation to an assessment;

(b) the way in which an assessment is to be carried out, by whom and when;

(c) the recording of the results of an assessment;

(d) the considerations to which the local authority are to have regard in carrying out an assessment.

(7) The authority shall keep the pathway plan under regular review.

(8) The responsible local authority shall safeguard and promote the child's welfare and, unless they are satisfied that his welfare does not require it, support him by –
- (a) maintaining him;
- (b) providing him with or maintaining him in suitable accommodation; and
- (c) providing support of such other descriptions as may be prescribed.

(9) Support under subsection (8) may be in cash.

(10) The Secretary of State may by regulations make provision about the meaning of 'suitable accommodation' and in particular about the suitability of landlords or other providers of accommodation.

(11) If the local authority have lost touch with a relevant child, despite taking reasonable steps to keep in touch, they must without delay –
- (a) consider how to re-establish contact; and
- (b) take reasonable steps to do so,

and while the child is still a relevant child must continue to take such steps until they succeed.

(12) Subsections (7) to (9) of section 17 apply in relation to support given under this section as they apply in relation to assistance given under that section.

(13) Subsections (4) and (5) of section 22 apply in relation to any decision by a local authority for the purposes of this section as they apply in relation to the decisions referred to in that section.

Continuing functions in respect of former relevant children

23C(1) Each local authority shall have the duties provided for in this section towards –
- (a) a person who has been a relevant child for the purposes of section 23A (and would be one if he were under eighteen), and in relation to whom they were the last responsible authority; and
- (b) a person who was being looked after by them when he attained the age of eighteen, and immediately before ceasing to be looked after was an eligible child,

and in this section such a person is referred to as a 'former relevant child'.

(2) It is the duty of the local authority to take reasonable steps –
- (a) to keep in touch with a former relevant child whether he is within their area or not; and
- (b) if they lose touch with him, to re-establish contact.

(3) It is the duty of the local authority –
- (a) to continue the appointment of a personal adviser for a former relevant child; and
- (b) to continue to keep his pathway plan under regular review.

(4) It is the duty of the local authority to give a former relevant child –
- (a) assistance of the kind referred to in section 24B(1), to the extent that his welfare requires it;
- (b) assistance of the kind referred to in section 24B(2), to the extent that his welfare and his educational or training needs require it;
- (c) other assistance, to the extent that his welfare requires it.

(5) The assistance given under subsection (4)(c) may be in kind or, in exceptional circumstances, in cash.

(6) Subject to subsection (7), the duties set out in subsections (2), (3) and (4) subsist until the former relevant child reaches the age of twenty-one.

(7) If the former relevant child's pathway plan sets out a programme of education or training which extends beyond his twenty-first birthday –

    (a) the duty set out in subsection (4)(b) continues to subsist for so long as the former relevant child continues to pursue that programme; and

    (b) the duties set out in subsections (2) and (3) continue to subsist concurrently with that duty.

(8) For the purposes of subsection (7)(a) there shall be disregarded any interruption in a former relevant child's pursuance of a programme of education or training if the local authority are satisfied that he will resume it as soon as is reasonably practicable.

(9) Section 24B(5) applies in relation to a person being given assistance under subsection (4)(b) as it applies in relation to a person to whom section 24B(3) applies.

(10) Subsections (7) to (9) of section 17 apply in relation to assistance given under this section as they apply in relation to assistance given under that section.

Personal advisers

23D(1) The Secretary of State may by regulations require local authorities to appoint a personal adviser for children or young persons of a prescribed description who have reached the age of sixteen but not the age of twenty-one who are not –

    (a) children who are relevant children for the purposes of section 23A;

    (b) the young persons referred to in section 23C; or

    (c) the children referred to in paragraph 19C of Schedule 2.

(2) Personal advisers appointed under or by virtue of this Part shall (in addition to any other functions) have such functions as the Secretary of State prescribes.

Pathway plans

23E(1) In this Part, a reference to a 'pathway plan' is to a plan setting out –

    (a) in the case of a plan prepared under paragraph 19B of Schedule 2 –

        (i) the advice, assistance and support which the local authority intend to provide a child under this Part, both while they are looking after him and later; and

        (ii) when they might cease to look after him; and

    (b) in the case of a plan prepared under section 23B, the advice, assistance and support which the local authority intend to provide under this Part,

    and dealing with such other matters (if any) as may be prescribed.

(2) The Secretary of State may by regulations make provision about pathway plans and their review.

Persons qualifying for advice and assistance

24[(1) In this Part 'a person qualifying for advice and assistance' means a person who –

    (a) is under twenty-one; and

(b) at any time after reaching the age of sixteen but while still a child was, but is no longer, looked after, accommodated or fostered.]

(1) In this Part 'a person qualifying for advice and assistance' means a person to whom subsection (1A) or (1B) applies.

(1A) This subsection applies to a person –

> *(a) who has reached the age of 16 but not the age of 21;*
>
> *(b) with respect to whom a special guardianship order is in force (or, if he has reached the age of 18, was in force when he reached that age); and*
>
> *(c) who was, immediately before the making of that order, looked after by a local authority.*

(1B) This subsection applies to a person to whom subsection (1A) does not apply, and who –

> *(a) is under 21; and*
>
> *(b) at any time after reaching the age of sixteen but while still a child was, but is no longer, looked after, accommodated or fostered.*[40]

(2) In subsection (1)(b),[41] 'looked after, accommodated or fostered' means –

> (a) looked after by a local authority;
>
> (b) accommodated by or on behalf of a voluntary organisation;
>
> (c) accommodated in a private children's home;
>
> (d) accommodated for a consecutive period of at least three months –
>
> > (i) by any Health Authority, Special Health Authority, Primary Care Trust or local education authority, or
> >
> > (ii) in any care home or independent hospital or in any accommodation provided by a National Health Service trust; or
>
> (e) privately fostered.

(3) Subsection (2)(d) applies even if the period of three months mentioned there began before the child reached the age of sixteen.

(4) In the case of a person qualifying for advice and assistance by virtue of subsection (2)(a), it is the duty of the local authority which last looked after him to take such steps as they think appropriate to contact him at such times as they think appropriate with a view to discharging their functions under sections 24A and 24B.

(5) In each of sections 24A and 24B, the local authority under the duty or having the power mentioned there ('the relevant authority') is –

> *(za) in the case of a person to whom subsection (1A) applies, a local authority determined in accordance with regulations made by the Secretary of State;*[42]
>
> (a) in the case of a person qualifying for advice and assistance by virtue of subsection (2)(a), the local authority which last looked after him; or
>
> (b) in the case of any other person qualifying for advice and assistance, the

---

40 Subsection (1), in square brackets, is to be substituted by subsections (1), (1A) and (1B), from a date to be appointed, by the Adoption and Children Act 2002 s139 (1), Sch 3 paras 54, 60(a).

41 Subsection (1)(b) to be subsection (1B)(b). See above.

42 Paragraph (za) inserted by the Adoption and Children Act 2002 s139 (1), Sch 3 paras 54, 60(c), from a date to be appointed.

local authority within whose area the person is (if he has asked for help of a kind which can be given under section 24A or 24B).

Advice and assistance

24A(1) The relevant authority shall consider whether the conditions in subsection (2) are satisfied in relation to a person qualifying for advice and assistance.

(2) The conditions are that –

- (a) he needs help of a kind which they can give under this section or section 24B; and
- (b) in the case of a person *to whom section 24(1A) applies, or to whom section 24(1B) applies and*[43] who was not being looked after by any local authority, they are satisfied that the person by whom he was being looked after does not have the necessary facilities for advising or befriending him.

(3) If the conditions are satisfied –

- (a) they shall advise and befriend him if *he is a person to whom section 24(1A) applies, or he is a person to whom section 24(1B) applies and*[44] he was being looked after by a local authority or was accommodated by or on behalf of a voluntary organisation; and
- (b) in any other case they may do so.

(4) Where as a result of this section a local authority are under a duty, or are empowered, to advise and befriend a person, they may also give him assistance.

(5) The assistance may be in kind [and, in exceptional circumstances, assistance may be given –

- (a) by providing accommodation, if in the circumstances assistance may not be given in respect of the accommodation under section 24B, or
- (b) in cash.

(6) Subsections (7) to (9) of section 17 apply in relation to assistance given under this section or section 24B as they apply in relation to assistance given under that section.

Employment, education and training

24B(1) The relevant local authority may give assistance to any person who qualifies for advice and assistance by virtue of *section 24(1A) or*[45] section 24(2)(a) by contributing to expenses incurred by him in living near the place where he is, or will be, employed or seeking employment.

(2) The relevant local authority may give assistance to a person to whom subsection (3) applies by –

- (a) contributing to expenses incurred by the person in question in living near the place where he is, or will be, receiving education or training; or

---

43 Words in italics inserted by the Adoption and Children Act 2002 s139(1), Sch 3 paras 54, 61(a) from a date to be appointed.

44 Words in italics inserted by the Adoption and Children Act 2002 s139(1), Sch 3 paras 54, 61(a) from a date to be appointed.

45 Words in italics inserted by the Adoption and Children Act 2002 s139(1), Sch 3 paras 54, 62 from a date to be appointed.

    (b) making a grant to enable him to meet expenses connected with his education or training.

(3) This subsection applies to any person who –

    (a) is under twenty-four; and

    (b) qualifies for advice and assistance by virtue of *section 24(1A) or*[46] section 24(2)(a), or would have done so if he were under twenty-one.

(4) Where a local authority are assisting a person under subsection (2) they may disregard any interruption in his attendance on the course if he resumes it as soon as is reasonably practicable.

(5) Where the local authority are satisfied that a person to whom subsection (3) applies who is in full-time further or higher education needs accommodation during a vacation because his term-time accommodation is not available to him then, they shall give him assistance by –

    (a) providing him with suitable accommodation during the vacation; or

    (b) paying him enough to enable him to secure such accommodation himself.

(6) The Secretary of State may prescribe the meaning of 'full-time', 'further education', 'higher education' and 'vacation' for the purposes of subsection (5).

SCHEDULE 2 – LOCAL AUTHORITY SUPPORT FOR CHILDREN AND FAMILIES
Preparation for ceasing to be looked after

19A It is the duty of the local authority looking after a child to advise, assist and befriend him with a view to promoting his welfare when they have ceased to look after him.

19B(1) A local authority shall have the following additional functions in relation to an eligible child whom they are looking after.

(2) In sub-paragraph (1) 'eligible child' means, subject to sub-paragraph (3), a child who –

    (a) is aged sixteen or seventeen; and

    (b) has been looked after by a local authority for a prescribed period, or periods amounting in all to a prescribed period, which began after he reached a prescribed age and ended after he reached the age of sixteen.

(3) The Secretary of State may prescribe –

    (a) additional categories of eligible children; and

    (b) categories of children who are not to be eligible children despite falling within sub-paragraph (2).

(4) For each eligible child, the local authority shall carry out an assessment of his needs with a view to determining what advice, assistance and support it would be appropriate for them to provide him under this Act –

    (a) while they are still looking after him; and

    (b) after they cease to look after him,

and shall then prepare a pathway plan for him.

---

46 Words in italics inserted by the Adoption and Children Act 2002 s139(1), Sch 3 paras 54, 62 from a date to be appointed.

(5) The local authority shall keep the pathway plan under regular review.

(6) Any such review may be carried out at the same time as a review of the child's case carried out by virtue of section 26.

(7) The Secretary of State may by regulations make provision as to assessments for the purposes of sub-paragraph (4).

(8) The regulations may in particular provide for the matters set out in section 23B(6).

Personal advisers

19C   A local authority shall arrange for each child whom they are looking after who is an eligible child for the purposes of paragraph 19B to have a personal adviser.

NATIONAL HEALTH SERVICE AND COMMUNITY CARE ACT 1990 ss46(3), 47

GENERAL PROVISIONS CONCERNING COMMUNITY CARE SERVICES

Local authority plans for community care services

46 (3) In this section –

'local authority' means the council of a county, a county borough, a metropolitan district or a London borough or the Common Council of the City of London;

'community care services' means services which a local authority may provide or arrange to be provided under any of the following provisions –

(a) Part III of the National Assistance Act 1948;

(b) section 45 of the Health Services and Public Health Act 1968;

(c) section 21 of and Schedule 8 to the National Health Service Act 1977; and

(d) section 117 of the Mental Health Act 1983; and

'private carer' means a person who is not employed to provide the care in question by any body in the exercise of its function under any enactment.

Assessment of needs for community care services

47 (1) Subject to subsections (5) and (6) below, where it appears to a local authority that any person for whom they may provide or arrange for the provision of community care services may be in need of any such services, the authority –

(a) shall carry out an assessment of his needs for those services; and

(b) having regard to the results of that assessment, shall then decide whether his needs call for the provision by them of any such services.

(2) If at any time during the assessment of the needs of any person under subsection (1)(a) above it appears to a local authority that he is a disabled person, the authority –

(a) shall proceed to make such a decision as to the services he requires as is mentioned in section 4 of the Disabled Persons (Services, Consultation and Representation) Act 1986 without his requesting them to do so under that section; and

(b) shall inform him that they will be doing so and of his rights under that Act.

(3) If at any time during the assessment of the needs of any person under subsection (1)(a) above, it appears to a local authority –

(a) that there may be a need for the provision to that person by such Primary Care Trust or Health Authority as may be determined in accordance with regulations of any services under the National Health Service Act 1977, or

(b) that there may be the need for the provision to him of any services which fall within the functions of a local housing authority (within the meaning of the Housing Act 1985) which is not the local authority carrying out the assessment,

the local authority shall notify that Primary Care Trust, Health Authority or local housing authority and invite them to assist, to such extent as is reasonable in the circumstances, in the making of the assessment; and, in making their decision as to the provision of services needed for the person in question, the local authority shall take into account any services which are likely to be made available for him by that Primary Care Trust, Health Authority or local housing authority.

(4) The Secretary of State may give directions as to the manner in which an assessment under this section is to be carried out or the form it is to take but, subject to any such directions and to subsection (7) below, it shall be carried out in such manner and take such form as the local authority consider appropriate.

(5) Nothing in this section shall prevent a local authority from temporarily providing or arranging for the provision of community care services for any person without carrying out a prior assessment of his needs in accordance with the preceding provisions of this section if, in the opinion of the authority, the condition of that person is such that he requires those services as a matter of urgency.

(6) If, by virtue of subsection (5) above, community care services have been provided temporarily for any person as a matter of urgency, then, as soon as practicable thereafter, an assessment of his needs shall be made in accordance with the preceding provisions of this section.

(7) This section is without prejudice to section 3 of the Disabled Persons (Services, Consultation and Representation) Act 1986.

(8) In this section –

'disabled person' has the same meaning as in that Act; and

'local authority' and 'community care services' have the same meanings as in section 46 above.

LOCAL GOVERNMENT ACT 2000 ss2–4

PROMOTION OF WELL-BEING
Promotion of well-being

2 (1) Every local authority are to have power to do anything which they consider is likely to achieve any one or more of the following objects –
   (a) the promotion or improvement of the economic well-being of their area;
   (b) the promotion or improvement of the social well-being of their area, and
   (c) the promotion or improvement of the environmental well-being of their area.

(2) The power under subsection (1) may be exercised in relation to or for the benefit of –
   (a) the whole or any part of a local authority's area, or
   (b) all or any persons resident or present in a local authority's area.

(3) In determining whether or how to exercise the power under subsection (1), a local authority must have regard to their strategy under section 4.

(4) The power under subsection (1) includes power for a local authority to –
   (a) incur expenditure,
   (b) give financial assistance to any person,
   (c) enter into arrangements or agreements with any person,
   (d) co-operate with, or facilitate or co-ordinate the activities of, any person,
   (e) exercise on behalf of any person any functions of that person, and
   (f) provide staff, goods, services or accommodation to any person.

(5) The power under subsection (1) includes power for a local authority to do anything in relation to, or for the benefit of, any person or area situated outside their area if they consider that it is likely to achieve any one or more of the objects in that subsection.

(6) Nothing in subsection (4) or (5) affects the generality of the power under subsection (1).

Limits on power to promote well-being

3 (1) The power under section 2(1) does not enable a local authority to do anything which they are unable to do by virtue of any prohibition, restriction or limitation on their powers which is contained in any enactment (whenever passed or made).

(2) The power under section 2(1) does not enable a local authority to raise money (whether by precepts, borrowing or otherwise).

(3) The Secretary of State may by order make provision preventing local authorities from doing, by virtue of section 2(1), anything which is specified, or is of a description specified, in the order.

(4) Before making an order under subsection (3), the Secretary of State must consult such representatives of local government and such other persons (if any) as he considers appropriate.

(5) Before exercising the power under section 2(1), a local authority must have regard to any guidance for the time being issued by the Secretary of State about the exercise of that power.

(6) Before issuing any guidance under subsection (5), the Secretary of State must consult such representatives of local government and such other persons (if any) as he considers appropriate.

(7) In its application to Wales, this section has effect as if for any reference to the Secretary of State there were substituted a reference to the National Assembly for Wales.

(8) In this section 'enactment' includes an enactment comprised in subordinate legislation (within the meaning of the Interpretation Act 1978).

Strategies for promoting well-being

4 (1) Every local authority must prepare a strategy (referred to in this section as a community strategy) for promoting or improving the economic, social and environmental well-being of their area and contributing to the achievement of sustainable development in the United Kingdom.

(2) A local authority may from time to time modify their community strategy.

(3) In preparing or modifying their community strategy, a local authority –
   (a) must consult and seek the participation of such persons as they consider appropriate, and
   (b) must have regard to any guidance for the time being issued by the Secretary of State.

(4) Before issuing any guidance under this section, the Secretary of State must consult such representatives of local government and such other persons (if any) as he considers appropriate.

(5) In its application to Wales, this section has effect as if for any reference to the Secretary of State there were substituted a reference to the National Assembly for Wales.

Human rights

HUMAN RIGHTS ACT 1998

LEGISLATION

Interpretation of legislation

3 (1) So far as it is possible to do so, primary legislation and subordinate legislation must be read and given effect in a way which is compatible with the Convention rights.

(2) This section –

(a) applies to primary legislation and subordinate legislation whenever enacted;

(b) does not affect the validity, continuing operation or enforcement of any incompatible primary legislation; and

(c) does not affect the validity, continuing operation or enforcement of any incompatible subordinate legislation if (disregarding any possibility of revocation) primary legislation prevents removal of the incompatibility.

Declaration of incompatibility

4 (1) Subsection (2) applies in any proceedings in which a court determines whether a provision of primary legislation is compatible with a Convention right.

(2) If the court is satisfied that the provision is incompatible with a Convention right, it may make a declaration of that incompatibility.

(3) Subsection (4) applies in any proceedings in which a court determines whether a provision of subordinate legislation, made in the exercise of a power conferred by primary legislation, is compatible with a Convention right.

(4) If the court is satisfied –

(a) that the provision is incompatible with a Convention right, and

(b) that (disregarding any possibility of revocation) the primary legislation concerned prevents removal of the incompatibility,

it may make a declaration of that incompatibility.

(5) In this section 'court' means –

(a) the House of Lords;

(b) the Judicial Committee of the Privy Council;

(c) the Courts-Martial Appeal Court;

(d) in Scotland, the High Court of Justiciary sitting otherwise than as a trial court or the Court of Session;

(e) in England and Wales or Northern Ireland, the High Court or the Court of Appeal.

(6) A declaration under this section ('a declaration of incompatibility') –

(a) does not affect the validity, continuing operation or enforcement of the provision in respect of which it is given; and

(b) is not binding on the parties to the proceedings in which it is made.

PUBLIC AUTHORITIES
Acts of public authorities

6 (1) It is unlawful for a public authority to act in a way which is incompatible with a Convention right.

(2) Subsection (1) does not apply to an act if –

    (a) as the result of one or more provisions of primary legislation, the authority could not have acted differently; or

    (b) in the case of one or more provisions of, or made under, primary legislation which cannot be read or given effect in a way which is compatible with the Convention rights, the authority was acting so as to give effect to or enforce those provisions.

(3) In this section 'public authority' includes –

    (a) a court or tribunal, and

    (b) any person certain of whose functions are functions of a public nature,

but does not include either House of Parliament or a person exercising functions in connection with proceedings in Parliament.

(4) In subsection (3) 'Parliament' does not include the House of Lords in its judicial capacity.

(5) In relation to a particular act, a person is not a public authority by virtue only of subsection (3)(b) if the nature of the act is private.

(6) 'An act' includes a failure to act but does not include a failure to –

    (a) introduce in, or lay before, Parliament a proposal for legislation; or

    (b) make any primary legislation or remedial order.

SCHEDULE 1: THE ARTICLES

PART I: THE CONVENTION: RIGHTS AND FREEDOMS
Article 2: Right to life

1 Everyone's right to life shall be protected by law. No one shall be deprived of his life intentionally save in the execution of a sentence of a court following his conviction of a crime for which this penalty is provided by law.

2 Deprivation of life shall not be regarded as inflicted in contravention of this Article when it results from the use of force which is no more than absolutely necessary:

    (a) in defence of any person from unlawful violence;

    (b) in order to effect a lawful arrest or to prevent the escape of a person lawfully detained;

    (c) in action lawfully taken for the purpose of quelling a riot or insurrection.

Article 3: Prohibition of torture

No one shall be subjected to torture or to inhuman or degrading treatment or punishment.

Article 4: Prohibition of slavery and forced labour

1 No one shall be held in slavery or servitude.

2 No one shall be required to perform forced or compulsory labour.

3 For the purpose of this Article the term 'forced or compulsory labour' shall not include:

(a) any work required to be done in the ordinary course of detention imposed according to the provisions of Article 5 of this Convention or during conditional release from such detention;

(b) any service of a military character or, in case of conscientious objectors in countries where they are recognised, service exacted instead of compulsory military service;

(c) any service exacted in case of an emergency or calamity threatening the life or well-being of the community;

(d) any work or service which forms part of normal civic obligations.

Article 5: Right to liberty and security

1 Everyone has the right to liberty and security of person. No one shall be deprived of his liberty save in the following cases and in accordance with a procedure prescribed by law:

(a) the lawful detention of a person after conviction by a competent court;

(b) the lawful arrest or detention of a person for non-compliance with the lawful order of a court or in order to secure the fulfilment of any obligation prescribed by law;

(c) the lawful arrest or detention of a person effected for the purpose of bringing him before the competent legal authority on reasonable suspicion of having committed an offence or when it is reasonably considered necessary to prevent his committing an offence or fleeing after having done so;

(d) the detention of a minor by lawful order for the purpose of educational supervision or his lawful detention for the purpose of bringing him before the competent legal authority;

(e) the lawful detention of persons for the prevention of the spreading of infectious diseases, of persons of unsound mind, alcoholics or drug addicts or vagrants;

(f) the lawful arrest or detention of a person to prevent his effecting an unauthorised entry into the country or of a person against whom action is being taken with a view to deportation or extradition.

2 Everyone who is arrested shall be informed promptly, in a language which he understands, of the reasons for his arrest and of any charge against him.

3 Everyone arrested or detained in accordance with the provisions of paragraph 1(c) of this Article shall be brought promptly before a judge or other officer authorised by law to exercise judicial power and shall be entitled to trial within a reasonable time or to release pending trial. Release may be conditioned by guarantees to appear for trial.

4 Everyone who is deprived of his liberty by arrest or detention shall be entitled to take proceedings by which the lawfulness of his detention shall be decided speedily by a court and his release ordered if the detention is not lawful.

5 Everyone who has been the victim of arrest or detention in contravention of the provisions of this Article shall have an enforceable right to compensation.

Article 6: Right to a fair trial

1 In the determination of his civil rights and obligations or of any criminal charge against him, everyone is entitled to a fair and public hearing within a reasonable time by an independent and impartial tribunal established by law. Judgment shall be pronounced publicly but the press and public may be excluded from all or part of the trial in the interest of morals, public order or national security in a democratic society, where the interests of juveniles or the protection of the private life of the parties so require, or to the extent strictly necessary in the opinion of the court in special circumstances where publicity would prejudice the interests of justice.

2 Everyone charged with a criminal offence shall be presumed innocent until proved guilty according to law.

3 Everyone charged with a criminal offence has the following minimum rights:
   (a) to be informed promptly, in a language which he understands and in detail, of the nature and cause of the accusation against him;
   (b) to have adequate time and facilities for the preparation of his defence;
   (c) to defend himself in person or through legal assistance of his own choosing or, if he has not sufficient means to pay for legal assistance, to be given it free when the interests of justice so require;
   (d) to examine or have examined witnesses against him and to obtain the attendance and examination of witnesses on his behalf under the same conditions as witnesses against him;
   (e) to have the free assistance of an interpreter if he cannot understand or speak the language used in court.

Article 7: No punishment without law

1 No one shall be held guilty of any criminal offence on account of any act or omission which did not constitute a criminal offence under national or international law at the time when it was committed. Nor shall a heavier penalty be imposed than the one that was applicable at the time the criminal offence was committed.

2 This Article shall not prejudice the trial and punishment of any person for any act or omission which, at the time when it was committed, was criminal according to the general principles of law recognised by civilised nations.

Article 8: Right to respect for private and family life

1 Everyone has the right to respect for his private and family life, his home and his correspondence.

2 There shall be no interference by a public authority with the exercise of this right except such as is in accordance with the law and is necessary in a democratic society in the interests of national security, public safety or the economic well-being of the country, for the prevention of disorder or crime, for the protection of health or morals, or for the protection of the rights and freedoms of others.

Article 9: Freedom of thought, conscience and religion

1 Everyone has the right to freedom of thought, conscience and religion; this right includes freedom to change his religion or belief and freedom, either

alone or in community with others and in public or private, to manifest his religion or belief, in worship, teaching, practice and observance.

2 Freedom to manifest one's religion or beliefs shall be subject only to such limitations as are prescribed by law and are necessary in a democratic society in the interests of public safety, for the protection of public order, health or morals, or for the protection of the rights and freedoms of others.

Article 10: Freedom of expression

1 Everyone has the right to freedom of expression. This right shall include freedom to hold opinions and to receive and impart information and ideas without interference by public authority and regardless of frontiers. This Article shall not prevent States from requiring the licensing of broadcasting, television or cinema enterprises.

2 The exercise of these freedoms, since it carries with it duties and responsibilities, may be subject to such formalities, conditions, restrictions or penalties as are prescribed by law and are necessary in a democratic society, in the interests of national security, territorial integrity or public safety, for the prevention of disorder or crime, for the protection of health or morals, for the protection of the reputation or rights of others, for preventing the disclosure of information received in confidence, or for maintaining the authority and impartiality of the judiciary.

Article 11: Freedom of assembly and association

1 Everyone has the right to freedom of peaceful assembly and to freedom of association with others, including the right to form and to join trade unions for the protection of his interests.

2 No restrictions shall be placed on the exercise of these rights other than such as are prescribed by law and are necessary in a democratic society in the interests of national security or public safety, for the prevention of disorder or crime, for the protection of health or morals or for the protection of the rights and freedoms of others. This Article shall not prevent the imposition of lawful restrictions on the exercise of these rights by members of the armed forces, of the police or of the administration of the State.

Article 12: Right to marry

Men and women of marriageable age have the right to marry and to found a family, according to the national laws governing the exercise of this right.

Article 14: Prohibition of discrimination

The enjoyment of the rights and freedoms set forth in this Convention shall be secured without discrimination on any ground such as sex, race, colour, language, religion, political or other opinion, national or social origin, association with a national minority, property, birth or other status.

Article 16: Restrictions on political activity of aliens

Nothing in Articles 10, 11 and 14 shall be regarded as preventing the High Contracting Parties from imposing restrictions on the political activity of aliens.

Article 17: Prohibition of abuse of rights

Nothing in this Convention may be interpreted as implying for any State, group or person any right to engage in any activity or perform any act aimed at the destruction of any of the rights and freedoms set forth herein or at their limitation to a greater extent than is provided for in the Convention.

Article 18: Limitation on use of restrictions on rights

The restrictions permitted under this Convention to the said rights and freedoms shall not be applied for any purpose other than those for which they have been prescribed.

PART II: THE FIRST PROTOCOL
Article 1: Protection of property

Every natural or legal person is entitled to the peaceful enjoyment of his possessions. No one shall be deprived of his possessions except in the public interest and subject to the conditions provided for by law and by the general principles of international law.

The preceding provisions shall not, however, in any way impair the right of a State to enforce such laws as it deems necessary to control the use of property in accordance with the general interest or to secure the payment of taxes or other contributions or penalties.

Article 2: Right to education

No person shall be denied the right to education. In the exercise of any functions which it assumes in relation to education and to teaching, the State shall respect the right of parents to ensure such education and teaching in conformity with their own religious and philosophical convictions.

Article 3: Right to free elections

The High Contracting Parties undertake to hold free elections at reasonable intervals by secret ballot, under conditions which will ensure the free expression of the opinion of the people in the choice of the legislature.

PART III: THE SIXTH PROTOCOL
Article 1: Abolition of the death penalty

The death penalty shall be abolished. No one shall be condemned to such penalty or executed.

Article 2: Death penalty in time of war

A State may make provision in its law for the death penalty in respect of acts committed in time of war or of imminent threat of war; such penalty shall be applied only in the instances laid down in the law and in accordance with its provisions. The State shall communicate to the Secretary General of the Council of Europe the relevant provisions of that law.

Directions and guidance

Asylum support

HOME OFFICE GUIDANCE ON SECTION 4 HARD CASES

CRITERIA FOR SUPPORT UNDER SECTION 4 OF THE IMMIGRATION AND ASYLUM ACT 1999

As a matter of policy the Secretary of State has decided that a person who meets all of the following criteria may be provided with support under section 4 of the 1999 Act:

Whose claim for asylum has been determined (within the meaning of Part VI of the 1999 Act);

Who has been supported by the National Asylum Support Service or by a local authority under Schedule 9 to the 1999 Act;

Who is no longer an asylum seeker within the meaning of Part VI of the Act;

Who appears to the Secretary of State to be destitute within the meaning of Part VI of the Act; and

Who has no other avenue of support.

Each case is considered on its merits, but support will not normally be made available to a person unless they are:

Unable to leave the United Kingdom by reason of a physical impediment to travel e.g. through illness or late pregnancy;

Complying with an attempt to obtain a travel document to facilitate return; (this includes a person who has elected to return voluntarily under the Voluntary Assisted Returns and Reintegration Programme (VARRP) administered by the International Organisation for Migration (IOM) but who cannot leave immediately because they require a travel document);

Unable to leave because there is no viable route of return available;

Applying for judicial review of the decision to refuse them asylum and have been granted permission to proceed or in Scotland have applied for judicial review (Scotland does not have a formal permission to proceed stage); or

The circumstances of the case are otherwise wholly exceptional or compassionate.

SECTION 4 SUPPORT TERMS

Support under section 4 of the Act is normally provided as basic full board accommodation mostly outside of London and the south-east. There is no separate financial support and the accommodation will be offered on a no choice basis. While every effort will be made, to provide accommodation in the area a claimant was previously dispersed to, it may be necessary for claimants to relocate.

If the conduct of a supported person causes an accommodation provider to refuse to continue to provide accommodation, Section 4 support will be withdrawn.

Those supported may be required to subject themselves to regular reviews and, other than in cases where judicial proceedings are outstanding, be able to show that they are taking all reasonable steps to leave the United Kingdom and in any event are complying fully with efforts to remove them.

Home Office

Immigration and Nationality Directorate
National Asylum Support Service

2nd Floor, Voyager House, 30 Wellesley Road, Croydon CR0 2AD

Fax: 020 8633 0455   E-Mail: Section4@homeoffice.gsi.gov.uk

REQUEST FOR SECTION 4 SUPPORT

THIS IS A REQUEST FORM AND DOES NOT GUARANTEE SUPPORT UNDER SECTION 4 OF THE IMMIGRATION & ASYLUM ACT 1999. THOSE REQUESTING SUPPORT MUST HAVE BEEN REFUSED LEAVE TO REMAIN IN THE UK AS AN ASYLUM SEEKER. THEY MUST SHOW REASON WHY THEY CANNOT NOW LEAVE THE UK AND THAT THEY ARE DESTITUTE WITH NO OTHER MEANS OF SUPPORT. REQUESTS NOT ACCOMPANIED BY SUPPORTING EVIDENCE ARE LIKELY TO BE REFUSED.

DATE OF REQUEST:

APPLICANTS DETAILS:

NAME: D.O.B:

NATIONALITY: HO REF:

NASS REF:

CURRENT ADDRESS (inc Tel No.):

REPRESENTATIVE DETAILS:

NAME: ORGANISATION:

ADDRESS:

TEL: FAX:

If support is provided any travel tickets should be sent to: Applicant/Representative

                                                                  (Delete as appropriate)

I CONSIDER I MEET THE CRITERIA FOR SECTION 4 SUPPORT BECAUSE:
(Tick box as appropriate)

❏ **I am unfit to travel from the United Kingdom.**
(Note: Support will not be granted for this reason unless you provide medical evidence that clearly shows that you are unfit to travel to your country and indicates, where possible, when you are expected to be fit to travel)

❏ **I cannot return to my country voluntarily because there is no safe route of return available.**
(Note: You should indicate why you believe this to be the case)

❏ **I am taking steps to leave the United Kingdom but need time to obtain a travel document and complete other arrangements.**
(Note: You should provide information to support this, for example that you have made an application for assistance to the International Organisation of Migration)

❏ **I have applied for judicial review on a matter connected to the decision to refuse my asylum application and the decision is outstanding.**
(Note: You should provide conformation from your legal representative that permission to seek judicial review has been obtained)

❏ **The circumstances of my case are exceptional or compassionate**.
(Note: Support will not be granted solely on the grounds that you are a failed asylum seeker and without access to support. All requests are considered on their merits and you should make your case on a separate sheet of paper and submit it together with

your completed request form and supporting evidence. The fact that you may disagree with the reasons why you were refused asylum will not be taken into account when considering a grant of Section 4 support)

You should set out below details of any circumstances that may affect your request for support and provide supporting evidence, for example: special accommodation requirements due to care needs/disability, husband/wife's or partner's details, requests to stay in the area where you are currently living.

SECTION 4 SUPPORT ACCEPTANCE FORM

In order that we can promptly arrange accommodation for you if your request for support is successful, please complete the acceptance form below and return it together with the request form.

To: Section 4 Support Team

    National Asylum Support Service

I ....confirm that I have understood the attached criteria and conditions under which Section 4 accommodation is offered and accept that if I am offered support I may have to relocate. I also understand that if I am provided with accommodation my receipt of support will be subject to review. I agree that I will inform NASS of any change to my circumstances and that I will comply with any reasonable request to provide information while I continue to receive support.

Signed ....

Dated ....

DIRECTIONS Nos 1–4 MADE UNDER PARAGRAPH 14(1) OF SCHEDULE 15 TO THE IMMIGRATION AND ASYLUM ACT 1999

Direction No 1

The Secretary of State, in exercise of the powers conferred upon him by paragraph 14(1) of Schedule 15 to the Immigration and Asylum Act 1999 ('the Act'), hereby makes the following direction to any local authority to whom Schedule 9 to the Act applies:

In relation to an asylum-seeker within the meaning of Part VI of the Act who –

(a) makes, on or after 3rd April 2000, a claim on his arrival (other than on his re-entry) in the United Kingdom from a country outside the Channel Islands, the Isle of Man or the Republic of Ireland; or

(b) becomes, while present in the United Kingdom, an asylum-seeker when–

(i) the Secretary of State makes a declaration to the effect that the country of which he is a national is subject to such a fundamental change of circumstances that he would not normally order the return of a person to that country, and

(ii) he makes, on or after 3rd April 2000, his claim for asylum within the period of three months from the date that declaration was made; or

(c) would fall within a category specified under paragraph (a) or (b) above but for the fact he makes his claim for asylum before 3rd April 2000, and has not received a notice from the Secretary of State of his decision on that claim; or

(d) does not fall within a category specified under any paragraphs (a) to (c) above but makes a claim for asylum on or after 3rd April 2000 and has at any time thereafter been detained at Oakington Reception Centre,

the local authority is to treat the interim period fixed by regulation 2(5) of the Asylum Support (Interim Provision) Regulations 1999 as coming to an end on 2nd April 2000.

Home Office
13 March 2000

Direction No 2

The Secretary of State, in exercise of the powers conferred upon him by paragraph 14(1) of Schedule 15 to the Immigration and Asylum Act 1999 ('the Act'), hereby makes the following direction to any local authority, except Kent County Council and Medway District Council, to whom Schedule 9 to the Act applies:

In relation to an asylum-seeker within the meaning of Part VI of the Act who –

(a) while in Kent or Medway , makes a claim for asylum on or after 17th April 2000; or

(b) on or after that date, receives while in Kent or Medway a notice from the Secretary of State of his decision on his claim for asylum, and would fall within paragraph (a) or (b) of the Direction dated 13th March 2000 but for the fact that that claim was made before 3rd April 2000, the local authority is to treat the interim period by regulation 2(5) of the Asylum Support (Interim Provisions) Regulations 1999 as coming to an end on 16th April 2000.

Home Office
10 April 2000

Direction No 2A

The Secretary of State, in exercise of the powers conferred upon him by paragraph 14(1) of Schedule 15 to the Immigration and Asylum Act 1999 ('the Act'), hereby makes the following direction to Kent County Council and Medway District Council:

In relation to an asylum-seeker within the meaning of Part VI of the Act who –

(a) makes a claim for asylum on or after 17th April 2000; or

(b) on or after that date, receives notice from the Secretary of State of his decision on his claim for asylum and would fall within paragraph (a) or (b) of the Direction dated 13th March 2000 but for the fact that that claim was made before 3rd April 2000,

the council is to treat the interim period fixed by regulation 2(5) of the Asylum Support (Interim Provisions) Regulations 1999 as coming to an end on 16th April 2000.

Home Office
10 April 2000

Direction No 3

The Secretary of State, in exercise of the powers conferred upon him by paragraph 14(1) of Schedule 15 to the Immigration and Asylum Act 1999 ('the Act'), hereby makes the following direction to any local authority, except Kent County Council and Medway District Council, to whom Schedule 9 to the Act applies:

1. In relation to any asylum-seeker within the meaning of Part VI of the Act who makes a claim for asylum on or after 24th July 2000, each London Borough Council and the Common Council of the City of London is to treat the interim period fixed by regulation 2(5) of the Asylum Support (Interim Provisions) Regulations 1999 ('the Interim Regulations') as coming to an end on 23rd July 2000.

2. In relation to any asylum-seeker within the meaning of Part VI of the Act who makes a claim for asylum on or after 31st July 2000, each local authority mentioned in Part I of the Schedule is to treat the interim period fixed by regulation 2(5) if the Interim Regulations as coming to an end on 30th July 2000.

3. In relation to any asylum-seeker within the meaning of Part VI of the Act who makes a claim for asylum on or after 14th August 2000, each local authority mentioned in Part II of the Schedule is to treat the interim period fixed by regulation 2(5) if the Interim Regulations as coming to an end on 13th August 2000.

4. In relation to any asylum-seeker within the meaning of Part VI of the Act who makes a claim for asylum on or after 29th August 2000, each local authority mentioned in Part III of the Schedule is to treat the interim period fixed by regulation 2(5) if the Interim Regulations as coming to an end on 28th August 2000.

5. In relation to any asylum-seeker within the meaning of Part VI of the Act who would fall within paragraph (a) or (b) of the direction dated 13th March 2000 but for the fact that his claim for asylum was made before 3rd April 2000 where–

   (a) he abandons that claim on or after 25th September 2000; or
   (b) the Secretary of State, on or after that date, records his decision on that claim,

   each local authority to whom this direction is made is to treat the interim period fixed by regulation 2(5) of the Interim Regulations as coming to an end on 24th September 2000.

Home Office
11th July 2000

SCHEDULE – LOCAL AUTHORITIES TO WHOM PARAGRAPHS 2 TO 4 OF THIS DIRECTION APPLY

Part I – Local authorities to whom paragraph 2 applies

Darlington Borough Council
Durham County Council
Gateshead Metropolitan Borough Council
Hartlepool Borough Council
Middlesborough Borough Council
Newcastle upon Tyne City Council
North Tyneside Metropolitan Borough Council
Northumberland County Council
Redcar and Cleveland Borough Council
South Tyneside Metropolitan Borough Council
Stockton on Tees Borough Council
Sunderland City Council

Barnsley Metropolitan Borough Council
City of Bradford Council
Calderdale Metropolitan Borough Council
Doncaster Metropolitan Borough Council
East Riding of Yorkshire Council
Kingston upon Hull City Council
Kirklees Metropolitan Borough Council
Leeds City Council
North Yorkshire County Council
Rotherham Metropolitan Borough Council

Sheffield City Council
Wakefield Metropolitan District Council
City of York Council

Blaenau Gwent County Borough Council
Bridgend County Borough Council
Caerphilly County Borough Council
City and County of Cardiff Council
Carmarthenshire County Borough Council
Ceredigion County Council
Conwy County Borough Council
Denbighshire County Council
Flintshire County Council
Gwynedd County Council
Isle of Anglesey County Council
Merthyr Tydfil County Borough Council
Monmouthshire County Council
Neath Port Talbot County Borough Council
Newport County Borough Council
Pembrokeshire County Council
Powys County Council
Rhondda Cynon Taff County Borough Council
City and County of Swansea Council
Torfaen County Borough Council
Vale of Glamorgan Council
Wrexham County Borough Council

Part II – Local authorities to whom paragraph 3 applies

Blackburn with Darwen Borough Council
Blackpool Borough Council
Bolton Metropolitan Borough Council
Bury Metropolitan Borough Council
Cheshire County Council
Cumbria County Council
Halton Borough Council
Knowsley Metropolitan Borough Council
Lancashire County Council
Liverpool City Council
Manchester City Council
Oldham Metropolitan Borough Council
Rochdale Metropolitan Borough Council
St Helens Metropolitan Borough Council
Salford City Council
Sefton Metropolitan Borough Council
Stockport Metropolitan Borough Council

Tameside Metropolitan Borough Council
Trafford Metropolitan Borough Council
Warrington Borough Council
Wigan Metropolitan Borough Council
Wirral Metropolitan Borough Council

Derby City Council
Derbyshire County Council
Leicester City Council
Leicestershire County Council
Lincolnshire County Council
North East Lincolnshire County Council
North Lincolnshire County Council
Northamptonshire County Council
Nottingham City Council
Nottinghamshire County Council
Rutland County Council

Bedfordshire County Council
Cambridgeshire County Council
Essex County Council
Hertfordshire County Council
Norfolk County Council
Luton Borough Council
Peterborough City County
Southend on Sea Borough Council
Suffolk County Council
Thurrock Borough Council

Bath and North East Somerset Council
Bristol City Council
Cornwall County Council
Devon County Council
Dorset County Council
Gloucestershire County Council
Council of the Isles of Scilly
North Somerset County Council
Plymouth City Council
South Gloucestershire Council
Swindon Borough Council
Torbay Council
Wiltshire County Council

Bournemouth Borough Council
Bracknell Forest Borough Council

Buckinghamshire County Council
Hampshire County Council
Hertfordshire County Council
Isle of Wight Council
Milton Keynes Council
Oxfordshire County Council
Borough of Poole Council
Portsmouth City Council
Reading Borough Council
Slough Borough Council
Southampton City Council
Surrey County Council
West Berkshire Council
Royal Borough of Windsor and Maidenhead Council
Wokingham District Council

Part III – Local authorities to whom paragraph 4 applies
Birmingham City Council
Coventry City Council
Dudley Metropolitan Borough Council
Herefordshire Council
Sandwell Metropolitan Borough Council
Shropshire Country Council
Solihull Metropolitan Borough Council
Staffordshire County Council
Stoke on Trent City Council
Telford & Wrekin Council
Walsall Metropolitan Borough Council
Warwickshire County Council
Wolverhampton Metropolitan Borough Council
Worcester County Council

Brighton & Hove Council
East Sussex County Council
West Sussex County Council

Direction No 4

The Secretary of State, in exercise of the powers conferred upon him by paragraph 14(1) of Schedule 15 to the Immigration and Asylum Act 1999 ('the Act'), hereby makes the following direction to any local authority to whom Schedule 9 to the Act applies:

1. Where paragraph 2 applies, a local authority shall not treat the interim period fixed by regulation 2(5) of the Asylum Support (Interim Provisions) Regulations 1999 ('the Interim Regulations') as coming to an end on any date which is so provided for in Directions No 2, 2A or 3 ('the relevant date') is respect of a claim for asylum made in any of the circumstances specified in those Directions.

2. This paragraph applies where an asylum-seeker has been provided with, or at any time been eligible for, support under the Interim Regulations and where: (i) he has made a claim for asylum after the relevant date; (ii) at the time of that claim his household included a child under 18; and (iii) he and the child have remained in the United Kingdom at all times since being provided with, or having been eligible for, support under the Interim Regulations.

Home Office
9 August 2001

NASS POLICY BULLETINS

These are available at: http://www.ind.homeoffice.gov.uk/ind/en/home/ applying/national_asylum_support/policy_bulletin.html

Access to support

PB 79   Section 57 (Application for support: False or incomplete information) 2002 Act guidance

PB 76   Asylum support for asylum seekers and dependants who are nationals of an European Economic Area (EEA) state or who have refugee status abroad

PB 75   Section 55 (Late claims) 2002 Act guidance

PB 73   Admittance to Emergency Accommodation

PB 69   Accommodation and Subsistence to Subsistence Only

PB 24   Subs Only

PB 12   Refusals

PB 11   Mixed Households

PB 70   Domestic Violence

Provision of support

PB78   Additional payments to pregnant women and children aged under 3

PB67   Overpayments

PB65   Assessing Capital or Other Income

PB37   Maternity Payment

PB34   Additional Single Payments

PB4   Threshold Table – v1.2

PB3   Supercal (Superseded – Deleted)

PB71   Section 4 of the Immigration and Asylum Act 1999

PB80   Backpayment of asylum support

Disbenefited

PB53   Temporary Support for NASS Eligible Disbenefited Singles

PB52   Funding for Disbenefited Families With Children

PB51   Disbenefited Cases

Dispersal

PB31   Dispersal Guidelines

Travel

PB66   Providing Travelling Expenses to Persons in Emergency Accommodation

PB56   Reimbursing Asylum Seekers Their Essential Travel Costs

PB28   Travel

PB25   Failure to Travel (Addendum)

PB17   Failure to Travel

Children
PB63 Education
PB33 Age Disputes
PB29 Transition at Age 18

Medical
PB61 Pregnancy
PB59 Funerals
PB43 HC2 Certificates
PB19 Medical Foundation for the care of victims of torture

End of support
PB77 Failure to comply with removal directions
PB38 Grace Periods
PB22 Discontinuation

General
PB72 Employment
PB81 Racist Incidents
PB41 Dealing With Representations in Respect of an Asylum Claim
PB23 Asylum support appeals process (Revised v5)
PB30 The Human Rights Act 1998
PB7 Judicial Review
PB64 Application for support from people detained under the Immigration Act 1971 or who have been granted Immigration bail

NASS is conducting a comprehensive review of Policy Bulletins. Numbers 9, 10, 18, 15, 26, 27, 44, 45, 46, 48, 49, 54, 57, 58, 60 and 62 have recently been withdrawn as they are procedural (rather than policy) documents, are outdated, or the information they contain is provided elsewhere.

ASYLUM SUPPORT ADJUDICATORS REASONS STATEMENT 00/11/0095 (DISPERSAL)

Appeal Number: 00/11/0095
NASS Ref Number: 00/09/03545/001
Appellant's Ref Number:

ASYLUM SUPPORT ADJUDICATORS
Christopher Wren House
113 High Street Croydon CR0 1QG
Telephone: 020 8688 3977
Fax: 020 8688 6075

**IMMIGRATION AND ASYLUM ACT 1999
ASYLUM SUPPORT APPEALS (PROCEDURE) RULES 2000**

Adjudicator Mrs Sehba Haroon Storey
Appellant (s)
Respondent Secretary of State

REASONS STATEMENT

1. This Reasons Statement is made in accordance with rule 13 of the Asylum Support Appeals (Procedure) Rules 2000 ('the Rules'), and gives reasons for the Adjudication given on Thursday the 16th day of November 2000 allowing the above mentioned appeal.

2. The appellant a 69 year old citizen of Poland appeals against the decision of the Secretary of State who on 25 October 2000 decided to discontinue support to the appellant under regulation 20(1)(a) of the Asylum Support Regulations 2000 ('the Regulations') on the grounds that the Secretary of State is satisfied that the appellant has breached his conditions of support by failing to travel as arranged.

3. The appellant resides with his wife who is 72 years of age. They live with their son, Jan and his family which consists of a wife and five children. The property has two bedrooms and two living rooms.

4. It is not disputed that both the appellant and his wife suffer from numerous medical conditions stated in some detail on their application form for support. The appellant is hard of hearing, blind in one eye, a diabetic, suffers from rheumatism, has a twisted spine and problems with his leg. His diabetes is poorly controlled through diet and also regular medication which he takes three times daily. He is fearful of fainting as a result and tells me that he cannot go anywhere alone and is accompanied by his granddaughter at all times whether this is for shopping or visits to the doctor. The appellant's wife suffers from ischaemic heart disease, angina, abdominal pains and a deformed spine which causes backache. I am told that she spends much of her time resting in bed and relies heavily upon the day to day care provided by her son and his family. Neither of them speak English and are therefore

heavily reliant upon their relatives to act as interpreter at GP/hospital appointments.

5. I have before me a letter from the appellant's general practitioner. He describes both the appellant and his dependant wife as chronically ill with multiple health problems, some of which are under hospital investigation. He describes the appellant's diabetes as very poorly controlled and states that they are very dependent upon the support of family members. With regards to the appellant, the general practitioner also makes reference to vascular problems for which the appellant has been referred for further investigations. I am also in receipt of a note from Dr Keen, the NASS doctor, who expressed the view on 28 September 2000 that there are services available throughout the UK to deal adequately with the applicant's established medical conditions. He considered that proximity to London is not essential and that dispersal is reasonable to accommodation either on the first floor or with lift facilities.

6. The appellant informs me that he is old and frail as indeed is his wife and that in the light of their medical conditions, they do not wish to be dispersed outside London. This is because they have an extensive family network in London consisting of two sons, one daughter and several grandchildren all of whom are both able and willing to provide physical, moral and emotional support which would otherwise have to be provided by a local authority.

7. I found the appellant a credible witness. He appeared more concerned about his wife than himself and told me that she had a heart problem as a result of which she was unable to climb stairs unless she did so very slowly. She also required help from female members of the family to get in and out of the bath. He said that she had problems walking, sitting, standing, bending and kneeling and described her as being doubled up with pain regularly. He said that caring for his wife was like looking after a child and I am satisfied that that care is at present being provided by the relatives. I am equally satisfied that the appellant is not able to provide adequate care for his wife in the light of his age and medical conditions.

8. At the conclusion of the hearing, I asked the respondent's representative, Ms Tracey Brown, to address me on the applicability of NASS Policy 30, paragraph 8.22 and Policy 31, paragraph 4.

9. Policy 30 deals with the merits of dispersing asylum seekers to an area different to a family member. It states '... as a general rule an asylum seeker would have to demonstrate that there exists close personal ties between themselves and their relative, before a decision could be made to place him/her in a particular area simply because that family member lives there'.

10. Policy 31, paragraph 4, deals with the issue of family ties and the applicability of Article 8 of the European Convention on Human Rights to asylum seekers wishing to be allocated accommodation near or with relatives or friends. Paragraph 4.3 states 'An asylum seeker may request to be allocated accommodation in London or the South East because they have a relative there. The person's individual circumstances and the nature of the relationship with that relative should always be carefully taken into account. But in the absence of exceptional circumstances dispersal will generally be appropriate'.

11. Paragraph 4.5 alerts caseworkers to be mindful of exceptional circumstances of individual cases where it might be appropriate to depart from general

guidelines and directs such cases should be referred to HEO level and be accompanied by a written proposal.

12. Ms Brown for the respondent confirmed that there was no specific reference on file to suggest that consideration has been given to the applicability of Article 8 of the Convention to this case as required by Policies 30 and 31.

13. Section 97(2)(a) of the Immigration and Asylum Act 1999 ('the Act') states that when exercising his power under section 95 to provide accommodation, the Secretary of State may not have regard to any preference of the supported person or his dependants (if any) may have as to the locality in which the accommodation is to be provided. This means that accommodation is given on a no-choice basis and appellants are required as a condition of their support to travel to their dispersal address when notified.

14. Regulation 19(1) of the Regulations states that when deciding:
    (a) whether to provide, or to continue to provide, asylum support for any person or persons, . . .
    the Secretary of State may take into account the extent to which any relevant condition has been complied with.
    Regulation 20(1) of the Regulations states that asylum support for a supported person and his dependants (if any) or for one or more dependants of a supported person, may be suspended or discontinued, if –
    (a) the Secretary of State has reasonable grounds to suspect that the supported person or any dependant of his has failed without reasonable excuse to comply with any condition subject to which the asylum support is provided;

15. Section 3(1) of the Human Rights Act 1998 states:
    'So far as it is possible to do so, primary legislation and subordinate legislation must be read and given effect in a way which is compatible with the Convention Rights'.

16. The Secretary of State's Policy Bulletins numbers 30 and 31 are designed to ensure the compatibility of primary and subordinate legislation with the Human Rights Act and Convention Rights. It is for this reason that notwithstanding the requirements of section 97, Policies 30 and 31 direct caseworkers to consider whether the decision to disperse is compatible with the Human Rights Act 1998 and in particular that they should have regard to Article 8 of the European Convention on Human Rights and consider the exceptional circumstances of individual cases in deciding whether dispersal outside of London is appropriate.

17. I am therefore satisfied that in deciding this case, I am bound to consider whether the Secretary of State has exercised his discretion under his published policies to consider whether the appellant's individual circumstances are such that they merit a departure from the applicability of section 97 generally to dispersal cases on the grounds that failure to do so would result in a breach of the appellant's rights under Article 8 of the Convention.

18. I have given careful consideration to all the evidence before me, including medical reports submitted by the appellant and respondent, the oral evidence of the appellant and submissions made by the Secretary of State's representative.

19. The appellant clearly failed to travel to his dispersal address in Nelson, Lancashire. His excuse for this is that he needed to be near his family without whose help he cannot manage given his and his wife's chronic ill-health.

20. I have no hesitation in stating that this is a case meriting exceptional compassionate consideration in the light of the particular circumstances of this case. The appellant and his wife are both elderly, sick and frail. Whilst individually their medical conditions may not appear to be serious in nature, the cumulative effect of the various complaints renders them (especially the appellant's wife) virtually incapable of caring for themselves in any meaningful way. In addition, I am satisfied that were they to be dispersed outside of London, they would require substantial and comprehensive social services support at considerable cost to the public purse. I accept that the appellant and his wife can receive medical treatment for their conditions in other parts of the UK, but I do not accept that they will receive the high quality personal, practical and emotional support they require daily and which is presently provided free of charge by their family, from any other source.

21. I am satisfied the appellant has demonstrated that there exists a very close personal tie between him, his wife and his carers which is both personal and emotional. Applying the relevant law as above stated to the appellant's exceptional, compassionate circumstances, I am satisfied that the appellant did have reasonable excuse for failing to disperse to Lancashire. In addition, I am satisfied that to disperse the appellant and his wife away from their extensive and close family network in London would amount an interference to their right to private and family life. I am satisfied that such interference is not in accordance with the law applying the principles of Secretary of State for the Home Department v Abdi [1996] Imm AR 148 (CA). Whilst I am satisfied that the Secretary of State's dispersal policy pursues a legitimate aim, I find that in the case of the appellant, the decision to disperse him away from his family in London was neither necessary nor proportionate.

22. On the totality of the evidence before me, I am satisfied on a balance of probabilities that the decision of the Secretary of State is not in accordance with the law. The appeal is allowed.

Signed .... Date ....

Chief Asylum Support Adjudicator

Community care

LAC(93)10 WITH APPENDICES 1–3

LOCAL AUTHORITY CIRCULAR   LAC(93) 10

DEPARTMENT OF HEALTH

To: The Chief Executive
    Metropolitan District Councils)   - In England
    County Councils   )
    London Borough Councils
    Common Council of the City of London
    Council of the Isles of Scilly

    Directors of Social Services   - for information

                                               March 1993

APPROVALS AND DIRECTIONS FOR ARRANGEMENTS FROM 1 APRIL 1993
MADE UNDER SCHEDULE 8 TO THE NATIONAL HEALTH SERVICE ACT 1977 AND SECTIONS 21
AND 29 OF THE NATIONAL ASSISTANCE ACT 1948

SUMMARY

This circular contains guidance on the consolidated approvals and directions made by the Secretary of
State for Health on local authorities continuing responsibilities, from 1 April 1993, to provide residential
accommodation and welfare services, insofar as they are provided under sections 21 and 29 of the
National Assistance Act, 1948 and paragraphs 1 and 2 of Schedule 8 of the NHS Act, 1977.

ACTION

1.   This circular contains approvals and directions made by the Secretary of State in exercise of the
powers conferred by sections 21 (1) and 29 (1) of the National Assistance Act 1948 and paragraphs 1
and 2 of Schedule 8 to the National Health Service Act 1977.

2.   It consolidates the existing approvals and directions contained in LAC13/74, LAC19/74, LAC(74)28
and Annexes 1 and 2 of LAC(91)12. This circular does not of itself create any additional responsibilities
which have not previously been expected of local social services authorities. This circular also updates
existing guidance on registration practice and related statistics.

BACKGROUND

3.   Social services authorities' powers under sections 21 and 29 of the 1948 Act and under Schedule
8 to the 1977 Act are subject to the requirement to act with the approval and under the direction of the
Secretary of State. The relevant information is at:

     - Appendix 1 = Approvals and Directions under section 21(1) of the 1948 Act.
     - Appendix 2 = Approvals and Directions under section 29(1) of the 1948 Act.
     - Appendix 3 = Approvals and Directions under paras 1 and 2 of Schedule 8 of the 1977 Act.

4.   The approvals and directions contained in this circular take account of the amendments made to
Part III of the 1948 Act and Schedule 8 of the 1977 Act by the Mental Health Act 1983, the Children Act
1989, the National Health Service and Community Care Act 1990 and the Community Care (Residential
Accommodation) Act 1992.

24721B+/OR/WEL–1

It is the view of the Department that the amendments introduced into the 1948 Act by section 1 of the Community Care (Residential Accommodation) Act 1992 will require authorities to make some direct provision for residential care under Part 111 of the 1948 Act.

5.   From 1 April 1993, when section 43 of the 1990 Act comes into force, authorities will not be able to provide accommodation to people ordinarily resident in independent homes immediately before that date with preserved rights to the higher levels of Income Support. The new section 26A(3) of the 1948 Act, inserted by section 43 of the 1990 Act, gives the Secretary of State power to make exceptions. These are set out in LAC(93)6 together with SI 1993 No 477.

6.   Paragraphs 1 and 2 of the Schedule 8 to the National Health Service Act 1977 will remain in force after 1 April 1993, but they will be amended so that local authorities will no longer be able to provide residential accommodation under them. For convenience, the approvals and directions previously contained in Circulars 19/74 and 74/28, which related to services other than the provision of accommodation have been included in this Circular.

7.   The opportunity has been taken to consolidate and update circulars 25/61, 17/74, (74)37 and (78)20 concerning registration practice and statistics. Appendix 4 refers.

WHITE PAPER AND POLICY GUIDANCE

8.   It will be the responsibility of Social Services Departments to make maximum possible use of private and voluntary providers and so increase the available range of options and widen consumer choice (paragraph 1.11 of the White Paper "Caring for People" (Cm 849)). The Government welcomes the action being taken by authorities to review the range of services they are currently providing, as part of a comprehensive review of the needs and services available in their area. Social services authorities will continue to play a valuable role in the provision of services, but in those cases where they are currently the main or sole providers of services, they will be expected to take all reasonable steps to secure diversity of provision (paragraph 3.4.1). Regarding the circumstances in which direct provision may be needed the White Paper said (paragraph 3.4.11) that the Government will expect local authorities to retain the ability to act as direct service providers, if other forms of service provision are unforthcoming or unsuitable. This is likely to be particularly important in services for people with high levels of dependency, or particularly challenging patterns of behaviour, whose care it is essential to safeguard.

9.   The role of housing and social services authorities in relation to housing and community care is set out in the joint circular from the Departments of Health (LAC(92)12) and the Environment (10/92). This circular has also been issued to housing associations by the Housing Corporation.

10.   By virtue of Section 2 of the Chronically Sick and Disabled Persons Act 1970 the matters dealt with in sub section (1) of that section do not need to be included in the arrangements contained in Appendix 2.

11.   It is not necessary for the arrangements contained in this circular to cover the provision by local authorities of sheltered employment as this is provided under powers deriving from the Disabled Persons (Employment) Acts 1944 and 1958.

12.   The Secretary of State hopes that authorities will keep in mind the needs of individuals, families and groups to ensure that the services provided are administered flexibly and in accordance with changing needs. For the purpose of any of these arrangements, where no express statutory power exists for authorities to use outside service providers, the Secretary of State has also approved the use by authorities of suitable accommodation, services or facilities made available by another authority, voluntary body or person on such conditions as may be agreed. Thus, for example, authorities may continue to make use on a repayment basis of suitable residential or training places made available by other authorities, though they are asked nevertheless to bear in mind the importance of such services being provided as near to the person's home place as is practicable.

13.   Social services authorities' powers to prevent mental disorder or provide care for those who are or have been suffering from mental disorder are embraced in their wider powers under paragraph 2 of Schedule 8 to the 1977 Act to prevent illness and provide care for those who are or have been suffering from it. In addition, if authorities wish to provide services other than accommodation specifically for persons who are alcoholic or drug-dependent, the Secretary of State has approved them so doing. Because authorities' powers to provide accommodation under paragraph 2 of Schedule 8 are being repealed, the approvals and directions in relation to the provision of accommodation for the prevention of mental disorder or for persons who are or who have been suffering from mental disorder, or specifically for persons who are alcoholic or drug-dependent, have all been transferred to section 21(1) of the 1948 Act. Further guidance on the provision of alcohol and drug services within community care is contained in LAC(93)2.

EFFECTIVE DATE

14. The Approvals and Directions are effective from 1 April 1993.

CANCELLATION OF CIRCULARS

15. This circular cancels LAC13/74, LAC19/74, LAC(74)28, LAC17/74, LAC(74)37 and LAC(78)20. It also cancels Annexes 1 and 2 of LAC (91)12. Authorities should note however the saving provision contained in paragraph 6(3) of Appendix 1 to this circular in relation to the directions contained in Annexes 1 and 2 of Circular LAC(91)12.

ENQUIRIES

16. Enquiries about this circular should be made to CS1 Division, Department of Health on 071 972 4237.

From:

CS1 Division
Wellington House
133-155 Waterloo Road
LONDON   SE1 8UG

Tel: 071 972 4237   EAR 100

Further copies of this circular may be obtained from DH Store, Health Publications Unit, No 2 Site, Manchester Road, Heywood. Lancs OL10 2PZ quoting the code and serial number appearing on the top right-hand corner.

This circular may be freely reproduced by all to whom it is addressed.

SECRETARY OF STATE'S APPROVALS AND DIRECTIONS

UNDER SECTION 21(1) OF THE NATIONAL ASSISTANCE ACT 1948

The Secretary of State for Health, in exercise of the powers conferred on her by section 21(1) of the National Assistance Act 1948(a), hereby makes the following Approvals and Directions:-

Commencement, interpretation and extent

1.-(1)   These Approvals and Directions shall come into force on 1st April 1993.

(2)   In these Approvals and Directions, unless the context otherwise requires, "the Act" means the National Assistance Act 1948.

(3)   The Interpretation Act 1978(b) applies to these Approvals and Directions as it applies to an Act of Parliament.

(4)   These Approvals and Directions shall apply only to England and Wales.

Residential accommodation for persons in need of care and attention

2.-(1)   The Secretary of State hereby-

(a)   1948 c.29; amended by paragraph 2(1) of Schedule 23 to the Local Government Act 1972 (c.70) and section 42(1) of the National Health Service and Community Care Act 1990 (c.19).

(b)   1978 c.30.

(a) approves the making by local authorities of arrangements under section 21(1)(a) of the Act in relation to persons with no settled residence and, to such extent as the authority may consider desirable, in relation to persons who are ordinarily resident in the area of another local authority, with the consent of that other authority; and

(b) directs local authorities to make arrangements under section 21(1)(a) of the Act in relation to persons who are ordinarily resident in their area and other persons who are in urgent need thereof,

to provide residential accommodation for persons aged 18 or over who by reason of age, illness, disability or any other circumstance are in need of care and attention not otherwise available to them.

(2) Without prejudice to the generality of sub-paragraph (1), the Secretary of State hereby directs local authorities to make arrangements under section 21(1)(a) of the Act to provide temporary accommodation for persons who are in urgent need thereof in circumstances where the need for that accommodation could not reasonably have been foreseen.

(3) Without prejudice to the generality of sub-paragraph (1), the Secretary of State hereby directs local authorities to make arrangements under section 21(1)(a) of the Act to provide accommodation-

(a) in relation to persons who are or have been suffering from mental disorder, or

(b) for the purposes of the prevention of mental disorder,

for persons who are ordinarily resident in their area and for persons with no settled residence who are in the authority's area.

(4)   Without prejudice to the generality of sub-paragraph (1) and subject to section 24(4) of the Act(a), the Secretary of State hereby approves the making by local authorities of arrangements under section 21(1)(a) of the Act to provide residential accommodation–

> (a)   in relation to persons who are or have been suffering from mental disorder; or
>
> (b)   for the purposes of the prevention of mental disorder,

for persons who are ordinarily resident in the area of another local authority but who following discharge from hospital have become resident in the authority's area;

(5)   Without prejudice to the generality of sub-paragraph (1), the Secretary of State hereby approves the making by local authorities of arrangements under section 21(1)(a) of the Act to provide accommodation to meet the needs of persons for–

> (a)   the prevention of illness;
>
> (b)   the care of those suffering from illness; and
>
> (c)   the aftercare of those so suffering.

(6)   Without prejudice to the generality of sub-paragraph (1), the Secretary of State hereby approves the making by local authorities of arrangements under section 21(1)(a) of the Act specifically for persons who are alcoholic or drug-dependent.

(a)   Amended by section 195(6) of paragraph 2(2) of Schedule 23 to the Local Government Act 1972.

Residential accommodation for expectant and nursing mothers

3. The Secretary of State hereby approves the making by local authorities of arrangements under section 21(1)(aa) of the Act(a) to provide residential accommodation (in particular mother and baby homes) for expectant and nursing mothers (of any age) who are in need of care and attention which is not otherwise available to them.

Arrangements to provide services for residents

4. The Secretary of State hereby directs local authorities to make arrangements in relation to persons provided with accommodation under section 21(1) of the Act for all or any of the following purposes-

(a) for the welfare of all persons for whom accommodation is provided;

(b) for the supervision of the hygiene of the accommodation so provided;

(c) to enable persons for whom accommodation is provided to obtain-

(i) medical attention,

(ii) nursing attention during illnesses of a kind which are ordinarily nursed at home, and

(iii) the benefit of any services provided by the National Health Service of which they may from time to time be in need,

---

(a) Inserted by section 42(1) of the National Health Service and Community Care Act 1990.

but nothing in this paragraph shall require a local
authority to make any provision authorised or
required to be provided under the National Health
Service Act 1977(a);

(d) for the provision of board and such other services,
amenities and requisites provided in connection with
the accommodation, except where in the opinion of the
authority managing the premises their provision is
unnecessary(b);

(e) to review regularly the provision made under the
arrangements and to make such improvements as the
authority considers necessary.

Arrangements for the conveyance of residents

5.   The Secretary of State hereby approves the making by local
authorities of arrangements under section 21(1) of the Act to
provide, in such cases as the authority considers appropriate,
for the conveyance of persons to and from premises in which
accommodation is provided for them under Part III of the Act.

Duties in respect of residents in transferred accommodation

6.-(1)   Where a person is provided with accommodation
pursuant to section 21(1) of the Act, and-

(a) the residential accommodation is local authority

(a) See section 21(8) of the Act, as amended by section 66(1)
and (2) of, and paragraph 5(3) of Schedule 9 and Schedule 10
to, the National Health Service and Community Care Act 1990.

(b) See section 21(5) of the Act; see also section 26(4A) of
the Act, inserted by section 66(1) of and paragraph 5(5)(b) of
Schedule 9 to the National Health Service and Community Care
Act 1990.

accommodation provided pursuant to section 21(4) of the 1948 Act(a);

   (b)   the local authority transfer the management of the residential accommodation to a voluntary organisation who—

      (i)   manages it as a residential care home within the meaning of Part I of the Registered Homes Act 1984(b), and

      (ii)   is registered under that Part or is not required to be so registered by virtue of being an exempt body; and

   (c)   the person is accommodated in the residential accommodation immediately before and after the transfer,

while that person remains accommodated in that residential accommodation, the local authority shall remain under a duty to make arrangements to provide accommodation for him after any transfer to which paragraph (b) of this sub-paragraph refers.

   (2)   For the purposes of paragraph (c) of sub-paragraph (1), a person shall be regarded as accommodated in residential accommodation if—

   (a)   he is temporarily absent from such accommodation (including circumstances in which he is in hospital or on holiday);

   (b)   before 1st April 1993, that accommodation was

(a) Amended by section 195(6) of and paragraph 2(1) of Schedule 23 to the Local Government Act 1972, and section 66(1) of and paragraph 5(1) of Schedule 9 to the National Health Service and Community Care Act 1990.

(b) 1984 c.23.

provided under paragraph 2(1) of Schedule 8 to the National Health Service Act 1977(a).

(3)   Where immediately before these Approvals and Directions come into force a local authority was under a duty to provide a person with accommodation by virtue of-

(a)   the Secretary of State's former Directions under Section 21(1) of the National Assistance Act 1948 contained in Annex 1 of Department of Health Circular LAC(91)12; or

(b)   the Secretary of State's former Directions under paragraph 2 of Schedule 8 to the National Health Service Act 1977 contained in Annex 2 of Department of Health Circular LAC(91)12,

while that person remains accommodated in that residential accommodation, the local authority shall remain under a duty to make arrangements to provide that person with accommodation from the date on which these Directions come into force.

Powers to make arrangements with other local authorities and voluntary organisations etc.

7.   For the avoidance of doubt, these Approvals and Directions are without prejudice to any of the powers conferred on local authorities by section 21(4) and section 26(1) of the Act(b) (arrangements with voluntary organisations etc.).

(a)   As amended by section 148 of and paragraph 47 of Schedule 4 to the Mental Health Act 1983 (c.20).

(b)   Section 26(1) of the Act was substituted by a new subsection (1) for that section contained in section 1(1) of the Community Care (Residential Accommodation) Act 1992 (c.49).

Ann de Peyer

ANN DE PEYER

Dated 17/3/1993

Signed on behalf of the

Secretary of State for Health

LAC(93)10 Appendix 2

SECRETARY OF STATE'S APPROVALS AND DIRECTIONS

UNDER SECTION 29(1) OF THE NATIONAL ASSISTANCE ACT 1948

The Secretary of State for Health, in exercise of the powers conferred on her by section 29(1) of the National Assistance Act 1948(a), hereby makes the following Approvals and Directions:-

Commencement, interpretation and extent

1.-(1)   These Approvals and Directions shall come into force on 1st April 1993.

(2)   In these Approvals and Directions, unless the context otherwise requires, "the Act" means the National Assistance Act 1948.

(3)   The Interpretation Act 1978(b) applies to these Approvals and Directions as it applies to an Act of Parliament.

(4)   These Approvals and Directions shall apply only to England and Wales.

Powers and duties to make welfare arrangements

2.-(1)   The Secretary of State hereby approves the making by

---

(a)   1948 c.29; amended by section 113(1) of and Schedule 4 to the Mental Health (Scotland) Act 1960 (c.61), section 195(6) of and paragraph 2(4) of Schedule 23 to the Local Government Act 1972 (c.70), and section 108(5) of and paragraph 11 of Schedule 13 to the Children Act 1989 (c.41).

(b)   1978 c.30.

local authorities of arrangements under section 29(1) of the Act for all persons to whom that subsection applies and directs local authorities to make arrangements under section 29(1) of the Act in relation to persons who are ordinarily resident in their area for all or any of the following purposes-

    (a)   to provide a social work service and such advice and support as may be needed for people in their own homes or elsewhere;

    (b)   to provide, whether at centres or elsewhere, facilities for social rehabilitation and adjustment to disability including assistance in overcoming limitations of mobility or communication;

    (c)   to provide, whether at centres or elsewhere, facilities for occupational, social, cultural and recreational activities and, where appropriate, the making of payments to persons for work undertaken by them(a);

    (2)   The Secretary of State hereby directs local authorities to make the arrangements referred to in section 29(4)(g) of the Act (compiling and maintaining registers) in relation to persons who are ordinarily resident in their area.

    (3)   The Secretary of State hereby approves the making by local authorities of arrangements under section 29(1) of the Act for all persons to whom that subsection applies for the following purposes-

    (a)   to provide holiday homes;

    (b)   to provide free or subsidised travel for all or any persons who do not otherwise qualify for travel

---

(a) <u>See</u> section 29(4)(d) and (6)(a) of the Act.

concessions, but only in respect of travel arrangements for which concessions are available;

(c) to assist a person in finding accommodation which will enable him to take advantage of any arrangements made under section 29(1) of the Act;

(d) to contribute to the cost of employing a warden on welfare functions in warden assisted housing schemes;

(e) to provide warden services for occupiers of private housing.

(4) Save as is otherwise provided for under this paragraph, the Secretary of State hereby approves the making by local authorities of all or any of the arrangements referred to in section 29(4) of the Act(a) (welfare arrangements etc.) for all persons to whom section 29(1) applies.

Welfare arrangements with another local authority

3. The Secretary of State hereby approves the making by local authorities of arrangements under section 29(1) of the Act, where appropriate, with another local authority for the provision of any of the services referred to in these Approvals and Directions.

Welfare arrangements with voluntary organisations and otherwise

4. For the avoidance of doubt, these Approvals and Directions are without prejudice to the powers conferred on local

---

(a) Amended by the section 14(1) of and paragraph 3 of Schedule 3 to the Employment and Training Act 1973 (c.50), and section 44(7) of the National Health Service and Community Care Act 1990 (c.19).

authorities by section 30(1) of the Act(a) (voluntary organisations for disabled persons welfare).

ANN DE PEYER

Dated   17/3/1993   Signed on behalf of the
                                            Secretary of State for Health

---

(a) Amended by section 195(6) of and paragraph 2(5) of Schedule 23 to Local Government Act 1972 (c.70), and section 42(6) of the National Health Service and Community Care Act 1990.

SECRETARY OF STATE'S APPROVALS AND DIRECTIONS

UNDER PARAGRAPHS 1 AND 2 OF SCHEDULE 8

TO THE NATIONAL HEALTH SERVICE ACT 1977

The Secretary of State for Health, in exercise of the powers conferred on her by paragraphs 1(1) and 2(1) of Schedule 8 to the National Health Service Act 1977(a), hereby makes the following Approvals and Directions:-

Commencement, interpretation and extent

1.-(1)   These Approvals and Directions shall come into force on 1st April 1993.

(2)   In these Approvals and Directions, unless the context otherwise requires, "the Act" means the National Health Service Act 1977.

(3)   The Interpretation Act 1978(b) applies to these Approvals and Directions as it applies to an Act of Parliament.

(4)   For the avoidance of doubt, these Approvals and

(a)   1977 c.49; paragraph 1(1) was amended by section 237 of and paragraph 22 of Schedule 12 to the Education Reform Act 1988 (c.40), section 108(7) of and Schedule 15 to the Children Act 1989 (c.41), and section 66(1) of and paragraph 14(a) of Schedule 9 to the National Health Service and Community Care Act 1990 (c.19); and paragraph 2(1) was amended by section 148 of and paragraph 47 of Schedule 4 to the Mental Health Act 1983 (c.20), and section 66(1) and (2) of, and paragraph 14(b)(i) of Schedule 9 and Schedule 10 to, the National Health Service and Community Care Act 1990.

(b)   1978 c.30.

Directions apply only to England and Wales.

Services for expectant and nursing mothers

2. The Secretary of State hereby approves the making of arrangements under paragraph 1(1) of Schedule 8 to the Act for the care of expectant and nursing mothers (of any age) other than the provision of residential accommodation for them.

Services for the purpose of the prevention of illness etc.

3.-(1) The Secretary of State hereby approves the making by local authorities of arrangements under paragraph 2(1) of Schedule 8 to the Act for the purpose of the prevention of illness, and the care of persons suffering from illness and for the aftercare of persons who have been so suffering and in particular for-

    (a) the provision, for persons whose care is undertaken with a view to preventing them becoming ill, persons suffering from illness and persons who have been so suffering, of centres or other facilities for training them or keeping them suitably occupied and the equipment and maintenance of such centres;

    (b) the provision, for the benefit of such persons as are mentioned in paragraph (a) above, of ancillary or supplemental services.

    (2)   The Secretary of State hereby directs local authorities to make arrangements under paragraph 2(1) of Schedule 8 to the Act for the purposes of the prevention of mental disorder, or in relation to persons who are or who have been suffering from mental disorder-

(a)   for the provision of centres (including training centres and day centres) or other facilities (including domiciliary facilities), whether in premises managed by the local authority or otherwise, for training or occupation of such persons;

(b)   for the appointment of sufficient social workers in their area to act as approved social workers for the purposes of the Mental Health Act 1983(a);

(c)   for the exercise of the functions of the authority in respect of persons suffering from mental disorder who are received into guardianship under Part II or III of the Mental Health Act 1983 (whether the guardianship of the local social services authority or of other persons);

(d)   for the provision of social work and related services to help in the identification, diagnosis, assessment and social treatment of mental disorder and to provide social work support and other domiciliary and care services to people living in their homes and elsewhere.

(3)   Without prejudice to the generality of sub-paragraph (1), the Secretary of State hereby approves the making by local authorities of arrangements under paragraph 2(1) of Schedule 8 to the Act for the provision of-

(a)   meals to be served at the centres or other facilities referred to in sub-paragraphs (1)(a) and (2)(a) above and meals-on-wheels for house-bound people not provided for-

---

(a)   1983 c.20.

(i)   under section 45(1) of the Health Services and Public Health Act 1968(a), or

(ii) by a district council under paragraph 1 of Part II of Schedule 9 to the Health and Social Services and Social Security Adjudications Act 1983(b);

(b)   remuneration for persons engaged in suitable work at the centres or other facilities referred to in sub-paragraphs (1)(a) and (2)(a) above, subject to paragraph 2(2)(a) of Schedule 8 to the Act(c);

(c)   social services (including advice and support) for the purposes of preventing the impairment of physical or mental health of adults in families where such impairment is likely, and for the purposes of preventing the break-up of such families, or for assisting in their rehabilitation;

(d)   night-sitter services;

(e)   recuperative holidays;

(f)   facilities for social and recreational activities;

(g)   services specifically for persons who are alcoholic or drug-dependent.

Services made available by another local authority etc.

4. For the purposes of any arrangements made under these

(a) 1968 c.46; amended by S.I. 1968/1699. <u>See</u> Paragraph 4(a) of Department of Health and Social Security Circular No. 19/71.

(b) 1983 c.41.

(c) As amended by section 108(7) of and Schedule 15 to the Children Act 1989.

Approvals and Directions, the Secretary of State hereby approves the use by local authorities of services or facilities made available by another authority, voluntary body or person on such conditions as may be agreed, but in making such arrangements, a local authority shall have regard to the importance of services being provided as near to a person's home as is practicable.

ANN DE PEYER

Dated   17/3/1993   Signed on behalf of the

Secretary of State for Health

DH FAIR ACCESS TO CARE SERVICES – GUIDANCE ON ELIGIBILITY CRITERIA FOR ADULT SOCIAL CARE

OVERVIEW

This guidance provides councils with social services responsibilities (hereafter referred to as 'councils') with a framework for determining eligibility for adult social care. It covers how councils should carry out assessments and reviews, and support individuals through these processes. Councils should ensure that they can provide or commission services to meet eligible needs, subject to their resources and, that within a council area, individuals in similar circumstances receive services capable of achieving broadly similar outcomes. Councils should implement the guidance by 7 April 2003. Through using the same framework to determine eligibility, local implementation should lead to a more consistent approach to eligibility and fairer access to care services across the country. Councils should be aware that this guidance neither says that different councils should make identical decisions about eligibility, nor prescribes what services should be available to service users who have similar needs.

A fundamental aspect of this guidance is for individual councils to make only one eligibility decision with respect to adults seeking social care support; that is, whether they are eligible for help or not. This decision should be made following an assessment of an individual's **presenting needs**. Councils should not operate eligibility criteria for specific types of assessment; rather, the scale and depth of the assessment should be proportionate to the individual's presenting needs and circumstances. Neither should councils operate eligibility criteria for different services to meet **eligible needs**. The most appropriate and cost-effective help should be determined by matching services to eligible needs through the use of statements of purpose.

Councils should assess an individual's presenting needs, and prioritise their eligible needs, according to the risks to their independence in both the short- and longer-term were help not to be provided. Councils should make changes in their practice to take a longer-term preventative view of individuals' needs and circumstances. With regard to their resources and other local factors, councils should focus help on those in greatest immediate or longer-term need.

Reviews should be undertaken at regular intervals to ensure that the care provided to individuals is still required and achieving the agreed outcomes. These reviews should include a re-assessment of an individual's needs.

The guidance advises councils on work to tackle age discrimination as outlined in the National Service Framework (NSF) for Older People (Department of Health, 2001).

The guidance is issued under section 7(1) of the Local Authority Social Services Act 1970. Practice guidance, offering suggestions and good practice models, will be published separately (Department of Health, forthcoming).

LINKS TO OTHER LEGISLATION
Health and social care
Local health bodies and councils were requested to agree their respective responsibilities for continuing health and social care services by 1 March 2002 (HSC 2001/015; LAC (2001)18). Once there is agreement about local responsibilities for NHS care and social care, councils should use this Fair Access guidance to determine eligibility for the services for which they are responsible by 1 October 2002 where possible, but no later than 7 April 2003. Continuing care criteria need to be agreed at a Strategic Health Authority level by 1 October 2002. As the framework for determining eligibility focuses on risks to independence, including health risks, this guidance may also be used as a starting point for eligibility criteria for packages of continuing health and social care.

For similar reasons, where local health bodies and councils are operating partnership arrangements under section 31 of the Health Act 1999, this guidance should be used by those agencies as a starting point to help them determine joint eligibility.

Children and Families
In the course of assessing an individual's needs, councils should recognise that adults, who have parenting responsibilities for a child under 18 years, may require help with these responsibilities. In this respect, in addition to the provision of adult care assessment and support, councils should be prepared to address their duty under the Children Act 1989 to safeguard and promote the welfare of children in their area. Where appropriate, councils should consider the use of the 'Framework for the Assessment of Children in Need and their Families' (or 'Assessment Framework') (Department of Health, 2000) to explore whether there are any issues relating to children in need and their parenting. The Assessment Framework should be used if it appears that there are children in need. On occasions, within one family, it may be necessary to concurrently assess the needs of an adult parent using the appropriate format for adult assessment, and the needs of the children and related parenting issues using the Assessment Framework.

Carers
This Fair Access guidance focuses on adults using, or seeking to use, social services. However, for many individuals the help and support of family members or other carers is essential to them remaining independent. Often carers should, and need to be, involved in the assessments and subsequent decisions about the help that is provided to the individual. Carers' own needs may be assessed within the framework of 'The Carers and Disabled Children Act 2000: A practitioners guide to carers' assessments' (Department of Health, 2001) where the focus is the carer's needs and the sustainability of the caring role.

Road Traffic Act 2000
The provision of services, such as travel concessions, and disabled persons parking badges for motor vehicles, is covered by regulations and guidance under the Road Traffic Act 2000, which give prescribed eligible categories and

descriptions of disabled people who may receive such services. As such, these services are outside the scope of this Fair Access guidance.

Rights and discrimination

When drawing up eligibility criteria for adult social care, councils should have regard to the Sex Discrimination Act 1975, the Disability Discrimination Act 1995, the Human Rights Act 1998, and the Race Relations (Amendment) Act 2000.

INTERPRETATION

In this guidance the issues and problems that are identified when individuals contact, or are referred to, councils seeking social care support are defined as 'presenting needs'. Those presenting needs for which a council will provide help because they fall within the council's eligibility criteria, are defined as 'eligible needs'. 'Eligibility criteria' describe the full range of eligible needs that will be met by councils having taken their resources into account.

Setting the eligibility criteria

In general, councils may provide community care services to individual adults with needs arising from physical, sensory, learning or cognitive disabilities and impairments, or from mental health difficulties. In this regard, councils' responsibilities to provide such services are principally set out in the:

National Assistance Act 1948.

Health Services and Public Health Act 1968.

Chronically Sick and Disabled Persons Act 1970.

National Health Service Act 1977.

Mental Health Act 1983.

Disabled Persons (Services, Consultation and Representation) Act 1986.

Councils should use the following eligibility framework to specify their eligibility criteria. In other words, they should use the framework to describe those circumstances that make individuals, with the disabilities, impairments and difficulties described in paragraph 14, eligible for help. The eligibility framework is based on the impact of needs on factors that are key to maintaining an individual's independence over time. The framework makes no reference to age, gender, ethnic group, religion, disabilities, impairments or similar difficulties, personal relationships, location, living and caring arrangements, and similar factors. In themselves, these factors do not threaten independence; however, they may need to be taken into account as needs are assessed and services considered.

The eligibility framework is graded into four bands, which describe the seriousness of the risk to independence or other consequences if needs are not addressed. The four bands are as follows:

Critical – when
life is, or will be, threatened; and/or
significant health problems have developed or will develop; and/or
there is, or will be, little or no choice and control over vital aspects of the immediate environment; and/or

serious abuse or neglect has occurred or will occur; and/or

there is, or will be, an inability to carry out vital personal care or domestic routines; and/or

vital involvement in work, education or learning cannot or will not be sustained; and/or

vital social support systems and relationships cannot or will not be sustained; and/or

vital family and other social roles and responsibilities cannot or will not be undertaken.

Substantial – when

there is, or will be, only partial choice and control over the immediate environment; and/or

abuse or neglect has occurred or will occur; and/or

there is, or will be, an inability to carry out the majority of personal care or domestic routines; and/or

involvement in many aspects of work, education or learning cannot or will not be sustained; and/or

the majority of social support systems and relationships cannot or will not be sustained; and/or

the majority of family and other social roles and responsibilities cannot or will not be undertaken.

Moderate – when

there is, or will be, an inability to carry out several personal care or domestic routines; and/or

involvement in several aspects of work, education or learning cannot or will not be sustained; and/or

several social support systems and relationships cannot or will not be sustained; and/or

several family and other social roles and responsibilities cannot or will not be undertaken.

Low – when

there is, or will be, an inability to carry out one or two personal care or domestic routines; and/or

involvement in one or two aspects of work, education or learning cannot or will not be sustained; and/or

one or two social support systems and relationships cannot or will not be sustained; and/or

one or two family and other social roles and responsibilities cannot or will not be undertaken.

In constructing and using their eligibility criteria, and also in determining eligibility for individuals, councils should prioritise needs that have immediate and longer-term critical consequences for independence ahead of needs with substantial consequences. Similarly, needs that have substantial consequences should be placed before needs with moderate consequences; and so on.

In setting their eligibility criteria councils should take account of their resources, local expectations, and local costs. Councils should take account of agreements with the NHS, including those covering transfers of care and hospital discharge. They should also take account of other agreements with other agencies, as well as other local and national factors.

Councils should review their eligibility criteria in line with their usual budget cycles. Such reviews may be brought forward if there are major or unexpected changes, including those with significant resource consequences.

Although final decisions remain with councils, they should consult service users, carers and appropriate local agencies and organisations about their eligibility criteria and how information about the criteria is presented and made available. Eligibility criteria should be published in local 'Better Care, Higher Standards' charters, and made readily available and accessible to service users, the public more generally, and other relevant local bodies.

Preventative approaches

With respect to prevention:

Councils should develop methods of risk assessment to help them identify those individuals where risks to independence appear relatively low, but are likely to become more serious over time. In doing so, they should refer to LAC(99)13 and LAC(99)14, issued in support of the Prevention Special Grant (subsequently the Promoting Independence Grant). Councils should also consider the benefits of preventative action to support carers, and refer to the Carers and Disabled Children Act 2000 in this regard.

Councils may become involved with other agencies in wider community development, 'Supporting People' or health promotion approaches, where there is widespread social disadvantage, or evidence that particular groups of people are socially excluded, or are geographically isolated. They should be prepared to act where it is difficult to estimate the likely benefit to a particular individual, but where there is evidence of the likely preventative benefits from non-intensive or other help to certain populations or groups.

Councils' published eligibility criteria should state explicitly how they approach the preventative issues set out above.

COMMISSIONING SERVICES

On determining their eligibility criteria for any given period, councils should ensure that services are in place to meet eligible needs. Councils should not adhere so rigidly to budget headings for specific services that resources cannot move from one budget heading to another, if necessary. Neither should they have blanket policies not to provide specific services. In particular, as noted in the NSF for Older People, they should consider whether age-based services for adults are in the best interests of service users, and be able to justify commissioning or providing services that, for example, separate older users from other adults.

Councils should develop strategies to fill service gaps and improve the range, accessibility and effectiveness of current service options, ensuring that services are sensitive to, and respect, the culture and faith, and communication and sensory attributes, of service users. Services should also be accessible to those who live in remote and isolated rural areas. To assist them in their commissioning, councils should follow the good practice outlined in 'Building capacity and partnership in care' (Department of Health, 2001).

For each service that councils directly provide or commission from others, there should be a statement of purpose. For registered services, statements of purpose will have been provided to the National Care Standards Commission. For non-registered services, councils should secure similar statements of purpose when finalising contracts or service agreements. These should set out the objectives and philosophy of care, nature of services, facilities, physical and geographical access, and likely charges. They should also describe the types of circumstances and the people for whom the service is designed. The statements of purpose should be used at the care planning stage to match services to eligible needs and desired outcomes.

Councils should use the framework of Best Value to ensure that services are reviewed and developed in a cost-effective, fair and transparent manner. Councils will be assisted in these reviews by the collection and analysis of information for the purposes of self-audit and monitoring, as described in paragraph 73.

Councils should ensure that commissioning arrangements are consistent with the objective of promoting direct payments. If a council chooses to set aside a budget for direct payments, separate from other budgets for non-residential care, it should be prepared to act flexibly if direct payments prove a more popular way than expected of meeting individuals' needs. Moreover, councils should prevent inflexible internal budget management procedures from hindering the commencement of a direct payments package.

GENERAL PRINCIPLES OF ASSESSMENT

Appropriate assessment lies at the heart of effective service delivery for a whole range of health and social care provision. Its purpose is to identify and evaluate an individual's presenting needs and how they constrain or support his/her capacity to live a full and independent life. Councils should ensure that individuals are active partners in the assessment of their needs. Appropriate service provision can then be planned both in the immediate and the longer-term to promote or preserve independence. Information from an individual's assessment should be used to inform decisions on eligibility and services that may be offered.

Councils should help individuals who may wish to approach them for support by publishing and disseminating information about access, eligibility and services, in a range of languages and formats. The information should also say what usually happens during assessment and care management processes, related time-scales, and how individuals might access direct payments. Local 'Better Care, Higher Standards' charters will be the means for providing this information and for setting standards and targets. Councils should promote the development of services that provide interpreters, translators, advocates, and supporters to help individuals access and make best use of the assessment process.

With reference to section 47(1) of the NHS and Community Care Act 1990, before starting a community care assessment councils should first ascertain whether a person appears to be in need of community care services. In exercising this judgement councils should set a low threshold, and avoid screening individuals out of the assessment process before sufficient information is known about them.

The presenting needs and circumstances of adults should be assessed with reference to this general assessment guidance, which builds on the 'Care management and assessment: practitioners' guide' issued by the Social Services Inspectorate (SSI) of the Department of Health and the Social Work Services Group of the Scottish Office in 1991.

In addition, reference should be made to the relevant policy and practice guidance for assessment and care planning for particular groups:

The NSF for Mental Health (Department of Health, 1999) and 'Effective Care Co-ordination in Mental Health Services – Modernising the Care Programme Approach' (Department of Health, 1999).

The NSF for Older People, and the detailed guidance on the single assessment process (Department of Health, 2002).

'Valuing people: a new strategy for learning disability for the 21st century' (Department of Health, 2001).

'The Carers and Disabled Children Act 2000: a practitioners guide to carers' assessments' (Department of Health, 2001).

Where individuals of working age are subject to an assessment, councils should ensure that practices and protocols are developed that reflect the local 'Welfare to Work' Joint Investment Plans for disabled people.

Whichever assessment framework is used, councils should not operate eligibility criteria to determine the complexity of the assessment offered; rather the depth and breadth of the assessment should be proportionate to individuals' presenting needs and circumstances. Based on their judgement, professionals may wish to carry out initial assessments, or assessments to take stock of wider needs, or specialist assessments of particular needs, or comprehensive assessment across all potential needs. In many cases, combinations of these assessment types may be used.

It is important for assessment to be rounded and person-centred, and for the evaluation of assessment information to lead to appropriate eligibility decisions and services that promote independence. In addition to social care problems, where appropriate, assessment should take account of health and other problems such as housing, but at the same time aim to be as simple and timely as possible. Councils should recognise that individuals are the experts on their own situation and encourage a partnership approach to assessment. They should help them prepare for the assessment process and find the best way for each individual to state their views. The use of interpreters, translators, advocates or supporters can be critical in this regard.

Assessment should be carried out in such a way, and be sufficiently transparent, for individuals to:

Gain a better understanding of their situation.

Identify the options that are available for managing their own lives.

Identify the outcomes required from any help that is provided.

Understand the basis on which decisions are reached.

In responding to the individual's account of his/her presenting needs, professionals should explore the intensity of particular needs including the physical pain, distress or disruption they cause, and the instability and predictability of problems, both on a day-to-day basis and over longer periods of time. They should consider with the individual any external and environmental factors that have caused, or exacerbate, the difficulties the individual is experiencing. The number of different needs faced by individuals, how needs interact, and how individuals react to the difficulties facing them are also important. Together, the individual and professional should look at the strengths and abilities that the individual can bring to bear on the presenting needs.

Assessment should be co-ordinated and integrated across local agencies relevant to the service user group. Agencies should share and agree the values that will underpin their work on assessment and care planning. They should ensure that information from assessment and related activities is shared among professionals, with due regard to informed consent, in such a way that duplication of assessment is minimised for service users and professionals alike. The content of the assessment process, and the systems and protocols for how agencies interact with each other should be agreed. The result will be an assessment process that individuals experience as consistent and timely

Assessment should not unfairly discriminate against individuals on the grounds of their age, gender, ethnic group, religion, disabilities, personal relationships, or living and caring arrangements, or whether they live in an urban or rural area. However, councils should take account of these factors in so far as they have a bearing on either presenting needs or the type and intensity of any care that is provided.

As presenting needs are fully described and explored, the individual and professional should consider and evaluate the risks to independence that result from the needs both in the immediate and longer-term. This evaluation should take full account of how needs and risks might change over time and the likely outcome if help were not to be provided. The evaluation of risks should focus on the following aspects that are central to an individual's independence:

Autonomy and freedom to make choices.

Health and safety including freedom from harm, abuse and neglect, and taking wider issues of housing and community safety into account.

The ability to manage personal and other daily routines.

Involvement in family and wider community life, including leisure, hobbies, unpaid and paid work, learning, and volunteering.

Individuals and professionals should consider risks faced not only by individuals but also those close to them, such as carers. They should consider which risks cause serious concern, and which risks may be acceptable or viewed as a natural and healthy part of independent living.

DETERMINING ELIGIBILITY IN RESPECT OF INDIVIDUALS

Eligibility for an individual is determined following assessment. As part of the assessment, information about an individual's presenting needs and related circumstances is established, and should be recorded. This information is then evaluated against the risks to his/ her autonomy, health and safety, ability to manage daily routines, and involvement in family and wider community life. Councils may wish to facilitate the risk evaluation by asking their professionals to identify risks using the framework in paragraph 16 above. These identified risks to independence will then be compared to the council's eligibility criteria. Through identifying the risks that fall within the eligibility criteria, professionals should identify eligible needs.

Once eligible needs are identified, councils should meet them. However, services may also be provided to meet some presenting needs as a consequence of, or to facilitate, eligible needs being met.

The determination of eligibility in individual cases should take account of the support from carers, family members, friends and neighbours which individuals can access to help them meet presenting needs. If, for example, an individual cannot perform several personal care tasks, but can do so without difficulty with the help of a carer, and the carer is happy to sustain their caring role in this way, both currently and in the longer-term, then the individual should not be perceived as having needs calling for community care services. That is, they should not be perceived as having eligible needs. However, during the actual assessment, no assumptions should be made about the level and quality of such support without the agreement of the relevant parties. Even where carers and others are providing support to an individual, the nature of the individual's needs, and the level of care, could be such as to make the individual eligible for community care services.

Councils should also be ready to support carers and others whenever necessary and appropriate, and in doing so consider a separate assessment of their circumstances.

Where eligible needs, and associated risks to independence, have been identified for an individual, they should be recorded, and agreed wherever possible, by them or their representatives. Councils should refer to paragraphs 65 to 68 for action they should take following decisions not to provide community care services as a consequence of either first assessments or subsequent reviews.

CARE PLANNING

If an individual is eligible for help then, together with the individual, councils should develop a care plan. The written record of the care plan should include as a minimum:

A note of the eligible needs and associated risks.

The preferred outcomes of service provision.

Contingency plans to manage emergency changes.

Details of services to be provided, and any charges the individual is assessed to pay, or if direct payments have been agreed.

Contributions which carers and others are willing and able to make.

A review date.

Appropriate services should be identified with reference to the statements of purpose requested from providers and, where appropriate, with reference to local continuing care agreements. Wherever applicable, the use of direct payments should also be considered and a decision made about their use.

Councils should aim to agree care plans with the service user, and should provide them with a copy of the care plan. Service users should be made aware of the arrangements for review and, where appropriate, advised that services may be withdrawn or changed as a result of the review.

Specific service user groups are subject to particular arrangements for care planning. Reference should be made to the documents listed in paragraph 32.

Councils are reminded that they should consider potential outcomes for individuals, and the cost-effectiveness of providing care to them, on the merits of each case. In doing so they should tailor services to each individual's circumstances, and should only use upper-cost parameters for care packages as a guide. Councils who only provide certain services to particular groups of adult service users including age-groups, or who have blanket policies about not providing other services including those geared towards prevention (see LAC(99)13 and LAC(99)14), should review their policies.

Councils are also reminded that they may take their resources into account when drawing up their eligibility criteria against which they assess individuals' needs, and when deciding which services will be provided to meet those needs. However, this does not mean that councils can take decisions on the basis of resources alone. Once a council has decided it is necessary to provide services to meet the eligible needs of an individual, it is under a duty to provide those services. For fuller details see LASSL(97)13 'Responsibilities of council social services departments: implications of recent judgments'.

Councils should provide services promptly once they have agreed to do so, but where waiting is unavoidable they should ensure alternative services are in place to meet eligible needs.

A council should ensure that all service users in its area with similar eligible needs, receive packages of care that are capable of achieving broadly similar outcomes, even though the particular form of help offered will be tailored to the individual service user.

Transitions

Councils should have in place arrangements to identify individuals who, as they move from youth to adulthood and then into older age, may need different kinds of service. In these situations, councils may wish to re-assess their needs, but in responding should note that marked changes in the type, level and location of support are usually not in service users' best interests.

When a service user permanently moves from one council area to another, the 'receiving' council should, pending an assessment, take account of the services that were previously received and the effect of any substantial changes on the service user when reaching an interim decision about what services to provide. The 'receiving' council should have regard to these factors, as well as the outcomes that were previously pursued, when carrying out the assessment and reaching longer-term decisions about what services will be provided. Where 'receiving' councils intend to pursue significantly different outcomes, or provide significantly different services, they should produce clear and written explanations for service users.

REVIEWS

From 7 April 2003, councils should begin to review the circumstances of all individuals in receipt of social care services, provided or commissioned by the council or purchased with direct payments. Notwithstanding closure, the circumstances of all service users in receipt of services on 7 April 2003 should have been reviewed at least once by the beginning of April 2004, and further reviews should be planned in accordance with this guidance.

Reviews should:

Establish how far the services provided have achieved the outcomes, set out in the care plan.

Re-assess the needs and circumstances of individual service users.

Help determine individuals' continued eligibility for support.

Confirm or amend the current care plan, or lead to closure.

Comment on the effectiveness of direct payments, where appropriate.

If not covered by the NSFs for Mental Health and Older People, or other guidance, the re-assessment part of the review should follow the general principles of assessment in this guidance.

There should be an initial review within three months of help first being provided or major changes made to current services. Thereafter, reviews should be scheduled at least annually or more often if individuals' circumstances appear to warrant it. Reviews may be considered on request from service users, providers of services and other appropriate individuals or agencies.

Reviews should be co-ordinated by council professionals who are competent in assessment and are in a position to determine eligibility and plan care services. Councils should bear in mind that council professionals involved in providing particular residential or community care services may not be best placed to carry out these functions, and that many users would prefer reviews to be independent of those actually providing their care. Such providers, as well as those in the independent sector, can however, provide useful information for use in the review.

In addition to the service user, reviews should involve: carers and representatives of the service user where appropriate; agencies that have purchased services for the service user; and key providers of those services. Reviews should consist of a meeting between the individual service user and the council professional responsible for the review, and may involve key others from those just listed. In exceptional circumstances reviews may be undertaken without direct face-to-face contact with the service user; however, councils need to be assured that this is feasible, particularly with respect to the re-assessment part of the review.

One-off pieces of assistive equipment provided to meet eligible needs for personal care, or to help service users manage their environment, do not need reviewing after initial confirmation of suitability. Major items of equipment should be reviewed as to their suitability and safety on an annual basis. The suitability and effectiveness of periodic services such as short-term breaks should be reviewed shortly after the first period and annually thereafter.

Councils should record the results of reviews with reference to the functions in paragraph 58. For those service users who remain eligible councils should update the care plan. For those people who are no longer eligible, councils should record the reasons for closure and share these with the individual.

SUPPORTING INDIVIDUALS WHOSE NEEDS ARE NOT ELIGIBLE FOR HELP

Following assessment, councils may decide not to provide help because an individual's needs are not eligible for support. In reaching its conclusion, the council should have satisfied itself that needs would not significantly worsen or increase in the foreseeable future for the lack of help, and thereby compromise key aspects of independence, including involvement in employment, training and education and parenting responsibilities, set out in paragraph 40 above. Similarly, when following a review it is planned to withdraw services from an individual, councils should be certain that needs will not worsen or increase and become eligible for help again in the foreseeable future as independence is undermined. (In helping to evaluate needs in this way, see paragraph 21 above.) When considering needs in this context, councils should not make assumptions about the capacity of family members or close friends to offer support. As with other key decisions, it will be particularly important when councils are considering significantly reducing or withdrawing services that service users fully appreciate what is happening and the consequences. In this regard, the use of interpreters, translators, advocates and supporters will be essential where appropriate.

Councils should exercise considerable caution and sensitivity when considering the withdrawal of services, following implementation of the Fair Access guidance, where reviews of needs and services have not been carried out for some time. In some individual cases it may not be practicable or safe to withdraw services, even though needs and associated risks may initially appear to fall outside eligibility criteria. In addition, before proceeding with closure, councils should check any commitments they gave to service users at the outset about the longevity of service receipt.

Where councils do not offer direct help following assessment, or feel able to withdraw services after review, they should put such decisions and reasons in writing, and make a written record available to the individual. Councils should be prepared to provide individuals with useful information and advice about other sources of support to address outstanding issues and problems. Councils should make individuals aware that they may use the complaints procedures to challenge decisions to withhold or withdraw services. Councils should tell individuals who are not eligible for help that if their circumstances change, they should renew contact at which time their needs may be reassessed. A contact number in the council should be given.

If individuals need other services, officers of the council should help them to find the right person to talk to in the relevant agency or organisation, and make contact on their behalf (see 'Better Care, Higher Standards'). Councils may also consider that a cross-council or cross-agency approach in support of wider community development, 'Supporting People' or health promotion is appropriate to certain individuals, and should facilitate access to relevant services.

EMERGENCIES AND CRISES

Councils should provide an immediate response to those individuals who approach them, or are referred, for social care support in emergencies and crises. After this initial response, they should inform the individual that a fuller assessment will follow, and services may be withdrawn or changed as a result of this assessment.

INDIVIDUALS' RESOURCES AND CAPACITY

An individual's financial circumstances should have no bearing on whether a council carries out a community care assessment or not. Neither should the individual's finances affect the level or detail of the assessment process. Once an individual's care needs have been assessed and a decision made about the care to be provided, an assessment of their ability to pay charges should be carried out promptly, and written information about any charges payable, and how they have been calculated, should be communicated to the individual.

CARE HOME RESIDENTS

Residents of care homes are important consumers of services. When planning to move into a care home, councils should inform individuals of suitable homes and provide them with statements of purpose for these homes including information on facilities, fees, charging arrangements, and NHS-funded nursing care where appropriate. Throughout their stay, care home residents should be kept informed of changes and developments that affect them. (For fuller details refer to 'Care Homes for Older People: National Minimum Standards', Department of Health, 2001.)

If an individual is to move to residential accommodation, and has both the 'capacity' (that is, mental ability) and the financial resources to arrange and pay for this care, the council should, if requested, provide information and advice to help him/her find an appropriate care home. However, generally, in these circumstances any contract for the residential accommodation will be between the individual and the provider of service. (There are exceptions. For example, during the 12-weeks property disregard, the contract should be agreed between the council and care home.)

SELF-AUDIT AND MANAGEMENT INFORMATION

Councils should ensure that they audit and monitor their performance with respect to fair access. In particular, they should be able to:

Monitor the extent to which different groups are referred, which groups receive an assessment and, following assessment, which groups go on to receive services.

Monitor the quality of the assessment and the eligibility decisions of their staff.

Monitor which presenting needs are evaluated as eligible needs and which are not.

Audit service effectiveness with reference to care plans and reviews.

Monitor the speed of assessment and subsequent service delivery in accordance with local 'Better Care, Higher Standards' charters.

Monitor the timing and frequency of reviews.

Monitor the extent to which residents of different geographical areas within the council's boundary receive an assessment and which go on to receive services.

Once information has been collected and analysed, results from all the above analyses should be shared with a range of interested parties including service users, elected members, and other local agencies.

MONITORING PROGRESS

While the primary responsibility for monitoring fair access to services lies with councils, the Department of Health will check the implementation of this Fair Access guidance through SSI monitoring and inspections, and other means. Councils whose eligibility criteria are most out of line will be expected to justify their positions.

STAFF LEARNING AND UNDERSTANDING

Councils should put in place training and development activities to enable an organisational culture that promotes person-centred care and independence. In particular, training on the assessment process should focus on improving risk assessments to identify the longer-term consequences of individuals' circumstances. Training should build on councils' achievements in this area and draw on the expertise and experience of particular service user and professional groups, anti-discriminatory practice and effective multi-disciplinary working. Training should involve staff from other agencies who may be involved in social care assessments and contribute to eligibility decisions. Training with other agencies will be essential where eligibility criteria have been developed jointly with other agencies and operate across agency boundaries.

COST OF IMPLEMENTATION

For the most part this guidance confirms and consolidates the 1990 Caring for People policy guidance and the 1991 'Care management and assessment: practitioners' guide'. As such this guidance has limited resource consequences. The guidance is fully consistent with the financial settlements for Personal Social Services resulting from the Government's Spending Reviews in 2000 and 2002. Nothing in it alters each council's responsibility to determine the level of resources allocated to social care for adults.

SUMMARY OF IMPLEMENTATION

Councils should use this guidance to review and revise their eligibility criteria and related arrangements including case reviews for adult social care. Prior to 7 April 2003, councils should review and consult on their eligibility criteria for adult social care in line with this Fair Access guidance. From 7 April 2003, they should apply eligibility criteria based on this guidance to all new referrals and requests for help, and schedule and conduct reviews if and as appropriate. All cases open on 7 April 2003 should be reviewed and reassessed by the beginning of April 2004, and further reviews should be planned for cases that remain open.

ROOTING OUT AGE DISCRIMINATION

Through implementing this Fair Access guidance, councils will fulfil the first stage requirement of Standard One of the NSF for Older People with respect to rooting out age discrimination. Namely, they will achieve the milestone, originally set for April 2002, for reviewing their 'eligibility criteria for adult social care to ensure that they do not discriminate against older people'. Implementation will also assist councils to review wider policies for, and access to, adult social care in pursuit of Standard One.

The next milestone, for October 2002, in the NSF for Older People with respect to tackling age discrimination relates to the analysis of levels and patterns of services, particularly in the NHS. More detailed guidance will be issued in 2002. Councils are encouraged to engage in this process, through their local NSF for Older People implementation teams, and to apply it to their own services.

COPIES AND ENQUIRIES

This guidance can be accessed on the Internet at www.doh.gov.uk/scg/facs. Further copies of the guidance may be obtained from the Department of Health, PO Box 777, London SE1 6XH, telephone 0870 155 5455 or fax 01623 724 524.

Enquiries about this guidance, apart from requests for copies, can be made to:

Department of Health (FACS)
Older Peoples Services CC3
Area 221
Wellington House
133–155 Waterloo Road
London SE1 8UG

DH CHILDREN (LEAVING CARE) ACT 2000 – REGULATIONS AND GUIDANCE (EXTRACTS)

Full text is available at: http://www.dh.gov.uk/PublicationsAndStatistics/ Publications/PublicationsLegislation/PublicationsLegislationArticle/fs/en? CONTENT_ID=4005283&chk=RfuTEG

Chapter 2
Unaccompanied asylum-seeking children (UASC)

7. Unaccompanied asylum-seeking children (UASC) are covered by the Children Act 1989 and the new provisions introduced by the Children (Leaving Care) Act in exactly the same way as other children in this country. However they will also have an immigration status – applying for asylum, acceptance as a refugee, granted exceptional leave to remain or refused leave to remain – which will need to be taken into account by councils providing services for them.

8. The Home Office has responsibility for immigration issues and it has stringent targets for dealing with cases. It aims to resolve all asylum applications within six months; that is, two months for the initial application and four months for any subsequent appeals. Any young person who enters the country as an unaccompanied minor claiming asylum should therefore normally have their case resolved while they are still a minor. While they are under 18 the local authority will be responsible under the Children Act for their care and accommodation. Depending on the council's assessment of their need, applying the Framework for the Assessment of Children in Need and their Families, this will normally mean either accommodating them under section 20 of the Children Act 1989, or helping them under section 17. In the former case, these young people will then come within the scope of the 2000 Act.

9. However it is possible that someone entering the country might reach the age of 18 without having received a final decision on their asylum application – for example, they might arrive and make their claim shortly before their 18th birthday. In such a case, the young person might expect to move on to the support arrangements for adult asylum seekers under the National Asylum Support Service (NASS) (the question of whether the person should apply to NASS or the local authority for support would depend on the date and location of their asylum claim). This might be vouchers only – for example, where they can live with family or friends; accommodation and vouchers; or accommodation only – for example, where they have been given permission to work but their income is insufficient to meet accommodation costs. At the same time, the responsible authority might have continuing duties towards the young person under the Children Act as amended by the Children (Leaving Care) Act, as a former relevant child, or as a qualifying person under section 24.

10. One aspect of the NASS arrangements is that asylum seekers may be dispersed around the country. However NASS will treat such 18 year-old asylum seekers sympathetically, and will not seek to disperse them, except in exceptional circumstances. In such a case NASS would contribute up to a pre-set limit to the cost of accommodation and utilities in the area where the young person was living, and if possible the same accommodation which he was already occupying. The responsible authority would be responsible for identi-

fying and managing suitable accommodation. The responsible authority would invoice NASS for the cost of accommodation and utilities at a rate agreed by the Home Office and the Department of Health. If the actual costs exceeded this agreed amount, the responsible authority would pay the balance using section 23C in the same way as for any other former relevant child, or section 24 for a qualifying person. However, before NASS can make any payment to the local authority it will need to ensure that a valid application has been made using a NASS application form.

11. If the young person requires vouchers for support, these will be provided by NASS on receipt of a valid NASS application form. The Children (Leaving Care) Act (Section 23C) gives the responsible authority continuing duties to assist former relevant children with the expenses associated with education and training, with employment and in general. Although the Benefits Agency disregards payments under Section 23C and Section 24 when determining benefits entitlement for former relevant children, because of its duty to consider whether an applicant is destitute, NASS cannot automatically disregard such payments. Where the responsible authority advises NASS that further assistance may or will be provided in accordance with Section 23C the Assessment Caseworker will need to establish as precisely as possible the nature of that support, and whether it has any impact on the young person's entitlement to NASS support. For example, if they are receiving assistance solely and specifically for travel expenses in connection with their education or training, it should not be treated as other income. However, where the responsible authority makes cash payments for essential living needs, they may be treated as income.

Benefits

DWP DECISION MAKER'S GUIDE TO THE PROVISION OF NATIONAL INSURANCE NUMBERS (AMENDMENT 13 – MAY 2003)

The Decision Maker's Guide is available in full from the DWP website at: http://www.dwp.gov.uk/publications/dwp/dmg/index.asp

Volume 1
Chapter 2 – Claims and applications
Provision of National Insurance numbers

. . .

02154   There is no entitlement to the benefits affected unless the claim is accompanied by sufficient information or evidence
1. to confirm the NI number quoted belongs to the claimant and any adult affected by the provisions,
2. to enable the NI number to be traced where the NI number is unknown,
3. to enable a NI number to be allocated where the claimant or adult does not have a NI number and they apply for one.[2]

02155   The [decision maker] DM should consider all three provisions in DMG 02154.

Example

A claimant mistakenly provides an incorrect NI number which cannot be confirmed using Departmental records. The NI number cannot be traced using the claimant's details. The claimant does not hold an NI number. The claimant should make an application for an NI number and provide sufficient information and evidence to enable a number to be traced or allocated.

02156   The NI number provisions are considered each time a relevant claim to benefit is made. The DM should not accept the conditions as satisfied simply because they were accepted as satisfied on an earlier claim. Conflicts in the evidence from the claimant and Departmental records should be resolved before the claim is referred to the DM.

02157   If the provisions are not satisfied the DM decides that there is no entitlement because a condition of entitlement is not met. If the NI number is produced after a disallowance, or there is a doubt about a number during an award, reconsideration may be appropriate (see DMG Chapters 03 and 04).

02158   Where a claim is made for a personal benefit and an adult dependency increase the NI number provisions must be satisfied for the claimant and the adult dependant. If the conditions are not satisfied for either the claimant or the adult the personal benefit and the adult dependency increase are disallowed. Personal benefit may already be in payment when an adult dependency increase is claimed. If the NI number provisions are not satisfied for the adult the award of personal benefit should be reconsidered (see DMG Chapters 03 and 04).

---

2   Social Security (National Insurance Number Information: Exemption) Regulations 1997 SI No 2676; Social Security Administration Act 1992 s1(1A) and (1B).

02159   Where JSA or IS are claimed the NI number provisions must be satisfied by the claimant and any adult included in the claim. If the condition is not satisfied for the claimant or the adult the claim is disallowed. JSA or IS may already be in payment when the claimant claims for another adult. If the NI number provisions are not satisfied for the adult the award of JSA or IS should be reconsidered (see DMG Chapters 03 and 04).

DWP LEAFLET 'HOW TO PROVE YOUR IDENTITY FOR SOCIAL SECURITY' GL25 OCTOBER 2003

Proving your identity

Benefit fraud costs the country millions of pounds. We need to make sure benefits are paid to the right people at the right time.

If you are claiming social security benefits you must be able to prove your identity.

This leaflet tells you about the ways you can prove your identity and the main papers you can show us to help. Check the list on page 3.

You will need to prove your identity if:

- You are claiming benefit
- You are starting work and need a National Insurance (NI) number
- You are actively seeking work and will need an NI number. Evidence that you are actively seeking work could include:
  – letters from employers
  – details of employment agencies you are registered with
  – confirmation of registration with a Jobcentre.

If you are claiming benefit for your partner, or for an adult dependant, you will need to prove their identity as well. If the partner/dependant has an NI number, you will need to provide this number.

If you do not have papers to help prove your identity, you should explain this to us. We may need to arrange an interview to help you prove your identity.

- If you have an NI number you should bring it with you.
- You can find this number on your NI number card, letters from social security or payslips.
- If you do not have an NI number we will arrange an interview. We will give you a number if necessary, but not always at the same time as your interview.
- An NI number is always made up of numbers and letters, like this: AC 12 34 56 C.

Your NI number is not proof of your identity.

Other formats

This leaflet is also available in large print, braille, on audio cassette and in the following languages:

• Arabic • Bengali • Chinese • Gujarati • Punjabi • Somali • Urdu • Vietnamese. You can also get these from your social security office.

Social security interviews

- Interviews can help us to help you prove your identity.
- You should bring as many papers as you can from the following list. Any other papers showing your name, address, date of birth or a photograph may also help.
- You cannot normally make a claim on behalf of someone else. If you want

more information get GL21 *A helping hand for benefits* from your social security office.

Papers you can use

These are some of the papers you can use to help prove your identity. You need to provide as much information as possible to confirm your identity. We cannot usually accept photocopies:

- Valid Passport/ID card
- Two or more passports if of dual/multi-nationality
- Home Office documents
- Work Permit
- Letter from employer/contract of employment
- Evidence of actively seeking work
- Payslips
- Mortgage/rental agreement of letter confirming where residing
- Marriage/birth certificate/deed poll
- Student loan documentation
- Certificate of incorporation
- Memorandum of association
- Articles of association
- Stock transfer form
- Schedule D Taxation form
- Services contract
- Invoices
- Letter from accountant
- Letter from clients
- Letter from college, including details of type and length of course and weekly hours
- Student ID card
- Full driving licence

Where to get help and advice

To get more information or other leaflets, get in touch with your social security office. For your nearest social security office look for the **Jobcentre Plus**, **social security** or **Jobcentre** display advert in the business numbers section of the phone book.

If you are able to use the internet, you can get more information from the DWP website. The address is:

www.dwp.gov.uk

To contact us by email see the *Contact Us* section of the website.

Remember that this leaflet is a general guide and is not a full and authoritative statement of the law. We have made every effort to ensure that the information in this leaflet is correct at the date shown on the cover. However, changes in the law may make the leaflet become gradually less accurate.

Leaflet GL25 October 2003. Replaces leaflet GL25 from April 2002
Produced by DWP Communications (Leeds).

International instruments

COUNCIL DIRECTIVE 2003/9/EEC[1]
Laying down minimum standards for the reception of asylum seekers

THE COUNCIL OF THE EUROPEAN UNION,

Having regard to the Treaty establishing the European Community, and in particular point (1)(b) of the first subparagraph of Article 63 thereof,

Having regard to the proposal from the Commission,[2]

Having regard to the opinion of the European Parliament,[3]

Having regard to the opinion of the Economic and Social Committee,[4]

Having regard to the opinion of the Committee of the Regions,[5]

Whereas:

(1) A common policy on asylum, including a Common European Asylum System, is a constituent part of the European Union's objective of progressively establishing an area of freedom, security and justice open to those who, forced by circumstances, legitimately seek protection in the Community.

(2) At its special meeting in Tampere on 15 and 16 October 1999, the European Council agreed to work towards establishing a Common European Asylum System, based on the full and inclusive application of the Geneva Convention relating to the Status of Refugees of 28 July 1951, as supplemented by the New York Protocol of 31 January 1967, thus maintaining the principle of non-refoulement.

(3) The Tampere Conclusions provide that a Common European Asylum System should include, in the short term, common minimum conditions of reception of asylum seekers.

(4) The establishment of minimum standards for the reception of asylum seekers is a further step towards a European asylum policy.

(5) This Directive respects the fundamental rights and observes the principles recognised in particular by the Charter of Fundamental Rights of the European Union. In particular, this Directive seeks to ensure full respect for human dignity and to promote the application of Articles 1 and 18 of the said Charter.

---

1 Comes into force in February 2005.
2 OJ C 213 E, 31 July 2001, p286.
3 Opinion delivered on 25 April 2002 (not yet published in the Official Journal).
4 OJ C 48, 21 February 2002, p63.
5 OJ C 107, 3 May 2002, p85.

(6) With respect to the treatment of persons falling within the scope of this Directive, Member States are bound by obligations under instruments of international law to which they are party and which prohibit discrimination.

(7) Minimum standards for the reception of asylum seekers that will normally suffice to ensure them a dignified standard of living and comparable living conditions in all Member States should be laid down.

(8) The harmonisation of conditions for the reception of asylum seekers should help to limit the secondary movements of asylum seekers influenced by the variety of conditions for their reception.

(9) Reception of groups with special needs should be specifically designed to meet those needs.

(10) Reception of applicants who are in detention should be specifically designed to meet their needs in that situation.

(11) In order to ensure compliance with the minimum procedural guarantees consisting in the opportunity to contact organisations or groups of persons that provide legal assistance, information should be provided on such organisations and groups of persons.

(12) The possibility of abuse of the reception system should be restricted by laying down cases for the reduction or withdrawal of reception conditions for asylum seekers.

(13) The efficiency of national reception systems and co-operation among Member States in the field of reception of asylum seekers should be secured.

(14) Appropriate co-ordination should be encouraged between the competent authorities as regards the reception of asylum seekers, and harmonious relationships between local communities and accommodation centres should therefore be promoted.

(15) It is in the very nature of minimum standards that Member States have the power to introduce or maintain more favourable provisions for third-country nationals and stateless persons who ask for international protection from a Member State.

(16) In this spirit, Member States are also invited to apply the provisions of this Directive in connection with procedures for deciding on applications for forms of protection other than that emanating from the Geneva Convention for third country nationals and stateless persons.

(17) The implementation of this Directive should be evaluated at regular intervals.

(18) Since the objectives of the proposed action, namely to establish minimum standards on the reception of asylum seekers in Member States, cannot be sufficiently achieved by the Member States and can therefore, by reason of the scale and effects of the proposed action, be better achieved by the Community, the Community may adopt measures in accordance with the principles of subsidiarity as set out in Article 5 of the Treaty. In accordance with the principle of proportionality, as set out in that Article, this Directive does not go beyond what is necessary in order to achieve those objectives.

(19) In accordance with Article 3 of the Protocol on the position of the United Kingdom and Ireland, annexed to the Treaty on European Union and to the Treaty establishing the European Community, the United Kingdom gave notice, by letter of 18 August 2001, of its wish to take part in the adoption and application of this Directive.

(20) In accordance with Article 1 of the said Protocol, Ireland is not participating in the adoption of this Directive. Consequently, and without prejudice to Article 4 of the aforementioned Protocol, the provisions of this Directive do not apply to Ireland.

(21) In accordance with Articles 1 and 2 of the Protocol on the position of Denmark, annexed to the Treaty on European Union and to the Treaty establishing the European Community, Denmark is not participating in the adoption of this Directive and is therefore neither bound by it nor subject to its application,

HAS ADOPTED THIS DIRECTIVE:

CHAPTER I
PURPOSE, DEFINITIONS AND SCOPE

Article 1
Purpose

The purpose of this Directive is to lay down minimum standards for the reception of asylum seekers in Member States.

Article 2
Definitions

For the purposes of this Directive:

(a) 'Geneva Convention' shall mean the Convention of 28 July 1951 relating to the status of refugees, as amended by the New York Protocol of 31 January 1967;

(b) 'application for asylum' shall mean the application made by a third-country national or a stateless person which can be understood as a request for international protection from a Member State, under the Geneva Convention. Any application for international protection is presumed to be an application for asylum unless a third-country national or a stateless person explicitly requests another kind of protection that can be applied for separately;

(c) 'applicant' or 'asylum seeker' shall mean a third country national or a stateless person who has made an application for asylum in respect of which a final decision has not yet been taken;

(d) 'family members' shall mean, in so far as the family already existed in the country of origin, the following members of the applicant's family who are present in the same Member State in relation to the application for asylum:

  (i) the spouse of the asylum seeker or his or her unmarried partner in a stable relationship, where the legislation or practice of the Member State concerned treats unmarried couples in a way comparable to married couples under its law relating to aliens;

  (ii) the minor children of the couple referred to in point (i) or of the applicant, on condition that they are unmarried and dependent and regardless of whether they were born in or out of wedlock or adopted as defined under the national law;

(e) 'refugee' shall mean a person who fulfils the requirements of Article 1(A) of the Geneva Convention;

(f) 'refugee status' shall mean the status granted by a Member State to a person who is a refugee and is admitted as such to the territory of that Member State;

(g) 'procedures' and 'appeals', shall mean the procedures and appeals established by Member States in their national law;

(h) 'unaccompanied minors' shall mean persons below the age of eighteen who arrive in the territory of the Member States unaccompanied by an adult responsible for them whether by law or by custom, and for as long as they are not effectively taken into the care of such a person; it shall include minors who are left unaccompanied after they have entered the territory of Member States;

(i) 'reception conditions' shall mean the full set of measures that Member States grant to asylum seekers in accordance with this Directive;

(j) 'material reception conditions' shall mean the reception conditions that include housing, food and clothing, provided in kind, or as financial allowances or in vouchers, and a daily expenses allowance;

(k) 'detention' shall mean confinement of an asylum seeker by a Member State within a particular place, where the applicant is deprived of his or her freedom of movement;

(l) 'accommodation centre' shall mean any place used for collective housing of asylum seekers.

Article 3
Scope

1. This Directive shall apply to all third country nationals and stateless persons who make an application for asylum at the border or in the territory of a Member State as long as they are allowed to remain on the territory as asylum seekers, as well as to family members, if they are covered by such application for asylum according to the national law.

2. This Directive shall not apply in cases of requests for diplomatic or territorial asylum submitted to representations of Member States.

3. This Directive shall not apply when the provisions of Council Directive 2001/55/EC of 20 July 2001 on minimum standards for giving temporary protection in the event of a mass influx of displaced persons and on measures promoting a balance of efforts between Member States in receiving such persons and bearing the consequences thereof[6] are applied.

4. Member States may decide to apply this Directive in connection with procedures for deciding on applications for kinds of protection other than that emanating from the Geneva Convention for third-country nationals or stateless persons who are found not to be refugees.

Article 4
More favourable provisions

Member States may introduce or retain more favourable provisions in the field of reception conditions for asylum seekers and other close relatives of the applicant who are present in the same Member State when they are dependent on him or for humanitarian reasons insofar as these provisions are compatible with this Directive.

6   OJ L 212, 7 August 2001, p12.

CHAPTER II
GENERAL PROVISIONS ON RECEPTION CONDITIONS

Article 5
Information

1. Member States shall inform asylum seekers, within a reasonable time not exceeding fifteen days after they have lodged their application for asylum with the competent authority, of at least any established benefits and of the obligations with which they must comply relating to reception conditions.

   Member States shall ensure that applicants are provided with information on organisations or groups of persons that provide specific legal assistance and organisations that might be able to help or inform them concerning the available reception conditions, including health care.

2. Member States shall ensure that the information referred to in paragraph 1 is in writing and, as far as possible, in a language that the applicants may reasonably be supposed to understand. Where appropriate, this information may also be supplied orally.

Article 6
Documentation

1. Member States shall ensure that, within three days after an application is lodged with the competent authority, the applicant is provided with a document issued in his or her own name certifying his or her status as an asylum seeker or testifying that he or she is allowed to stay in the territory of the Member State while his or her application is pending or being examined.

   If the holder is not free to move within all or a part of the territory of the Member State, the document shall also certify this fact.

2. Member States may exclude application of this Article when the asylum seeker is in detention and during the examination of an application for asylum made at the border or within the context of a procedure to decide on the right of the applicant legally to enter the territory of a Member State. In specific cases, during the examination of an application for asylum, Member States may provide applicants with other evidence equivalent to the document referred to in paragraph 1.

3. The document referred to in paragraph 1 need not certify the identity of the asylum seeker.

4. Member States shall adopt the necessary measures to provide asylum seekers with the document referred to in paragraph 1, which must be valid for as long as they are authorised to remain in the territory of the Member State concerned or at the border thereof.

5. Member States may provide asylum seekers with a travel document when serious humanitarian reasons arise that require their presence in another State.

Article 7
Residence and freedom of movement

1. Asylum seekers may move freely within the territory of the host Member State or within an area assigned to them by that Member State. The assigned area

shall not affect the unalienable sphere of private life and shall allow sufficient scope for guaranteeing access to all benefits under this Directive.

2. Member States may decide on the residence of the asylum seeker for reasons of public interest, public order or, when necessary, for the swift processing and effective monitoring of his or her application.

3. When it proves necessary, for example for legal reasons or reasons of public order, Member States may confine an applicant to a particular place in accordance with their national law.

4. Member States may make provision of the material reception conditions subject to actual residence by the applicants in a specific place, to be determined by the Member States. Such a decision, which may be of a general nature, shall be taken individually and established by national legislation.

5. Member States shall provide for the possibility of granting applicants temporary permission to leave the place of residence mentioned in paragraphs 2 and 4 and/or the assigned area mentioned in paragraph 1. Decisions shall be taken individually, objectively and impartially and reasons shall be given if they are negative.

   The applicant shall not require permission to keep appointments with authorities and courts if his or her appearance is necessary.

6. Member States shall require applicants to inform the competent authorities of their current address and notify any change of address to such authorities as soon as possible.

Article 8
Families
Member States shall take appropriate measures to maintain as far as possible family unity as present within their territory, if applicants are provided with housing by the Member State concerned. Such measures shall be implemented with the asylum seeker's agreement.

Article 9
Medical screening
Member States may require medical screening for applicants on public health grounds.

Article 10
Schooling and education of minors
1. Member States shall grant to minor children of asylum seekers and to asylum seekers who are minors access to the education system under similar conditions as nationals of the host Member State for so long as an expulsion measure against them or their parents is not actually enforced. Such education may be provided in accommodation centres.

   The Member State concerned may stipulate that such access must be confined to the State education system.

   Minors shall be younger than the age of legal majority in the Member State in which the application for asylum was lodged or is being examined. Member States shall not withdraw secondary education for the sole reason that the minor has reached the age of majority.

2. Access to the education system shall not be postponed for more than three months from the date the application for asylum was lodged by the minor or the minor's parents. This period may be extended to one year where specific education is provided in order to facilitate access to the education system.
3. Where access to the education system as set out in paragraph 1 is not possible due to the specific situation of the minor, the Member State may offer other education arrangements.

Article 11
Employment

1. Member States shall determine a period of time, starting from the date on which an application for asylum was lodged, during which an applicant shall not have access to the labour market.
2. If a decision at first instance has not been taken within one year of the presentation of an application for asylum and this delay cannot be attributed to the applicant, Member States shall decide the conditions for granting access to the labour market for the applicant.
3. Access to the labour market shall not be withdrawn during appeals procedures, where an appeal against a negative decision in a regular procedure has suspensive effect, until such time as a negative decision on the appeal is notified.
4. For reasons of labour market policies, Member States may give priority to EU citizens and nationals of States parties to the Agreement on the European Economic Area and also to legally resident third-country nationals.

Article 12
Vocational training

Member States may allow asylum seekers access to vocational training irrespective of whether they have access to the labour market.

Access to vocational training relating to an employment contract shall depend on the extent to which the applicant has access to the labour market in accordance with Article 11.

Article 13
General rules on material reception conditions and health care

1. Member States shall ensure that material reception conditions are available to applicants when they make their application for asylum.
2. Member States shall make provisions on material reception conditions to ensure a standard of living adequate for the health of applicants and capable of ensuring their subsistence.

   Member States shall ensure that that standard of living is met in the specific situation of persons who have special needs, in accordance with Article 17, as well as in relation to the situation of persons who are in detention.
3. Member States may make the provision of all or some of the material reception conditions and health care subject to the condition that applicants do not have sufficient means to have a standard of living adequate for their health and to enable their subsistence.

4. Member States may require applicants to cover or contribute to the cost of the material reception conditions and of the health care provided for in this Directive, pursuant to the provision of paragraph 3, if the applicants have sufficient resources, for example if they have been working for a reasonable period of time.

   If it transpires that an applicant had sufficient means to cover material reception conditions and health care at the time when these basic needs were being covered, Member States may ask the asylum seeker for a refund.

5. Material reception conditions may be provided in kind, or in the form of financial allowances or vouchers or in a combination of these provisions.

   Where Member States provide material reception conditions in the form of financial allowances or vouchers, the amount thereof shall be determined in accordance with the principles set out in this Article.

Article 14
Modalities for material reception conditions

1. Where housing is provided in kind, it should take one or a combination of the following forms:
   (a) premises used for the purpose of housing applicants during the examination of an application for asylum lodged at the border;
   (b) accommodation centres which guarantee an adequate standard of living;
   (c) private houses, flats, hotels or other premises adapted for housing applicants.

2. Member States shall ensure that applicants provided with the housing referred to in paragraph 1(a), (b) and (c) are assured:
   (a) protection of their family life;
   (b) the possibility of communicating with relatives, legal advisers and representatives of the United Nations High Commissioner for Refugees (UNHCR) and non-governmental organisations (NGOs) recognised by Member States.

   Member States shall pay particular attention to the prevention of assault within the premises and accommodation centres referred to in paragraph 1(a) and (b).

3. Member States shall ensure, if appropriate, that minor children of applicants or applicants who are minors are lodged with their parents or with the adult family member responsible for them whether by law or by custom.

4. Member States shall ensure that transfers of applicants from one housing facility to another take place only when necessary. Member States shall provide for the possibility for applicants to inform their legal advisers of the transfer and of their new address.

5. Persons working in accommodation centres shall be adequately trained and shall be bound by the confidentiality principle as defined in the national law in relation to any information they obtain in the course of their work.

6. Member States may involve applicants in managing the material resources and non-material aspects of life in the centre through an advisory board or council representing residents.

7. Legal advisors or counsellors of asylum seekers and representatives of the

United Nations High Commissioner for Refugees or non-governmental organisations designated by the latter and recognised by the Member State concerned shall be granted access to accommodation centres and other housing facilities in order to assist the said asylum seekers. Limits on such access may be imposed only on grounds relating to the security of the centres and facilities and of the asylum seekers.

8. Member States may exceptionally set modalities for material reception conditions different from those provided for in this Article, for a reasonable period which shall be as short as possible, when:
   - an initial assessment of the specific needs of the applicant is required,
   - material reception conditions, as provided for in this Article, are not available in a certain geographical area,
   - housing capacities normally available are temporarily exhausted,
   - the asylum seeker is in detention or confined to border posts.

These different conditions shall cover in any case basic needs.

Article 15
Health care

1. Member States shall ensure that applicants receive the necessary health care which shall include, at least, emergency care and essential treatment of illness.
2. Member States shall provide necessary medical or other assistance to applicants who have special needs.

CHAPTER III
REDUCTION OR WITHDRAWAL OF RECEPTION CONDITIONS

Article 16
Reduction or withdrawal of reception conditions

1. Member States may reduce or withdraw reception conditions in the following cases:
   (a) where an asylum seeker:
       - abandons the place of residence determined by the competent authority without informing it or, if requested, without permission, or
       - does not comply with reporting duties or with requests to provide information or to appear for personal interviews concerning the asylum procedure during a reasonable period laid down in national law, or
       - has already lodged an application in the same Member State.

       When the applicant is traced or voluntarily reports to the competent authority, a duly motivated decision, based on the reasons for the disappearance, shall be taken on the reinstallation of the grant of some or all of the reception conditions;
   (b) where an applicant has concealed financial resources and has therefore unduly benefited from material reception conditions.

   If it transpires that an applicant had sufficient means to cover material reception conditions and health care at the time when these basic needs were being covered, Member States may ask the asylum seeker for a refund.

2. Member States may refuse conditions in cases where an asylum seeker has failed to demonstrate that the asylum claim was made as soon as reasonably practicable after arrival in that Member State.

3. Member States may determine sanctions applicable to serious breaching of the rules of the accommodation centres as well as to seriously violent behaviour.

4. Decisions for reduction, withdrawal or refusal of reception conditions or sanctions referred to in paragraphs 1, 2 and 3 shall be taken individually, objectively and impartially and reasons shall be given. Decisions shall be based on the particular situation of the person concerned, especially with regard to persons covered by Article 17, taking into account the principle of proportionality. Member States shall under all circumstances ensure access to emergency health care.

5. Member States shall ensure that material reception conditions are not withdrawn or reduced before a negative decision is taken.

CHAPTER IV
PROVISIONS FOR PERSONS WITH SPECIAL NEEDS

Article 17
General principle

1. Member States shall take into account the specific situation of vulnerable persons such as minors, unaccompanied minors, disabled people, elderly people, pregnant women, single parents with minor children and persons who have been subjected to torture, rape or other serious forms of psychological, physical or sexual violence, in the national legislation implementing the provisions of Chapter II relating to material reception conditions and health care.

2. Paragraph 1 shall apply only to persons found to have special needs after an individual evaluation of their situation.

Article 18
Minors

1. The best interests of the child shall be a primary consideration for Member States when implementing the provisions of this Directive that involve minors.

2. Member States shall ensure access to rehabilitation services for minors who have been victims of any form of abuse, neglect, exploitation, torture or cruel, inhuman and degrading treatment, or who have suffered from armed conflicts, and ensure that appropriate mental health care is developed and qualified counselling is provided when needed.

Article 19
Unaccompanied minors

1. Member States shall as soon as possible take measures to ensure the necessary representation of unaccompanied minors by legal guardianship or, where necessary, representation by an organisation which is responsible for the care and well-being of minors, or by any other appropriate representation. Regular assessments shall be made by the appropriate authorities.

2. Unaccompanied minors who make an application for asylum shall, from the moment they are admitted to the territory to the moment they are obliged to leave the host Member State in which the application for asylum was made or is being examined, be placed:
   (a) with adult relatives;
   (b) with a foster-family;
   (c) in accommodation centres with special provisions for minors;
   (d) in other accommodation suitable for minors.
   Member States may place unaccompanied minors aged 16 or over in accommodation centres for adult asylum seekers.
   As far as possible, siblings shall be kept together, taking into account the best interests of the minor concerned and, in particular, his or her age and degree of maturity. Changes of residence of unaccompanied minors shall be limited to a minimum.
3. Member States, protecting the unaccompanied minor's best interests, shall endeavour to trace the members of his or her family as soon as possible. In cases where there may be a threat to the life or integrity of the minor or his or her close relatives, particularly if they have remained in the country of origin, care must be taken to ensure that the collection, processing and circulation of information concerning those persons is undertaken on a confidential basis, so as to avoid jeopardising their safety.
4. Those working with unaccompanied minors shall have had or receive appropriate training concerning their needs, and shall be bound by the confidentiality principle as defined in the national law, in relation to any information they obtain in the course of their work.

Article 20
Victims of torture and violence
Member States shall ensure that, if necessary, persons who have been subjected to torture, rape or other serious acts of violence receive the necessary treatment of damages caused by the aforementioned acts.

CHAPTER V
APPEALS

Article 21
Appeals
1. Member States shall ensure that negative decisions relating to the granting of benefits under this Directive or decisions taken under Article 7 which individually affect asylum seekers may be the subject of an appeal within the procedures laid down in the national law. At least in the last instance the possibility of an appeal or a review before a judicial body shall be granted.
2. Procedures for access to legal assistance in such cases shall be laid down in national law.

CHAPTER VI
ACTIONS TO IMPROVE THE EFFICIENCY OF THE RECEPTION SYSTEM

Article 22
Co-operation
Member States shall regularly inform the Commission on the data concerning the number of persons, broken down by sex and age, covered by reception conditions and provide full information on the type, name and format of the documents provided for by Article 6.

Article 23
Guidance, monitoring and control system
Member States shall, with due respect to their constitutional structure, ensure that appropriate guidance, monitoring and control of the level of reception conditions are established.

Article 24
Staff and resources
1. Member States shall take appropriate measures to ensure that authorities and other organisations implementing this Directive have received the necessary basic training with respect to the needs of both male and female applicants.
2. Member States shall allocate the necessary resources in connection with the national provisions enacted to implement this Directive.

CHAPTER VII
FINAL PROVISIONS

Article 25
Reports
By 6 August 2006, the Commission shall report to the European Parliament and the Council on the application of this Directive and shall propose any amendments that are necessary.

Member States shall send the Commission all the information that is appropriate for drawing up the report, including the statistical data provided for by Article 22 by 6 February 2006.

After presenting the report, the Commission shall report to the European Parliament and the Council on the application of this Directive at least every five years.

Article 26
Transposition
1. Member States shall bring into force the laws, regulations and administrative provisions necessary to comply with this Directive by 6 February 2005. They shall forthwith inform the Commission thereof.

When the Member States adopt these measures, they shall contain a reference to this Directive or shall be accompanied by such a reference on the occasion of their official publication. Member States shall determine how such a reference is to be made.

2. Member States shall communicate to the Commission the text of the provisions of national law which they adopt in the field relating to the enforcement of this Directive.

Article 27
Entry into force

This Directive shall enter into force on the day of its publication in the Official Journal of the European Union.

Article 28
Addressees

This Directive is addressed to the Member States in accordance with the Treaty establishing the European Union.

Done at Brussels, 27 January 2003.

For the Council
The President
G Papandreou

EUROPEAN CONVENTION ON SOCIAL AND MEDICAL ASSISTANCE AND PROTOCOL 1953

SECTION I: GENERAL PROVISIONS

Article 1

Each of the Contracting Parties undertakes to ensure that nationals of the other Contracting Parties who are lawfully present in any part of its territory to which this Convention applies, and who are without sufficient resources, shall be entitled equally with its own nationals and on the same conditions to social and medical assistance (hereinafter referred to as 'assistance') provided by the legislation in force from time to time in that part of its territory.

SECTION III: RESIDENCE

Article 11

(a) Residence by an alien in the territory of any of the Contracting Parties shall be considered lawful within the meaning of this Convention so long as there is in force in his case a permit or such other permission as is required by the laws and regulations of the country concerned to reside therein. Failure to renew any such permit, if due solely to the inadvertence of the person concerned, shall not cause him to cease to be entitled to assistance.

(b) Lawful residence shall become unlawful from the date of any deportation order made out against the person concerned, unless a stay of execution is granted.

Article 12

The commencing date of the period of residence laid down in Article 7 shall in each country be established, in the absence of evidence to the contrary, on the basis of evidence supplied by official investigation or by the documents listed in Annex III or any documents recognised by the laws and regulations of the country as affording proof of residence.

Article 13

(a) Proof of continuity of residence may be shown by the production of any evidence acceptable in the country of residence, such as proof of occupational activity or the production of rent receipts.

(b) (i)   Residence shall be regarded as continuous notwithstanding periods of absence of less than three months, provided that the absence is not caused by repatriation or deportation.

(ii)   Periods of absence of six months or more shall be held to interrupt the continuity of residence.

(iii) In order to determine whether a period of absence of between three and six months shall interrupt the continuity of residence, regard shall be had to the intention or otherwise of the person concerned to return to the country of residence and to the extent to which he has preserved his connection therewith during the period of his absence.

(iv)   Service in ships registered in the country of residence shall not be held to interrupt the continuity of residence. Service in other ships shall be treated in accordance with the provisions of sub-paragraphs (i) to (iii) above.

Article 14

There shall be excluded in the calculation of length of residence those periods during which the person concerned has been in receipt of assistance from public monies as laid down in the legislative measures mentioned in Annex I, except in the case of medical treatment for acute illness or short-term medical treatment.

SECTION IV: MISCELLANEOUS PROVISIONS

Article 18

The provisions of this Convention shall not limit the provisions of any national laws or regulations, international conventions or bilateral or multilateral agreements which are more favourable for the beneficiary.

Article 19

Annexes I, II and III shall constitute an integral part of this Convention.

PROTOCOL (signed but not yet ratified)

Article 1

For the purposes of this Protocol the term 'refugee' shall have the meaning ascribed to it in Article 1 of the Geneva Convention, provided that each Contracting Party shall make a declaration at the time of signature or ratification hereof or accession hereto, specifying which of the meanings set out in paragraph B of Article 1 of that Convention it applies for the purpose of its obligations under this Protocol, unless such Party has already made such a declaration at the time of its signature or ratification of that Convention.

Article 2

The provisions of Section I of the Assistance Convention shall apply to refugees under the same conditions as they apply to the nationals of the Contracting Parties thereto.

Article 3

1 The provisions of Section II of the Assistance Convention shall not apply to refugees.
2 In the case of a person who has ceased to qualify for the benefits of the Geneva Convention in accordance with the provisions of paragraph C of Article 1 thereof, the period for repatriation laid down in Article 7(a)(i) of the Assistance Convention shall begin from the date when he has thus ceased to qualify.

Article 4

As between the Contracting Parties, the provisions of Articles 1, 2 and 3 of this Protocol shall be regarded as additional articles to the Assistance Convention, and the remaining provisions of that Convention shall apply accordingly.

1 This Protocol shall be open to the signature of the members of the Council of Europe who have signed the Assistance Convention. It shall be ratified.
2 Any State which has acceded to the Assistance Convention may accede to this Protocol.
3 This Protocol shall come into force on the first day of the month following the

date of deposit of the second instrument of ratification.

4 As regards any signatory ratifying subsequently, or any acceding State, the Protocol shall come into force on the first day of the month following the date of the deposit of its instrument of ratification or accession.

5 Instruments of ratification and accession shall be deposited with the Secretary General of the Council of Europe, who shall notify the members of the Council and acceding States of the names of those who have ratified or acceded.

Annex I – Legislative measures regarding assistance referred to in Article 1 of the Convention

United Kingdom of Great Britain and Northern Ireland

Great Britain: The Social Security Act 1986 and regulations made thereunder so far as the Act and regulations relate to Income Support and Family Credit; and the Social Security Act 1986 and regulations made and directions given thereunder so far as the Act, regulations and directions relate to payments payable out of the Social Fund referred to in the directions as Crisis Loans.

Northern Ireland: The Social Security (Northern Ireland) Order 1986 and regulations made thereunder so far as the Order and regulations relate to the Income Support and Family Credit; and the Social Security (Northern Ireland) Order 1986 and regulations made and directions given thereunder so far as the Order, regulations and directions relate to payments payable out of the Social Fund referred to in the directions as Crisis Loans.

Laws and regulations concerning Great Britain, Northern Ireland and the Isle of Ma establishing National health services.

Annex II – Reservations formulated by the Contracting Parties
The Government of the United Kingdom has formulated the following reservation:

Her Majesty's Government reserve the right to free themselves from their obligation under Article 1 in respect of any person who may be repatriated by virtue of the provisions of Article 7 but who fails to take advantage of the facilities offered for his repatriation (including free transport to the frontier of his country of origin).

Annex III – List of documents recognised as affording proof of residence, referred to in article 11 of the Convention
United Kingdom of Great Britain and Northern Ireland
An endorsement in the passport or other travel document; a residence permit issued to nationals of EEC member states; or a police certificate of registration.

European Social Charter 1961

PART II

The Contracting Parties undertake, as provided for in Part III, to consider themselves bound by the obligations laid down in the following articles and paragraphs.

Article 1: The right to work

With a view to ensuring the effective exercise of the right to work, the Contracting Parties undertake:

1 To accept as one of their primary aims and responsibilities the achievement and maintenance of as high and stable a level of employment as possible, with a view to the attainment of full employment;
2 To protect effectively the right of the worker to earn his living in an occupation freely entered upon;
3 To establish or maintain free employment services for all workers;
4 To provide or promote appropriate vocational guidance, training and rehabilitation.

Article 12: The right to social security

With a view to ensuring the effective exercise of the right to social security, the Contracting Parties undertake:

1 To establish or maintain a system of social security;
2 To maintain the social security system at a satisfactory level at least equal to that required for ratification of the International Labour Convention (No 102) Concerning Minimum Standards of Social Security;
3 To endeavour to raise progressively the system of social security to a higher level;
4 To take steps, by the conclusion of appropriate bilateral and multilateral agreements or by other means, and subject to the conditions laid down in such agreements, in order to ensure:
   (a) Equal treatment with their own nationals of the nationals of other Contracting Parties in respect of social security rights, including the retention of benefits arising out of social security legislation, whatever movements the persons protected may undertake between the territories of the Contracting Parties;
   (b) The granting, maintenance and resumption of social security rights by such means as the accumulation of insurance or employment periods completed under the legislation of each of the Contracting Parties.

Article 13: The right to social and medical assistance

With a view to ensuring the effective exercise of the right to social and medical assistance, the Contracting Parties undertake:

1 To ensure that any person who is without adequate resources and who is unable to secure such resources either by his own efforts or from other sources, in particular by benefits under a social security scheme, be granted adequate assistance, and, in case of sickness, the care necessitated by his condition;

2 To ensure that persons receiving such assistance shall not, for that reason, suffer from a diminution of their political or social rights;

3 To provide that everyone may receive by appropriate public or private services such advice and personal help as may be required to prevent, to remove, or to alleviate personal or family want;

4 To apply the provisions referred to in paragraphs 1, 2 and 3 of this article on an equal footing with their nationals to nationals of other Contracting Parties lawfully within their territories, in accordance with their obligations under the European Convention on Social and Medical Assistance, signed at Paris on 11 December 1953.

Article 14: The right to benefit from social welfare services

With a view to ensuring the effective exercise of the right to benefit from social welfare services, the Contracting Parties undertake:

1 To promote or provide services which, by using methods of social work, would contribute to the welfare and development of both individuals and groups in the community, and to their adjustment to the social environment;

2 To encourage the participation of individuals and voluntary or other organisations in the establishment and maintenance of such services.

Article 15: The right of physically or mentally disabled persons to vocational training, rehabilitation and social resettlement

With a view to ensuring the effective exercise of the right of the physically or mentally disabled to vocational training, rehabilitation and resettlement, the Contracting Parties undertake:

1 To take adequate measures for the provision of training facilities, including, where necessary, specialised institutions, public or private;

2 To take adequate measures for the placing of disabled persons in employment, such as specialised placing services, facilities for sheltered employment and measures to encourage employers to admit disabled persons to employment.

Article 16: The right of the family to social, legal and economic protection

With a view to ensuring the necessary conditions for the full development of the family, which is a fundamental unit of society, the Contracting Parties undertake to promote the economic, legal and social protection of family life by such means as social and family benefits, fiscal arrangements, provision of family housing, benefits for the newly married and other appropriate means.

Article 17: The right of mothers and children to social and economic protection

With a view to ensuring the effective exercise of the right of mothers and children to social and economic protection, the Contracting Parties will take all appropriate and necessary measures to that end, including the establishment or maintenance of appropriate institutions or services.

Article 18: The right to engage in a gainful occupation in the territory of other Contracting Parties

With a view to ensuring the effective exercise of the right to engage in a gainful occupation in the territory of any other Contracting Party, the Contracting Parties undertake:

1 To apply existing regulations in a spirit of liberality;
2 T o simplify existing formalities and to reduce or abolish chancery dues and other charges payable by foreign workers or their employers;
3 To liberalise, individually or collectively, regulations governing the employment of foreign workers;
and recognise:
4 The right of their nationals to leave the country to engage in a gainful occupation in the territories of the other Contracting Parties.

Article 19: The right of migrant workers and their families to protection and assistance

With a view to ensuring the effective exercise of the right of migrant workers and their families to protection and assistance in the territory of any other Contracting Party, the Contracting Parties undertake:

1 To maintain or to satisfy themselves that there are maintained adequate and free services to assist such workers, particularly in obtaining accurate information, and to take all appropriate steps, so far as national laws and regulations permit, against misleading propaganda relating to emigration and immigration;
2 To adopt appropriate measures within their own jurisdiction to facilitate the departure, journey and reception of such workers and their families, and to provide, within their own jurisdiction, appropriate services for health, medical attention and good hygienic conditions during the journey;
3 To promote co-operation, as appropriate, between social services, public and private, in emigration and immigration countries;
4 To secure for such workers lawfully within their territories, insofar as such matters are regulated by law or regulations or are subject to the control of administrative authorities, treatment not less favourable than that of their own nationals in respect of the following matters:
   (a) remuneration and other employment and working conditions;
   (b) membership of trade unions and enjoyment of the benefits of collective bargaining;
   (c) accommodation;
5 To secure for such workers lawfully within their territories treatment not less favourable than that of their own nationals with regard to employment taxes, dues or contributions payable in respect of employed persons;
6 To facilitate as far as possible the reunion of the family of a foreign worker permitted to establish himself in the territory;
7 To secure for such workers lawfully within their territories treatment not less favourable than that of their own nationals in respect of legal proceedings relating to matters referred to in this article;
8 To secure that such workers lawfully residing within their territories are not

expelled unless they endanger national security or offend against public interest or morality;

9 To permit, within legal limits, the transfer of such parts of the earnings and savings of such workers as they may desire;

10 To extend the protection and assistance provided for in this article to self-employed migrants insofar as such measures apply;

Article 20: Undertakings

1 Each of the Parties undertakes:

(a) to consider Part I of this Charter as a declaration of the aims which it will pursue by all appropriate means, as stated in the introductory paragraph of that part;

(b) to consider itself bound by at least five of the following articles of Part II of this Charter:

Articles 1, 5, 6, 12, 13, 16 and 19;

(c) in addition to the articles selected by it in accordance with the preceding sub-paragraph, to consider itself bound by such a number of articles or numbered paragraphs of Part II of the Charter as it may select, provided that the total number of articles or numbered paragraphs by which it is bound is not less than 10 articles or 45 numbered paragraphs.

2 The articles or paragraphs selected in accordance with sub-paragraphs b and c of paragraph 1 of this article shall be notified to the Secretary General of the Council of Europe at the time when the instrument of ratification or approval of the Contracting Party concerned is deposited.

3 Any Contracting Party may, at a later date, declare by notification addressed to the Secretary General that it considers itself bound by any articles or any numbered paragraphs of Part II of the Charter which it has not already accepted under the terms of paragraph 1 of this article. Such undertakings subsequently given shall be deemed to be an integral part of the ratification or approval and shall have the same effect as from the thirtieth day after the date of the notification.

4 The Secretary General shall communicate to all the signatory governments and to the Director General of the International Labour Office any notification which he shall have received pursuant to this part of the Charter.

5 Each Contracting Party shall maintain a system of labour inspection appropriate to national conditions.

TABLE SHOWING WHICH COUNTRIES ARE MEMBERS OF THE EUROPEAN UNION AND EUROPEAN ECONOMIC AREA AND SIGNATORIES/RATIFICATIONS OF THE COUNCIL OF EUROPE SOCIAL CHARTER AND THE EUROPEAN CONVENTION ON SOCIAL AND MEDICAL ASSISTANCE

Country	EU	EEA	ECSMA Date of signature	CESC Date of signature	CESC Date of ratification
Austria	x	x	–	22/7/63	29/10/69
Belgium	x	x	11/12/53	18/10/61	16/10/90
Croatia			–	8/3/99	–
Cyprus	x	x	–	22/5/67	7/3/68
Czech Republic*	x	x	–	27/5/92	3/11/99
Denmark	x	x	11/12/53	18/10/61	3/3/65
Estonia	x	x	1/12/99	–	–
Finland	x	x	–	9/2/90	29/4/91
France	x	x	11/12/53	18/10/61	9/3/73
Germany	x	x	11/12/53	18/10/61	27/1/65
Greece	x	x	11/12/53	18/10/61	6/6/84
Hungary	x	x	–	13/12/91	8/7/99
Iceland		x	11/12/53	15/1/76	15/1/76
Ireland	x	x	11/12/53	18/10/61	7/10/64
Italy	x	x	11/12/53	18/10/61	22/10/65
Latvia	x	x	–	29/5/97	–
Liechtenstein		x	–	9/10/91	–
Luxembourg	x	x	11/12/53	18/10/61	10/10/91
Lithuania	x	x			
Macedonia (Former Republic of Yugoslavia)			–	5/5/98	–
Malta	x	x	7/5/68	26/5/88	4/10/88
Netherlands	x	x	11/12/53	18/10/61	22/4/82
Norway		x	11/12/53	18/10/61	26/10/62
Poland	x	x	–	26/11/91	25/6/97
Portugal	x	x	27/4/77	1/6/82	30/9/91
Romania			–	4/10/94	–
Slovakia*	x	x	–	27/5/92	22/6/98
Slovenia	x	x	–	11/10/97	–
Spain	x	x	9/2/81	27/4/98	6/5/80
Sweden	x	x	11/12/53	18/10/61	17/12/62
Switzerland			–	6/5/76	–
Turkey			11/12/53	18/10/61	24/11/89
Ukraine			–	2/5/96	–
United Kingdom	x	x	11/12/53	18/10/61	11/7/62

* CESC signature date is the date of signing by the former Czech and Slovak Federal Republic (Czechoslovakia).

EU: European Union; EEA: European Economic Area; ECSMA: European Convention on Social and Medical Assistance; CESC: Council of Europe Social Charter. Note that 10 countries have ratified the revised CESC: Bulgaria, Cyprus, Estonia, France, Ireland, Italy, Norway, Romania, Slovenia and Sweden (not UK).

Up-to-date to May 2004.

Immigration Status documents

APPLICATION REGISTRATION CARD (ARC)

IS96: NOTIFICATION OF TEMPORARY ADMISSION TO A PERSON WHO IS LIABLE TO BE DETAINED

Home Office

Port Ref:
HO Ref:

IS96 ENF NW

Communications House Enforcement Unit
UK Immigration Service
Communications House
210 Old Street
London, EC1V 9BR
Telephone 020 7324 6529 Fax 020 7324 6548

IMMIGRATION ACT 1971 – NOTIFICATION OF TEMPORARY ADMISSION TO A PERSON
WHO IS LIABLE TO BE DETAINED

To: Date of Birth: September 1980   Nationality: Eritrea

X _____

LIABILITY TO DETENTION

A   You are a person who is liable to be detained*

TEMPORARY ADMISSION RESTRICTIONS

B   I hereby authorise your (further) temporary admission to the United Kingdom subject to the following restrictions **:

- You **must** reside at the address shown at X above
- You **must** report to an **Immigration** Officer at:

UK Immigration Service
Communications House
210 Old Street
London
EC1V 9BR

On 04 September 2003   at 11:00 – 14:00   hrs

And then monthly on the 04th between 11:00 and 14:00   hrs

YOU MAY NOT ENTER EMPLOYMENT, PAID OR UNPAID, OR ENGAGE IN ANY BUSINESS OR PROFESSION.

ANY CHANGE OF RESTRICTION

If these restrictions are to be changed, an Immigration Officer will write to you.
- **Although you have been temporarily admitted, you remain liable to be detained**
- You have NOT been given leave to enter the United Kingdom within the meaning of the Immigration Act 1971

Date 04 August 2003   ‾‾‾‾Immigration Officer

* Paragraph 16 of Schedule 2 to the Act
** Paragraph 21 of Schedule 2 to the Act

[IS 96 ENF NW Temporary Admission]

RESIDENT PERMITS

The UK residence permit

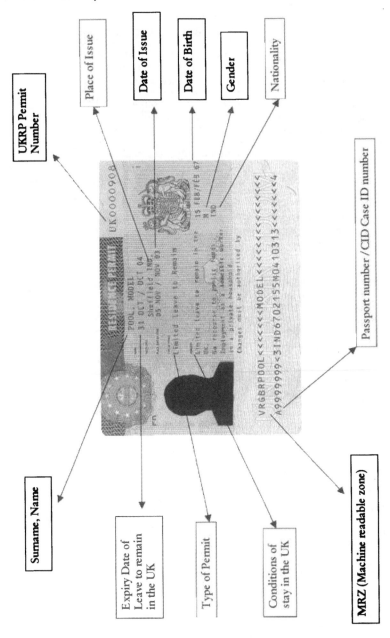

UKRP Permit Number

Place of Issue

Date of Issue

Date of Birth

Gender

Nationality

Passport number / CID Case ID number

Surname, Name

Expiry Date of Leave to remain in the UK

Type of Permit

Conditions of stay in the UK

MRZ (Machine readable zone)

Remarks for UKRP Vignettes

Leave To Remain Codes	Remarks to be printed on UKRP vignette
Code 1	Limited leave to remain in the UK. No recourse to public funds.
Code 1 **(Requirement to register with police)**	Limited leave to remain in the UK No recourse to public funds. Register at once with the police.
Code 1 **(Requirement to continue registration with police)**	Limited leave to remain in the UK. No recourse to public funds. Report extension to the police.
Code 2	Limited leave to remain in the UK. No recourse to public funds. Able to work as authorised by Secretary of State.
Code 2 **(Requirement to register with police)**	Limited leave to remain in the UK. No recourse to public funds. Able to work as authorised by Secretary of State. Register at once with the police.
Code 2 **(Requirement to continue registration with police)**	Limited leave to remain in the UK No recourse to public funds. Able to work as authorised by Secretary of State. Report extension to the police.
Code 3	Limited leave to remain in the UK. No recourse to public funds. No work or engaging in business.
Code 3 **(Requirement to register with police)**	Limited leave to remain in the UK. No recourse to public funds. No work or engaging in business. Register at once with the police.
Code 3 **(Requirement to continue registration with police)**	Limited leave to remain in the UK. No recourse to public funds. No work or engaging in business. Report extension to the police.
ILR	Indefinite leave to remain in the UK.
NTL	No time limit on holder's stay in the UK.
LOTR	Leave to remain outside the Rules

Leave To Remain Code 4	Remarks to be printed on UKRP vignette
Au pairs	Limited leave to remain in the UK. No recourse to public funds. Employment as an Au pair. Changes must be authorised by the Secretary of State.
Au pairs **(Requirement to register with police)**	Limited leave to remain in the UK. No recourse to public funds. Employment as an Au pair. Changes must be authorised by the Secretary of State. Register at once with the police
Au pairs **(Requirement to continue registration with police)**	Limited leave to remain in the UK. No recourse to public funds. Employment as an Au pair. Changes must be authorised by the Secretary of State. Report extension to the police.
Working Holidaymakers	Limited leave to remain in the UK. No recourse to public funds. Employed as a working holidaymaker. Changes must be authorised by the Secretary of State.
Overseas Domestic worker in private households.	Limited leave to remain in the UK. No recourse to public funds. Employment as a domestic worker in a private household. Changes must be authorised by the Secretary of State.
Overseas Domestic worker in private households. **(Requirement to register with police)**	Limited leave to remain in the UK No recourse to public funds Employment as a domestic worker Changes must be authorised by the Secretary of State Register at once with the police
Overseas Domestic worker in private households. **(Requirement to continue registration with police)**	Limited leave to remain in the UK No recourse to public funds. Employment as a domestic worker. Changes must be authorised by the Secretary of State. Report extension to the police.

Leave To Remain Code 4	Remarks to be printed on UKRP vignette
Domestic workers in diplomatic households	Limited leave to remain in the UK. No recourse to public funds. Employment as a domestic worker in a diplomatic household. Changes must be authorised by the Secretary of State.
Seasonal Agricultural Workers	Limited leave to remain in the UK. No recourse to public funds. Employment as a Seasonal Agricultural Worker. Changes must be authorised by the Secretary of State.
Voluntary workers	Limited leave to remain in the UK. No recourse to public funds. Employment as a voluntary worker Changes must be authorised by the Secretary of State.
Voluntary workers **(Requirement to register with police)**	Limited leave to remain in the UK. No recourse to public funds. Employment as a voluntary worker. Changes must be authorised by the Secretary of State. Register at once with the police
Voluntary workers **(Requirement to continue registration with police)**	Limited leave to remain in the UK. No recourse to public funds. Employment as a voluntary worker. Changes must be authorised by the Secretary of State. Report extension to the police.
Overseas government employees	Limited leave to remain in the UK. No recourse to public funds Employment as an overseas government employee. Changes must be authorised by the Secretary of State.
Overseas government employees **(Requirement to register with police)**	Limited LTR in the UK. No recourse to public funds. Employed by an overseas government in the UK. Changes must be authorised by The Secretary of State. Register at once with the police

Leave To Remain Code 4	Remarks to be printed on UKRP vignette
Overseas government employees **(Requirement to continue registration with police)**	Limited LTR in the UK. No recourse to public funds. Employed by an overseas government in the UK. Changes must be authorised by the Secretary of State. Report extension to the police.
Ministers of religion	Limited leave to remain in the UK No recourse to public funds. Employment as a Minister of Religion. Changes must be authorised by the Secretary of State.
Sole representatives	Limited LTR in the UK. No recourse to public funds. Employed under the sole rep immigration provisions. Changes must be authorised by the Secretary of State.
Sole representatives **(Requirement to register with police)**	Limited LTR in the UK. No recourse to public funds. Employed under the sole representatives immigration provisions. Changes must be authorised by the Secretary of State. Register at once with the police.
Sole representatives **(Requirement to continue registration with police)**	Limited LTR in the UK. No recourse to public funds. Employed under the sole representatives immigration provisions. Changes must be authorised by the Secretary of State. Report extension to the police.
Operational ground staff of overseas owned airlines	Limited LTR in the UK. No recourse to public funds. Employed as operational ground staff of an overseas owned airline. Changes must be authorised by the Secretary of State

Leave To Remain Code 4	Remarks to be printed on UKRP vignette
Operational ground staff of overseas owned airlines **(Requirement to register with police)**	Limited LTR in the UK. No recourse to public funds. Employed as operational ground staff of an overseas owned airline. Changes must be authorised by the Secretary of State. Register with the police.
Operational ground staff of overseas owned airlines **(Requirement to continue registration with police)**	Limited LTR in the UK. No recourse to public funds. Employed as operational ground staff of an overseas owned airline. Changes must be authorised by the Secretary of State. Report extension to the police.
Exchange teachers and language assistants	Limited LTR in the UK. No recourse to public funds. Employed as Exchange Teacher or Assistant. Changes must be authorised by the Secretary of State.
Exchange teachers and language assistants **(Requirement to register with police)**	Limited LTR in the UK. No recourse to public funds. Employed as Exchange Teacher or Assistant. Changes must be authorised by the Secretary of State. Register at once with the police.
Exchange teachers and language assistants **(Requirement to continue registration with police)**	Limited LTR in the UK. No recourse to public funds. Employed as Exchange Teacher or Assistant. Changes must be authorised the Secretary of State. Report extension to the police.
BUNAC	Limited leave to remain in the UK. No recourse to public funds. Employment as a BUNAC Scheme participant. Changes must be authorised by the Secretary of State.
BUNAC **(Requirement to register with police)**	Limited LTR in the UK. No recourse to public funds. Employed as a BUNAC participant. Changes must be authorised by the Secretary of State. Register at once with the police.

Leave To Remain Code 4	Remarks to be printed on UKRP vignette
BUNAC **(Requirement to continue registration with police)**	Limited LTR in the UK. No recourse to public funds. Employed as a BUNAC participant. Changes must be authorised by the Secretary of State. Report extension to the police.
Representatives of overseas newspapers, news agencies and broadcasting organisations	Limited LTR in the UK. No recourse to public funds. Employed as representative of overseas newspaper, news agency or broadcast organisation. Changes must be authorised by the Secretary of State.
Representatives of overseas newspapers, news agencies and broadcasting organisations **(Requirement to register with police)**	Limited LTR in the UK. No recourse to public funds. Employed as representative of overseas newspaper, news agency or broadcast organisation. Changes must be authorised by the Secretary of State. Register at once with the police.
Representatives of overseas newspapers, news agencies and broadcasting organisations **(Requirement to continue registration with police)**	Limited LTR in the UK. No recourse to public funds. Employed as representative of overseas newspaper, news agency or broadcast organisation. Changes must be authorised by the Secretary of State. Report extension to the police.
LTE/LTR Codes for (Asylum)	**Remarks to be printed on UKRP vignette**
Code 1A	Limited leave to enter the UK.
Code 1A	Limited leave to remain in the UK.
ILE	Indefinite leave to enter the UK.
ILR	Indefinite leave to remain in the UK.

ACD.2151: ISSUED TO ASYLUM CLAIMANTS AND THEIR DEPENDANTS GRANTED REFUGEE STATUS

Home Office

Error! AutoText entry not defined.
Asylum Casework Directorate

Address for correspondence (unless otherwise advised):
Lunar House, 40 Wellesley Road, Croydon, CR9 2BY
Telephone 0870 606 7766 Fax On Request

FORENAMES SURNAME	Our Ref	Our Ref
Date of Birth **DATE**	Your Ref	Your Ref
Nationality: **NATIONALITY**	Case ID	CID Case ID
	Date	Date

Dear Salutation

GRANT OF ASYLUM

You have been recognised as a refugee as defined by the 1951 Geneva Convention relating to the Status of Refugees and its Protocol and have been granted asylum in accordance with the Immigration Rules. You have been granted indefinite leave to enter/remain in the United Kingdom and this means that you are free to stay in this country permanently.

THIS LETTER IN ITSELF CONFERS NO LEAVE TO ENTER OR REMAIN IN THE UNITED KINGDOM AND DOES NOT CONSTITUTE PROOF OF YOUR STATUS.

Please find enclosed your Immigration Status Document. This has been endorsed with indefinite leave to enter/remain in the United Kingdom. It is this endorsement that constitutes proof of your immigration status in the United Kingdom.

ENTITLEMENTS
You are free to take a job and do not need the permission of any Government Department before doing so. You are free to use the National Health Service and the social services, and other services provided by local authorities as you need them.

POLICE REGISTRATION
You no longer need to report changes of address or other details to the police. Please find enclosed your police registration certificate endorsed to show that you no longer need to register.

TRAVEL ABROAD
You may travel out of the Common Travel Area any number of times during the validity of the leave you have been granted. The Common Travel Area comprises the United Kingdom, the Channel Islands, the Isle of Man and the Republic of Ireland. On your return, you will be re-admitted to the United Kingdom without having to obtain fresh leave to enter unless

ACD.0725 02/04

1 of 2

BUILDING A SAFE, JUST AND TOLERANT SOCIETY

you have been absent from the United Kingdom for a continuous period of more than two years, or

* you are seeking admission in a different capacity from the one in which this leave has been granted.

Nevertheless, an investigation into your circumstances may be carried out upon your return to the United Kingdom, in order to determine whether or not the leave you have been granted should be revoked.

Using your national passport to travel outside the United Kingdom or returning to your country of origin may result in the loss of your refugee status and could lead to the revocation of your indefinite leave to enter/remain in the United Kingdom. If you want to travel abroad you should apply for a Refugee Convention Travel Document from the Travel Document Section, Immigration and Nationality Directorate, Lunar House, 40 Wellesley Road, Croydon, CR9 2BY (telephone 0870 241 0645). If you leave the United Kingdom with a Refugee Convention Travel Document, you will be allowed back into the country at any time while it is still valid, subject to the above.

DEPENDANTS

If you are the principal sponsor and you are married and/or have children under the age of 18, the leave to enter/remain you have been granted entitles your spouse and minor children (who formed part of the family unit prior to you leaving your country of origin and seeking asylum) to join you in the United Kingdom. It is current Home Office policy that the sponsor is not expected to meet the normal support and accommodation requirements of the Immigration Rules. If your spouse and minor children wish to apply for family reunion, they will need to approach a British Embassy, High Commission or Consulate abroad to make an application for entry clearance to the United Kingdom. Dependants are required to make their application for family reunion before travelling to the United Kingdom.

CAUTION

You should understand, however, that you may not be allowed to remain in the United Kingdom if, during your stay, you take part in any criminal activities or activities such as support for or encouragement of terrorist organisations, or you otherwise endanger national security or public order. You may also not be allowed to remain in the United Kingdom if it is decided for some other reason that your presence here is not conducive to the public good.

Yours sincerely

Name
<u>Asylum Casework Directorate</u>
acting on behalf of the Secretary of State

BUILDING A SAFE, JUST AND TOLERANT SOCIETY

Home Office
Immigration and Nationality Directorate

IMMIGRATION
STATUS
DOCUMENT

Personal Details

Full Name
SURNAME, FORENAME(S)

Nationality
NATIONALITY

Date of Birth
DATE OF BIRTH

Place of Birth
PLACE OF BIRTH

Gender
MALE / FEMALE

Case ID
CID CASE ID

Refugee Status

The person named on this document has been recognised by the Secretary of State as a refugee as defined by the 1951 Geneva Convention relating to the Status of Refugees and its Protocol.

The period for which leave to enter or remain in the United Kingdom has been granted is indicated in the endorsement.

While the period of leave indicated remains valid, the holder is able to work in the United Kingdom without any immigration restrictions limiting the type of work they can undertake.

This Immigration Status Document has been endorsed in place of a valid national passport or travel document and confers upon the person named leave to enter or remain in the United Kingdom for the period indicated. It does not certify the accuracy of the personal particulars, which are those supplied by the person who made the application. It remains the property of Her Majesty's Government and may be withdrawn at any time. It should not be tampered with or passed to an unauthorised person. Any case of loss or destruction should be immediately reported to the nearest police station and to the Immigration and Nationality Directorate at the address below; only after exhaustive enquiries can a replacement be issued in such circumstances. The Immigration Status Document of a deceased person should be returned to the Immigration and Nationality Directorate for cancellation.

Enquiries about the purpose, use, or validity of this document should be made to the Immigration and Nationality Directorate at:
Lunar House, 40 Wellesley Road, Croydon, CR9 2BY (telephone 0870 606 7766)

ACD.2151

VIGNETTE

ACD.2152: ISSUED TO ASYLUM CLAIMANTS AND THEIR DEPENDANTS GRANTED HUMANITARIAN PROTECTION BUT ONLY WHERE A NATIONAL PASSPORT IS NOT AVAILABLE

Home Office

Error! AutoText entry not defined
Asylum Casework Directorate

Address for correspondence (unless otherwise advised):
Lunar House, 40 Wellesley Road, Croydon, CR9 2BY
Telephone 0870 606 7766 Fax On Request

FORENAMES SURNAME	Our Ref	Our Ref
Date of Birth: **DATE**	Your Ref	Your Ref
Nationality: **NATIONALITY**	Case ID	CID Case ID
	Date	Date

Dear Salutation

GRANT OF HUMANITARIAN PROTECTION

You have/Your claim has been reviewed and you have been granted limited leave to enter/remain in the United Kingdom for a reason not covered by the Immigration Rules.

THIS LETTER IN ITSELF CONFERS NO LEAVE TO ENTER OR REMAIN IN THE UNITED KINGDOM AND DOES NOT CONSTITUTE PROOF OF YOUR STATUS.

Please find enclosed your Immigration Status Document/Passport. This has been endorsed with your leave to enter/remain in the United Kingdom. The date this leave to enter or remain expires is shown on the endorsement. It is this endorsement that constitutes proof of your immigration status in the United Kingdom.

You have been granted this leave in accordance with the published Home Office Asylum Policy Instruction on Humanitarian Protection.

ENTITLEMENTS

You are free to take a job and do not need the permission of any Government Department before doing so. You are free to use the National Health Service and the social services, and other services provided by local authorities as you need them.

POLICE REGISTRATION

You no longer need to report changes of address or other details to the police. Please find enclosed your police registration certificate endorsed to show that you no longer need to register.

TRAVEL ABROAD

You may travel out of the Common Travel Area any number of times during the validity of the leave you have been granted. The Common Travel Area comprises the United Kingdom, the Channel Islands, the Isle of Man and the Republic of Ireland. On your

ACD.2158 02/04

BUILDING A SAFE, JUST AND TOLERANT SOCIETY

return, you will be re-admitted to the United Kingdom without having to obtain fresh leave to enter unless

you have been absent from the United Kingdom for a continuous period of more than two years, or

- you are seeking admission for a different purpose from the one for which this leave has been granted.

Nevertheless, an investigation into your circumstances may be carried out upon your return to the United Kingdom, in order to determine whether or not the leave you have been granted should be varied or cancelled.

If you travel abroad during the period of leave you have been granted, this leave will lapse. Any subsequent application you make to return to this country will be considered as an application for fresh leave. For the purposes of this paragraph, 'abroad' means outside the Common Travel Area, which comprises the United Kingdom, the Channel Islands, the Isle of Man and the Republic of Ireland.

DEPENDANTS

If you are the principal sponsor and you are married and/or have children under the age of 18, the leave to enter/remain you have been granted does not entitle your spouse or minor children (who formed part of the family unit prior to you leaving your country of origin and seeking asylum) to join you in the United Kingdom. An application for them to join you will not normally be considered until you have applied for, and been granted, indefinite leave to remain. In addition, the normal requirements of the Immigration Rules regarding support and accommodation of dependants would have to be satisfied. However, an application for family reunion may be granted at an earlier point if there are compelling compassionate circumstances. In the event that you are granted indefinite leave to remain, and your spouse and minor children wish to apply for family reunion, they will need to approach a British Embassy, High Commission of Consulate abroad to make an application for entry clearance to the United Kingdom. Dependants are required to make their application for family reunion before travelling to the United Kingdom.

APPLYING FOR AN EXTENSION

Before the period of leave that you have been granted expires, you should either leave the United Kingdom or apply for an extension of stay, explaining the reasons on which you are seeking further leave. Any application will be considered in the light of the circumstances prevailing at that time. If your application to extend your stay is refused, you will be advised of the reasons for this and of any right of appeal against that decision. Applications to extend your stay must be made on the correct form, which is available from this office or by calling 0870 241 0645.

CAUTION

You should understand, however, that you may not be allowed to remain in the United Kingdom if, during your stay, you take part in any criminal activities or activities such as support for or encouragement of terrorist organisations, or you otherwise endanger national security or public order. You may also not be allowed to remain in the United Kingdom if it is decided for some other reason that your presence here is not conducive to the public good.

IMMIGRATION STATUS DOCUMENT

Home Office
Immigration and Nationality Directorate

Personal Details

Full Name
SURNAME, FORENAME(S)

Nationality
NATIONALITY

Date of Birth
DATE OF BIRTH

Place of Birth
PLACE OF BIRTH

Gender
MALE/FEMALE

Case ID
CID CASE ID

VIGNETTE

Humanitarian Protection

The Secretary of State has granted the person named on this document limited leave to enter or remain in the United Kingdom for a reason not covered by the Immigration Rules, in accordance with the Home Office Asylum Policy Instruction on Humanitarian Protection.

The period for which leave to enter or remain in the United Kingdom has been granted is indicated in the endorsement.

While the period of leave indicated remains valid, the holder is able to work in the United Kingdom without any immigration restrictions limiting the type of work they can undertake.

This Immigration Status Document has been endorsed in place of a valid national passport or travel document and confers upon the person named leave to enter or remain in the United Kingdom for the period indicated. It does not certify the accuracy of the personal particulars, which are those supplied by the person who made the application. It remains the property of Her Majesty's Government and may be withdrawn at any time. It should not be tampered with or passed to an unauthorised person. Any case of loss or destruction should be immediately reported to the nearest police station and to the Immigration and Nationality Directorate at the address below only after exhaustive enquiries can a replacement be issued in such circumstances. The Immigration Status Document of a deceased person should be returned to the Immigration and Nationality Directorate for cancellation.

Enquiries about the purpose, use, or validity of this document should be made to the Immigration and Nationality Directorate at:
Lunar House, 40 Wellesley Road, Croydon, CR9 2BY (telephone 0870 606 7766)

ACD.2152

ACD.2373: ISSUED TO ASYLUM CLAIMANTS AND THEIR DEPENDANTS GRANTED DISCRETIONARY LEAVE BUT ONLY WHERE A NATIONAL PASSPORT IS NOT AVAILABLE

Home Office

Error! AutoText entry not defined.
Asylum Casework Directorate

Address for correspondence (unless otherwise advised):
Lunar House, 40 Wellesley Road, Croydon, CR9 2BY
Telephone 0870 606 7766 Fax On Request

FORENAMES SURNAME	Our Ref	Our Ref
Date of Birth: **DATE**	Your Ref	Your Ref
Nationality: **NATIONALITY**	Case ID	CID Case ID
	Date	Date

Dear Salutation

DISCRETIONARY GRANT OF LEAVE TO ENTER/REMAIN

It/Your claim has been reviewed and it has been decided that the Secretary of State's discretion should be exercised in your favour and you have been granted limited leave to enter/remain in the United Kingdom for a reason not covered by the Immigration Rules.

THIS LETTER IN ITSELF CONFERS NO LEAVE TO ENTER OR REMAIN IN THE UNITED KINGDOM AND DOES NOT CONSTITUTE PROOF OF YOUR STATUS.

Please find enclosed your Immigration Status Document/Passport. This has been endorsed with your leave to enter/remain in the United Kingdom. The date this leave to enter/remain expires is shown on the endorsement. It is this endorsement that constitutes proof of your immigration status in the United Kingdom.

You have been granted this leave in accordance with the published Home Office Asylum Policy Instruction on Discretionary Leave.

ENTITLEMENTS
You are free to take a job and do not need the permission of any Government Department before doing so. You are free to use the National Health Service and the social services, and other services provided by local authorities as you need them.

POLICE REGISTRATION
You no longer need to report changes of address or other details to the police. Please find enclosed your police registration certificate endorsed to show that you no longer need to register.

TRAVEL ABROAD
You may travel out of the Common Travel Area any number of times during the validity of the leave you have been granted. The Common Travel Area comprises the United Kingdom, the Channel Islands, the Isle of Man and the Republic of Ireland. On your

ACD.2155 02/04   1 of 3

BUILDING A SAFE, JUST AND TOLERANT SOCIETY

return, you will be re-admitted to the United Kingdom without having to obtain fresh leave to enter unless

- you have been absent from the United Kingdom for a continuous period of more than two years, or

- you are seeking admission for a different purpose from the one for which this leave has been granted.

Nevertheless, an investigation into your circumstances may be carried out upon your return to the United Kingdom, in order to determine whether or not the leave you have been granted should be varied or cancelled.

If you travel abroad during the period of leave you have been granted, this leave will lapse. Any subsequent application you make to return to this country will be considered as an application for fresh leave. For the purposes of this paragraph, 'abroad' means outside the Common Travel Area, which comprises the United Kingdom, the Channel Islands, the Isle of Man and the Republic of Ireland.

DEPENDANTS

If you are the principal sponsor and you are married and/or have children under the age of 18, the leave to enter/remain you have been granted does not entitle your spouse or minor children (who formed part of the family unit prior to you leaving your country of origin and seeking asylum) to join you in the United Kingdom. An application for them to join you will not normally be considered until you have applied for, and been granted, indefinite leave to remain. In addition, the normal requirements of the Immigration Rules regarding support and accommodation of dependants would have to be satisfied. However, an application for family reunion may be granted at an earlier point if there are compelling compassionate circumstances. In the event that you are granted indefinite leave to remain, and your spouse and minor children wish to apply for family reunion, they will need to approach a British Embassy, High Commission or Consulate abroad to make an application for entry clearance to the United Kingdom. Dependants are required to make their application for family reunion before travelling to the United Kingdom.

APPLYING FOR AN EXTENSION

Before the period of leave that you have been granted expires, you should either leave the United Kingdom or apply for an extension of stay, explaining the reasons on which you are seeking further leave. Any application will be considered in the light of the circumstances prevailing at that time. If your application to extend your stay is refused, you will be advised of the reasons for this and of any right of appeal against that decision. Applications to extend your stay must be made on the correct form, which is available from this office or by calling 0870 241 0645.

CAUTION

The leave you have been granted may be subject to review before it expires if the circumstances which led to your grant of leave change. You should also understand that you may not be allowed to remain in the United Kingdom if, during your stay, you take part in any criminal activities or activities such as support for or encouragement of terrorist organisations, or you otherwise endanger national security or public order. Furthermore you may not be allowed to remain in the United Kingdom if it is decided for some other reason that your presence here is not conducive to the public good.

Yours sincerely

ACD.2155 01/04   2 of 3

IMMIGRATION STATUS DOCUMENT

Home Office
Immigration and Nationality Directorate

Personal Details

Full Name
SURNAME, FORENAME(S)

Nationality
NATIONALITY

Date of Birth
DATE OF BIRTH

Place of Birth
PLACE OF BIRTH

Gender
MALE / FEMALE

Case ID
CID CASE ID

Discretionary Leave

The Secretary of State has granted the person named on this document limited leave to enter or remain in the United Kingdom for a reason not covered by the Immigration Rules, in accordance with the Home Office Asylum Policy Instruction on Discretionary Leave.

The period for which leave to enter or remain in the United Kingdom has been granted is indicated in the endorsement.

While the period of leave indicated remains valid, the holder is able to work in the United Kingdom without any immigration restrictions limiting the type of work they can undertake.

This Immigration Status Document has been endorsed in place of a valid national passport or travel document and confers upon the person named leave to enter or remain in the United Kingdom for the period indicated. It does not certify the accuracy of the personal particulars, which are those supplied by the person who made the application. It remains the property of Her Majesty's Government and may be withdrawn at any time. It should not be tampered with or passed to an unauthorised person. Any case of loss or destruction should be immediately reported to the nearest police station and to the Immigration and Nationality Directorate at the address below; only after exhaustive enquiries can a replacement be issued in such circumstances. The Immigration Status Document of a deceased person should be returned to the Immigration and Nationality Directorate for cancellation.

Enquiries about the purpose, use, or validity of this document should be made to the Immigration and Nationality Directorate at:
Lunar House, 40 Wellesley Road, Croydon, CR9 2BY (telephone 0870 606 7766)

ACD.2373

VIGNETTE

ACD.2150: ISSUED TO THOSE PERSONS UNABLE TO MAKE USE OF A NATIONAL PASSPORT WHO ARE GRANTED LEAVE FOR REASONS OTHER THAN ASYLUM

Home Office

Error! AutoText entry not defined.
Asylum Casework Directorate

Address for correspondence (unless otherwise advised):
Lunar House, 40 Wellesley Road, Croydon, CR9 2BY
Telephone 0870 606 7766 Fax On Request

FORENAMES SURNAME	Our Ref	Our Ref
Date of Birth **DATE**	Your Ref	Your Ref
Nationality: **NATIONALITY**	Case ID	CID Case ID
	Date	Date

Dear Salutation

GRANT OF INDEFINITE LEAVE TO REMAIN

You have been granted indefinite leave to remain in the United Kingdom and this means that you are free to stay in this country permanently.

THIS LETTER IN ITSELF CONFERS NO LEAVE TO ENTER OR REMAIN IN THE UNITED KINGDOM AND DOES NOT CONSTITUTE PROOF OF YOUR STATUS.

Please find enclosed your Immigration Status Document/Passport. This has been endorsed with indefinite leave to remain in the United Kingdom. It is this endorsement that constitutes proof of your immigration status in the United Kingdom.

ENTITLEMENTS
You are free to take a job and do not need the permission of any Government Department before doing so. You are free to use the National Health Service and the social services, and other services provided by local authorities as you need them.

POLICE REGISTRATION .
You no longer need to report changes of address or other details to the police. Please find enclosed your police registration certificate endorsed to show that you no longer need to register.

TRAVEL ABROAD
You may travel out of the Common Travel Area any number of times during the validity of the leave you have been granted. The Common Travel Area comprises the United Kingdom, the Channel Islands, the Isle of Man and the Republic of Ireland. On your return, you will be re-admitted to the United Kingdom without having to obtain fresh leave to enter unless

- you have been absent from the United Kingdom for a continuous period of more than two years, or

ACD.2374 01/04   1 of 2

BUILDING A SAFE, JUST AND TOLERANT SOCIETY

- you are seeking admission in a different capacity from the one in which this leave has been granted.

Nevertheless, an investigation into your circumstances may be carried out upon your return to the United Kingdom, in order to determine whether or not the leave you have been granted should be revoked.

CAUTION
You should understand, however, that you may not be allowed to remain in the United Kingdom if, during your stay, you take part in any criminal activities or activities such as support for or encouragement of terrorist organisations, or you otherwise endanger national security or public order. You may also not be allowed to remain in the United Kingdom if it is decided for some other reason that your presence here is not conducive to the public good.

Yours sincerely

Name
Asylum Casework Directorate
acting on behalf of the Secretary of State

Home Office
Immigration and Nationality Directorate

IMMIGRATION
STATUS
DOCUMENT

Personal Details

Full Name
SURNAME, FORENAME(S)

Nationality
NATIONALITY

Date of Birth
DATE OF BIRTH

Place of Birth
PLACE OF BIRTH

Gender
MALE/FEMALE

Case ID
CID CASE ID

The period for which leave to enter or remain in
the United Kingdom has been granted is indicated
in the endorsement.

This Immigration Status Document has been endorsed in place of a valid national
passport or travel document and confers upon the person named leave to enter or
remain in the United Kingdom for the period indicated. It does not certify the
accuracy of the personal particulars, which are those supplied by the person who
made the application. It remains the property of Her Majesty's Government and
may be withdrawn at any time. It should not be tampered with or passed to an
unauthorised person. Any case of loss or destruction should be immediately
reported to the nearest police station and to the Immigration and Nationality
Directorate at the address below; only after exhaustive enquiries can a
replacement be issued in such circumstances. The Immigration Status Document
of a deceased person should be returned to the Immigration and Nationality
Directorate for cancellation.

Enquiries about the purpose, use, or validity of this document should be made to
the Immigration and Nationality Directorate at:
Lunar House, 40 Wellesley Road, Croydon, CR9 2BY (telephone 0870 606
7766)

ACD.2150

VIGNETTE

Outline of interim support

Introduction

The first edition of this handbook included a chapter on 'interim support'. Since then, the numbers of asylum-seekers supported under the interim scheme have significantly reduced since many of them have been, or will soon be, granted leave to remain. The scheme is due to end on 4 April 2005 (the Asylum Support (Interim Provisions) (Amendment) Regulations 2004 SI No 566). The interim scheme has many similarities with the NASS scheme which is covered in chapters 3 and 4. This appendix will provide a brief outline and highlight some differences. The table below explains who is entitled to interim support or NASS asylum support.

The scheme

Interim support is the 'interim scheme' of support provided by local authorities. It is governed by Immigration and Asylum Act (IAA) 1999 Part VI as amended by Nationality, Immigration and Asylum Act (NIAA) 2002. The Asylum Support (Interim Provisions) Regulations 1999 SI No 3056, referred to here as 'the Interim Regs' were made under Schedule 9 of the Act. The detail of how the scheme works is contained in the regulations rather than the statute. They came into force on the 6 December 1999, requiring local authorities to continue supporting asylum-seeker households who they had previously supported under National Assistance Act s21 and Children Act 1989 s17.

Eligibility

Local Authorities have a duty to provide support to 'eligible persons'. An eligible person is an asylum-seeker or their dependant(s) who 'appear to be destitute or likely to become destitute within 14 days'. Either the asylum-seeker or the dependant may make the claim, for example, if the asylum-seeker is in detention. The definition of 'dependant' and 'destitute' are different from the definition in NASS cases.

Exclusions (Interim reg 7)

An asylum-seeker is excluded from interim support if he or she is eligible for benefits. An asylum-seeker may not apply to a local authority for interim support if he or she has previously been supported by another authority within the past 12 months. There are a number of Asylum Support Adjudicator decisions where NASS support has been withdrawn because the appellant was eligible for interim support (these decisions are available from www.asylum-support-adjudicators.org.uk.

Asylum-seeker

'An asylum-seeker' for interim support purposes is as defined in IAA 1999 s94(1), as for NASS cases see chapter 3.

Dependant

The classes of dependant are defined by Interim reg 2(1) (see appendix A). The definition seems to encompass same-sex couples since unlike the Asylum Support Regs, 'unmarried couple' is not defined as a man and woman. It also allows a dependant of an asylum-seeker to claim support for their own dependants even if they are not dependant on the asylum claim, for example, a grandchild of the asylum-seeker.

Mixed households

Where a family member joins a household in receipt of interim support he or she will become entitled to support under the Interim Regs if he or she is a dependant of the main claimant (see also 'mixed households' in chapters 2 and 3). In this case he or she will not be entitled to NASS support unless claiming asylum and living in a separate household.

Different destitution test

A local authority must reach its own decision on whether or not an asylum-seeker household appears to be destitute without the benefit of the detailed guidance applicable to NASS cases. The definition of destitution in IAA 1999 s95(3)–(8) applies but there is no list of prescribed matters in the Interim Regs. The starting point for assessing destitution is the test applied in *R v Hammersmith and Fulham LBC ex p M* (1997) 1 CCLR 85 CA.

Assessment process and dispersal

The Local Government Association (LGA) has produced guidance on the interim scheme for local authorities covering assessment procedures and dispersal (see Appendix G for website). The procedures for dispersing or transferring asylum-seekers between authorities are outlined in chapter 5.

Service provision

Unlike NASS cases, when considering the adequacy of support, the local authority must take into account 'the welfare' of the assisted person as a relevant factor (Interim reg 6(1)(c)), which may enable inadequate accommodation or subsistence to be challenged. The regulations do not generally allow for subsistence only support to be provided for childless asylum-seekers, requiring local authorities to provide them with both accommodation and essential living needs. A childless asylum-seeker who was living with her husband who had leave to remain applied to Barnet LBC for cash only support. He was claiming housing benefit for his one bedroom flat but could not support her from the £33 per week in income support he received. The council agreed to provide her with subsistence under regulation 5(4) which provides that 'where the circumstances of a particular case are exceptional, support is to be provided in such other ways as are necessary.'

Level of support

There are no fixed amounts of support to be provided under the interim scheme which has led to discrepancies between different authorities. Unlike the NASS scheme, many authorities have not provided for regular increases, so in 2004 there were single people supported under the interim scheme who continued to receive only £30 per week, the same rate as that applied in 1996 regardless of their age or particular needs. This is significantly lower than the rate of benefit paid to a UK national who is a pensioner or with long-term sickness. See chapter 4 for details of attempts to challenge the inadequate level of interim support, arguing that it is irrational and in breach of the Human Rights Convention, so far with limited success.

Refusal, suspension or withdrawal of support

A decision to refuse support must be made under Interim reg 7 and is drafted as a duty, unlike decisions to withdraw or suspend support which are mainly discretionary. Local authorities have a discretion to withdraw or suspend support under Interim reg 8 for breach of conditions or leaving accommodation for seven days without reasonable excuse. Reg 8 provides a duty to withdraw/ suspend where it would have been refused under Interim Reg 7 if the local authority had been aware of circumstances when the claim was made. Advisers should check that the local authority has correctly approached their decision by reference to these regulations. For example if an asylum-seeker were to set fire to their accommodation without justification, support should probably be withdrawn on the basis of breach of conditions (Reg 8) rather than intentional destitution (Reg 7). If a local authority is considering the refusal or withdrawal of support, it will need to consider the case of *R v Kensington and Chelsea RLBC ex p Kujtim* (1999) 2 CCLR 340, CA (see para 3.161), and Human Rights Convention considerations (see para 3.259). It may also need to carry out a Children Act or Community Care assessment.

End of support after asylum decision

As with NASS support, there is a grace period of 21 or 28 days respectively after notification of the asylum or appeal decision before support is withdrawn (amendment by Asylum Support (Interim Provisions) (Amendment) Regulations 2002 SI No 471, reg 4 (6)).

Remedies and complaints

Complaints may be made through the local authority's ordinary complaints procedure since the statutory social services complaints procedure does not apply to the interim scheme. A complaint may be made to the Local Government Ombudsman (see Appendix G) if internal procedures are inadequate. A copy of the asylum-seeker's file could first be requested under Data Protection Act 1998 s7 (see para 3.154). Judicial review can be brought to challenge a decision to refuse or withdraw support as well as to challenge the adequacy of support. There is no right of appeal to the Asylum Support Adjudicators against a local authority decision relating to interim support.

Asylum support or interim support?[1]

Asylum-seekers awaiting a final decision who are eligible to claim asylum support from NASS	Asylum-seekers awaiting a final decision who are eligible to claim interim support from a local authority
Applied for asylum on arrival in the UK on or after 3 April 2000.	
	Applied for asylum on arrival before 3 April 2000, and received a negative asylum decision before 25 September 2000 (so losing eligibility for income support).
Applied for asylum in-country on or after 3 April while living in Scotland or Northern Ireland.	
Applied for asylum in-country on or after 3 April 2000, was detained at Oakington Detention Centre and then released.	
Living in the area of Kent County Council or Medway Council and applied for asylum in-country or received asylum refusal decision on or after 17 April 2000.	All in-country applicants who claimed asylum in England or Wales before 24 July 2000 (except for those living in Kent who were only eligible to claim interim support before 17 April 2000).
Applied for asylum in-country from London on or after 24 July 2000.	
Applied for asylum in-country from the north-east, Yorkshire, Humberside or Wales on or after 31 July 2000.	In-country asylum-seekers who claimed asylum before 31 July 2000 while living in the north-east, Humberside or Wales.
Applied for asylum in-country from the south-west, south central, north eastern or East Midlands regions on or after 14 August 2000.	Applied for asylum in-country before 14 August 2000 from the south-west, south central, eastern or East Midlands regions.
Applied for asylum from the West Midlands or Sussex on or after 29 August 2000.	In country asylum-seekers who claimed asylum before 29 August 2000 while living in the West Midlands or Sussex.
'Disbenefited' cases in England or Wales who were notified of a refusal of asylum on or after 25 September 2000, ie, applicants who are refused income support due to a negative decision on their asylum claim (applies to on-arrival and 'country of upheaval' cases).	Disbenefited 'in-country' asylum-seekers who have lost entitlement to benefits, eg, those who have been receiving benefit since before 5 February 1996.
Asylum-seekers who ceased to be entitled to interim support because their asylum claim was finally determined and who then made a fresh asylum or article 3 claim after the above relevant dates, unless their household includes a child under 18.	Asylum-seekers who ceased to be entitled to interim support because their asylum claim was finally determined and who then made a fresh asylum or article 3 claim after the above relevant dates, provided their household included a child

---

1   Table showing whether entitlement is under the Asylum Support Regulations 2000 or the Asylum Support (Interim Provisions) Regulations 1999 as interpreted by Directions 1–4 made under IAA 1999 Schedule 15, para 14(1). Note that the interim support scheme is due to end on 4 April 2005. The Directions are set out at appendix B.

How to contact NASS and 'one-stop' services

HOW TO CONTACT NASS

NASS's main office is at:

> Voyager House
> 30 Wellesley Road
> Croydon
> CR0 2AD

NASS has pages on the Home Office website for Policy Bulletins and latest news from NASS: www.ind.homeoffice.gov.uk/ind/en/home/applying/national_asylum_support.html

Type of Problem	Contact
General public enquiries Obtaining NASS application forms Progress of new applications Notifying change of circumstances/absences Help with travel/health costs Harassment	NASS telephone enquiry bureau 0845 602 1739
Termination of or sudden interruption in support.	NASS Support Enquiry Line 0845 600 0914.
Stolen/missing ARC card, missing emergency vouchers.	Sodexho Helpline 01252 369 799.
Emergency vouchers haven't arrived by next day delivery.	Royal Mail special delivery 0345 001 200.
Lost or stolen support notification.	Fax NASS 0208 633 0653.
Backdating/extra payments.	Write to Exceptional Payments, NASS at above address.
Renewal of HC2 exemption from NHS charges	Tel: 0208 633 0266 or fax: 0113 386 5700.
Maternity payment requests	Fax: 020 8633 0213/0129 or write to above address, c/o PAC (Post Allocation Casework), Team 3.
S4 Hard Cases Support Applications	020 8633 0204/0209.

Note that NASS's structure, telephone and fax numbers may change at short notice.

NASS regional offices

Region	Address	Telephone	Fax
Greater London	1st Floor, Quest House 11 Cross Rd Croydon CR9 6EL	0208 6330503	0208 6330896
South West	Unit 1 Greystoke Business Centre High Street Portishead Bristol BS20 6PY	01275 815300	01275 815301
South East & Central	Units 4&6 Whitfield Court, White Cliffs Business Park, Honeywood Road, Whitfield, Dover CT16 3PX	01304 873111	01304 873133
East of England	Ground Floor, Silvaco Technology Centre Compass Point St.Ives Cambs PE27 5JL	01480 309341	01480 309375
East Midlands	Regus House, Herald Way Pegasus Business Park Castle Donnington Derbyshire DE74 2TZ	01332 638617	01332 63829
West Midlands	Regus Building 2nd Floor, Blythe Valley Business Park Central Boulevard Solihull, West Midlands B90 8AG	01564 711751	01564 711347

Region	Address	Telephone	Fax
North West	PO Box 191 4th Floor Concorde Offices 4M Building Manchester Airport M90 3WZ	0161 261 1307	0161 261 1323
Yorkshire and Humberside	Waterside Court, Kirkstall Road LEEDS LS4 2QB	0113 386 5654	0113 386 5700
North East	Rotterdam House 116 Quayside Newcastle Upon Tyne NE1 3DY	0191 2064540	0191 2064276
Wales	Room 216, Regus House Falcon Drive Cardiff Bay CF10 4RY	02920 504001	02920 504211
Scotland	c/o IS Scottish Enforcement Unit Festival Court 200 Brand Street Glasgow G51 1DH	0141 4191308	0141 4191329
Northern Ireland	11B Merrion Business Centre, 58 Howard Street BELFAST BT1 6PJ	02890 585971	02890 500888

ONE STOP SERVICES FOR AGENCIES

S = Surgery Services

Note: a part time outreach service is provided by many One-stop services (OSSs) in their local area – contact the nearest OSS for information.

Scotland

23–Glasgow

6–Newcastle
7–Wallsend
8–Sunderland

10–Belfast

N. Ireland

9–Middlesbrough

England

22–Leeds
14–Manchester
13–Liverpool
27–Wrexham

11–Nottingham
12–Leicester
Wales   21–Birmingham

25–Swansea 24–Cardiff
26–Newport   20–London 4–Thanet
16–Bristol   18–Hounslow 1 & 2–Dover
15–Southampton 3–Hastings
5–Brighton

17–Plymouth

Map Ref	Organisation	Address	Tel/fax
1	MIGRANT HELPLINE Kent	The Rendezvous Building Freight Service Approach Road Eastern Docks Dover CT16 1JA	T: 01304 203 977 F: 01304 203 995
2 Mon, Tue & Fri: 09.30–15.30 Thurs: 9.30–13.00	MIGRANT HELPLINE Kent	89 Folkestone Road Dover Kent CT17 9SD	T: 01304 203 074 F: 01304 204 036
S Wed: 9.30–15.00	MIGRANT HELPLINE Kent	Ashford Christian Fellowship Solid Rock Norwood Street Ashford Kent TN23 1QU	Contact main office
S Mon: 9.30–15.30	MIGRANT HELPLINE Kent	The Friends Meeting House 6 The Friars Canterbury Kent CT1 2AS	Contact main office
S Tues, Wed & Fri: 9.30–15.30	MIGRANT HELPLINE Kent	53 The Old High Street Folkestone Kent CT20 1RN	Contact main office
S Fri: 10.30–15.30	MIGRANT HELPLINE Kent	The Methodist Church Hall Wilfred Street Gravesend Kent DA12 2RE	Mobile: 07976 450324
3 Mon–Fri: 9.30–16.00 Except Wed: 11.00–16.00	MIGRANT HELPLINE East Sussex	48 Havelock Road Hastings TN34 1BE	T: 01424 717 011 F: 01424 717 098
4 Mon–Fri: 9.30–15.30 Except Thurs: 9.30–13.00	MIGRANT HELPLINE Thanet	1 Cecil Street Margate Kent CT9 1NX	T: 01843 292 921 F: 01843 232 085

Map Ref	Organisation	Address	Tel/fax
5	MIGRANT HELPLINE West Sussex	7a Church Street Brighton BN1 1US	T: 01273 671 711 F: 01273 695 830
6	NERS (North of England Refugee Service)	19 The Bigg Market Newcastle NE1 1UN	T: 0191 222 0406 F: 0191 222 0239
7	NERS	3rd Floor Forum House The Forum Wallsend Tyne & Wear NE28 8LX	T: 0191 200 1109 F: 0191 200 5929
8	NERS	19 Villiers Street Sunderland Tyne & Wear SR1 1EJ	T: 0191 510 8685 F: 0191 510 8697
9	NERS	27 Borough Road Middlesbrough TS1 4AD	T: 01642 217 447 F: 01642 210 200
10	NICEM Belfast	3rd Floor Ascott House 24/31 Shaftesbury Square Belfast BT2 7DB	T: 02890 238 645 F: 02890 319 485
11	REFUGEE ACTION East Midlands	3rd Floor Albion House. 5–13 Canal Street Nottingham NG1 7EG	T: 0115 941 8552 F: 0115 950 9980
12	REFUGEE ACTION East Midlands	Muslim Community Resource Centre Melbourne Centre Melbourne Road Leicester LE2 0GU	T: 0116 261 4830 F: 0116 262 7162
13	REFUGEE ACTION North West	34 Princes Road Liverpool L8 1TH	T: 0151 702 6300 F: 0151 709 6684
S Fri: 13.00–15.00	REFUGEE ACTION North West	Great Homer Street Medical Centre 25 Conway Street Liverpool L5	Contact main office

Map Ref	Organisation	Address	Tel/fax
14	REFUGEE ACTION North West	Dale House 4th Floor 35 Dale Street Manchester M12 2HF	T: 0161 233 1200 F: 0161 236 4285
15	REFUGEE ACTION South Central	50 Oxford Street Southampton SO14 3DP	T: 02380 248130 F: 02380 632995
16	REFUGEE ACTION South West	Senate House, 36 Stokes Croft Bristol BS1 3QD	T: 0117 989 2100 F: 0117 924 8576
17	REFUGEE ACTION South West	Virginia House 40 Looe Street Plymouth PL4 0EB	T: 01752 519 860 F: 01752 519 861
18	RAP (Refugee Arrivals Project) London Airports	41b Cross Lances Road Hounslow, Middlesex TW3 2AD	T: 020 8607 6888 F: 020 8607 6851
19	REFUGEE COUNCIL Eastern Region	1st Floor, 4–8 Museum Stree Ipswich IP1 1HT	T: 01473 221 560 F: 01473 217334
20	REFUGEE COUNCIL London	240–250 Ferndale Road Brixton London SW9 8BB	T: 020 7346 6770 F: 020 7346 6778
21	REFUGEE COUNCIL West Midlands	1st Floor Smithfield House Digbeth Birmingham B5 6BS	T: 0121 622 1515 F: 0121 622 4061
22	REFUGEE COUNCIL Yorkshire & Humberside	Ground Floor Hurley House 1 Dewsbury Road Leeds LS11 5DQ	T: 0113 244 9404 F: 0113 246 5229
23	SCOTTISH REFUGEE COUNCIL	5 Cadogan Square (170 Blythswood Court) Cadogan Street Glasgow G2 7PH	0800 0856087 (advice line for asylum seekers) T: 0141 248 9799 F: 0141 243 2499

Map Ref	Organisation	Address	Tel/fax
S Mon: 14.30–18.00	SCOTTISH REFUGEE COUNCIL	Women's Group Quaker Meeting House 38 Elmbank Crescent Glasgow	Contact main office
S Thurs: 13.00–18.00	SCOTTISH REFUGEE COUNCIL	Drop in Club@Elmbank Crescent Quaker Meeting House 38 Elmbank Crescent Glasgow	Contact main office
S Thursday	SCOTTISH REFUGEE COUNCIL	Scottish Refugee Council 200 Cowgate Edinburgh EH1 1NQ	Contact main office
24	WELSH REFUGEE COUNCIL	Phoenix House 389 Newport Road Cardiff CF24 1TP	T: 02920 489800 F: 02920 432980
25	WELSH REFUGEE COUNCIL	3rd Floor, C/o Swansea Bay Race Equality Council Grove House Grove Place Swansea SA1 5DF	Mobile: 07950 704746 or contact the Cardiff office
26	WELSH REFUGEE COUNCIL	High Street Chambers 51 High Street Newport NP20 1GB	T: 01633 266420 F: 01633 266421
27	WELSH REFUGEE COUNCIL	Trinity House Trinity Stree Wrexham LL11 1NL	T: 01978 363240 F: 01978 313424

APPENDIX G

Resources

ASYLUM AND IMMIGRATION LAW RESOURCES (CHAPTER 1)

Publications

- *Butterworths' Immigration Law Service,* Butterworths
- Coker, Finch and Stanley, *Putting children first: a guide for immigration practitioners,* Legal Action Group, 2002
- Macdonald and Blake, *Macdonald's Immigration Law and Practice,* Butterworths, 5th edn, 2001
- Phelan and Gillespie *Immigration Law Handbook,* Oxford University Press, 3rd edn, 2003
- Symes and Jorro, *Asylum Law & Practice,* Butterworths, 2003

Advice and information

Asylum Aid
28 Commercial Street
London E1 6LS
Tel: 020 7377 5123
www.asylumaid.org.uk
campaigns and provides
immigration advice

Immigration Advisory Service (IAS)
County House
190 Great Dover Street
London SE1 4YB
Tel:020 7967 1200
E-mail: advice@ias.org
www.iasuk.org

Government funded advice and representation

Greater Manchester Immigration Aid
Unit 400
Cheetham Hill Road
Manchester M8 7EL
Tel: 0161 740 7722
www.hlminfo.net/content2/gmiau
www.ein.org.uk/gmiau
Immigration advice and
campaigning

Joint Council for the Welfare of Immigrants (JCWI)
115 Old Street
London EC1V 9RT
Advice line for general civil contract
holders: 0845 602 1020
Advice line for public:
020 7251 8706
Legal advice on immigration and
nationality law

Refugee Legal Centre (RLC)
153–157 Commercial Road,
London E8 2DA
Tel: 020 7780 3200
www.refugee-legal-centre.org.uk
Advice and representation on
asylum and asylum appeals
(government-funded).

*UK Lesbian and Gay Immigration
Group* (UKLGIG)
c/o Gay.com
22/23 Carnaby Street
London W1F 7DB
Tel: 020 7734 3705
www.stonewall-immigration.org.uk
(formerly known as the Stonewall
Immigration Group). Campaigns
for immigration rights for same-sex
couples and asylum-seekers.

Terrence Higgins Trust (THT)
Terrence Higgins Trust
(national office)
52–54 Gray's Inn Road
London WC1X 8JU
Helpline: 0845 1221 200
E-mail: info@tht.org.uk
www.tht.org.uk
Advice and information on asylum,
immigration and asylum support
for people with HIV

General information and government bodies

Electronic Immigration Network
Tel: 0845 458 4151/0161 2737515
E-mail: info@ein.org.uk
www.ein.org.uk
Electronic Immigration Network
has extensive links to organisations
and legal sources.

UN Refugee Agency
United Nations High
Commissioner for Refugees
Case Postale 2500
CH-1211 Genève 2 Dépôt
Suisse
Tel: +41 22 739 8111
(automatic switchboard)
www.unhcr.ch

United Nations High
Commissioner for Refugees
The Office of the Representative for
the United Kingdom
21st Floor, Millbank Tower
Millbank
London SW1P 4QP
Tel: 020 7828 9191
www.unhcr.org.uk
UN High Commissioner for
Refugees' website holds
international refugee law, up-to-date
country and guidance on the
protection of refugees.

Home Office Immigration and Nationality Directorate
Home Office Immigration and Nationality Department (IND)
Lunar House
40 Wellesley Road
Croydon CR9 2BY
Tel: 0870 606 7766
www.ind.homeoffice.gov.uk
Home Office's website publishes immigration law, policy and guidance including full text of the Immigration rules, country assessments, prescribed application forms and NASS policy bulletins

Home Office Research Development Statistics
www.homeoffice.gov.uk/rds
Home Office statistics, research and publications on asylum and immigration. Quarterly statistics showing asylum and NASS applications

Office of the Immigration Services Commissioner (OISC)
5th Floor
Counting House
53 Tooley Street
London SE1 2QN
Tel: 020 7211 1500
General enquiries: 0845 000 0046
www.oisc.gov.uk
Regulates provision of immigration advice

Parliamentary Ombudsman
Office of the Parliamentary Commissioner
Millbank Tower
21–24 Millbank
London SW1P 4QP
Helpline: 0845 015 4033
E-mail: opca.enquiries @ombudsman.gsi.gov.uk
www.parliament.ombudsman. org.uk
Considers complaints about Home Office maladministration.

Immigration Law Practitioners' Association (ILPA)
Lindsey House
40–42 Charterhouse Street
London EC1M 6JH
Tel: 020 7251 8363
www.ilpa.org.uk
Professional association of immigration lawyers and academics

BENEFITS RESOURCES (CHAPTER 2)

Publications

- Bonner, Hooker and White, Social Security Legislation 2003, Sweet and Maxwell, 2003 (Published annually in September)
- Welfare Benefits and Tax Credits Handbook 2004/2005, 6th edn, CPAG, 2004 (published annually)
- Migration and Social Security Handbook , 3rd edn, CPAG, 2002
- Findlay, George, Poynter and Stagg, CPAG's Housing Benefit and Council Tax Benefit Legislation 2003/2004, 16th edn, CPAG, 2003

Advice and information

London Advice Services Alliance (LASA)
Universal House
88–94 Wentworth Street
London E1 7SA
Tel: 020 7377 2738
www.rightsnet.org.uk
Welfare benefits information and training. LASA's welfare rights website contains discussion and current information about asylum support issues. Contains good links to other legal sites.

Child Poverty Action Group (CPAG)
94 White Lion Street
London N1 9PF
Tel: 020 7837 7979
Advice line (for advisers only)
020 7833 4627 Mon–Fri 2pm–4pm
www.cpag.org.uk
Welfare benefits information, training and publications including *Welfare Rights Bulletin*

Citizens Advice
Middleton House
115–123 Pentonville Road
London N1 9LZ
Tel: 020 7833 2181
www.citizensadvice.org.uk
For details of the local Citizens' Advice Bureau

Government offices and agencies

Department for Work and Pensions
(benefits)
Public Enquiry Office
Correspondence Unit
Room 539
The Adelphi
1–11 John Adam Street
London WC2N 6HT
Tel: 020 7712 2171
Benefits enquiry line for sick or
disabled people 0800 882200
www.dwp.gov.uk
The DWP website lists all the local
offices and contact details

*Complaints and claims for ex-gratia
payments*
Chief Executive
Ms Alexis Cleveland
Quarry House
Quarry Hill
Leeds LS2 7UA
Tel: 0113 232 4000

*Independent Review Service for the
Social Fund*
4th Floor
Centre City Podium
5 Hill St
Birmingham B5 4UB
Tel: 0121 606 2100
www.irs-review.org.uk
Carries out independent reviews
for dissatisfied customers of the
discretionary social fund.

*National Insurance Contributions
Office*
Inland Revenue
Benton Park View
Newcastle upon Tyne NE98 1ZZ
Tel: 0191 213 5000

*Offices of the Social Security and
Child Support Commissioners*
3rd Floor
Procession House
55 Ludgate Hill
London EC4A 7JW
Tel: 020 7029 9850
www.osscsc.org.uk
Commissioners' decisions and
guidance.

Tax Credit Office Guidance Team
Inland Revenue
Room 312, Block 3
Norcross
Blackpool FY5 3TA
Tel: 0845 300 3900

ASYLUM SUPPORT RESOURCES (CHAPTERS 3–4)

Publications/websites

There are numerous publications about the effect of the NASS scheme and other aspects of support on asylum-seekers Many of these can be accessed via the websites and organisations below:

- www.icar.org.uk
  Information Centre about Asylum and Refugees in the UK.
- www.asylumsupport.info
  Regularly updated site with latest policy guidance, links to other useful sites and news of case-law developments.
- www.niknicol.co.uk
  Barrister's overview of immigration and asylum support law
- www.refugeecouncil.org.uk
  The Refugee Council's website has numerous research publications and resources including translated leaflets and guides about asylum support.
- www.ind.homeoffice.gov.uk
  NASS pages on Home Office website for NASS Policy Bulletins and latest developments.
- www.lga.gov.uk/lga/asylum
  Local Government Association website, containing guidance on interim support scheme, information about legal and policy development, particularly useful for local authority staff.
- www.westminster.gov.uk/socialservices/lasc
  The London Asylum-seekers consortium co-ordinates London local authorities' work on asylum support and refugee integration. The website includes statistical information.
- www.publications.parliament.uk
  Past and current Parliamentary debates on the support provisions are published on this site in Hansard.

Advice and information (see also list of national 'one-stop' services)

Refugee Council
3 Bondway
London SW8 1SJ
Tel: 020 7820 3000
E-mail: info@refugeecouncil.org.uk
www.refugeecouncil.org.uk
Information, advice, training and publications.

Advisory Centre for Education (ACE)
Unit 1C Aberdeen Studios
22 Highbury Grove
London N5 2DQ
Tel: 020 7354 8321
www.ace-ed.org.uk
Advice about education rights.

Commission for Racial Equality (CRE)
Elliott House
10–12 Allington Street
London SW1E 5EH
Tel: 020 7828 7022
www.cre.gov.uk
Advice and information about tackling race discrimination.

Language Line
Tel: 020 7520 1400
info@language line.co.uk
Commercial telephone interpreting service

Law Centres' Federation (LCF)
Duchess House
18–19 Warren Street
London W1P 5DB
Tel: 020 7387 8570
www.lawcentres.org.uk
Details of local Law Centres.

Government offices and agencies

Asylum Support Adjudicators
Christopher Wren House
113 High Street
Croydon CR1 1GQ
Tel: 020 8688 3977
Fax: 020 8688 6075
www.asylum-support-adjudicators.org.uk
ASAs hear asylum support appeals at the above address. Website includes directions, appeal form and all their decisions

Department of Health
www.dh.gov.uk
Guidance on rights to healthcare, Prescription Pricing Authority for forms and information about free prescriptions and health benefits

Health Service Ombudsman
www.ombudsman.org.uk
Tel: 020 7217 4051

Local Government Ombudsman
Advice line 0845 6021983
www.lgo.gov.uk
Considers complaints about local authority maladministration.

National Asylum Support Service (NASS)
(see above, Appendix F 'how to contact NASS')
Voyager House
30 Wellesley Road
Croydon CR0 2AD
Telephone Enquiry Bureau: 0845 602 1739
www.ind.homeoffice.gov.uk

Office of the Information Commissioner
Helpline 01625 545745 333
www.informationcommissioner.gov.uk
Considers complaints about the handling of information under the Data Protection Act 1998.

Parliamentary Ombudsman
Tel: 0845 015 4033
www.ombudsman.org.uk
Considers complaints against NASS (as part of the Home Office).

Sodexho Helpline
Tel: 01252 369 799
Private company which administers the NASS voucher scheme.

Treasury Solicitor
25 Queen Anne's Gate
London SW1 9BU
Tel: 0207 210 3000
Fax: 0207 210 3433
Solicitors for service of legal
proceedings on NASS (Secretary
of State).

Websites/legislation

- www.justask.org.uk
  Community Legal Service (CLS) site for details of local CLS advisers.
- www.legislation.hmso.gov.uk
  Acts of Parliament and statutory instruments.
- www.parliament.the-stationery-office.co.uk
  Parliamentary debates (Hansard).
- www.direct.gov.uk
  For information about government departments.
- www.venables.co.uk
  Legislation and case-law

HOUSING RESOURCES (CHAPTER 5)

Publications

- Arden (ed), *Encyclopedia of Housing Law and Practice*, Sweet and Maxwell
- Garvie, *Far From Home: the housing of asylum-seekers in private rented accommodation*, Shelter, 2001
- Arden and Hunter, *Homelessness and Allocations*, revised 6th edn, Legal Action Group, 2003
- Luba and Davies, *The Homelessness Act 2002: special bulletin*, Jordans, 2002
- Luba and Knafler, *Repairs: tenants' rights*, 3rd edn, Legal Action Group, 1999

Advice and information (see also general advice)

Shelter
88 Old Street
London EC1V 9HU
Tel: 020 7505 2000
Shelterline advice line:
0808 800 4444
www.shelter.org.uk (includes
an online advice service)

Government offices and agencies

Independent Housing Ombudsman
Norman House
105–109 The Strand
London WC2R 0AA
Tel: 020 7836 3630
E-mail: ombudsman@ihos.org.uk
www.ihos.org.uk

Office of the Deputy Prime Minister
www.odpm.gov.uk
Website of the ODPM publishes
housing regulations and guidance,
eg, relating to the dispersal scheme.

COMMUNITY CARE/HEALTH RESOURCES (CHAPTER 6)

Community care

Publications and guidance

- Clements, *Community Care and the Law*, 3rd edn, Legal Action Group, 2004
- *Community Care Law Reports*, Legal Action Group (quarterly)
- Levenson and Sharma, *The Health of Refugee Children – Guidelines for Paediatricians*, Royal College of Paediatrics and Child Health. *See also* www.rcph.ac.uk for assistance in assessing the age of unaccompanied minors
- *Guidance on Support for Asylum-seekers with care needs*, April 2004, see www.alg.gov.uk

Advice and information

Public Law Project
Tel (advisers only): 0808 800 4546
or 020 7697 2194
www.publiclawproject.org.uk
Specialist legal advice about public law and Human Rights Act issues.

Health resources

Publications and guidance

- Burnett and Fassil, 'Meeting the health needs of refugee and asylum seekers in the UK – an information and resource pack for health workers', Department of Health, 2003. www.dh.gov.uk/publicationsandstatistics/ publications/publicationspolicyandguidance

Advice and information

Department of Health
www.dh.gov.uk
For wide range of resources and publications.

Health Benefits Division
Prologistics
Department of Health
PO Box 777
London SE1 6XN
Help desk Tel: 0191 203 5555.
Processes applications for exemption from prescription charges for asylum-seekers (and others) on a low income who are not supported by NASS.

Department of Health Overseas Visitors Policy Unit
www.gov.uk/overseasvisitors
For queries about charges for GP or hospital treatment.

Health Services Ombudsman
Tel: 0845 015 4033
E-mail: OHSC.Enquiries @ombudsman.gsi.gov.uk
www.ombudsman.org.uk
For complaints about the NHS.

Prescription Pricing Authority
Tel: 0191 203 5100
www.ppa.org.uk
For enquiries about exemption from
prescription and other charges.

HARP
www.harpweb.org.uk
Information about health issues
affecting asylum-seekers and
refugees includes standard letters
interpreted into various languages.

Medact
Tel: 0207 271 2020
www.medact.org.uk
A network of health workers
who exchange information and
resources to improve conditions
for asylum-seekers and refugees.

*Medical Foundation for the Care of
Victims of Torture*
Tel: 0207 813 7777
www.torturecare.org.uk
Provides counseling and other
services for torture survivors.

Terrence Higgins Trust
Tel: 0845 1221200
 www.tht.org.uk
Offers support and information
including legal advice to people
affected by HIV/AIDS throughout
the UK.

*All Party Parliamentary Group on
HIV and AIDS*
www.appg-aids.org.uk

HUMAN RIGHTS/EUROPEAN/INTERNATIONAL RESOURCES

Publications

- Starmer, *European Human Rights Law*, Legal Action Group, 1999
- Luba, *Housing and the Human Rights Act*, Jordans, 2000
- Baker, Carter and Hunter, *Housing and human rights law*, Legal Action Group, 2001
- Luba, *Human Rights Act: special bulletin*, forthcoming, Jordans, 2004

Websites

- www.europa.eu.int
  Comprehensive European law site with legislation and case-law.
- www.conventions.coe.int
  Council of Europe site with European treaties, conventions and list of signatories, eg, of Council of Europe Social Charter.
- www.echr.coe.int/
  Judgments of European Court of Human Rights and other human rights materials.
- www.beagle.org.uk/hra/

Advice and information

Advice on Individual Rights in Europe (AIRE Centre)
Advice line 0207 831 3850
www.airecentre.org.uk
Advice/information about EC law.

Liberty (National Council for Civil Liberties)
Tel: 0808 808 4546
www.liberty-human-rights.org.uk
Advisers' helpline on human rights.

Interrights
Tel: 020 7278 3230
www.interrights.org.
Advice and information about European and international human rights law.

section 55 materials

SOLICITOR'S CHECKLIST OF PRACTICAL STEPS IN A SECTION 55 OR ASYLUM SUPPORT JUDICIAL REVIEW

See also attached list of documents and useful telephone numbers.

Although this checklist was prepared mainly for use in s55 cases, it can be used as guidance to solicitors for other urgent asylum support judicial review cases.

Before seeing the client

1. At point of referral, encourage any referring agency to send you a copy of any written representations or to fax some to NASS if none have been written.
Has the client seen or been referred to a doctor?
Is an interpreter needed?
If the client is under 18, or has care needs, they should first be referred to a local authority for assessment.

2. Previous solicitor?
Ensure client doesn't already have a solicitor representing (or a current public funding certificate) in relation to asylum support. Unless there has been a significant change in circumstances, the new solicitor may need to apply to transfer the certificate (APP 8).

3. Consider the timetable and availability of staff.
If an urgent paper application is to be considered on the same day, papers need to be filed at Admin Court by 2pm to ensure a duty judge will consider the application on the papers between 5 and 6pm.

4. Ensure counsel available to give oral advice for CLS certificate purposes/ draft N461 if needed/ make phone application.

Client arrives

5. Explain process (need to reassure client as accurate instructions including sensitive information are needed). Client should understand this info may be passed to IND so should be consistent with their asylum claim.

6. Assess urgency LSC guidance (Focus, December 2003) required representations to have been sent 24 hours before the grant of public funding in s55 cases.

Take instructions/ check and copy client's documents (see questionnaire. below).
• Do they have the following:
NASS decision letter?
Application registration card (ARC)?

IND documents eg SEF, One-Stop notice?
- Check client's age and special needs – is it an age dispute or community care case?
- Check they have an outstanding asylum claim/ appeal.
- Do they have an immigration solicitor? If so do they have a copy of their asylum statement? If not consider contacting immigration solicitor to ask them to fax it (it may include details of journey to UK which will save time on your witness statement).

7. FAX letter before action to NASS with detailed representations in s55 cases if none have been sent. The letter should contain enough detail to justify reconsideration and should raise article 3 grounds. If NASS fails to provide a positive response after 24 hours and client is street homeless/ without food.

8. Obtain emergency public funding
Consider devolved powers under housing/ community care/ public law/ franchise. Firms without devolved powers experiencing difficulty in obtaining certificates or where the case appears borderline could consider obtaining extra evidence or counsel's opinion as to the merits of the application. The LSC Contract Support services may be able to assist with this.

9. Draft witness statement.
In s55 cases, statement should include:

date of birth
port/ IND reference
nationality
brief details of asylum claim/ reason for leaving home country
details of journey to UK
personal circumstances in port of arrival
details of movements since entering UK to explain any delay including whether he or she can speak English
where he or she has stayed/ any nights sleeping rough
access to food/ money
process of asylum claim, eg did they present to police before being referred to Croydon IND
what occurred at IND?
effect of sleeping rough etc, any health problems, friends or family in UK.

The statement should exhibit relevant documents which may include the client's asylum statement or some evidence of asylum seeker status, eg the ARC card, medical evidence, referral letters showing where he or she has been, letters from charities saying that they can't help. The statement should be countersigned by any interpreter.

Preparation and issue

Instruct counsel

Fax or e-mail witness statement for counsel to draft N461/N463/draft order/ make telephone application. Some solicitors may decide to draft some or all of the pleadings, particularly in urgent or straightforward cases.

The Permission bundle must include the N461, N463 draft order and witness statement, decision letter and reps. It should be paginated and indexed and identify essential reading. See Appendix A for statutory materials to be considered for authorities bundle.

10. Paper applications:

- Fax N463 certificate of urgency signed by counsel and completed N461 and the draft order to the Treasury Solicitor and then file at Admin Court office. The court office may accept an undertaking to file a fully indexed bundle at a later stage in urgent cases provided there is sufficient evidence for the judge to make a decision.
- Solicitors unable to arrange filing in person, may phone the Admin Court general office to ask if they will accept a faxed application with an undertaking to file papers and fee lodged eg next day.
- Remember to complete the N463 with the time and date when you served the papers on Treasury. If you can show the Admin Court issue office a £30 cheque made payable to HMPG, they may accept the papers before you produce them at Fee Room.
- Urgent paper applications should be filed by 2pm so that the duty judge can consider them at the end of the afternoon.
- Telephone the Admin Court Paper Applications section 020 7947 7806 at 4.30-5pm to check if the paper application is being considered.
- The resulting order should be faxed to the solicitor around 5–6pm. If not and the case is exceptional the solicitor should discuss with counsel whether a phone application is feasible.

11. Telephone applications

- Telephone duty judge from 5pm via Security at the Royal Courts of Justice, it may be a few hours before the order is granted and then an additional period to finalise accommodation arrangements.
- The solicitor or counsel should contact the Royal Courts of Justice 0207 947 6000 from 5pm with counsel's name and contact number for the evening.
- Clerk will later phone counsel to check: client's name, IND and port reference, date of birth, nationality, date entered UK and brief facts.
- Judge will later phone counsel for the application to be made. If it is granted, the judge will give instructions eg to fax a draft order to judge's clerk that night or next day.
- The signed order needs to be filed at the Admin Court office for sealing within time-scale given by judge (usually the next day).

12. After the application is granted   In London the client may go to Migrant Helpline or RAP office up to 11pm and the sealed order may be faxed there. Alternatively or where outside London phone NASS out of hours team. They will house for one night only and send client to a voluntary sector provider the next day. Tell them client's name, date of birth, Home Office reference and cultural details i.e. gender/language/ religion. They should make enquiries about where client should go and call you back with details. If it's a telephone order, they will accept it for one night, provided the signed/sealed order is faxed following day.

13. Explain next steps to client   Address, cost of travel, map and travel arrangements to get to address. If possible give client copy of draft or signed order and compliment slip or letter stating order granted. Ask client to notify you asap of their new address.

14. After filing and service   Remember to file the certificate of service N215 at court to confirm that you have served a full copy of the permission bundle and the sealed order on the Treasury Solicitor within 7 days of issue. NB 5 days for CLS forms to reach LSC. If permission is granted on the papers, remember to pay the £180 fee

Section 55 Resource list:

Treasury Solicitor
tel: 020 7210 3000
fax: 020 7210 3433

Serve proceedings against the Secretary of State for the Home Department (NASS) on:
Team D2, Treasury Solicitor
Queen Anne Chambers
28 Broadway
London SW1H 9JS
DX 123242 St. James Park

Royal Courts of Justice (High Court)
general tel (for security/ out of hours service from 5pm): 020 7947 6000
Administrative Court office tel: 020 7947 6205/ 7410
fax: 020 7947 6802
DX 44450, The Strand

Admin Court Paper Applications
tel:020 7947 7806/7824

www.courtservice.gov.uk has information about contacting the Administrative Court, its procedures and court forms.

NASS
Out of hours number NASS emergency accommodation
tel: 07789 272059

RANS post-refusal casework team
tel: 0208 760 4517
fax: 020 8760 3820

Voyager House
30 Wellesley Road
Croydon CR0 2AD

Voluntary Sector (see also Appendix G)

Other Section 55 Resources
1 NASS Policy Bulletin 47 regarding judicial reviews
   (www.ind.homeoffice.gov.uk)

2 NASS Policy Bulletin 75 regarding late claims
   (www.ind.homeoffice.gov.uk)
3 Immigration and Asylum Act 1999 ss94, 95 and 98
4 Nationality, Immigration and Asylum Act 2002
5 Practice direction 54 issued 31 August 2000
6 Judicial review protocol: see www.dca.gov.uk
7 Mr Justice Maurice Kay's guidance in R (Q, D and others) v (Shelter
   intervening party) SSHD, 24 October 2003

Documents
Guidance and forms available on www.courtservice.gov.uk:
1 N461 judicial review claim form
2 N463 certificate of urgency
3 Draft court order
4 N215 certificate of service

Section 55 questionnaire

Name:

Sex:

DoB:

Country of Origin and Nationality:

HO Ref. No:

Details (dates, methods) of any detention, torture, other traumatic circumstances in country of origin/nationality:

Time/Place of Departure:

Date/Time of Arrival:

Place/Method of Arrival:

With agent/alone:

Name of agent:

Nationality/Colour of Passport:

Travel ID:

Did applicant know he had to claim asylum (a) at port, (b) at all?

What advice/threats came from agent?

What were dealings with Immigration Officer?

Date/Place of Asylum Claim:

Date of Start of Emergency Support:

Date of s55 refusal letter:

Date refusal letter handed over:

Date of eviction from NASS accommodation:

Letter of further representations:

Reply:

At what stage is asylum claim (give details):

Sleeping circumstances since eviction (places, bedding etc – also, has applicant been subjected to any harassment whilst homeless):

Food circumstances since eviction:

Has applicant ever begged for accommodation or for food or for money if so provide details:

Washing/Bathing:

Toileting:

Clothes Washing:

Does applicant have spare clothes?

Attempts to find charitable support in respect of accommodation, food or other provision. Give details.

Physical consequences:

Mental consequences:

Medical evidence:

APPENDIX I

Summary of entitlements for asylum-seekers, refugees and those granted leave to remain and their dependants[1]

Services	Asylum-seeker supported by NASS (see Chapter 3)	Asylum-seeker supported under interim scheme	Asylum-seeker supported by Social Services or other means (eg relatives)	Failed asylum-seeker awaiting removal directions	Former asylum-seeker granted indefinite leave to remain as a refugee	Former asylum-seeker granted discretionary or other leave to remain	Former asylum-seeker now A8 national
NHS hospital treatment	yes	yes	yes	yes if resident in the UK for 12 months, or needs treatment for emergency or specified illnesses or if treatment needed to avoid a breach of ECHR, article 2 or 3 (see chapter 4). Otherwise may be charged	yes	yes	yes but from 2005 form E111, E119 or E128 may be needed as proof of entitlement
NHS GP treatment	yes	yes	yes	yes if in the UK for at least 12 months. Otherwise law may change in 2004 to empower charges for primary care. Treatment should be provided to avoid a breach ECHR, article 2 or 3 (see chapter 4).	yes	yes	yes but from 2005 form E111, E119 or E128 may be needed as proof of entitlement
Free prescriptions	yes with HC2 certificate	Yes, should get local authority help with HC2 application	need to apply on form HC1 on basis of low income	yes, may apply on form HC1 on basis of low income	if on benefits/low income	if on benefits/low income	If on benefits/ low income
Early years provision	Yes, unless in accommodation centre where there may be alternative provision	yes	yes	yes	yes	yes	yes
School provision 5-16	yes unless in accommodation centre where there may be alternative provision	yes	yes	yes	yes	yes	yes
Free school meals	yes	yes	no	no	if on income support	if on income support	if on income support

[1] This table is intended as a basic outline. Please refer to relevant chapters for a fuller explanation

Further education	yes	yes	yes	Learning and Skills Council does not cover fees	yes	yes	yes if self-supporting
Higher education (university)	no funding and overseas student fees	no funding and overseas student fees	no funding and overseas student fees	no	eligible for any loan/ grant funding on same basis as British Citizen without waiting for a qualifying period	3-year qualifying period for any grant funding	yes if self-supporting
Social Security benefits	eligible for contributory benefits if it has permission to work and has paid sufficient contributions but income must be below NASS destitution threshold to retain NASS entitlement.	eligible for contributory benefits if it has permission to work and has paid sufficient contributions but income must be below interim support threshold to retain support entitlement.	eligible for relevant contributory benefits if it has permission to work and has paid sufficient contributions	no	may also claim backdated child benefit and child tax credit within 3 months of leave decision	yes	If s/he has right to reside eg is working and registered to work, or has been working and registered for a continuous period of 12 months or is dependant of the above or is self-employed
Social Housing	no, except as part of an eligible household	no, except as part of an eligible household	no, except as part of an eligible household	no, except as part of an eligible household	yes	yes	If s/he has right to reside eg is working and registered to work, or has been working and registered for a continuous period of 12 months or is self-employed
Social Services help (community care)	yes for 'non-destitution needs'	yes for 'non-destitution needs'	yes for 'non-destitution needs'	yes for 'non-destitution needs', but excluded if Schedule 3 applies (see chapter 6)	yes	yes	Only if provision is necessary to avoid a breach of rights under EU treaty or Human Rights Convention
Asylum support	yes	yes	yes, eg for family members not supported by Social Services	yes if has dependent child under 18 who was in household during asylum application/ appeal, unless refusing to co-operate with departure. Otherwise s4 'hard cases' support if meet criteria	ends 28 days after notice of decision	ends 28 days after notice of decision	Ends after 1 May 2004 unless support is necessary to avoid a breach of Human Rights Convention Rights, or s/he is awaiting and 'amnesty decision' granting indefinite leave to remain (chapter 1)

Index